CrimeLine
Magistrates' Courts Criminal Practice 2013

First published in 2012 by CrimeLine Training Limited
Registered office: 1st and 2nd Floor, 7-9 Mesnes St, Wigan WN1 1QP
Tel: 01942 40 52 61
Email: admin@crimeline.info
Website: http://www.crimeline.info

For further information on our products please visit:
www.crimeline.info
© CrimeLine Training Ltd

ISBN 978-1-291-01616-1
Typeset by Hope Services, Abingdon

Contents

Contents

Contents

Contents

Contents

Contents

Contents

Contents

Contents

Contents

Contents

Contents

Contents

Contents

Contents

Contents

Contents

Cases

Contents

Contents

Contents

Contents

Contents

Contents

Contents

Contents

Contents

Contents

Contents

Contents

Contents

Contents

Contents

Contents

Contents

Contents

Contents

Contents

PART A OFFENCES

ANIMALS AND WILDLIFE

ANIMAL CRUELTY

The Animal Welfare Act 2006 creates a number of offences relating to animal cruelty in sections 4–9. All offences are triable summarily only, with a maximum sentence of 6 months' imprisonment and/or a fine of £5,000 (£20,000 for offences under sections 4, 5, 6(1) and (2), 7 and 8). Section 31 allows for offences to be laid outside of the usual 6 months' limitation period, but any defect in procedure in this respect is likely to prove fatal to the prosecution (see *RSPCA v King* [2010] EWHC 637 (Admin)) and *RSPCA v Johnson* [2009] EWHC 2702 (Admin)). In *Lamont-Perkins v RSPCA* [2012] EWHC 1002 (Admin) the court held that the phrase "the prosecutor" in section 31 of the 2006 Act is not limited to prosecutors who prosecute pursuant to a power conferred by some statutory provision but applies to anyone who initiates a prosecution under the Act. The court further held that any challenge to the validity of the section 31 certificate ought to be heard by the trial court, and not brought in the High Court by way of satellite litigation (reversing statements to the opposite effect in *Johnson*).

Offence seriousness (culpability and harm)
A. Identify the appropriate starting point
Starting points based on first time offender pleading not guilty

Examples of nature of activity	Starting point	Range
One impulsive act causing little or no injury; short-term neglect	Band C fine	Band B fine to medium level community order
Several incidents of deliberate ill-treatment/frightening animal(s); medium-term neglect	High level community order	Medium level community order to 12 weeks custody
Attempt to kill/torture; animal baiting/conducting or permitting cock-fighting etc; prolonged neglect	18 weeks custody	12 to 26 weeks custody

---

Offence seriousness (culpability and harm)
B. Consider the effect of aggravating and mitigating factors (other than those within examples above)
The following may be particularly relevant but these lists are not exhaustive

Factors indicating higher culpability	Factors indicating lower culpability
1. Offender in position of special responsibility	1. Offender induced by others
2. Adult involves children in offending	2. Ignorance of appropriate care
3. Animal(s) kept for livelihood	3. Offender with limited capacity
4. Use of weapon	
5. Offender ignored advice/warnings	
6. Offence committed for commercial gain	

Factors indicating greater degree of harm	Factors indicating lower culpability
1. Serious injury or death	1. Offender induced by others
2. Several animals affected	2. Ignorance of appropriate care
	3. Offender with limited capacity

There are several ancillary orders frequently encountered in these cases: Deprivation (s. 33), Disqualification (s. 34) and Destruction orders (ss. 37, 38). A court can amend a defective order under the provisions of section 142 MCA 1980 (*King v RSPCA* [2007] EWHC 637 (Admin)).

When considering the making of a disqualification order regard can properly be had to previous convictions (*Ward v RSPA* [2010] EWHC 347 (Admin)).

An application for costs can encompass the costs of investigating the offences (*Associated Octel ltd* [1997] 1 Cr App R(S) 435), including costs incurred as a result of action taken pursuant to s. 18 of the Act (see *James* [2011] EWHC 1642 (Admin)).

Animal Welfare Act 2006, ss 4, 5, 6, 7, 8, 9, 33, 34, 37 and 38

4 Unnecessary suffering

(1) A person commits an offence if—

    (a) an act of his, or a failure of his to act, causes an animal to suffer,

    (b) he knew, or ought reasonably to have known, that the act, or failure to act, would have that effect or be likely to do so,

    (c) the animal is a protected animal, and

    (d) the suffering is unnecessary.

(2) A person commits an offence if—

    (a) he is responsible for an animal,

    (b) an act, or failure to act, of another person causes the animal to suffer,

    (c) he permitted that to happen or failed to take such steps (whether by way of supervising the other person or otherwise) as were reasonable in all the circumstances to prevent that happening, and

    (d) the suffering is unnecessary.

5 Mutilation

(1) A person commits an offence if—

    (a) he carries out a prohibited procedure on a protected animal;

    (b) he causes such a procedure to be carried out on such an animal.

(2) A person commits an offence if—

    (a) he is responsible for an animal,

    (b) another person carries out a prohibited procedure on the animal, and

    (c) he permitted that to happen or failed to take such steps (whether by way of supervising the other person or otherwise) as were reasonable in all the circumstances to prevent that happening.

    [...]

(6) Nothing in this section applies to the removal of the whole or any part of a dog's tail.

6 Docking of dogs' tails

(1) A person commits an offence if—

    (a) he removes the whole or any part of a dog's tail, otherwise than for the purpose of its medical treatment;

    (b) he causes the whole or any part of a dog's tail to be removed by another person, otherwise than for the purpose of its medical treatment.

(2)   A person commits an offence if—

    (a) he is responsible for a dog,

    (b) another person removes the whole or any part of the dog's tail, otherwise than for the purpose of its medical treatment, and

    (c) he permitted that to happen or failed to take such steps (whether by way of supervising the other person or otherwise) as were reasonable in all the circumstances to prevent that happening.

(3)   Subsections (1) and (2) do not apply if the dog is a certified working dog that is not more than 5 days old.

(4)   For the purposes of subsection (3), a dog is a certified working dog if a veterinary surgeon has certified, in accordance with regulations made by the appropriate national authority, that the first and second conditions mentioned below are met.

(5)   The first condition referred to in subsection (4) is that there has been produced to the veterinary surgeon such evidence as the appropriate national authority may by regulations require for the purpose of showing that the dog is likely to be used for work in connection with—

    (a) law enforcement,

    (b) activities of Her Majesty's armed forces,

    (c) emergency rescue,

    (d) lawful pest control, or

    (e) the lawful shooting of animals.

(6)   The second condition referred to in subsection (4) is that the dog is of a type specified for the purposes of this subsection by regulations made by the appropriate national authority.

(7)   It is a defence for a person accused of an offence under subsection (1) or (2) to show that he reasonably believed that the dog was one in relation to which subsection (3) applies.

(8)   A person commits an offence if—

    (a) he owns a subsection (3) dog, and

    (b) fails to take reasonable steps to secure that, before the dog is 3 months old, it is identified as a subsection (3) dog in accordance with regulations made by the appropriate national authority.

(9)   A person commits an offence if—

    (a) he shows a dog at an event to which members of the public are admitted on payment of a fee,

    (b) the dog's tail has been wholly or partly removed (in England and Wales or elsewhere), and

    (c) removal took place on or after the commencement day.

(10)   Where a dog is shown only for the purpose of demonstrating its working ability, subsection (9) does not apply if the dog is a subsection (3) dog.

(11)   It is a defence for a person accused of an offence under subsection (9) to show that he reasonably believed—

    (a) that the event was not one to which members of the public were admitted on payment of an entrance fee,

    (b) that the removal took place before the commencement day, or

    (c) that the dog was one in relation to which subsection (10) applies.

(12)   A person commits an offence if he knowingly gives false information to a veterinary surgeon in connection with the giving of a certificate for the purposes of this section.

7 Administration of poisons etc.

(1) A person commits an offence if, without lawful authority or reasonable excuse, he—

   (a) administers any poisonous or injurious drug or substance to a protected animal, knowing it to be poisonous or injurious, or

   (b) causes any poisonous or injurious drug or substance to be taken by a protected animal, knowing it to be poisonous or injurious.

(2) A person commits an offence if—

   (a) he is responsible for an animal,

   (b) without lawful authority or reasonable excuse, another person administers a poisonous or injurious drug or substance to the animal or causes the animal to take such a drug or substance, and

   (c) he permitted that to happen or, knowing the drug or substance to be poisonous or injurious, he failed to take such steps (whether by way of supervising the other person or otherwise) as were reasonable in all the circumstances to prevent that happening.

(3) In this section, references to a poisonous or injurious drug or substance include a drug or substance which, by virtue of the quantity or manner in which it is administered or taken, has the effect of a poisonous or injurious drug or substance.

8 Fighting etc.

(1) A person commits an offence if he—

   (a) causes an animal fight to take place, or attempts to do so;

   (b) knowingly receives money for admission to an animal fight;

   (c) knowingly publicises a proposed animal fight;

   (d) provides information about an animal fight to another with the intention of enabling or encouraging attendance at the fight;

   (e) makes or accepts a bet on the outcome of an animal fight or on the likelihood of anything occurring or not occurring in the course of an animal fight;

   (f) takes part in an animal fight;

   (g) has in his possession anything designed or adapted for use in connection with an animal fight with the intention of its being so used;

   (h) keeps or trains an animal for use for in connection with an animal fight;

   (i) keeps any premises for use for an animal fight.

(2) A person commits an offence if, without lawful authority or reasonable excuse, he is present at an animal fight.

(3) A person commits an offence if, without lawful authority or reasonable excuse, he—

   (a) knowingly supplies a video recording of an animal fight,

   (b) knowingly publishes a video recording of an animal fight,

   (c) knowingly shows a video recording of an animal fight to another, or

   (d) possesses a video recording of an animal fight, knowing it to be such a recording, with the intention of supplying it.

(4) Subsection (3) does not apply if the video recording is of an animal fight that took place—

   (a) outside Great Britain, or

   (b) before the commencement date.

(5) Subsection (3) does not apply—

   (a) in the case of paragraph (a), to the supply of a video recording for inclusion in a programme service;

   (b) in the case of paragraph (b) or (c), to the publication or showing of a video recording by means of its inclusion in a programme service;

(c) in the case of paragraph (d), by virtue of intention to supply for inclusion in a programme service.

...

(7) In this section—

'animal fight' means an occasion on which a protected animal is placed with an animal, or with a human, for the purpose of fighting, wrestling or baiting;

...;

'programme service' has the same meaning as in the Communications Act 2003 (c. 21);

'video recording' means a recording, in any form, from which a moving image may by any means be reproduced and includes data stored on a computer disc or by other electronic means which is capable of conversion into a moving image.

(8) In this section—

(a) references to supplying or publishing a video recording are to supplying or publishing a video recording in any manner, including, in relation to a video recording in the form of data stored electronically, by means of transmitting such data;

(b) references to showing a video recording are to showing a moving image reproduced from a video recording by any means.

[Note. Subsections 3, 4, 5, and 6 were not in force at the time of writing.]

9 Duty of person responsible for animal to ensure welfare

(1) A person commits an offence if he does not take such steps as are reasonable in all the circumstances to ensure that the needs of an animal for which he is responsible are met to the extent required by good practice.

(2) For the purposes of this Act, an animal's needs shall be taken to include—

(a) its need for a suitable environment,

(b) its need for a suitable diet,

(c) its need to be able to exhibit normal behaviour patterns,

(d) any need it has to be housed with, or apart from, other animals, and

(e) its need to be protected from pain, suffering, injury and disease.

(3) The circumstances to which it is relevant to have regard when applying subsection (1) include, in particular—

(a) any lawful purpose for which the animal is kept, and

(b) any lawful activity undertaken in relation to the animal.

(4) Nothing in this section applies to the destruction of an animal in an appropriate and humane manner.

33 Deprivation order

(1) If the person convicted of an offence under any of sections 4, 5, 6(1) and (2), 7, 8 and 9 is the owner of an animal in relation to which the offence was committed, the court by or before which he is convicted may, instead of or in addition to dealing with him in any other way, make an order depriving him of ownership of the animal and for its disposal.

(2) Where the owner of an animal is convicted of an offence under section 34(9) because ownership of the animal is in breach of a disqualification under section 34(2), the court by or before which he is convicted may, instead of or in addition to dealing with him in any other way, make an order depriving him of ownership of the animal and for its disposal.

(3) Where the animal in respect of which an order under subsection (1) or (2) is made has any dependent offspring, the order may include provision depriving the person to whom it relates of ownership of the offspring and for its disposal.

(4) Where a court makes an order under subsection (1) or (2), it may—

    (a) appoint a person to carry out, or arrange for the carrying out of, the order;

    (b) require any person who has possession of an animal to which the order applies to deliver it up to enable the order to be carried out;

    (c) give directions with respect to the carrying out of the order;

    (d) confer additional powers (including power to enter premises where an animal to which the order applies is being kept) for the purpose of, or in connection with, the carrying out of the order;

    (e) order the offender to reimburse the expenses of carrying out the order.

(5) Directions under subsection (4)(c) may—

    (a) specify the manner in which an animal is to be disposed of, or

    (b) delegate the decision about the manner in which an animal is to be disposed of to a person appointed under subsection (4)(a).

(6) Where a court decides not to make an order under subsection (1) or (2) in relation to an offender, it shall—

    (a) give its reasons for the decision in open court, and

    (b) if it is a magistrates' court, cause them to be entered in the register of its proceedings.

(7) Subsection (6) does not apply where the court makes an order under section 34(1) in relation to the offender.

(8) In subsection (1), the reference to an animal in relation to which an offence was committed includes, in the case of an offence under section 8, an animal which took part in an animal fight in relation to which the offence was committed.

(9) In this section, references to disposing of an animal include destroying it.

34 Disqualification order

(1) If a person is convicted of an offence to which this section applies, the court by or before which he is convicted may, instead of or in addition to dealing with him in any other way, make an order disqualifying him under any one or more of subsections (2) to (4) for such period as it thinks fit.

(2) Disqualification under this subsection disqualifies a person—

    (a) from owning animals,

    (b) from keeping animals,

    (c) from participating in the keeping of animals, and

    (d) from being party to an arrangement under which he is entitled to control or influence the way in which animals are kept.

(3) Disqualification under this subsection disqualifies a person from dealing in animals.

(4) Disqualification under this subsection disqualifies a person—

    (a) from transporting animals, and

    (b) from arranging for the transport of animals.

(5) Disqualification under subsection (2), (3) or (4) may be imposed in relation to animals generally, or in relation to animals of one or more kinds.

(6) The court by which an order under subsection (1) is made may specify a period during which the offender may not make an application under section 43(1) for termination of the order.

...

(10) This section applies to an offence under any of sections 4, 5, 6(1) and (2), 7, 8, 9 and 13(6) and subsection (9).

37 Destruction in the interests of the animal

(1) The court by or before which a person is convicted of an offence under any of sections 4, 5, 6(1) and (2), 7, 8(1) and (2) and 9 may order the destruction of an animal in relation to

which the offence was committed if it is satisfied, on the basis of evidence given by a veterinary surgeon, that it is appropriate to do so in the interests of the animal.

(2) A court may not make an order under subsection (1) unless—

   (a) it has given the owner of the animal an opportunity to be heard, or
   (b) it is satisfied that it is not reasonably practicable to communicate with the owner.

(3) Where a court makes an order under subsection (1), it may—

   (a) appoint a person to carry out, or arrange for the carrying out of, the order;
   (b) require a person who has possession of the animal to deliver it up to enable the order to be carried out;
   (c) give directions with respect to the carrying out of the order (including directions about how the animal is to be dealt with until it is destroyed);
   (d) confer additional powers (including power to enter premises where the animal is being kept) for the purpose of, or in connection with, the carrying out of the order;
   (e) order the offender or another person to reimburse the expenses of carrying out the order.

(4) Where a court makes an order under subsection (1), each of the offender and, if different, the owner of the animal may—

   (a) in the case of an order made by a magistrates' court, appeal against the order to the Crown Court;
   (b) in the case of an order made by the Crown Court, appeal against the order to the Court of Appeal.

(5) Subsection (4) does not apply if the court by which the order is made directs that it is appropriate in the interests of the animal that the carrying out of the order should not be delayed.

(6) In subsection (1), the reference to an animal in relation to which an offence was committed includes, in the case of an offence under section 8(1) or (2), an animal which took part in an animal fight in relation to which the offence was committed.

38 Destruction of animals involved in fighting offences

(1) The court by or before which a person is convicted of an offence under section 8(1) or (2) may order the destruction of an animal in relation to which the offence was committed on grounds other than the interests of the animal.

(2) A court may not make an order under subsection (1) unless—

   (a) it has given the owner of the animal an opportunity to be heard, or
   (b) it is satisfied that it is not reasonably practicable to communicate with the owner.

(3) Where a court makes an order under subsection (1), it may—

   (a) appoint a person to carry out, or arrange for the carrying out of, the order;
   (b) require a person who has possession of the animal to deliver it up to enable the order to be carried out;
   (c) give directions with respect to the carrying out of the order (including directions about how the animal is to be dealt with until it is destroyed);
   (d) confer additional powers (including power to enter premises where the animal is being kept) for the purpose of, or in connection with, the carrying out of the order;
   (e) order the offender or another person to reimburse the expenses of carrying out the order.

(4) Where a court makes an order under subsection (1) in relation to an animal which is owned by a person other than the offender, that person may—

   (a) in the case of an order made by a magistrates' court, appeal against the order to the Crown Court;

(b) in the case of an order made by the Crown Court, appeal against the order to the Court of Appeal.

(5) In subsection (1), the reference to an animal in relation to which the offence was committed includes an animal which took part in an animal fight in relation to which the offence was committed.

BADGERS

All offences under the 1992 Act are triable summarily only. Section 1(1), (3), 2 and 3 carry a penalty of 6 months imprisonment/£5,000; All other offences carry a fine of £5,000 save for an offence under s 1(3) where the fine is £1,000. Where an offence was committed in respect of more than one badger the maximum fine which may be imposed shall be determined as if the person convicted had been convicted of a separate offence in respect of each badger. The court shall order the forfeiture of any badger or badger skin in respect of which the offence was committed and may, if they think fit, order the forfeiture of any weapon or article in respect of or by means of which the offence was committed.

Where a dog has been used in or was present at the commission of an offence under sections 1(1), 2 or 3 of the Act the court can order the destruction of the dog and/or disqualify the offender from having the custody of a dog (s 13).

Badgers' sett is defined at section 14 as any structure or place indicating current use by a badger. In *Green and Others v Director of Public Prosecutions* (2000) 164 JP 477 the High Court said that the phrase "badger sett" refers to the tunnels and chambers constructed by badgers and the entrance holes to those tunnels and chambers. It does not however include the cover above those tunnels and chambers up to and including the surface (but note that an offence under section 2 is likely to be charged in this situation). It may apply to other structures; where badgers, for example, occupy culverts or disused sheds as their shelter or refuge.

Protection of Badgers Act 1992, s 1, 2, 3, 4, 5, 6, 7, 8, 9, 11A and 13

Taking, injuring or killing badgers, s 1

(1) A person is guilty of an offence if, except as permitted by or under this Act, he wilfully kills, injures or takes, or attempts to kill, injure or take, a badger.

(2) If, in any proceedings for an offence under subsection (1) above consisting of attempting to kill, injure or take a badger, there is evidence from which it could reasonably be concluded that at the material time the accused was attempting to kill, injure or take a badger, he shall be presumed to have been attempting to kill, injure or take a badger unless the contrary is shown.

(3) A person is guilty of an offence if, except as permitted by or under this Act, he has in his possession or under his control any dead badger or any part of, or anything derived from, a dead badger.

(4) A person is not guilty of an offence under subsection (3) above if he shows that—

(a) the badger had not been killed, or had been killed otherwise than in contravention of the provisions of this Act or of the Badgers Act 1973; or

(b) the badger or other thing in his possession or control had been sold (whether to him or any other person) and, at the time of the purchase, the purchaser had had no reason to believe that the badger had been killed in contravention of any of those provisions.

(5) If a person is found committing an offence under this section on any land it shall be lawful for the owner or occupier of the land, or any servant of the owner or occupier, or any constable, to require that person forthwith to quit the land and also to give his name and address; and if that person on being so required wilfully remains on the land or refuses to give his full name or address he is guilty of an offence.

Cruelty, s 2

(1) A person is guilty of an offence if—

    (a) he cruelly ill-treats a badger;

    (b) he uses any badger tongs in the course of killing or taking, or attempting to kill or take, a badger;

    (c) except as permitted by or under this Act, he digs for a badger; or

    (d) he uses for the purpose of killing or taking a badger any firearm other than a smooth bore weapon of not less than 20 bore or a rifle using ammunition having a muzzle energy not less than 160 footpounds and a bullet weighing not less than 38 grains.

(2) If in any proceedings for an offence under subsection (1)(c) above there is evidence from which it could reasonably be concluded that at the material time the accused was digging for a badger he shall be presumed to have been digging for a badger unless the contrary is shown.

Interfering with badger setts, s 3

A person is guilty of an offence if, except as permitted by or under this Act, he interferes with a badger sett by doing any of the following things—

    (a) damaging a badger sett or any part of it;

    (b) destroying a badger sett;

    (c) obstructing access to, or any entrance of, a badger sett;

    (d) causing a dog to enter a badger sett; or

    (e) disturbing a badger when it is occupying a badger sett,

intending to do any of those things or being reckless as to whether his actions would have any of those consequences.

Selling and possession of live badgers, s 4

A person is guilty of an offence if, except as permitted by or under this Act, he sells a live badger or offers one for sale or has a live badger in his possession or under his control.

Marking and ringing, s 5

A person is guilty of an offence if, except as authorised by a licence under section 10 below, he marks, or attaches any ring, tag or other marking device to, a badger other than one which is lawfully in his possession by virtue of such a licence.

General exceptions, s 6

A person is not guilty of an offence under this Act by reason only of—

    (a) taking or attempting to take a badger which has been disabled otherwise than by his act and is taken or to be taken solely for the purpose of tending it;

    (b) killing or attempting to kill a badger which appears to be so seriously injured or in such a condition that to kill it would be an act of mercy;

    (c) unavoidably killing or injuring a badger as an incidental result of a lawful action;

    (d) doing anything which is authorised under the Animals (Scientific Procedures) Act 1986.

Exceptions from s. 1, s 7

(1) Subject to subsection (2) below, a person is not guilty of an offence under section 1(1) above by reason of—

    (a) killing or taking, or attempting to kill or take, a badger; or

    (b) injuring a badger in the course of taking it or attempting to kill or take it,

if he shows that his action was necessary for the purpose of preventing serious damage to land, crops, poultry or any other form of property.

(2) The defence provided by subsection (1) above does not apply in relation to any action taken at any time if it had become apparent, before that time, that the action would prove necessary for the purpose there mentioned and either—

    (a) a licence under section 10 below authorising that action had not been applied for as soon as reasonably practicable after that fact had become apparent; or

    (b) an application for such a licence had been determined.

Exceptions from s. 3, s 8

(1) Subject to subsection (2) below, a person is not guilty of an offence under section 3 above if he shows that his action was necessary for the purpose of preventing serious damage to land, crops, poultry or any other form of property.

(2) Subsection (2) of section 7 above applies to the defence in subsection (1) above as it applies to the defence in subsection (1) of that section.

(3) A person is not guilty of an offence under section 3(a), (c) or (e) above if he shows that his action was the incidental result of a lawful operation and could not reasonably have been avoided.

Exceptions from s. 4, s 9

A person is not guilty of an offence under section 4 above by reason of having a live badger in his possession or under his control if—

    (a) it is in his possession or under his control, as the case may be, in the course of his business as a carrier; or

    (b) it has been disabled otherwise than by his act and taken by him solely for the purpose of tending it and it is necessary for that purpose for it to remain in his possession or under his control, as the case may be.

Attempts, s 11A

(1) A person who attempts to commit an offence under this Act is guilty of the offence and is liable to be proceeded against and punished accordingly.

(2) A person who is in possession, for the purposes of committing an offence under this Act, of anything capable of being used for committing the offence is guilty of the offence and is liable to be proceeded against and punished accordingly.

(3) If, in any proceedings for an offence under section 1(1) above or section 1(6) above consisting of or involving an attempt to kill, injure or take a badger, there is evidence from which it could reasonably be concluded that at the material time a person was attempting to kill, injure or take a badger, he shall be presumed to have been attempting to kill, injure or take a badger unless the contrary is shown.

Powers of court where dog used or present at commission of offence, s 13

(1) Where a dog has been used in or was present at the commission of an offence under sections 1(1), 2 or 3 above, the court, on convicting the offender, may, in addition to or in substitution for any other punishment, make either or both of the following orders—

    (a) an order for the destruction or other disposal of the dog;

    (b) an order disqualifying the offender, for such period as it thinks fit, for having custody of a dog.

(2) Where the court makes an order under subsection (1)(a) above, it may—

    (a) appoint a person to undertake the destruction or other disposal of the dog and require any person having custody of the dog to deliver it up for that purpose; and

    (b) order the offender to pay such sum as the court may determine to be the reasonable expenses of destroying or otherwise disposing of the dog and of keeping it pending its destruction or disposal.

(3) Where an order under subsection (1)(a) above is made in relation to a dog owned by a person other than the offender, the owner of the dog may appeal to the Crown Court against the order.

(4) A dog shall not be destroyed pursuant to an order under subsection (1)(a) above—

(a) until the end of the period within which notice of appeal to the Crown Court against the order can be given; and

(b) if notice of appeal is given in that period, until the appeal is determined or withdrawn,

unless the owner of the dog gives notice to the court which made the order that he does not intend to appeal against it.

(5) A person who is disqualified for having custody of a dog by virtue of an order made under subsection (1)(b) above may, at any time after the end of the period of one year beginning with the date of the order, apply to the court that made it (or any magistrates' court acting [in the same local justice] 1 area as that court) for a direction terminating the disqualification.

(6) On an application under subsection (5) above the court may—

(a) having regard to the applicant's character, his conduct since the disqualification was imposed and any other circumstances of the case, grant or refuse the application; and

(b) order the applicant to pay all or any part of the costs of the application;

and where an application in respect of an order is refused no further application in respect of that order shall be entertained if made before the end of the period of one year beginning with the date of the refusal.

(7) Any person who—

(a) has custody of a dog in contravention of an order under subsection (1)(b) above; or

(b) fails to comply with a requirement imposed on him under subsection (2)(a) above,

is guilty of an offence.

DANGEROUS DOGS–CIVIL DESTRUCTION ORDER

There is no legal aid funding available to defend an application made under the 1871 Act, nor can costs be awarded from central funds if an application is successfully defended. An application for civil costs could be made under section 64 MCA 1980, but on ordinary principles of costs recovery it is likely to be refused. Provided the dog is within the jurisdiction a court can deal with an allegation that the behaviour complained of occurred outside the jurisdiction (*R (Shufflebottom) v CC Greater Manchester* [2003] EWHC 246 (Admin)). It should be noted that since 1 April 2005 the concept of petty sessional jurisdiction has been abolished, but the above case remains of interest in relation to national territorial jurisdiction. Proceedings must be commenced within 6 months of the behaviour complained of, and be proved to the civil standard.

Dangerous: ...in an exceptional case "a single act may... reveal a dangerous disposition." In other cases it may be that the Justices would not be satisfied if evidence was only produced of a single act, but would require further evidence to satisfy them that the dog was dangerous within the meaning of the 1871 Act. At any event, I am satisfied that the meaning of the word "dangerous" should not be confined as meaning dangerous to mankind or dangerous to the livestock identified for particular protection by Parliament in relation to the law of England. Dangerous is a word which the Magistrates are entitled to apply whatever the evidence is before them (*Briscoe v Shattock* (1998) 163 JP 201).

Dangerous Dogs Act 1871, s 2

Dangerous dogs may be destroyed, s 2

Any court of summary jurisdiction may take cognizance of a complaint that a dog is dangerous, and not kept under proper control, and if it appears to the court having cognizance of such complaint that such dog is dangerous, the court may make an order in a summary way directing the dog to be kept by the owner under proper control or destroyed.

DANGEROUS DOGS–CRIMINAL OFFENCES

The Dangerous Dogs Act 1991 creates a number of offences in relation to the ownership and control of certain breeds of dog. Sections 1 and 3 are summary only, carrying a maximum sentence of 6 months' imprisonment/£5000 fine, save where an offence under section 3 is aggravated by injury having been caused to a person. Aggravated offences under sections 3(1) and (3) are triable either-way and carry a maximum sentence of 2 years imprisonment.

Appointed day: 30 November 1991. **Control:** Plain evidence is required to show that control has passed to another (*Huddart* [1999] Crim LR 568), the passing of the dog lead to another may simply lead to a conclusion that there is joint control (*L v CPS*, unreported, 10 February 2010).

Dangerously out of control: defined in section 10(3): a dog shall be regarded as dangerously out of control on any occasion on which there are grounds for reasonable apprehension that it will injure any person, whether or not it actually does so. A danger to other dogs alone suffices (*Briscoe v Shattock* (1998) 163 JP 201), but normal hunting behaviour (killing rabbits etc) does not make a dog dangerous (*Sansom v Chief Constable of Kent* [1981] Crim LR 617). The fact that a dog had not previously displayed bad traits was a relevant but not determinative consideration (*Gedminintaite* [2008] EWCA Crim 814). It is irrelevant that the bad behaviour was not anticipated by the owner (*Bezzina* (1994) 158 JP 671).

Defence to section 1: There are no defences available under s 1, e.g. intoxication (*Director of Public Prosecutions v Kellett* (1994) 158 JP 1138) and unmuzzling for medical reasons (*Cichon v Director of Public Prosecutions* [1994] Crim LR 918).

Owner defence: s 3(2): It is not sufficient to leave control to a group (e.g. family unit), only when left with a named person will the defence be made out (*Huddart* [1999] Crim LR 568).

Public place: The inside of a vehicle which itself was in a public place, amounts to a public place (*Bates v Director of Public Prosecutions* [1994] 157 JP 1004). A driveway shared by neighbouring private properties was not a public place (*Bogdal* [2008] EWCA Crim 1).

Type: See *Crown Court at Knightsbridge, ex p Dune* [1993] 4 All ER 491.

Sentencing: A sentencing guideline applies in relation to all offenders sentenced on or after 20 August 2012 in relation to offences under section 3 of the Act. The guideline distinguishes between the basic and aggravated offences.

Ancillary orders of destruction and disqualification are available to the prosecution. In order to avoid destruction it was not sufficient simply to adduce petitions or letters of support from those with knowledge of the dog (*Holland* [2002] EWCA Crim 1585)). A court should not consider destruction under either s 1(3) or 3(1) unless it had first considered whether a contingent destruction order (s 4(A)(1) might be more appropriate (*Baballa* [2010] EWCA Crim 1950). Principles relating to contingent destruction orders can be found in *Flack* [2008] EWCA Crim 204). In R (Sandhu) v Isleworth Crown Court, Unreported 23 May 2012 the court held that there was no power to attach conditions to a contingent destruction order. Veterinary evidence or evidence from an animal behaviourist will normally be required describing the dog's general temperament and courts should ordinarily allow for an adjournment in order that such evidence can be placed before it (see *Harry* [2010] EWCA Crim 673).

Dangerous Dogs Act 1991, ss 3(1), 3(3)(a), where injury is caused

Step one–determining offence category

Category 1	Greater harm and higher culpability
Category 2	Greater harm and lower culpability; or lesser harm and higher culpability
Category 3	Lesser harm and lower culpability

The court should determine culpability and harm caused or intended, by reference only to the factors below, which comprise the principal factual elements of the offence. Where an offence does not fall squarely into a category, individual factors may require a degree of weighting before making an overall assessment and determining the appropriate offence category.

Factors indicating greater harm	Factors indicating higher culpability
Serious injury (which includes disease transmission and/or psychological harm) Sustained or repeated attack Victim is a child or otherwise vulnerable because of personal circumstances	**Statutory aggravating factors:** Offence racially or religiously aggravated Offence motivated by, or demonstrating, hostility to the victim based on his or her sexual orientation (or presumed sexual orientation) Offence motivated by, or demonstrating, hostility to the victim based on the victim's disability (or presumed disability) **Other aggravating factors:** Failure to respond to warnings or concerns expressed by others about the dog's behaviour Goading, or allowing goading, of dog Dog used as weapon or to intimidate victim Offence motivated by, or demonstrating, hostility based on the victim's age, sex, gender identity (or presumed gender identity)
Factors indicating lesser harm	**Factors indicating lower culpability**
Minor injury	Attempts made to regain control of dog and/or intervene Provocation of dog without fault of the offender Evidence of safety or control measures having been taken Mental disorder or learning disability, where linked to the commission of the offence

Step two–starting point and category range

Offence category	Starting point (applicable to all offenders)	Category range (applicable to all offenders)
Category 1	26 weeks' custody	Medium level community order–Crown Court (18 months' custody)
Category 2	Medium level community order	Band B fine–26 weeks' custody
Category 3	Band B fine	Discharge–Band C fine

The table below contains a non-exhaustive list of additional factual elements providing the context of the offence and factors relating to the offender. Identify whether any combination of these, or other relevant factors, should result in an upward or downward adjustment from the starting point. In some cases, having considered these factors, it may be appropriate to move outside the identified category range. When sentencing category 1 or 2 offences, the court should also consider the custody threshold as follows:

- has the custody threshold been passed?
- if so, is it unavoidable that a custodial sentence be imposed?
- if so, can that sentence be suspended?

When sentencing category 2 offences, the court should also consider the community order threshold as follows:

- has the community order threshold been passed?

Factors increasing seriousness	Factors reducing seriousness or reflecting personal mitigation
Statutory aggravating factors: Previous convictions, having regard to a) the nature of the offence to which the conviction relates and its relevance to the current offence; and b) the time that has elapsed since the conviction Offence committed whilst on bail **Other aggravating factors include:** Injury to another animal(s) Location of the offence Ongoing effect upon the victim and/or others Failure to take adequate precautions to prevent dog escaping Allowing person insufficiently experienced or trained, to be in charge of dog Ill treatment or failure to ensure welfare needs of dog, where not charged separately Dog known to be prohibited Lack or loss of control of dog due to influence of alcohol or drugs Offence committed against those working in the public sector or providing a service to the public Established evidence of community impact Failure to comply with current court orders Offence committed whilst on licence	No previous convictions or no relevant/recent convictions Isolated incident No previous complaints against, or incidents involving, the dog Remorse Good character and/or exemplary conduct Evidence of responsible ownership Determination and/or demonstration of steps taken to address addiction or offending behaviour Serious medical conditions requiring urgent, intensive or long-term treatment Age and/or lack of maturity where it affects the responsibility of the offender Mental disorder or learning disability, where not linked to the commission of the offence Sole or primary carer for dependent relatives

Additional steps:

Consider any factors which indicate a reduction, such as assistance to the prosecution; reduction for guilty plea; dangerousness; totality principle; compensation and ancillary orders; reasons; consideration for remand time.

Dangerous Dogs Act 1991, ss 3(1), 3(3)(b), where no injury is caused

Step one–determining offence category

Category 1	Greater harm and higher culpability
Category 2	Greater harm and lower culpability; or lesser harm and higher culpability
Category 3	Lesser harm and lower culpability

The court should determine culpability and harm caused or intended, by reference only to the factors below, which comprise the principal factual elements of the offence. Where an offence does not fall squarely into a category, individual factors may require a degree of weighting before making an overall assessment and determining the appropriate offence category.

Factors indicating greater harm	Factors indicating higher culpability
Presence of children or others who are vulnerable because of personal circumstances Injury to another animal(s)	**Statutory aggravating factors:** Offence racially or religiously aggravated Offence motivated by, or demonstrating, hostility to the victim based on his or her sexual orientation (or presumed sexual orientation) Offence motivated by, or demonstrating, hostility to the victim based on the victim's disability (or presumed disability) **Other aggravating factors:** Failure to respond to warnings or concerns expressed by others about the dog's behaviour Goading, or allowing goading, of dog Dog used as weapon or to intimidate victim Offence motivated by, or demonstrating, hostility based on the victim's age, sex, gender identity (or presumed gender identity)
Factors indicating lesser harm	**Factors indicating lower culpability**
Low risk to the public	Attempts made to regain control of dog and/or intervene Provocation of dog without fault of the offender Evidence of safety or control measures having been taken Mental disorder or learning disability, where linked to the commission of the offence

Step two—starting point and category range

Offence category	Starting point (applicable to all offenders)	Category range (applicable to all offenders)
Category 1	Medium level community order	Band C fine–26 weeks' custody
Category 2	Band B fine	Band A fine–Low level community order
Category 3	Band A fine	Discharge–Band B fine

The table below contains a non-exhaustive list of additional factual elements providing the context of the offence and factors relating to the offender. Identify whether any combination of these, or other relevant factors, should result in an upward or downward adjustment from the starting point. In some cases, having considered these factors, it may be appropriate to move outside the identified category range. When sentencing category 1 or 2 offences, the court should also consider the custody threshold as follows:

- has the custody threshold been passed?
- if so, is it unavoidable that a custodial sentence be imposed?
- if so, can that sentence be suspended?

When sentencing category 2 offences, the court should also consider the community order threshold as follows:

- has the community order threshold been passed?

Factors increasing seriousness	Factors reducing seriousness or reflecting personal mitigation
Statutory aggravating factors: Previous convictions, having regard to a) the nature of the offence to which the conviction relates and its relevance to the current offence; and b) the time that has elapsed since the conviction Offence committed whilst on bail **Other aggravating factors include:** Location of the offence Ongoing effect upon the victim and/or others Failure to take adequate precautions to prevent dog escaping Allowing person insufficiently experienced or trained, to be in charge of dog Ill treatment or failure to ensure welfare needs of dog, where not charged separately Dog known to be prohibited Lack or loss of control of dog due to the influence of alcohol or drugs Offence committed against those working in the public sector or providing a service to the public Established evidence of community impact Failure to comply with current court orders Offence committed whilst on licence	No previous convictions or no relevant/recent convictions Isolated incident No previous complaints against, or incidents involving, the dog Remorse Good character and/or exemplary conduct Evidence of responsible ownership Determination and/or demonstration of steps taken to address addiction or offending behaviour Serious medical conditions requiring urgent, intensive or long-term treatment Age and/or lack of maturity where it affects the responsibility of the offender Mental disorder or learning disability, where not linked to the commission of the offence Sole or primary carer for dependent relatives

Additional steps:

Consider any factors which indicate a reduction, such as assistance to the prosecution; reduction for guilty plea; dangerousness; totality principle; compensation and ancillary orders; reasons; consideration for remand time.

Dangerous Dogs Act 1991, ss 1, 3, 4, and 4A

Dogs bred for fighting, s 1

(1) This section applies to—

    (a) any dog of the type known as the pit bull terrier;

    (b) any dog of the type known as the Japanese tosa; and

    (c) any dog of any type designated for the purposes of this section by an order of the Secretary of State, being a type appearing to him to be bred for fighting or to have the characteristics of a type bred for that purpose.

(2) No person shall—

    (a) breed, or breed from, a dog to which this section applies;

    (b) sell or exchange such a dog or offer, advertise or expose such a dog for sale or exchange;

    (c) make or offer to make a gift of such a dog or advertise or expose such a dog as a gift;

    (d) allow such a dog of which he is the owner or of which he is for the time being in charge to be in a public place without being muzzled and kept on a lead; or

    (e) abandon such a dog of which he is the owner or, being the owner or for the time being in charge of such a dog, allow it to stray.

(3) After such day as the Secretary of State may by order appoint for the purposes of this subsection no person shall have any dog to which this section applies in his possession or custody except—

    (a) in pursuance of the power of seizure conferred by the subsequent provisions of this Act; or

    (b) in accordance with an order for its destruction made under those provisions;

but the Secretary of State shall by order make a scheme for the payment to the owners of such dogs who arrange for them to be destroyed before that day of sums specified in or determined under the scheme in respect of those dogs and the cost of their destruction.

  (4) Subsection (2)(b) and (c) above shall not make unlawful anything done with a view to the dog in question being removed from the United Kingdom before the day appointed under subsection (3) above.

  (5) The Secretary of State may by order provide that the prohibition in subsection (3) above shall not apply in such cases and subject to compliance with such conditions as are specified in the order and any such provision may take the form of a scheme of exemption containing such arrangements (including provision for the payment of charges or fees) as he thinks appropriate.

  (6) A scheme under subsection (3) or (5) above may provide for specified functions under the scheme to be discharged by such persons or bodies as the Secretary of State thinks appropriate.

  (7) Any person who contravenes this section is guilty of an offence and liable on summary conviction to imprisonment for a term not exceeding six months or a fine not exceeding level 5 on the standard scale or both except that a person who publishes an advertisement in contravention of subsection (2)(b) or (c)—

    (a) shall not on being convicted be liable to imprisonment if he shows that he published the advertisement to the order of someone else and did not himself devise it; and

    (b) shall not be convicted if, in addition, he shows that he did not know and had no reasonable cause to suspect that it related to a dog to which this section applies.

  (8) An order under subsection (1)(c) above adding dogs of any type to those to which this section applies may provide that subsections (3) and (4) above shall apply in relation to those dogs with the substitution for the day appointed under subsection (3) of a later day specified in the order.

Keeping dogs under proper control, s 3

  (1) If a dog is dangerously out of control in a public place—

    (a) the owner; and

    (b) if different, the person for the time being in charge of the dog,

is guilty of an offence, or, if the dog while so out of control injures any person, an aggravated offence, under this subsection.

  (2) In proceedings for an offence under subsection (1) above against a person who is the owner of a dog but was not at the material time in charge of it, it shall be a defence for the accused to prove that the dog was at the material time in the charge of a person whom he reasonably believed to be a fit and proper person to be in charge of it.

  (3) If the owner or, if different, the person for the time being in charge of a dog allows it to enter a place which is not a public place but where it is not permitted to be and while it is there—

    (a) it injures any person; or

    (b) there are grounds for reasonable apprehension that it will do so,

he is guilty of an offence, or, if the dog injures any person, an aggravated offence, under this subsection.

  (4) A person guilty of an offence under subsection (1) or (3) above other than an aggravated offence is liable on summary conviction to imprisonment for a term not exceeding six

months or a fine not exceeding level 5 on the standard scale or both; and a person guilty of an aggravated offence under either of those subsections is liable—

   (a) on summary conviction, to imprisonment for a term not exceeding six months or a fine not exceeding the statutory maximum or both;

   (b) on conviction on indictment, to imprisonment for a term not exceeding two years or a fine or both.

(5) It is hereby declared for the avoidance of doubt that an order under section 2 of the Dogs Act 1871 (order on complaint that dog is dangerous and not kept under proper control)—

   (a) may be made whether or not the dog is shown to have injured any person; and

   (b) may specify the measures to be taken for keeping the dog under proper control, whether by muzzling, keeping on a lead, excluding it from specified places or otherwise.

(6) If it appears to a court on a complaint under section 2 of the said Act of 1871 that the dog to which the complaint relates is a male and would be less dangerous if neutered the court may under that section make an order requiring it to be neutered.

(7) The reference in section 1(3) of the Dangerous Dogs Act 1989 (penalties) to failing to comply with an order under section 2 of the said Act of 1871 to keep a dog under proper control shall include a reference to failing to comply with any other order made under that section; but no order shall be made under that section by virtue of subsection (6) above where the matters complained of arose before the coming into force of that subsection.

Destruction and disqualification orders, s 4

(1) Where a person is convicted of an offence under section 1 or 3(1) or (3) above or of an offence under an order made under section 2 above the court—

   (a) may order the destruction of any dog in respect of which the offence was committed and, subject to subsection (1A) below, shall do so in the case of an offence under section 1 or an aggravated offence under section 3(1) or (3) above; and

   (b) may order the offender to be disqualified, for such period as the court thinks fit, for having custody of a dog.

(1A) Nothing in subsection (1)(a) above shall require the court to order the destruction of a dog if the court is satisfied—

   (a) that the dog would not constitute a danger to public safety; and

   (b) where the dog was born before 30th November 1991 and is subject to the prohibition in section 1 (3) above, that there is a good reason why the dog has not been exempted from that prohibition.

(2) Where a court makes an order under subsection (1)(a) above for the destruction of a dog owned by a person other than the offender, the owner may appeal to the Crown Court against the order.

(3) A dog shall not be destroyed pursuant to an order under subsection (1)(a) above—

   (a) until the end of the period for giving notice of appeal against the conviction or, against the order; and

   (b) if notice of appeal is given within that period, until the appeal is determined or withdrawn,

unless the offender and, in a case to which subsection (2) above applies, the owner of the dog give notice to the court that made the order that there is to be no appeal.

(4) Where a court makes an order under subsection (1)(a) above it may—

   (a) appoint a person to undertake the destruction of the dog and require any person having custody of it to deliver it up for that purpose; and

    (b) order the offender to pay such sum as the court may determine to be the reasonable expenses of destroying the dog and of keeping it pending its destruction.

(5) Any sum ordered to be paid under subsection (4)(b) above shall be treated for the purposes of enforcement as if it were a fine imposed on conviction.

(6) Any person who is disqualified for having custody of a dog by virtue of an order under subsection (1)(b) above may, at any time after the end of the period of one year beginning with the date of the order, apply to the court that made it (or a magistrates' court acting in the same local justice area as that court) for a direction terminating the disqualification.

(7) On an application under subsection (6) above the court may—

    (a) having regard to the applicant's character, his conduct since the disqualification was imposed and any other circumstances of the case, grant or refuse the application; and

    (b) order the applicant to pay all or any part of the costs of the application;

and where an application in respect of an order is refused no further application in respect of that order shall be entertained if made before the end of the period of one year beginning with the date of the refusal.

(8) Any person who—

    (a) has custody of a dog in contravention of an order under subsection (1)(b) above; or

    (b) fails to comply with a requirement imposed on him under subsection (4)(a) above,

is guilty of an offence and liable on summary conviction to a fine not exceeding level 5 on the standard scale.

Contingent destruction orders, s 4A

(1) Where—

    (a) a person is convicted of an offence under section 1 above or an aggravated offence under section 3(1) or (3) above;

    (b) the court does not order the destruction of the dog under section 4(1)(a) above; and

    (c) in the case of an offence under section 1 above, the dog is subject to the prohibition in section 1(3) above.

the court shall order that, unless the dog is exempted from that prohibition within the requisite period, the dog shall be destroyed.

(2) Where an order is made under subsection (1) above in respect of a dog, and the dog is not exempted from the prohibition in section 1(3) above within the requisite period, the court may extend that period.

(3) Subject to subsection (2) above, the requisite period for the purposes of such an order is the period of two months beginning with the date of the order.

(4) Where a person is convicted of an offence under section 3(1) or (3) above, the court may order that, unless the owner of the dog keeps it under proper control, the dog shall be destroyed.

(5) An order under subsection (4) above—

    (a) may specify the measures to be taken for keeping the dog under proper control, whether by muzzling, keeping on a lead, excluding it from specified places or otherwise; and

    (b) if it appears to the court that the dog is a male and would be less dangerous if neutered, may require it to be neutered.

(6) Subsections (2) to (4) of section 4 above shall apply in relation to an order under subsection (1) or (4) above as they apply in relation to an order under subsection (1)(a) of that section.

DOG WORRYING LIVESTOCK

Dogs (Protection of Livestock) Act 1953, s 1

(1) Subject to the provisions of this section, if a dog worries livestock on any agricultural land, the owner of the dog, and, if it is in the charge of a person other than its owner, that person also, shall be guilty of an offence under this Act.

(2) For the purposes of this Act worrying livestock means—

    (a) attacking livestock, or

    (b) chasing livestock in such a way as may reasonably be expected to cause injury or suffering to the livestock or, in the case of females, abortion, or loss of or diminution in their produce, or

    (c) being at large (that is to say not on a lead or otherwise under close control) in a field or enclosure in which there are sheep.

(2A) Subsection (2)(c) of this section shall not apply in relation to—

    (a) a dog owned by, or in the charge of, the occupier of the field or enclosure or the owner of the sheep or a person authorised by either of those persons; or

    (b) a police dog, a guide dog, trained sheep dog, a working gun dog or a pack of hounds.

(3) A person shall not be guilty of an offence under this Act by reason of anything done by a dog, if at the material time the livestock are trespassing on the land in question and the dog is owned by, or in the charge of, the occupier of that land or a person authorised by him, except in a case where the said person causes the dog to attack the livestock.

(4) The owner of a dog shall not be convicted of an offence under this Act in respect of the worrying of livestock by the dog if he proves that at the time when the dog worried the livestock it was in the charge of some other person, whom he reasonably believed to be a fit and proper person to be in charge of the dog.

(5) Where the Minister is satisfied that it is inexpedient that subsection (1) of this section should apply to land in any particular area, being an area appearing to him to consist wholly or mainly of mountain, hill, moor, heath or down land, he may by order direct that subsection shall not apply to land in that area.

(6) A person guilty of an offence under this Act shall be liable on summary conviction—

    (a) except in a case falling within the succeeding paragraph, to a fine not exceeding level 3 on the standard scale;

    (b) in a case where the person in question has previously been convicted of an offence under this Act in respect of the same dog, to a fine not exceeding level 3 on the standard scale.

GUARD DOGS

Offences under sections 1 and 2 of the Act are triable summarily only; both with a maximum penalty of a level 5 fine (£5,000).

Guard Dogs Act 1975, ss 1, 2, and 7

Control of guard dogs, s 1

(1) A person shall not use or permit the use of a guard dog at any premises unless a person ("the handler") who is capable of controlling the dog is present on the premises and the dog is under the control of the handler at all times while it is being so used except while it is secured so that it is not at liberty to go freely about the premises.

(2) The handler of a guard dog shall keep the dog under his control at all times while it is being used as a guard dog at any premises except—

    (a) while another handler has control over the dog; or

(b) while the dog is secured so that it is not at liberty to go freely about the premises.

(3) A person shall not use or permit the use of a guard dog at any premises unless a notice containing a warning that a guard dog is present is clearly exhibited at each entrance to the premises.

Restriction on keeping guard dogs without a licence, s 2

(1) A person shall not keep a dog at guard dog kennels unless he holds a licence under section 3 of this Act in respect of the kennels.

(2) A person shall not use or permit the use at any premises of a guard dog if he knows or has reasonable cause to suspect that the dog (when not being used as a guard dog) is normally kept at guard dog kernels in breach of subsection (1) of this section.

Interpretation, s 7

In this Act, unless the context otherwise requires—

"agricultural land" has the same meaning as in the Dogs (Protection of Livestock) Act 1953;

"guard dog" means a dog which is being used to protect—

(a) premises; or
(b) property kept on the premises; or
(c) a person guarding the premises or such property;

"guard dog kennels" means a place where a person in the course of business keeps a dog which (notwithstanding that it is used for other purposes) is used as a guard dog elsewhere, other than a dog which is used as a guard dog only at premises belonging to its owner;

"premises" means land other than agricultural land and land within the curtilage of a dwelling-house, and buildings, including parts of buildings, other than dwelling-houses.

WILD MAMMALS

All section 1 offences are triable summarily only with a maximum sentence of 6 months' imprisonment and/or £5,000 fine. If the offence was committed against more than one wild mammal a fine of up to £5,000 can be imposed in respect to each mammal (s 5(2)).Vehicles or equipment used in the commission of the offence may be confiscated (s 6(1))).

Wild Mammals (Protection) Act 1996, s 1

Offences, s 1

If, save as permitted by this Act, any person mutilates, kicks, beats, nails or otherwise impales, stabs, burns, stones, crushes, drowns, drags or asphyxiates any wild mammal with intent to inflict unnecessary suffering he shall be guilty of an offence.

CORRUPTION AND JUSTICE

BAIL, FAILING TO SURRENDER

Triable either-way, 3 months/£5,000 for summary proceedings, 12 month imprisonment for offence on indictment. In the event that the defendant facing bail proceedings has been extradited back to the United Kingdom it is important to ensure that any Bail Act charge was specified in the extradition warrant, otherwise the rule of speciality (Extradition Act 2003, s 151) will apply (*Jones* [2011] EWCA Crim 107). A decision to lay a charge in relation to court imposed bail lies ultimately with the court itself.

De minimis: In *Scott* [2007] EWCA Crim 2757 the court rejected an argument that surrendering to bail 30 minutes late was de minimis so as to make proceeding with a Bail Act charge Wednesbury unreasonable. The court held: 'We are prepared for the sake of argument to accept the possibility that there could be circumstances where a defendant's late arrival at court was so truly marginal that it would be Wednesbury unreasonable to pursue it but it would be a rare case.' In *Gateshead Justices, ex p Usher* [1981] Crim LR 491, a period of seven minutes was held to be de minimis; however, in Scott the court said that no gloss should be placed on the clear wording in the Bail Act and Usher established no clear principle of law, observing that: '... there could be circumstances where a defendant's late arrival at court was so truly marginal that it would be Wednesbury unreasonable to pursue it but it would be a rare case... Even if a delay is small it can still cause inconvenience and waste of time. If a culture of lateness is tolerated the results can be cumulative and bad for the administration of justice.'

Reasonable excuse: In *Liverpool Justices, ex p Santos* The Times, 23 January 1997 the court held that reliance on mistaken information provided by a solicitor may be found a reasonable excuse for failing to surrender. The court went on to say that all relevant factors would need to be considered and a mistake on the part of a solicitor in calculating the bail date did not automatically excuse the defendant's non-attendance. A failure to give the defendant a written bail notice does not amount to a reasonable excuse. A genuine, albeit mistaken, belief that bail was to another date would not amount to a reasonable excuse (*Laidlaw v Atkinson* The Times, 2 August 1986). A reasonable excuse need only be proved to the civil standard (*Carr-Bryant* (1944) 29 Cr App R 76). **Surrender:** A person who had overtly [subjected] himself to the court's direction (see *Central Criminal Court, ex p Guney* [1995] 2 All ER 577), or reported to court officials as directed, had surrendered to custody (see *Director of Public Prosecutions v Richards* [1988] QB 701). If the defendant later left court, no offence would be committed (although the court could issue a warrant for arrest). It is not essential that there be a formal surrender to an official (*Rumble* [2003] EWCA Crim 770), but simply arriving at the court at the proper time may not be enough (*Render* (1987) 84 Cr App R 294). For a more recent analysis of the authorities in relation to this issue see *Evans* [2011] EWCA Crim 2842. **Mitigation:** Being acquitted of the offence which he was on bail for does not mitigate the penalty for failing to surrender (*Maguire* [1993] RTR 306).

Offence seriousness (culpability and harm)		
A. Identify the appropriate starting point		
Starting points based on first time offender pleading not guilty		
Example of nature of activity	**Starting point**	**Range**
Surrenders late on day but case proceeds as planned	Band A fine	Band A fine to band B fine
Negligent or non-deliberate failure to attend causing delay and/or interference with the administration of justice	Band C fine	Band B fine to medium level community order
Deliberate failure to attend causing delay and/or interference with the administration of justice The type and degree of harm actually caused will affect where in the range the case falls	14 days custody	Low level community order to 10 weeks custody

Offence seriousness (culpability and harm) **B. Consider the effect of aggravating and mitigating factors** (other than those within examples above) The following may be particularly relevant but **these lists are not exhaustive**	
Factors indicating higher culpability	**Factors indicating lower culpability**
1. Serious attempts to evade justice	Where not amounting to a defence:
2. Determined attempt seriously to undermine the course of justice	1. Misunderstanding
	2. Failure to comprehend bail significance or requirements
3. Previous relevant convictions and/or breach of court orders or police bail	3. Caring responsibilities
Factor indicating greater degree of harm	**Factor indicating lesser degree of harm**
1. Lengthy absence	1. Prompt voluntary surrender

Magistrates' Courts Act 1980, s 135

(1) A magistrates' court that has power to commit to prison a person convicted of an offence, or would have that power but for section 82 or 88 above, may order him to be detained within the precincts of the court-house or at any police station until such hour, not later than 8 o'clock in the evening of the day on which the order is made, as the court may direct, and, if it does so, shall not, where it has power to commit him to prison or detention if aged 18–20 years, exercise that power.

(2) A court shall not make such an order under this section as will deprive the offender of a reasonable opportunity of returning to his abode on the day of the order.

Bail Act 1976, s 6(1)–(2)

(1) If a person who has been released on bail in criminal proceedings fails without reasonable cause to surrender to custody he shall be guilty of an offence.

(2) If a person who—

    (a) has been released on bail in criminal proceedings, and

    (b) having reasonable cause therefor [sic], has failed to surrender to custody, fails to surrender to custody at the appointed place as soon after the appointed time as is reasonably practicable he shall be guilty of an offence.

BRIBERY

Sentence: See section 11. See *Patel* [2012] EWCA Crim 1243 for sentencing in the first case prosecuted under the Act.

Bribery Act 2010, ss 1–15

1 Offences of bribing another person

(1) A person ("P") is guilty of an offence if either of the following cases applies.

(2) Case 1 is where—

    (a) P offers, promises or gives a financial or other advantage to another person, and

    (b) P intends the advantage—

        (iii) to induce a person to perform improperly a relevant function or activity, or

        (ii) to reward a person for the improper performance of such a function or activity.

(3) Case 2 is where—

    (a) P offers, promises or gives a financial or other advantage to another person, and

    (b) P knows or believes that the acceptance of the advantage would itself constitute the improper performance of a relevant function or activity.

(4) In case 1 it does not matter whether the person to whom the advantage is offered, promised or given is the same person as the person who is to perform, or has performed, the function or activity concerned.

(5) In cases 1 and 2 it does not matter whether the advantage is offered, promised or given by P directly or through a third party.

2 Offences relating to being bribed

(1) A person ("R") is guilty of an offence if any of the following cases applies.

(2) Case 3 is where R requests, agrees to receive or accepts a financial or other advantage intending that, in consequence, a relevant function or activity should be performed improperly (whether by R or another person).

(3) Case 4 is where—

   (a) R requests, agrees to receive or accepts a financial or other advantage, and
   (b) the request, agreement or acceptance itself constitutes the improper performance by R of a relevant function or activity.

(4) Case 5 is where R requests, agrees to receive or accepts a financial or other advantage as a reward for the improper performance (whether by R or another person) of a relevant function or activity.

(5) Case 6 is where, in anticipation of or in consequence of R requesting, agreeing to receive or accepting a financial or other advantage, a relevant function or activity is performed improperly—

   (a) by R, or
   (b) by another person at R's request or with R's assent or acquiescence.

(6) In cases 3 to 6 it does not matter—

   (a) whether R requests, agrees to receive or accepts (or is to request, agree to receive or accept) the advantage directly or through a third party,
   (b) whether the advantage is (or is to be) for the benefit of R or another person.

(7) In cases 4 to 6 it does not matter whether R knows or believes that the performance of the function or activity is improper.

(8) In case 6, where a person other than R is performing the function or activity, it also does not matter whether that person knows or believes that the performance of the function or activity is improper.

3 Function or activity to which bribe relates

(1) For the purposes of this Act a function or activity is a relevant function or activity if—

   (a) it falls within subsection (2), and
   (b) meets one or more of conditions A to C.

(2) The following functions and activities fall within this subsection—

   (a) any function of a public nature,
   (b) any activity connected with a business,
   (c) any activity performed in the course of a person's employment,
   (d) any activity performed by or on behalf of a body of persons (whether corporate or unincorporate).

(3) Condition A is that a person performing the function or activity is expected to perform it in good faith.

(4) Condition B is that a person performing the function or activity is expected to perform it impartially.

(5) Condition C is that a person performing the function or activity is in a position of trust by virtue of performing it.

(6) A function or activity is a relevant function or activity even if it—

    (a) has no connection with the United Kingdom, and

    (b) is performed in a country or territory outside the United Kingdom.

(7) In this section "business" includes trade or profession.

4 Improper performance to which bribe relates

(1) For the purposes of this Act a relevant function or activity—

    (a) is performed improperly if it is performed in breach of a relevant expectation, and

    (b) is to be treated as being performed improperly if there is a failure to perform the function or activity and that failure is itself a breach of a relevant expectation.

(2) In subsection (1) "relevant expectation"—

    (a) in relation to a function or activity which meets condition A or B, means the expectation mentioned in the condition concerned, and

    (b) in relation to a function or activity which meets condition C, means any expectation as to the manner in which, or the reasons for which, the function or activity will be performed that arises from the position of trust mentioned in that condition.

(3) Anything that a person does (or omits to do) arising from or in connection with that person's past performance of a relevant function or activity is to be treated for the purposes of this Act as being done (or omitted) by that person in the performance of that function or activity.

5 Expectation test

(1) For the purposes of sections 3 and 4, the test of what is expected is a test of what a reasonable person in the United Kingdom would expect in relation to the performance of the type of function or activity concerned.

(2) In deciding what such a person would expect in relation to the performance of a function or activity where the performance is not subject to the law of any part of the United Kingdom, any local custom or practice is to be disregarded unless it is permitted or required by the written law applicable to the country or territory concerned.

(3) In subsection (2) "written law" means law contained in—

    (a) any written constitution, or provision made by or under legislation, applicable to the country or territory concerned, or

    (b) any judicial decision which is so applicable and is evidenced in published written sources.

6 Bribery of foreign public officials

(1) A person ("P") who bribes a foreign public official ("F") is guilty of an offence if P's intention is to influence F in F's capacity as a foreign public official.

(2) P must also intend to obtain or retain—

    (a) business, or

    (b) an advantage in the conduct of business.

(3) P bribes F if, and only if—

    (a) directly or through a third party, P offers, promises or gives any financial or other advantage—

        (i) to F, or

        (ii) to another person at F's request or with F's assent or acquiescence, and

    (b) F is neither permitted nor required by the written law applicable to F to be influenced in F's capacity as a foreign public official by the offer, promise or gift.

(4) References in this section to influencing F in F's capacity as a foreign public official mean influencing F in the performance of F's functions as such an official, which includes—

(a) any omission to exercise those functions, and

(b) any use of F's position as such an official, even if not within F's authority.

(5) "Foreign public official" means an individual who—

    (a) holds a legislative, administrative or judicial position of any kind, whether appointed or elected, of a country or territory outside the United Kingdom (or any subdivision of such a country or territory),

    (b) exercises a public function—

        (i) for or on behalf of a country or territory outside the United Kingdom (or any subdivision of such a country or territory), or

        (ii) for any public agency or public enterprise of that country or territory (or subdivision), or

    (c) is an official or agent of a public international organisation.

(6) "Public international organisation" means an organisation whose members are any of the following—

    (a) countries or territories,

    (b) governments of countries or territories,

    (c) other public international organisations,

    (d) a mixture of any of the above.

(7) For the purposes of subsection (3)(b), the written law applicable to F is—

    (a) where the performance of the functions of F which P intends to influence would be subject to the law of any part of the United Kingdom, the law of that part of the United Kingdom,

    (b) where paragraph (a) does not apply and F is an official or agent of a public international organisation, the applicable written rules of that organisation,

    (c) where paragraphs (a) and (b) do not apply, the law of the country or territory in relation to which F is a foreign public official so far as that law is contained in—

        (i) any written constitution, or provision made by or under legislation, applicable to the country or territory concerned, or

        (ii) any judicial decision which is so applicable and is evidenced in published written sources.

(8) For the purposes of this section, a trade or profession is a business.

7 Failure of commercial organisations to prevent bribery

(1) A relevant commercial organisation ("C") is guilty of an offence under this section if a person ("A") associated with C bribes another person intending—

    (a) to obtain or retain business for C, or

    (b) to obtain or retain an advantage in the conduct of business for C.

(2) But it is a defence for C to prove that C had in place adequate procedures designed to prevent persons associated with C from undertaking such conduct.

(3) For the purposes of this section, A bribes another person if, and only if, A—

    (a) is, or would be, guilty of an offence under section 1 or 6 (whether or not A has been prosecuted for such an offence), or

    (b) would be guilty of such an offence if section 12(2)(c) and (4) were omitted.

(4) See section 8 for the meaning of a person associated with C and see section 9 for a duty on the Secretary of State to publish guidance.

(5) In this section—

"partnership" means—

    (a) a partnership within the Partnership Act 1890, or

(b) a limited partnership registered under the Limited Partnerships Act 1907,

or a firm or entity of a similar character formed under the law of a country or territory outside the United Kingdom,

"relevant commercial organisation" means—

    (a) a body which is incorporated under the law of any part of the United Kingdom and which carries on a business (whether there or elsewhere),

    (b) any other body corporate (wherever incorporated) which carries on a business, or part of a business, in any part of the United Kingdom,

    (c) a partnership which is formed under the law of any part of the United Kingdom and which carries on a business (whether there or elsewhere), or

    (d) any other partnership (wherever formed) which carries on a business, or part of a business, in any part of the United Kingdom,

and, for the purposes of this section, a trade or profession is a business.

8 Meaning of associated person

(1) For the purposes of section 7, a person ("A") is associated with C if (disregarding any bribe under consideration) A is a person who performs services for or on behalf of C.

(2) The capacity in which A performs services for or on behalf of C does not matter.

(3) Accordingly A may (for example) be C's employee, agent or subsidiary.

(4) Whether or not A is a person who performs services for or on behalf of C is to be determined by reference to all the relevant circumstances and not merely by reference to the nature of the relationship between A and C.

(5) But if A is an employee of C, it is to be presumed unless the contrary is shown that A is a person who performs services for or on behalf of C.

9 Guidance about commercial organisations preventing bribery

(1) The Secretary of State must publish guidance about procedures that relevant commercial organisations can put in place to prevent persons associated with them from bribing as mentioned in section 7(1).

(2) The Secretary of State may, from time to time, publish revisions to guidance under this section or revised guidance.

(3) The Secretary of State must consult the Scottish Ministers before publishing anything under this section.

(4) Publication under this section is to be in such manner as the Secretary of State considers appropriate.

(5) Expressions used in this section have the same meaning as in section 7.

10 Consent to prosecution

(1) No proceedings for an offence under this Act may be instituted in England and Wales except by or with the consent of—

    (a) the Director of Public Prosecutions ,

    (b) the Director of the Serious Fraud Office, or

    (c) the Director of Revenue and Customs Prosecutions.

(2) No proceedings for an offence under this Act may be instituted in Northern Ireland except by or with the consent of—

    (a) the Director of Public Prosecutions for Northern Ireland, or

    (b) the Director of the Serious Fraud Office.

(3) No proceedings for an offence under this Act may be instituted in England and Wales or Northern Ireland by a person—

(a) who is acting—

    (i) under the direction or instruction of the Director of Public Prosecutions, the Director of the Serious Fraud Office or the Director of Revenue and Customs Prosecutions, or

    (ii) on behalf of such a Director, or

(b) to whom such a function has been assigned by such a Director, except with the consent of the Director concerned to the institution of the proceedings.

(4) The Director of Public Prosecutions, the Director of the Serious Fraud Office and the Director of Revenue and Customs Prosecutions must exercise personally any function under subsection (1), (2) or (3) of giving consent.

(5) The only exception is if—

(a) the Director concerned is unavailable, and

(b) there is another person who is designated in writing by the Director acting personally as the person who is authorised to exercise any such function when the Director is unavailable.

(6) In that case, the other person may exercise the function but must do so personally.

(7) Subsections (4) to (6) apply instead of any other provisions which would otherwise have enabled any function of the Director of Public Prosecutions , the Director of the Serious Fraud Office or the Director of Revenue and Customs Prosecutions under subsection (1), (2) or (3) of giving consent to be exercised by a person other than the Director concerned.

(8) No proceedings for an offence under this Act may be instituted in Northern Ireland by virtue of section 36 of the Justice (Northern Ireland) Act 2002 (delegation of the functions of the Director of Public Prosecutions for Northern Ireland to persons other than the Deputy Director) except with the consent of the Director of Public Prosecutions for Northern Ireland to the institution of the proceedings.

(9) The Director of Public Prosecutions for Northern Ireland must exercise personally any function under subsection (2) or (8) of giving consent unless the function is exercised personally by the Deputy Director of Public Prosecutions for Northern Ireland by virtue of section 30(4) or (7) of the Act of 2002 (powers of Deputy Director to exercise functions of Director).

(10) Subsection (9) applies instead of section 36 of the Act of 2002 in relation to the functions of the Director of Public Prosecutions for Northern Ireland and the Deputy Director of Public Prosecutions for Northern Ireland under, or (as the case may be) by virtue of, subsections (2) and (8) above of giving consent.

11 Penalties

(1) An individual guilty of an offence under section 1, 2 or 6 is liable—

(a) on summary conviction, to imprisonment for a term not exceeding 12 months, or to a fine not exceeding the statutory maximum, or to both,

(b) on conviction on indictment, to imprisonment for a term not exceeding 10 years, or to a fine, or to both.

(2) Any other person guilty of an offence under section 1, 2 or 6 is liable—

(a) on summary conviction, to a fine not exceeding the statutory maximum,

(b) on conviction on indictment, to a fine.

(3) A person guilty of an offence under section 7 is liable on conviction on indictment to a fine.

(4) The reference in subsection (1)(a) to 12 months is to be read—

(a) in its application to England and Wales in relation to an offence committed before the commencement of section 154(1) of the Criminal Justice Act 2003, and

(b) in its application to Northern Ireland, as a reference to 6 months.

12 Offences under this Act: territorial application

(1) An offence is committed under section 1, 2 or 6 in England and Wales, Scotland or Northern Ireland if any act or omission which forms part of the offence takes place in that part of the United Kingdom.

(2) Subsection (3) applies if—

    (a) no act or omission which forms part of an offence under section 1, 2 or 6 takes place in the United Kingdom,

    (b) a person's acts or omissions done or made outside the United Kingdom would form part of such an offence if done or made in the United Kingdom, and

    (c) that person has a close connection with the United Kingdom.

(3) In such a case—

    (a) the acts or omissions form part of the offence referred to in subsection (2)(a), and

    (b) proceedings for the offence may be taken at any place in the United Kingdom.

(4) For the purposes of subsection (2)(c) a person has a close connection with the United Kingdom if, and only if, the person was one of the following at the time the acts or omissions concerned were done or made—

    (a) a British citizen,

    (b) a British overseas territories citizen,

    (c) a British National (Overseas),

    (d) a British Overseas citizen,

    (e) a person who under the British Nationality Act 1981 was a British subject,

    (f) a British protected person within the meaning of that Act,

    (g) an individual ordinarily resident in the United Kingdom,

    (h) a body incorporated under the law of any part of the United Kingdom,

    (i) a Scottish partnership.

(5) An offence is committed under section 7 irrespective of whether the acts or omissions which form part of the offence take place in the United Kingdom or elsewhere.

(6) Where no act or omission which forms part of an offence under section 7 takes place in the United Kingdom, proceedings for the offence may be taken at any place in the United Kingdom.

(7) Subsection (8) applies if, by virtue of this section, proceedings for an offence are to be taken in Scotland against a person.

(8) Such proceedings may be taken—

    (a) in any sheriff court district in which the person is apprehended or in custody, or

    (b) in such sheriff court district as the Lord Advocate may determine.

(9) In subsection (8) "sheriff court district" is to be read in accordance with section 307(1) of the Criminal Procedure (Scotland) Act 1995.

13 Defence for certain bribery offences etc.

(1) It is a defence for a person charged with a relevant bribery offence to prove that the person's conduct was necessary for—

    (a) the proper exercise of any function of an intelligence service, or

    (b) the proper exercise of any function of the armed forces when engaged on active service.

(2) The head of each intelligence service must ensure that the service has in place arrangements designed to ensure that any conduct of a member of the service which would otherwise be a relevant bribery offence is necessary for a purpose falling within subsection (1)(a).

(3) The Defence Council must ensure that the armed forces have in place arrangements designed to ensure that any conduct of—

(a) a member of the armed forces who is engaged on active service, or

(b) a civilian subject to service discipline when working in support of any person falling within paragraph (a),which would otherwise be a relevant bribery offence is necessary for a purpose falling within subsection (1)(b).

(4) The arrangements which are in place by virtue of subsection (2) or (3) must be arrangements which the Secretary of State considers to be satisfactory.

(5) For the purposes of this section, the circumstances in which a person's conduct is necessary for a purpose falling within subsection (1)(a) or (b) are to be treated as including any circumstances in which the person's conduct—

(a) would otherwise be an offence under section 2, and

(b) involves conduct by another person which, but for subsection (1)(a) or (b), would be an offence under section 1.

(6) In this section—

"active service" means service in—

(a) an action or operation against an enemy,

(b) an operation outside the British Islands for the protection of life or property, or

(c) the military occupation of a foreign country or territory,

"armed forces" means Her Majesty's forces (within the meaning of the Armed Forces Act 2006),

"civilian subject to service discipline" and "enemy" have the same meaning as in the Act of 2006,

"GCHQ" has the meaning given by section 3(3) of the Intelligence Services Act 1994,

"head" means—

(a) in relation to the Security Service, the Director General of the Security Service,

(b) in relation to the Secret Intelligence Service, the Chief of the Secret Intelligence Service, and

(c) in relation to GCHQ, the Director of GCHQ,

"intelligence service" means the Security Service, the Secret Intelligence Service or GCHQ,

"relevant bribery offence" means—

(a) an offence under section 1 which would not also be an offence under section 6,

(b) an offence under section 2,

(c) an offence committed by aiding, abetting, counselling or procuring the commission of an offence falling within paragraph (a) or (b),

(d) an offence of attempting or conspiring to commit, or of inciting the commission of, an offence falling within paragraph (a) or (b), or

(e) an offence under Part 2 of the Serious Crime Act 2007 (encouraging or assisting crime) in relation to an offence falling within paragraph (a) or (b).

14 Offences under sections 1, 2 and 6 by bodies corporate etc.

(1) This section applies if an offence under section 1, 2 or 6 is committed by a body corporate or a Scottish partnership.

(2) If the offence is proved to have been committed with the consent or connivance of—

(a) a senior officer of the body corporate or Scottish partnership, or

(b) a person purporting to act in such a capacity, the senior officer or person (as well as the body corporate or partnership) is guilty of the offence and liable to be proceeded against and punished accordingly.

(3) But subsection (2) does not apply, in the case of an offence which is committed under section 1, 2 or 6 by virtue of section 12(2) to (4), to a senior officer or person purporting to act in such a capacity unless the senior officer or person has a close connection with the United Kingdom (within the meaning given by section 12(4)).

(4) In this section—

"director", in relation to a body corporate whose affairs are managed by its members, means a member of the body corporate,

"senior officer" means—

    (a) in relation to a body corporate, a director, manager, secretary or other similar officer of the body corporate, and

    (b) in relation to a Scottish partnership, a partner in the partnership.

15 Offences under section 7 by partnerships

(1) Proceedings for an offence under section 7 alleged to have been committed by a partnership must be brought in the name of the partnership (and not in that of any of the partners).

(2) For the purposes of such proceedings—

    (a) rules of court relating to the service of documents have effect as if the partnership were a body corporate, and

    (b) the following provisions apply as they apply in relation to a body corporate—

        (i) section 33 of the Criminal Justice Act 1925 and Schedule 3 to the Magistrates' Courts Act 1980,

        (ii) section 18 of the Criminal Justice Act (Northern Ireland) 1945 (c. 15 (N.I.)) and Schedule 4 to the Magistrates' Courts (Northern Ireland) Order 1981 (S.I. 1981/1675 (N.I.26)),

        (iii) section 70 of the Criminal Procedure (Scotland) Act 1995.

(3) A fine imposed on the partnership on its conviction for an offence under section 7 is to be paid out of the partnership assets.

(4) In this section "partnership" has the same meaning as in section 7.

WITNESS INTIMIDATION

Triable either-way, 6 months/£5,000 (5 years).

Intimidation: In *Patrascu* [2004] EWCA Crim 2417 it was held:

"A person does an act which intimidates another person within section 51(1)(a), if he puts the victim in fear. He also does so if he seeks to deter the victim from some relevant action by threat or violence. A threat unaccompanied by violence may be sufficient, and the threat need not necessarily be a threat of violence. The act must be intended to intimidate. The person doing the act has to know or believe that the victim is assisting in the investigation of an offence or is a witness or potential witness or juror or potential juror in proceedings for an offence. He has to do the act intending thereby to cause the investigation or the course of justice to be obstructed, perverted or interfered with. If the other ingredients are established, this intention is presumed unless the contrary is proved (sub-section (7)). The intimidation does not necessarily have to be successful in the sense that the victim does not have actually to be deterred or put in fear. But it will obviously be material evidence if the victim was not in fact deterred or put in fear. A person may intimidate another person without the victim being intimidated. This apparent contradiction arises from different shades of meaning of the active and passive use of the verb. An act may amount to intimidation and thus intimidate, even though the victim is sufficiently steadfast not to be intimidated".

Investigation: An investigation must be underway at the time of the offence (*Singh* [1999] Crim LR 681). **Physical harm:** Harm which causes injury (physical or psychiatric) (*Normanton* [1998] Crim LR 220, where spitting on the complainant was held to be insufficient).

Offence seriousness (culpability and harm)		
A. Identify the appropriate starting point		
Starting points based on first time offender pleading not guilty		
Examples of nature of activity	Starting point	Range
Sudden outburst in chance encounter	6 weeks custody	Medium level community order to 18 weeks custody
Conduct amounting to a threat; staring at, approaching, or following witnesses; talking about the case; trying to alter or stop evidence	18 weeks custody	12 weeks custody to Crown Court
Threats of violence to witnesses and/or their families; deliberately seeking out witnesses	Crown Court	Crown Court

Offence seriousness (culpability and harm)	
B. Consider the effect of aggravating and mitigating factors (other than those within examples above) The following may be particularly relevant but these lists are not exhaustive	
Factors indicating higher culpability 1. Breach of bail conditions 2. Offender involves others **Factors indicating greater degree of harm** 1. Detrimental impact on administration of justice 2. Contact made at or in vicinity of victim's home	

Criminal Justice and Public Order Act 1994, s 51

(1) A person commits an offence if—

    (a) he does an act which intimidates, and is intended to intimidate, another person ("the victim"),

    (b) he does the act knowing or believing that the victim is assisting in the investigation of an offence or is a witness or potential witness or a juror or potential juror in proceedings for an offence, and

    (c) he does it intending thereby to cause the investigation or the course of justice to be obstructed, perverted or interfered with.

(2) A person commits an offence if—

    (a) he does an act which harms, and is intended to harm, another person or, intending to cause another person to fear harm, he threatens to do an act which would harm that other person,

    (b) he does or threatens to do the act knowing or believing that the person harmed or threatened to be harmed ("the victim"), or some other person, has assisted in an investigation into an offence or has given evidence or particular evidence in proceedings for an offence, or has acted as a juror or concurred in a particular verdict in proceedings for an offence, and

    (c) he does or threatens to do it because of that knowledge or belief.

(3) For the purposes of subsections (1) and (2) it is immaterial that the act is or would be done, or that the threat is made—

    (a) otherwise than in the presence of the victim, or

    (b) to a person other than the victim.

(4) The harm that may be done or threatened may be financial as well as physical (whether

to the person or a person's property) and similarly as respects an intimidatory act which consists of threats.

(5) The intention required by subsection (1)(c) and the motive required by subsection (2)(c) above need not be the only or the predominating intention or motive with which the act is done or, in the case of subsection (2), threatened.

(6) A person guilty of an offence under this section shall be liable—

    (a) on conviction on indictment, to imprisonment for a term not exceeding five years or a fine or both;

    (b) on summary conviction, to imprisonment for a term not exceeding six months or a fine not exceeding the statutory maximum or both.

(7) If, in proceedings against a person for an offence under subsection (1) above, it is proved that he did an act falling within paragraph (a) with the knowledge or belief required by paragraph (b), he shall be presumed, unless the contrary is proved, to have done the act with the intention required by paragraph (c) of that subsection.

(8) If, in proceedings against a person for an offence under subsection (2) above, it is proved that he did or threatened to do an act falling within paragraph (a) within the relevant period—

    (a) he did an act which harmed, and was intended to harm, another person, or

    (b) intending to cause another person fear of harm, he threatened to do an act which would harm that other person,

and that he did the act, or (as the case may be) threatened to do the act with the knowledge or belief required by paragraph (b), he shall be presumed, unless the contrary is proved, to have done the act or (as the case may be) threatened to do the act with the motive required by paragraph (c) of that subsection.

(9) In this section—

"investigation into an offence" means such an investigation by the police or other person charged with the duty of investigating offences or charging offenders;

"offence" includes an alleged or suspected offence;

"potential", in relation to a juror, means a person who has been summoned for jury service at the court at which proceedings for the offence are pending; and

"the relevant period"—

    (a) in relation to a witness or juror in any proceedings for an offence, means the period beginning with the institution of the proceedings and ending with the first anniversary of the conclusion of the trial or, if there is an appeal or a reference under section 9 or 11 of the Criminal Appeal Act 1995, of the conclusion of the appeal;

    (b) in relation to a person who has, or is believed by the accused to have, assisted in an investigation into an offence, but was not also a witness in proceedings for an offence, means the period of one year beginning with any act of his, or any act believed by the accused to be an act of his, assisting in the investigation; and

    (c) in relation to a person who both has, or is believed by the accused to have, assisted in the investigation into an offence and was a witness in proceedings for the offence, means the period beginning with any act of his, or any act believed by the accused to be an act of his, assisting in the investigation and ending with the anniversary mentioned in paragraph (a) above.

(10) For the purposes of the definition of the relevant period in subsection (9) above—

    (a) proceedings for an offence are instituted at the earliest of the following times—

        (i) when a justice of the peace issues a summons or warrant under section 1 of the Magistrates' Courts Act 1980 in respect of the offence;

(ii) when a person is charged with the offence after being taken into custody without a warrant;

(iii) when a bill of indictment is preferred by virtue of section 2(2)(b) of the Administration of Justice (Miscellaneous Provisions) Act 1933;

(b) proceedings at a trial of an offence are concluded with the occurrence of any of the following, the discontinuance of the prosecution, the discharge of the jury without a finding otherwise than in circumstances where the proceedings are continued without a jury, the acquittal of the accused or the sentencing of or other dealing with the accused for the offence of which he was convicted; and

(c) proceedings on an appeal are concluded on the determination of the appeal or the abandonment of the appeal.

(11) This section is in addition to, and not in derogation of, any offence subsisting at common law.

CRIMINAL DAMAGE

ANCIENT MONUMENTS AND ARCHAEOLOGICAL AREAS

Ancient Monuments and Archaeological Areas Act 1979, ss 9E, 28, and 42

Section	Mode of trial	Sentence
9E Offence where scheduled monument enforcement notice not complied with	Either-way	£20,000 (unlimited on indictment) S 9E(7) states: In determining the amount of any fine to be imposed, the court is in particular to have regard to any financial benefit which has accrued or appears likely to accrue to the person in consequence of the offence.
28 Offence of damaging certain ancient monuments	Either-way	6 months/£5,000 (2 years)
42 Restrictions on use of metal detectors	Summary only	£1,000 (£5,000 for an offence under s 42(3))

CRIMINAL DAMAGE ACT, GENERAL PRINCIPLES

Mode of trial: In respect to simple criminal damage (but not arson) if the damage is less than £5,000 the offence must be tried summarily (Magistrates' Courts Act 1980, s 22). If the court is unable to quantify the damage the defendant must be offered trial on indictment. There is no prescribed procedure for determining disputes as to value, and there is no right to call or challenge witness evidence (*Canterbury Justices ex p Klisiak* [1982] QB 398), the court generally proceeding by way of documentary evidence or clear inference. Value means open market value and no regard can be had to any consequential loss (*R (Abbott) v Colchester Justices* [2001] EWHC (Admin) 136) If the defendant faces two or more charges charged on the same occasion and it appears to the court that they constitute or form part of a series of two or more offences of the same or a similar character, then it is the aggregate value of the damaged property that is considered when determining whether the damage exceeds £5,000. It is submitted that charged on the same occasion means the charges being put to the defendant on the same occasion. Attempted criminal damage can be charged where the value is less than £5,000 (*Bristol Justices ex p E* [1999] 1 WLR 390). There is no right of appeal against the courts determination as to value of damage, but judicial review or case stated might lie in an exceptional case.

Consent to prosecute: Proceedings shall not be instituted against a person for any offence of stealing or doing unlawful damage to property which at the time of the offence belongs to that person's wife or husband or civil partner, or for any attempt, incitement or conspiracy to commit such an offence, unless the proceedings are instituted by or with the consent of the Director of Public Prosecutions (Theft Act 1968, s 30(4)). Consent is not required in relation to proceedings against a person for an offence (i) if that person is charged with committing the offence jointly with the wife or husband or civil partner; (ii) if by virtue of any judicial decree or order (wherever made) that person and the wife or husband are at the time of the offence under no obligation to cohabit; or (iii) an order (wherever made) is in force providing for the separation of that person and his or her civil partner. **Damage**: Determining whether something has been damaged is a matter of fact and degree to be determined by the magistrates or jury (*Roe v Kingerlee* [1986] Crim LR 735). Damage does not need to be destruction and encompasses not permanent harm, such as graffiti. If expense or inconvenience is involved in putting right the matter then damage will have been caused (eg stamping on a policeman's helmet so that it had to be pushed back into shape). Damaging something that can be restored (eg deleting a computer program) constitutes damage (*Cox v Riley* (1986) 83 Cr App R 54). Spitting on a police officer's uniform is unlikely to cause damage (*A v R* [1978] Crim LR 689). The soaking of a blanket and the flooding of the floor of a police cell was held to amount to damage in *Fiak* [2005] EWCA 2381, and the daubing of water-soluble paint on a pavement was equally found to amount to damage in *Hardman v Chief Constable of Avon and Somerset* [1986] Crim LR 330. **Danger to life**: The danger must have resulted from the destruction of or damage to the property (*Steer* (1988) AC 111). **Joint ownership**: It is an offence to damage property in joint ownership. A person having custody, control, proprietary right or interest or having a charge on property has property belonging to him (Criminal Damage Act 1971, s 10). In relation to simple arson the property must belong to another, but for aggravated arson (s 1(2)) it suffices even if the property belongs solely to the defendant. **Lawful excuse**: See s 5. Intoxication does not negate lawful excuse (*Jaggard v Dickinson* (1981) 72 Cr App R 33). **Mens rea**: Provided that the prosecution can prove an intention or recklessness as to whether damage would be caused by an act, it was not necessary for the prosecution to further prove recklessness as to whether that damage amounted to damage in law (*Seray-Wurie v Director of Public Prosecutions* [2012] EWHC 208 (Admin)). The prosecution will have proved that the defendant was reckless if, having regard to all the available evidence the court is sure: that he was aware of a risk that property would be destroyed/damaged; and that in the circumstances which were known to him it was unreasonable for him to take that risk. This test allows for some of the personal characteristics of a defendant to be taken into account (*G* [2003] UKHL 50). It is sufficient for intent to be conditional (*Buckingham* (1976) 63 Cr App R 159). **Threat**: This must be objectively assessed, considering the words and actions of the defendant (*Cakmak* [2002] EWCA Crim 500).

CRIMINAL DAMAGE ACT 1971, SS 1, 3 DESTROY/DAMAGE PROPERTY

Overview

Offence	Mode of trial	Penalty
S 1 Destroying or damaging property	Venue dictated by value (see below). Racially/ religiously aggravated offences are triable either-way.	Damage below £5,000: 3 months/£2500 Damage above £5,000: 6 months' imprisonment if tried summarily, 10 years on indictment. Racially/religiously aggravated (Crime and Disorder Act 1988, s 30): 6 months/£5,000; 14 years on indictment).
S 1(2) Endangering life S 1(3) Destroying or damaging property by fire (Arson)	Triable either-way, save where there is reckless or intentional endangerment to life (s 1(2)) in which case the offence is indictable only.	6 months' imprisonment/£5,000 (life).
S 2 Threats to destroy or damage property	Triable either-way.	6 months' imprisonment/£5,000 (14 years on indictment)
S 3 Possessing anything with intent to destroy or damage property	Triable either-way.	6 months' imprisonment/£5,000 (10 years on indictment)

Sentencing: criminal damage

Offence seriousness (culpability and harm) **A. Identify the appropriate starting point** Starting points bases on first time offender pleading not guilty		
Examples of nature of activity	**Starting point**	**Range**
Minor damage eg breaking small window; small amount of graffiti	Band B fine	Conditional discharge to band C fine
Moderate damage eg breaking large plate-glass or shop window; widespread graffiti	Low level community order	Band C fine to medium level community order
Significant damage up to £5,000 eg damage caused as part of a spree	High level community order	Medium level community order to 12 weeks custody
Damage between £5,000 and £10,000	12 weeks custody	6 to 26 weeks custody
Damage over £10,000	Crown Court	Crown Court

Offence seriousness (culpability and harm)
B. Consider the effect of aggravating and mitigating factors (other than those within examples above) The following may be particularly relevant but **these lists are not exhaustive**

Factors indicating higher culpability	Factors indicating lower culpability
1. Revenge attack	1. Damage caused recklessly
2. Targeting vulnerable victim	2. Provocation
Factors indicating greater degree of harm	
1. Damage to emergency equipment	
2. Damage to public amenity	
3. Significant public or private fear caused eg in domestic context	

Sentencing: arson

Offence seriousness (culpability and harm)

A. Identify the appropriate starting point

Starting points based on first time offender pleading not guilty

Examples of nature of activity	Starting point	Range
Minor damage by fire	High level community order	Medium level community order to 12 weeks custody
Moderate damage by fire	12 weeks custody	6 to 26 weeks custody
Significant damage by fire	Crown Court	Crown Court

Offence seriousness (culpability and harm)

B. Consider the effect of aggravating and mitigating factors (other than those within examples above)

The following may be particularly relevant but **these lists are not exhaustive**

Factors indicating higher culpability	Factor indicating lower culpability
1. Revenge attack	1. Damage caused recklessly
2. Targeting vulnerable victim	
Factors indicating greater degree of harm	
1. Damage to emergency equipment	
2. Damage to public amenity	
3. Significant public or private fear caused eg in domestic context	

Criminal Damage Act 1971, ss 1, 2, 3, and 5

Destroying or damaging property, s 1

(1) A person who without lawful excuse destroys or damages any property belonging to another intending to destroy or damage any such property or being reckless as to whether any such property would be destroyed or damaged shall be guilty of an offence.

(2) A person who without lawful excuse destroys or damages any property, whether belonging to himself or another—

 (a) intending to destroy or damage any property or being reckless as to whether any property would be destroyed or damaged; and

 (b) intending by the destruction or damage to endanger the life of another or being reckless as to whether the life of another would be thereby endangered;

shall be guilty of an offence.

(3) An offence committed under this section by destroying or damaging property by fire shall be charged as arson.

Threats to destroy or damage property, s 2

A person who without lawful excuse makes to another a threat, intending that that other would fear it would be carried out,—

  (a) to destroy or damage any property belonging to that other or a third person; or
  (b) to destroy or damage his own property in a way which he knows is likely to endanger the life of that other or third person;

shall be guilty of an offence.

Possessing anything with intent to destroy or damage property, s 3(a)

A person who has anything in his custody or under his control intending without lawful excuse to use it or cause or permit another to use it—

  (a) to destroy or damage any property belonging to some other person; or
  (b) to destroy or damage his own or the user's property in a way which he knows is likely to endanger the life of some other person;

shall be guilty of an offence.

Without lawful excuse, s 5(2)–(5)

  (2) A person charged with an offence to which this section applies, shall, whether or not he would be treated for the purposes of this Act as having a lawful excuse apart from this subsection, be treated for those purposes as having a lawful excuse—

  (a) if at the time of the act or acts alleged to constitute the offence he believed that the person or persons whom he believed to be entitled to consent to the destruction of or damage to the property in question had so consented, or would have so consented to it if he or they had known of the destruction or damage and its circumstances; or
  (b) if he destroyed or damaged or threatened to destroy or damage the property in question or, in the case of a charge of an offence under section 3 above, intended to use or cause or permit the use of something to destroy or damage it, in order to protect property belonging to himself or another or a right or interest in property which was or which he believed to be vested in himself or another, and at the time of the act or acts alleged to constitute the offence he believed—
    (i) that the property, right or interest was in immediate need of protection; and
    (ii) that the means of protection adopted or proposed to be adopted were or would be reasonable having regard to all the circumstances.

  (3) For the purposes of this section it is immaterial whether a belief is justified or not if it is honestly held.
  (4) For the purposes of subsection (2) above a right or interest in property includes any right or privilege in or over land, whether created by grant, licence or otherwise.
  (5) This section shall not be construed as casting doubt on any defence recognised by law as a defence to criminal charges.

CRIMINAL DAMAGE ACT 1971,
S 2 THREATS TO DESTROY OR DAMAGE PROPERTY

Either-way, 6 months/£5,000 (10 years)

Criminal Damage Act 1971, s 2

A person who without lawful excuse makes to another a threat, intending that that other would fear it would be carried out,—

  (a) to destroy or damage any property belonging to that other or a third person; or
  (b) to destroy or damage his own property in a way which he knows is likely to endanger the life of that other or third person;

shall be guilty of an offence.

CRIMINAL DAMAGE ACT 1971, S 3(A) POSSESSING ANYTHING WITH INTENT TO DESTROY OR DAMAGE PROPERTY

Either-way, 6 months/£5,000 (10 years)

Criminal Damage Act 1971, s 3(a)

A person who has anything in his custody or under his control intending without lawful excuse to use it or cause or permit another to use it—

(a) to destroy or damage any property belonging to some other person; or
(b) to destroy or damage his own or the user's property in a way which he knows is likely to endanger the life of some other person;

shall be guilty of an offence.

CRIMINAL DAMAGE, RACIALLY OR RELIGIOUSLY AGGRAVATED

Either-way, 6 months/£5,000 (14 years)

See above for the Magistrates' Court Sentencing Guideline for this offence. In *Saunders* [2000] 1 Cr App R 458 the court held:

"One of the most important lessons of this century, as it nears its end, is that racism must not be allowed to flourish. The message must be received and understood, in every corner of our society, in our streets and prisons, in the services, in the workplace, on public transport, in our hospitals, public houses and clubs, that racism is evil. It cannot coexist with fairness and justice. It is incompatible with democratic civilisation. The courts must do all they can, in accordance with Parliament's recently expressed intention, to convey that message clearly, by the sentences which they pass in relation to racially aggravated offences. Those who indulge in racially aggravated violence must expect to be punished severely, in order to discourage the repetition of that behaviour, by them or others. It will often be helpful if the sentencing judge first considers, though he or she need not express it, the appropriate sentence for the offence in the absence of racial aggravation and then adds a further term for the racial element, so that the total sentence reflects the overall criminality. Even if the basic offence would not cross the custody threshold so as to merit imprisonment, the element of racial aggravation may well result in the custody threshold being passed. At what level in the sentencing scale a case falls, having regard to the possible maximum addition of two years, will depend on all the circumstances of the particular case. Relevant factors will include the nature of the hostile demonstration, whether by language, gestures or weapons; its length, whether isolated, repeated, or persistent; its location, whether public or private; the number both of those demonstrating and those demonstrated against; and the presence or absence of other features—for example, the same offensive remark is likely to attract a heavier penalty if uttered in a crowded church, mosque or synagogue than if uttered in an empty public house. A discount will be appropriate in accordance with general sentencing principles for, among other things, genuine remorse, a plea of guilty and previous good character".

Crime and Disorder Act 1998, s 30

(1) A person is guilty of an offence under this section if he commits an offence under section 1(1) of the Criminal Damage Act 1971 (destroying or damaging property belonging to another) which is racially or religiously aggravated for the purposes of this section.
(2) [...]
(3) For the purposes of this section, section 28(1)(a) above shall have effect as if the person to whom the property belongs or is treated as belonging for the purposes of that Act were the victim of the offence.

DRUGS

DEFINITIONS

Controlled drug: In order to establish guilt the prosecution must prove that the prohibited substance is in the possession of the defendant. If it is an offence to have the drug in one form but not an offence to have the drug in another form the prosecution must prove that the drug is in the prohibited form for otherwise no offence is established (*Hunt* [1987] 1 All ER 1). An admission from a drug user that the exhibit is a controlled drug amounts to prima facie evidence of that fact (*Chatwood* [1980] 1 All ER 467). **Possession and knowledge of possession:** If a defendant consumes a drug he is no longer in possession of it (*Hambleton v Callinan* [1968] 2 All ER 943). The defendant must know or suspect that he is in possession of drugs–see section 28 of the Act. A person who 'forgot' that he had drugs would still be in possession of those drugs, but a person who had no knowledge at all would not (*Martindale* [1986] 3 All ER 25). A person need not be in physical possession of a drug provided he is in control (sole or joint): see Misuse of Drugs Act 1971, s 37(3). It is not sufficient that the defendant might have knowledge of a confederate's possession of drugs; the test is whether the drugs were part of a common pool from which all could draw (*Searle* [1971] Crim LR 592). The fact that the quantity of drug was so miniscule as to be incapable of being used does not amount to a defence (*Boyesen* [1982] AC 768), it is merely an indication that the defendant may not have knowledge of its presence. If a person is in possession of a container and he knows there is something inside, he will be in possession of the contents, even if he does not know their characteristics (*Lambert* [2002] 2 AC 545). If, however, the defendant had no right to open the container he may not be in possession of its contents (*Warner v Metropolitan Police Commissioner* [1969] 2 AC 256), nor if he believed the contents to be different from what in fact they were (*McNamara* (1988) 87 Cr App R 246). **Defences:** Defences are provided by sections 5 and 28 of the Act. In considering a defence under section 28(3)(b), self-induced intoxication should not be considered (*Young* [1984] 2 All ER 164). Once sufficient evidence is raised in relation to the defence under section 28, it is for the crown to disprove it to the criminal standard (*Lambert* [2001] 2 All ER 577). The defence of necessity (commonly pleaded by sufferers of certain illnesses) is not a defence available in law for this charge (*Quayle and others* [2006] 1 All ER 988). Possession of drugs for religious purposes is not afforded any special protection under the European Convention (*Taylor* [2002] 1 Cr App R 519). **Destruction:** Burying a drug is not sufficient to amount to destruction, to destroy is "to undo, break into useless pieces or reduce into useless form, consume or dissolve any material, structure or object". (*Murphy* (2002) Crim LR 819). **Cultivation of cannabis:** It is the plant that must be cultivated, not the cannabis produced from the plant. The accused does not need to know that the plant was in fact cannabis (*Champ* (1981) 73 Cr App R 267). **Concerned in:** The prosecution has to prove (1) the supply of a drug to another, or as the case may be the making of an offer to supply a drug to another, in contravention of section 4(1) of the Act; (2) participation by the defendant in an enterprise involving such supply or, as the case may be, such offer to supply; and (3) knowledge by the defendant of the nature of the enterprise, i.e. that it involved supply of a drug or, as the case may be, offering to supply a drug (*Hughes* (1985) 81 Cr App R 344). **Permitting:** For an offence under section 8 of the Act the prosecution must establish that the prohibited act occurred on the actual premises (*McGee* [2012] EWCA Crim 613). **Produced/Production:** Means producing it by manufacture, cultivation or any other method, and 'production' has a corresponding meaning (see s 37(1)). **Offer to supply:** This also incorporates an act of distributing a drug. **Supply:** The word should be given its everyday meaning (*Holmes v Chief Constable of Merseyside* [1976] Crim LR 125). A person who places drugs in the hands of a third party merely for safekeeping does not supply drugs (*Maginnis* [1987] AC 303). An offer to supply can be made by words or conduct, and once made cannot be withdrawn. Purchasing drugs on behalf of a third party, and passing those drugs to that party, even for no profit, amounts to supply. So-called social supply should be charged as simple possession, in *Denslow* [1998] Crim LR 566 the court said:

"We wonder why it was thought necessary to charge supply in the circumstances of this case. How could it possibly serve the interests of the public that there should be either a trial or if not a trial as conventionally understood a hearing to determine this matter of law? It was inevitable that the appellant would be dealt with at worst as though he were in possession of the drugs and, as turned out in this case, as though he were without any criminal responsibility for that particular part of the transaction. We are told that a plea had been offered to a charge of possession. It ought to have been accepted. We hope that those words will be borne in mind by prosecuting authorities in the future."

Misuse of Drugs Act 1971, ss 5, 28

5.— Restriction of possession of controlled drugs.

(1)   Subject to any regulations under section 7 of this Act for the time being in force, it shall not be lawful for a person to have a controlled drug in his possession.

(2)   Subject to section 28 of this Act and to subsection (4) below, it is an offence for a person to have a controlled drug in his possession in contravention of subsection (1) above.

(2A)   Subsections (1) and (2) do not apply in relation to a temporary class drug.

(3)   Subject to section 28 of this Act, it is an offence for a person to have a controlled drug in his possession, whether lawfully or not, with intent to supply it to another in contravention of section 4(1) of this Act.

(4)   In any proceedings for an offence under subsection (2) above in which it is proved that the accused had a controlled drug in his possession, it shall be a defence for him to prove—

    (a)   that, knowing or suspecting it to be a controlled drug, he took possession of it for the purpose of preventing another from committing or continuing to commit an offence in connection with that drug and that as soon as possible after taking possession of it he took all such steps as were reasonably open to him to destroy the drug or to deliver it into the custody of a person lawfully entitled to take custody of it; or

    (b)   that, knowing or suspecting it to be a controlled drug, he took possession of it for the purpose of delivering it into the custody of a person lawfully entitled to take custody of it and that as soon as possible after taking possession of it he took all such steps as were reasonably open to him to deliver it into the custody of such a person.

    [...]

(6)   Nothing in subsection (4) above shall prejudice any defence which it is open to a person charged with an offence under this section to raise apart from that subsection.

28.— Proof of lack of knowledge etc. to be a defence in proceedings for certain offences.

(1)   This section applies to offences under any of the following provisions of this Act, that is to say section 4(2) and (3), section 5(2) and (3), section 6(2) and section 9.

(2)   Subject to subsection (3) below, in any proceedings for an offence to which this section applies it shall be a defence for the accused to prove that he neither knew of nor suspected nor had reason to suspect the existence of some fact alleged by the prosecution which it is necessary for the prosecution to prove if he is to be convicted of the offence charged.

(3)   Where in any proceedings for an offence to which this section applies it is necessary, if the accused is to be convicted of the offence charged, for the prosecution to prove that some substance or product involved in the alleged offence was the controlled drug which the prosecution alleges it to have been, and it is proved that the substance or product in question was that controlled drug, the accused—

   (a) shall not be acquitted of the offence charged by reason only of proving that he neither knew nor suspected nor had reason to suspect that the substance or product in question was the particular controlled drug alleged; but

   (b) shall be acquitted thereof—

      (i) if he proves that he neither believed nor suspected nor had reasons to suspect that the substance or product in question was a controlled drug; or

      (ii) if he proves that he believed the substance or product in question to be a controlled drug, or a controlled drug of a description, such that, if it had in fact been that controlled drug or a controlled drug of that description, he would not at the material time have been committing any offence to which this section applies.

(4) Nothing in this section shall prejudice any defence which it is open to a person charged with an offence to which this section applies to raise apart from this section.

FAIL/REFUSE TO PROVIDE A SAMPLE

Summary only, 3 months/£2,500

Police and Criminal Evidence Act 1984, s 63B

(1) A sample of urine or a non-intimate sample may be taken from a person in police detention for the purpose of ascertaining whether he has any specified Class A drug in his body if—

   (a) either the arrest condition or the charge condition is met;

   (b) both the age condition and the request condition are met; and

   (c) the notification condition is met in relation to the arrest condition, the charge condition or the age condition (as the case may be).

(1A) The arrest condition is that the person concerned has been arrested for an offence but has not been charged with that offence and either—

   (a) the offence is a trigger offence; or

   (b) a police officer of at least the rank of inspector has reasonable grounds for suspecting that the misuse by that person of a specified Class A drug caused or contributed to the offence and has authorised the sample to be taken.

(2) The charge condition is either—

   (a) that the person concerned has been charged with a trigger offence; or

   (b) that the person concerned has been charged with an offence and a police officer of at least the rank of inspector, who has reasonable grounds for suspecting that the misuse by that person of any specified Class A drug caused or contributed to the offence and has authorised the sample to be taken.

(3) The age condition is—

   (a) if the arrest condition is met, that the person concerned has attained the age of 18;

   (b) if the charge condition is met, that he has attained the age of 14.

(4) The request condition is that a police officer has requested the person concerned to give the sample.

[....]

(5) Before requesting the person concerned to give a sample, an officer must—

   (a) warn him that if, when so requested, he fails without good cause to do so he may be liable to prosecution, and

   (b) in a case within subsection (1A)(b) or (2)(b) above, inform him of the giving of the authorisation and of the grounds in question.

(5A) In the case of a person who has not attained the age of 17—

    (a) the making of the request under subsection (4) above;

    (b) the giving of the warning and (where applicable) the information under subsection (5) above; and

    (c) the taking of the sample,

may not take place except in the presence of an appropriate adult.

(5B) ...

(5C) Despite subsection (1)(a) above, a sample may be taken from a person under this section if—

    (a) he was arrested for an offence (the first offence),

    (b) the arrest condition is met but the charge condition is not met,

    (c) before a sample is taken by virtue of subsection (1) above he would (but for his arrest as mentioned in paragraph (d) below) be required to be released from police detention,

    (d) he continues to be in police detention by virtue of his having been arrested for an offence not falling within subsection (1A) above, and

    (e) the sample is taken before the end of the period of 24 hours starting with the time when his detention by virtue of his arrest for the first offence began.

(5D) A sample must not be taken from a person under this section if he is detained in a police station unless he has been brought before the custody officer.

(6) A sample may be taken under this section only by a person prescribed by regulations made by the Secretary of State by statutory instrument.

[...]

(8) A person who fails without good cause to give any sample which may be taken from him under this section shall be guilty of an offence.

Offence seriousness (culpability and harm)		
A. Identify the appropriate starting point		
Starting points based on first time offender pleading not guilty		
Examples of nature of activity	**Starting point**	**Range**
Refusal to provide sample without good cause when required by police officer	Medium level community order	Band C fine to high level community order

Offence seriousness (culpability and harm)	
B. Consider the effect of aggravating and mitigating factors	
(other than those within examples above)	
The following may be particularly relevant but **these lists are not exhaustive**	
Factor indicating greater degree of harm	**Factors indicating lower culpability**
1. Threats or abuse to staff	1. Subsequent voluntary contact with drug workers
	2. Subsequent compliance with testing on arrest/ charge

FAIL TO ATTEND/REMAIN FOR INITIAL ASSESSMENT

Summary only, 3 months/£2,500

Drugs Act 2005, s 12(1)–(3)

(1) This section applies if a person is required to attend an initial assessment and remain for its duration by virtue of section 9(2).

(2) The initial assessor must inform a police officer or a police support officer if the person—

    (a) fails to attend the initial assessment at the specified time and place, or

    (b) attends the assessment at the specified time and place but fails to remain for its duration.

(3) A person is guilty of an offence if without good cause—

    (a) he fails to attend an initial assessment at the specified time and place, or

    (b) he attends the assessment at the specified time and place but fails to remain for its duration.

Offence seriousness (culpability and harm)		
A. Identify the appropriate starting point		
Starting points based on first time offender pleading not guilty		
Examples of nature of activity	**Starting point**	**Range**
Failure to attend at the appointed place and time	Medium level community order	Band C fine to high level community order

Offence seriousness (culpability and harm)	
B. Consider the effect of aggravating and mitigating factors (other than those within examples above)	
The following may be particularly relevant but **these lists are not exhaustive**	
Factor indicating greater degree of harm	**Factors indicating lower culpability**
1. Threats or abuse to assessor or other staff	1. Offender turns up but at wrong place or time or fails to remain for duration of appointment 2. Subsequent voluntary contact to rearrange appointment

FRAUDULENT EVASION OF A PROHIBITION BY BRINGING INTO OR TAKING OUT OF THE UK A CONTROLLED DRUG

Either-way, 6 months/£5,000 (or 3 times the value of the goods concerned). On indictment the offence carries 7 years increased to 10 years for some items (see s 170(4A) of the 1979 Act) and 14 years for others (s 170(4C)).

Step 1: Determining the offence category

Culpability demonstrated by offender's role. One or more of these characteristics may demonstrate the offender's role. The list is not exhaustive.	Category of harm. Indicative output or potential output (upon which the starting point is based):
LEADING role: • directing or organising production on a commercial scale; • substantial links to, and influence on, others in a chain; • expectation of substantial financial gain; • uses business as cover; • abuses a position of trust or responsibility.	Category 1 • heroin, cocaine–5kg; • ecstasy–10,000 tablets; • LSD–250,000 tablets; • amphetamine–20kg; • cannabis–200kg; • ketamine–5kg.

SIGNIFICANT role:

- operational or management function within a chain;
- involves others in the operation whether by pressure, influence, intimidation or reward;
- motivated by financial or other advantage, whether or not operating alone;
- some awareness and understanding of scale of operation.

LESSER role:

- performs a limited function under direction;
- engaged by pressure, coercion, intimidation;
- involvement through naivety/exploitation;
- no influence on those above in a chain;
- very little, if any, awareness or understanding of the scale of operation;
- if own operation, solely for own use (considering reasonableness of account in all the circumstances).

Category 2

- heroin, cocaine–1kg;
- ecstasy–2,000 tablets;
- LSD–25,000 squares;
- amphetamine–4kg;
- cannabis–40kg;
- ketamine–1kg.

Category 3

- heroin, cocaine–150g;
- ecstasy–300 tablets;
- LSD–2,500 squares;
- amphetamine–750g;
- cannabis–6kg
- ketamine–150g.

Category 4

- heroin, cocaine–5g;
- ecstasy–20 tablets;
- LSD–170 squares;
- amphetamine–20g;
- cannabis–100g
- ketamine–5g

Step 2: Starting point and category range

CLASS A	Leading role	Significant role	Lesser role
Category 1	Crown Court	Crown Court	Crown Court
Category 2	Crown Court	Crown Court	Crown Court
Category 3	Crown Court	Crown Court	Crown Court
Category 4	Crown Court	Crown Court	Crown Court

CLASS B	Leading role	Significant role	Lesser role
Category 1	Crown Court	Crown Court	Crown Court
Category 2	Crown Court	Crown Court	1 year's custody. Range: 26 weeks'–3 years' custody
Category 3	Crown Court	Crown Court	Crown Court
Category 4	Crown Court	Crown Court	1 year's custody. Range: 12 weeks' custody–18 months' custody

CLASS C	Leading role	Significant role	Lesser role
Category 1	Crown Court	Crown Court	Crown Court
Category 2	Crown Court	Crown Court	26 weeks' custody. Range: 12 weeks'–18 months' custody

Category 3	Crown Court	26 weeks' custody. Range: 12 weeks'–18 months' custody	High level community order. Range: Medium level community order–12 weeks' custody
Category 4	*	*	*

* Where the quantity falls below the indicative amount set out in the guideline for category 4, first identify the role for the importation offence, then refer to the starting point and ranges for possession or supply offences, depending on intent. Where the quantity is significantly larger than the indicative amounts for category 4 but below category 3 amounts, refer to the category 3 ranges.

Factors increasing seriousness	Factors reducing seriousness or reflecting personal mitigation
Statutory aggravating factors:	Lack of sophistication as to nature of concealment
Previous convictions, having regard to a) nature of the offence to which conviction relates and relevance to current offence; and b) time elapsed since Offender used or permitted a person under 18 to deliver a controlled drug to a third person	Involvement due to pressure, intimidation or coercion falling short of duress, except where already taken into account at step 1
	Mistaken belief of the offender regarding the type of drug, taking into account the reasonableness of such belief in all the circumstances
Offence committed on bail	Isolated incident
	Low purity
Other aggravating factors include:	No previous convictions or no relevant or recent convictions
Sophisticated nature of concealment and/or attempts to avoid detection	Offender's vulnerability was exploited
Attempts to conceal or dispose of evidence, where not charged separately	Remorse
	Good character and/or exemplary conduct
Exposure of others to more than usual danger, for example drugs cut with harmful substances	Determination and/or demonstration of steps having been taken to address addiction or offending behaviour
Presence of weapon, where not charged separately	Serious medical conditions requiring urgent, intensive or long-term treatment
High purity	Age and/or lack of maturity where it affects the responsibility of the offender
Failure to comply with current court orders	Mental disorder or learning disability
Offence committed on licence	Sole or primary carer for dependent relatives

Additional steps:

Consider any factors which indicate a reduction, such as assistance to the prosecution; reduction for guilty plea; dangerousness; totality principle; compensation and ancillary orders; reasons; consideration for remand time.

Customs and Excise Management Act 1979, s 170

(1) Without prejudice to any other provision of the Customs and Excise Acts 1979, if any person—

    (a) knowingly acquires possession of any of the following goods, that is to say—

        (i) goods which have been unlawfully removed from a warehouse or Queen's warehouse;

      (ii)   goods which are chargeable with a duty which has not been paid;

      (iii) goods with respect to the importation or exportation of which any prohibition or restriction is for the time being in force under or by virtue of any enactment; or

    (b) is in any way knowingly concerned in carrying, removing, depositing, harbouring, keeping or concealing or in any manner dealing with any such goods,

and does so with intent to defraud Her Majesty of any duty payable on the goods or to evade any such prohibition or restriction with respect to the goods he shall be guilty of an offence under this section and may be arrested.

(2)   Without prejudice to any other provision of the Customs and Excise Acts 1979, if any person is, in relation to any goods, in any way knowingly concerned in any fraudulent evasion or attempt at evasion—

    (a) of any duty chargeable on the goods;

    (b) of any prohibition or restriction for the time being in force with respect to the goods under or by virtue of any enactment; or

    (c) of any provision of the Customs and Excise Acts 1979 applicable to the goods,

he shall be guilty of an offence under this section and may be arrested.

(3)   Subject to subsection (4), (4A), (4B) or (4C) below, a person guilty of an offence under this section shall be liable—

    (a) on summary conviction, to a penalty of the prescribed sum or of three times the value of the goods, whichever is the greater, or to imprisonment for a term not exceeding 6 months, or to both; or

    (b) on conviction on indictment, to a penalty of any amount, or to imprisonment for a term not exceeding 7 years, or to both.

(4)   In the case of an offence under this section in connection with prohibition or restriction on importation or exportation having effect by virtue of section 3 of the Misuse of Drugs Act 1971, subsection (3) above shall have effect subject to the modifications specified in Schedule 1 to this Act.

(4A) In the case of—

    (a) an offence under subsection (2) or (3) above committed in Great Britain in connection with a prohibition or restriction on the importation or exportation of any weapon or ammunition that is of a kind mentioned in section 5(1)(a), (ab), (aba), (ac), (ad), (ae), (af) or (c) or (1A)(a) of the Firearms Act 1968,

    (b) any such offence committed in Northern Ireland in connection with a prohibition or restriction on the importation or exportation of any weapon or ammunition that is of a kind mentioned in Article 6(1)(a), (ab), (ac), (ad), (ae) or (c) or (1A)(a) of the Firearms (Northern Ireland) Order 1981, or

    (c) any such offence committed in connection with the prohibitions contained in sections 20 and 21 of the Forgery and Counterfeiting Act 1981,

subsection (3)(b) above shall have effect as if for the words "7 years" there were substituted the words "10 years".

(4B) In the case of an offence under subsection (1) or (2) above in connection with the prohibition contained in regulation 2 of the Import of Seal Skins Regulations 1996, subsection (3) above shall have effect as if–

    (a) for paragraph (a) there were substituted the following-

"(a) on summary conviction, to a fine not exceeding the statutory maximum or to imprisonment for a term not exceeding three months, or to both"

; and

(b) in paragraph (b) for the words "7 years" there were substituted the words "2 years".

(4C) In the case of an offence under subsection (1) or (2) above in connection with a prohibition or restriction relating to the importation, exportation or shipment as stores of nuclear material, subsection (3)(b) above shall have effect as if for the words "7 years" there were substituted the words "14 years".

(5) In any case where a person would, apart from this subsection, be guilty of—

(a) an offence under this section in connection with a prohibition or restriction; and

(b) a corresponding offence under the enactment or other instrument imposing the prohibition or restriction, being an offence for which a fine or other penalty is expressly provided by that enactment or other instrument,

he shall not be guilty of the offence mentioned in paragraph (a) of this subsection.

(6) Where any person is guilty of an offence under this section, the goods in respect of which the offence was committed shall be liable to forfeiture.

PERMITTING PREMISES TO BE USED

Either-way, 6 months/£5,000 (Class A and B), 3 months/£2,500 (Class C); 14 years in indictment.

Misuse of Drugs Act 1971, s 8

Step 1: Determining the offence category.

Category 1: Higher culpability and greater harm

Category 2: lower culpability and greater harm; or higher culpability and lesser harm

Category 3: Lower culpability and lesser harm

Factors indicating culpability (non-exhaustive)	Factors indicating harm (non-exhaustive)
Higher culpability: Permits premises to be used primarily for drug activity, for example crack house Permits use in expectation of substantial financial gain Uses legitimate business premises to aid and/or conceal illegal activity, for example public house or club **Lower culpability:** Permits use for limited or no financial gain No active role in any supply taking place Involvement through naivety	**Greater harm:** Regular drug-related activity Higher quantity of drugs, for example: • heroin, cocaine–more than 5g; • cannabis–more than 50g. **Lesser harm:** Infrequent drug-related activity Lower quantity of drugs, for example: • heroin, cocaine–up to 5g; • cannabis–up to 50g.

Step 2: Starting point and category range

Class A

Offence category	Starting point	Category range
Category 1	Crown court	Crown court
Category 2	36 weeks' custody	High level community order –18 months' custody
Category 3	Medium level community order	Low level community order–high level community order

Class B

Offence category	Starting point	Category range
Category 1	1 year's custody	26 weeks'–18 months' custody
Category 2	High level community order	Low level community order–26 weeks' custody
Category 3	Band C fine	Band A fine–low level community order

Class C

Offence category	Starting point	Category range
Category 1	12 weeks' custody	High level community order–26 weeks custody (maz 12 weeks when tried summarily)
Category 2	Low level community order	Band C fine–high level community order
Cateogry 3	Band A fine	Discharge–band C fine

Factors increasing seriousness	Factors reducing seriousness or reflecting personal mitigation
Statutory aggravating factors: Previous convictions, having regard to a) nature of the offence to which conviction relates and relevance to current offence; and b) time elapsed since conviction Offence committed on bail **Other aggravating factors include:** Length of time over which premises used for drug activity Volume of drug activity permitted Premises adapted to facilitate drug activity Location of premises, for example proximity to school Attempts to conceal or dispose of evidence, where not charged separately Presence of others, especially children and/or non-users High purity Presence of weapons, where not charged separately Failure to comply with current court orders Offence committed on licence Established evidence of community impact	Involvement due to pressure, intimidation or coercion falling short of duress Isolated incident Low purity No previous convictions or no relevant or recent convictions Offender's vulnerability was exploited Remorse Good character and/or exemplary conduct Determination and/or demonstration of steps having been taken to address addiction or offending behaviour Serious medical conditions requiring urgent, intensive or long-term treatment Age and/or lack of maturity where it affects the responsibility of the offender Mental disorder or learning disability Sole or primary carer for dependent relatives

Additional steps:

Consider any factors which indicate a reduction, such as assistance to the prosecution; reduction for guilty plea; dangerousness; totality principle; compensation and ancillary orders; reasons; consideration for remand time.

POSSESSION OF A CONTROLLED DRUG

Either-way, 6 months/£5,000 Class A, 3 months/£2,500 Class B, 3 months/£1,000 Class C (7 years Class A, 5 years Class B, 2 years Class C)

Misuse of Drugs Act 1971, s 5(2)

Step 1: Determine the offence category

Category 1: Class A drug

Category 2: Class B drug

Category 3: Class C drug

Step 2: Starting point and range

Offence category	Starting point	Category range
Category 1 (class A)	Band C fine	Band A fine–51 weeks' custody
Category 2 (class B)	Band B fine	Discharge–26 weeks' custody
Cateogry 3 (class C)	Band A fine	Discharge–medium level community order

Factors increasing seriousness	Factors reducing seriousness or reflecting personal mitigation
Statutory aggravating factors: Previous convictions, having regard to a) nature of theoffence to which conviction relates and relevance to current offence; and b) time elapsed since conviction	No previous convictions or no relevant or recent convictions
Offence committed on bail	Remorse
Other aggravating factors include:	Good character and/or exemplary conduct
Possession of drug in prison	Offender is using cannabis to help with a diagnosed medical condition
Presence of others, especially children and/or non-users	Determination and/or demonstration of steps having been taken to address addiction or offending behaviour
Possession of drug in a school or licensed premises	Serious medical conditions requiring urgent, intensive or long-term treatment
Failure to comply with current court orders	Isolated incident
Offence committed on licence	Age and/or lack of maturity where it affects the responsibility of the offender
Attempts to conceal or dispose of evidence, where notcharged separately	Mental disorder or learning disability
Charged as importation of a very small amount	Sole or primary carer for dependent relatives
Established evidence of community impact	

Additional steps:

Consider any factors which indicate a reduction, such as assistance to the prosecution; reduction for guilty plea; dangerousness; totality principle; compensation and ancillary orders; reasons; consideration for remand time.

PRODUCTION OF A CONTROLLED DRUG AND CULTIVATION OF CANNABIS

Either-way, 6 months/£5,000 (Life–Class A, 14 years otherwise (section 6(2) offence is 14 years on indictment))

Misuse of Drugs Act 1971, ss 4(2)(a) or (b), 6(2)

Step 1: Determining the offence category

Culpability demonstrated by offender's role. One or more of these characteristics may demonstrate the offender's role. The list is not exhaustive.	Category of harm. Indicative output or potential output (upon which the starting point is based):
LEADING role: • directing or organising production on a commercial scale; • substantial links to, and influence on, others in a chain; • expectation of substantial financial gain; • uses business as cover; • abuses a position of trust or responsibility. **SIGNIFICANT role:** • operational or management function within a chain; • involves others in the operation whether by pressure, influence, intimidation or reward; • motivated by financial or other advantage, whether or not operating alone; • some awareness and understanding of scale of operation. LESSER role: • performs a limited function under direction; • engaged by pressure, coercion, intimidation; • involvement through naivety/exploitation; • no influence on those above in a chain; • very little, if any, awareness or understanding of the scale of operation; • if own operation, solely for own use (considering reasonableness of account in all the circumstances).	**Category 1** • heroin, cocaine–5kg; • ecstasy–10,000 tablets; • LSD–250,000 tablets; • amphetamine–20kg; • cannabis–operation capable of producing industrial quantities for commercial use; • ketamine–5kg. **Category 2** • heroin, cocaine–1kg; • ecstasy–2,000 tablets; • LSD–25,000 squares; • amphetamine–4kg; • cannabis–operation capable of producing significant quantities for commercial use; • ketamine–1kg. **Category 3** • heroin, cocaine–150g; • ecstasy–300 tablets; • LSD–2,500 squares; • amphetamine–750g; • cannabis–28 plants;* • ketamine–150g. Category 4 • heroin, cocaine–5g; • ecstasy–20 tablets; • LSD–170 squares; • amphetamine–20g; • cannabis–9 plants (domestic operation);* • ketamine–5g *with an assumed yield of 40g per plant

Step 2: Starting point and category range

CLASS A	Leading role	Significant role	Lesser role
Category 1	Crown Court	Crown Court	Crown Court
Category 2	Crown Court	Crown Court	Crown Court
Category 3	Crown Court	Crown Court	Crown Court
Category 4	Crown Court	Crown Court	Starting point 18 months' custody. Range: High level community order–3 years' custody

CLASS B	Leading role	Significant role	Lesser role
Category 1	Crown Court	Crown Court	Crown Court
Category 2	Crown Court	Crown Court	1 year's custody. Range: 26 weeks'– 3 years' custody
Category 3	Crown Court	1 year's custody. Range: 26 weeks' –3 years' custody	High level community order. Range: low level community order–26 weeks' custody
Category 4	1 year's custody. Range: High level cimmunityorder –3 years' custody	High level community order. Range: Medium level community order –26 weeks' custody	Band C fine. Range: Discharge –medium level community penalty

CLASS C	Leading role	Significant role	Lesser role
Category 1	Crown Court	Crown Court	Crown Court
Category 2	Crown Court	Crown Court	26 weeks' custody. Range: High level community order–18 months' custody
Category 3	Crown Court	26 weeks' custody. Range: High level community order–18 months' custody	High level community order. Range: low level community order–12 weeks' custody
Category 4	26 weeks' custody. Range: High level community order–18 months' custody	High level community order. Range: low level community order–12 weeks' custody	Band C fine. Range: Discharge–medium level community penalty

Factors increasing seriousness	Factors reducing seriousness or reflecting personal mitigation
Statutory aggravating factors: Previous convictions, having regard to a) nature of theoffence to which conviction relates and relevance to current offence; and b) time elapsed since conviction Offence committed on bail **Other aggravating factors include:** Nature of any likely supply Level of any profit element Use of premises accompanied by unlawful access to electricity/other utility supply of others Ongoing/large scale operation as evidenced by presenceand nature of specialist equipment Exposure of others to more than usual danger, for exampledrugs cut with harmful substances	Involvement due to pressure, intimidation or coercion falling short of duress, except where already taken into account at step 1 Isolated incident Low purity No previous convictions or no relevant or recent convictions Offender's vulnerability was exploited Remorse Good character and/or exemplary conduct Determination and/or demonstration of steps having been taken to address addiction or offending behaviour Serious medical conditions requiring urgent, intensive or long-term treatment

Attempts to conceal or dispose of evidence, where not charged separately	Age and/or lack of maturity where it affects the responsibility of the offender
Presence of others, especially children and/or non-users	Mental disorder or learning disability
Presence of weapon, where not charged separately	Sole or primary carer for dependent relatives
High purity or high potential yield	
Failure to comply with current court orders	
Offence committed on licence	
Established evidence of community impact	

Additional steps:

Consider any factors which indicate a reduction, such as assistance to the prosecution; reduction for guilty plea; dangerousness; totality principle; compensation and ancillary orders; reasons; consideration for remand time.

SUPPLYING OR OFFERING TO SUPPLY A CONTROLLED DRUG; POSSESSION OF A CONTROLLED DRUG WITH INTENT TO SUPPLY IT TO ANOTHER

Either-way, 6 months/£5,000 (Life–Class A, otherwise 14 years).Note that if an offence under section 4(3) is committed on or near school premises (by an adult offender), that must be treated as an aggravating factor (see s 4A below)

Misuse of Drugs Act 1971, s 4(3), 5(3)

Step 1: Determining the offence category

Culpability demonstrated by offender's role. One or more of these characteristics may demonstrate the offender's role. The list is not exhaustive.	Category of harm. Indicative output or potential output (upon which the starting point is based):
LEADING role: • directing or organising production on a commercial scale; • substantial links to, and influence on, others in a chain; • expectation of substantial financial gain; • uses business as cover; • abuses a position of trust or responsibility. **SIGNIFICANT role:** • operational or management function within a chain; • involves others in the operation whether by pressure, influence, intimidation or reward; • motivated by financial or other advantage, whether or not operating alone; • some awareness and understanding of scale of operation.	**Category 1** • heroin, cocaine–5kg; • ecstasy–10,000 tablets; • LSD–250,000 tablets; • amphetamine–20kg; • cannabis–200kg; • ketamine–5kg. **Category 2** • heroin, cocaine–1kg; • ecstasy–2,000 tablets; • LSD–25,000 squares; • amphetamine–4kg; • cannabis–40kg; • ketamine–1kg.

LESSER role:
- performs a limited function under direction;
- engaged by pressure, coercion, intimidation;
- involvement through naivety/exploitation;
- no influence on those above in a chain;
- very little, if any, awareness or understanding of the scale of operation;
- if own operation, solely for own use (considering reasonableness of account in all the circumstances).

Category 3

Where the offence is selling directly to users* ('street dealing'), the starting point is not based on quantity,

OR

Where the offence is suppy of drugs in prison by a prison employee, the starting point is not based on quantity.
- heroin, cocaine–150g;
- ecstasy–300 tablets;
- LSD–2,500 squares;
- amphetamine–750g;
- cannabis–6kg
- ketamine–150g.

Category 4
- heroin, cocaine–5g;
- cstasy–20 tablets;
- LSD–170 squares;
- amphetamine–20g;
- cannabis–100g
- ketamine–5g

OR

Where the offence is selling directly to users* ('street dealing') the starting point is not based on quantity–go to category 3

*including test purchase officers

Step 2: Starting point and category range

CLASS A	Leading role	Significant role	Lesser role
Category 1	Crown Court	Crown Court	Crown Court
Category 2	Crown Court	Crown Court	Crown Court
Category 3	Crown Court	Crown Court	Crown Court
Category 4	Crown Court	Crown Court	18 months' custody. Range: High level community order–3 years' custody

CLASS B	Leading role	Significant role	Lesser role
Category 1	Crown Court	Crown Court	Crown Court
Category 2	Crown Court	Crown Court	1 year's custody. Range: 26 weeks'–3 years' custody
Category 3	Crown Court	1 year's custody. Range: 26 weeks'–3 years' custody	High level community order. Range: Band B fine–medium level community order
Category 4	18 months' custody. Range: 16 weeks'–3 years custody	High level community order. Range: medium level community order–26 weeks' custody	Low level community order. Range: Band B fine–medium level community order

CLASS C	Leading role	Significant role	Lesser role
Category 1	Crown Court	Crown Court	Crown Court
Category 2	Crown Court	Crown Court	26 weeks' custody. Range: 12 weeks'–18 months' custody
Category 3	Crown Court	26 weeks' custody. Range: 12 weeks'–18 months' custody	High level community order. Range: low level community order–12 weeks' custody
Category 4	26 weeks' custody. Range: high level community order–18 months' custody	High level community order. Range: low level community order–12 weeks' custody	Low level community order. Range: Band A fine–medium level community order

Factors increasing seriousness	Factors reducing seriousness or reflecting personal mitigation
Statutory aggravating factors:	Involvement due to pressure, intimidation or coercion falling short of duress, except where already taken into account at step 1
Previous convictions, having regard to a) nature of theoffence to which conviction relates and relevance to current offence; and b) time elapsed since conviction	Supply only of drug to which offender addicted
Offender used or permitted a person under 18 to deliver acontrolled drug to a third person	Mistaken belief of the offender regarding the type of drug, taking into account the reasonableness of such belief in all the circumstances
Offender 18 or over supplies or offers to supply a drug on,or in the vicinity of, school premises either when school in use as such or at a time between one hour before and one hour after they are to be used	Isolated incident
Offence committed on bail	Low purity
Other aggravating factors include:	No previous convictions or no relevant or recent convictions
Targeting of any premises intended to locate vulnerableindividuals or supply to such individuals and/or supply to those under 18	Offender's vulnerability was exploited
Exposure of others to more than usual danger, for example drugs cut with harmful substances	Remorse
Attempts to conceal or dispose of evidence, where not charged separately	Good character and/or exemplary conduct
Presence of others, especially children and/or non-users	Determination and/or demonstration of steps having been taken to address addiction or offending behaviour
Presence of weapon, where not charged separately	Serious medical conditions requiring urgent, intensive or long-term treatment
Charged as importation of a very small amount	Age and/or lack of maturity where it affects the responsibility of the offender
High purity	
Failure to comply with current court orders	Mental disorder or learning disability
Offence committed on licence	Sole or primary carer for dependent relatives
Established evidence of community impact	

Additional steps:

Consider any factors which indicate a reduction, such as assistance to the prosecution; reduction for guilty plea; dangerousness; totality principle; compensation and ancillary orders; reasons; consideration for remand time.

Misuse of Drugs Act 1971, s 4A

4A Aggravation of offence of supply of controlled drug

(1) This section applies if–

(a) a court is considering the seriousness of an offence under section 4(3) of this Act, and

(b) at the time the offence was committed the offender had attained the age of 18.

(2) If either of the following conditions is met the court–

(a) must treat the fact that the condition is met as an aggravating factor (that is to say, a factor that increases the seriousness of the offence), and

(b) must state in open court that the offence is so aggravated.

(3) The first condition is that the offence was committed on or in the vicinity of school premises at a relevant time.

(4) The second condition is that in connection with the commission of the offence the offender used a courier who, at the time the offence was committed, was under the age of 18.

(5) In subsection (3), a relevant time is–

(a) any time when the school premises are in use by persons under the age of 18;

(b) one hour before the start and one hour after the end of any such time.

(6) For the purposes of subsection (4), a person uses a courier in connection with an offence under section 4(3) of this Act if he causes or permits another person (the courier)–

(a) to deliver a controlled drug to a third person, or

(b) to deliver a drug related consideration to himself or a third person.

(7) For the purposes of subsection (6), a drug related consideration is a consideration of any description which–

(a) is obtained in connection with the supply of a controlled drug, or

(b) is intended to be used in connection with obtaining a controlled drug.

(8) In this section–

"school premises" means land used for the purposes of a school excluding any land occupied solely as a dwelling by a person employed at the school; and

"school" has the same meaning–

(a) in England and Wales, as in section 4 of the Education Act 1996;

(b) in Scotland, as in section 135(1) of the Education (Scotland) Act 1980;

(c) in Northern Ireland, as in Article 2(2) of the Education and Libraries (Northern Ireland) Order 1986.

EDUCATION

SCHOOL ATTENDANCE ORDER, FAILURE TO COMPLY

Summary only, Fine £1000.

Burden: The burden of proving the defence under s 443(1) lies on the parent (*Oxfordshire County Council v L* [2010] EWHC 798 (Admin)).

Education Act 1996, s 443(1) and (2)

(1) If a parent on whom a school attendance order is served fails to comply with the requirements of the order, he is guilty of an offence, unless he proves that he is causing the child to receive suitable education otherwise than at school.

(2) If, in proceedings for an offence under this section, the parent is acquitted, the court may direct that the school attendance order shall cease to be in force.

SCHOOL NON-ATTENDANCE

Summary only. £1,000 fine (s 444(1), 3 months/£2500 fine (s 444(1A)).

Alternative verdict: If, on the trial of an offence under subsection (1A), the court finds the defendant not guilty of that offence but is satisfied that he is guilty of an offence under subsection (1), the court may find him guilty of that offence (s 444(8B), but see *Sutton London Borough Council v K* [2004] EWHC 2876 (Admin). **Burden of proof**: Once reasonable justification is raised by the defence (evidential standard) it falls upon the crown to disprove the defence to the criminal standard (*R(P) v Liverpool City Magistrates' Court* [2006] EWHC 2732 (Admin)). **Duress**: It is doubtful whether a defence of duress of circumstance is available (*Hampshire County Council v E* [2007] EWHC 2584 (Admin)). **Mens rea**: Section 444(1) is strict liability, and not contrary to article 6(2) ECHR (*Barnfather v Islington Education Authority* [2003] 1 WLR 2318). **Unavoidable cause**: A child's behavioural or psychological difficulties which contributed to a parent's difficulty in securing the child's attendance at school were insufficient to provide a defence under section 444(2A) (*Islington Borough Council v D* [2011] EWHC 990 (Admin)). A deliberate decision on the part of a child to leave the family home and refuse to tell a parent her whereabouts, was not capable of being an "unavoidable case" of the child's absence from school (*Warman v Bath District Council*, Unreported 19/11/1998). In the same case the court doubted the appropriateness of prosecuting the case given that the child was almost 16 years of age and of some maturity and whilst remitting the case back to the magistrates' court the High Court opined that an absolute discharge might be appropriate.

Education Act 1996, s 444(1), (1A), (1B), (2), (2A), and (3)

(1) If a child of compulsory school age who is a registered pupil at a school fails to attend regularly at the school, his parent is guilty of an offence.

(1A) If in the circumstances mentioned in subsection (1) the parent knows that his child is failing to attend regularly at the school and fails to cause him to do so, he is guilty of an offence.

(1B) It is a defence for a person charged with an offence under subsection (1A) to prove that he had a reasonable justification for his failure to cause the child to attend regularly at the school.

(2) Subsections (2A) to (6) below apply in proceedings for an offence under this section in respect of a child who is not a boarder at the school at which he is a registered pupil.

(2A) The child shall not be taken to have failed to attend regularly at the school by reason of his absence from the school at any time if the parent proves that at that time the child was prevented from attending by reason of sickness or any unavoidable cause.

(3) The child shall not be taken to have failed to attend regularly at the school by reason of his absence from the school—

(a) with leave, or

(b) [repealed]

(c) on any day exclusively set apart for religious observance by the religious body to which his parent belongs.

Offence seriousness (culpability and harm)		
A. Identify the appropriate starting point		
Starting points based on first time offender pleading not guilty		
Example of nature of activity	**Starting point**	**Range**
Short period following previous good attendance (s 444(1))	Band A fine	Conditional discharge to band A fine
Erratic attendance for long period (s 444(1))	Band B fine	Band B fine to band C fine
Colluding in and condoning non-attendance or deliberately instigating non-attendance (s 444(1A))	Medium level community order	Low level community order to high level community order

Offence seriousness (culpability and harm)	
B. Consider the effect of aggravating and mitigating factors (other than those within examples above)	
The following may be particularly relevant but **these lists are not exhaustive**	
Factors indicating higher culpability	**Factors indicating lower culpability**
1. Parental collusion (s 444(1) only)	1. Parent unaware of child's whereabouts
2. Lack of parental effort to ensure attendance (s 444(1) only)	2. Parent tried to ensure attendance
3. Threats to teachers and/or officials	3. Parent concerned by child's allegations of bullying/unable to get school to address bullying
4. Refusal to cooperate with school and/or officials	
Factors indicating greater degree of harm	
1. More than one child	
2. Harmful effect on other children in family	

FIREARMS

DEFINITIONS

See Firearms Act 1968, s 57 for general definitions. **Lawful authority:** This is not defined in the Act but is taken to mean those who have the right to possess firearms without a certificate (eg police, armed forces). A firearm certificate is only valid when the firearm is being carried in public in accordance with the terms of that certificate (*Jones* [1995] 1 Cr App R 262). **The proof whereof shall lie on him:** The civil standard of proof applies (*Carr-Briant* [1943] 2 All ER 156). **Has with him:** Means knowingly has with him (*Cugullere* [1961] 2 All ER 343). The firearm does not have to be in his personal possession, it is enough that there is a close physical link between him and the firearm (*Kelt* [1977] 1 WLR 1365).

Loaded: It is not necessary to prove that the defendant knew that the firearm was loaded (*Harrison* [1996] Crim LR 200). Ammunition in the chamber, barrel or magazine will be deemed to be loaded if it is capable of being manually or automatically fed into the chamber or barrel. **Imitation:** 'anything which has the appearance of being a firearm (other than such a weapon as is mentioned in section 5(1) (b) of this Act), whether or not it is capable of discharging any shot, bullet or other missile' (Firearms Act 1968, s 57(4)). If an item looked like a firearm at the time of its use then it is an imitation firearm (*Morris and King* (1984) 149 JP 60). A body part (in this case fingers being pointed under clothing) could not constitute an imitation firearm as the act required it to be a 'thing' distinct from the defendant himself (*Bentham* [2005] UKHL 18).

Firearms act 1968, s 57

(1) In this Act, the expression "firearm" means a lethal barrelled weapon of any description from which any shot, bullet or other missile can be discharged and includes—

    (a) any prohibited weapon, whether it is such a lethal weapon as aforesaid or not; and

    (b) any component part of such a lethal or prohibited weapon; and

    (c) any accessory to any such weapon designed or adapted to diminish the noise or flash caused by firing the weapon;

and so much of section 1 of this Act as excludes any description of firearm from the category of firearms to which that section applies shall be construed as also excluding component parts of, and accessories to, firearms of that description.

...

(2) In this Act, the expression "ammunition" means ammunition for any firearm and includes grenades, bombs and other like missiles, whether capable of use with a firearm or not, and also includes prohibited ammunition.

(2A) In this Act "self-loading" and "pump-action" in relation to any weapon mean respectively that it is designed or adapted (otherwise than as mentioned in section 5(1)(a)) so that it is automatically reloaded or that it is so designed or adapted that it is reloaded by the manual operation of the fore-end or forestock of the weapon.

(2B) In this Act "revolver", in relation to a smooth-bore gun, means a gun containing a series of chambers which revolve when the gun is fired.

(3) For purposes of sections 45, 46, 50, 51(4) and 52 of this Act, the offences under this Act relating specifically to air weapons are those under sections 22(4), 22(5), 23(1), 24(4) and 24ZA(1).

(4) In this Act—

"acquire" means hire, accept as a gift or borrow and "acquisition" shall be construed accordingly;

"air weapon" has the meaning assigned to it by section 1(3)(b) of this Act;

"another member State" means a member State other than the United Kingdom, and "other member States" shall be construed accordingly;

"area" means a police area;

"Article 7 authority" means a document issued by virtue of section 32A(1)(b) or (2) of this Act;

...

"certificate" (except in a context relating to the registration of firearms dealers) and "certificate under this Act" mean a firearm certificate or a shot gun certificate and—

    (a) "firearm certificate" means a certificate granted by a chief officer of police under this Act in respect of any firearm or ammunition to which section 1 of this Act applies and includes a certificate granted in Northern Ireland under section 1 of the Firearms Act 1920 or under an enactment of the Parliament of Northern Ireland amending or substituted for that section; and

    (b) "shot gun certificate" means a certificate granted by a chief officer of police under this Act and authorising a person to possess shot guns;

"civilian officer" means—

    (a) as respects England and Wales—

        (i) a person employed by a police authority established under section 3 of the Police Act 1996 who is under the direction and control of a chief officer of police,

      (ii)   a person employed by the Commissioner of Police of the Metropolis, or

      (iii) a person employed by the Corporation of the City of London who is under the direction and control of the Commissioner of Police for the City of London;

   (b) as respects Scotland, a person employed by a police authority who is under the direction and control of a chief officer of police;

"European firearms pass" means a document to which the holder of a certificate under this Act is entitled by virtue of section 32A(1)(a) of this Act;

"European weapons directive" means the directive of the Council of the European Communities No. 91/477/EEC (directive on the control of the acquisition and possession of weapons);

"firearms dealer" means [a person who, by way of trade or business—

   (a) manufactures, sells, transfers, repairs, tests or proves firearms or ammunition to which section 1 of this Act applies or shot guns; or

   (b) sells or transfers air weapons;

"imitation firearm" means anything which has the appearance of being a firearm (other than such a weapon as is mentioned in section 5(1)(b) of this Act) whether or not it is capable of discharging any shot, bullet or other missile;

...

"premises" includes any land;

"prescribed" means prescribed by rules made by the Secretary of State under section 53 of this Act;

"prohibited weapon" and "prohibited ammunition" have the meanings assigned to them by section 5(2) of this Act;

"public place" includes any highway and any other premises or place to which at the material time the public have or are permitted to have access, whether on payment or otherwise;

"registered", in relation to a firearms dealer, means registered either—

   (a) in Great Britain, under section 33 of this Act, or

   (b) in Northern Ireland, under section 8 of the Firearms Act 1920 or any enactment of the Parliament of Northern Ireland amending or substituted for that section,

and references to "the register", "registration" and a "certificate of registration" shall be construed accordingly, except in section 40;

"rifle" includes carbine;

"shot gun" has the meaning assigned to it by section 1(3)(a) of this Act and, in sections 3(1) and 45(2) of this Act and in the definition of "firearms dealer", includes any component part of a shot gun and any accessory to a shot gun designed or adapted to diminish the noise or flash caused by firing the gun;

"slaughtering instrument" means a firearm which is specially designed or adapted for the instantaneous slaughter of animals or for the instantaneous stunning of animals with a view to slaughtering them; and

"transfer" includes let on hire, give, lend and part with possession, and "transferor" and "transferee" shall be construed accordingly.

  (4A) For the purposes of any reference in this Act to the use of any firearm or ammunition for a purpose not authorised by the European weapons directive, the directive shall be taken to authorise the use of a firearm or ammunition as or with a slaughtering instrument and the use of a firearm and ammunition-

   (a) for sporting purposes;

   (b) for the shooting of vermin, or, in the course of carrying on activities in connection with the management of any estate, of other wildlife; and

(c) for competition purposes and target shooting outside competitions.

(5) The definitions in subsections (1) to (3) above apply to the provisions of this Act except where the context otherwise requires.

(6) For purposes of this Act—

(a) the length of the barrel of a firearm shall be measured from the muzzle to the point at which the charge is exploded on firing; and

(b) a shot gun or an air weapon shall be deemed to be loaded if there is ammunition in the chamber or barrel or in any magazine or other device which is in such a position that the ammunition can be fed into the chamber or barrel by the manual or automatic operation of some part of the gun or weapon.

AIR WEAPONS AND AMMUNITION

It is an offence for a person under the age of 18 to have with him an air weapon or ammunition for an air weapon (Firearms Act 1968, s 22(4)). The offence is triable summarily only, £1000 fine. Section 23 provides for a number of defences (see below).

It is an offence to prevent minors from having access to air weapons (Firearms Act 1968, s 24ZA). The offence is triable summarily only, £1000 fine.

Firearms Act 1968, s 23

(1) It is not an offence under section 22(4) of this Act for a person to have with him an air weapon or ammunition while he is under the supervision of a person of or over the age of twenty-one; but where a person has with him an air weapon on any premises in circumstances where he would be prohibited from having it with him but for this subsection, it is an offence for the person under whose supervision he is to allow him to use it for firing any missile beyond those premises.

...

(1A) In proceedings against a person for an offence under subsection (1) it shall be a defence for him to show that the only premises into or across which the missile was fired were premises the occupier of which had consented to the firing of the missile (whether specifically or by way of a general consent).

(2) It is not an offence under section 22(4) of this Act for a person to have with him an air weapon or ammunition at a time when—

(a) being a member of a rifle club or miniature rifle club for the time being approved by the Secretary of State for the purposes of this section or section 15 of the Firearms (Amendment) Act 1988, he is engaged as such a member ... in connection with target shooting; or

(b) he is using the weapon or ammunition at a shooting gallery where the only firearms used are either air weapons or miniature rifles not exceeding .23 inch calibre.

(3) It is not an offence under section 22(4) of this Act for a person of or over the age of fourteen to have with him an air weapon or ammunition on private premises with the consent of the occupier.

Firearms Act 1968, s 24ZA

(1) It is an offence for a person in possession of an air weapon to fail to take reasonable precautions to prevent any person under the age of eighteen from having the weapon with him.

(2) Subsection (1) does not apply where by virtue of section 23 of this Act the person under the age of eighteen is not prohibited from having the weapon with him.

(3) In proceedings for an offence under subsection (1) it is a defence to show that the person charged with the offence—

(a) believed the other person to be aged eighteen or over; and

(b) had reasonable ground for that belief.

(4) For the purposes of this section a person shall be taken to have shown the matters specified in subsection (3) if—

(a) sufficient evidence of those matters is adduced to raise an issue with respect to them; and

(b) the contrary is not proved beyond a reasonable doubt.

FIREARM, CARRYING IN A PUBLIC PLACE

Triable either-way unless the weapon is an air weapon (summary only). 6 months/£5,000 (7 years on indictment, or 12 months if an imitation weapon)

Loaded: It is not necessary for the prosecution to prove that the defendant knew that the firearm was loaded (*Harrison* [1996] Crim LR 200). **Imitation firearm:** An item is an imitation firearm if it 'looked like' a firearm at the time of its use (*Morris and King* (1984) 149 JP 60). A part of the body (eg fingers pointed under clothing) could not constitute an imitation firearm (*Bentham* [2005] UKHL 18).

Offence seriousness (culpability and harm)		
A. Identify the appropriate starting point		
Starting points based on first time offender pleading not guilty		
Examples of nature of activity	Starting point	Range
Carrying an unloaded air weapon	Low level community order	Band B fine to medium level community order
Carrying loaded air weapon/ imitation firearm/unloaded shot gun without ammunition	High level community order	Medium level community order to 26 weeks custody (air weapon) Medium level community order to Crown Court (imitation firearm, unloaded shot gun)
Carrying loaded shot gun/ carrying shot gun or any other firearm together with ammunition for it	Crown Court	Crown Court

Offence seriousness (culpability and harm)	
B. Consider the effect of aggravating and mitigating factors (other than those within examples above)	
The following may be particularly relevant but **these lists are not exhaustive**	
Factors indicating higher culpability	**Factors indicating lower culpability**
1. Brandishing firearm	1. Firearm not in sight
2. Carrying firearm in a busy place	2. No intention to use firearm
3. Planned illegal use	3. Firearm to be used for lawful purpose (not amounting to defence)
Factors indicating greater degree of harm	
1. Person or people put in fear	
2. Offender participating in violent incident	

Firearms Act 1968, s 19

A person commits an offence if, without lawful authority or reasonable excuse (the proof whereof lies on him) he has with him in a public place—

(a) a loaded shot gun,

(b) an air weapon (whether loaded or not),

(c) any other firearm (whether loaded or not) together with ammunition suitable for use in that firearm, or

(d) an imitation firearm.

FIRING AIR WEAPON

Summary only, £1,000 fine.

Firearms Act 1968, s 21A

(1) A person commits an offence if–

(a) he has with him an air weapon on any premises; and

(b) he uses it for firing a missile beyond those premises.

(2) In proceedings against a person for an offence under this section it shall be a defence for him to show that the only premises into or across which the missile was fired were premises the occupier of which had consented to the firing of the missile (whether specifically or by way of a general consent).

SHOTGUN OR FIREARM CERTIFICATES

Either-way, 6 months/£5,000 (Section 1(1) 5 years, or 7 years if aggravated; Section 2(1) 3 years or 5 years). Sections 1(2) and 2(2) offences are summary only.

Strict liability: The offences are strict liability (*Zahid* [2010] EWCA Crim 2158). **Necessity:** In *Gregory* [2011] EWCA Crim 1712 the court held:

"The defence of duress of circumstances is of strictly limited ambit. Nevertheless, it is possible to envisage circumstances in which, in the context of possession of a firearm, it, or a defence of necessity, might arise. In argument Walker J invited consideration of a situation in which a member of the public, witnessing a man firing a gun in a school room, disarms him and seizes hold of the weapon. A similar situation would arise if a bank robber drops his gun and a member of the public seizes hold of it and runs away with it to a safe place to keep it until the police arrive. We do not propose to give a ruling on these hypothetical cases. They must be decided in the light of their individual facts when they arise. We simply observe that in such extreme circumstances it may not be sufficient or fair to the public-spirited citizen to assume that because he or she would never be prosecuted and that, if a prosecution were mounted, the case would be disposed of by an absolute discharge, the possible duress/necessity defence would be bound to fail. But even these hypothetical facts do not exist here. There is and never has been any doubt that there was a time when the appellant was voluntarily in possession of the firearm, and that he remained in possession of it, intending to keep it for his own use. For a time, at any rate, even on the best possible view of his account, he had no altruistic or public-spirited intention, and there were no circumstances which created the slightest duress. None was suggested in his interview; none was suggested on his behalf prior to the judge's ruling; and in reality, even when he gave evidence at the Newton hearing, he did not suggest any duress of circumstances."

Firearms Act 1968, ss 1–2

1.— Requirement of firearms certificate.

(1) Subject to any exemption under this Act, it is an offence for a person—

(a) to have in his possession, or to purchase or acquire, a firearm to which this section applies without holding a firearm certificate in force at the time, or otherwise than as authorised by such a certificate;

(b) to have in his possession, or to purchase or acquire, any ammunition to which this section applies without holding a firearm certificate in force at the time, or otherwise than as authorised by such a certificate, or in quantities in excess of those so authorised.

(2) It is an offence for a person to fail to comply with a condition subject to which a firearm certificate is held by him.

(3) This section applies to every firearm except—

(a) a shot gun within the meaning of this Act, that is to say a smooth-bore gun (not being an air gun) which—

(i) has a barrel not less than 24 inches in length and does not have any barrel with a bore exceeding 2 inches in diameter;

(ii) either has no magazine or has a non-detachable magazine incapable of holding more than two cartridges; and

(iii) is not a revolver gun; and

(b) an air weapon (that is to say, an air rifle, air gun or air pistol which does not fall within section 5(1) and which is not of a type declared by rules made by the Secretary of State under section 53 of this Act to be specially dangerous).

(3A) A gun which has been adapted to have such a magazine as is mentioned in subsection (3)(a)(ii) above shall not be regarded as falling within that provision unless the magazine bears a mark approved by the Secretary of State for denoting that fact and that mark has been made, and the adaptation has been certified in writing as having been carried out in a manner approved by him, either by one of the two companies mentioned in section 58(1) of this Act or by such other person as may be approved by him for that purpose.

(4) This section applies to any ammunition for a firearm, except the following articles, namely:—

(a) cartridges containing five or more shot, none of which exceeds .36 inch in diameter;

(b) ammunition for an air gun, air rifle or air pistol; and

(c) blank cartridges not more than one inch in diameter measured immediately in front of the rim or cannelure of the base of the cartridge.

2.— Requirement of certificate for possession of shot guns.

(1) Subject to any exemption under this Act, it is an offence for a person to have in his possession, or to purchase or acquire, a short gun without holding a certificate under this Act authorising him to possess shot guns.

(2) It is an offence for a person to fail to comply with a condition subject to which a shot gun certificate is held by him.

SUPPLYING IMITATION FIREARMS

Summary only, 6 months/£5,000.

Firearms Act 1968, s 24A

(1) It is an offence for a person under the age of eighteen to purchase an imitation firearm.

(2) It is an offence to sell an imitation firearm to a person under the age of eighteen.

(3) In proceedings for an offence under subsection (2) it is a defence to show that the person charged with the offence–

(a) believed the other person to be aged eighteen or over; and

(b) had reasonable ground for that belief.

(4) For the purposes of this section a person shall be taken to have shown the matters specified in subsection (3) if–

(a) sufficient evidence of those matters is adduced to raise an issue with respect to them; and

(b) the contrary is not proved beyond a reasonable doubt.

IMMIGRATION OFFENCES

GENERAL

Extended time limits: Certain summary offences can be commenced greater than 6 months from commission:

Immigration Act 1971, s 28

(1) Where the offence is one to which, under section 24 or 26 above, an extended time limit for prosecutions is to apply, then—

(a) an information relating to the offence may in England and Wales be tried by a magistrates' court if it is laid within six months after the commission of the offence, or if it is laid within three years after the commission of the offence and not more than two months after the date certified by an officer of police above the rank of chief superintendent to be the date on which evidence sufficient to justify proceedings came to the notice of an officer of the police force to which he belongs; and

(b) summary proceedings for the offence may in Scotland be commenced within six months after the commission of the offence, or within three years after the commission of the offence and not more than two months after the date on which evidence sufficient in the opinion of the Lord Advocate to justify proceedings came to his knowledge; and

(c) a complaint charging the commission of the offence may in Northern Ireland be heard and determined by a magistrates' court if it is made within six months after the commission of the offence, or if it is made within three years after the commission of the offence and not more than two months after the date certified by an officer of police not below the rank of assistant chief constable to be the date on which evidence sufficient to justify the proceedings came to the notice of the police in Northern Ireland.

(2) For purposes of subsection (1)(b) above proceedings shall be deemed to be commenced on the date on which a warrant to apprehend or to cite the accused is granted, if such warrant is executed without undue delay; and a certificate of the Lord Advocate as to the date on which such evidence as is mentioned in subsection (1)(b) came to his knowledge shall be conclusive evidence.

(3) For the purposes of the trial of a person for an offence under this Part of this Act, the offence shall be deemed to have been committed either at the place at which it actually was committed or at any place at which he may be.

(4) Any powers exercisable under this Act in the case of any person may be exercised notwithstanding that proceedings for an offence under this Part of this Act have been taken against him.

ASSISTING UNLAWFUL ENTRY

Either-way 6 months/£5,000 (14 years)

Distinction between section 25 and 25A: "It is not possible to conclude, by reading Section 25 and 25A together, that only Section 25A covers a case where the third party is an asylum seeker. Section 25A would in my judgment apply in the case of an asylum seeker who arrives in or enters the United Kingdom without any breach of immigration law being committed by the third party at all. It is plainly principally directed at traffickers of asylum seekers ... Section 25, by contrast, is concerned with facilitation of the commission of breaches of immigration law" (*Sternaj v Director of Public Prosecutions* [2011] EWHC 1094 (Admin)). **Immigration law:** A law which determined whether a person was lawfully or unlawfully either entering the United Kingdom, or in transit or being in the UK (*Kapoor* [2012] EWCA 435).

Immigration Act 1971, ss 25, 25A, and 25B

25 **Assisting unlawful immigration to member State**

(1) A person commits an offence if he—

   (a) does an act which facilitates the commission of a breach of immigration law by an individual who is not a citizen of the European Union,

   (b) knows or has reasonable cause for believing that the act facilitates the commission of a breach of immigration law by the individual, and

   (c) knows or has reasonable cause for believing that the individual is not a citizen of the European Union.

25A **Helping asylum-seeker to enter United Kingdom**

(1) A person commits an offence if—

   (a) he knowingly and for gain facilitates the arrival in, or the entry into, the United Kingdom of an individual, and

   (b) he knows or has reasonable cause to believe that the individual is an asylum-seeker.

25B **Assisting entry to United Kingdom in breach of deportation or exclusion order**

(1) A person commits an offence if he—

   (a) does an act which facilitates a breach of a deportation order in force against an individual who is a citizen of the European Union, and

   (b) knows or has reasonable cause for believing that the act facilitates a breach of the deportation order.

ILLEGAL ENTRY AND SIMILAR OFFENCES

Section 24: Summary only, 6 months/£5,000; Section 24A Either-way, 6 months/£5,000 (2 years)

Time limit: An extended time limit for prosecution applies to section 24(1)(a) and (c). **Proving legality of entry:** The burden of proving that entry was legal falls upon the defendant in relation to prosecutions commenced within six months of that entry (s 24(4)(b)).

Immigration Act 1971, s 24, 24A

24 **Illegal entry and similar offences**

(1) It is an offence—

   (a) if contrary to this Act he knowingly enters the United Kingdom in breach of a deportation order or without leave;

   (b) if, having only a limited leave to enter or remain in the United Kingdom, he knowingly either—

       (i) remains beyond the time limited by the leave; or

      (ii)   fails to observe a condition of the leave;

    (c) if, having lawfully entered the United Kingdom without leave by virtue of section 8(1) above, he remains without leave beyond the time allowed by section 8(1);

    (d) if, without reasonable excuse, he fails to comply with any requirement imposed on him under Schedule 2 to this Act to report to a medical officer of health, or to attend, or submit to a test or examination, as required by such an officer;

    (e) if, without reasonable excuse, he fails to observe any restriction imposed on him under Schedule 2 or 3 to this Act as to residence, as to his employment or occupation or as to reporting to the police, to an immigration officer or to the Secretary of State;

    (f) if he disembarks in the United Kingdom from a ship or aircraft after being placed on board under Schedule 2 or 3 to this Act with a view to his removal from the United Kingdom;

    (g) if he embarks in contravention of a restriction imposed by or under an Order in Council under section 3(7) of this Act.

(1A)   A person commits an offence under subsection (1)(b)(i) above on the day when he first knows that the time limited by his leave has expired and continues to commit it throughout any period during which he is in the United Kingdom thereafter; but a person shall not be prosecuted under that provision more than once in respect of the same limited leave.

(3)   The extended time limit for prosecutions which is provided for by section 28 below shall apply to offences under subsection (1)(a) and (c) above.

(4)   In proceedings for an offence against subsection (1)(a) above of entering the United Kingdom without leave,—

    (a) any stamp purporting to have been imprinted on a passport or other travel document by an immigration officer on a particular date for the purpose of giving leave shall be presumed to have been duly so imprinted, unless the contrary is proved;

    (b) proof that a person had leave to enter the United Kingdom shall lie on the defence if, but only if, he is shown to have entered within six months before the date when the proceedings were commenced.

24A Deception

(1)   A person who is not a British citizen is guilty of an offence if, by means which include deception by him—

    (a) he obtains or seeks to obtain leave to enter or remain in the United Kingdom; or

    (b) he secures or seeks to secure the avoidance, postponement or revocation of enforcement action against him.

(2)   "Enforcement action", in relation to a person, means—

    (a) the giving of directions for his removal from the United Kingdom ("directions") under Schedule 2 to this Act or section 10 of the Immigration and Asylum Act 1999;

    (b) the making of a deportation order against him under section 5 of this Act; or

    (c) his removal from the United Kingdom in consequence of directions or a deportation order.

POSSESSING FALSE PASSPORTS, WORK PERMITS, REGISTRATION CARDS, ETC

Section 26 summary only, 6 months/£5,000; Section 26A either-way, 6 months/£5,000 (10 years) (subsection (3)(a), (b), (d), (e), (f) or (g)); 6 months/£5,000 (2 years) (subsection (3)(c) or (h)); Section 26B either-way, 6 months/£5,000

Time limit: An extended time limit for prosecution applies to section 26(1)(c) and (d).

Immigration Act 1971, ss 26, 26A and 26B

26 General offences in connection with administration of Act

(1) A person shall be guilty of an offence [...] in any of the following cases—

(a) if, without reasonable excuse, he refuses or fails to submit to examination under Schedule 2 to this Act;

(b) if, without reasonable excuse, he refuses to fails to furnish or produce any information in his possession, or any documents in his possession or control, which he is on an examination under that Schedule required to furnish or produce;

(c) if on any such examination or otherwise he makes or causes to be made to an immigration officer or other person lawfully acting in the execution of a relevant enactment a return, statement or representation which he knows to be false or does not believe to be true;

(d) if, without lawful authority, he alters any certificate of entitlement, entry clearance, work permit or other document issued or made under or for the purposes of this Act, or uses for the purposes of this Act, or has in his possession for such use, any passport, certificate of entitlement, entry clearance, work permit or other document which he knows or has reasonable cause to believe to be false;

(e) if, without reasonable excuse, he fails to complete and produce a landing or embarkation card in accordance with any order under Schedule 2 to this Act;

(f) if, without reasonable excuse, he fails to comply with any requirement of regulations under section 4(3) or of an order under section 4(4) above;

(g) if, without reasonable excuse, he obstructs an immigration officer or other person lawfully acting in the execution of this Act.

26A Registration card

...

(3) A person commits an offence if he—

(a) makes a false registration card,

(b) alters a registration card with intent to deceive or to enable another to deceive,

(c) has a false or altered registration card in his possession without reasonable excuse,

(d) uses or attempts to use a false registration card for a purpose for which a registration card is issued,

(e) uses or attempts to use an altered registration card with intent to deceive,

(f) makes an article designed to be used in making a false registration card,

(g) makes an article designed to be used in altering a registration card with intent to deceive or to enable another to deceive, or

(h) has an article within paragraph (f) or (g) in his possession without reasonable excuse.

(4) In subsection (3) "false registration card" means a document which is designed to appear to be a registration card.

26B Possession of immigration stamp

(1) A person commits an offence if he has an immigration stamp in his possession without reasonable excuse.

(2) A person commits an offence if he has a replica immigration stamp in his possession without reasonable excuse.

(3) In this section—

(a) "immigration stamp" means a device which is designed for the purpose of stamping documents in the exercise of an immigration function,

(b) "replica immigration stamp" means a device which is designed for the purpose of stamping a document so that it appears to have been stamped in the exercise of an immigration function, and

(c) "immigration function" means a function of an immigration officer or the Secretary of State under the Immigration Acts.

OFFENCES AGAINST THE PERSON

ASSAULT OCCASIONING ACTUAL BODILY HARM

Either-way, 6 months/£5,000 (5 years; 7 years if racially or religiously aggravated).

Degree: Injury must be more than merely transient or trifling, but need not be permanent (*Donovan* [1934] 2 KB 498). **Hair:** Cutting off someone's hair amounts to actual bodily harm (*Director of Public Prosecutions v Smith* [2006] 1 WLR 1571).

Offences Against the Person Act 1861, s 47

Step 1: Determining the offence category

Category 1: Greater harm (serious injury must normally be present) and higher culpability

Category 2: Greater harm (serious injury must normally be present) and lower culpability or lesser harm and higher culpability

Category 3: Lesser harm and lower culpability

Factors indicating greater harm	Factors indicating higher culpability
Injury (which includes disease transmission and/or psychological harm) which is serious in the context of the offence (must normally be present) Victim is particularly vulnerable because of personal circumstances Sustained or repeated assault on the same victim	**Statutory aggravating factors:** Offence motivated by, or demonstrating, hostility to the victim based on his or her sexual orientation (or presumed sexual orientation) Offence motivated by, or demonstrating, hostility to the victim based on the victim's disability (or presumed disability) **Other aggravating factors:** A significant degree of premeditation Use of weapon or weapon equivalent (for example, shod foot, headbutting, use of acid, use of animal) Intention to commit more serious harm than actually resulted from the offence Deliberately causes more harm than is necessary for commission of offence Deliberate targeting of vulnerable victim Leading role in group or gang Offence motivated by, or demonstrating, hostility based on the victim's age, sex, gender identity (or presumed gender identity)
Factors indicating lesser harm	**Factors indicating lower culpability**

Injury which is less serious in the context of the offence	Subordinate role in group or gang
	A greater degree of provocation than normally expected
	Lack of premeditation
	Mental disorder or learning disability, where linked to commission of the offence
	Excessive self defence

Step 2: Starting point and category range

Offence category	Starting point	Category Range
Category 1	Crown court	Crown court
Category 2	26 weeks' custody	Low level community order–crown court (51 weeks' custody)
Category 3	Medium level community order	Band A fine–high level community order

Factors increasing seriousness	Factors reducing seriousness or reflecting personal mitigation
Statutory aggravating factors: Previous convictions, having regard to a) the nature of the offence to which the conviction relates and its relevance to the current offence; and b) the time that has elapsed since the conviction	No previous convictions or no relevant/recent convictions
Offence committed whilst on bail	Single blow
Other aggravating factors include:	Remorse
Location of the offence	Good character and/or exemplary conduct
Timing of the offence	Determination and/or demonstration of steps taken to address addiction or offending behaviour
Ongoing effect upon the victim	
Offence committed against those working in the public sector or providing a service to the public	Serious medical conditions requiring urgent, intensive or long-term treatment
Presence of others including relatives, especially childrenor partner of the victim	Isolated incident
Gratuitous degradation of victim	Age and/or lack of maturity where it affects the responsibility of the offender
In domestic violence cases, victim forced to leave their home	
Failure to comply with current court orders	
Offence committed whilst on licence	Lapse of time since the offence where this is not the fault of the offender
An attempt to conceal or dispose of evidence	
Failure to respond to warnings or concerns expressed by others about the offender's behaviour	Mental disorder or learning disability, where not linked to the commission of the offence
Commission of offence whilst under the influence of alcohol or drugs	
Abuse of power and/or position of trust	Sole or primary carer for dependent relatives
Exploiting contact arrangements with a child to commit an offence	
Established evidence of community impact	
Any steps taken to prevent the victim reporting an incident, obtaining assistance and/or from assisting or supporting the prosecution	
Offences taken into consideration (TICs)	

Additional steps:

Consider any factors which indicate a reduction, such as assistance to the prosecution; reduction for guilty plea; dangerousness; totality principle; compensation and ancillary orders; reasons; consideration for remand time.

ASSAULT WITH INTENT TO RESIST ARREST

Either-way, 6 months/£5,000 (2 years).

Lawful arrest: A defendant's honest but mistaken belief as to the lawfulness of the arrest does not afford him a defence as it is not one relating to fact (*Lee* [2000] Crim LR 991; *Hewitt v Director of Public Prosecutions* [2002] EWHC 2801 (QB)). **Police officers:** In the case of an arrest by a police officer, the prosecution does not need to prove that the defendant was aware that the arresting person was a police officer (*Brightling* [1991] Crim LR 364). **Offence:** Offence means criminal offence and does not extend to breach of the peace or exercise of police powers generally (*Kenlin v Gardener* [1967] 2 WLR 129; *Wood v Director of Public Prosecutions* [2008] EWHC 1056 (Admin)).

Step 1: Determining the offence category

Category 1: Greater harm and higher culpability

Category 2: Greater harm and lower culpability; or lesser harm and higher culpability

Category 3: Lesser harm and lower culpability

Factors indicating greater harm	Factors indicating higher culpability
Sustained or repeated assault on the same victim	**Statutory aggravating factors:** Offence racially or religiously aggravated Offence motivated by, or demonstrating, hostility to the victim based on his or her sexual orientation(or presumed sexual orientation) Offence motivated by, or demonstrating, hostility to the victim based on the victim's disability (or presumed disability) **Other aggravating factors:** A significant degree of premeditation Use of weapon or weapon equivalent (for example, shod foot, headbutting, use of acid, use of animal) Intention to commit more serious harm than actually resulted from the offence Deliberately causes more harm than is necessary for commission of offence Leading role in group or gang Offence motivated by, or demonstrating, hostility based on the victim's age, sex, gender identity (or presumed gender identity)
Factors indicating lesser harm	**Factors indicating lower culpability**
Injury which is less serious in the context of the offence	Subordinate role in group or gang Lack of premeditation Mental disorder or learning disability, where linked to commission of the offence

Step 2: Starting point and category range

Offence category	Starting point	Category Range
Category 1	26 weeks' custody	12 weeks' custody–crown court (51 weeks' custody)
Category 2	Medium level community order	Low level community order–High level community order
Category 3	Band B fine	Band A fine–Band C fine

Factors increasing seriousness	Factors reducing seriousness or reflecting personal mitigation
Statutory aggravating factors: Previous convictions, having regard to a) the nature of the offence to which the conviction relates and its relevance to the current offence; and b) the time that has elapsed since the conviction Offence committed whilst on bail **Other aggravating factors include:** Location of the offence Timing of the offence Ongoing effect upon the victim Gratuitous degradation of victim Failure to comply with current court orders Offence committed whilst on licence An attempt to conceal or dispose of evidence Failure to respond to warnings or concerns expressed by others about the offender's behaviour Commission of offence whilst under the influence of alcohol or drugs Established evidence of community impact Any steps taken to prevent the victim reporting an incident, obtaining assistance and/or from assisting or supporting the prosecution Offences taken into consideration (TICs)	No previous convictions or no relevant/recent convictions Single blow Remorse Good character and/or exemplary conduct Determination and/or demonstration of steps taken to address addiction or offending behaviour Serious medical conditions requiring urgent, intensive or long-term treatment Isolated incident Age and/or lack of maturity where it affects the responsibility of the defendant Mental disorder or learning disability, where not linked to the commission of the offence Sole or primary carer for dependent relatives

Additional steps:

Consider any factors which indicate a reduction, such as assistance to the prosecution; reduction for guilty plea; dangerousness; totality principle; compensation and ancillary orders; reasons; consideration for remand time.

Offences Against the Person Act 1861, s 38

Whosoever shall assault any person with intent to resist or prevent the lawful apprehension or detainer of himself or of any other person for any offence, shall be guilty of an offence.

ASSAULTING A COURT SECURITY OFFICER

Summary only, 6 months/£5,000.

Courts Act 2003, s 57.

A court officer must be appointed by the Lord Chancellor, and designated in that role (Courts Act 2003, s 51). Section 51(3) provides that '…a court security officer who is not readily identifiable as such (whether by means of his uniform or badge or otherwise), is not to be regarded as acting in the execution of his duty'.

ASSAULTING A POLICE CONSTABLE OR RESISTING OR OBSTRUCTING A POLICE CONSTABLE

Summary only, 6 months/£5,000 (assaults), 1 month/£1,000 (resist/obstruct).

The constable must be acting lawfully (ie in execution of his duty) and the prosecution should adduce evidence to establish the lawfulness of the officer's actions, although in some cases it could be readily inferred from the circumstances (*R (Odewale) v Director of Public Prosecutions*, unreported, 28 November 2000, see *Bristol* [2007] EWCA Crim 3214 and *Fiak* [2005] EWCA Crim 2381 for a good illustration of this issue). **Knowledge:** The prosecution does not need to prove that the defendant knew that the person was a police officer (*Brightling* [1991] Crim LR 364). **Lawfully:** If an officer is not acting lawfully in arresting a suspect, any other officer who in good faith seeks to assist officer A will also be acting unlawfully (*Cumberbatch v Crown Prosecution Service* [2009] EWHC 3353 (Admin)). If a suspect is accused of trying to impede the arrest of a third party, it must be shown that the arrest of that third party was lawful (*Riley v Director of Public Prosecutions* 91 Cr App R 14). For the lawfulness of a police officer entering premises to save life or limb, see *Baker v Crown Prosecution Service* [2009] EWHC 299 (Admin). For the situation where a police officer has had a licence to remain on property revoked, see *R (Fullard) v Woking Magistrates' Court* [2005] EWHC 2922 (Admin) where it was said that the issue of revocation was to be objectively judged. An officer who had not yet established grounds for arrest was acting unlawfully in restraining a suspect (*Wood v Director of Public Prosecutions* [2008] EWHC 1056 (Admin)). **Recklessness:** The court is entitled to convict on the basis of recklessness even where the Crown puts its case on the basis of an intentional assault (*D v Director of Public Prosecutions* [2005] Crim LR 962). **Obstruction:** This means making the officer's task more difficult (*Hinchcliffe v Sheldon* [1955] 1 WLR 1207). Warning a driver that there is a 'speed trap' might amount to obstruction if it could be established that the person warned was or was likely to be, speeding (*Director of Public Prosecutions v Glendinning* [2005] EWHC 2333 (Admin)).

Step 1: Determining the offence category

Category 1: Greater harm and higher culpability

Category 2: Greater harm and lower culpability; or lesser harm and higher culpability

Category 3: Lesser harm and lower culpability

Factors indicating greater harm	Factors indicating higher culpability
Sustained or repeated assault on the same victim	**Statutory aggravating factors:** Offence racially or religiously aggravated Offence motivated by, or demonstrating, hostility to the victim based on his or her sexual orientation (or presumed sexual orientation) Offence motivated by, or demonstrating, hostility to the victim based on the victim's disability(or presumed disability) **Other aggravating factors:** A significant degree of premeditation Use of weapon or weapon equivalent (for example, shod foot, headbutting, use of acid, use of animal) Intention to commit more serious harm than actually resulted from the offence

	Deliberately causes more harm than is necessary for commission of offence Leading role in group or gang Offence motivated by, or demonstrating, hostility based on the victim's age, sex, gender identity (or presumed gender identity)
Factors indicating lesser harm	**Factors indicating lower culpability**
Injury which is less serious in the context of the offence	Subordinate role in group or gang Lack of premeditation Mental disorder or learning disability, where linked to commission of the offence

Step 2: Starting point and category range

Offence category	Starting point	Category Range
Category 1	12 weeks' custody	Low level community order–26 weeks' custody
Category 2	Medium level community order	Low level community order–high level community order
Category 3	Band B fine	Band A fine–Band C fine

Factors increasing seriousness	Factors reducing seriousness or reflecting personal mitigation
Statutory aggravating factors: Previous convictions, having regard to a) the nature of the offence to which the conviction relates and its relevance to the current offence; and b) the time that has elapsed since the conviction Offence committed whilst on bail **Other aggravating factors include:** Location of the offence Timing of the offence Ongoing effect upon the victim Gratuitous degradation of victim Failure to comply with current court orders Offence committed whilst on licence An attempt to conceal or dispose of evidence Failure to respond to warnings or concerns expressed by others about the offender's behaviour Commission of offence whilst under the influence of alcohol or drugs Established evidence of community impact Any steps taken to prevent the victim reporting an incident, obtaining assistance and/or from assisting or supporting the prosecution Offences taken into consideration (TICs)	No previous convictions or no relevant/recent convictions Single blow Remorse Good character and/or exemplary conduct Determination and/or demonstration of steps taken to address addiction or offending behaviour Serious medical conditions requiring urgent, intensive or long-term treatment Isolated incident Age and/or lack of maturity where it affects the responsibility of the offender Lapse of time since the offence where this is not the fault of the offender Mental disorder or learning disability, where not linked to the commission of the offence Sole or primary carer for dependent relatives

Additional steps:

Consider any factors which indicate a reduction, such as assistance to the prosecution; reduction for guilty plea; dangerousness; totality principle; compensation and ancillary orders; reasons; consideration for remand time.

Police Act 1996, s 89(1)–(2)

(1) Any person who assaults a constable in the execution of his duty, or a person assisting a constable in the execution of his duty, shall be guilty of an offence…

(2) Any person who resists or wilfully obstructs a constable in the execution of his duty, or a person assisting a constable in the execution of his duty, shall be guilty of an offence.

COMMON ASSAULT

Summary only (unless racially or religiously aggravated when it is triable either-way). 6 months/£5,000 (2 years if racially/religiously aggravated).

Criminal Justice Act 1988, s 39.

Consent: Evidence of a lack of consent can be inferred from evidence in the case and need not come from the complainant (see *Director of Public Prosecutions v Shabbir* [2009] EWHC 2754 (Admin)), where the court was scathing as to the raising of lack of consent as being an arguable point). **Battery:** Spitting on someone's face is sufficient to constitute a battery (*Lynsey* [1995] 2 Cr App R 667). **Duplicity:** A charge that alleges both assault and battery is duplicitous (*Norman* [1994] Crim LR 518).

Step 1: Determining the offence category

Category 1: Greater harm (injury or fear of injury must normally be present) and higher culpability

Category 2: Greater harm (injury or fear of injury must normally be present) and lower culpability; or lesser harm and higher culpability

Category 3: Lesser harm and lower culpability

Factors indicating greater harm	Factors indicating higher culpability
Injury or fear of injury which is serious in the context of the offence (must normally be present) Victim is particularly vulnerable because of personal circumstances Sustained or repeated assault on the same victim	**Statutory aggravating factors:** Offence motivated by, or demonstrating, hostility to the victim based on his or her sexual orientation (or presumed sexual orientation) Offence motivated by, or demonstrating, hostility to the victim based on the victim's disability (or presumed disability) **Other aggravating factors:** A significant degree of premeditation Threatened or actual use of weapon or weapon equivalent (for example, shod foot, headbutting, use of acid, use of animal) Intention to commit more serious harm than actually resulted from the offence Deliberately causes more harm than is necessary for commission of offence Deliberate targeting of vulnerable victim Leading role in group or gang Offence motivated by, or demonstrating, hostility based on the victim's age, sex, gender identity (or presumed gender identity)

Factors indicating lesser harm	Factors indicating lower culpability
Injury which is less serious in the context of the offence	Subordinate role in group or gang
	A greater degree of provocation than normally expected
	Lack of premeditation
	Mental disorder or learning disability, where linked to commission of the offence
	Excessive self defence

Step 2: Starting point and category range

Offence category	Starting point	Category Range
Category 1	High level community order	Low level community order–23 weeks' custody
Category 2	Medium level community order	Band A fine–high level community order
Category 3	Band A fine	Discharge–Band C fine

Factors increasing seriousness	Factors reducing seriousness or reflecting personal mitigation
Statutory aggravating factors:	
Previous convictions, having regard to a) the nature of the offence to which the conviction relates and its relevance to the current offence; and b) the time that has elapsed since the conviction	No previous convictions or no relevant/recent convictions
Offence committed whilst on bail	Single blow
Other aggravating factors include:	Remorse
Location of the offence	Good character and/or exemplary conduct
Timing of the offence	
Ongoing effect upon the victim	Determination and/or demonstration of steps taken to address addiction or offending behaviour
Offence committed against those working in the public sector or providing a service to the public	
Presence of others including relatives, especially children or partner of the victim	
Gratuitous degradation of victim	Serious medical conditions requiring urgent, intensive or long-term treatment
In domestic violence cases, victim forced to leave their home	
Failure to comply with current court orders	
Offence committed whilst on licence	Isolated incident
An attempt to conceal or dispose of evidence	Age and/or lack of maturity where it affects the responsibility of the offender
Failure to respond to warnings or concerns expressed by others about the offender's behaviour	
Commission of offence whilst under the influence of alcohol or drugs	
Abuse of power and/or position of trust	Lapse of time since the offence where this is not the fault of the offender
Exploiting contact arrangements with a child to commit an offence	Mental disorder or learning disability, where not linked to the commission of the offence
Established evidence of community impact	
Any steps taken to prevent the victim reporting an incident, obtaining assistance and/or from assisting or supporting the prosecution	
Offences taken into consideration (TICs	Sole or primary carer for dependent relative

Additional steps:

Consider any factors which indicate a reduction, such as assistance to the prosecution; reduction for guilty plea; dangerousness; totality principle; compensation and ancillary orders; reasons; consideration for remand time.

CHILD ABANDONMENT

Either-way, 6 months/£5,000 (5 years).

Abandonment: This means 'leaving a child to its fate' or 'wipe his hands clear of [them]' (*Boulden* 41 Cr App R 105).

Offences Against the Person Act 1861, s 27

Whosoever shall unlawfully abandon or expose any child, being under the age of two years, whereby the life of such child shall be endangered, or the health of such child shall have been or shall be likely to be permanently injured, shall be guilty...

CHILD ABDUCTION

Either-way, 6 months/£5,000 (7 years).

Consent: The Director of Public Prosecutions consent is required in relation to an offence under section 1. **Necessity:** This defence is not available (*S* [2012] EWCA Crim 389). **Overstay:** Where a person had been given consent to take a child out of the UK but then did not return with that child, no offence was committed under section 1 (*R (Nicolaou v Redbridge Magistrates' Court* [2012] EWHC 1647 (Admin)).

Child Abduction Act 1982, ss 1–2

1.— Offence of abduction of child by parent, etc.

(1)   Subject to subsections (5) and (8) below, a person connected with a child under the age of sixteen commits an offence if he takes or sends the child out of the United Kingdom without the appropriate consent.

(2)   A person is connected with a child for the purposes of this section if—

(a)   he is a parent of the child; or

(b)   in the case of a child whose parents were not married to each other at the time of his birth, there are reasonable grounds for believing that he is the father of the child; or

(c)   he is a guardian of the child; or

(ca) he is a special guardian of the child; or

(d)   he is a person in whose favour a residence order is in force with respect to the child; or

(e)   he has custody of the child.

(3)   In this section 'the appropriate consent', in relation to a child, means —

(a)   the consent of each of the following—

(i)   the child's mother;

(ii)   the child's father, if he has parental responsibility for him;

(iii)   any guardian of the child;

(iiia) any special guardian of the child;

(iv)   any person in whose favour a residence order is in force with respect to the child;

(v)   any person who has custody of the child; or

(b)   the leave of the court granted under or by virtue of any provision of Part II of the Children Act 1989; or

(c) if any person has custody of the child, the leave of the court which awarded custody to him.

(4) A person does not commit an offence under this section by taking or sending a child out of the United Kingdom without obtaining the appropriate consent if—

(a) he is a person in whose favour there is a residence order in force with respect to the child, and he takes or sends the child out of the United Kingdom for a period of less than one month; or

(b) he is a special guardian of the child and he takes or sends the child out of the United Kingdom for a period of less than three months.

(4A) Subsection (4) above does not apply if the person taking or sending the child out of the United Kingdom does so in breach of an order under Part II of the Children Act 1989.

(5) A person does not commit an offence under this section by doing anything without the consent of another person whose consent is required under the foregoing provisions if—

(a) he does it in the belief that the other person—

(i)   has consented; or

(ii) would consent if he was aware of all the relevant circumstances; or

(b) he has taken all reasonable steps to communicate with the other person but has been unable to communicate with him; or

(c) the other person has unreasonably refused to consent,

[...]

(5A) Subsection (5)(c) above does not apply if—

(a) the person who refused to consent is a person—

(i)   in whose favour there is a residence order in force with respect to the child;

(ia) who is a special guardian of the child; or

(ii) who has custody of the child; or

(b) the person taking or sending the child out of the United Kingdom is, by so acting, in breach of an order made by a court in the United Kingdom.

(6) Where, in proceedings for an offence under this section, there is sufficient evidence to raise an issue as to the application of subsection (5) above, it shall be for the prosecution to prove that that subsection does not apply.

(7) For the purposes of this section—

(a) 'guardian of a child', 'special guardian', 'residence order' and 'parental responsibility' have the same meaning as in the Children Act 1989; and

(b) a person shall be treated as having custody of a child if there is in force an order of a court in the United Kingdom awarding him (whether solely or jointly with another person) custody, legal custody or care and control of the child.

(8) This section shall have effect subject to the provisions of the Schedule to this Act in relation to a child who is in the care of a local authority detained in a place of safety, remanded to a local authority accommodation or the subject of proceedings or an order relating to adoption.

2.— Offence of abduction of child by other persons.

(1) Subject to subsection (3) below, a person, other than one mentioned in subsection (2) below, commits an offence if, without lawful authority or reasonable excuse, he takes or detains a child under the age of sixteen—

(a) so as to remove him from the lawful control of any person having lawful control of the child; or

(b) so as to keep him out of the lawful control of any person entitled to lawful control of the child.

(2) The persons are—

    (a) where the father and mother of the child in question were married to each other at the time of his birth, the child's father and mother;

    (b) where the father and mother of the child in question were not married to each other at the time of his birth, the child's mother; and

    (c) any other person mentioned in section 1(2)(c) to (e) above.

(3) In proceedings against any person for an offence under this section, it shall be a defence for that person to prove—

    (a) where the father and mother of the child in question were not married to each other at the time of his birth—

        (i) that he is the child's father; or

        (ii) that, at the time of the alleged offence, he believed, on reasonable grounds, that he was the child's father; or

    (b) that, at the time of the alleged offence, he believed that the child had attained the age of sixteen.

CRUELTY TO A CHILD

Either-way, 6 months/£5,000 (10 years).

A parent or other person legally liable to maintain a child or young person, or the legal guardian of a child or young person, shall be deemed to have neglected him in a manner likely to cause injury to his health if he has failed to provide adequate food, clothing, medical aid, or lodging for him, or if, having been unable otherwise to provide such food, clothing, medical aid, or lodging, he has failed to take steps to procure it to be provided under the enactments applicable in that behalf. **Suffocation:** Where it is proved that the death of an infant under three years of age was caused by suffocation (not being suffocation caused by disease or the presence of any foreign body in the throat or air passages of the infant) while the infant was in bed with some other person who has attained the age of 16 years, that other person shall, if he was, when he went to bed, under the influence of drink, be deemed to have neglected the infant in a manner likely to cause injury to its health.

A person may be convicted of an offence under this section: (1) notwithstanding that actual suffering or injury to health, or the likelihood of actual suffering or injury to health, was obviated by the action of another person; (2) notwithstanding the death of the child or young person in question.

Sentencing:

The same starting point and sentencing range are proposed for offences which might fall into the four categories (assault, ill-treatment or neglect, abandonment, and failure to protect). These are designed to take into account the fact that the victim is particularly vulnerable, assuming an abuse of trust or power and the likelihood of psychological harm, and are designed to reflect the seriousness with which society as a whole regards these offences. The starting points have been calculated to reflect the likelihood of psychological harm and this cannot be treated as an aggravating factor. Where there is an especially serious physical or psychological effect on the victim, even if unintended, this should increase sentence. The normal sentencing starting point for an offence of child cruelty should be a custodial sentence. The length of that sentence will be influenced by the circumstances in which the offence took place. However, in considering whether a custodial sentence is the most appropriate disposal, the court should take into account any available information concerning the future care of the child. Where the offender is the sole or primary carer of the victim or other dependants, this potentially should be taken into account for sentencing purposes, regardless of whether the offender is male or female. In such cases, an immediate custodial sentence may not be appropriate. The most relevant areas of personal mitigation are likely to be:

- mental illness/depression;
- inability to cope with pressures of parenthood;
- lack of support;
- sleep deprivation;
- offender dominated by an abusive or stronger partner;
- extreme behavioural difficulties in the child, often coupled with a lack of support;
- inability to secure assistance or support services in spite of every effort having been made by the offender.

Some of the factors identified above, in particular sleep deprivation, lack of support, and an inability to cope, could be regarded as an inherent part of caring for children, especially when a child is very young and could be put forward as mitigation by most carers charged with an offence of child cruelty. It follows that, before being accepted as mitigation, there must be evidence that these factors were present to a high degree and had an identifiable and significant impact on the offender's behaviour.

Offence seriousness (culpability and harm)
A. Identify the appropriate starting point
Starting points based on first time offender pleading not guilty

Example of nature of activity		Starting point	Range
(i)	Short-term neglect or ill-treatment	12 weeks custody	Low level community order to 26 weeks custody
(ii)	Single incident of short-term abandonment		
(iii)	Failure to protect a child from any of the above		
(i)	Assault(s) resulting in injuries consistent with ABH	Crown Court	26 weeks custody to Crown Court
(ii)	More than one incident of neglect or ill-treatment (but not amounting to long-term behaviour)		
(iii)	Single incident of long-term abandonment OR regular incidents of short-term abandonment (the longer the period of long-term abandonment or the greater the number of incidents of short-term abandonment, the more serious the offence)		
(iv)	Failure to protect a child from any of the above		
(i)	Series of assaults	Crown Court	Crown Court
(ii)	Protracted neglect or ill-treatment		
(iii)	Serious cruelty over a period of time		
(iv)	Failure to protect a child from any of the above		

Offence seriousness (culpability and harm)
B. Consider the effect of aggravating and mitigating factors
(other than those within examples above)
The following may be particularly relevant but **these lists are not exhaustive**

Factors indicating higher culpability	Factor indicating lower culpability
1. Targeting one particular child from the family	1. Seeking medical help or bringing the situation to the notice of the authorities
2. Sadistic behaviour	
3. Threats to prevent the victim from reporting the offence	
4. Deliberate concealment of the victim from the authorities	
5. Failure to seek medical help	

Children and Young Persons Act 1933, s 1(1)

(1) If any person who has attained the age of sixteen years and has responsibility for any child or young person under that age, wilfully assaults, ill-treats, neglects, abandons, or exposes him, or causes or procures him to be assaulted, ill-treated, neglected, abandoned, or exposed, in a manner likely to cause him unnecessary suffering or injury to health (including injury to or loss of sight, or hearing, or limb, or organ of the body, and any mental derangement), that person shall be guilty of an offence.

GRIEVOUS BODILY HARM/UNLAWFUL WOUNDING

Either-way, 6 months/£5,000 (5 years, 7 years if racially/religiously aggravated).

Grievous bodily harm: This means really serious harm and the jury should give the term its normal meaning (*Smith* [1961] AC 290). For psychiatric injury see *Ireland* [1998] AC 147. **Inflict:** This does not require the direct application of force (eg *Burstow* [1997] 1 Cr App R 144, where psychiatric harm was caused by the making of malicious telephone calls). **Wound:** Requires a break in the continuity of the skin (*Morris* [2005] EWCA Crim 609).

Step 1: Determining the offence category

Category 1: Greater harm (serious injury must normally be present) and higher culpability

Category 2: Greater harm (serious injury must normally be present) and lower culpability; or lesser harm and higher culpability

Category 3: Lesser harm and lower culpability

Factors indicating greater harm	Factors indicating higher culpability
Injury (which includes disease transmission and/or psychological harm) which is serious in the context of the offence (must normally be present)	**Statutory aggravating factors:** Offence motivated by, or demonstrating, hostility to the victim based on his or her sexual orientation (or presumed sexual orientation) Offence motivated by, or demonstrating, hostility to the victim based on the victim's disability (or presumed disability)
Victim is particularly vulnerable because of personal circumstances	**Other aggravating factors:** A significant degree of premeditation Use of weapon or weapon equivalent (for example, shod foot, headbutting, use of acid, use of animal)
Sustained or repeated assault on the same victim	Intention to commit more serious harm than actually resulted from the offence Deliberately causes more harm than is necessary for commission of offence Deliberate targeting of vulnerable victim Leading role in group or gang Offence motivated by, or demonstrating, hostility based on the victim's age, sex, gender identity (or presumed gender identity
Factors indicating lesser harm	**Factors indicating lower culpability**
Injury which is less serious in the context of the offence	

Step 2: Starting point and category range

Offence category	Starting point	Category Range
Category 1	Crown court	Crown court
Category 2	Crown court	Crown court
Category 3	High level community order	Low level community order–crown court (51 weeks' custody)

Factors increasing seriousness	Factors reducing seriousness or reflecting personal mitigation
Statutory aggravating factors: Previous convictions, having regard to a) the nature of the offence to which the conviction relates and its relevance to the current offence; and b) the time that has elapsed since the conviction Offence committed whilst on bail **Other aggravating factors include:** Location of the offence Timing of the offence Ongoing effect upon the victim Offence committed against those working in the public sector or providing a service to the public Presence of others including relatives, especially children or partner of the victim Gratuitous degradation of victim In domestic violence cases, victim forced to leave their home Failure to comply with current court orders Offence committed whilst on licence An attempt to conceal or dispose of evidence Failure to respond to warnings or concerns expressed by others about the offender's behaviour Commission of offence whilst under the influence of alcohol or drugs Abuse of power and/or position of trust Exploiting contact arrangements with a child to commit an offence Established evidence of community impact Any steps taken to prevent the victim reporting an incident, obtaining assistance and/or from assisting or supporting the prosecution Offences taken into consideration (TICs)	No previous convictions or no relevant/recent convictions Single blow Remorse Good character and/or exemplary conduct Determination and/or demonstration of steps taken to address addiction or offending behaviour Serious medical conditions requiring urgent, intensive or long-term treatment Isolated incident Age and/or lack of maturity where it affects the responsibility of the offender Lapse of time since the offence where this is not the fault of the offender Mental disorder or learning disability, where not linked to the commission of the offence Sole or primary carer for dependent relatives

Additional steps:

Consider any factors which indicate a reduction, such as assistance to the prosecution; reduction for guilty plea; dangerousness; totality principle; compensation and ancillary orders; reasons; consideration for remand time.

Offences Against the Person Act 1861, s 20

Whosoever shall unlawfully and maliciously wound or inflict any grievous bodily harm upon any other person, either with or without any weapon or instrument, shall be guilty of an offence.

HARASSMENT

Course of conduct: As few as 2 incidents can amount to a course of conduct, and this is so even where the complainant has been subject to distress on one occasion only (for example listening to a series of voice messages: *Kelly v Director of Public Prosecutions* (2002) 166 JP 621). In *R v Curtis* [2010] EWCA 123 the court allowed an appeal where the defendant, in the context of there being a volatile relationship, had been responsible for six incidents over a period of nine months. The court held that the conduct must be unacceptable to a degree which would sustain criminal liability and also must be oppressive, and went on to say:

> "Courts are well able to separate the wheat from the chaff at an early stage of the proceedings. They should be astute to do so. In most cases courts should have little difficulty in applying the 'close connection' test. Where the claim meets that requirement, and the quality of the conduct said to constitute harassment is being examined, courts will have in mind that irritations, annoyances, even a measure of upset, arise at times in everybody's day-to-day dealings with other people. Courts are well able to recognise the boundary between conduct which is unattractive, even unreasonable, and conduct which is oppressive and unacceptable. To cross the boundary from the regrettable to the unacceptable the gravity of the misconduct must be of an order which would sustain criminal liability under section 2."

Harassment: In *Curtis* the court observed:

> "To harass as defined in the Concise Oxford Dictionary, Tenth Edition, is to "torment by subjecting to constant interference or intimidation". The conduct must be unacceptable to a degree which would sustain criminal liability and also must be oppressive. Section 7 of the 1997 Act does not purport to provide a comprehensive definition of harassment. There are many actions that foreseeably alarm or cause a person distress that could not possibly be described as harassment. "Harassment" is, however, a word which has a meaning which is generally understood. It describes conduct targeted at an individual which is calculated to produce the consequences described in s.7 and which is oppressive and unreasonable. The practice of stalking is a prime example of such conduct. It is to be borne in mind that the state of affairs which was relied upon by the prosecution was miles away from the "stalking" type of offence for which the Act was intended. That is not to say that it is never appropriate so to charge a person who is making a nuisance of himself to his partner or wife when they have become estranged. However, in a situation such as this, when they were frequently coming back together and intercourse was taking place (apparently a video was taken of them having intercourse) it is unrealistic to think that this fell within the stalking category which either postulates a stranger or an estranged spouse".

Limitation period: Provided that at least one incident occurs within 6 months of charge, other incidents alleged outside of that period do not offend the limitation period in relation to a charge under section 2 of the 1997 Act (*Director of Public Prosecutions v Baker* (2005) 169 JPN 78).
Multiple complainants: The naming of two complainants in one charge is not duplicitous, but at least one of the complainants must have feared violence on at least two occasions (*Caurti v Director of Public Prosecutions* [2002] EWHC 867 (Admin)).

Harassment (without violence) (s 2)

Summary only if not aggravated, 6 months/£5,000; Either-way if racially/religiously aggravated, 6 months/£5,000 (2 years).

Offence seriousness (culpability and harm)
A. Identify the appropriate starting point
Starting points based on first time offender pleading not guilty

Examples of nature of activity	Starting point	Range
Small number of incidents	Medium level community order	Band C fine to high level community order
Constant contact at night, trying to come into workplace or home, involving others	6 weeks custody	Medium level community order to 12 weeks custody
Threatening violence, taking personal photographs, sending offensive material	18 weeks custody	12 to 26 weeks custody

Offence seriousness (culpability and harm)
B. Consider the effect of aggravating and mitigating factors
(other than those within examples above)
The following may be particularly relevant but **these lists are not exhaustive**

Factors indicating higher culpability	Factors indicating lower culpability
1. Planning	1. Limited understanding of effect on victim
2. Offender ignores obvious distress	2. Initial provocation
3. Offender involves others	
4. Using contact arrangements with a child to instigate offence	
Factors indicating greater degree of harm	
1. Victim needs medical help/counselling	
2. Action over long period	
3. Children frightened	
4. Use or distribution of photographs	

Harassment, putting people in fear of violence (s 4)

Either-way, 6 months/£5,000 (5 years) (7 years if racially or religiously aggravated).

Protection from Harassment Act 1997, s 2 and 4

2.— Offence of harassment.

(1) A person who pursues a course of conduct in breach of section 1(1) or (1A) is guilty of an offence.

4.— Putting people in fear of violence.

(1) A person whose course of conduct causes another to fear, on at least two occasions, that violence will be used against him is guilty of an offence if he knows or ought to know that his course of conduct will cause the other so to fear on each of those occasions.

(2) For the purposes of this section, the person whose course of conduct is in question ought to know that it will cause another to fear that violence will be used against him on any occasion if a reasonable person in possession of the same information would think the course of conduct would cause the other so to fear on that occasion.

(3) It is a defence for a person charged with an offence under this section to show that—

    (a) his course of conduct was pursued for the purpose of preventing or detecting crime,

    (b) his course of conduct was pursued under any enactment or rule of law or to comply with any condition or requirement imposed by any person under any enactment, or

    (c) the pursuit of his course of conduct was reasonable for the protection of himself or another or for the protection of his or another's property.

HARASSMENT, DIRECTIONS STOPPING

Summary only, see ss 42(7)–(7C).

Criminal Justice and Police Act 2001, s 42

(1) Subject to the following provisions of this section, a constable who is at the scene may give a direction under this section to any person if–

    (a) that person is present outside or in the vicinity of any premises that are used by any individual ("the resident") as his dwelling;

    (b) that constable believes, on reasonable grounds, that that person is present there for the purpose (by his presence or otherwise) of representing to the resident or another individual (whether or not one who uses the premises as his dwelling), or of persuading the resident or such another individual–

        (i) that he should not do something that he is entitled or required to do; or

        (ii) that he should do something that he is not under any obligation to do;

and

    (c) that constable also believes, on reasonable grounds, that the presence of that person (either alone or together with that of any other persons who are also present)–

        (i) amounts to, or is likely to result in, the harassment of the resident; or

        (ii) is likely to cause alarm or distress to the resident.

(2) A direction under this section is a direction requiring the person to whom it is given to do all such things as the constable giving it may specify as the things he considers necessary to prevent one or both of the following–

    (a) the harassment of the resident; or

    (b) the causing of any alarm or distress to the resident.

(3) A direction under this section may be given orally; and where a constable is entitled to give a direction under this section to each of several persons outside, or in the vicinity of, any premises, he may give that direction to those persons by notifying them of his requirements either individually or all together.

(4) The requirements that may be imposed by a direction under this section include—

    (a) a requirement to leave the vicinity of the premises in question, and

    (b) a requirement to leave that vicinity and not to return to it within such period as the constable may specify, not being longer than 3 months;

and (in either case) the requirement to leave the vicinity may be to do so immediately or after a specified period of time.

(5) A direction under this section may make exceptions to any requirement imposed by the direction, and may make any such exception subject to such conditions as the constable giving the direction thinks fit; and those conditions may include–

    (a) conditions as to the distance from the premises in question at which, or otherwise as to the location where, persons who do not leave their vicinity must remain; and

    (b) conditions as to the number or identity of the persons who are authorised by the exception to remain in the vicinity of those premises.

(6) The power of a constable to give a direction under this section shall not include–

    (a) any power to give a direction at any time when there is a more senior-ranking police officer at the scene; or

    (b) any power to direct a person to refrain from conduct that is lawful under section 220 of the Trade Union and Labour Relations (Consolidation) Act 1992 (c. 52) (right peacefully to picket a work place);

but it shall include power to vary or withdraw a direction previously given under this section.

(7) Any person who knowingly fails to comply with a requirement in a direction given to him under this section (other than a requirement under subsection (4)(b)) shall be guilty of an offence and liable, on summary conviction, to imprisonment for a term not exceeding three months or to a fine not exceeding level 4 on the standard scale, or to both.

(7A) Any person to whom a constable has given a direction including a requirement under subsection (4)(b) commits an offence if he—

(a) returns to the vicinity of the premises in question within the period specified in the direction beginning with the date on which the direction is given; and
(b) does so for the purpose described in subsection (1)(b).

(7B) A person guilty of an offence under subsection (7A) shall be liable, on summary conviction, to imprisonment for a term not exceeding 51 weeks or to a fine not exceeding level 4 on the standard scale, or to both.

(7C) In relation to an offence committed before the commencement of section 281(5) of the Criminal Justice Act 2003 (alteration of penalties for summary offences), the reference in subsection (7B) to 51 weeks is to be read as a reference to 6 months.

[...]

(9) In this section "dwelling" has the same meaning as in Part 1 of the Public Order Act 1986 (c. 64).

HARASSMENT IN THE HOME

Summary only, 6 months/£2,500.

Criminal Justice and Police Act 2001, s 42A

(1) A person commits an offence if—

(a) that person is present outside or in the vicinity of any premises that are used by any individual ("the resident") as his dwelling;
(b) that person is present there for the purpose (by his presence or otherwise) of representing to the resident or another individual (whether or not one who uses the premises as his dwelling), or of persuading the resident or such another individual—
  (i) that he should not do something that he is entitled or required to do; or
  (ii) that he should do something that he is not under any obligation to do;
(c) that person—
  (i) intends his presence to amount to the harassment of, or to cause alarm or distress to, the resident; or
  (ii) knows or ought to know that his presence is likely to result in the harassment of, or to cause alarm or distress to, the resident; and
(d) the presence of that person—
  (i) amounts to the harassment of, or causes alarm or distress to, any person falling within subsection (2); or
  (ii) is likely to result in the harassment of, or to cause alarm or distress to, any such person.

(2) A person falls within this subsection if he is—

(a) the resident,
(b) a person in the resident's dwelling, or
(c) a person in another dwelling in the vicinity of the resident's dwelling.

(3) The references in subsection (1)(c) and (d) to a person's presence are references to his presence either alone or together with that of any other persons who are also present.

(4) For the purposes of this section a person (A) ought to know that his presence is likely to result in the harassment of, or to cause alarm or distress to, a resident if a reasonable

person in possession of the same information would think that A's presence was likely to have that effect.

HARASSMENT OF DEBTORS

Summary only, Fine £5,000.

Calculated: The word 'calculated' in section 40(1)(a) means "likely to subject", and not "intended to subject" (*Norweb PLC v Dixon* [1995] 1 WLR 636). **Contract:** A conviction against an electricity company was quashed as an agreement for the supply of electricity was not pursuant to a contract (*Norweb PLC v Dixon*).

Administration of Justice Act 1970, s 40

(1) A person commits an offence if, with the object of coercing another person to pay money claimed from the other as a debt due under a contract, he—

    (a) harasses the other with demands for payment which, in respect of their frequency or the manner or occasion of making any such demand, or of any threat or publicity by which any demand is accompanied, are calculated to subject him or members of his family or household to alarm, distress or humiliation;

    (b) falsely represents, in relation to the money claimed, that criminal proceedings lie for failure to pay it;

    (c) falsely represents himself to be authorised in some official capacity to claim or enforce payment; or

    (d) utters a document falsely represented by him to have some official character or purporting to have some official character which he knows it has not.

(2) A person may be guilty of an offence by virtue of subsection (1)(a) above if he concerts with others in the taking of such action as is described in that paragraph, notwithstanding that his own course of conduct does not by itself amount to harassment.

(3) Subsection (1)(a) above does not apply to anything done by a person which is reasonable (and otherwise permissible in law) for the purpose—

    (a) of securing the discharge of an obligation due, or believed by him to be due, to himself or to persons for whom he acts, or protecting himself or them from future loss; or

    (b) of the enforcement of any liability by legal process.

(3A) Subsection (1) above does not apply to anything done by a person to another in circumstances where what is done is a commercial practice within the meaning of the Consumer Protection from Unfair Trading Regulations 2008 and the other is a consumer in relation to that practice.

OBSTRUCTION OF EMERGENCY WORKERS

Summary only, Fine £5,000.

Emergency Workers (Obstruction) Act 2006, ss 1-3

1 Obstructing or hindering certain emergency workers responding to emergency circumstances

(1) A person who without reasonable excuse obstructs or hinders another while that other person is, in a capacity mentioned in subsection (2) below, responding to emergency circumstances, commits an offence.

(2) The capacity referred to in subsection (1) above is–

    (a) that of a person employed by a fire and rescue authority in England and Wales;

    (b) in relation to England and Wales, that of a person (other than a person falling within paragraph (a)) whose duties as an employee or as a servant of the Crown involve–

      (i)   extinguishing fires; or

      (ii)   protecting life and property in the event of a fire;

  (c) that of a person employed by a relevant NHS body in the provision of ambulance services (including air ambulance services), or of a person providing such services pursuant to arrangements made by, or at the request of, a relevant NHS body;

  (d) that of a person providing services for the transport of organs, blood, equipment or personnel pursuant to arrangements made by, or at the request of, a relevant NHS body;

  (e) that of a member of Her Majesty's Coastguard;

  (f) that of a member of the crew of a vessel operated by–

      (i)   the Royal National Lifeboat Institution, or

      (ii)   any other person or organisation operating a vessel for the purpose of providing a rescue service,

or a person who musters the crew of such a vessel or attends to its launch or recovery.

(3) For the purposes of this section and section 2 of this Act, a person is responding to emergency circumstances if the person–

  (a) is going anywhere for the purpose of dealing with emergency circumstances occurring there; or

  (b) is dealing with emergency circumstances or preparing to do so.

(4) For the purposes of this Act, circumstances are "emergency" circumstances if they are present or imminent and–

  (a) are causing or are likely to cause–

      (i)   serious injury to or the serious illness (including mental illness) of a person;

      (ii)   serious harm to the environment (including the life and health of plants and animals);

      (iii) serious harm to any building or other property; or

      (iv) a worsening of any such injury, illness or harm; or

  (b) are likely to cause the death of a person.

(5) In subsection (2) above "relevant NHS body" means–

  (a) in relation to England and Wales, an NHS foundation trust, National Health Service trust, Special Health Authority, Primary Care Trust or Local Health Board;

  (b) in relation to Northern Ireland, a Health and Social Services trust or Health and Social Services Board.

2 Obstructing or hindering persons assisting emergency workers

(1) A person who without reasonable excuse obstructs or hinders another in the circumstances described in subsection (2) below commits an offence.

(2) Those circumstances are where the person being obstructed or hindered is assisting another while that other person is, in a capacity mentioned in section 1(2) of this Act, responding to emergency circumstances.

3 Provisions supplementary to sections 1 and 2

(1) A person may be convicted of the offence under section 1 or 2 of this Act notwithstanding that it is–

  (a) effected by means other than physical means; or

  (b) effected by action directed only at any vehicle, vessel, apparatus, equipment or other thing or any animal used or to be used by a person referred to in that section.

(2) For the purposes of sections 1 and 2 of this Act, circumstances to which a person is responding are to be taken to be emergency circumstances if the person believes and has reasonable grounds for believing they are or may be emergency circumstances.

OFFENCES AGAINST DESIGNATED AND ACCREDITED PERSONS

Summary only, see section 46(3) for penalties.

Police Reform Act 2002, s 46

(1) Any person who assaults—

    (a) a designated person in the execution of his duty,

    (b) an accredited person in the execution of his duty,

    (ba) an accredited inspector in the execution of his duty, or

    (c) a person assisting a designated or accredited person or an accredited inspector in the execution of his duty,

is guilty of an offence and shall be liable, on summary conviction, to imprisonment for a term not exceeding six months or to a fine not exceeding level 5 on the standard scale, or to both.

(2) Any person who resists or wilfully obstructs—

    (a) a designated person in the execution of his duty,

    (b) an accredited person or an accredited inspector in the execution of his duty,

    (ba) an accredited inspector in the execution of his duty, or

    (c) a person assisting a designated or accredited person in the execution of his duty,

is guilty of an offence and shall be liable, on summary conviction, to imprisonment for a term not exceeding one month or to a fine not exceeding level 3 on the standard scale, or to both.

(3) Any person who, with intent to deceive—

    (a) impersonates a designated person, an accredited person or an accredited inspector,

    (b) makes any statement or does any act calculated falsely to suggest that he is a designated person, that he is an accredited person or that he is an accredited inspector, or

    (c) makes any statement or does any act calculated falsely to suggest that he has powers as a designated or accredited person or as an accredited inspector that exceed the powers he actually has,

is guilty of an offence and shall be liable, on summary conviction, to imprisonment for a term not exceeding six months or to a fine not exceeding level 5 on the standard scale, or to both.

(4) In this section references to the execution by a designated person, accredited person or accredited inspector of his duty are references to his exercising any power or performing any duty which is his by virtue of his designation or accreditation.

RACIALLY OR RELIGIOUSLY AGGRAVATED OFFENCES

Crime and Disorder Act 1998, ss 28, 29, 32

28.— Meaning of " racially or religiously aggravated ".

(1) An offence is racially or religiously aggravated for the purposes of sections 29 to 32 below if—

    (a) at the time of committing the offence, or immediately before or after doing so, the offender demonstrates towards the victim of the offence hostility based on the victim's membership (or presumed membership) of a [racial or religious group; or

    (b) the offence is motivated (wholly or partly) by hostility towards members of a racial or religious group based on their membership of that group.

(2) In subsection (1)(a) above—

"membership", in relation to a racial or religious group, includes association with members of that group;

"presumed" means presumed by the offender.

(3) It is immaterial for the purposes of paragraph (a) or (b) of subsection (1) above whether or not the offender's hostility is also based, to any extent, [on any other factor not mentioned in that paragraph.

29.— Racially or religiously aggravated assaults.

(1) A person is guilty of an offence under this section if he commits—

(a) an offence under section 20 of the Offences Against the Person Act 1861 (malicious wounding or grievous bodily harm);

(b) an offence under section 47 of that Act (actual bodily harm); or

(c) common assault,

which is racially or religiously aggravated for the purposes of this section.

32.— Racially or religiously aggravated harassment etc.

(1) A person is guilty of an offence under this section if he commits—

(a) an offence under section 2 of the Protection from Harassment Act 1997 (offence of harassment); or

(b) an offence under section 4 of that Act (putting people in fear of violence),

which is racially or religiously aggravated for the purposes of this section.

STALKING

Section 2A, summary only–6 months'/£5,000; Section 4A, either-way–6 months'/£5,000 (5 years).

Alternative verdict: If on the trial on indictment of a person charged with an offence under this section the jury find the person not guilty of the offence charged, they may find the person guilty of an offence under section 2 or 2A. The Crown Court has the same powers and duties in relation to a person who is convicted before it of a lesser offence under section 2 or 2A as a magistrates' court would have on convicting the person of the offence.

Protection from Harassment Act 1997, s 2A and 4A

2A Offence of stalking

(1) A person is guilty of an offence if—

(a) the person pursues a course of conduct in breach of section 1(1), and

(b) the course of conduct amounts to stalking.

(2) For the purposes of subsection (1)(b) (and section 4A(1)(a)) a person's course of conduct amounts to stalking of another person if—

(a) it amounts to harassment of that person,

(b) the acts or omissions involved are ones associated with stalking, and

(c) the person whose course of conduct it is knows or ought to know that the course of conduct amounts to harassment of the other person.

(3) The following are examples of acts or omissions which, in particular circumstances, are ones associated with stalking—

(a) following a person,

(b) contacting, or attempting to contact, a person by any means,

(c) publishing any statement or other material—

(i) relating or purporting to relate to a person, or

(ii) purporting to originate from a person,

(d) monitoring the use by a person of the internet, email or any other form of electronic communication,

    (e) loitering in any place (whether public or private),

    (f) interfering with any property in the possession of a person,

    (g) watching or spying on a person.

    ...

(6) This section is without prejudice to the generality of section 2.

4A Stalking involving fear of violence or serious alarm or distress

(1) A person ("A") whose course of conduct—

    (a) amounts to stalking, and

    (b) either—

        (i) causes another ("B") to fear, on at least two occasions, that violence will be used against B, or

        (ii) causes B serious alarm or distress which has a substantial adverse effect on B's usual day-to-day activities, is guilty of an offence if A knows or ought to know that A's course of conduct will cause B so to fear on each of those occasions or (as the case may be) will cause such alarm or distress.

(2) For the purposes of this section A ought to know that A's course of conduct will cause B to fear that violence will be used against B on any occasion if a reasonable person in possession of the same information would think the course of conduct would cause B so to fear on that occasion.

(3) For the purposes of this section A ought to know that A's course of conduct will cause B serious alarm or distress which has a substantial adverse effect on B's usual day-to-day activities if a reasonable person in possession of the same information would think the course of conduct would cause B such alarm or distress.

(4) It is a defence for A to show that—

    (a) A's course of conduct was pursued for the purpose of preventing or detecting crime,

    (b) A's course of conduct was pursued under any enactment or rule of law or to comply with any condition or requirement imposed by any person under any enactment, or

    (c) the pursuit of A's course of conduct was reasonable for the protection of A or another or for the protection of A's or another's property.

    ...

(9) This section is without prejudice to the generality of section 4.

THREATS TO KILL

Either-way, 6 months/£5,000 (10 years).

Lawful excuse: Includes self-defence and prevention of crime (*Cousins* (1982) 74 Cr App R 363). **Maliciously:** Means wilfully or intentionally and without lawful excuse (*Solanke* (1970) 54 Cr App R 30). **Previous act of violence:** Such incidents may be admissible in order to demonstrate that the defendant intended the current threat to be taken seriously (*Williams* (1987) 84 Cr App R 299).

Offences Against the Person Act 1861, s 16

A person who without lawful excuse makes to another a threat, intending that that other would fear it would be carried out, to kill that other or a third person shall be guilty of an offence.

Offence seriousness (culpability and harm)		
A. Identify the appropriate starting point		
Starting points based on first time offender pleading not guilty		
Examples of nature of activity	**Starting point**	**Range**
One threat uttered in the heat of the moment, no more than fleeting impact on victim	Medium level community order	Low level community order to high level community order
Single calculated threat or victim fears that threat will be carried out	12 weeks custody	6 to 26 weeks custody
Repeated threats or visible weapon	Crown Court	Crown Court

Offence seriousness (culpability and harm)	
B. Consider the effect of aggravating and mitigating factors	
(other than those within examples above)	
The following may be particularly relevant but **these lists are not exhaustive**	
Factors indicating higher culpability	**Factor indicating lower culpability**
1. Planning	1. Provocation
2. Offender deliberately isolates victim	
3. Group action	
4. Threat directed at victim because of job	
5. History of antagonism towards victim	
Factors indicating greater degree of harm	
1. Vulnerable victim	
2. Victim needs medical help/counselling	

PRISONS

CONVEYANCE OF ARTICLES INTO PRISONS

Conveyance of an A list article is triable on indictment only. Conveyance of a B list article is triable either-way, 6 months/£5,000 (2 years on indictment) (Prison Act 1952, s 40C). Conveyance of a C list item is triable summarily only, £1,000 fine (Prison Act 1952, s 40C).

The Prison Act 1952 lists the following prohibited articles (Prison Act 1952, s 40A):

List A articles	List B articles
(a) a controlled drug (as defined for the purposes of the Misuse of Drugs Act 1971); (b) an explosive;	(a) alcohol (as defined for the purposes of the Licensing Act 2003); (b) a mobile telephone; (c) a camera; (d) a sound-recording device.

| (c) any firearm or ammunition (as defined in section 57 of the Firearms Act 1968);

(d) any other offensive weapon (as defined in section 1(9) of the Police and Criminal Evidence Act 1984). | "camera" includes any device by means of which a photograph (as defined in section 40E) can be produced;
 "sound-recording device" includes any device by means of which a sound-recording (as defined in section 40E) can be made.

(5) The reference in paragraph (b), (c) or (d) of List B to a device of any description includes a reference to–

(a) a component part of a device of that description; or

(b) an article designed or adapted for use with a device of that description (including any disk, film or other separate article on which images, sounds or information may be recorded). |

A List C article is any article or substance prescribed for the purposes of this subsection by prison rules.

Prison Act 1952, s 40C

(1) A person who, without authorisation–

  (a) brings, throws or otherwise conveys a List B article into or out of a prison,

  (b) causes another person to bring, throw or otherwise convey a List B article into or out of a prison,

  (c) leaves a List B article in any place (whether inside or outside a prison) intending it to come into the possession of a prisoner, or

  (d) knowing a person to be a prisoner, gives a List B article to him,

is guilty of an offence.

(2) A person who, without authorisation–

  (a) brings, throws or otherwise conveys a List C article into a prison intending it to come into the possession of a prisoner,

  (b) causes another person to bring, throw or otherwise convey a List C article into a prison intending it to come into the possession of a prisoner,

  (c) brings, throws or otherwise conveys a List C article out of a prison on behalf of a prisoner,

  (d) causes another person to bring, throw or otherwise convey a List C article out of a prison on behalf of a prisoner,

  (e) leaves a List C article in any place (whether inside or outside a prison) intending it to come into the possession of a prisoner, or

  (f) while inside a prison, gives a List C article to a prisoner,

is guilty of an offence.

(3) A person who attempts to commit an offence under subsection (2) is guilty of that offence.

(4) In proceedings for an offence under this section it is a defence for the accused to show that–

  (a) he reasonably believed that he had authorisation to do the act in respect of which the proceedings are brought, or

  (b) in all the circumstances there was an overriding public interest which justified the doing of that act.

OTHER OFFENCES RELATING TO PRISON DISCIPLINE

Section 40D relates to recording devices and those capable of transmission (mobile phones). The offence is triable either-way, 6 months/£5,000 (2 years on indictment).

Prison Act 1952, s 40D

(1)   A person who, without authorisation–

    (a) takes a photograph, or makes a sound-recording, inside a prison, or

    (b) transmits, or causes to be transmitted, any image, sound or information from inside a prison by electronic communications for simultaneous reception outside the prison,

is guilty of an offence.

(2)   It is immaterial for the purposes of subsection (1)(a) where the recording medium is located.

(3)   A person who, without authorisation–

    (a) brings or otherwise conveys a restricted document out of a prison or causes such a document to be brought or conveyed out of a prison, ...

    ...

is guilty of an offence.

(3A) A person who, without authorisation, is in possession of any of the items specified in subsection (3B) inside a prison is guilty of an offence.

(3B) The items referred to in subsection (3A) are—

    (a) a device capable of transmitting or receiving images, sounds or information by electronic communications (including a mobile telephone);

    (b) a component part of such a device;

    (c) an article designed or adapted for use with such a device (including any disk, film or other separate article on which images, sounds or information may be recorded).

(4)   In proceedings for an offence under this section it is a defence for the accused to show that–

    (a) he reasonably believed that he had authorisation to do the act in respect of which the proceedings are brought, or

    (b) in all the circumstances there was an overriding public interest which justified the doing of that act.

PRISON LICENCE, BREACH OF

Triable summarily only, maximum £1000 fine and imprisonment for a maximum of the 'relevant period'. Relevant period means a period equal in length to the period between the date on which the failure occurred or began and the date of the expiry of the licence (Criminal Justice Act 1991, s 40A(4)).

The following principles emerge from *West Midlands Probation Board v French* [2008] EWHC 2631 (Admin): (1) Any challenge to the validity of the order must be made by way of judicial review and not by way of collateral challenge as part of any defence, (2) If there was to be any challenge to the validity of the order the appropriate application would be to adjourn the proceedings in order that this could be done. The actual prison licence is admissible by virtue of a number of statutory provisions (and at common law), if this matter is to be put in issue the judgment at paragraph 39–54 will need to be carefully considered by all parties.

Criminal Justice Act 1991, s 40A(4)

If the person fails to comply with such conditions as may for the time being be specified in the licence, he shall be liable on summary conviction—

(a) to a fine not exceeding level 3 on the standard scale; or

(b) to a sentence of imprisonment for a term not exceeding the relevant period,

but not liable to be dealt with in any other way.

… 'the relevant period' means a period which is equal in length to the period between the date on which the failure occurred or began and the date of the expiry of the licence.

PROPERTY OFFENCES

COMPUTER MISUSE

Section 1: Either-way, 6 months/£5,000 (2 years); **Section 2**: Either-way, 6 months/£5,000 (5 years); **Section 3**: Either-way, 6 months/£5,000 (10 years)

Meaning: Section 1(1)(a) is to be given a plain and natural meaning (*Attorney General's Reference (No 1 of 1991)* [1992] 3 WLR 432). **Modification:** Arranging for a computer to send bulk emails, without consent, amounts to a modification where the sending computer receives data back as a result; Section 3(4) requires that it be established not only that the modifications caused to the complainant's computer should be unauthorised, but that the defendant had knowledge that they were unauthorised. (*Lennon v Director of Public Prosecutions* [2006] EWHC 1201 (Admin)). **Hacking with intent (sentence):** In *Mangham* [2012] EWHC Crim 973 the court held:

"We would identify a number of aggravating factors which will bear on sentence in this type of case: firstly, whether the offence is planned and persistent and then the nature of the damage caused to the system itself and to the wider public interest such as national security, individual privacy, public confidence and commercial confidentiality. The other side of the coin to the damage caused will be the cost of remediation, although we do not regard that as a determining factor. Next, motive and benefit are also relevant. Revenge […] is a serious aggravating factor. Further, the courts are likely to take a very dim view where a hacker attempts to reap financial benefit by the sale of information which has been accessed. Whether or not the information is passed onto others is another factor to be taken into account. The value of the intellectual property involved may also be relevant to sentencing. Among the mitigating factors the psychological profile of an offender will deserve close attention".

General sentencing: In *Lindesay* [2001] EWCA Crim 1720, the court upheld a sentence of 9 months' imprisonment: that was imposed on an offender who had, in revenge for his dismissal, gained unauthorised entry into three websites and deleted certain data to cause inconvenience. There was no damage to the software or direct revenue loss. The appellant had pleaded guilty and had strong personal mitigation. The court regarded the use of confidential passwords, the inconvenience to the company and its clients, the appellant's motive and the breach of trust as justifying the sentence the judge imposed. In *Vallor* [2003] EWCA Crim 2288, the appellant unsuccessfully appealed a sentence of 2 years' imprisonment. He had imported a number of viruses into the Internet. The first was detected in 42 different countries and apparently led to computers stopping some 27,000 times. The court regarded that behaviour as disruptive, albeit not destructive. The second and third viruses were worms in email messages, which caused computers to stop and delete unsaved material. The damage was unknown but may have affected material on 200 to 300 computers. The court said the offending was planned and calculated to cause disruption on a grand scale. In *Baker* [2011] EWCA Crim 928, the sentence of 4 months' imprisonment on a person of good character was upheld. On 20 occasions, over a week, the appellant had used a remote dial-up connection from his home computer to gain unauthorised access to the Welsh Assembly computer system. The appellant had read a number of sensitive emails up to the restricted level. He had been dismissed and said he was searching for material relevant to that".

Computer Misuse Act 1990, ss 1, 2, 3

1.— Unauthorised access to computer material.

(1)   A person is guilty of an offence if—

    (a)   he causes a computer to perform any function with intent to secure access to any program or data held in any computer, or to enable any such access to be secured;

    (b)   the access he intends to secure, or to enable to be secured, is unauthorised; and

    (c)   he knows at the time when he causes the computer to perform the function that that is the case.

(2)   The intent a person has to have to commit an offence under this section need not be directed at—

    (a)   any particular program or data;

    (b)   a program or data of any particular kind; or

    (c)   a program or data held in any particular computer.

2.— Unauthorised access with intent to commit or facilitate commission of further offences.

(1)   A person is guilty of an offence under this section if he commits an offence under section 1 above ("the unauthorised access offence") with intent—

    (a)   to commit an offence to which this section applies; or

    (b)   to facilitate the commission of such an offence (whether by himself or by any other person);

and the offence he intends to commit or facilitate is referred to below in this section as the further offence.

(2)   This section applies to offences—

    (a)   for which the sentence is fixed by law; or

    (b)   for which a person of twenty-one years of age or over (not previously convicted) may be sentenced to imprisonment for a term of five years (or, in England and Wales, might be so sentenced but for the restrictions imposed by section 33 of the Magistrates' Courts Act 1980).

(3)   It is immaterial for the purposes of this section whether the further offence is to be committed on the same occasion as the unauthorised access offence or on any future occasion.

(4)   A person may be guilty of an offence under this section even though the facts are such that the commission of the further offence is impossible.

3 Unauthorised acts with intent to impair, or with recklessness as to impairing, operation of computer, etc.

(1)   A person is guilty of an offence if–

    (a)   he does any unauthorised act in relation to a computer;

    (b)   at the time when he does the act he knows that it is unauthorised; and

    (c)   either subsection (2) or subsection (3) below applies.

(2)   This subsection applies if the person intends by doing the act–

    (a)   to impair the operation of any computer;

(b) to prevent or hinder access to any program or data held in any computer;

(c) to impair the operation of any such program or the reliability of any such data; or

(d) to enable any of the things mentioned in paragraphs (a) to (c) above to be done.

(3) This subsection applies if the person is reckless as to whether the act will do any of the things mentioned in paragraphs (a) to (d) of subsection (2) above.

(4) The intention referred to in subsection (2) above, or the recklessness referred to in subsection (3) above, need not relate to–

(a) any particular computer;

(b) any particular program or data; or

(c) a program or data of any particular kind.

(5) In this section–

(a) a reference to doing an act includes a reference to causing an act to be done;

(b) "act" includes a series of acts;

(c) a reference to impairing, preventing or hindering something includes a reference to doing so temporarily.

SCRAP METAL, BUYING FOR CASH

Summary only, Fine £5,000.

Scrap Metal Dealers Act 1964, s 3A

(1) A scrap metal dealer must not pay for scrap metal except—

(a) by a cheque which under section 81A of the Bills of Exchange Act 1882 is not transferable, or

(b) by an electronic transfer of funds (authorised by credit or debit card or otherwise).

(2) The Secretary of State may by order amend subsection (1) to permit other methods of payment.

(3) In this section paying includes paying in kind (with goods or services).

(4) If a scrap metal dealer pays for scrap metal in breach of subsection (1), each of the following is guilty of an offence—

(a) the scrap metal dealer;

(b) a person who makes the payment acting for the dealer;

(c) a manager who fails to take reasonable steps to prevent the payment being made in breach of subsection (1).

(5) In subsection (4)(c) "manager" means a person who works in the carrying on of the dealer's business as a scrap metal dealer in a capacity, whether paid or unpaid, which authorises the person to prevent the payment being made in breach of subsection (1).

(6) Subsection (1) does not apply if—

(a) the payment is made in the carrying on of the dealer's business as a scrap metal dealer as part of the business of an itinerant collector, and

(b) at the time of the payment an order under section 3(1) is in force in relation to the dealer.

USE OR THREAT OF VIOLENCE TO SECURE ENTRY TO PREMISES

Summary only, 6 months/£5,000.

Protected intended occupier: For the position of an excluded freeholder see *Wakolo v DPP* [2012] EWHC 611 (Admin).

Criminal Law Act 1977, s 6

(1) Subject to the following provisions of this section, any person who, without lawful authority, uses or threatens violence for the purpose of securing entry into any premises for himself or for any other person is guilty of an offence, provided that—

    (a) there is someone present on those premises at the time who is opposed to the entry which the violence is intended to secure; and

    (b) the person using or threatening the violence knows that that is the case.

(1A) Subsection (1) above does not apply to a person who is a displaced residential occupier or a protected intending occupier of the premises in question or who is acting on behalf of such an occupier; and if the accused adduces sufficient evidence that he was, or was acting on behalf of, such an occupier he shall be presumed to be, or to be acting on behalf of, such an occupier unless the contrary is proved by the prosecution.

(2) Subject to subsection (1A) above, The fact that a person has any interest in or right to possession or occupation of any premises shall not for the purposes of subsection (1) above constitute lawful authority for the use or threat of violence by him or anyone else for the purpose of securing his entry into those premises.

[...]

(4) It is immaterial for the purposes of this section—

    (a) whether the violence in question is directed against the person or against property; and

    (b) whether the entry which the violence is intended to secure is for the purpose of acquiring possession of the premises in question or for any other purpose.

    [...]

(7) Section 12 below contains provisions which apply for determining when any person is to be regarded for the purposes of this Part of this Act as a displaced residential occupier of any premises or of any access to any premises and section 12A below contains provisions which apply for determining when any person is to be regarded for the purposes of this Part of this Act as a protected intending occupier of any premises or of any access to any premises.

PROTECTIVE ORDERS

ANTI-SOCIAL BEHAVIOUR ORDER, BREACH OF

Triable either-way, 6 months' imprisonment/£5,000, 5 years on indictment.

Reasonable excuse: The prosecution bears the burden of negating reasonable excuse (*Charles* [2009] EWCA Crim 1570). Forgetfulness, misunderstanding or ignorance of the terms of the order are capable of amounting to reasonable excuse (*Nicholson* [2006] EWCA Crim 1518). A defendant's state of mind is relevant to the issue of breach, notwithstanding the fact that the offence is one of strict liability (*JB v CPS* [2012] EWHC 72 (Admin)). The fact that an appeal has been lodged against the order cannot amount to a reasonable excuse (*West Midlands Probation Board v Daly* [2008] EWHC 15 (Admin)), but a belief that the order had ended, when in fact it was still current can (*Barber v CPS* [2004] EWHC 2605 (Admin)). It is not open to a court to find that the original order (or a term within in) was void or otherwise unenforceable, although such matters may well be relevant to sentence (*CPS v T* [2005] EWHC 728 (Admin)). A lack of clarity in relation to a prohibition may lead the court to conclude that there was no breach, or that it provided a reasonable excuse (*Crown Prosecution Service v T* [2005] EWHC 728 (Admin)).

Crime and Disorder Act 1998, s 1(10)

If without reasonable excuse a person does anything which he is prohibited from doing by an anti-social behaviour order, he is guilty of an offence.

Sentencing guideline

Nature of failure and harm	Starting point	Sentencing range
Serious harassment, alarm, or distress has been caused or where such harm was intended	26 weeks custody	Custody threshold—2 years custody
Lesser degree of harassment, alarm, or distress, where such harm was intended, or where it would have been likely if the offender had not been apprehended	6 weeks custody	Medium level community order to 26 weeks custody
No harassment, alarm, or distress was actually caused by the breach and none was intended by the offender	Low level community order	Band B fine to medium level community order

Aggravating factors	Mitigating factors
1. Offender has a history of disobedience to court orders 2. Breach was committed immediately or shortly after the order was made 3. Breach was committed subsequent to earlier breach proceedings arising from the same order 4. Targeting of a person the order was made to protect or a witness in the original proceedings	1. Breach occurred after a long period of compliance 2. The prohibition(s) breached was not fully understood, especially where an interim order was made without notice

Where the breach amounts in itself to a criminal offence, the court is not bound by the maximum penalty that would have been available had the defendant faced the alternative charge (*Stevens* [2006] EWCA Crim 255), it is not however appropriate for the prosecution to charge breach of an order purely to circumvent a lower maximum sentence. Breach of an interim order or a final order is equally serious and the same approach to sentencing should be taken.

Where a defendant under the age of 16 years is convicted of breaching an ASBO the court must make a parenting order in respect of a person who is a parent or guardian of the person convicted, unless it is of the opinion that there are exceptional circumstances that would make a parenting order inappropriate (Crime and Disorder Act 1998, s 8A(2)).

PROTECTIVE ORDER, BREACH OF

The 2 main orders are: Non-molestation order (Family Law Act 1996, s 42A) and restraining orders (Protection from Harassment Act 1997 (s 5). Both offences are triable either-way (6 months/£5,000 (5 years)).

Offence seriousness (culpability and harm)		
A. Identify the appropriate starting point		
Starting points based on first time offender pleading not guilty		
Examples of nature of activity	**Starting point**	**Range**
Single breach involving no/minimal direct contact	Low level community order	Band C fine to medium level community order
More than one breach involving no/minimal contact or some direct contact	Medium level community order	Low level community order to high level community order
Single breach involving some violence and/or significant physical or psychological harm to the victim	18 weeks custody	13 to 26 weeks custody
More than one breach involving some violence and/or significant physical or psychological harm to the victim	Crown Court	26 weeks custody to Crown Court
Breach (whether one or more) involving significant physical violence and significant physical or psychological harm to the victim	Crown Court	Crown Court

Offence seriousness (culpability and harm)	
B. Consider the effect of aggravating and mitigating factors (other than those within examples above)	
The following may be particularly relevant but **these lists are not exhaustive**	
Factors indicating higher culpability	**Factors indicating lower culpability**
1. Proven history of violence or threats by the offender	1. Breach occurred after long period of compliance
2. Using contact arrangements with a child to instigate offence	2. Victim initiated contact
3. Offence is a further breach, following earlier breach proceedings	
4. Offender has history of disobedience to court orders	
5. Breach committed immediately or shortly after order made	
Factors indicating greater degree of harm	
1. Victim is particularly vulnerable	
2. Impact on children	
3. Victim is forced to leave home	

Family Law Act 1996, s 42A

(1) A person who without reasonable excuse does anything that he is prohibited from doing by a non-molestation order is guilty of an offence.

(2) In the case of a non-molestation order made by virtue of section 45(1), a person can be guilty of an offence under this section only in respect of conduct engaged in at a time when he was aware of the existence of the order.

(3) Where a person is convicted of an offence under this section in respect of any conduct, that conduct is not punishable as a contempt of court.

(4) A person cannot be convicted of an offence under this section in respect of any conduct which has been punished as a contempt of court.

Protection from Harassment Act 1997, s 5(5)

(5) If without reasonable excuse the defendant does anything which he is prohibited from doing by an order under this section, he is guilty of an offence.

SEX OFFENDER NOTIFICATION, BREACH OF REQUIREMENTS

Either-way, 6 months'/£5,000 (5 years on indictment).

It is an offence to fail, without reasonable excuse to (a) make an initial notification, (b) notify a change in details, (c) make an annual renotification, (d) comply with foreign travel requirements, (e) notify that a change did not happen as predicted when it had been notified in advance, (f) allow a police officer to take photograph/fingerprints, (g) ensure that a young offender on whose behalf he is required by a parental direction to comply with the notification requirements attends a police station when a notification is made, and (h) in the first four cases set out above, if he knowingly provides false information. A breach is a continuing offence, but only one instance should be charged. Proceedings may be commenced in any court having jurisdiction in any place where the person charged with the offence resides or is found.

Sentencing guideline

Offence seriousness (culpability and harm)		
A. Identify the appropriate starting point		
Starting points based on first time offender (see note below) pleading not guilty		
Example of nature of activity	**Starting point**	**Range**
Negligent or inadvertent failure to comply with requirements	Medium level community order	Band C fine to high level community order
Deliberate failure to comply with requirements OR Supply of information known to be false	6 weeks custody	High level community order to 26 weeks custody
Conduct as described in box above AND Long period of non-compliance OR Attempts to avoid detection	18 weeks custody	6 weeks custody to Crown Court

Offence seriousness (culpability and harm)	
B. Consider the effect of aggravating and mitigating factors	
(other than those within examples above)	
The following may be particularly relevant but **these lists are not exhaustive**	
Factor indicating higher culpability	**Factor indicating lower culpability**
1. Long period of non-compliance (where not in the examples above)	1. Genuine misunderstanding
Factors indicating greater degree of harm	
1. Alarm or distress caused to victim	
2. Particularly serious original offence	

A court is prohibited from imposing a conditional discharge.

Sexual Offences Act 2003, s 91(1)

(1)   A person commits an offence if he—

    (a) fails, without reasonable excuse, to comply with section 83(1), 84(1), 4(4)(b), 85(1), 87(4) or 89(2)(b) or any requirement imposed by regulations made under section 86(1); or

    (b) notifies to the police, in purported compliance with section 83(1), 4(1) or 85(1) or any requirement imposed by regulations made under section 86(1), any information which he knows to be false.

VIOLENT OFFENDER ORDER, BREACH OF REQUIREMENTS

All offences triable either-way, 6 months/£5,000 (5 years).

Criminal Justice and Immigration Act 2008, s 113

(1) If a person fails, without reasonable excuse, to comply with any prohibition, restriction or condition contained in—

    (a) a violent offender order, or

    (b) an interim violent offender order,

the person commits an offence.

(2) If a person fails, without reasonable excuse, to comply with—

    (a) section 108(1), 109(1) or (6)(b), 110(1) or 112(4), or

    (b) any requirement imposed by regulations made under section 111(1),

the person commits an offence.

(3) If a person notifies to the police, in purported compliance with—

    (a) section 108(1), 109(1) or 110(1), or

    (b) any requirement imposed by regulations made under section 111(1),

any information which the person knows to be false, the person commits an offence.

(4) As regards an offence under subsection (2), so far as it relates to non-compliance with—

    (a) section 108(1), 109(1) or 110(1), or

    (b) any requirement imposed by regulations made under section 111(1),

a person commits such an offence on the first day on which the person first fails, without reasonable excuse, to comply with the provision mentioned in paragraph (a) or (as the case may be) the requirement mentioned in paragraph (b), and continues to commit it throughout any period during which the failure continues.

(5) But a person must not be prosecuted under subsection (2) more than once in respect of the same failure.

(6) A person guilty of an offence under this section is liable—

    (a) on summary conviction, to imprisonment for a term not exceeding the relevant period or a fine not exceeding the statutory maximum or both;

    (b) on conviction on indictment, to imprisonment for a term not exceeding 5 years or a fine or both.

(7) In subsection (6)(a) "the relevant period" means—

    (a) in relation to England and Wales and Scotland, 12 months;

    (b) in relation to Northern Ireland, 6 months.

(8) Proceedings for an offence under this section may be commenced in any court having jurisdiction in any place where the person charged with the offence resides or is found.

PUBLIC ORDER OFFENCES

AFFRAY

Either-way, 6 months/£5,000 (3 years).

Place: An affray may be committed in both public and private places. **Words alone:** Are not sufficient.

Fights in public: See: *Plavecz* [2002] EWCA Crim 1802 and *Sanchez* (1996) 160 JP 321 where it was said:

> "The offence of affray envisages at least three persons: (i) the person using or threatening unlawful violence; (ii) a person towards whom the violence or threat is directed; and (iii) a person of reasonable firmness who need not actually be, or be likely to be, present at the scene. Thus the question in the present case was not whether a person of reasonable firmness in [the victim's] shoes would have feared for his personal safety but whether this hypothetical person, present in the room and seeing [the defendant's] conduct towards [the victim] would have so feared."

In *Leeson v Director of Public Prosecutions* [2010] EWHC 994 (Admin) a conviction was quashed where L, who was drunk, had threatened a person with a knife in the bathroom of a private dwelling. The court held that an hypothetical bystander would have viewed the threat as being restricted to the parties involved due to the turbulence of their relationship.

Together: In *NW* [2010] EWCA Crim 404 the court held:

> "Three or more people using or threatening violence in the same place at the same time, whether for the same purpose or different purposes, are capable of creating a daunting prospect for those who may encounter them simply by reason of the fact that they represent a breakdown of law and order which has unpredictable consequences. [The court is unable] to accept that the phrase requires any degree of cooperation between those who are using or threatening violence; all that is required is that they be present in the same place at the same time. The section is concerned with public disorder and is deliberately worded in a way that is apt to apply to anyone who uses or threatens violence of the requisite nature in a particular context, namely, in a public place where others are engaged in the same activity.... the requirement that the conduct of the participants taken together should be such as to cause members of the public to fear for their safety was included in order to direct attention to the overall effect of what may otherwise be unrelated acts or threats of violence."

Offence seriousness (culpability and harm) A. Identify the appropriate starting point Starting points based on first time offender pleading not guilty		
Example of nature of activity	Starting point	Range
Brief offence involving low level violence, no substantial fear created	Low level community order	Band C fine to medium level community order
Degree of fighting or violence that causes substantial fear	High level community order	Medium level community order to 12 weeks custody

Fight involving a weapon/throwing objects, or conduct causing risk of serious injury	18 weeks custody	12 weeks custody to Crown Court

Offence seriousness (culpability and harm)

B. Consider the effect of aggravating and mitigating factors (other than those within examples above)

The following may be particularly relevant but **these lists are not exhaustive**

Factors indicating higher culpability	Factors indicating lower culpability
1. Group action	1. Did not start the trouble
2. Threats	2. Provocation
3. Lengthy incident	3. Stopped as soon as police arrived

Factors indicating greater degree of harm	
1. Vulnerable person(s) present	
2. Injuries caused	
3. Damage to property	

Public Order Act 1986, s 3(1), (2), and (4)

(1) A person is guilty of affray if he uses or threatens unlawful violence towards another and his conduct is such as would cause a person of reasonable firmness present at the scene to fear for his personal safety.

(2) Where 2 or more persons use or threaten the unlawful violence, it is the conduct of them taken together that must be considered for the purposes of subsection (1).

(3) ...

(4) No person of reasonable firmness need actually be, or be likely to be, present at the scene.

ALCOHOL AT SPORTING EVENTS

Summary only, Section 2(1) 3 months/£1,000, Section 2(2) Fine £500.

Offence seriousness (culpability and harm)

A. Identify the appropriate starting point

Starting points based on first time offender pleading not guilty

Examples of nature of activity	Starting point	Range
Being drunk in, or whilst trying to enter, ground	Band A fine	Conditional discharge to band B fine
Possession of alcohol whilst entering or trying to enter ground	Band C fine	Band B fine to high level community order

Offence seriousness (culpability and harm)

B. Consider the effect of aggravating and mitigating factors (other than those within examples above)

The following may be particularly relevant but **these lists are not exhaustive**

Factors indicating higher culpability	
1. Commercial ticket operation; potential high cash value; counterfeit tickets	
2. Inciting others to misbehave	
3. Possession of large quantity of alcohol	
4. Offensive language or behaviour (where not an element of the offence)	

Factor indicating greater degree of harm	
1. Missile likely to cause serious injury eg coin, glass, bottle, stone	

Sporting Events (Control of Alcohol etc.) Act 1985, s 2(1), 2(2)

(1)   A person who has alcohol or an article to which this section applies in his possession—

   (a) at any time during the period of a designated sporting event when he is in any area of a designated sports ground from which the event may be directly viewed, or

   (b) while entering or trying to enter a designated sports ground at any time during the period of a designated sporting event at that ground,

is guilty of an offence.

(1A) Subsection (1)(a) above has effect subject to section 5A(1) of this Act.

(2)   A person who is drunk in a designated sports ground at any time during the period of a designated sporting event at that ground or is drunk while entering or trying to enter such a ground at any time during the period of a designated sporting event at that ground is guilty of an offence.

ALCOHOL ON COACHES AND TRAINS

Summary only, Fine level 4 (s 1(2) offence), 3 months/fine level 3 (s 1(3) offence), fine level 2 (s 1(4) offence).

Sporting Events (Control of Alcohol etc.) Act 1985, s 1(1)–(4)

(1)   This section applies to a vehicle which—

   (a) is a public service vehicle or railway passenger vehicle, and

   (b) is being used for the principal purpose of carrying passengers for the whole or part of a journey to or from a designated sporting event.

(2)   A person who knowingly causes or permits alcohol to be carried on a vehicle to which this section applies is guilty of an offence—

   (a) if the vehicle is a public service vehicle and he is the operator of the vehicle or the servant or agent of the operator, or

   (b) if the vehicle is a hired vehicle and he is the person to whom it is hired or the servant or agent of that person.

(3)   A person who has alcohol in his possession while on a vehicle to which this section applies is guilty of an offence.

(4)   A person who is drunk on a vehicle to which this section applies is guilty of an offence.

(5)   In this section 'public service vehicle' and 'operator' have the same meaning as in the Public Passenger Vehicles Act 1981.

ALCOHOL SALE OFFENCES

Summary only, £1,000 fine (ss 140, 141), £5,000 fine (ss 146 and 147), £10,000 fine (s 147A).

Licensing Act 2003, s 140 (allowing disorderly conduct) s 141 (sale of alcohol to drunk person), s 146 (sale of alcohol to children), s 147 (allowing sale of alcohol to children), S147A (persistently selling alcohol to children).

Offence seriousness (culpability and harm)		
A. Identify the appropriate starting point		
Starting points based on first time offender pleading not guilty		
Examples of nature of activity	**Starting point**	**Range**
Sale to a child (ie person under 18)/to a drunk person	Band B fine	Band A fine to band C fine

Offence seriousness (culpability and harm)	
B. Consider the effect of aggravating and mitigating factors (other than those within examples above)	
The following may be particularly relevant but **these lists are not exhaustive**	

Factors indicating higher culpability	
1. No attempt made to establish age	
2. Spirits/high alcohol level of drink	
3. Drunk person highly intoxicated	
4. Large quantity of alcohol supplied	
5. Sale intended for consumption by group of children/drunk people	
6. Offender in senior or management position	

Factors indicating greater degree of harm	
1. Younger child/children	
2. Drunk person causing distress to others	
3. Drunk person aggressive	

Licensing Act 2003, ss 140, 141, 146, 147, 147A

140 Allowing disorderly conduct on licensed premises etc.

(1) A person to whom subsection (2) applies commits an offence if he knowingly allows disorderly conduct on relevant premises.

(2) This subsection applies—

   (a) to any person who works at the premises in a capacity, whether paid or unpaid, which authorises him to prevent the conduct,

   (b) in the case of licensed premises, to—

      (i) the holder of a premises licence in respect of the premises, and

      (ii) the designated premises supervisor (if any) under such a licence,

   (c) in the case of premises in respect of which a club premises certificate has effect, to any member or officer of the club which holds the certificate who at the time the conduct takes place is present on the premises in a capacity which enables him to prevent it, and

   (d) in the case of premises which may be used for a permitted temporary activity by virtue of Part 5, to the premises user in relation to the temporary event notice in question.

141 Sale of alcohol to a person who is drunk

(1) A person to whom subsection (2) applies commits an offence if, on relevant premises, he knowingly—

   (a) sells or attempts to sell alcohol to a person who is drunk, or

   (b) allows alcohol to be sold to such a person.

(2) This subsection applies—

   (a) to any person who works at the premises in a capacity, whether paid or unpaid, which gives him authority to sell the alcohol concerned,

   (b) in the case of licensed premises, to—

      (i) the holder of a premises licence in respect of the premises, and

      (ii) the designated premises supervisor (if any) under such a licence,

   (c) in the case of premises in respect of which a club premises certificate has effect, to any member or officer of the club which holds the certificate who at the time the sale (or attempted sale) takes place is present on the premises in a capacity which enables him to prevent it, and

(d) in the case of premises which may be used for a permitted temporary activity by virtue of Part 5, to the premises user in relation to the temporary event notice in question.

(3) This section applies in relation to the supply of alcohol by or on behalf of a club to or to the order of a member of the club as it applies in relation to the sale of alcohol.

146 Sale of alcohol to children

(1) A person commits an offence if he sells alcohol to an individual aged under 18.
(2) A club commits an offence if alcohol is supplied by it or on its behalf—

(a) to, or to the order of, a member of the club who is aged under 18, or
(b) to the order of a member of the club, to an individual who is aged under 18.

(3) A person commits an offence if he supplies alcohol on behalf of a club—

(a) to, or to the order of, a member of the club who is aged under 18, or
(b) to the order of a member of the club, to an individual who is aged under 18.

(4) Where a person is charged with an offence under this section by reason of his own conduct it is a defence that—

(a) he believed that the individual was aged 18 or over, and
(b) either—

(i) he had taken all reasonable steps to establish the individual's age, or
(ii) nobody could reasonably have suspected from the individual's appearance that he was aged under 18.

(5) For the purposes of subsection (4), a person is treated as having taken all reasonable steps to establish an individual's age if—

(a) he asked the individual for evidence of his age, and
(b) the evidence would have convinced a reasonable person.

(6) Where a person ("the accused") is charged with an offence under this section by reason of the act or default of some other person, it is a defence that the accused exercised all due diligence to avoid committing it.

147 Allowing the sale of alcohol to children

(1) A person to whom subsection (2) applies commits an offence if he knowingly allows the sale of alcohol on relevant premises to an individual aged under 18.
(2) This subsection applies to a person who works at the premises in a capacity, whether paid or unpaid, which authorises him to prevent the sale.
(3) A person to whom subsection (4) applies commits an offence if he knowingly allows alcohol to be supplied on relevant premises by or on behalf of a club—

(a) to or to the order of a member of the club who is aged under 18, or
(b) to the order of a member of the club, to an individual who is aged under 18.

(4) This subsection applies to—

(a) a person who works on the premises in a capacity, whether paid or unpaid, which authorises him to prevent the supply, and
(b) any member or officer of the club who at the time of the supply is present on the relevant premises in a capacity which enables him to prevent it.

147A Persistently selling alcohol to children

(1) A person is guilty of an offence if–

(a) on 2 or more different occasions within a period of 3 consecutive months alcohol is unlawfully sold on the same premises to an individual aged under 18;

(b) at the time of each sale the premises were either licensed premises or premises authorised to be used for a permitted temporary activity by virtue of Part 5; and

(c) that person was a responsible person in relation to the premises at each such time.

(2) For the purposes of this section alcohol sold to an individual aged under 18 is unlawfully sold to him if–

(a) the person making the sale believed the individual to be aged under 18; or

(b) that person did not have reasonable grounds for believing the individual to be aged 18 or over.

(3) For the purposes of subsection (2) a person has reasonable grounds for believing an individual to be aged 18 or over only if–

(a) he asked the individual for evidence of his age and that individual produced evidence that would have convinced a reasonable person; or

(b) nobody could reasonably have suspected from the individual's appearance that he was aged under 18.

(4) A person is, in relation to premises and a time, a responsible person for the purposes of subsection (1) if, at that time, he is–

(a) the person or one of the persons holding a premises licence in respect of the premises; or

(b) the person or one of the persons who is the premises user in respect of a temporary event notice by reference to which the premises are authorised to be used for a permitted temporary activity by virtue of Part 5.

(5) The individual to whom the sales mentioned in subsection (1) are made may, but need not be, the same in each case.

(6) The same sale may not be counted in respect of different offences for the purpose–

(a) of enabling the same person to be convicted of more than one offence under this section; or

(b) of enabling the same person to be convicted of both an offence under this section and an offence under section 146 or 147.

(7) In determining whether an offence under this section has been committed, the following shall be admissible as evidence that there has been an unlawful sale of alcohol to an individual aged under 18 on any premises on any occasion–

(a) the conviction of a person for an offence under section 146 in respect of a sale to that individual on those premises on that occasion;

(b) the giving to a person of a caution (within the meaning of Part 5 of the Police Act 1997) in respect of such an offence; or

(c) the payment by a person of a fixed penalty under Part 1 of the Criminal Justice and Police Act 2001 in respect of such a sale.

(8) A person guilty of an offence under this section shall be liable, on summary conviction, to a fine not exceeding £20,000.

(9) The Secretary of State may by order amend subsection (8) to increase the maximum fine for the time being specified in that subsection.

BOMB HOAX

Either-way, 6 months/£5,000 (7 years).

Sentence: The custody threshold is met in most cases (*Philipson* [2008] 2 Cr App R (S) 110, *Wareham*, Unreported, 11 February 2000).

Criminal Law Act 1977, s 51

(1) A person who—

    (a) places any article in any place whatever; or

    (b) dispatches any article by post, rail or any other means whatever of sending things from one place to another,

with the intention (in either case) of inducing in some other person a belief that it is likely to explode or ignite and thereby cause personal injury or damage to property is guilty of an offence.

In this subsection "article"includes substance.

(2) A person who communicates any information which he knows or believes to be false to another person with the intention of inducing in him or any other person a false belief that a bomb or other thing liable to explode or ignite is present in any place or location whatever is guilty of an offence.

(3) For a person to be guilty of an offence under subsection (1) or (2) above it is not necessary for him to have any particular person in mind as the person in whom he intends to induce the belief mentioned in that subsection.

DEMONSTRATIONS IN VICINITY OF PARLIAMENT

Serious Organised Crime and Police Act 2005, ss 132, 134-136.

These offences were repealed on 30 March 2012. See Parliament Square Controlled Area for new offences.

DISORDERLY BEHAVIOUR WITH INTENT TO CAUSE HARASSMENT, ALARM, OR DISTRESS

Summary only unless racially or religiously aggravated, 6 months/£5,000 (2 years on indictment if racially or religiously aggravated).

Place: An offence under this section may be committed in a public or a private place, except that no offence is committed where the words or behaviour are used, or the writing, sign or other visible representation is displayed, by a person inside a dwelling and the person who is harassed, alarmed, or distressed is also inside that or another dwelling. **Defence:** The Public Order Act 1986, s 4A(3) provides:

It is a defence for the accused to prove—

    (a) that he was inside a dwelling and had no reason to believe that the words or behaviour used, or the writing, sign or other visible representation displayed, would be heard or seen by a person outside that or any other dwelling, or

    (b) that his conduct was reasonable.

Offence seriousness (culpability and harm)		
A. Identify the appropriate starting point		
Starting points based on first time offender pleading not guilty		
Examples of nature of activity	**Starting point**	**Range**
Threats, abuse, or insults made more than once but on same occasion against the same person eg while following down the street	Band C fine	Band B fine to low level community order
Group action or deliberately planned action against targeted victim	Medium level community order	Low level community order to 12 weeks custody

Weapon brandished or used or threats against vulnerable victim—course of conduct over longer period	12 weeks custody	High level community order to 26 weeks custody

Offence seriousness (culpability and harm)	
B. Consider the effect of aggravating and mitigating factors (other than those within examples above)	
The following may be particularly relevant but **these lists are not exhaustive**	

Factors indicating higher culpability	Factors indicating lower culpability
1. High degree of planning	1. Very short period
2. Offender deliberately isolates victim	2. Provocation
Factors indicating greater degree of harm	
1. Offence committed in vicinity of victim's home	
2. Large number of people in vicinity	
3. Actual or potential escalation into violence	
4. Particularly serious impact on victim	

Public Order Act 1986, s 4A(1)

(1) A person is guilty of an offence if, with intent to cause a person harassment, alarm or distress, he—

   (a) uses threatening, abusive or insulting words or behaviour, or disorderly behaviour, or
   (b) displays any writing, sign or other visible representation which is threatening, abusive or insulting,

thereby causing that or another person harassment, alarm or distress.

DISORDERLY BEHAVIOUR (HARASSMENT, ALARM, OR DISTRESS)

Summary only, £1,000 fine; £2,500 fine if racially or religiously aggravated.

Place: Offence may be committed in a public or a private place, except that no offence is committed where the words or behaviour are used, or the writing, sign, or other visible representation is displayed, by a person inside a dwelling and the other person is also inside that or another dwelling. Concern for others: The conduct need not be directed at the complainant and it is enough that he should be concerned for another (*Lodge v Director of Public Prosecutions*, The Times October 26 1998). **Harassment:** Emotional upset is not a necessary result of any harassment *Southard v Director of Public Prosecutions* [2006] EWHC 3449 (Admin), however the act should not be trivial eg *R (R) v Director of Public Prosecutions* [2006] EWHC 1375 (Admin) and *Harvey v Director of Public Prosecutions* [2011] EWHC 3992 (Admin) [both cases involving swearing at police officers]. **Disorderly behaviour:** Concealing a video camera in a changing room can amount to disorderly behaviour (*Vigon v Director of Public Prosecutions* (1997) 162 JP 115). **ECHR considerations:** In *Abdul and Others v Crown Prosecution Service* [2011] EWHC 247 (Admin)). The following principles emerge from Article 10 jurisprudence (para. 49 of the judgment):

   i)   The starting point is the importance of the right to freedom of expression.
   ii)   In this regard, it must be recognised that legitimate protest can be offensive at least to some—and on occasions must be, if it is to have impact. Moreover, the right to freedom of expression would be unacceptably devalued if it did no more than protect those holding popular, mainstream views; it must plainly extend beyond that so that minority views can be freely expressed, even if distasteful. [The context of the remarks is a key factor.]
   iii) The justification for interference with the right to freedom of expression must be convincingly established. Accordingly, while Art. 10 does not confer an unqualified right

to freedom of expression, the restrictions contained in Art. 10.2 are to be narrowly construed.

iv) There is not and cannot be any universal test for resolving when speech goes beyond legitimate protest, so attracting the sanction of the criminal law. The justification for invoking the criminal law is the threat to public order. Inevitably, the context of the particular occasion will be of the first importance.

v) The relevance of the threat to public order should not be taken as meaning that the risk of violence by those reacting to the protest is, without more, determinative; sometimes it may be that protesters are to be protected. That said, in striking the right balance when determining whether speech is "threatening, abusive or insulting", the focus on minority rights should not result in overlooking the rights of the majority.

vi) Plainly, if there is no prima facie case that speech was "threatening, abusive or insulting" or that the other elements of the s.5 offence can be made good, then no question of prosecution will arise. However, even if there is otherwise a prima facie case for contending that an offence has been committed under s.5, it is still for the Crown to establish that prosecution is a proportionate response, necessary for the preservation of public order.

vii) If the line between legitimate freedom of expression and a threat to public order has indeed been crossed, freedom of speech will not have been impaired by "ruling ...out" threatening, abusive or insulting speech.

Offence seriousness (culpability and harm)
A. Identify the appropriate starting point
Starting points based on first time offender pleading not guilty

Examples of nature of activity	Starting point	Range
Shouting, causing disturbance for some minutes	Band A fine	Conditional discharge to band B fine
Substantial disturbance caused	Band B fine	Band A fine to band C fine

Offence seriousness (culpability and harm)
B. Consider the effect of aggravating and mitigating factors (other than those within examples above)
The following may be particularly relevant but **these lists are not exhaustive**

Factors indicating higher culpability	Factors indicating lower culpability
1. Group action	1. Stopped as soon as police arrived
2. Lengthy incident	2. Brief/minor incident
Factors indicating greater degree of harm	3. Provocation
1. Vulnerable person(s) present	
2. Offence committed at school, hospital, or other place where vulnerable persons may be present	
3. Victim providing public service	

Public Order Act 1986, ss 5, 6(4)

5.— Harassment, alarm or distress.

(1) A person is guilty of an offence if he—

(a) uses threatening, abusive or insulting words or behaviour, or disorderly behaviour, or

(b) displays any writing, sign or other visible representation which is threatening, abusive or insulting,

within the hearing or sight of a person likely to be caused harassment, alarm or distress thereby.

(2) An offence under this section may be committed in a public or a private place, except that no offence is committed where the words or behaviour are used, or the writing, sign or other visible representation is displayed, by a person inside a dwelling and the other person is also inside that or another dwelling.

(3) It is a defence for the accused to prove—

(a) that he had no reason to believe that there was any person within hearing or sight who was likely to be caused harassment, alarm or distress, or

(b) that he was inside a dwelling and had no reason to believe that the words or behaviour used, or the writing, sign or other visible representation displayed, would be heard or seen by a person outside that or any other dwelling, or

(c) that his conduct was reasonable.

6.— Mental element: miscellaneous.

(4) A person is guilty of an offence under section 5 only if he intends his words or behaviour, or the writing, sign or other visible representation, to be threatening, abusive or insulting, or is aware that it may be threatening, abusive or insulting or (as the case may be) he intends his behaviour to be or is aware that it may be disorderly.

DRUNK AND DISORDERLY

Summary only £1,000 fine

Definition: In *Carroll v Director of Public Prosecutions* [2009] EWHC 554 (Admin) the court held that the offence requires proof of three elements, namely that (1) the defendant was drunk; (2) he was in a public place; and (3) he was guilty of disorderly behaviour. Only the first and third elements call for further comment: As to the first element in *Neale v RMJE* (1985) 80 Cr App R 20, this court (Robert Goff LJ and Mann J, as they each then were) decided that the word 'drunk' should be given its ordinary and natural meaning. In the end, therefore, whether a defendant was drunk is a simple question of fact in each case. On familiar principles it is the voluntary consumption of alcohol which is the requisite mens rea, such as it is, of this most basic offence. If that voluntary consumption results in the defendant becoming drunk then the first element of the offence is proved. As to the third element, there is no requirement for mens rea at all. What is required is proof that objectively viewed the defendant was guilty of disorderly behaviour. Specific drunken intent and recklessness are nothing to the point. The words 'disorderly behaviour' are again to be given their ordinary and natural meaning. In the end, therefore, it is a simple question of fact in each case: whether the defendant is guilty of disorderly behaviour. **Substances:** The defendant must be drunk as a result of the voluntary consumption of alcohol, other substances such as glue would not be sufficient to found a conviction (*Neale v RMJE* (1985) 80 Cr App R 20).

Offence seriousness (culpability and harm)		
A. Identify the appropriate starting point		
Starting points based on first time offender pleading not guilty		
Examples of nature of activity	**Starting point**	**Range**
Shouting, causing disturbance for some minutes	Band A fine	Conditional discharge to band B fine
Substantial disturbance caused	Band B fine	Band A fine to band C fine

Offence seriousness (culpability and harm)
B. Consider the effect of aggravating and mitigating factors (other than those within examples above)
The following may be particularly relevant but **these lists are not exhaustive**

Factors indicating higher culpability	Factors indicating lower culpability
1. Brandishing firearm	1. Firearm not in sight
2. Carrying firearm in a busy place	2. No intention to use firearm
3. Planned illegal use	3. Firearm to be used for lawful purpose (not amounting to defence)
Factors indicating greater degree of harm	
1. Person or people put in fear	
2. Offender participating in violent incident	

Criminal Justice Act 1967, s 91(1), (2), and (4)

(1) Any person who in any public place is guilty, while drunk, of disorderly behaviour ... shall be liable on summary conviction to a fine not exceeding level 3 on the standard scale.

(2) The foregoing subsection shall have effect instead of any corresponding provision contained in section 12 of the Licensing Act 1872, section 58 of the Metropolitan Police Act 1839, section 37 of the City of London Police Act 1839, and section 29 of the Town Police Clauses Act 1847 (being enactments which authorise the imposition of a short term of imprisonment or of a fine not exceeding £10 or both for the corresponding offence) and instead of any corresponding provision contained in any local Act.

(3) ...

(4) In this section 'public place' includes any highway and any other premises or place to which at the material time the public have or are permitted to have access, whether on payment or otherwise.

GOING ONTO THE PLAYING AREA

Summary only, Fine £1,000.

Offence seriousness (culpability and harm)
A. Identify the appropriate starting point
Starting points based on first time offender pleading not guilty

Examples of nature of activity	Starting point	Range
Going onto playing or other prohibited area; unauthorized sale or attempted sale of tickets	Band B fine	Band A fine to band C fine

Offence seriousness (culpability and harm)
B. Consider the effect of aggravating and mitigating factors (other than those within examples above)
The following may be particularly relevant but **these lists are not exhaustive**

Factors indicating higher culpability
1. Commercial ticket operation; potential high cash value; counterfeit tickets
2. Inciting others to misbehave
3. Possession of large quantity of alcohol
4. Offensive language or behaviour (where not an element of the offence)

Factor indicating greater degree of harm
1. Missile likely to cause serious injury eg coin, glass, bottle, stone

Football Offences Act 1991, s 4

It is an offence for a person at a designated football match to go onto the playing area, or any area adjacent to the playing area to which spectators are not generally admitted, without lawful authority or lawful excuse (which shall be for him to prove).

IMPROPER USE OF PUBLIC ELECTRONIC COMMUNICATIONS NETWORK

Summary only, 6 months and/or £5,000 fine.

Intent: In *Director of Public Prosecutions v Collins* [2006] UKHL 40 the court held that to be guilty of an offence under section 127: (1) The defendant must have intended his words to be offensive to those to whom they related, or (2) be aware that they might be taken to be so. In *Chambers v Director of Public Prosecutions* [2012] EWHC 2157 (Admin) the court, in commenting on the mental element of the offence as described in *Collins* added: "We would merely emphasise that even expressed in these terms, the mental element of the offence is directed exclusively to the state of the mind of the offender, and that if he may have intended the message as a joke, even if a poor joke in bad taste, it is unlikely that the mens rea required before conviction for the offence of sending a message of a menacing character will be established." **Menacing:** In *Chambers* the court emphasised that whilst a menacing message will contain a threat, "[Before] concluding that a message is criminal on the basis that it represents a menace, its precise terms, and any inferences to be drawn from its precise terms, need to be examined in the context in and the means by which the message was sent." **Offensive:** The question of whether something is in fact offensive is to be determined by reference to whether or not reasonable persons would find the message grossly offensive, judged by the standards of an open and just multiracial society. It is irrelevant whether or not the message is actually received (*Collins*). Parliament cannot have intended to criminalize the conduct of a person using language which is, for reasons unknown to him, grossly offensive to those to whom it relates, or which may even be thought, however wrongly, to represent a polite or acceptable usage. On the other hand, a culpable state of mind will ordinarily be found where a message is couched in terms showing an intention to insult those to whom the message relates or giving rise to the inference that a risk of doing so must have been recognized by the sender. The same will be true where facts known to the sender of a message about an intended recipient render the message peculiarly offensive to that recipient, or likely to be so, whether or not the message in fact reaches the recipient (*Collins*). **ECHR:** European Convention rights to freedom of expression will rarely provide a defence (see *Connolly v Director of Public Prosecutions* [2007] EWHC 237 (Admin), a case concerned with a different statute).

Offence seriousness (culpability and harm)
A. Identify the appropriate starting point
Starting points based on first time offender pleading not guilty

Sending grossly offensive, indecent, obscene, or menacing messages (s 127(1))

Example of nature of activity	Starting point	Range
Single offensive, indecent, obscene, or menacing call of short duration, having no significant impact on receiver	Band B fine	Band A fine to band C fine
Single call where extreme language used, having only moderate impact on receiver	Medium level community order	Low level community order to high level community order
Single call where extreme language used and substantial distress or fear caused to receiver; OR One of a series of similar calls as described in box above	6 weeks custody	High level community order to 12 weeks custody

Sending false message/persistent use of communications network for purpose of causing annoyance, inconvenience, or needless anxiety (s 127(2))		
Examples of nature of activity	**Starting point**	**Range**
Persistent silent calls over short period to private individual, causing inconvenience or annoyance	Band B fine	Band A fine to band C fine
Single hoax call to public or private organization resulting in moderate disruption or anxiety	Medium level community order	Low level community order to high level community order
Single hoax call resulting in major disruption or substantial public fear or distress; OR One of a series of similar calls as described in box above	12 weeks custody	High level community order to 18 weeks custody

Communications Act 2003, s 127(1)–(2)

(1) A person is guilty of an offence if he—

    (a) sends by means of a public electronic communications network a message or other matter that is grossly offensive or of an indecent, obscene or menacing character; or

    (b) causes any such message or matter to be so sent.

(2) A person is guilty of an offence if, for the purpose of causing annoyance, inconvenience or needless anxiety to another, he—

    (a) sends by means of a public electronic communications network, a message that he knows to be false,

    (b) causes such a message to be sent; or

    (c) persistently makes use of a public electronic communications network.

INDECENT OR OFFENSIVE OR THREATENING LETTERS ETC

Summary only 6 months/£5,000 (Note that in *Byrne* [2011] EWCA Crim 3230 the Court of Appeal quashed a sentence of imprisonment on the erroneous basis that section 1(4) was still in force in its original form. That section was amended on May 11 2001 and the offence carries the penalties cited).

ECHR: see *Connolly v Director of Public Prosecutions* [2007] EWHC 237 (Admin).

Malicious Communications Act 1988, s 1

(1) Any person who sends to another person—

    (a) a letter, electronic communication or article of any description which conveys—

        (i) a message which is indecent or grossly offensive;

        (ii) a threat; or

        (iii) information which is false and known or believed to be false by the sender; or

    (b) any article or electronic communication which is, in whole or part, of an indecent or grossly offensive nature,

is guilty of an offence if his purpose, or one of his purposes, in sending it is that it should, so far as falling within paragraph (a) or (b) above, cause distress or anxiety to the recipient or to any other person to whom he intends that it or its contents or nature should be communicated.

(2) A person is not guilty of an offence by virtue of subsection (1)(a)(ii) above if he shows—

    (a) that the threat was used to reinforce a demand made by him on reasonable grounds; and

    (b) that he believed, and had reasonable grounds for believing, that the use of the threat was a proper means of reinforcing the demand.

(2A) In this section "electronic communication" includes—

    (a) any oral or other communication by means of an electronic communications network; and

    (b) any communication (however sent) that is in electronic form.

(3) In this section references to sending include references to delivering or transmitting and to causing to be sent, delivered or transmitted and "sender" shall be construed accordingly.

INDECENT OR RACIALIST CHANTING

Summary only, Fine £1,000.

Offence seriousness (culpability and harm) **A. Identify the appropriate starting point** Starting points based on first time offender pleading not guilty		
Examples of nature of activity	**Starting point**	**Range**
Throwing missile; indecent or racialist chanting	Band C fine	Band C fine

Offence seriousness (culpability and harm) **B. Consider the effect of aggravating and mitigating factors (other than those within examples above)** The following may be particularly relevant but **these lists are not exhaustive**	
Factors indicating higher culpability 1. Commercial ticket operation; potential high cash value; counterfeit tickets 2. Inciting others to misbehave 3. Possession of large quantity of alcohol 4. Offensive language or behaviour (where not an element of the offence)	
Factor indicating greater degree of harm 1. Missile likely to cause serious injury eg coin, glass, bottle, stone	

Football Offences Act 1991, s 3

(1) It is an offence to engage or take part in chanting of an indecent or racialist nature at a designated football match.

(2) For this purpose—

    (a) 'chanting' means the repeated uttering of any words or sounds (whether alone or in concert with one or more others); and

    (b) 'of a racialist nature' means consisting of or including matter which is threatening, abusive or insulting to a person by reason of his colour, race, nationality (including citizenship) or ethnic or national origins.

NUISANCE OR DISTURBANCE ON NHS PREMISES

Summary only, Fine £1,000.

Generally: "A nuisance or disturbance can include any form of non-physical behaviour which breaches the peace, such as verbal aggression or intimidating gestures towards NHS staff. A person will not commit the offence if he or she has a reasonable excuse for causing the nuisance or disturbance or refusing to leave the premises. Behaviour consequential to the receipt of upsetting news or bereavement may, for example, constitute a reasonable excuse. A nuisance or disturbance must be caused to an NHS staff member, rather than any other person. At the time the nuisance or disturbance is caused, the NHS staff member must either be working at the premises or be there for some other purpose relating to his work, such as travelling to work, walking between buildings or taking a break. The nuisance or disturbance must be caused on NHS premises. ... A reasonable excuse for not leaving the premises may, for example, include a situation where a dependent is on the premises concerned and the person causing a nuisance or disturbance has a responsibility to remain on the premises with this dependent." (Explanatory note).

Criminal Justice and Immigration Act 2008, s 119

(1)   A person commits an offence if—

    (a)   the person causes, without reasonable excuse and while on NHS premises, a nuisance or disturbance to an NHS staff member who is working there or is otherwise there in connection with work,

    (b)   the person refuses, without reasonable excuse, to leave the NHS premises when asked to do so by a constable or an NHS staff member, and

    (c)   the person is not on the NHS premises for the purpose of obtaining medical advice, treatment or care for himself or herself.

(2)   [...]

(3)   For the purposes of this section—

    (a)   a person ceases to be on NHS premises for the purpose of obtaining medical advice, treatment or care for himself or herself once the person has received the advice, treatment or care, and

    (b)   a person is not on NHS premises for the purpose of obtaining medical advice, treatment or care for himself or herself if the person has been refused the advice, treatment or care during the last 8 hours.

(4)   In this section—

"English NHS premises" means—

    (a)   any hospital vested in, or managed by, a relevant English NHS body,

    (b)   any building or other structure, or vehicle, associated with the hospital and situated on hospital grounds (whether or not vested in, or managed by, a relevant English NHS body), and

    (c)   the hospital grounds,

"hospital grounds" means land in the vicinity of a hospital and associated with it,

"NHS premises" means English NHS premises or Welsh NHS premises,

"NHS staff member" means a person employed by a relevant English NHS body, or a relevant Welsh NHS body, or otherwise working for such a body (whether as or on behalf of a contractor, as a volunteer or otherwise),

"relevant English NHS body" means—

    (a)   a National Health Service trust (see section 25 of the National Health Service Act 2006 (c. 41)), all or most of whose hospitals, establishments and facilities are situated in England,

    (b)   a Primary Care Trust (see section 18 of that Act), or

    (c)   an NHS foundation trust (see section 30 of that Act),

"relevant Welsh NHS body" means—

    (a)   a National Health Service trust (see section 18 of the National Health Service (Wales) Act 2006 (c. 42)), all or most of whose hospitals, establishments and facilities are situated in Wales, or

    (b)   a Local Health Board (see section 11 of that Act),

"vehicle" includes an air ambulance,

"Welsh NHS premises" means—

    (a) any hospital vested in, or managed by, a relevant Welsh NHS body,

    (b) any building or other structure, or vehicle, associated with the hospital and situated on hospital grounds (whether or not vested in, or managed by, a relevant Welsh NHS body), and

    (c) the hospital grounds.

PARLIAMENT SQUARE CONTROLLED AREA

Summary only, Fine £5,000. Note the power to make ancillary orders under section 146.

Police Reform and Social Responsibility Act 2011, ss 142-148

142 Controlled area of Parliament Square

(1) For the purposes of this Part, the "controlled area of Parliament Square" means the area of land that is comprised in—

    (a) the central garden of Parliament Square, and

    (b) the footways that immediately adjoin the central garden of Parliament Square.

(2) In subsection (1)—

"the central garden of Parliament Square" means the site in Parliament Square on which the Minister of Works was authorised by the Parliament Square (Improvements) Act 1949 to lay out the garden referred to in that Act as "the new central garden";

"footway" has the same meaning as in the Highways Act 1980 (see section 329(1) of that Act).

143 Prohibited activities in controlled area of Parliament Square

(1) A constable or authorised officer who has reasonable grounds for believing that a person is doing, or is about to do, a prohibited activity may direct the person—

    (a) to cease doing that activity, or

    (b) (as the case may be) not to start doing that activity.

(2) For the purposes of this Part, a "prohibited activity" is any of the following—

    (a) operating any amplified noise equipment in the controlled area of Parliament Square;

    (b) erecting or keeping erected in the controlled area of Parliament Square—

        (i) any tent, or

        (ii) any other structure that is designed, or adapted, (solely or mainly) for the purpose of facilitating sleeping or staying in a place for any period;

    (c) using any tent or other such structure in the controlled area of Parliament Square for the purpose of sleeping or staying in that area;

    (d) placing or keeping in place in the controlled area of Parliament Square any sleeping equipment with a view to its use (whether or not by the person placing it or keeping it in place) for the purpose of sleeping overnight in that area;

    (e) using any sleeping equipment in the controlled area of Parliament Square for the purpose of sleeping overnight in that area.

(3) But an activity is not to be treated as a "prohibited activity" within subsection (2) if it is done—

    (a) for police, fire and rescue authority or ambulance purposes,

    (b) by or on behalf of a relevant authority, or

    (c) by a person so far as authorised under section 147 to do it (authorisation for operation of amplified noise equipment).

(4) In subsection (2)(a) "amplified noise equipment" means any device that is designed or adapted for amplifying sound, including (but not limited to)—

    (a) loudspeakers, and

    (b) loudhailers.

(5) In subsection (3)(b) "relevant authority" means any of the following—

    (a) a Minister of the Crown or a government department,

    (b) the Greater London Authority, or

    (c) Westminster City Council.

(6) It is immaterial for the purposes of a prohibited activity—

    (a) in the case of an activity within subsection (2)(b) or (c) of keeping a tent or similar structure erected or using a tent or similar structure, whether the tent or structure was first erected before or after the coming into force of this section;

    (b) in the case of an activity within subsection (2)(d) or (e) of keeping in place any sleeping equipment or using any such equipment, whether the sleeping equipment was first placed before or after the coming into force of this section.

(7) In this section "sleeping equipment" means any sleeping bag, mattress or other similar item designed, or adapted, (solely or mainly) for the purpose of facilitating sleeping in a place.

(8) A person who fails without reasonable excuse to comply with a direction under subsection (1) commits an offence and is liable on summary conviction to a fine not exceeding level 5 on the standard scale.

144 Directions under section 143: further provision

(1) A direction requiring a person to cease doing a prohibited activity may include a direction that the person does not start doing that activity again after having ceased it.

(2) A direction requiring a person not to start doing a prohibited activity continues in force until—

    (a) the end of such period beginning with the day on which the direction is given as may be specified by the constable or authorised officer giving the direction, or

    (b) if no such period is specified, the end of the period of 90 days beginning with the day on which the direction is given.

(3) A period specified under subsection (2)(a) may not be longer than 90 days.

(4) A direction may be given to a person to cease operating, or not to start operating, any amplified noise equipment only if it appears to the constable or authorised officer giving the direction that the following condition is met.

(5) The condition is that the person is operating, or is about to operate, the equipment in such a manner as to produce sound that other persons in or in the vicinity of the controlled area of Parliament Square can hear or are likely to be able to hear.

(6) A direction—

    (a) may be given orally,

    (b) may be given to any person individually or to two or more persons together, and

    (c) may be withdrawn or varied by the person who gave it.

(7) In this section—

"amplified noise equipment" has the meaning given by section 143(4);

"direction" means a direction given under section 143(1).

145 Power to seize property

(1) A constable or authorised officer may seize and retain a prohibited item that is on any land in the controlled area of Parliament Square if it appears to that constable or officer that the item is being, or has been, used in connection with the commission of an offence under section 143.

(2) A constable may seize and retain a prohibited item that is on any land outsideof the controlled area of Parliament Square if it appears to the constable that the item has been used in connection with the commission of an offence under section 143.

(3) A "prohibited item"is any item of a kind mentioned in section 143(2).

(4) A constable may use reasonable force, if necessary, in exercising a power of seizure under this section.

(5) An item seized under this section must be returned to the person from whom it was seized—

(a) no later than the end of the period of 28 days beginning with the day on which the item was seized, or

(b) if proceedings are commenced against the person for an offence under section 143 before the return of the item under paragraph (a), at the conclusion of those proceedings.

(6) If it is not possible to return an item under subsection (5) because the name or address of the person from whom it was seized is not known—

(a) the item may be returned to any other person appearing to have rights in the property who has come forward to claim it, or

(b) if there is no such person, the item may be disposed of or destroyed at any time after the end of the period of 90 days beginning with the day on which the item was seized.

(7) Subsections (5)(b) and (6) do not apply if a court makes an order under section 146(1)(a) for the forfeiture of the item.

(8) The references in subsections (1) and (2) to an item that is "on" any land include references to an item that is in the possession of a person who is on any such land.

146 Power of court on conviction

(1) The court may do either or both of the following on the conviction of a person ("P") of an offence under section 143—

(a) make an order providing for the forfeiture of any item of a kind mentioned in subsection (2) of that section that was used in the commission of the offence;

(b) make such other order as the court considers appropriate for the purpose of preventing P from engaging in any prohibited activity in the controlled area of Parliament Square.

(2) An order under subsection (1)(b) may (in particular) require P not to enter the controlled area of Parliament Square for such period as may be specified in the order.

(3) Power of the court to make an order under this section is in addition to the court's power to impose a fine under section 143(8).

147 Authorisation for operation of amplified noise equipment

(1) The responsible authority for any land in the controlled area of Parliament Square may authorise a person in accordance with this section to operate on that land any amplified noise equipment (as defined by section 143(4)).

(2) An application for authorisation must be made to the responsible authority by or on behalf of the person (or persons) seeking the authorisation.

(3) The responsible authority may—

(a) determine the form in which, and the manner in which, an application is to be made;

(b) specify the information to be supplied in connection with an application;

(c) require a fee to be paid for determining an application.

(4) If an application is duly made to a responsible authority, the authority must—

(a) determine the application, and

(b) give notice in writing to the applicant of the authority's decision within the period of 21 days beginning with the day on which the authority receives the application.

(5) The notice must specify—

    (a) the person (or persons) authorised (whether by name or description),

    (b) the kind of amplified noise equipment to which the authorisation applies,

    (c) the period to which the authorisation applies, and

    (d) any conditions to which the authorisation is subject.

(6) The responsible authority may at any time—

    (a) withdraw an authorisation given to a person under this section, or

    (b) vary any condition to which an authorisation is subject.

(7) Variation under subsection (6)(b) includes—

    (a) imposing a new condition,

    (b) removing an existing condition, or

    (c) altering any period to which a condition applies.

(8) The exercise of a power under subsection (6) to withdraw an authorisation or to vary a condition is effected by the responsible authority giving notice in writing to the applicant.

148 Meaning of "authorised officer" and "responsible authority"

(1) This section applies for the purposes of this Part.

(2) "Authorised officer", in relation to any land in the controlled area of Parliament Square, means—

    (a) an employee of the responsible authority for that land who is authorised in writing by the authority for the purposes of this Part, and

    (b) any other person who, under arrangements made with the responsible authority (whether by that or any other person), is so authorised for the purposes of this Part.

(3) "Responsible authority", in relation to any land in the controlled area of Parliament Square, means—

    (a) the Greater London Authority, for any land comprised in the central garden of Parliament Square (as defined by section 142(2)), and

    (b) Westminster City Council, for any other land.

PUBLIC PROCESSIONS

Summary only, Section 11: Fine £1,000; Section 12(4) 3 months/£2,500, Section 12(5) Fine £1,000, Section 12(6) 3 months/£2,500 (notwithstanding the effect of Magistrates' Courts Act 1980, s 45(3)); Section 13(7) 3 months/£2,500, Section 13(8) Fine £1,000, Section 13(9) 3 months/£2,500 (notwithstanding the effect of Magistrates' Courts Act 1980, s 45(3)).

Public Order Act 1986, ss 11-13

11.— Advance notice of public processions.

(1) Written notice shall be given in accordance with this section of any proposal to hold a public procession intended—

    (a) to demonstrate support for or opposition to the views or actions of any person or body of persons,

    (b) to publicise a cause or campaign, or

    (c) to mark or commemorate an event,

unless it is not reasonably practicable to give any advance notice of the procession.

(2) Subsection (1) does not apply where the procession is one commonly or customarily held in the police area (or areas) in which it is proposed to be held or is a funeral procession organised by a funeral director acting in the normal course of his business.

(3) The notice must specify the date when it is intended to hold the procession, the time when it is intended to start it, its proposed route, and the name and address of the person (or of one of the persons) proposing to organise it.

(4) Notice must be delivered to a police station—

(a) in the police area in which it is proposed the procession will start, or

(b) where it is proposed the procession will start in Scotland and cross into England, in the first police area in England on the proposed route.

(5) If delivered not less than 6 clear days before the date when the procession is intended to be held, the notice may be delivered by post by the recorded delivery service; but section 7 of the Interpretation Act 1978 (under which a document sent by post is deemed to have been served when posted and to have been delivered in the ordinary course of post) does not apply.

(6) If not delivered in accordance with subsection (5), the notice must be delivered by hand not less than 6 clear days before the date when the procession is intended to be held or, if that is not reasonably practicable, as soon as delivery is reasonably practicable.

(7) Where a public procession is held, each of the persons organising it is guilty of an offence if—

(a) the requirements of this section as to notice have not been satisfied, or

(b) the date when it is held, the time when it starts, or its route, differs from the date, time or route specified in the notice.

(8) It is a defence for the accused to prove that he did not know of, and neither suspected nor had reason to suspect, the failure to satisfy the requirements or (as the case may be) the difference of date, time or route.

(9) To the extent that an alleged offence turns on a difference of date, time or route, it is a defence for the accused to prove that the difference arose from circumstances beyond his control or from something done with the agreement of a police officer or by his direction.

12.— Imposing conditions on public processions.

(1) If the senior police officer, having regard to the time or place at which and the circumstances in which any public procession is being held or is intended to be held and to its route or proposed route, reasonably believes that—

(a) it may result in serious public disorder, serious damage to property or serious disruption to the life of the community, or

(b) the purpose of the persons organising it is the intimidation of others with a view to compelling them not to do an act they have a right to do, or to do an act they have a right not to do,

he may give directions imposing on the persons organising or taking part in the procession such conditions as appear to him necessary to prevent such disorder, damage, disruption or intimidation, including conditions as to the route of the procession or prohibiting it from entering any public place specified in the directions.

(2) In subsection (1) "the senior police officer" means —

(a) in relation to a procession being held, or to a procession intended to be held in a case where persons are assembling with a view to taking part in it, the most senior in rank of the police officers present at the scene, and

(b) in relation to a procession intended to be held in a case where paragraph (a) does not apply, the chief officer of police.

(3) A direction given by a chief officer of police by virtue of subsection (2)(b) shall be given in writing.

(4) A person who organises a public procession and knowingly fails to comply with a condition imposed under this section is guilty of an offence, but it is a defence for him to prove that the failure arose from circumstances beyond his control.

(5) A person who takes part in a public procession and knowingly fails to comply with a condition imposed under this section is guilty of an offence, but it is a defence for him to prove that the failure arose from circumstances beyond his control.

(6) A person who incites another to commit an offence under subsection (5) is guilty of an offence.

13.— Prohibiting public processions.

(1) If at any time the chief officer of police reasonably believes that, because of particular circumstances existing in any district or part of a district, the powers under section 12 will not be sufficient to prevent the holding of public processions in that district or part from resulting in serious public disorder, he shall apply to the council of the district for an order prohibiting for such period not exceeding 3 months as may be specified in the application the holding of all public processions (or of any class of public procession so specified) in the district or part concerned.

(2) On receiving such an application, a council may with the consent of the Secretary of State make an order either in the terms of the application or with such modifications as may be approved by the Secretary of State.

(3) Subsection (1) does not apply in the City of London or the metropolitan police district.

(4) If at any time the Commissioner of Police for the City of London or the Commissioner of Police of the Metropolis reasonably believes that, because of particular circumstances existing in his police area or part of it, the powers under section 12 will not be sufficient to prevent the holding of public processions in that area or part from resulting in serious public disorder, he may with the consent of the Secretary of State make an order prohibiting for such period not exceeding 3 months as may be specified in the order the holding of all public processions (or of any class of public procession so specified) in the area or part concerned.

(5) An order made under this section may be revoked or varied by a subsequent order made in the same way, that is, in accordance with subsections (1) and (2) or subsection (4), as the case may be.

(6) Any order under this section shall, if not made in writing, be recorded in writing as soon as practicable after being made.

(7) A person who organises a public procession the holding of which he knows is prohibited by virtue of an order under this section is guilty of an offence.

(8) A person who takes part in a public procession the holding of which he knows is prohibited by virtue of an order under this section is guilty of an offence.

(9) A person who incites another to commit an offence under subsection (8) is guilty of an offence.

SENDING INDECENT MATERIAL THROUGH POST

Either-way, £5,000 (12 months).

Indecent/Obscene: The words "indecent" and "obscene" are ordinary words of the English language. They will be readily understood by members of the jury. It is unnecessary and may be misleading to give to a jury any interpretation of them which uses other words which may either narrow or enlarge their meaning. A simple direction using those words is sufficient. Things which are shocking or lewd might be classed indecent or obscene (*Anderson* [1972] 1 QB 304). **ECHR:** Article 10 guarantees freedom of speech. Freedom of speech has always been an element and an important element of our democracy upheld by common law...If section 85 of the Postal Service Act 2000 is correctly construed and applied, there is no wrongful infringement on the right of free speech (*Kirk* [2006] EWCA Crim 725). **Sentencing:** In *Kirk* a 3 months sentence of imprisonment, following trial was upheld. In *Littleford* (1984) 6 Cr App R (S) 272 the court held: "the facts of this case, which involve no corruption and relate to offences by a man of mature years and good character, do not fall into the category where a sentence of imprisonment is required for a first offender".

Postal Services Act 2000, s 85

(1) A person commits an offence if he sends by post a postal packet which encloses any creature, article or thing of any kind which is likely to injure other postal packets in course of their transmission by post or any person engaged in the business of a postal operator.

(2) Subsection (1) does not apply to postal packets which enclose anything permitted (whether generally or specifically) by the postal operator concerned.

(3) A person commits an offence if he sends by post a postal packet which encloses—

  (a) any indecent or obscene print, painting, photograph, lithograph, engraving, cinematograph film or other record of a picture or pictures, book, card or written communication, or

  (b) any other indecent or obscene article (whether or not of a similar kind to those mentioned in paragraph (a)).

(4) A person commits an offence if he sends by post a postal packet which has on the packet, or on the cover of the packet, any words, marks or designs which are of an indecent or obscene character.

SQUATTING IN A RESIDENTIAL BUILDING

Summary only 6 months and/or £5,000 fine.

This provision was brought in to force on 1 September 2012 (SI 2012/1956).

Legal Aid, Sentencing and Punishment of Offenders Act 2012, s 144

(1) A person commits an offence if—

  (a) the person is in a residential building as a trespasser having entered it as a trespasser,

  (b) the person knows or ought to know that he or she is a trespasser, and

  (c) the person is living in the building or intends to live there for any period.

(2) The offence is not committed by a person holding over after the end of a lease or licence (even if the person leaves and re-enters the building).

(3) For the purposes of this section—

  (a) "building" includes any structure or part of a structure (including a temporary or moveable structure), and

  (b) a building is "residential" if it is designed or adapted, before the time of entry, for use as a place to live.

(4) For the purposes of this section the fact that a person derives title from a trespasser, or has the permission of a trespasser, does not prevent the person from being a trespasser.

THREATENING BEHAVIOUR

Summary only (unless racially or religiously aggravated), 6 months/£5,000 (2 years on indictment when aggravated offence charged).

Unlawful violence: It is not necessary that the victim actually fear violence, it is the intent of the defendant that is the key issue (*Swanston v Director of Public Prosecutions* (1997) 161 JP 203; *Knight v Director of Public Prosecutions* [2012] EWHC 606 (Admin)). In *Hughes v Director of*

Public Prosecutions [2012] EWHC 606 (Admin) a conviction was quashed where the defendant had allegedly attacked the complainant from behind, the complainant being unaware of the attack happening.

Offence seriousness (culpability and harm)
A. Identify the appropriate starting point
Starting points based on first time offender pleading not guilty

Examples of nature of activity	Starting point	Range
Fear or threat of low level immediate unlawful violence such as push, shove, or spit	Low level community order	Band B fine to medium level community order
Fear or threat of medium level immediate unlawful violence such as punch	High level community order	Low level community order to 12 weeks custody
Fear or threat of high level immediate unlawful violence such as use of weapon; missile thrown; gang involvement	12 weeks custody	6 to 26 weeks custody

Offence seriousness (culpability and harm)
B. Consider the effect of aggravating and mitigating factors (other than those within examples above)
The following may be particularly relevant but **these lists are not exhaustive**

Factors indicating higher culpability	Factors indicating lower culpability
1. Planning	1. Impulsive action
2. Offender deliberately isolates victim	2. Short duration
3. Group action	3. Provocation
4. Threat directed at victim because of job	
5. History of antagonism towards victim	
Factors indicating greater degree of harm	
1. Offence committed at school, hospital, or other place where vulnerable persons may be present	
2. Offence committed on enclosed premises such as public transport	
3. Vulnerable victim(s)	
4. Victim needs medical help/counselling	

Public Order Act 1986, s 4(1)

(1) A person is guilty of an offence if he—

    (a) uses towards another person threatening, abusive or insulting words or behaviour, or

    (b) distributes or displays to another person any writing, sign or other visible representation which is threatening, abusive or insulting,

with intent to cause that person to believe that immediate unlawful violence will be used against him or another by any person, or to provoke the immediate use of unlawful violence by that person or another, or whereby that person is likely to believe that such violence will be used or it is likely that such violence will be provoked.

THROWING MISSILES

Summary only, Fine £1,000.

Offence seriousness (culpability and harm)		
A. Identify the appropriate starting point		
Starting points based on first time offender pleading not guilty		
Examples of nature of activity	**Starting point**	**Range**
Throwing missile; indecent or racialist chanting	Band C fine	Band C fine

Offence seriousness (culpability and harm)	
B. Consider the effect of aggravating and mitigating factors (other than those within examples above)	
The following may be particularly relevant but **these lists are not exhaustive**	
Factors indicating higher culpability 1. Commercial ticket operation; potential high cash value; counterfeit tickets 2. Inciting others to misbehave 3. Possession of large quantity of alcohol 4. Offensive language or behaviour (where not an element of the offence)	
Factor indicating greater degree of harm 1. Missile likely to cause serious injury eg coin, glass, bottle, stone	

Football Offences Act 1991, s 2

It is an offence for a person at a designated football match to throw anything at or towards—

    (a)   the playing area, or any area adjacent to the playing area to which spectators are not generally admitted, or

    (b)   any area in which spectators or other persons are or may be present,

without lawful authority or lawful excuse (which shall be for him to prove).

TICKET TOUTING

Summary only, Fine £5,000.

Offence seriousness (culpability and harm)		
A. Identify the appropriate starting point		
Starting points based on first time offender pleading not guilty		
Examples of nature of activity	**Starting point**	**Range**
Going onto playing or other prohibited area; unauthorized sale or attempted sale of tickets	Band B fine	Band A fine to band C fine

Offence seriousness (culpability and harm)	
B. Consider the effect of aggravating and mitigating factors (other than those within examples above)	
The following may be particularly relevant but **these lists are not exhaustive**	
Factors indicating higher culpability 1. Commercial ticket operation; potential high cash value; counterfeit tickets 2. Inciting others to misbehave 3. Possession of large quantity of alcohol 4. Offensive language or behaviour (where not an element of the offence)	
Factor indicating greater degree of harm 1. Missile likely to cause serious injury eg coin, glass, bottle, stone	

Criminal Justice and Public Order Act 1994, s 166

(1) It is an offence for an unauthorised person to—

    (a) sell a ticket for a designated football match, or

    (b) otherwise to dispose of such a ticket to another person.

(2) For this purpose—

    (a) a person is 'unauthorised' unless he is authorised in writing to sell or otherwise dispose of tickets for the match by the organisers of the match;

    (aa) a reference to selling a ticket includes a reference to—

        (i) offering to sell a ticket;

        (ii) exposing a ticket for sale;

        (iii) making a ticket available for sale by another;

        (iv) advertising that a ticket is available for purchase; and

        (v) giving a ticket to a person who pays or agrees to pay for some other goods or services or offering to do so.

    (b) a 'ticket' means anything which purports to be a ticket.

VIOLENT DISORDER

Either-way, 6 months/£5,000 (5 years).

Offence seriousness (culpability and harm)
A. Identify the appropriate starting point
Starting points based on first time offender pleading not guilty
The offences should normally be dealt with in the Crown Court
However, there may be rare cases involving minor violence or threats of violence leading to no or minor injury, with few people involved and no weapon or missiles, in which a custodial sentence within the jurisdiction of a magistrates' court may be appropriate.

Public Order Act 1986, s 2(1)–(3)

(1) Where 3 or more persons who are present together use or threaten unlawful violence and the conduct of them (taken together) is such as would cause a person of reasonable firmness present at the scene to fear for his personal safety, each of the persons using or threatening unlawful violence is guilty of violent disorder.

(2) It is immaterial whether or not the 3 or more use or threaten unlawful violence simultaneously.

REGULATORY OFFENCES

CONSUMER PROTECTION FROM UNFAIR TRADING

Either-way, 6 months/£5,000 (2 years).

Generally: "It is important to bear in mind that 'trader', for the purpose of the 2008 Regulations, extends to any person who in relation to a commercial practice is acting for purposes relating to his business. The words 'any', 'in relation to', 'acting' and 'relating to' are all words of width and elasticity. As to the definition of 'commercial practice' that is likewise broadly framed. It is amply sufficient to cover involvement in or supervision or control of training, in appropriate circumstances, as being directly connected with the promotion or sale or supply of a product; and it is also to be noted that the definition of 'commercial practice' carefully avoids saying that the promotion or sale or supply has to be made by the trader itself." (*Scottish and Southern Energy Plc* [2012] EWCA Crim 539).

Sentence: Cases are of course fact specific but custodial sentences are common and are consecutive in appropriate cases (eg *Stone* [2012] EWCA Crim 186, reducing sentences of 4 and 3 years to 30 months and 2 years respectively).

Consumer Protection from Unfair Trading Regulations 2008, regs 3-18 and Sch 1

Prohibition of unfair commercial practices

3.—(1) Unfair commercial practices are prohibited.
  (2) Paragraphs (3) and (4) set out the circumstances when a commercial practice is unfair.
  (3) A commercial practice is unfair if—

    (a) it contravenes the requirements of professional diligence; and
    (b) it materially distorts or is likely to materially distort the economic behaviour of the average consumer with regard to the product.

  (4) A commercial practice is unfair if—

    (a) it is a misleading action under the provisions of regulation 5;
    (b) it is a misleading omission under the provisions of regulation 6;
    (c) it is aggressive under the provisions of regulation 7; or
    (d) it is listed in Schedule 1.

Prohibition of the promotion of unfair commercial practices

4. The promotion of any unfair commercial practice by a code owner in a code of conduct is prohibited.

Misleading actions

5.—(1) A commercial practice is a misleading action if it satisfies the conditions in either paragraph (2) or paragraph (3).
  (2) A commercial practice satisfies the conditions of this paragraph—

    (a) if it contains false information and is therefore untruthful in relation to any of the matters in paragraph (4) or if it or its overall presentation in any way deceives or is likely to deceive the average consumer in relation to any of the matters in that paragraph, even if the information is factually correct; and
    (b) it causes or is likely to cause the average consumer to take a transactional decision he would not have taken otherwise.

  (3) A commercial practice satisfies the conditions of this paragraph if—

    (a) it concerns any marketing of a product (including comparative advertising) which creates confusion with any products, trade marks, trade names or other distinguishing marks of a competitor; or
    (b) it concerns any failure by a trader to comply with a commitment contained in a code of conduct which the trader has undertaken to comply with, if—
      (i) the trader indicates in a commercial practice that he is bound by that code of conduct, and
      (ii) the commitment is firm and capable of being verified and is not aspirational,

and it causes or is likely to cause the average consumer to take a transactional decision he would not have taken otherwise, taking account of its factual context and of all its features and circumstances.

  (4) The matters referred to in paragraph (2)(a) are—

    (a) the existence or nature of the product;

    (b) the main characteristics of the product (as defined in paragraph 5);

    (c) the extent of the trader's commitments;

    (d) the motives for the commercial practice;

    (e) the nature of the sales process;

    (f) any statement or symbol relating to direct or indirect sponsorship or approval of the trader or the product;

    (g) the price or the manner in which the price is calculated;

    (h) the existence of a specific price advantage;

    (i) the need for a service, part, replacement or repair;

    (j) the nature, attributes and rights of the trader (as defined in paragraph 6);

    (k) the consumer's rights or the risks he may face.

(5) In paragraph (4)(b), the "main characteristics of the product" include—

    (a) availability of the product;

    (b) benefits of the product;

    (c) risks of the product;

    (d) execution of the product;

    (e) composition of the product;

    (f) accessories of the product;

    (g) after-sale customer assistance concerning the product;

    (h) the handling of complaints about the product;

    (i) the method and date of manufacture of the product;

    (j) the method and date of provision of the product;

    (k) delivery of the product;

    (l) fitness for purpose of the product;

    (m) usage of the product;

    (n) quantity of the product;

    (o) specification of the product;

    (p) geographical or commercial origin of the product;

    (q) results to be expected from use of the product; and

    (r) results and material features of tests or checks carried out on the product.

(6) In paragraph (4)(j), the "nature, attributes and rights" as far as concern the trader include the trader's—

    (a) identity;

    (b) assets;

    (c) qualifications;

    (d) status;

    (e) approval;

    (f) affiliations or connections;

    (g) ownership of industrial, commercial or intellectual property rights; and

    (h) awards and distinctions.

(7) In paragraph (4)(k) "consumer's rights" include rights the consumer may have under Part 5A of the Sale of Goods Act 1979(1) or Part 1B of the Supply of Goods and Services Act 1982(2).

Misleading omissions

6.—(1) A commercial practice is a misleading omission if, in its factual context, taking account of the matters in paragraph (2)—

    (a) the commercial practice omits material information,

    (b) the commercial practice hides material information,

    (c) the commercial practice provides material information in a manner which is unclear, unintelligible, ambiguous or untimely, or

(d) the commercial practice fails to identify its commercial intent, unless this is already apparent from the context,

and as a result it causes or is likely to cause the average consumer to take a transactional decision he would not have taken otherwise.

(2) The matters referred to in paragraph (1) are—

    (a) all the features and circumstances of the commercial practice;

    (b) the limitations of the medium used to communicate the commercial practice (including limitations of space or time); and

    (c) where the medium used to communicate the commercial practice imposes limitations of space or time, any measures taken by the trader to make the information available to consumers by other means.

(3) In paragraph (1) "material information" means—

    (a) the information which the average consumer needs, according to the context, to take an informed transactional decision; and

    (b) any information requirement which applies in relation to a commercial communication as a result of a Community obligation.

(4) Where a commercial practice is an invitation to purchase, the following information will be material if not already apparent from the context in addition to any other information which is material information under paragraph (3)—

    (a) the main characteristics of the product, to the extent appropriate to the medium by which the invitation to purchase is communicated and the product;

    (b) the identity of the trader, such as his trading name, and the identity of any other trader on whose behalf the trader is acting;

    (c) the geographical address of the trader and the geographical address of any other trader on whose behalf the trader is acting;

    (d) either—

        (i) the price, including any taxes; or

        (ii) where the nature of the product is such that the price cannot reasonably be calculated in advance, the manner in which the price is calculated;

    (e) where appropriate, either—

        (i) all additional freight, delivery or postal charges; or

        (ii) where such charges cannot reasonably be calculated in advance, the fact that such charges may be payable;

    (f) the following matters where they depart from the requirements of professional diligence—

        (i) arrangements for payment,

        (ii) arrangements for delivery,

        (iii) arrangements for performance,

        (iv) complaint handling policy;

    (g) for products and transactions involving a right of withdrawal or cancellation, the existence of such a right.

Aggressive commercial practices

7.—(1) A commercial practice is aggressive if, in its factual context, taking account of all of its features and circumstances—

    (a) it significantly impairs or is likely significantly to impair the average consumer's freedom of choice or conduct in relation to the product concerned through the use of harassment, coercion or undue influence; and

    (b) it thereby causes or is likely to cause him to take a transactional decision he would not have taken otherwise.

(2) In determining whether a commercial practice uses harassment, coercion or undue influence account shall be taken of—

    (a) its timing, location, nature or persistence;

    (b) the use of threatening or abusive language or behaviour;

    (c) the exploitation by the trader of any specific misfortune or circumstance of such gravity as to impair the consumer's judgment, of which the trader is aware, to influence the consumer's decision with regard to the product;

    (d) any onerous or disproportionate non-contractual barrier imposed by the trader where a consumer wishes to exercise rights under the contract, including rights to terminate a contract or to switch to another product or another trader; and

    (e) any threat to take any action which cannot legally be taken.

(3) In this regulation—

    (a) "coercion" includes the use of physical force; and

    (b) "undue influence" means exploiting a position of power in relation to the consumer so as to apply pressure, even without using or threatening to use physical force, in a way which significantly limits the consumer's ability to make an informed decision.

Offences relating to unfair commercial practices

8.—(1) A trader is guilty of an offence if—

    (a) he knowingly or recklessly engages in a commercial practice which contravenes the requirements of professional diligence under regulation 3(3)(a); and

    (b) the practice materially distorts or is likely to materially distort the economic behaviour of the average consumer with regard to the product under regulation 3(3)(b).

(2) For the purposes of paragraph (1)(a) a trader who engages in a commercial practice without regard to whether the practice contravenes the requirements of professional diligence shall be deemed recklessly to engage in the practice, whether or not the trader has reason for believing that the practice might contravene those requirements.

9. A trader is guilty of an offence if he engages in a commercial practice which is a misleading action under regulation 5 otherwise than by reason of the commercial practice satisfying the condition in regulation 5(3)(b).

10. A trader is guilty of an offence if he engages in a commercial practice which is a misleading omission under regulation 6.

11. A trader is guilty of an offence if he engages in a commercial practice which is aggressive under regulation 7.

12. A trader is guilty of an offence if he engages in a commercial practice set out in any of paragraphs 1 to 10, 12 to 27 and 29 to 31 of Schedule 1.

Penalty for offences

13. A person guilty of an offence under regulation 8, 9, 10, 11 or 12 shall be liable—

    (a) on summary conviction, to a fine not exceeding the statutory maximum; or

    (b) on conviction on indictment, to a fine or imprisonment for a term not exceeding two years or both.

Time limit for prosecution

14.—(1) No proceedings for an offence under these Regulations shall be commenced after—

    (a) the end of the period of three years beginning with the date of the commission of the offence, or

    (b) the end of the period of one year beginning with the date of discovery of the offence by the prosecutor, whichever is earlier.

(2) For the purposes of paragraph (1)(b) a certificate signed by or on behalf of the prosecutor and stating the date on which the offence was discovered by him shall be conclusive evidence of that fact and a certificate stating that matter and purporting to be so signed shall be treated as so signed unless the contrary is proved.

(3) Notwithstanding anything in section 127(1) of the Magistrates' Courts Act 1980(1), an information relating to an offence under these Regulations which is triable by a magistrates' court in England and Wales may be so tried if it is laid at any time before the end of the period of twelve months beginning with the date of the commission of the offence.

(4) Notwithstanding anything in section 136 of the Criminal Procedure (Scotland) Act 1995(2) summary proceedings in Scotland for an offence under these Regulations may be commenced at any time before the end of the period of twelve months beginning with the date of the commission of the offence.

(5) For the purposes of paragraph (4), section 136(3) of the Criminal Procedure (Scotland) Act 1995 shall apply as it applies for the purposes of that subsection.

(6) Notwithstanding anything in Article 19(1) of the Magistrates' Courts (Northern Ireland) Order 1981(3) a complaint charging an offence under these Regulations which is triable by a magistrates' court in Northern Ireland may be so tried if it is made at any time before the end of the period of twelve months beginning with the date of the commission of the offence.

Offences committed by bodies of persons

15.—(1) Where an offence under these Regulations committed by a body corporate is proved—

(a) to have been committed with the consent or connivance of an officer of the body, or

(b) to be attributable to any neglect on his part,

the officer as well as the body corporate is guilty of the offence and liable to be proceeded against and punished accordingly.

(2) In paragraph (1) a reference to an officer of a body corporate includes a reference to—

(a) a director, manager, secretary or other similar officer; and

(b) a person purporting to act as a director, manager, secretary or other similar officer.

(3) Where an offence under these Regulations committed by a Scottish partnership is proved—

(a) to have been committed with the consent or connivance of a partner, or

(b) to be attributable to any neglect on his part,

the partner as well as the partnership is guilty of the offence and liable to be proceeded against and punished accordingly.

(4) In paragraph (3) a reference to a partner includes a person purporting to act as a partner.

Offence due to the default of another person

16.—(1) This regulation applies where a person "X"—

(a) commits an offence under regulation 9, 10, 11 or 12, or

(b) would have committed an offence under those regulations but for a defence under regulation 17 or 18,

and the commission of the offence, or of what would have been an offence but for X being able to rely on a defence under regulation 17 or 18, is due to the act or default of some other person "Y".

(2) Where this regulation applies Y is guilty of the offence, subject to regulations 17 and 18, whether or not Y is a trader and whether or not Y's act or default is a commercial practice.

(3) Y may be charged with and convicted of the offence by virtue of paragraph (2) whether or not proceedings are taken against X.

Due diligence defence

17.—(1) In any proceedings against a person for an offence under regulation 9, 10, 11 or 12 it is a defence for that person to prove—

> (a) that the commission of the offence was due to—
>> (i)   a mistake;
>> (ii) reliance on information supplied to him by another person;
>> (iii) the act or default of another person;
>> (iv) an accident; or
>> (v)   another cause beyond his control; and
>
> (b) that he took all reasonable precautions and exercised all due diligence to avoid the commission of such an offence by himself or any person under his control.

(2) A person shall not be entitled to rely on the defence provided by paragraph (1) by reason of the matters referred to in paragraph (ii) or (iii) of paragraph (1)(a) without leave of the court unless—

> (a) he has served on the prosecutor a notice in writing giving such information identifying or assisting in the identification of that other person as was in his possession; and
>
> (b) the notice is served on the prosecutor at least seven clear days before the date of the hearing.

Innocent publication of advertisement defence

18.—(1) In any proceedings against a person for an offence under regulation 9, 10, 11 or 12 committed by the publication of an advertisement it shall be a defence for a person to prove that—

> (a) he is a person whose business it is to publish or to arrange for the publication of advertisements;
>
> (b) he received the advertisement for publication in the ordinary course of business; and
>
> (c) he did not know and had no reason to suspect that its publication would amount to an offence under the regulation to which the proceedings relate.

(2) In paragraph (1) "advertisement" includes a catalogue, a circular and a price list.

SCHEDULE 1

Commercial practices which are in all circumstances considered unfair

1. Claiming to be a signatory to a code of conduct when the trader is not.

2. Displaying a trust mark, quality mark or equivalent without having obtained the necessary authorisation.

3. Claiming that a code of conduct has an endorsement from a public or other body which it does not have.

4. Claiming that a trader (including his commercial practices) or a product has been approved, endorsed or authorised by a public or private body when the trader, the commercial practices or the product have not or making such a claim without complying with the terms of the approval, endorsement or authorisation.

5. Making an invitation to purchase products at a specified price without disclosing the existence of any reasonable grounds the trader may have for believing that he will not be able to offer for supply, or to procure another trader to supply, those products or equivalent products at that price for a period that is, and in quantities that are, reasonable having regard to the product, the scale of advertising of the product and the price offered (bait advertising).

6. Making an invitation to purchase products at a specified price and then—

    (a)   refusing to show the advertised item to consumers,

    (b)   refusing to take orders for it or deliver it within a reasonable time, or

    (c)   demonstrating a defective sample of it,

with the intention of promoting a different product (bait and switch).

7. Falsely stating that a product will only be available for a very limited time, or that it will only be available on particular terms for a very limited time, in order to elicit an immediate decision and deprive consumers of sufficient opportunity or time to make an informed choice.

8. Undertaking to provide after-sales service to consumers with whom the trader has communicated prior to a transaction in a language which is not an official language of the EEA State where the trader is located and then making such service available only in another language without clearly disclosing this to the consumer before the consumer is committed to the transaction.

9. Stating or otherwise creating the impression that a product can legally be sold when it cannot.

10. Presenting rights given to consumers in law as a distinctive feature of the trader's offer.

11. Using editorial content in the media to promote a product where a trader has paid for the promotion without making that clear in the content or by images or sounds clearly identifiable by the consumer (advertorial).

12. Making a materially inaccurate claim concerning the nature and extent of the risk to the personal security of the consumer or his family if the consumer does not purchase the product.

13. Promoting a product similar to a product made by a particular manufacturer in such a manner as deliberately to mislead the consumer into believing that the product is made by that same manufacturer when it is not.

14. Establishing, operating or promoting a pyramid promotional scheme where a consumer gives consideration for the opportunity to receive compensation that is derived primarily from the introduction of other consumers into the scheme rather than from the sale or consumption of products.

15. Claiming that the trader is about to cease trading or move premises when he is not.

16. Claiming that products are able to facilitate winning in games of chance.

17. Falsely claiming that a product is able to cure illnesses, dysfunction or malformations.

18. Passing on materially inaccurate information on market conditions or on the possibility of finding the product with the intention of inducing the consumer to acquire the product at conditions less favourable than normal market conditions.

19. Claiming in a commercial practice to offer a competition or prize promotion without awarding the prizes described or a reasonable equivalent.

20. Describing a product as 'gratis', 'free', 'without charge' or similar if the consumer has to pay anything other than the unavoidable cost of responding to the commercial practice and collecting or paying for delivery of the item.

21. Including in marketing material an invoice or similar document seeking payment which gives the consumer the impression that he has already ordered the marketed product when he has not.

22. Falsely claiming or creating the impression that the trader is not acting for purposes relating to his trade, business, craft or profession, or falsely representing oneself as a consumer.

23. Creating the false impression that after-sales service in relation to a product is available in an EEA State other than the one in which the product is sold.

24. Creating the impression that the consumer cannot leave the premises until a contract is formed.

25. Conducting personal visits to the consumer's home ignoring the consumer's request to leave or not to return, except in circumstances and to the extent justified to enforce a contractual obligation.

26. Making persistent and unwanted solicitations by telephone, fax, e-mail or other remote media except in circumstances and to the extent justified to enforce a contractual obligation.

27. Requiring a consumer who wishes to claim on an insurance policy to produce documents which could not reasonably be considered relevant as to whether the claim was valid, or failing systematically to respond to pertinent correspondence, in order to dissuade a consumer from exercising his contractual rights.

28. Including in an advertisement a direct exhortation to children to buy advertised products or persuade their parents or other adults to buy advertised products for them.

29. Demanding immediate or deferred payment for or the return or safekeeping of products supplied by the trader, but not solicited by the consumer, except where the product is a substitute supplied in accordance with regulation 19(7) of the Consumer Protection (Distance Selling) Regulations 2000 (inertia selling)(1).

30. Explicitly informing a consumer that if he does not buy the product or service, the trader's job or livelihood will be in jeopardy.

31. Creating the false impression that the consumer has already won, will win, or will on doing a particular act win, a prize or other equivalent benefit, when in fact either—

(a) there is no prize or other equivalent benefit, or

(b) taking any action in relation to claiming the prize or other equivalent benefit is subject to the consumer paying money or incurring a cost.

FOOD, OFFENCES RELATING TO

Acts of employees: An employer is vicariously liable (eg *Goodfellow v Johnson* [1966] 1 QB 83; *United Dairies Ltd v Beckenham* [1963] 1 QB 434. See *Nottingham City Council v Wolverhampton and Dudley Breweries* [2003] EWHC 2847 (Admin) for the liability of a brewery that owned premises from which poor quality drink was sold. **Due diligence defence:** See section 21. **Limitation period:** See section 34. **Mode of trial and sentence:** See section 35. **Person:** This includes a limited company (*ICR Haulage Ltd* [1944] KB 551). **Purchaser's prejudice:** A person is not prejudiced if the matter (nature/substance/quality) is brought to his attention (*Sandys v Jackson* (1905) 69 JP 171).

Food Safety Act 1990, ss 1, 14, 15, 16, 20, 21, 22, 34, 35, 36

1.— Meaning of "food" and other basic expressions.

(1) In this Act "food"has the same meaning as it has in Regulation (EC) No. 178/2002.

(2) In this Act "Regulation (EC) No. 178/2002" means Regulation (EC) No. 178/2002 of the European Parliament and of the Council laying down the general principles and requirements of food law, establishing the European Food Safety Authority and laying down procedures in matters of food safety.

(3) In this Act, unless the context otherwise requires—

"business"includes the undertaking of a canteen, club, school, hospital or institution, whether carried on for profit or not, and any undertaking or activity carried on by a public or local authority;

"commercial operation", in relation to any food or contact material, means any of the following, namely—

(a) selling, possessing for sale and offering, exposing or advertising for sale;

(b) consigning, delivering or serving by way of sale;

(c) preparing for sale or presenting, labelling or wrapping for the purpose of sale;

(d) storing or transporting for the purpose of sale;

(e) importing and exporting;

and, in relation to any food source, means deriving food from it for the purpose of sale or for purposes connected with sale;

"contact material" means any article or substance which is intended to come into contact with food;

"food business" means any business in the course of which commercial operations with respect to food or food sources are carried out;

"food premises" means any premises used for the purposes of a food business;

"food source" means any growing crop or live animal, bird or fish from which food is intended to be derived (whether by harvesting, slaughtering, milking, collecting eggs or otherwise);

"premises" includes any place, any vehicle, stall or moveable structure and, for such purposes as may be specified in an order made by the Secretary of State, any ship or aircraft of a description so specified.

(4) The reference in subsection (3) above to preparing for sale shall be construed, in relation to any contact material, as a reference to manufacturing or producing for the purpose of sale.

14.— Selling food not of the nature or substance or quality demanded.

(1) Any person who sells to the purchaser's prejudice any food which is not of the nature or substance or quality demanded by the purchaser shall be guilty of an offence.

(2) In subsection (1) above the reference to sale shall be construed as a reference to sale for human consumption; and in proceedings under that subsection it shall not be a defence that the purchaser was not prejudiced because he bought for analysis or examination.

15.— Falsely describing or presenting food.

(1) Any person who gives with any food sold by him, or displays with any food offered or exposed by him for sale or in his possession for the purpose of sale, a label, whether or not attached to or printed on the wrapper or container, which—

(a) falsely describes the food; or

(b) is likely to mislead as to the nature or substance or quality of the food,

shall be guilty of an offence.

(2) Any person who publishes, or is a party to the publication of, an advertisement (not being such a label given or displayed by him as mentioned in subsection (1) above) which—

(a) falsely describes any food; or

(b) is likely to mislead as to the nature or substance or quality of any food,

shall be guilty of an offence.

(3) Any person who sells, or offers or exposes for sale, or has in his possession for the purpose of sale, any food the presentation of which is likely to mislead as to the nature or substance or quality of the food shall be guilty of an offence.

(4) In proceedings for an offence under subsection (1) or (2) above, the fact that a label or advertisement in respect of which the offence is alleged to have been committed contained an accurate statement of the composition of the food shall not preclude the court from finding that the offence was committed.

(5) In this section references to sale shall be construed as references to sale for human consumption.

16.— Food safety and consumer protection.

(1) The Secretary of State may by regulations make—

    (a) provision for requiring, prohibiting or regulating the presence in food or food sources of any specified substance, or any substance of any specified class, and generally for regulating the composition of food;

    (b) provision for securing that food is fit for human consumption and meets such microbiological standards (whether going to the fitness of the food or otherwise) as may be specified by or under the regulations;

    (c) provision for requiring, prohibiting or regulating the use of any process or treatment in the preparation of food;

    (d) provision for securing the observance of hygienic conditions and practices in connection with the carrying out of commercial operations with respect to food or food sources;

    (e) provision for imposing requirements or prohibitions as to, or otherwise regulating, the labelling, marking, presenting or advertising of food, and the descriptions which may be applied to food; and

    (f) such other provision with respect to food or food sources, including in particular provision for prohibiting or regulating the carrying out of commercial operations with respect to food or food sources, as appears to them to be necessary or expedient—

        (i) for the purpose of securing that food complies with food safety requirements or in the interests of the public health; or

        (ii) for the purpose of protecting or promoting the interests of consumers.

(2) The Secretary of State may also by regulations make provision—

    (a) for securing the observance of hygienic conditions and practices in connection with the carrying out of commercial operations with respect to contact materials which are intended to come into contact with food intended for human consumption;

    (b) for imposing requirements or prohibitions as to, or otherwise regulating, the labelling, marking or advertising of such materials, and the descriptions which may be applied to them; and

    (c) otherwise for prohibiting or regulating the carrying out of commercial operations with respect to such materials.

(3) Without prejudice to the generality of subsection (1) above, regulations under that subsection may make any such provision as is mentioned in Schedule 1 to this Act.

(4) In making regulations under subsection (1) above, the Secretary of State shall have regard to the desirability of restricting, so far as practicable, the use of substances of no nutritional value as foods or as ingredients of foods.

(5) In subsection (1) above and Schedule 1 to this Act, unless the context otherwise requires—

    (a) references to food shall be construed as references to food intended for sale for human consumption; and

    (b) references to food sources shall be construed as references to food sources from which such food is intended to be derived.

20. Offences due to fault of another person.

Where the commission by any person of an offence under any of the preceding provisions of this Part is due to an act or default of some other person, that other person shall be guilty of the offence; and a person may be charged with and convicted of the offence by virtue of this section whether or not proceedings are taken against the first-mentioned person.

21.— Defence of due diligence.

(1) In any proceedings for an offence under any of the preceding provisions of this Part (in this section referred to as "the relevant provision"), it shall, subject to subsection (5)

below, be a defence for the person charged to prove that he took all reasonable precautions and exercised all due diligence to avoid the commission of the offence by himself or by a person under his control.

(2) Without prejudice to the generality of subsection (1) above, a person charged with an offence under section 14 or 15 above who neither—

(a) prepared the food in respect of which the offence is alleged to have been committed; nor

(b) imported it into Great Britain,

shall be taken to have established the defence provided by that subsection if he satisfies the requirements of subsection (3) or (4) below.

(3) A person satisfies the requirements of this subsection if he proves—

(a) that the commission of the offence was due to an act or default of another person who was not under his control, or to reliance on information supplied by such a person;

(b) that he carried out all such checks of the food in question as were reasonable in all the circumstances, or that it was reasonable in all the circumstances for him to rely on checks carried out by the person who supplied the food to him; and

(c) that he did not know and had no reason to suspect at the time of the commission of the alleged offence that his act or omission would amount to an offence under the relevant provision.

(4) A person satisfies the requirements of this subsection if he proves—

(a) that the commission of the offence was due to an act or default of another person who was not under his control, or to reliance on information supplied by such a person;

(b) that the sale or intended sale of which the alleged offence consisted was not a sale or intended sale under his name or mark; and

(c) that he did not know, and could not reasonably have been expected to know, at the time of the commission of the alleged offence that his act or omission would amount to an offence under the relevant provision.

(5) If in any case the defence provided by subsection (1) above involves the allegation that the commission of the offence was due to an act or default of another person, or to reliance on information supplied by another person, the person charged shall not, without leave of the court, be entitled to rely on that defence unless—

(a) at least seven clear days before the hearing; and

(b) where he has previously appeared before a court in connection with the alleged offence, within one month of his first such appearance,

he has served on the prosecutor a notice in writing giving such information identifying or assisting in the identification of that other person as was then in his possession.

(6) In subsection (5) above any reference to appearing before a court shall be construed as including a reference to being brought before a court.

22. Defence of publication in the course of business.

In proceedings for an offence under any of the preceding provisions of this Part consisting of the advertisement for sale of any food, it shall be a defence for the person charged to prove—

(a) that he is a person whose business it is to publish or arrange for the publication of advertisements; and

(b) that he received the advertisement in the ordinary course of business and did not know and had no reason to suspect that its publication would amount to an offence under that provision.

34. Time limit for prosecutions.

No prosecution for an offence under this Act which is punishable under section 35(2) below shall be begun after the expiry of—

(a) three years from the commission of the offence; or

(b) one year from its discovery by the prosecutor,

whichever is the earlier.

35.— Punishment of offences.

(1) A person guilty of an offence under section 33(1) above shall be liable on summary conviction to a fine not exceeding level 5 on the standard scale or to imprisonment for a term not exceeding three months or to both.

(2) A person guilty of any other offence under this Act shall be liable—

(a) on conviction on indictment, to a fine or to imprisonment for a term not exceeding two years or to both;

(b) on summary conviction, to a fine not exceeding the relevant amount or to imprisonment for a term not exceeding six months or to both.

(3) In subsection (2) above "the relevant amount" means —

(a) in the case of an offence under section 7 or 14 above, £20,000;

(b) in any other case, the statutory maximum.

(4) If a person who is—

(a) licensed under section 1 of the Slaughterhouses Act 1974 to keep a knacker's yard;

(b) registered under section 4 of the Slaughter of Animals (Scotland) Act 1980 in respect of any premises for use as a slaughterhouse; or

(c) licensed under section 6 of the Slaughter of Animals (Scotland) Act 1980 to use any premises as a knacker's yard,

is convicted of an offence under Part II of this Act, the court may, in addition to any other punishment, cancel his licence or registration.

36.— Offences by bodies corporate.

(1) Where an offence under this Act which has been committed by a body corporate is proved to have been committed with the consent or connivance of, or to be attributable to any neglect on the part of—

(a) any director, manager, secretary or other similar officer of the body corporate; or

(b) any person who was purporting to act in any such capacity,

he as well as the body corporate shall be deemed to be guilty of that offence and shall be liable to be proceeded against and punished accordingly.

(2) In subsection (1) above "director", in relation to any body corporate established by or under any enactment for the purpose of carrying on under national ownership any industry or part of an industry or undertaking, being a body corporate whose affairs are managed by its members, means a member of that body corporate.

TRADE MARK, UNAUTHORIZED USE OF

Either-way, 6 months/£5,000 (10 years).

It is a defence for a person charged with an offence under this section to show that he believed on reasonable grounds that the use of the sign in the manner in which it was used, or was to be used, was not an infringement of the registered trade mark. In order to be able to satisfy the statutory defence under section 95(2) of the Trade Marks Act 1994, the defendant must show that not only did he have an honest belief that the trade marks did not infringe registered trade marks, but also that he had reasonable grounds for so believing (*Essex Trading Standards v Singh*, unreported, 3 March 2009). It is not a defence to argue that the trade marks were of such poor quality that no confusion would be caused (*Boulter* [2008] EWCA Crim 2375).

Offence seriousness (culpability and harm)		
A. Identify the appropriate starting point		
Starting points based on first time offender pleading not guilty		
Examples of nature of activity	**Starting point**	**Range**
Small number of counterfeit items	Band C fine	Band B fine to low level community order
Larger number of counterfeit items but no involvement in wider operation	Medium level community order, plus fine*	Low level community order to 12 weeks custody, plus fine*
High number of counterfeit items or involvement in wider operation eg manufacture or distribution	12 weeks custody	6 weeks custody to Crown Court
Central role in large-scale operation	Crown Court	Crown Court

* this may be an offence where it is appropriate to combine a fine with a community order.

Offence seriousness (culpability and harm)	
B. Consider the effect of aggravating and mitigating factors	
(other than those within examples above)	
The following may be particularly relevant but **these lists are not exhaustive**	
Factors indicating higher culpability	**Factor indicating lower culpability**
1. High degree of professionalism 2. High level of profit	1. Mistake or ignorance about provenance of goods
Factor indicating greater degree of harm	
1. Purchasers at risk of harm eg from counterfeit drugs	

Trade Marks Act 1994, s 92(1)–(4)

(1) A person commits an offence who with a view to gain for himself or another, or with intent to cause loss to another, and without the consent of the proprietor—

   (a) applies to goods or their packaging a sign identical to, or likely to be mistaken for, a registered trade mark, or

   (b) sells or lets for hire, offers or exposes for sale or hire or distributes goods which bear, or the packaging of which bears, such a sign, or

   (c) has in his possession, custody or control in the course of a business any such goods with a view to the doing of anything, by himself or another, which would be an offence under paragraph (b).

(2) A person commits an offence who with a view to gain for himself or another, or with intent to cause loss to another, and without the consent of the proprietor—

   (a) applies a sign identical to, or likely to be mistaken for, a registered trade mark to material intended to be used—

   (i) for labelling or packaging goods,

   (ii) as a business paper in relation to goods, or

       (iii) for advertising goods, or

(b) uses in the course of a business material bearing such a sign for labelling or packaging goods, as a business paper in relation to goods, or for advertising goods, or

(c) has in his possession, custody or control in the course of a business any such material with a view to the doing of anything, by himself or another, which would be an offence under paragraph (b).

(3) A person commits an offence who with a view to gain for himself or another, or with intent to cause loss to another, and without the consent of the proprietor—

(a) makes an article specifically designed or adapted for making copies of a sign identical to, or likely to be mistaken for, a registered trade mark, or

(b) has such an article in his possession, custody or control in the course of a business,

knowing or having reason to believe that it has been, or is to be, used to produce goods, or material for labelling or packaging goods, as a business paper in relation to goods, or for advertising goods.

(4) A person does not commit an offence under this section unless—

(a) the goods are goods in respect of which the trade mark is registered, or

(b) the trade mark has a reputation in the United Kingdom and the use of the sign takes or would take unfair advantage of, or is or would be detrimental to, the distinctive character or the repute of the trade mark.

TV LICENCE PAYMENT EVASION

Summary only, £1,000 fine.

Communications Act 2003, s 363.

Offence seriousness (culpability and harm) A. Identify the appropriate starting point Starting points based on first time offender pleading not guilty		
Examples of nature of activity	**Starting point**	**Range**
Up to 6 months unlicensed use	Band A fine	Band A fine
Over 6 months unlicensed use	Band B fine	Band A fine to band B fine

Offence seriousness (culpability and harm) B. Consider the effect of aggravating and mitigating factors (other than those within examples above) The following may be particularly relevant but **these lists are not exhaustive**	
	Factors indicating lower culpability 1. Accidental oversight or belief licence held 2. Confusion of responsibility 3. Licence immediately obtained

ROAD TRAFFIC AND VEHICULAR OFFENCES

DEFINITIONS

Inquests: If death has resulted from the driving any trial should await the conclusion of any inquest (*Smith v Director of Public Prosecutions* [2000] RTR 36).

Accident: Accident is to be given its ordinary meaning (*Chief Constable of West Midlands v Billingham* [1979] 1 WLR 747). A deliberate act can amount to an accident (*Chief Constable of Staffordshire v Lees* [1981] RTR 506). A physical impact is not necessary (*Currie* [2007] EWCA Crim 927), but the de minimis principle applies (*Morris* [1972] 1 WLR 228).

Causing: Causing requires a positive act (*Ross Hillman Ltd v Bond* [1974] QB 435) committed with prior knowledge.

Driver: Section 192 of the Road Traffic Act 1988 provides:

Road Traffic Act 1988, s 192(1)

... 'driver', where a separate person acts as a steersman of a motor vehicle, includes (except for the purposes of section 1 of this Act) that person as well as any other person engaged in the driving of the vehicle, and 'drive' is to be interpreted accordingly.

A person supervising a driver will not be a driver unless they exercise some control over the vehicle (dual controls, for example) (*Evans v Walkden* [1956] 1 WLR 1019).

Driving: In *MacDonagh* [1974] QB 448 defined driving as use of the driver's controls for the purpose of directing the movement of the vehicle. The court gave the following guidance:

There are an infinite number of ways in which a person may control the movement of a motor vehicle, apart from the orthodox one of sitting in the driving seat and using the engine for propulsion. He may be coasting down a hill with the gears in neutral and the engine switched off; he may be steering a vehicle which is being towed by another. As has already been pointed out, he may be sitting in the driving seat whilst others push, or half sitting in the driving seat but keeping one foot on the road in order to induce the car to move. Finally, as in the present case, he may be standing in the road and himself pushing the car with or without using the steering wheel to direct it. Although the word 'drive' must be given a wide meaning, the Courts must be alert to see that the net is not thrown so widely that it includes activities which cannot be said to be driving a motor vehicle in any ordinary use of that word in the English language.

As a person may be driving a stationary vehicle, it is a matter of fact to be decided in each case and factors such as the reason for the vehicle stopping and the duration of the stop will be relevant (*Planton v Director of Public Prosecutions* [2002] RTR 107).

Steering a vehicle being towed would amount to driving where there was an operational breaking system (*McQuaid v Anderton* [1981] 1 WLR 154), as would freewheeling a vehicle down a hill while steering (*Saycell v Bool* [1948] 2 All ER 83. A person steering from the passenger seat is driving (*Tyler v Whatmore* [1976] RTR 83).

In charge: In cases where the matter is not clear, the case of *Director of Public Prosecutions v Watkins* (1989) 89 Cr App R 112 should be considered in detail. The court laid down the following broad guidance:

Broadly there are two distinct classes of case. (1) If the defendant is the owner or lawful possessor of the vehicle or has recently driven it, he will have been in charge of it, and the question for the Court will be whether he is still in charge or whether he has relinquished his charge. Usually such a defendant will be prima facie in charge unless he has put the vehicle in someone else's charge. However he would not be so if in all the circumstances he has ceased to be in actual control and there is no realistic possibility of his resuming actual control while unfit: eg if he is at home in bed for the night, if he is a great distance from the car, or if it is taken by another.

(2) If the defendant is not the owner, the lawful possessor, or recent driver but is sitting in the vehicle or is otherwise involved with it, the question for the Court is, as here, whether he has assumed being in charge of it. In this class of case the defendant will be in charge if, whilst unfit, he is voluntarily in de facto control of the vehicle or if, in the circumstances, including his position, his intentions and his actions, he may be expected imminently to assume control. Usually this will involve his having gained entry to the car and evinced an intention to take control of it. But gaining entry may not be necessary if he has manifested that intention some other way, eg by stealing the keys of a car in circumstances which show he means presently to drive it.

The circumstances to be taken into account will vary infinitely, but the following will be usually relevant:

(i)   Whether and where he is in the vehicle or how far he is from it.
(ii) What he is doing at the relevant time.
(iii) Whether he is in possession of a key that fits the ignition.
(iv) Whether there is evidence of an intention to take or assert control of the car by driving or otherwise
(v)   Whether any other person is in, at or near the vehicle and if so, the like particulars in respect of that person.

It will be for the Court to consider all the above factors with any others which may be relevant and reach its decision as a question of fact and degree.

Motor vehicle: There is no statutory definition of vehicle and therefore its ordinary meaning of a carriage or conveyance should apply. Where the statute uses the phrase 'motor vehicle', the definition to be found in section 185 of the Road Traffic Act 1988 states that it is a 'mechanically propelled vehicle intended or adapted for use on roads'. The maximum speed of the vehicle is not a relevant factor (*Director of Public Prosecutions v King* [2008] EWHC 447 (Admin)).

Owner: This includes a person in possession of a vehicle under a hire or hire purchase agreement.

Permitting: A person permits use when he allows or authorizes use, or fails to take reasonable steps to prevent use. For permitting no insurance the prosecution do not need to show that the person knew the driver to be uninsured. If, however, use is conditional (for example, on the person having insurance) the outcome would be different (*Newbury v Davis* [1974] RTR 367).

Public place: This is a place to which the public have access. However, the law draws a distinction between general public access, and access for a defined group of persons. The law in this area is complex and voluminous and advocates should always seek an adjournment where the answer is not clear.

Road: This is defined as any highway or road to which the public has access. The following have been held to be a road: Pedestrian pavement (*Randall v Motor Insurers' Bureau* [1968] 1 WLR 1900). Grass verge at the side of a road (*Worth v Brooks* [1959] Crim LR 855). Bridges over which a road passes. Trafalgar square in London (*Sadiku v Director of Public Prosecutions* [2000] RTR 155).

It will be a matter of fact and degree as to whether something is a road, and whether or not the public have access. A car park will not generally be a road, even if there are roads running through it. In *Barrett v Director of Public Prosecutions,* unreported, 10 February 2009 the court held that a roadway running through a private caravan park, and facilitating entry to a beach, constituted a road.

A vehicle will be 'on' a road when part of the vehicle protrudes over a road (*Avery v Crown Prosecution Service* [2011] EWHC 2388 (Admin)).

Highway: This is defined as land over which there is a right of way on foot, by riding or with vehicles and cattle. A highway includes: bridleways, footpaths, footways, walkways, carriageways and driftways.

Notice of intended prosecution:

Road Traffic Offenders Act 1988, ss 1–2

1.— Requirement of warning etc. of prosecutions for certain offences.

(1)   Subject to section 2 of this Act, a person shall not be convicted of an offence to which this section applies unless —

    (a) he was warned at the time the offence was committed that the question of prosecuting him for some one or other of the offences to which this section applies would be taken into consideration, or

    (b) within fourteen days of the commission of the offence a summons (or, in Scotland, a complaint) for the offence was served on him, or

    (c) within fourteen days of the commission of the offence a notice of the intended prosecution specifying the nature of the alleged offence and the time and place where it is alleged to have been committed, was—

        (i) in the case of an offence under section 28 or 29 of the Road Traffic Act 1988 (cycling offences), served on him,

        (ii) in the case of any other offence, served on him or on the person, if any, registered as the keeper of the vehicle at the time of the commission of the offence.

(1A) A notice required by this section to be served on any person may be served on that person—

    (a) by delivering it to him;

    (b) by addressing it to him and leaving it at his last known address; or

    (c) by sending it by registered post, recorded delivery service or first class post addressed to him at his last known address..

(2)   A notice shall be deemed for the purposes of subsection (1)(c) above to have been served on a person if it was sent by registered post or recorded delivery service addressed to him at his last known address, notwithstanding that the notice was returned as undelivered or was for any other reason not received by him.

(3)   The requirement of subsection (1) above shall in every case be deemed to have been complied with unless and until the contrary is proved.

(4)   Schedule 1 to this Act shows the offences to which this section applies.

2 .— Requirement of warning etc: supplementary.

(1)   The requirement of section 1(1) of this Act does not apply in relation to an offence if, at the time of the offence or immediately after it, an accident occurs owing to the presence on a road of the vehicle in respect of which the offence was committed.

(2)   The requirement of section 1(1) of this Act does not apply in relation to an offence in respect of which—

    (a) a fixed penalty notice (within the meaning of Part III of this Act) has been given or fixed under any provision of that Part, or

    (b) a notice has been given under section 54(4) of this Act.

(3)   Failure to comply with the requirement of section 1(1) of this Act is not a bar to the conviction of the accused in a case where the court is satisfied—

    (a) that neither the name and address of the accused nor the name and address of the registered keeper, if any, could with reasonable diligence have been ascertained in time for a summons or, as the case may be, a complaint to be served or for a notice to be served or sent in compliance with the requirement, or

(b) that the accused by his own conduct contributed to the failure.

(4) Failure to comply with the requirement of section 1(1) of this Act in relation to an offence is not a bar to the conviction of a person of that offence by virtue of the provisions of—

(a) section 24 of this Act, or

(b) any of the enactments mentioned in section 24(6);

but a person is not to be convicted of an offence by virtue of any of those provisions if section 1 applies to the offence with which he was charged and the requirement of section 1(1) was not satisfied in relation to the offence charged.

CARELESS DRIVING (DRIVE WITHOUT DUE CARE AND ATTENTION)

Summary only, Fine £5,000. Must endorse and may disqualify. 6–9 points must be endorsed if the court does not disqualify.

Careless driving:

Road Traffic Act 1988, s 3ZA

(2) A person is to be regarded as driving without due care and attention if (and only if) the way he drives falls below what would be expected of a competent and careful driver.

(3) In determining for the purposes of subsection (2) above what would be expected of a careful and competent driver in a particular case, regard shall be had not only to the circumstances of which he could be expected to be aware but also to any circumstances shown to have been within the knowledge of the accused.

(4) A person is to be regarded as driving without reasonable consideration for other persons only if those persons are inconvenienced by his driving.

Res ipsa: If the facts are such that in the absence of an explanation put forward by the defendant, or that explanation is objectively inadequate, and the only possible conclusion is that he was careless, he should be convicted (*Director of Public Prosecutions v Cox* (1993) 157 JP 1044). A court does not need to consider an alternative inference from facts, such as mechanical defect, without hearing evidence of the same (*Director of Public Prosecutions v Tipton* (1992) 156 JP 172).

Examples of careless driving:

- overtaking on the inside or driving inappropriately close to another vehicle,
- inadvertent mistakes such as driving through a red light or emerging from a side road into the path of another vehicle,
- short distractions such as tuning a car radio,
- Failing to adhere to relevant parts of the highway code.

Examples of inconsiderate driving:

- flashing of lights to force other drivers in front to give way,
- misuse of any lane to avoid queuing or gain some other advantage over other drivers,
- driving that inconveniences other road users or causes unnecessary hazards such as unnecessarily remaining in an overtaking lane, unnecessarily slow driving or braking without good cause, driving with undipped headlights which dazzle oncoming drivers or driving through a puddle causing pedestrians to be splashed
- Failing to adhere to relevant parts of the highway code.

Offence seriousness (culpability and harm)

A. Identify the appropriate starting point

Starting points based on first time offender pleading not guilty

Example of nature of activity	Starting point	Range
Momentary lapse of concentration or misjudgement at low speed	Band A fine	Band A fine 3–4 points
Loss of control due to speed, mishandling or insufficient attention to road conditions, or carelessly turning right across oncoming traffic	Band B fine	Band B fine 5–6 points
Overtaking manoeuvre at speed resulting in collision of vehicles, or driving bordering on the dangerous	Band C fine	Band C fine Consider disqualification OR 7–9 points

Offence seriousness (culpability and harm)

B. Consider the effect of aggravating and mitigating factors

(other than those within examples above)

The following may be particularly relevant but **these lists are not exhaustive**

Factors indicating higher culpability	Factors indicating lower culpability
1. Excessive speed	1. Minor risk
2. Carrying out other tasks while driving	2. Inexperience of driver
3. Carrying passengers or heavy load	3. Sudden change in road or weather conditions
4. Tiredness	
Factors indicating greater degree of harm	
1. Injury to others	
2. Damage to other vehicles or property	
3. High level of traffic or pedestrians in vicinity	
4. Location eg near school when children are likely to be present	

Road Traffic Act 1988, s 3

If a person drives a mechanically propelled vehicle on a road or other public place without due care and attention, or without reasonable consideration for other persons using the road or place, he is guilty of an offence.

CAUSING DEATH BY DRIVING

Either-way, 6 months/£5,000 (5 years' imprisonment (2 years for unlicensed, disqualified, or uninsured)), minimum disqualification of 12 months, discretionary re-test, 3–11 penalty points.

Causation: The driving must be more than a minimal cause of death, and death must result from the driving. It is not necessary that the driver be culpable or blameworthy in respect of an offence under section 3ZB. Where, therefore, a pedestrian walked in front of a vehicle and a collision occurred through no fault of the driver, a conviction would follow in the event that the driver was uninsured, disqualified or driving otherwise than in accordance with a licence (*Williams* [2010] EWCA Crim 2552). In *H* [2011] EWCA Crim 2367 the court certified a point of general public importance in respect to this issue, which may be determined by the Supreme Court during the lifetime of this edition. **Samples:** See *Coe* [2009] EWCA Crim 1452 in relation to the admission of samples taken in relation to alcohol.

Road Traffic Act 1988, ss 2B and 3ZB

2B Causing death by careless, or inconsiderate, driving

A person who causes the death of another person by driving a mechanically propelled vehicle on a road or other public place without due care and attention, or without reasonable consideration for other persons using the road or place, is guilty of an offence.

3ZB Causing death by driving: unlicensed, disqualified or uninsured drivers

A person is guilty of an offence under this section if he causes the death of another person by driving a motor vehicle on a road and, at the time when he is driving, the circumstances are such that he is committing an offence under—

    (a) section 87(1) of this Act (driving otherwise than in accordance with a licence),

    (b) section 103(1)(b) of this Act (driving while disqualified), or

    (c) section 143 of this Act (using motor vehicle while uninsured or unsecured against third party risks).

Nature of offence	Starting point	Sentencing range
Careless or inconsiderate driving falling not far short of dangerous driving	15 months custody	36 weeks–3 years custody
Other cases of careless or inconsiderate driving	36 weeks custody	Community order (HIGH)–2 years custody
Careless or inconsiderate driving arising from momentary inattention with no aggravating factors	Community order (MEDIUM)	Community order (LOW)–Community order (HIGH)

Additional aggravating factors	Additional mitigating factors
1. Other offences committed at the same time, such as driving other than in accordance with the terms of a valid licence; driving while disqualified; driving without insurance; taking a vehicle without consent; driving a stolen vehicle 2. Previous convictions for motoring offences, particularly offences that involve bad driving 3. More than one person was killed as a result of the offence 4. Serious injury to one or more persons in addition to the death(s) 5. Irresponsible behaviour, such as failing to stop or falsely claiming that one of the victims was responsible for the collision.	1. Offender was seriously injured in the collision 2. The victim was a close friend or relative 3. The actions of the victim or a third party contributed to the commission of the offence 4. The offender's lack of driving experience contributed significantly to the likelihood of a collision 5. The driving was in response to a proven and genuine emergency falling short of a defence

Causing death by unlicensed, disqualified or uninsured drivers

Nature of offence	Starting point	Sentencing range
The offender was disqualified from driving; OR The offender was unlicensed or uninsured plus two or more aggravating factors from the list below	12 months custody	36 weeks–2 years custody
The offender was unlicensed or uninsured plus at least one aggravating factor from the list below	26 weeks custody	Community order (HIGH)–36 weeks custody

The offender was unlicensed or uninsured—no aggravating factors	Community order (MEDIUM)	Community order (LOW)–Community order (HIGH)

Additional aggravating factors	Additional mitigating factors
1. Previous convictions for motoring offences, whether involving bad driving or involving an offence of the same kind that forms part of the present conviction (ie unlicensed, disqualified, or uninsured driving) 2. More than one person was killed as a result of the offence 3. Serious injury to one or more persons in addition to the death(s) 4. Irresponsible behaviour such as failing to stop or falsely claiming that someone else was driving	1. The decision to drive was brought about by a proven and genuine emergency falling short of a defence 2. The offender genuinely believed that he or she was insured or licensed to drive 3. The offender was seriously injured as a result of the collision 4. The victim was a close friend or relative

DANGEROUS DRIVING

Either-way, 6 months/£5,000 (2 years). Must endorse and disqualify for a minimum period of 12 months; must order extended re-test. Must disqualify for at least 2 years if offender has had two or more disqualifications for periods of 56 days or more in preceding 3 years.

Skill: The presence of a particular skill (in this case that of a police trained driver) is an irrelevant consideration when evaluating whether or not the driving is dangerous (*Bannister* [2009] EWCA Crim 1571). **Alcohol:** The fact that a driver had consumed alcohol (and by extension any other substance that might have a qualitative effect on the driving) is admissible (*Webster* [2006] 2 Cr App R 103). Where drink is a major plank of the prosecution case, advocates should have regard to *McBride* [1962] 2 QB 167. **Dangerous state:** Where a vehicle's dangerous state is due to its official design and not use, it will not usually be appropriate to prosecute (*Marchant* [2004] 1 All ER 1187). A vehicle is being driven in a dangerous state if the driver is aware that his ability to control the vehicle might be impaired such that the standard of his driving might fall below the requisite standard (*Marison* [1997] RTR 457).

Dangerous driving:

Road Traffic Act 1988, s 2A

(1) For the purposes of sections 1 and 2 above a person is to be regarded as driving dangerously if (and, subject to subsection (2) below, only if)—

    (a) the way he drives falls far below what would be expected of a competent and careful driver, and

    (b) it would be obvious to a competent and careful driver that driving in that way would be dangerous.

(2) A person is also to be regarded as driving dangerously for the purposes of sections 1 and 2 above if it would be obvious to a competent and careful driver that driving the vehicle in its current state would be dangerous.

(3) In subsections (1) and (2) above 'dangerous' refers to danger either of injury to any person or of serious damage to property; and in determining for the purposes of those subsections what would be expected of, or obvious to, a competent and careful driver in a particular case, regard shall be had not only to the circumstances of which he could be expected to be aware but also to any circumstances shown to have been within the knowledge of the accused.

(4) In determining for the purposes of subsection (2) above the state of a vehicle, regard may be had to anything attached to or carried on or in it and to the manner in which it is attached or carried.

Offence seriousness (culpability and harm)
A. Identify the appropriate starting point
Starting points based on first time offender pleading not guilty

Example of nature of activity	Starting point	Range
Single incident where little or no damage or risk of personal injury	Medium level community order	Low level community order to high level community order Disqualify 12–15 months
Incident(s) involving excessive speed or showing off, especially on busy roads or in built-up area; OR Single incident where little or no damage or risk of personal injury but offender was disqualified driver	12 weeks custody	High level community order to 26 weeks custody Disqualify 15–24 months
Prolonged bad driving involving deliberate disregard for safety of others; OR Incident(s) involving excessive speed or showing off, especially on busy roads or in built-up area, by disqualified driver; OR Driving as described in box above while being pursued by police	Crown Court	Crown Court

Offence seriousness (culpability and harm)
B. Consider the effect of aggravating and mitigating factors
(other than those within examples above)
The following may be particularly relevant but **these lists are not exhaustive**

Factors indicating higher culpability	Factors indicating lower culpability
1. Disregarding warnings of others	1. Genuine emergency
2. Evidence of alcohol or drugs	2. Speed not excessive
3. Carrying out other tasks while driving	3. Offence due to inexperience rather than irresponsibility of driver
4. Carrying passengers or heavy load	
5. Tiredness	
6. Aggressive driving, such as driving much too close to vehicle in front, racing, inappropriate attempts to overtake, or cutting in after overtaking	
7. Driving when knowingly suffering from a medical condition which significantly impairs the offender's driving skills	
8. Driving a poorly maintained or dangerously loaded vehicle, especially where motivated by commercial concerns	
Factors indicating greater degree of harm	
1. Injury to others	
2. Damage to other vehicles or property	

Road Traffic Act 1988, s 2

A person who drives a mechanically propelled vehicle dangerously on a road or other public place is guilty of an offence.

DRIVE WHILST DISQUALIFIED

Summary only, 6 month/£5,000. Must endorse and may disqualify. If no disqualification, impose 6 points.

Mens rea: The prosecution do not need to prove that the defendant was aware of the prosecution that led to him being disqualified (*Taylor v Kenyon* [1952] 2 All ER 726), this is the case even where a driving licence has been returned to the defendant by mistake (*Bowsher* [1973] RTR 202). **Proof:** Strict proof that the person disqualified by the court is the person now charged is required. This will normally arise from (a) admission, (b) fingerprints, (c) evidence of identity from someone in court when the disqualification was made (*R v Derwentside Justices, ex p Heaviside* [1996] RTR 384). Other evidence such as an unusual name will at least raise a prima facie case that the defendant will need to answer in order to avoid conviction (*Olakunori v Director of Public Prosecutions* [1998] COD 443).

An admission made whilst giving evidence is sufficient to prove a disqualification, even in the absence of a certificate of conviction (*Moran v Crown Prosecution Service* (2000) 164 JP 562). A defendant's silence in interview (where he did not later rely on any fact) and his general attitude to the management of the case in accordance with the Criminal Procedure Rules, could not provide sufficient proof (*Mills v Director of Public Prosecutions* [2008] EWHC 3304 (Admin)). Consistency of personal details will normally be sufficient to raise a prima facie case. If the defendant calls no evidence to contradict that prima facie case, it will be open to the court to be satisfied that identity is *proved* (*Pattison v Director of Public Prosecutions* [2006] RTR 13). A solicitor could be called as a witness to confirm identity (*R (Howe) v South Durham Magistrates' Court* [2005] RTR 4). **Mistaken belief:** A mistaken belief that he was not driving on a road will not amount to a defence (*R v Miller* [1975] 1 WLR 1222). **Successful appeal:** The fact that a disqualification was later quashed on appeal does not provide a defence (*R v Thames Magistrates' Court, ex p Levy* The Times, 17 July 1997). **Bad character:** A bad character application in relation to the disqualification is not necessary as it has to do with the facts of the alleged offence (Criminal Justice Act 2003, s 98) (*Director of Public Prosecutions v Agyemang* [2009] EWHC 1542 (Admin)).

Offence seriousness (culpability and harm)		
A. Identify the appropriate starting point		
Starting points based on first time offender pleading not guilty		
Example of nature of activity	**Starting point**	**Range**
Full period expired but re-test not taken	Low level community order	Band C fine to medium level community order 6 points or disqualify for 3–6 months
Lengthy period of ban already served	High level community order	Medium level community order to 12 weeks custody Lengthen disqualification for 6–12 months beyond expiry of current ban
Recently imposed ban	12 weeks custody	High level community order to 26 weeks custody Lengthen disqualification for 12–18 months beyond expiry of current ban

Road Traffic Act 1988, s 103

(1) A person is guilty of an offence if, while disqualified for holding or obtaining a licence, he—

(a) obtains a licence, or

(b) drives a motor vehicle on a road.

EXCESS ALCOHOL

Summary only, **Driving:** 6 months/£5,000. Must endorse and disqualify for at least 12 months. Must disqualify for at least 2 years if offender has had 2 or more disqualifications for periods of 56 days or more in preceding 3 years. Must disqualify for at least 3 years if offender has been convicted of a relevant offence in preceding 10 years. **In charge:** 3 months/£2,500. Must endorse and may disqualify. If no disqualification, impose 10 points.

Margin of error: There will be no prosecution unless the alcohol level is at least 40 microgrammes (Home Office Circular 46/1982); This 'allowance' is also provided for in blood or urine analysis.

Duress: Duress is available as a defence but only rarely will a driver be able to avail himself of it. The defence will only be available for so long as the threat is active and a sober and reasonable person would have driven (*Crown Prosecution Service v Brown* [2007] EWHC 3274 (Admin)).

Statutory presumption: Where there has been no consumption of alcohol between the incidence of driving and the testing, the alcohol reading is conclusive (Road Traffic Offenders Act 1988, s 15(2), and *Griffiths v Director of Public Prosecutions* [2002] EWHC 792 (Admin)). However, the presumption in section 15(2) applies only to trials and does not extend to a *Newton* hearing (*Goldsmith v Director of Public Prosecutions* [2009] EWHC 3010 (Admin)).

Road Traffic Offenders Act 1988, ss 15(2), (3)

(2) Evidence of the proportion of alcohol or any drug in a specimen of breath, blood or urine provided by or taken from the accused shall, in all cases (including cases where the specimen was not provided or taken in connection with the alleged offence), be taken into account and, subject to subsection (3) below, it shall be assumed that the proportion of alcohol in the accused's breath, blood or urine at the time of the alleged offence was not less than in the specimen.

(3) That assumption shall not be made if the accused proves—

    (a) that he consumed alcohol before he provided the specimen or had it taken from him and—

        (i) in relation to an offence under section 3A, after the time of the alleged offence, and

        (ii) otherwise, after he had ceased to drive, attempt to drive or be in charge of a vehicle on a road or other public place, and

    (b) that had he not done so the proportion of alcohol in his breath, blood or urine would not have exceeded the prescribed limit and, if it is alleged that he was unfit to drive through drink, would not have been such as to impair his ability to drive properly.

Back calculation: Where there is post driving consumption of alcohol the defendant is able to 'back calculate' to obtain a reading at the time of driving (Road Traffic offences Act 1988, s 15(3)). The prosecution is also entitled to rely upon back calculations but in practice rarely do so (*Gumbley v Cunningham* [1989] RTR 49).

No intention to drive: The burden of proof falls on the defendant to the civil standard (*Sheldrake v Director of Public Prosecutions* [2005] RTR 2):

Road Traffic Act 1988, s 5(2)–(3)

(2) It is a defence for a person charged with an offence under subsection (1) (b) above to prove that at the time he is alleged to have committed the offence the circumstances were such that there was no likelihood of his driving the vehicle whilst the proportion of alcohol in his breath, blood or urine remained likely to exceed the prescribed limit.

(3) The court may, in determining whether there was such a likelihood as is mentioned in subsection (2) above, disregard any injury to him and any damage to the vehicle.

Driving offence:

Offence seriousness (culpability and harm)
A. Identify the appropriate starting point
Starting points based on first time offender pleading not guilty

Level of alcohol			Starting point	Range	Disqualification	Disqual. 2nd offence in 10 years – see note above
Breath (mg)	Blood (ml)	Urine (ml)				
36–59	81–137	108–183	Band C fine	Band C fine	12–16 months	36–40 months
60–89	138–206	184–274	Band C fine	Band C fine	17–22 months	36–46 months
90–119	207–275	275–366	Medium level community order	Low level community order to high level community order	23–28 months	36–52 months
120–150 and above	276–345 and above	367–459 and above	12 weeks custody	High level community order to 26 weeks custody	29–36 months	36–60 months

Offence seriousness (culpability and harm)
B. Consider the effect of aggravating and mitigating factors
(other than those within examples above)
The following may be particularly relevant but **these lists are not exhaustive**

Factors indicating higher culpability	Factors indicating lower culpability
1. LGV, HGV, PSV, etc	1. Genuine emergency established*
2. Poor road or weather conditions	2. Spiked drinks*
3. Carrying passengers	3. Very short distance driven*
4. Driving for hire or reward	
5. Evidence of unacceptable standard of driving	* even where not amounting to special reasons
Factors indicating greater degree of harm	
1. Involved in accident	
2. Location eg near school	
3. High level of traffic or pedestrians in the vicinity	

In charge offence:

Offence seriousness (culpability and harm)				
A. Identify the appropriate starting point				
Starting points based on first time offender pleading not guilty				
Level of alcohol			**Starting point**	**Range**
Breath (mg)	**Blood (ml)**	**Urine (ml)**	**Band B fine**	**Band B fine 10 points**
36–59	81–137	108–183		
60–89	138–206	184–274	Band B fine	Band B fine 10 points OR consider disqualification
90–119	207–275	275–366	Band C fine	Band C fine to medium level community order Consider disqualification up to 6 months OR 10 points
120–150 and above	276–345 and above	367–459 and above	Medium level community order	Low level community order to 6 weeks custody Disqualify 6–12 months

Offence seriousness (culpability and harm)	
B. Consider the effect of aggravating and mitigating factors	
(other than those within examples above)	
The following may be particularly relevant but **these lists are not exhaustive**	
Factors indicating higher culpability	**Factor indicating lower culpability**
1. LGV, HGV, PSV, etc	1. Low likelihood of driving
2. Ability to drive seriously impaired	
3. High likelihood of driving	
4. Driving for hire or reward	

Road Traffic Act 1988, s 5(1)

(1) If a person—

    (a) drives or attempts to drive a motor vehicle on a road or other public place, or

    (b) is in charge of a motor vehicle on a road or other public place,

after consuming so much alcohol that the proportion of it in his breath, blood, or urine exceeds the prescribed limit he is guilty of an offence.

FAIL TO PROVIDE A PRELIMINARY SPECIMEN OF BREATH

Summary only, Fine £1,000, discretionary disqualification, endorseable with 4 penalty points.

Sentence: Starting point is level B fine.

Road Traffic Act 1988, s 6

(1) If any of subsections (2) to (5) applies a constable may require a person to co-operate with any one or more preliminary tests administered to the person by that constable or another constable.

(2) This subsection applies if a constable reasonably suspects that the person—

    (a) is driving, is attempting to drive or is in charge of a motor vehicle on a road or other public place, and

(b) has alcohol or a drug in his body or is under the influence of a drug.

(3) This subsection applies if a constable reasonably suspects that the person—

(a) has been driving, attempting to drive or in charge of a motor vehicle on a road or other public place while having alcohol or a drug in his body or while unfit to drive because of a drug, and

(b) still has alcohol or a drug in his body or is still under the influence of a drug.

(4) This subsection applies if a constable reasonably suspects that the person—

(a) is or has been driving, attempting to drive or in charge of a motor vehicle on a road or other public place, and

(b) has committed a traffic offence while the vehicle was in motion.

(5) This subsection applies if—

(a) an accident occurs owing to the presence of a motor vehicle on a road or other public place, and

(b) a constable reasonably believes that the person was driving, attempting to drive or in charge of the vehicle at the time of the accident.

(6) A person commits an offence if without reasonable excuse he fails to co-operate with a preliminary test in pursuance of a requirement imposed under this section.

(7) A constable may administer a preliminary test by virtue of any of subsections (2) to (4) only if he is in uniform.

(8) In this section—

(a) a reference to a preliminary test is to any of the tests described in sections 6A to 6C, and

(b) "traffic offence" means an offence under—

(i) a provision of Part II of the Public Passenger Vehicles Act 1981 (c. 14),

(ii) a provision of the Road Traffic Regulation Act 1984 (c. 27),

(iii) a provision of the Road Traffic Offenders Act 1988 (c. 53) other than a provision of Part III, or

(iv) a provision of this Act other than a provision of Part V.

FAIL TO PROVIDE SPECIMEN FOR ANALYSIS

Summary only, Driving/attempting to drive: 6 months/£5,000. Must endorse and disqualify for at least 12 months. Must disqualify for at least 2 years if offender has had 2 or more disqualifications for periods of 56 days or more in preceding 3 years Must disqualify for at least 3 years if offender has been convicted of a relevant offence in preceding 10 years. In-charge: 3 months/£2,500. Must endorse and may disqualify. If no disqualification, impose 10 points.

Reasonable excuse: A reasonable excuse for failing to provide must relate to inability due to physical or mental issues (*Lennard* [1973] RTR 252). Failure to mention a medical reason at the time of refusal does not preclude a court from finding that a reasonable excuse existed, although it was a factor to be taken into account (*Piggott v Director of Public Prosecutions* [2008] RTR 16). Once a reasonable excuse is raised it is for the prosecution to disprove it (*McKeon v Director of Public Prosecutions* [2008] RTR 14). A failure to understand the statutory warning relating to prosecution may amount to a reasonable excuse if the accused's understanding of English is poor. Failure to understand due to intoxication will not suffice. **Legal advice:** The taking of a specimen does not have to be delayed (over and above a couple of minutes) for the purpose of taking legal advice (*Gearing* [2008] EWHC 1695 (Admin)).

Offence seriousness (culpability and harm)

A. Identify the appropriate starting point

Starting points based on first time offender pleading not guilty

Examples of nature of activity	Starting point	Range	Disqual.	Disqual. 2nd offence in 10 years
Defendant refused test when had honestly held but unreasonable excuse	Band C fine	Band C fine	12–16 months	36–40 months
Deliberate refusal or deliberate failure	Low level community order	Band C fine to high level community order	17–28 months	36–52 months
Deliberate refusal or deliberate failure where evidence of serious impairment	12 weeks custody	High level community order to 26 weeks custody	29–36 months	36–60 months

Offence seriousness (culpability and harm)

B. Consider the effect of aggravating and mitigating factors

(other than those within examples above)

The following may be particularly relevant but **these lists are not exhaustive**

Factors indicating higher culpability	Factor indicating lower culpability
1. Evidence of unacceptable standard of driving 2. LGV, HGV, PSV, etc 3. Obvious state of intoxication 4. Driving for hire or reward **Factor indicating greater degree of harm** 1. Involved in accident	1. Genuine but unsuccessful attempt to provide specimen

C14.7.2 *Sentencing: in-charge*

Offence seriousness (culpability and harm)

A. Identify appropriate starting point

Starting points based on first time offender pleading not guilty

Examples of nature of activity	Starting point	Range
Defendant refused test when had honestly held but unreasonable excuse	Band B fine	Band B fine 10 points
Deliberate refusal or deliberate failure	Band C fine	Band C fine to medium level community order Consider disqualification OR 10 points
Deliberate refusal or deliberate failure where evidence of serious impairment	Medium level community order	Low level community order to 6 weeks custody Disqualify 6–12 months

Offence seriousness (culpability and harm)	
B. Consider the effect of aggravating and mitigating factors	
(other than those within examples above)	
The following may be particularly relevant but **these lists are not exhaustive**	
Factors indicating higher culpability	**Factors indicating lower culpability**
1. Obvious state of intoxication 2. LGV, HGV, PSV, etc 3. High likelihood of driving 4. Driving for hire of reward	1. Genuine but unsuccessful attempt to provide specimen 2. Low likelihood of driving

Road Traffic Act 1988, s 7(6)–(7)

(6) A person who, without reasonable excuse, fails to provide a specimen when required to do so in pursuance of this section is guilty of an offence.

(7) A constable must, on requiring any person to provide a specimen in pursuance of this section, warn him that a failure to provide it may render him liable to prosecution.

FAIL TO STOP/REPORT ROAD ACCIDENT

Summary only, 6 months/£5,000. Must endorse and may disqualify. If no disqualification, impose 5–10 points.

Stop: A driver must stop even if it is apparent that there is no-one who has witnessed an incident (*Lee v Knapp* [1966] 3 All ER 961), even if that is only for a very short time. There is no obligation to seek out potential people who might wish to receive the driver's details (*Mutton v Bates* [1984] RTR 256).

Offence seriousness (culpability and harm)		
A. Identify the appropriate starting point		
Starting points based on first time offender pleading not guilty		
Examples of nature of activity	**Starting point**	**Range**
Minor damage/injury or stopped at scene but failed to exchange particulars or report	Band B fine	Band B fine 5–6 points
Moderate damage/injury or failed to stop and failed to report	Band C fine	Band C fine 7–8 points Consider disqualification
Serious damage/injury and/or evidence of bad driving	High level community order	Band C fine to 26 weeks custody Disqualify 6–12 months OR 9–10 points

Offence seriousness (culpability and harm)	
B. Consider the effect of aggravating and mitigating factors	
(other than those within examples above)	
The following may be particularly relevant but **these lists are not exhaustive**	
Factors indicating higher culpability	**Factors indicating lower culpability**
1. Evidence of drink or drugs/evasion of test 2. Knowledge/suspicion that personal injury caused (where not an element of the offence) 3. Leaving injured party at scene 4. Giving false details	1. Believed identity known 2. Genuine fear of retribution 3. Subsequently reported

Road Traffic Act 1988, s 170

(1) This section applies in a case where, owing to the presence of a mechanically propelled vehicle on a road or other public place, an accident occurs by which—

    (a) personal injury is caused to a person other than the driver of that mechanically propelled vehicle, or

    (b) damage is caused—

        (i) to a vehicle other than that mechanically propelled vehicle or a trailer drawn by that mechanically propelled vehicle, or

        (ii) to an animal other than an animal in or on that mechanically propelled vehicle or a trailer drawn by that mechanically propelled vehicle, or

        (iii) to any other property constructed on, fixed to, growing in or otherwise forming part of the land on which the road or place in question is situated or land adjacent to such land.

(2) The driver of the mechanically propelled vehicle must stop and, if required to do so by any person having reasonable grounds for so requiring, give his name and address and also the name and address of the owner and the identification marks of the vehicle.

(3) If for any reason the driver of the mechanically propelled vehicle does not give his name and address under subsection (2) above, he must report the accident.

(4) A person who fails to comply with subsection (2) or (3) above is guilty of an offence.

(5) If, in a case where this section applies by virtue of subsection (1)(a) above, the driver of a motor vehicle does not at the time of the accident produce such a certificate of insurance or security, or other evidence, as is mentioned in section 165(2)(a) of this Act—

    (a) to a constable, or

    (b) to some person who, having reasonable grounds for so doing, has required him to produce it,

the driver must report the accident and produce such a certificate or other evidence.

This subsection does not apply to the driver of an invalid carriage.

(6) To comply with a duty under this section to report an accident or to produce such a certificate of insurance or security, or other evidence, as is mentioned in section 165(2)(a) of this Act, the driver—

    (a) must do so at a police station or to a constable, and

    (b) must do so as soon as is reasonably practicable and, in any case, within twenty-four hours of the occurrence of the accident.

(7) A person who fails to comply with a duty under subsection (5) above is guilty of an offence, but he shall not be convicted by reason only of a failure to produce a certificate or other evidence if, within seven days after the occurrence of the accident, the certificate or other evidence is produced at a police station that was specified by him at the time when the accident was reported.

(8) In this section 'animal' means horse, cattle, ass, mule, sheep, pig, goat or dog.

FAILING TO COMPLY WITH TRAFFIC SIGN

Summary only, Fine £1,000. Failure to comply with double white lines, pedestrian crossings, stop signs and traffic lights carries endorsement with 3 penalty points.

Properly placed: The burden of proving that a sign is defective by design or location falls on the defendant to the civil standard. De minimis variance with the regulations will be disregarded (*Canadine v DPP* [2007] EWHC 383 (Admin)).

Road Traffic Act 1988, s 36

(1) Where a traffic sign, being a sign—

    (a) of the prescribed size, colour and type, or

    (b) of another character authorised by the Secretary of State under the provisions in that behalf of the Road Traffic Regulation Act 1984,

has been lawfully placed on or near a road, a person driving or propelling a vehicle who fails to comply with the indication given by the sign is guilty of an offence.

(2) A traffic sign shall not be treated for the purposes of this section as having been lawfully placed unless either—

    (a) the indication given by the sign is an indication of a statutory prohibition, restriction or requirement, or

    (b) it is expressly provided by or under any provision of the Traffic Acts that this section shall apply to the sign or to signs of a type of which the sign is one;

and, where the indication mentioned in paragraph (a) of this subsection is of the general nature only of the prohibition, restriction or requirement to which the sign relates, a person shall not be convicted of failure to comply with the indication unless he has failed to comply with the prohibition, restriction or requirement to which the sign relates.

(3) For the purposes of this section a traffic sign placed on or near a road shall be deemed—

    (a) to be of the prescribed size, colour and type, or of another character authorised by the Secretary of State under the provisions in that behalf of the Road Traffic Regulation Act 1984, and

    (b) (subject to subsection (2) above) to have been lawfully so placed,

unless the contrary is proved.

(4) Where a traffic survey of any description is being carried out on or in the vicinity of a road, this section applies to a traffic sign by which a direction is given—

    (a) to stop a vehicle,

    (b) to make it proceed in, or keep to, a particular line of traffic, or

    (c) to proceed to a particular point on or near the road on which the vehicle is being driven or propelled,

being a direction given for the purposes of the survey (but not a direction requiring any person to provide any information for the purposes of the survey).

(5) Regulations made by the Secretary of State for the Environment, Transport and the Regions, the Secretary of State for Wales and the Secretary of State for Scotland acting jointly may specify any traffic sign for the purposes of column 5 of the entry in Schedule 2 to the Road Traffic Offenders Act 1988 relating to offences under this section (offences committed by failing to comply with certain signs involve discretionary disqualification).

FAILING TO GIVE INFORMATION OF DRIVER'S IDENTITY

Summary only, £1,000 Fine, discretionary disqualification, obligatory endorsement, 6 penalty points if not disqualifying.

In *Duff v Director of Public Prosecutions* [2009] EWHC 675 (Admin), D's wife was served with a notice under section 172 of the Road Traffic Act 1988 requiring her to identify the name of the driver. D in fact replied to the notice, naming himself as the driver. As a result a further section 172 notice was then served on D. Following legal advice D did not respond to that notice and was subsequently convicted of failing to provide information. It was held that the conviction was sound as the request to which he had in fact responded was a request of D's wife, not D himself.

Multiple addressees: A single notice addressed to more than one person living at the same address was a valid request under the act (*Lynes v Director of Public Prosecutions* [2012] EWHC 1300 (Admin)). In *Lynes* the court left open the question of whether each person had a responsibility to respond (see para 18). **Due diligence:** A driver is only to be judged in relation to s 172(4) by the actions they did or did not take from the time of the police request to ascertain the identity of the driver, not before (*Atkinson v Director of Public Prosecutions* [2011] EWHC 3363 (Admin)). **Section 172(7) defence:** For the defences available under s 172(7)(b) see: *Purnell v Snaresbrook Crown Court* [2011] EWHC 934 (Admin) and *Whiteside v Director of Public Prosecutions* [2011] EWHC 3471 (Admin) where the notice did not come to the attention of the driver as he worked abroad. The court held that as he had not (on the facts) made suitable arrangements for the processing of his post, he could not avail himself successfully of the defence).

Multiple requests: In *Thomson v Jackson* [2010] HCJAC 96 the Scottish High Court ruled that the police cannot make more than one request for information directed to the same person. It is doubted whether this decision would be followed by an English court, but prior to the point being decided practitioners should carefully consider its effect, particularly in relation to prosecutions being time-barred.

Road Traffic Act 1988, s 172

(1) This section applies—

    (a) to any offence under the preceding provisions of this Act except—

        (i) an offence under Part V, or

        (ii) an offence under section 13, 16, 51(2), 61(4), 67(9), 68(4), 96 or 120, and to an offence under section 178 of this Act,

    (b) to any offence under sections 25, 26 or 27 of the Road Traffic Offenders Act 1988,

    (c) to any offence against any other enactment relating to the use of vehicles on roads, and

    (d) to manslaughter, or in Scotland culpable homicide, by the driver of a motor vehicle.

(2) Where the driver of a vehicle is alleged to be guilty of an offence to which this section applies—

    (a) the person keeping the vehicle shall give such information as to the identity of the driver as he may be required to give by or on behalf of a chief officer of police, and

    (b) any other person shall if required as stated above give any information which it is in his power to give and may lead to identification of the driver.

(3) Subject to the following provisions, a person who fails to comply with a requirement under subsection (2) above shall be guilty of an offence.

(4) A person shall not be guilty of an offence by virtue of paragraph (a) of subsection (2) above if he shows that he did not know and could not with reasonable diligence have ascertained who the driver of the vehicle was. (5) Where a body corporate is guilty of an offence under this section and the offence is proved to have been committed with the consent or connivance of, or to be attributable to neglect on the part of, a director, manager, secretary or other similar officer of the body corporate, or a person who was purporting to act in any such capacity, he, as well as the body corporate, is guilty of that offence and liable to be proceeded against and punished accordingly.

(6) Where the alleged offender is a body corporate, or in Scotland a partnership or an unincorporated association, or the proceedings are brought against him by virtue of subsection (5) above or subsection (11) below, subsection (4) above shall not apply unless, in addition to the matters there mentioned, the alleged offender shows that no record was kept of the persons who drove the vehicle and that the failure to keep a record was reasonable.

(7) A requirement under subsection (2) may be made by written notice served by post; and where it is so made—

(a) it shall have effect as a requirement to give the information within the period of 28 days beginning with the day on which the notice is served, and

(b) the person on whom the notice is served shall not be guilty of an offence under this section if he shows either that he gave the information as soon as reasonably practicable after the end of that period or that it has not been reasonably practicable for him to give it.

(8) Where the person on whom a notice under subsection (7) above is to be served is a body corporate, the notice is duly served if it is served on the secretary or clerk of that body.

(9) For the purposes of section 7 of the Interpretation Act 1978 as it applies for the purposes of this section the proper address of any person in relation to the service on him of a notice under subsection (7) above is—

(a) in the case of the secretary or clerk of a body corporate, that of the registered or principal office of that body or (if the body corporate is the registered keeper of the vehicle concerned) the registered address, and

(b) in any other case, his last known address at the time of service.

(10) In this section—

'registered address', in relation to the registered keeper of a vehicle, means the address recorded in the record kept under the Vehicles Excise and Registration Act 1994 with respect to that vehicle as being that person's address, and 'registered keeper', in relation to a vehicle, means the person in whose name the vehicle is registered under that Act; and references to the driver of a vehicle include references to the rider of a cycle.

IMMOBILISING VEHICLES

Triable either-way, £5,000 fine (unlimited).

Protection of Freedoms Act 2012, s 54

(1) A person commits an offence who, without lawful authority—

(a) immobilises a motor vehicle by the attachment to the vehicle, or a part of it, of an immobilising device, or

(b) moves, or restricts the movement of, such a vehicle by any means,

intending to prevent or inhibit the removal of the vehicle by a person otherwise entitled to remove it.

(2) The express or implied consent (whether or not legally binding) of a person otherwise entitled to remove the vehicle to the immobilisation, movement or restriction concerned is not lawful authority for the purposes of subsection (1).

(3) But, where the restriction of the movement of the vehicle is by means of a fixed barrier and the barrier was present (whether or not lowered into place or otherwise restricting movement) when the vehicle was parked, any express or implied consent (whether or not legally binding) of the driver of the vehicle to the restriction is, for the purposes of subsection (1), lawful authority for the restriction.

(4) A person who is entitled to remove a vehicle cannot commit an offence under this section in relation to that vehicle.

(5)...

(6) In this section "motor vehicle" means a mechanically propelled vehicle or a vehicle designed or adapted for towing by a mechanically propelled vehicle.

MOTORWAY OFFENCES

Offence	Maximum	Points	Starting point	Special considerations
Drive in reverse or wrong way on slip road	£2,500	3	B	
Drive in reverse or wrong way on motorway	£2,500	3	C	
Drive off carriageway (central reservation or hard shoulder)	£2,500	3	B	
Make U turn	£2,500	3	C	
Learner driver or excluded vehicle	£2,500	3	B	
Stop on hard shoulder	£2,500	–	A	
Vehicle in prohibited lane	£2,500	3	A	
Walk on motorway, slip road or hard shoulder	£2,500	–	A	

NO INSURANCE, USING, CAUSING, OR PERMITTING

Section 143: Summary only. Fine £5,000, Discretionary disqualification, 6–8 penalty points. **Section 144A**: Summary only, Fine £1,000, not endorseable.

Burden of proof: It is for a defendant to show that he was insured once it is established that a motor vehicle was used on a road or other public place. **Limitation period**: Proceedings may be brought within six months of a prosecutor forming the opinion that there is sufficient evidence of an offence having been committed (subject to an overall three-year time bar). **State of vehicle**: It is not necessary that the vehicle be capable of being driven (*Pumbien v Vines* [1996] RTR 37). **Employees defence**: See Road Traffic Act 1988, s 143(3). **Voidable policies**: A policy which is voidable, for example because the driver gave false information to secure insurance is valid until voided by the insurance company (*Adams v Dunn* (1978) Crim LR 365).

Road Traffic Act 1988, ss 143, 144A, 144B

143.— Users of motor vehicles to be insured or secured against third-party risks.

(1) Subject to the provisions of this Part of this Act—

(a) a person must not use a motor vehicle on a road or other public place unless there is in force in relation to the use of the vehicle by that person such a policy of insurance or such a security in respect of third party risks as complies with the requirements of this Part of this Act, and

(b) a person must not cause or permit any other person to use a motor vehicle on a road or other public place unless there is in force in relation to the use of the vehicle by that other person such a policy of insurance or such a security in respect of third party risks as complies with the requirements of this Part of this Act.

(2) If a person acts in contravention of subsection (1) above he is guilty of an offence.

(3) A person charged with using a motor vehicle in contravention of this section shall not be convicted if he proves—

(a) that the vehicle did not belong to him and was not in his possession under a contract of hiring or of loan,

(b) that he was using the vehicle in the course of his employment, and

(c) that he neither knew nor had reason to believe that there was not in force in relation to the vehicle such a policy of insurance or security as is mentioned in subsection (1) above.

(4) This Part of this Act does not apply to invalid carriages.

144A Offence of keeping vehicle which does not meet insurance requirements

(1) If a motor vehicle registered under the Vehicle Excise and Registration Act 1994 does not meet the insurance requirements, the person in whose name the vehicle is registered is guilty of an offence.

(2) For the purposes of this section a vehicle meets the insurance requirements if–

    (a) it is covered by a such a policy of insurance or such a security in respect of third party risks as complies with the requirements of this Part of this Act, and

    (b) either of the following conditions is satisfied.

(3) The first condition is that the policy or security, or the certificate of insurance or security which relates to it, identifies the vehicle by its registration mark as a vehicle which is covered by the policy or security.

(4) The second condition is that the vehicle is covered by the policy or security because–

    (a) the policy or security covers any vehicle, or any vehicle of a particular description, the owner of which is a person named in the policy or security or in the certificate of insurance or security which relates to it, and

    (b) the vehicle is owned by that person.

(5) For the purposes of this section a vehicle is covered by a policy of insurance or security if the policy of insurance or security is in force in relation to the use of the vehicle.

144B Exceptions to section 144A offence

(1) A person ("the registered keeper") in whose name a vehicle which does not meet the insurance requirements is registered at any particular time ("the relevant time") does not commit an offence under section 144A of this Act at that time if any of the following conditions are satisfied.

(2) The first condition is that at the relevant time the vehicle is owned as described–

    (a) in subsection (1) of section 144 of this Act, or

    (b) in paragraph (a), (b), (da), (db), (dc) or (g) of subsection (2) of that section,

(whether or not at the relevant time it is being driven as described in that provision).

(3) The second condition is that at the relevant time the vehicle is owned with the intention that it should be used as described in paragraph (c), (d), (e) or (f) of section 144(2) of this Act.

(4) The third condition is that the registered keeper–

    (a) is not at the relevant time the person keeping the vehicle, and

    (b) if previously he was the person keeping the vehicle, he has by the relevant time complied with any requirements under subsection (7)(a) below that he is required to have complied with by the relevant or any earlier time.

(5) The fourth condition is that–

    (a) the registered keeper is at the relevant time the person keeping the vehicle,

    (b) at the relevant time the vehicle is not used on a road or other public place, and

    (c) the registered keeper has by the relevant time complied with any requirements under subsection (7)(a) below that he is required to have complied with by the relevant or any earlier time.

(6) The fifth condition is that–

    (a) the vehicle has been stolen before the relevant time,

    (b) the vehicle has not been recovered by the relevant time, and

    (c) any requirements under subsection (7)(b) below that, in connection with the theft, are required to have been complied with by the relevant or any earlier time have been complied with by the relevant time.

(6A) The sixth condition is that—

    (a) the registered keeper is at the relevant time the person keeping the vehicle,

    (b) neither a licence nor a nil licence under the Vehicle Excise and Registration Act 1994 was in force for the vehicle on 31st January 1998,

    (c) neither a licence nor a nil licence has been taken out for the vehicle for a period starting after that date, and

    (d) the vehicle has not been used or kept on a public road after that date.

(7) Regulations may make provision–

    (a) for the purposes of subsection (4)(b) and (5)(c) above, requiring a person in whose name a vehicle is registered to furnish such particulars and make such declarations as may be prescribed, and to do so at such times and in such manner as may be prescribed, and

    (b) for the purposes of subsection (6)(c) above, as to the persons to whom, the times at which and the manner in which the theft of a vehicle is to be notified.

(8) Regulations may make provision amending this section for the purpose of providing for further exceptions to section 144A of this Act (or varying or revoking any such further exceptions).

(9) A person accused of an offence under section 144A of this Act is not entitled to the benefit of an exception conferred by or under this section unless evidence is adduced that is sufficient to raise an issue with respect to that exception; but where evidence is so adduced it is for the prosecution to prove beyond reasonable doubt that the exception does not apply.

Offence seriousness (culpability and harm)

A. Identify the appropriate starting point

Starting points based on first time offender pleading not guilty

Examples of nature of activity	Starting point	Range
Using a motor vehicle on a road or other public place without insurance	Band C fine	Band C fine 6 points–12 months disqualification—see notes below

---

Offence seriousness (culpability and harm)

B. Consider the effect of aggravating and mitigating factors

(other than those within examples above)

The following may be particularly relevant but **these lists are not exhaustive**

Factors indicating higher culpability	Factors indicating lower culpability
1. Never passed test	1. Responsibility for providing insurance rests with another
2. Gave false details	2. Genuine misunderstanding
3. Driving LGV, HGV, PSV etc	3. Recent failure to renew or failure to transfer vehicle details where insurance was in existence
4. Driving for hire or reward	4. Vehicle not being driven
5. Evidence of sustained uninsured use	
Factors indicating greater degree of harm	
1. Involved in accident	
2. Accident resulting in injury	

PROPER CONTROL OF VEHICLE

Summary only, Fine £2,5000 (if a good vehicle or vehicle adapted to carry more than 8 passengers), otherwise £1,000. Discretionary disqualification, 3 penalty points.

Sentence: Starting point is Band A fine.

Hand held: Section 41D(a) (unlike subsection (b)) does not require that the mobile phone be hand held, and also covers use of other equipment such as a radio or satellite navigation device.

Road Traffic Act 1988, s 41D

A person who contravenes or fails to comply with a construction and use requirement–

    (a) as to not driving a motor vehicle in a position which does not give proper control or a full view of the road and traffic ahead, or not causing or permitting the driving of a motor vehicle by another person in such a position, or

    (b) as to not driving or supervising the driving of a motor vehicle while using a hand-held mobile telephone or other hand-held interactive communication device, or not causing or permitting the driving of a motor vehicle by another person using such a telephone or other device,

is guilty of an offence.

SPEEDING

Summary only, Fine £1,000 (£2,500 if committed on motorway).

Adequate notice of speed limit applying: See *Jones v DPP* [2011] EWHC 50 (Admin), where the court held that the question to be asked was: "Whether by the point on the road where the alleged offence took place (the point of enforcement) the driver by reference to the route taken thereto has been given (or drivers generally have been given) adequate guidance of the speed limit to be observed at that point on the road by the signs on the relevant part of parts of the road in so far as (and thus to the extent that) those traffic signs comply with the 2002 Regulations?"

Road Traffic Regulation Act 1984, s 89(10).

Offence seriousness (culpability and harm)			
A. Identify the appropriate starting point			
Starting points based on first time offender pleading not guilty			
Speed limit (mph)	Recorded speed (mph)		
20	21–30	31–40	41–50
30	31–40	41–50	51–60
40	41–55	56–65	66–75
50	51–65	66–75	76–85
60	61–80	81–90	91–100
70	71–90	91–100	101–110
Starting point	**Band A fine**	**Band B fine**	**Band B fine**
Range	**Band A fine**	**Band B fine**	**Band B fine**
Points/disqualification	3 points	4–6 points OR Disqualify 7–28 days	Disqualify 7–56 days OR 6 points

Offence seriousness (culpability and harm)

B. Consider the effect of aggravating and mitigating factors

(other than those within examples above)

The following may be particularly relevant but **these lists are not exhaustive**

Factors indicating higher culpability	Factor indicating lower culpability
1. Poor road or weather conditions	1. Genuine emergency established
2. LGV, HGV, PSV, etc	
3. Towing caravan/trailer	
4. Carrying passengers or heavy load	
5. Driving for hire or reward	
6. Evidence of unacceptable standard of driving over and above speed	
Factors indicating greater degree of harm	
1. Location eg near school	
2. High level of traffic or pedestrians in the vicinity	

TAXI TOUTING/SOLICITING FOR HIRE

Summary only, £2,500 fine.

Solicit: Some form of invitation to a prospective hirer (*R (Oddy) v Bugbugs Ltd* [2003] EWHC 2865 (Admin)).

Offence seriousness (culpability and harm)

A. Identify the appropriate starting point

Starting points based on first time offender pleading not guilty

Examples of nature of activity	Starting point	Range
Licensed taxi-driver touting for trade (ie making approach rather than waiting for a person to initiate hiring)	Band A fine	Conditional discharge to band A fine and consider disqualification 1–3 months
PHV licence held but touting for trade rather than being booked through an operator; an accomplice to touting	Band B fine	Band A fine to band C fine and consider disqualification 3–6 months
No PHV licence held	Band C fine	Band B fine to band C fine and disqualification 6–12 months

Offence seriousness (culpability and harm)

B. Consider the effect of aggravating and mitigating factors (other than those within examples above)

The following may be particularly relevant but **these lists are not exhaustive**

Factors indicating higher culpability	Factor indicating lower culpability
1. Commercial business/large scale operation	1. Providing a service when no licensed taxi available
2. No insurance/invalid insurance	
3. No driving licence and/or no MOT	
4. Vehicle not roadworthy	
Factors indicating greater degree of harm	
1. Deliberately diverting trade from taxi rank	
2. PHV licence had been refused/offender ineligible for licence	

Criminal Justice and Public Order Act 1994, s 167

(1) Subject to the following provisions, it is an offence, in a public place, to solicit persons to hire vehicles to carry them as passengers.

(2) Subsection (1) above does not imply that the soliciting must refer to any particular vehicle nor is the mere display of a sign on a vehicle that the vehicle is for hire soliciting within that subsection.

(3) No offence is committed under this section where soliciting persons to hire licensed taxis is permitted by a scheme under section 10 of the Transport Act 1985 (schemes for shared taxis) whether or not supplemented by provision made under section 13 of that Act (modifications of the taxi code).

(4) It is a defence for the accused to show that he was soliciting for passengers to be carried at separate fares by public service vehicles on behalf of the holder of a PSV operator's licence for those vehicles whose authority he had at the time of the alleged offence.

UNFIT THROUGH DRINK OR DRUGS

Summary only. **Drive/attempt to drive:** 6 months/£5,000. Must endorse and disqualify for at least 12 months. Must disqualify for at least 2 years if offender has had 2 or more disqualifications for periods of 56 days or more in preceding 3 years. Must disqualify for at least 3 years if offender has been convicted of a relevant offence in preceding 10 years. **In-charge:** 3 months/£2,500. Must endorse and may disqualify. If no disqualification, impose 10 points.

No intention to drive:

Road Traffic Act 1988, s 4(3)–(4)

(3) For the purposes of subsection (2) above, a person shall be deemed not to have been in charge of a mechanically propelled vehicle if he proves that at the material time the circumstances were such that there was no likelihood of his driving it so long as he remained unfit to drive through drink or drugs.

(4) The court may, in determining whether there was such a likelihood as is mentioned in subsection (3) above, disregard any injury to him and any damage to the vehicle.

Driving or attempting to drive:

Offence seriousness (culpability and harm)				
A. Identify the appropriate starting point				
Starting points based on first time offender pleading not guilty				
Examples of nature of activity	Starting point	Range	Disqual.	Disqual. 2nd offence in 10 years
Evidence of moderate level of impairment and no aggravating factors	Band C fine	Band C fine	12–16 months	36–40 months
Evidence of moderate level of impairment and presence of one or more aggravating factors listed below	Band C fine	Band C fine	17–22 months	36–46 months
Evidence of high level of impairment and no aggravating factors	Medium level community order	Low level community order to high level community order	23–28 months	36–52 months

| Evidence of high level of impairment and presence of one or more aggravating factors listed below | 12 weeks custody | High level community order to 26 weeks custody | 29–36 months | 36–60 months |

Offence seriousness (culpability and harm)

B. Consider the effect of aggravating and mitigating factors

(other than those within examples above)

The following may be particularly relevant but **these lists are not exhaustive**

Factors indicating higher culpability	Factors indicating lower culpability
1. LGV, HGV, PSV, etc	1. Genuine emergency established*
2. Poor road or weather conditions	2. Spike drinks*
3. Carrying passengers	3. Very short distance driven*
4. Driving for hire or reward	* even where not amounting to special reasons
5. Evidence of unacceptable standard of driving	
Factors indicating greater degree of harm	
1. Involved in accident	
2. Location eg near school	
3. High level of traffic or pedestrians in the vicinity	

In charge:

Offence seriousness (culpability and harm)

A. Identify the appropriate starting point

Starting points based on first time offender pleading not guilty

Examples of nature of activity	Starting point	Range
Evidence of moderate level of impairment and no aggravating factors	Band B fine	Band B fine 10 points
Evidence of moderate level of impairment and presence of one or more aggravating factors listed below	Band B fine	Band B fine 10 points or consider disqualification
Evidence of high level of impairment and no aggravating factors	Band C fine	Band C fine to medium level community order 10 points OR consider disqualification
Evidence of high level of impairment and presence of one or more aggravating factors listed below	High level community order	Medium level community order to 12 weeks custody Consider disqualification OR 10 points

Offence seriousness (culpability and harm)

B. Consider the effect of aggravating and mitigating factors

(other than those within examples above)

The following may be particularly relevant but **these lists are not exhaustive**

Factors indicating higher culpability	Factor indicating lower culpability
1. LGV, HGV, PSV, etc	1. Low likelihood of driving
2. High likelihood of driving	
3. Driving for hire or reward	

Road Traffic Act 1988, s 4(1)–(2), and (5)

(1) A person who, when driving or attempting to drive a mechanically propelled vehicle on a road or other public place, is unfit to drive through drink or drugs is guilty of an offence.

(2) Without prejudice to subsection (1) above, a person who, when in charge of a mechanically propelled vehicle which is on a road or other public place, is unfit to drive through drink or drugs is guilty of an offence.

…

(5) … a person shall be taken to be unfit to drive if his ability to drive properly is for the time being impaired.

VEHICLE LICENCE/REGISTRATION FRAUD

Either-way, £5,000 (2 years)

Sentence: In *Weston* [2011] EWCA Crim 2334 the court quashed a sentence of 6 weeks imprisonment (late plea) imposed for fraudulent use of an excise licence and substituted a fine of £1,000. The court held:

"The applicant behaved with blatant dishonesty and it was a calculated offence of its type. It must however be remembered that the applicant's last conviction for dishonesty was more than 40 years ago and that the sentencing guideline starting point for offences of this nature is a fine. In our judgment, this was not a case which crossed the custody threshold and the sentence of imprisonment was wrong in principle. The fact that the applicant's assets are currently restrained does not, in our view, prevent the court from imposing a financial penalty, allowing a lengthy period of time for payment so that the applicant can make any application which may prove necessary."

Offence seriousness (culpability and harm)		
A. Identify the appropriate starting point		
Starting points based on first time offender pleading not guilty		
Examples of nature of activity	**Starting point**	**Range**
Use of unaltered licence from another vehicle	Band B fine	Band B fine
Forged licence bought for own use, or forged/altered for own use	Band C fine	Band C fine
Use of number plates from another vehicle; OR Licence/number plates forged or altered for sale to another	High level community order (in Crown Court)	Medium level community order to Crown Court (Note: community order and custody available only in Crown Court)

Offence seriousness (culpability and harm)	
B. Consider the effect of aggravating and mitigating factors	
(other than those within examples above)	
The following may be particularly relevant but **these lists are not exhaustive**	
Factors indicating higher culpability	**Factors indicating lower culpability**
1. LGV, PSV, taxi, etc	1. Licence/registration mark from another vehicle owned by defendant
2. Long-term fraudulent use	2. Short-term use
Factors indicating greater degree of harm	
1. High financial gain	
2. Innocent victim deceived	
3. Legitimate owner inconvenienced	

Vehicle Excise and Registration Act 1994, s 44

(1) A person is guilty of an offence if he forges, fraudulently alters, fraudulently uses, fraudulently lends or fraudulently allows to be used by another person anything to which subsection (2) applies.

(2) This subsection applies to—

(a) a vehicle licence,
(b) a trade licence,
(c) a nil licence,
(d) a registration mark,
(e) a registration document, and
(f) a trade plate (including a replacement trade plate).

VEHICLE OFFENCES

Offence	Maximum	Points	Starting point	Special considerations
No excise licence	£1,000 or 5 times annual duty, whichever is greater	–	A (1–3 months unpaid) B (4-6 months unpaid) C (7–12 months unpaid)	Add duty lost
Fail to notify change of ownership to DVLA	£1,000	–	A	If offence committed in course of business: A (driver) A* (owner-driver) B (owner-company)
No test certificate	£1,000	–	A	If offence committed in course of business: A (driver) A* (owner-driver) B (owner-company)
Brakes defective Key points: It is sufficient only to prove that *any* part of the braking system is defective (*Kennett v British Airports Authority* [1975] Crim LR 106). The fact that everything possible (eg servicing) has been done in order to ensure that the vehicle is in good condition does not amount to a defence (*Hawkins v Holmes* [1974] RTR 436), as maintenance of the braking system is an absolute obligation on the driver (*Green v Burnett* [1954] 3 All ER 273).	£2,500	3	B	If offence committed in course of business: B (driver) B* (owner-driver) C (owner-company) £5,000 if goods vehicle

Steering defective	£2,500	3	B	If offence committed in course of business: B (driver) B* (owner-driver) C (owner-company) £5,000 if goods vehicle
Tyres defective. It is a defence if the vehicle is not being used and there was no intention to use when the tyres were defective, regardless of the fact that the vehicle was on a road (*Eden v Mitchell* [1975] RTR 425). There is no requirement for the prosecution to have had the tyre examined by an authorized examiner as the issue was a simple question of fact (*Phillips v Thomas* [1974] RTR 28).	£2,500	3	B	If offence committed in course of business: B (driver) B* (owner-driver) C (owner-company) £5,000 if goods vehicle Penalty per tyre
Condition of vehicle/accessories/equipment involving danger of injury (Road Traffic Act 1988, s 40A)	£2,500	3	B	Must disqualify for at least 6 months if offender has one or more previous convictions for same offence within 3 years If offence committed in course of business: B (driver) B* (owner-driver) C (owner-company) £5,000 if goods vehicle
Exhaust defective	£1,000	–	A	If offence committed in course of business: A (driver) A* (owner-driver) B (owner-company)
Lights defective	£1,000	–	A	If offence committed in course of business: A (driver) A* (owner-driver) B (owner-company)

VEHICLES OVER 3.5 TONNES, OFFENCES

*The guidelines for some of the offences below differentiate between three types of offender when the offence is committed in the course of business: driver, owner-driver, and owner-company. For owner-driver, the starting point is the same as for driver; however, the court should consider an uplift of at least 25 per cent.

Offence	Maximum	Points	Starting point	Special considerations
No goods vehicle plating certificate	£1,000		A (driver) A* (owner-driver) B (owner-company)	
No goods vehicle test certificate	£2,500		B (driver) B* (owner-driver) C (owner-company)	
Brakes defective	£5,000	3	B (driver) B* (owner-driver) C (owner-company)	
Steering defective	£5,000	3	B (driver) B* (owner-driver) C (owner-company)	
Tyres defective	£5,000	3	B (driver) B* (owner-driver) C (owner-company)	Penalty per tyre
Exhaust emission	£2,500	–	B (driver) B* (owner-driver) C (owner-company)	
Condition of vehicle/accessories/equipment involving danger of injury (Road Traffic Act 1988, s 40A)	£5,000	3	B (driver) B* (owner-driver) C (owner-company)	Must disqualify for at least 6 months if offender has one or more previous convictions for same offence within 3 years
Number of passengers or way carried involving danger of injury (Road Traffic Act 1988, s 40A)	£5,000	3	B (driver) B* (owner-driver) C (owner-company)	Must disqualify for at least 6 months if offender has one or more previous convictions for same offence within 3 years
Weight, position, or distribution of load or manner in which load secured involving danger of injury (Road Traffic Act 1988, s 40A)	£5,000	3	B (driver) B* (owner-driver) C (owner-company)	Must disqualify for at least 6 months if offender has one or more previous convictions for same offence within 3 years
Position or manner in which load secured (not involving danger) (Road Traffic Act 1988, s 42)	£2,500	–	B (driver) B* (owner-driver) C (owner-company)	
Overloading/exceeding axle weight	£5,000	–	B (driver) B* (owner-driver) C (owner-company)	Starting points cater for cases where the overload is up to and including 10%. Thereafter, 10% should be added to the penalty for each additional 1% of overload. Penalty per axle

Offence	Maximum	Points	Starting point	Special considerations
No operators licence	£2,500	–	B (driver) B* (owner-driver) C (owner-company)	
Speed limiter not used or incorrectly calibrated	£2,500	–	B (driver) B* (owner-driver) C (owner-company)	
Tachograph not used/not working	£5,000	–	B (driver) B* (owner-driver) C (owner-company)	
Exceed permitted driving time/periods of duty	£2,500	–	B (driver) B* (owner-driver) C (owner-company)	
Fail to keep/return written record sheets	£2,500	–	B (driver) B* (owner-driver) C (owner-company)	
Falsify or alter records with intent to deceive	£5,000/2 years	–	B (driver) B* (owner-driver) C (owner-company)	Either-way offence

VEHICLE USE OFFENCES

*The guidelines for some of the offences below differentiate between three types of offender when the offence is committed in the course of business: driver, owner-driver, and owner-company. For owner-driver, the starting point is the same as for driver; however, the court should consider an uplift of at least 25 per cent.

Offence	Maximum	Points	Starting point	Special considerations
Weight, position, or distribution of load or manner in which load secured involving danger of injury (Road Traffic Act 1988, s 40A). Many cases involve unsecured passengers on the back of vehicles which is objectively often viewed as involving danger of injury (eg *Gray v Director of Public Prosecutions* [1999] RTR 339)	£2,500	3	B	Must disqualify for at least 6 months if offender has one or more previous convictions for same offence within 3 years If offence committed in course of business: A (driver) A* (owner-driver) B (owner-company) £5,000 if goods vehicle
Number of passengers or way carried involving danger of injury (Road Traffic Act 1988, s 40A)	£2,500	3	B	If offence committed in course of business: A (driver) A* (owner-driver) B (owner-company) £5,000 if goods vehicle

Position or manner in which load secured (not involving danger) (Road Traffic Act 1988, s 42)	£1,000	–	A	£2,500 if goods vehicle

SEXUAL OFFENCES

GENERAL PRINCIPLES

Consent: In *Bree* [2007] EWCA Crim 04 it was held:

"If, through drink (or for any other reason) the complainant has temporarily lost her capacity to choose whether to have intercourse on the relevant occasion, she is not consenting, and subject to questions about the defendant's state of mind, if intercourse takes place, this would be rape. However, where the complainant has voluntarily consumed even substantial quantities of alcohol, but nevertheless remains capable of choosing whether or not to have intercourse, and in drink agrees to do so, this would not be rape. We should perhaps underline that, as a matter of practical reality, capacity to consent may evaporate well before a complainant becomes unconscious. Whether this is so or not, however, is fact specific, or more accurately, depends on the actual state of mind of the individuals involved on the particular occasion."

Sexual Offences Act 2003, ss 74–76

74 "Consent"

For the purposes of this Part, a person consents if he agrees by choice, and has the freedom and capacity to make that choice.

75 Evidential presumptions about consent

(1) If in proceedings for an offence to which this section applies it is proved–

    (a) that the defendant did the relevant act,

    (b) that any of the circumstances specified in subsection (2) existed, and

    (c) that the defendant knew that those circumstances existed,

the complainant is to be taken not to have consented to the relevant act unless sufficient evidence is adduced to raise an issue as to whether he consented, and the defendant is to be taken not to have reasonably believed that the complainant consented unless sufficient evidence is adduced to raise an issue as to whether he reasonably believed it.

(2) The circumstances are that–

    (a) any person was, at the time of the relevant act or immediately before it began, using violence against the complainant or causing the complainant to fear that immediate violence would be used against him;

    (b) any person was, at the time of the relevant act or immediately before it began, causing the complainant to fear that violence was being used, or that immediate violence would be used, against another person;

    (c) the complainant was, and the defendant was not, unlawfully detained at the time of the relevant act;

    (d) the complainant was asleep or otherwise unconscious at the time of the relevant act;

    (e) because of the complainant's physical disability, the complainant would not have been able at the time of the relevant act to communicate to the defendant whether the complainant consented;

(f) any person had administered to or caused to be taken by the complainant, without the complainant's consent, a substance which, having regard to when it was administered or taken, was capable of causing or enabling the complainant to be stupefied or overpowered at the time of the relevant act.

(3) In subsection (2)(a) and (b), the reference to the time immediately before the relevant act began is, in the case of an act which is one of a continuous series of sexual activities, a reference to the time immediately before the first sexual activity began.

76 Conclusive presumptions about consent

(1) If in proceedings for an offence to which this section applies it is proved that the defendant did the relevant act and that any of the circumstances specified in subsection (2) existed, it is to be conclusively presumed–

(a) that the complainant did not consent to the relevant act, and
(b) that the defendant did not believe that the complainant consented to the relevant act.

(2) The circumstances are that–

(a) the defendant intentionally deceived the complainant as to the nature or purpose of the relevant act;
(b) the defendant intentionally induced the complainant to consent to the relevant act by impersonating a person known personally to the complainant.

ABUSE OF POSITION OF TRUST

All offences either-way, see individual offences for penalty.

Section 15 offence:

Type/Nature of activity	Starting Point	Range
Where the intent is to commit an assault by penetration or rape	4 years custody if the victim is under 13 2 years custody if the victim is 13 or over but under 16	3–7 years custody 1–4 years custody
Where the intent is to coerce the child into sexual activity	2 years custody is the victim is under 13 18 months custody if the victim is 13 or over but under 16	1–4 years custody 12 months-2 years 6 months custody

Additional aggravating factors:	Additional mitigating factors:
1. Background of intimidation or coercion 2. Use of drugs, alcohol or other substance to facilitate the offence 3. Offender aware that he or she is suffering from a sexually transmitted infection 4. Abduction or detention	

Section 16 and 17 offences:

Type/Nature of activity	Starting Point	Range
Penile penetration of the vagina, anus or mouth or penetration of the vagina or anus with another body part or an object	18 months custody	12 months–2 years 6 months
Other forms of non-penetrative activity	26 weeks custody	4 weeks–18 months custody
Contact between part of the offender's body (other than the genitalia) with part of the victim's body (other than the genitalia)	Community order	Any appropriate non-custodial sentence

Additional aggravating factors:	Additional mitigating factors:
1. Background of intimidation or coercion 2. Offender ejaculated or caused the victim to ejaculate 3. Use of drugs, alcohol or other substance to facilitate the offence 4. Offender aware that he or she is suffering from a sexually transmitted disease	1. Small disparity in age between victim and offender 2. Relationship of genuine affection 3. No element of corruption

Section 18 offence:

Type/Nature of activity	Starting Point	Range
Consensual intercourse or other forms of consensual penetration	2 years custody	1-4 years custody
Masturbation (of oneself or another person)	18 months custody	12 months–2 years 6 months custody
Consensual sexual touching involving naked genitalia	12 months custody	26 weeks–2 years custody
Consensual sexual touching of naked body parts but not involving naked genitalia	26 weeks custody	4 weeks–18 months custody

Additional aggravating factors:	Additional mitigating factors:
1. Background of intimidation or coercion 2. Use of drugs, alcohol or other substance to facilitate the offence 3. Threats to prevent the victim reporting the incident 4. Abduction or detention	

Section 19 offence:

Type/Nature of activity	Starting Point	Range
Live sexual activity	18 months custody	12 months–2 years custody
Moving or still images of people engaged in sexual activity involving penetration	32 weeks custody	26 weeks–12 months custody
Moving or still images of people engaging in sexual activity other than penetration	Community order	Community order–26 weeks custody

Additional aggravating factors:	Additional mitigating factors:
1. Background of intimidation or coercion 2. Use of drugs, alcohol or other substance to facilitate the offence 3. Threats to prevent the victim reporting the incident 4. Abduction or detention 5. Images of violent activity	1. Small disparity in age between victim and offender

Sexual Offences Act 2003, ss 15–22

15 Meeting a child following sexual grooming etc.

(1) A person aged 18 or over (A) commits an offence if—

  (a) A has met or communicated with another person (B) on at least two occasions and subsequently—

    (i) A intentionally meets B,

    (ii) A travels with the intention of meeting B in any part of the world or arranges to meet B in any part of the world, or

    (iii) B travels with the intention of meeting A in any part of the world,

  (b) A intends to do anything to or in respect of B, during or after the meeting mentioned in paragraph (a)(i) to (iii) and in any part of the world, which if done will involve the commission by A of a relevant offence,

  (c) B is under 16, and

  (d) A does not reasonably believe that B is 16 or over.

(2) In subsection (1)—

  (a) the reference to A having met or communicated with B is a reference to A having met B in any part of the world or having communicated with B by any means from, to or in any part of the world;

  (b) "relevant offence" means—

    (i) an offence under this Part,

    [...]

    (iii) anything done outside England and Wales which is not an offence within sub-paragraph (i) but would be an offence within sub-paragraph (i) if done in England and Wales.

(4) A person guilty of an offence under this section is liable—

  (a) on summary conviction, to imprisonment for a term not exceeding 6 months or a fine not exceeding the statutory maximum or both;

  (b) on conviction on indictment, to imprisonment for a term not exceeding 10 years.

16 Abuse of position of trust: sexual activity with a child

(1) A person aged 18 or over (A) commits an offence if—

  (a) he intentionally touches another person (B),

  (b) the touching is sexual,

  (c) A is in a position of trust in relation to B,

  (d) where subsection (2) applies, A knows or could reasonably be expected to know of the circumstances by virtue of which he is in a position of trust in relation to B, and

  (e) either—

    (i) B is under 18 and A does not reasonably believe that B is 18 or over, or

    (ii) B is under 13.

(2) This subsection applies where A—

  (a) is in a position of trust in relation to B by virtue of circumstances within section 21(2), (3), (4) or (5), and

(b) is not in such a position of trust by virtue of other circumstances.

(3) Where in proceedings for an offence under this section it is proved that the other person was under 18, the defendant is to be taken not to have reasonably believed that that person was 18 or over unless sufficient evidence is adduced to raise an issue as to whether he reasonably believed it.

(4) Where in proceedings for an offence under this section—

(a) it is proved that the defendant was in a position of trust in relation to the other person by virtue of circumstances within section 21(2), (3), (4) or (5), and

(b) it is not proved that he was in such a position of trust by virtue of other circumstances,

it is to be taken that the defendant knew or could reasonably have been expected to know of the circumstances by virtue of which he was in such a position of trust unless sufficient evidence is adduced to raise an issue as to whether he knew or could reasonably have been expected to know of those circumstances.

(5) A person guilty of an offence under this section is liable—

(a) on summary conviction, to imprisonment for a term not exceeding 6 months or a fine not exceeding the statutory maximum or both;

(b) on conviction on indictment, to imprisonment for a term not exceeding 5 years.

17 Abuse of position of trust: causing or inciting a child to engage in sexual activity

(1) A person aged 18 or over (A) commits an offence if—

(a) he intentionally causes or incites another person (B) to engage in an activity,

(b) the activity is sexual,

(c) A is in a position of trust in relation to B,

(d) where subsection (2) applies, A knows or could reasonably be expected to know of the circumstances by virtue of which he is in a position of trust in relation to B, and

(e) either—

(i) B is under 18 and A does not reasonably believe that B is 18 or over, or

(ii) B is under 13.

(2) This subsection applies where A—

(a) is in a position of trust in relation to B by virtue of circumstances within section 21(2), (3), (4) or (5), and

(b) is not in such a position of trust by virtue of other circumstances.

(3) Where in proceedings for an offence under this section it is proved that the other person was under 18, the defendant is to be taken not to have reasonably believed that that person was 18 or over unless sufficient evidence is adduced to raise an issue as to whether he reasonably believed it.

(4) Where in proceedings for an offence under this section—

(a) it is proved that the defendant was in a position of trust in relation to the other person by virtue of circumstances within section 21(2), (3), (4) or (5), and

(b) it is not proved that he was in such a position of trust by virtue of other circumstances,

it is to be taken that the defendant knew or could reasonably have been expected to know of the circumstances by virtue of which he was in such a position of trust unless sufficient evidence is adduced to raise an issue as to whether he knew or could reasonably have been expected to know of those circumstances.

(5) A person guilty of an offence under this section is liable—

(a) on summary conviction, to imprisonment for a term not exceeding 6 months or a fine not exceeding the statutory maximum or both;

(b) on conviction on indictment, to imprisonment for a term not exceeding 5 years.

18 Abuse of position of trust: sexual activity in the presence of a child

(1) A person aged 18 or over (A) commits an offence if–

    (a) he intentionally engages in an activity,

    (b) the activity is sexual,

    (c) for the purpose of obtaining sexual gratification, he engages in it–

        (i)   when another person (B) is present or is in a place from which A can be observed, and

        (ii) knowing or believing that B is aware, or intending that B should be aware, that he is engaging in it,

    (d) A is in a position of trust in relation to B,

    (e) where subsection (2) applies, A knows or could reasonably be expected to know of the circumstances by virtue of which he is in a position of trust in relation to B, and

    (f) either–

        (i)   B is under 18 and A does not reasonably believe that B is 18 or over, or

        (ii) B is under 13.

(2) This subsection applies where A–

    (a) is in a position of trust in relation to B by virtue of circumstances within section 21(2), (3), (4) or (5), and

    (b) is not in such a position of trust by virtue of other circumstances.

(3) Where in proceedings for an offence under this section it is proved that the other person was under 18, the defendant is to be taken not to have reasonably believed that that person was 18 or over unless sufficient evidence is adduced to raise an issue as to whether he reasonably believed it.

(4) Where in proceedings for an offence under this section–

    (a) it is proved that the defendant was in a position of trust in relation to the other person by virtue of circumstances within section 21(2), (3), (4) or (5), and

    (b) it is not proved that he was in such a position of trust by virtue of other circumstances,

it is to be taken that the defendant knew or could reasonably have been expected to know of the circumstances by virtue of which he was in such a position of trust unless sufficient evidence is adduced to raise an issue as to whether he knew or could reasonably have been expected to know of those circumstances.

(5) A person guilty of an offence under this section is liable–

    (a) on summary conviction, to imprisonment for a term not exceeding 6 months or a fine not exceeding the statutory maximum or both;

    (b) on conviction on indictment, to imprisonment for a term not exceeding 5 years.

19 Abuse of position of trust: causing a child to watch a sexual act

(1) A person aged 18 or over (A) commits an offence if–

    (a) for the purpose of obtaining sexual gratification, he intentionally causes another person (B) to watch a third person engaging in an activity, or to look at an image of any person engaging in an activity,

    (b) the activity is sexual,

    (c) A is in a position of trust in relation to B,

    (d) where subsection (2) applies, A knows or could reasonably be expected to know of the circumstances by virtue of which he is in a position of trust in relation to B, and

    (e) either–

        (i)   B is under 18 and A does not reasonably believe that B is 18 or over, or

        (ii) B is under 13.

(2) This subsection applies where A–

(a) is in a position of trust in relation to B by virtue of circumstances within section 21(2), (3), (4) or (5), and

(b) is not in such a position of trust by virtue of other circumstances.

(3) Where in proceedings for an offence under this section it is proved that the other person was under 18, the defendant is to be taken not to have reasonably believed that that person was 18 or over unless sufficient evidence is adduced to raise an issue as to whether he reasonably believed it.

(4) Where in proceedings for an offence under this section–

(a) it is proved that the defendant was in a position of trust in relation to the other person by virtue of circumstances within section 21(2), (3), (4) or (5), and

(b) it is not proved that he was in such a position of trust by virtue of other circumstances,

it is to be taken that the defendant knew or could reasonably have been expected to know of the circumstances by virtue of which he was in such a position of trust unless sufficient evidence is adduced to raise an issue as to whether he knew or could reasonably have been expected to know of those circumstances.

(5) A person guilty of an offence under this section is liable–

(a) on summary conviction, to imprisonment for a term not exceeding 6 months or a fine not exceeding the statutory maximum or both;

(b) on conviction on indictment, to imprisonment for a term not exceeding 5 years.

20 Abuse of position of trust: acts done in Scotland

Anything which, if done in England and Wales, would constitute an offence under any of sections 16 to 19 also constitutes that offence if done in Scotland or Northern Ireland].

21 Positions of trust

(1) For the purposes of sections 16 to 19, a person (A) is in a position of trust in relation to another person (B) if–

(a) any of the following subsections applies, or

(b) any condition specified in an order made by the Secretary of State is met.

(2) This subsection applies if A looks after persons under 18 who are detained in an institution by virtue of a court order or under an enactment, and B is so detained in that institution.

(3) This subsection applies if A looks after persons under 18 who are resident in a home or other place in which–

(a) accommodation and maintenance are provided by an authority in accordance with section 22C(6) of the Children Act 1989 (c. 41), or

(b) accommodation is provided by a voluntary organisation under section 59(1) of that Act,

and B is resident, and is so provided with accommodation and maintenance or accommodation, in that place.

(4) This subsection applies if A looks after persons under 18 who are accommodated and cared for in one of the following institutions–

(a) a hospital,

(b) in Wales, an independent clinic,

(c) a care home,

(d) a community home, voluntary home or children's home, or

(e) a home provided under section 82(5) of the Children Act 1989,

and B is accommodated and cared for in that institution.

(5) This subsection applies if A looks after persons under 18 who are receiving education at

an educational institution and B is receiving, and A is not receiving, education at that institution.

(7) This subsection applies if A is engaged in the provision of services under, or pursuant to anything done under–

   (a) sections 8 to 10 of the Employment and Training Act 1973 (c. 50), or

   (b) section 114 of the Learning and Skills Act 2000 (c. 21),

and, in that capacity, looks after B on an individual basis.

(8) This subsection applies if A regularly has unsupervised contact with B (whether face to face or by any other means)–

   (a) in the exercise of functions of a local authority under section 20 or 21 of the Children Act 1989 (c. 41),

(9) This subsection applies if A, as a person who is to report to the court under section 7 of the Children Act 1989 on matters relating to the welfare of B, regularly has unsupervised contact with B (whether face to face or by any other means).

(10) This subsection applies if A is a personal adviser appointed for B under–

   (a) section 23B(2) of, or paragraph 19C of Schedule 2 to, the Children Act 1989,

and, in that capacity, looks after B on an individual basis.

(11) This subsection applies if–

   (a) B is subject to a care order, a supervision order or an education supervision order, and

   (b) in the exercise of functions conferred by virtue of the order on an authorised person or the authority designated by the order, A looks after B on an individual basis.

(12) This subsection applies if A–

   (a) is an officer of the Service appointed for B under section 41(1) of the Children Act 1989,

   (b) is appointed a children's guardian of B under rule 6 or rule 18 of the Adoption Rules 1984 (S.I. 1984/265),

   (c) is appointed to be the guardian ad litem of B under rule 9.5 of the Family Proceedings Rules 1991 (S. I. 1991/1247), or

   (d) is appointed to be the children's guardian of B under rule 59 of the Family Procedure (Adoption) Rules 2005 (S.I. 2005/2795) or rule 16.3(1)(ii) or rule 16.4 of the Family Procedure Rules 2010 (S.I. 2010/2955),

and, in that capacity, regularly has unsupervised contact with B (whether face to face or by any other means).

(13) This subsection applies if–

   (a) B is subject to requirements imposed by or under an enactment on his release from detention for a criminal offence, or is subject to requirements imposed by a court order made in criminal proceedings, and

   (b) A looks after B on an individual basis in pursuance of the requirements.

22 Positions of trust: interpretation

(1) The following provisions apply for the purposes of section 21.

(2) Subject to subsection (3), a person looks after persons under 18 if he is regularly involved in caring for, training, supervising or being in sole charge of such persons.

(3) A person (A) looks after another person (B) on an individual basis if–

   (a) A is regularly involved in caring for, training or supervising B, and

   (b) in the course of his involvement, A regularly has unsupervised contact with B (whether face to face or by any other means).

(4) A person receives education at an educational institution if–

(a) he is registered or otherwise enrolled as a pupil or student at the institution, or

(b) he receives education at the institution under arrangements with another educational institution at which he is so registered or otherwise enrolled.

(5) In section 21–

"authority"–

(a) in relation to England and Wales, means a local authority;

[...]

"care home" means an establishment which is a care home for the purposes of the Care Standards Act 2000 (c. 14);

"care order"has–

(a) in relation to England and Wales, the same meaning as in the Children Act 1989 (c. 41) ,

"children's home"has–

(a) in relation to England and Wales, the meaning given by section 1 of the Care Standards Act 2000 ,

"community home"has the meaning given by section 53 of the Children Act 1989;

"education supervision order"has–

(a) in relation to England and Wales, the meaning given by section 36 of the Children Act 1989 ,

"hospital" means—

(a) a hospital as defined by section 275 of the National Health Service Act 2006, or section 206 of the National Health Service (Wales) Act 2006; or

(b) any other establishment—
   (i) in England, in which any of the services listed in subsection (6) are provided; and
   (ii) in Wales, which is a hospital within the meaning given by section 2(3) of the Care Standards Act 2000;

"independent clinic"has–

(a) the meaning given by section 2 of the Care Standards Act 2000;

"supervision order" has–

(a) in relation to England and Wales, the meaning given by section 31(11) of the Children Act 1989 (c. 41),

"voluntary home"has–

(a) in relation to England and Wales, the meaning given by section 60(3) of the Children Act 1989 ,

(6) The services referred to in paragraph (b)(i) of the definition of "hospital" are as follows—

(a) medical treatment under anaesthesia or intravenously administered sedation;

(b) dental treatment under general anaesthesia;

(c) obstetric services and, in connection with childbirth, medical services;

(d) termination of pregnancies;

(e) cosmetic surgery, other than—
   (i) ear and body piercing;
   (ii) tattooing;
   (iii) the subcutaneous injection of a substance or substances into the skin for cosmetic purposes; or

(iv) the removal of hair roots or small blemishes on the skin by the application of heat using an electric current.

ADMINISTERING A SUBSTANCE WITH INTENT

Either-way, 6 months/£5,000.

Sentence: This offence will rarely if ever be suitable for summary trial.

Sexual Offences Act 2003, s 61

(1) A person commits an offence if he intentionally administers a substance to, or causes a substance to be taken by, another person (B)–

(a) knowing that B does not consent, and

(b) with the intention of stupefying or overpowering B, so as to enable any person to engage in a sexual activity that involves B.

ARRANGING OR FACILITATING A CHILD SEX OFFENCE

Either-way, 6 months/£5,000 (14 years).

Sentence: This offence will rarely if ever be suitable for summary trial.

Agreement or arrangement: The section does not require an agreement or arrangement. It does not require the consent or acquiescence of anyone else. An arrangement may be made without the agreement or acquiescence of anyone else. A defendant may take steps by way of a plan with the criminal objective identified in the section without involving anyone else and the mere fact that no-one else is involved would not necessarily mean that no arrangement was made (*R* [2008] EWCA Crim 619). Reckless touching: See *Heard* [2007] EWCA Crim 125.

Sexual Offences Act 2003, s 14

(1) A person commits an offence if–

(a) he intentionally arranges or facilitates something that he intends to do, intends another person to do, or believes that another person will do, in any part of the world, and

(b) doing it will involve the commission of an offence under any of sections 9 to 13.

(2) A person does not commit an offence under this section if–

(a) he arranges or facilitates something that he believes another person will do, but that he does not intend to do or intend another person to do, and

(b) any offence within subsection (1)(b) would be an offence against a child for whose protection he acts.

(3) For the purposes of subsection (2), a person acts for the protection of a child if he acts for the purpose of–

(a) protecting the child from sexually transmitted infection,

(b) protecting the physical safety of the child,

(c) preventing the child from becoming pregnant, or

(d) promoting the child's emotional well-being by the giving of advice,

and not for the purpose of obtaining sexual gratification or for the purpose of causing or encouraging the activity constituting the offence within subsection (1)(b) or the child's participation in it.

CAUSING A CHILD TO WATCH A SEXUAL ACT

Either-way, 6 months/£5,000 (10 years).

Type/Nature of Activity	Starting Point	Range
Live sexual activity	18 months custody	12 months–2 years custody
Moving or still images of people engaged in sexual activity involving penetration	32 weeks custody	26 weeks–12 months custody
Moving or still images of people engaged in sexual activity other than penetration	Community order	Community order–26 weeks custody

Additional aggravating factors:	Additional mitigating factors:
1. Background of intimidation or coercion 2. Use of drugs, alcohol or other substance to facilitate the offence 3. Threats to prevent victim reporting the incident 4. Abduction or detention 5. Images of violent activity	1. Small disparity in age between victim and offender

Sexual Offences Act 2003, s 12

(1) A person aged 18 or over (A) commits an offence if–

(a) for the purpose of obtaining sexual gratification, he intentionally causes another person (B) to watch a third person engaging in an activity, or to look at an image of any person engaging in an activity,

(b) the activity is sexual, and

(c) either–

(i) B is under 16 and A does not reasonably believe that B is 16 or over, or

(ii) B is under 13.

CAUSING A PERSON TO ENGAGE IN SEXUAL ACTIVITY WITHOUT CONSENT

Either-way (save for s 4(4) which is indictable only), 6 months/£5,000 (10 years (life if s 4(4) applies)).

Sentencing: It will rarely be appropriate or a court to accept jurisdiction in relation to an adult offender. The following sentencing guideline might offer guidance in relation to a youth being sentenced in the youth court:

Type/nature of activity	Starting Point	Range
Contact between naked genitalia of offender and another part of victim's body, or causing two or more victims to engage in such activity with each other Contact with naked genitalia of victim by offender using part of the body other than the genitalia or an object, or causing two or more victims to engage in such activity with each other Contact between either the clothed genitalia of offender and naked genitalia of victim, between naked genitalia of offender and clothed genitalia of victim, or causing two or more victims to engage in such activity with each other	2 years custody if the victim is a child under 13 or a person with a mental disorder 12 months custody	1–4 years custody 26 weeks–2 years custody

Contact between part of offender's body (other than the genitalia) with part of victim's body (other than the genitalia)	26 weeks custody if the victim is a child under 13 or a person with a mental disorder Community order	4 weeks–18 months custody An appropriate non-custodial sentence*

* 'Non-custodial sentence' in this context suggests a community order or a fine. In most instances, an offence will have crossed the threshold for a community order. However, in accordance with normal sentencing practice, a court is not precluded from imposing a financial penalty where that is determined to be the appropriate sentence.

Sexual Offences Act 2003, s 4

(1) A person (A) commits an offence if–

    (a) he intentionally causes another person (B) to engage in an activity,

    (b) the activity is sexual,

    (c) B does not consent to engaging in the activity, and

    (d) A does not reasonably believe that B consents.

(2) Whether a belief is reasonable is to be determined having regard to all the circumstances, including any steps A has taken to ascertain whether B consents.

(3) Sections 75 and 76 apply to an offence under this section.

(4) A person guilty of an offence under this section, if the activity caused involved–

    (a) penetration of B's anus or vagina,

    (b) penetration of B's mouth with a person's penis,

    (c) penetration of a person's anus or vagina with a part of B's body or by B with anything else, or

    (d) penetration of a person's mouth with B's penis

CHILD PROSTITUTION AND PORNOGRAPHY

Either-way, 6 months/£5,000 (14 years).

Sexual Offences Act 2003, ss 48, 49, and 50.

Offence seriousness (culpability and harm)
A. Identify the appropriate starting point
Starting points based on first time offender pleading not guilty

These offences should normally be dealt with in the Crown Court.
However, there may be rare cases of non-penetrative activity involving a victim aged 16 or 17 where the offender's involvement is minimal and not perpetrated for gain in which a custodial sentence within the jurisdiction of a magistrates' court may be appropriate.

Offence seriousness (culpability and harm)	
B. Consider the effect of aggravating and mitigating factors	
The following may be particularly relevant but **these lists are not exhaustive**	
Factors indicating higher culpability	**Factor indicating lower culpability**
1. Background of threats or intimidation	1. Offender also being controlled in prostitution or pornography and subject to threats or intimidation
2. Large-scale commercial operation	
3. Use of drugs, alcohol, or other substance to secure the victim's compliance	
4. Forcing a victim to violate another person	
5. Abduction or detention	

6. Threats to prevent the victim reporting the activity
7. Threats to disclose victim's activity to friends/relatives
8. Image distributed to other children or persons known to the victim
9. Financial or other gain

Factors indicating greater degree of harm

1. Induced dependency on drugs
2. Victim has been manipulated into physical and emotional dependence on the offender
3. Storing, making available, or distributing images in such a way that they can be inadvertently accessed by others

CHILD SEX OFFENCES COMMITTED BY CHILDREN OR YOUNG PERSONS

Either-way, 6 months/£5,000 (5 years).

Purpose: The purpose of this section is to provide a lower penalty where the offender is aged under 18. In practice (although there is no provision about this in the Act) decisions on whether persons under 18 should be charged with child sex offences will be made by Crown Prosecutors in accordance with the principles set out in the Code for Crown Prosecutors. In deciding whether it is in the public interest to prosecute these offences, where there is enough evidence to provide a realistic prospect of conviction, prosecutors may take into consideration factors such as the ages of the parties; the emotional maturity of the parties; whether they entered into a sexual relationship willingly; any coercion or corruption by a person; and the relationship between the parties and whether there was any existence of a duty of care or breach of trust. **Sentence:** See G [2007] EWHC 1033 (Admin).

Sexual Offences Act 2003, s 13

(1) A person under 18 commits an offence if he does anything which would be an offence under any of sections 9 to 12 if he were aged 18.

ENGAGING IN EXPOSURE

Either-way, 6 months/£5,000 (2 years).

Gender: This offence is committed where an offender intentionally exposes his or her genitals and intends that someone will see them and be caused alarm or distress. It is gender neutral, covering exposure of male or female genitalia to a male or female witness. **Sentencing repeat offenders:** The Sentencing Guidelines Council guideline provides that, when dealing with a repeat offender, the starting point should be 12 weeks custody with a range of four to 26 weeks custody. The presence of aggravating factors may suggest that a sentence above the range is appropriate and that the case should be committed to the Crown Court.

Offence seriousness (culpability and harm)		
A. Identify the appropriate starting point		
Starting points based on first time offender pleading not guilty		
Examples of nature of activity	**Starting point**	**Range**
Basic offence as defined in the Act, assuming no aggravating or mitigating factors	Low level community order	Band B fine to medium level community order
Offence with an aggravating factor	Medium level community order	Low level community order to high level community order

Two or more aggravating factors	12 weeks custody	6 weeks custody to Crown Court

Offence seriousness (culpability and harm)	
B. Consider the effect of aggravating and mitigating factors (other than those within examples above) The following may be particularly relevant but **these lists are not exhaustive**	
Factors indicating higher culpability 1. Threats to prevent the victim reporting an offence 2. Intimidating behaviour/threats of violence **Factor indicating greater degree of harm** 1. Victim is a child	

Sexual Offences Act 2003, s 66(1)

(1) A person commits an offence if—

    (a) he intentionally exposes his genitals, and

    (b) he intends that someone will see them and be caused alarm or distress.

ENGAGING IN SEXUAL ACTIVITY IN THE PRESENCE OF A CHILD

Either-way, 6 months/£5,000 (10 years).

Type/nature of activity	Starting Point	Range
Consensual intercourse or other forms of consensual penetration	2 years custody	1–4 years custody
Masturbation (of oneself or another person)	18 months custody	12 months–2 years 6 months custody
Consensual sexual touching involving naked genitalia	12 months custody	26 weeks–18 months custody
Consensual sexual touching of naked body parts but not involving naked genitalia	26 weeks custody	4 weeks–18 months custody

Sexual Offences Act 2003, s 10

(1) A person aged 18 or over (A) commits an offence if–

    (a) he intentionally engages in an activity,

    (b) the activity is sexual,

    (c) for the purpose of obtaining sexual gratification, he engages in it–

        (i) when another person (B) is present or is in a place from which A can be observed, and

        (ii) knowing or believing that B is aware, or intending that B should be aware, that he is engaging in it, and

    (d) either–

        (i) B is under 16 and A does not reasonably believe that B is 16 or over, or

        (ii) B is under 13.

EXTREME PORNOGRAPHY

Either-way, 6 months/£5,000 (3 years (2 years if the offence relates to an image that does not portray any act within section 63(7)(a) or (b))).

Sentencing: Whilst cases are fact specific low sentences have been passed in many recent cases and absent aggravating factors many cases may not cross the custody threshold, see in particular *Oliver* [2011] EWCA Crim 3114 and *Burns* [2012] EWCA Crim 192.

Criminal Justice and Immigration Act 2008, s 63

(1)　It is an offence for a person to be in possession of an extreme pornographic image.

(2)　An 'extreme pornographic image' is an image which is both—

　　(a)　pornographic, and
　　(b)　an extreme image.

(3)　An image is 'pornographic' if it is of such a nature that it must reasonably be assumed to have been produced solely or principally for the purpose of sexual arousal.

(4)　Where (as found in the person's possession) an image forms part of a series of images, the question whether the image is of such a nature as is mentioned in subsection (3) is to be determined by reference to—

　　(a)　the image itself, and
　　(b)　(if the series of images is such as to be capable of providing a context for the image) the context in which it occurs in the series of images.

(5)　So, for example, where—

　　(a)　an image forms an integral part of a narrative constituted by a series of images, and
　　(b)　having regard to those images as a whole, they are not of such a nature that they must reasonably be assumed to have been produced solely or principally for the purpose of sexual arousal, the image may, by virtue of being part of that narrative, be found not to be pornographic, even though it might have been found to be pornographic if taken by itself.

(6)　An 'extreme image' is an image which—

　　(a)　falls within subsection (7), and
　　(b)　is grossly offensive, disgusting or otherwise of an obscene character.

(7)　An image falls within this subsection if it portrays, in an explicit and realistic way, any of the following—

　　(a)　an act which threatens a person's life,
　　(b)　an act which results, or is likely to result, in serious injury to a person's anus, breasts or genitals,
　　(c)　an act which involves sexual interference with a human corpse, or
　　(d)　a person performing an act of intercourse or oral sex with an animal (whether dead or alive),and a reasonable person looking at the image would think that any such person or animal was real.

(8)　In this section 'image' means—

　　(a)　a moving or still image (produced by any means); or
　　(b)　data (stored by any means) which is capable of conversion into an image within paragraph (a).

(9)　In this section references to a part of the body include references to a part surgically constructed (in particular through gender reassignment surgery).

(10)　Proceedings for an offence under this section may not be instituted—

　　(a)　in England and Wales, except by or with the consent of the Director of Public Prosecutions ;

INCITING A CHILD TO ENGAGE IN SEXUAL ACTIVITY

Indictable only where the offence involves penetration (Life), otherwise either-way: 6 months/ £5,000 (14 years).

Type/nature of activity	Starting Point	Range
Contact between naked genitalia of offender and another part of victim's body, or causing two or more victims to engage in such activity with each other Contact with naked genitalia of victim by offender using part of the body other than the genitalia or an object, or causing two or more victims to engage in such activity with each other Contact between either the clothed genitalia of offender and naked genitalia of victim, between naked genitalia of offender and clothed genitalia of victim, or causing two or more victims to engage in such activity with each other	12 months custody	26 weeks–2 years custody
Contact between part of offender's body (other than the genitalia) with part of victim's body (other than the genitalia)	Community order	An appropriate non-custodial sentence*

* 'Non-custodial sentence' in this context suggests a community order or a fine. In most instances, an offence will have crossed the threshold for a community order. However, in accordance with normal sentencing practice, a court is not precluded from imposing a financial penalty where that is determined to be the appropriate sentence.

Sexual Offences Act 2003, s 10

(1)   A person aged 18 or over (A) commits an offence if–

    (a)   he intentionally causes or incites another person (B) to engage in an activity,

    (b)   the activity is sexual, and

    (c)   either–

        (i)   B is under 16 and A does not reasonably believe that B is 16 or over, or

        (ii)   B is under 13.

(2)   A person guilty of an offence under this section, if the activity caused or incited involved–

    (a)   penetration of B's anus or vagina,

    (b)   penetration of B's mouth with a person's penis,

    (c)   penetration of a person's anus or vagina with a part of B's body or by B with anything else, or

    (d)   penetration of a person's mouth with B's penis,

is liable, on conviction on indictment, to imprisonment for a term not exceeding 14 years.

INDECENT PHOTOGRAPHS OF CHILDREN

See also: Prohibited Images of Children.

Either-way, 6 months/£5,000 (10 years (5 if s 160)).

Photograph: Photograph includes tracing or other image derived in whole or part from a photograph or pseudo-photograph. **Indecent:** Whether a photograph is indecent depends on normally recognized standards of propriety. The age of the child may be relevant to the issue of indecency (*Owen* (1988) 88 Cr App R 291). **Making:** The opening of an email, or viewing of an image on the screen would amount to the making of an image if the defendant has the requisite knowledge of what he is doing. **Child:** A child is a person under 18 years of age (Sexual offences Act 2003, s 45). **Image levels:** The levels of seriousness (in ascending order) for sentencing for offences involving pornographic images are: Level 1: Images depicting erotic posing with no sexual activity. Level 2: Non-penetrative sexual activity between children, or solo masturbation by a child. Level 3: Non-penetrative sexual activity between adults and children. Level 4: Penetrative sexual activity involving a child or children, or both children and adults. Level 5: Sadism or penetration of, or by, an animal. Pseudo-photographs generally should be treated less seriously than real photographs. Starting points should be higher where the subject of the indecent photograph(s) is a child under 13.

Offence seriousness (culpability and harm)

A. Identify the appropriate starting point

Starting points based on first time offender pleading not guilty

Examples of nature of activity	Starting point	Range
Possession of a large amount of level 1 material and/or no more than a small amount of level 2, and the material is for personal use and has not been distributed or shown to others	Medium level community order	Band C fine to high level community order
Offender in possession of a large amount of material at level 2 or a small amount at level 3 Offender has shown or distributed material at level 1 on a limited scale Offender has exchanged images at level 1 or 2 with other collectors, but with no element of financial gain	12 weeks custody	4 to 26 weeks custody
Possession of a large quantity of level 3 material for personal use Possession of a small number of images at level 4 or 5 Large number of level 2 images shown or distributed Small number of level 3 images shown or distributed	26 weeks custody	4 weeks custody to Crown Court
Possession of a large quantity of level 4 or 5 material for personal use only Large number of level 3 images shown or distributed Offender traded material at levels 1–3 Level 4 or 5 images shown or distributed	Crown Court	26 weeks custody to Crown Court
Offender involved in the production of material of any level	Crown Court	Crown Court

---

Offence seriousness (culpability and harm)

B. Consider the effect of aggravating and mitigating factors

(other than those within examples above)

The following may be particularly relevant but **these lists are not exhaustive**

Factors indicating higher culpability	Factors indicating lower culpability
1. Collection is systematically stored or organized, indicating a sophisticated approach to trading or a high level of personal interest 2. Use of drugs, alcohol, or other substance to facilitate the offence of making or taking 3. Background of intimidation or coercion 4. Threats to prevent victim reporting the activity	1. A few images held solely for personal use 2. Images viewed but not stored 3. A few images held solely for personal use and it is established that the subject is aged 16 or 17 and that he or she was consenting

5. Threats to disclose victim's activity to friends/relatives
6. Financial or other gain

Factors indicating greater degree of harm

1. Images shown or distributed to others, especially children
2. Images stored, made available, or distributed in such a way that they can be inadvertently accessed by others

Criminal Justice Act 1988, s 160

(1) Subject to section 160A, it is an offence for a person to have any indecent photograph or pseudo-photograph of a child in his possession.

(2) Where a person is charged with an offence under subsection (1) above, it shall be a defence for him to prove—

(a) that he had a legitimate reason for having the photograph or pseudo-photograph in his possession; or

(b) that he had not himself seen the photograph or pseudo-photograph and did not know, nor had any cause to suspect, it to be indecent; or

(c) that the photograph or pseudo-photograph was sent to him without any prior request made by him or on his behalf and that he did not keep it for an unreasonable time.

Protection of Children Act 1978, s 1

(1) Subject to sections 1A and 1B, it is an offence for a person—

(a) to take, or permit to be taken or to make, any indecent photograph or pseudo-photograph of a child; or

(b) to distribute or show such indecent photographs or pseudo-photographs; or

(c) to have in his possession such indecent photographs or pseudo-photographs, with a view to their being distributed or shown by himself or others; or

(d) to publish or cause to be published any advertisement likely to be understood as conveying that the advertiser distributes or shows such indecent photographs or pseudo-photographs, or intends to do so.

(2) For purposes of this Act, a person is to be regarded as distributing an indecent photograph or pseudo-photograph if he parts with possession of it to, or exposes or offers it for acquisition by, another person.

(3) Proceedings for an offence under this Act shall not be instituted except by or with the consent of the Director of Public Prosecutions .

(4) Where a person is charged with an offence under subsection (1)(b) or (c), it shall be a defence for him to prove—

(a) that he had a legitimate reason for distributing or showing the photographs or pseudo-photographs or (as the case may be) having them in his possession; or

(b) that he had not himself seen the photographs or pseudo-photographs and did not know, nor had any cause to suspect, them to be indecent.

INTERCOURSE WITH AN ANIMAL

Either-way, 6 months/£5,000 (2 years).

Type/nature of activity	Starting point	Range
Basic offence as defined in the act, assuming no aggravating or mitigating factors	Community order	An appropriate non-custodial sentence

Additional aggravating factors:	Additional mitigating factors:
Recording activity and/or circulating pictures or videos	Symptom of isolation rather than depravity

Sexual Offences Act 2003, s 69

(1) A person commits an offence if–

(a) he intentionally performs an act of penetration with his penis,

(b) what is penetrated is the vagina or anus of a living animal, and

(c) he knows that, or is reckless as to whether, that is what is penetrated.

(2) A person (A) commits an offence if–

(a) A intentionally causes, or allows, A's vagina or anus to be penetrated,

(b) the penetration is by the penis of a living animal, and

(c) A knows that, or is reckless as to whether, that is what A is being penetrated by.

KERB CRAWLING, LOITERING, AND SOLICITING

Summary only, Fine £1,000 (for first offence fine is limited to £500 for an offence under section 1 Street Offences Act).

Persistent: Conduct is persistent if it takes place on two or more occasions in any period of three months; **Prostitution:** Any reference to a person loitering or soliciting for the purposes of prostitution is a reference to a person loitering or soliciting for the purposes of offering services as a prostitute; **Definitions:** "street" includes any bridge, road, lane, footway, subway, square, court, alley or passage, whether a thoroughfare or not, which is for the time being open to the public; and the doorways and entrances of premises abutting on a street (as hereinbefore defined), and any ground adjoining and open to a street, shall be treated as forming part of the street. *Other order:* Under the 1959 Act the court has the power to require the offender to attend (3) meetings in order to address the causes of his offending (Street Offences Act 1959, ss 1(2A) and 1A).

Sexual Offences Act 1985, ss 1(1) and 2(1)

1 Kerb-crawling

(1) A person commits an offence if he solicits another person (or different persons) for the purpose of prostitution—

(a) from a motor vehicle while it is in a street or public place; or

(b) in a street or public place while in the immediate vicinity of a motor vehicle that he has just got out of or off,

persistently or in such manner or in such circumstances as to be likely to cause annoyance to the person (or any of the persons) solicited, or nuisance to other persons in the neighbourhood.

2 Persistent soliciting

(1) A person commits an offence if in a street or public place he persistently solicits another person (or different persons) for the purpose of prostitution.

Street Offences Act 1959, s 1

(1) It shall be an offence for a person (whether male or female) persistently to loiter or solicit in a street or public place for the purpose of prostitution.

Sexual Offences Act 2003, s 51A

(1) It is an offence for a person in a street or public place to solicit another (B) for the purpose of obtaining B's sexual services as a prostitute.

(2) The reference to a person in a street or public place includes a person in a vehicle in a street or public place.

MEETING A CHILD FOLLOWING SEXUAL GROOMING

Either-way, 6 months/£5,000 (10 years).

Sentence: This offence will rarely if ever be suitable for summary trial.

Sexual Offences Act 2003, s 15

(1) A person aged 18 or over (A) commits an offence if–

   (a) A has met or communicated with another person (B) on at least two occasions and subsequently—

   (i) A intentionally meets B,

   (ii) A travels with the intention of meeting B in any part of the world or arranges to meet B in any part of the world, or

   (iii) B travels with the intention of meeting A in any part of the world,

   (b) A intends to do anything to or in respect of B, during or after the meeting mentioned in paragraph (a)(i) to (iii) and in any part of the world, which if done will involve the commission by A of a relevant offence,

   (c) B is under 16, and

   (d) A does not reasonably believe that B is 16 or over.

(2) In subsection (1)–

   (a) the reference to A having met or communicated with B is a reference to A having met B in any part of the world or having communicated with B by any means from, to or in any part of the world;

   (b) "relevant offence" means–

   (i) an offence under this Part,

   [...]

   (iii) anything done outside England and Wales which is not an offence within sub-paragraph (i) but would be an offence within sub-paragraph (i) if done in England and Wales.

OUTRAGING PUBLIC DECENCY

Triable either-way, 6 months/£5,000 (Life imprisonment as the offence is contrary to common law).

The offence is committed when a person an act which is lewd, obscene or disgusting in public, which has the effect of outraging public decency.

Obscene: In *Stanley* [1965] 2 QB 327 the court held: "The words "indecent or obscene" convey one idea, namely, offending against the recognised standards of propriety, indecent being at the lower end of the scale and obscene at the upper end of the scale." **Disgusting:** In *Choi* [1999] EWCA Crim 1279 the court held: "Disgusting conduct is conduct which fills the onlooker with loathing or extreme distaste or causes the onlooker extreme annoyance." **Witnesses:** At least 2 people must either witness or be in a position to witness the act (regardless of whether they actually did) (*Hamilton* [2007] EWCA Crim 2062). If there was no evidence that people might have seen the act then there can be no conviction, see for example *Rose v Director of Public Prosecutions* [2006] EWHC 852. **Outraging public decency:** In *Knuller v Director of Public Prosecutions* [1973] AC 435 it was held: "Indecency is not confined to sexual indecency: indeed it is difficult to find any limit short of saying that it includes anything which an ordinary decent man or woman would find to be shocking, disgusting and revolting. And "in public" also has a wide meaning. It appears to cover exhibitions in all places to which the public have access either as of right or gratis or on payment." **Intent:** There is no requirement to prove that the defendant intended to outrage public decency (*Gibson* [1990] 91 Cr App R 341).

PROHIBITED IMAGES OF CHILDREN

See also: Indecent Photographs of Children.

Either-way, 6 months/Unlimited fine (3 years).

Defence: See section 64(1). **Definitions:** See section 65.

Coroners and Justice Act 2009, ss 63, 64(1), 65

Section 63

(1) It is an offence for a person to be in possession of a prohibited image of a child.

(2) A prohibited image is an image which—

    (a) is pornographic,

    (b) falls within subsection (6), and

    (c) is grossly offensive, disgusting or otherwise of an obscene character.

(3) An image is 'pornographic' if it is of such a nature that it must reasonably be assumed to have been produced solely or principally for the purpose of sexual arousal.

(4) Where (as found in the person's possession) an image forms part of a series of images, the question whether the image is of such a nature as is mentioned in subsection (3) is to be determined by reference to—

    (a) the image itself, and

    (b) (if the series of images is such as to be capable of providing a context for the image) the context in which it occurs in the series of images.

(5) So, for example, where—

    (a) an image forms an integral part of a narrative constituted by a series of images, and

    (b) having regard to those images as a whole, they are not of such a nature that they must reasonably be assumed to have been produced solely or principally for the purpose of sexual arousal, the image may, by virtue of being part of that narrative, be found not to be pornographic, even though it might have been found to be pornographic if taken by itself.

(6) An image falls within this subsection if it—

    (a) is an image which focuses solely or principally on a child's genitals or anal region, or

    (b) portrays any of the acts mentioned in subsection (7).

(7) Those acts are—

    (a) the performance by a person of an act of intercourse or oral sex with or in the presence of a child;

    (b) an act of masturbation by, of, involving or in the presence of a child;

    (c) an act which involves penetration of the vagina or anus of a child with a part of a person's body or with anything else;

    (d) an act of penetration, in the presence of a child, of the vagina or anus of a person with a part of a person's body or with anything else;

(e) the performance by a child of an act of intercourse or oral sex with an animal (whether dead or alive or imaginary);

(f) the performance by a person of an act of intercourse or oral sex with an animal (whether dead or alive or imaginary) in the presence of a child.

(8) For the purposes of subsection (7), penetration is a continuing act from entry to withdrawal.

(9) Proceedings for an offence under subsection (1) may not be instituted—

(a) in England and Wales, except by or with the consent of the Director of Public Prosecutions .

Section 64

(1) Where a person is charged with an offence under section 62(1), it is a defence for the person to prove any of the following matters—

(a) that the person had a legitimate reason for being in possession of the image concerned;

(b) that the person had not seen the image concerned and did not know, nor had any cause to suspect, it to be a prohibited image of a child;

(c) that the person—

(i) was sent the image concerned without any prior request having been made by or on behalf of the person, and

(ii) did not keep it for an unreasonable time.

Section 65

(1) The following apply for the purposes of sections 62 to 64.

(2) "Image" includes—

(a) a moving or still image (produced by any means), or

(b) data (stored by any means) which is capable of conversion into an image within paragraph (a).

(3) "Image" does not include an indecent photograph, or indecent pseudophotograph, of a child.

(4) In subsection (3) "indecent photograph" and "indecent pseudo-photograph" are to be construed—

(a) in relation to England and Wales, in accordance with the Protection of Children Act 1978 (c. 37), and

(b) in relation to Northern Ireland, in accordance with the Protection of Children (Northern Ireland) Order 1978 (S.I. 1978/1047 (N.I. 17)).

(5) "Child", subject to subsection (6), means a person under the age of 18.

(6) Where an image shows a person the image is to be treated as an image of a child if—

(a) the impression conveyed by the image is that the person shown is a child, or

(b) the predominant impression conveyed is that the person shown is a child despite the fact that some of the physical characteristics shown are not those of a child.

(7) References to an image of a person include references to an image of an imaginary person.

(8) References to an image of a child include references to an image of an imaginary child.

PROSTITUTION, EXPLOITATION OF

Either-way, 6 months/£5,000 (7 years).

Sexual Offences Act 2003, ss 52 and 53.

Control: In *Massey* [2007] EWCA Crim 2664 it was held:

"In our judgment, "control" includes but is not limited to one who forces another to carry out the relevant activity. "Control" may be exercised in a variety of ways. It is not necessary or appropriate for us to seek to lay down a comprehensive definition of an ordinary English word. It is certainly enough if a defendant instructs or directs the other person to carry out the relevant activity or do it in a particular way. There may be a variety of reasons why the other person does as instructed. It may be because of physical violence or threats of violence. It may be because of emotional blackmail, for example, being told that "if you really loved me, you would do this for me". It may be because the defendant has a dominating personality and the woman who acts under his direction is psychologically damaged and fragile. It may be because the defendant is an older person, and the other person is emotionally immature. It may be because the defendant holds out the lure of gain, or the hope of a better life. Or there may be other reasons.

Sex workers are often vulnerable young women with disturbed backgrounds, who have never known a stable relationship or respect from others and are therefore prey to pimps. It is all too easy for such a person to fall under the influence of a dominant male, who exploits that vulnerability for financial gain. Exploitation of prostitution for financial gain is the broad mischief against which section 53 is aimed, whether or not it involves intimidation of the prostitute or prostitutes concerned. At one stage it was submitted by Mr Gerasimidis that some degree of absence of free will on the part of the prostitute is an essential ingredient of control. But on the reflection he withdrew that submission and, in our judgment, he was right to do so. If, for example, a group recruits young women from overseas and puts them to work in organised prostitution in the United Kingdom, we do not see any ground for saying that the prosecution would have to prove absence of free will in order to be able to show that the organisers were controlling the activities of the women for gain.

Although, as we have stressed, we do not seek to substitute alternative words for the word "control" which Parliament has used, our approach to the interpretation of the word in its statutory content is consistent also with its ordinary English usage. The Concise Oxford Dictionary defines "in control of" as "directing an activity". It defines the noun "control" as "power of directing, command". By contrast, it does not includes the words "compel, force or coerce", although they would doubtless be forms of control."

Offence seriousness (culpability and harm)		
A. Identify the appropriate starting point		
Starting points based on first time offender pleading not guilty		
Examples of nature of activity	**Starting point**	**Range**
No evidence victim was physically coerced or corrupted, and the involvement of the offender was minimal	Medium level community order	Band C fine to high level community order
No coercion or corruption but the offender is closely involved in the victim's prostitution	Crown Court	26 weeks custody to Crown Court
Evidence of physical and/or mental coercion	Crown Court	Crown Court

Offence seriousness (culpability and harm)	
B. Consider the effect of aggravating and mitigating factors	
(other than those within examples above)	
Factors indicating higher culpability	**Factor indicating lower culpability**
1. Background of threats, intimidation or coercion 2. Large-scale commercial operation 3. Substantial gain (in the region of £5,000 and up)	1. Offender also being controlled in prostitution and subject to threats or intimidation

4. Use of drugs, alcohol, or other substance to secure the victim's compliance
5. Abduction or detention
6. Threats to prevent the victim reporting the activity
7. Threats to disclose victim's activity to friends/ relatives

Factor indicating greater degree of harm
1. Induced dependency on drugs

PROSTITUTION, KEEPING A BROTHEL

Either-way, 6 months/£5,000 (7 years).

Sexual Offences Act 1956, ss 33 and 33A.

Brothel: The offering of sexual services by a couple, operating from a domestic dwelling, did not fall into the definition of a brothel (disorderly house) (*Court* [2012] EWCA Crim 133).

Offence seriousness (culpability and harm)		
A. Identify the appropriate starting point		
Starting points based on first time offender pleading not guilty		
Examples of nature of activity	**Starting point**	**Range**
Involvement of the offender was minimal	Medium level community order	Band C fine to high level community order
Offender is the keeper of a brothel and is personally involved in its management	Crown Court	26 weeks to Crown Court
Offender is the keeper of a brothel and has made substantial profits in the region of £5,000 and upwards	Crown Court	Crown Court

Offence seriousness (culpability and harm)	
B. Consider the effect of aggravating and mitigating factors	
(other than those within examples above)	
The following may be particularly relevant but **these lists are not exhaustive**	
Factors indicating higher culpability	**Factors indicating lower culpability**
1. Background of threats, intimidation, or coercion 2. Large-scale commercial operation 3. Personal involvement in the prostitution of others 4. Abduction or detention 5. Financial or other gain	1. Using employment as a route out of prostitution and not actively involved in exploitation 2. Coercion by third party

RAPE AND ASSAULT BY PENETRATION

Indictable only–Life imprisonment.

Sexual Offences Act 2003, ss 1, 2

1 Rape

(1) A person (A) commits an offence if–

(a) he intentionally penetrates the vagina, anus or mouth of another person (B) with his penis,

(b) B does not consent to the penetration, and

(c) A does not reasonably believe that B consents.

(2) Whether a belief is reasonable is to be determined having regard to all the circumstances, including any steps A has taken to ascertain whether B consents.

(3) Sections 75 and 76 apply to an offence under this section.

2 Assault by penetration

(1) A person (A) commits an offence if–

(a) he intentionally penetrates the vagina or anus of another person (B) with a part of his body or anything else,

(b) the penetration is sexual,

(c) B does not consent to the penetration, and

(d) A does not reasonably believe that B consents.

(2) Whether a belief is reasonable is to be determined having regard to all the circumstances, including any steps A has taken to ascertain whether B consents.

(3) Sections 75 and 76 apply to an offence under this section.

SEXUAL ASSAULT

Either-way - Save for sections 4, 8 and 9 where penetration is involved and the offences become triable only on indictment with maximum sentences of life for both sections 4 and 8, and 14 years for section 9.

6 months/£5,000 (10 years (ss 3, 4) 14 years (ss 7, 8) 14 years (s 9), save for section 4 and 8 where penetration is involved and the offence is triable only on indictment with a maximum of life imprisonment)).

Knowledge of age: If a defendant does not reasonably know, or is mistaken about the age of the child, it affords a defence to a section 7 offence (*B v Director of Public* Prosecutions [2000] AC 428). **Mode of offence:** When charging an offence under section 8 the prosecution should specify on which basis it was proceeding (s 8(2)) (*Grout* [2011] EWCA Crim 299).

Offence seriousness (culpability and harm)		
A. Identify the appropriate starting point		
Starting points based on first time offender pleading not guilty		
Examples of nature of activity	**Starting point**	**Range**
Contact between part of offender's body (other than the genitalia) with part of the victim's body (other than the genitalia)	26 weeks custody if the victim is under 13 Medium level community order if the victim is aged 13 or over	4 weeks custody to Crown Court Band C fine to 6 weeks custody

Contact between naked genitalia of offender and another part of victim's body Contact with naked genitalia of victim by offender using part of his or her body other than the genitalia, or an object Contact between either the clothed genitalia of offender and naked genitalia of victim or naked genitalia of offender and clothed genitalia of victim	Crown Court if the victim is under 13 Crown Court if the victim is aged 13 or over	Crown Court 26 weeks custody to Crown Court
Contact between naked genitalia of offender and naked genitalia, face, or mouth of the victim	Crown Court	Crown Court

Offence seriousness (culpability and harm)

B. Consider the effect of aggravating and mitigating factors

(other than those within examples opposite)

The following may be particularly relevant but **these lists are not exhaustive**

Factors indicating higher culpability	Factors indicating lower culpability
1. Background of intimidation or coercion	1. Youth and immaturity of the offender
2. Use of drugs, alcohol, or other substance to facilitate the offence	2. Minimal or fleeting contact
3. Threats to prevent the victim reporting the incident	*Where the victim is aged 16 or over*
	3. Victim engaged in consensual activity with the offender on the same occasion and immediately before the offence
4. Abduction or detention	
5. Offender aware that he or she is suffering from a sexually transmitted infection	*Where the victim is under 16*
6. Prolonged activity or contact	4. Sexual activity between two children (one of whom is the offender) was mutually agreed and experimental
Factors indicating greater degree of harm	
1. Offender ejaculated or caused victim to ejaculate	
2. Physical harm caused	

Sexual Offences Act 2003, ss 3(1)–(3), 4, 7(1), 8, and 9

3 Sexual assault

(1) A person (A) commits an offence if—

    (a) he intentionally touches another person (B),

    (b) the touching is sexual,

    (c) B does not consent to the touching, and

    (d) A does not reasonably believe that B consents.

(2) Whether a belief is reasonable is to be determined having regard to all the circumstances, including any steps A has taken to ascertain whether B consents.

(3) Sections 75 and 76 apply to an offence under this section.

4 Causing a person to engage in sexual activity without consent

(1) A person (A) commits an offence if—

    (a) he intentionally causes another person (B) to engage in an activity,

    (b) the activity is sexual,

    (c) B does not consent to engaging in the activity, and

    (d) A does not reasonably believe that B consents.

(2) Whether a belief is reasonable is to be determined having regard to all the circumstances, including any steps A has taken to ascertain whether B consents.

(3) Sections 75 and 76 apply to an offence under this section.

(4) A person guilty of an offence under this section, if the activity caused involved—

    (a) penetration of B's anus or vagina,

    (b) penetration of B's mouth with a person's penis,

    (c) penetration of a person's anus or vagina with a part of B's body or by B with anything else, or

    (d) penetration of a person's mouth with B's penis,

is liable, on conviction on indictment, to imprisonment for life.

7 Sexual assault of a child under 13

(1) A person commits an offence if—

    (a) he intentionally touches another person,

    (b) the touching is sexual, and

    (c) the other person is under 13.

8 Causing or inciting a child under 13 to engage in sexual activity

(1) A person commits an offence if—

    (a) he intentionally causes or incites another person (B) to engage in an activity,

    (b) the activity is sexual, and

    (c) B is under 13.

(2) A person guilty of an offence under this section, if the activity caused or incited involved—

    (a) penetration of B's anus or vagina,

    (b) penetration of B's mouth with a person's penis,

    (c) penetration of a person's anus or vagina with a part of B's body or by B with anything else, or

    (d) penetration of a person's mouth with B's penis,

is liable, on conviction on indictment, to imprisonment for life.

9 Sexual activity with a child

(1) A person aged 18 or over (A) commits an offence if—

    (a) he intentionally touches another person (B),

    (b) the touching is sexual, and

    (c) either—

        (i) B is under 16 and A does not reasonably believe that B is 16 or over, or

        (ii) B is under 13.

(2) A person guilty of an offence under this section, if the touching involved—

    (a) penetration of B's anus or vagina with a part of A's body or anything else,

    (b) penetration of B's mouth with A's penis,

    (c) penetration of A's anus or vagina with a part of B's body, or

    (d) penetration of A's mouth with B's penis.

SEXUAL ACTIVITY IN A PUBLIC LAVATORY

Summary only, 6 months/£5,000.

Offence seriousness (culpability and harm) A. Identify the appropriate starting point Starting points based on first time offender pleading not guilty		
Examples of nature of activity	Starting point	Range
Basic offence as defined in the Act, assuming no aggravating or mitigating factors	Band C fine	Band C fine
Offence with aggravating factors	Low level community order	Band C fine to medium level community order
Offence seriousness (culpability and harm) B. Consider the effect of aggravating and mitigating factors (other than those within examples above) The following may be particularly relevant but these lists are not exhaustive		
Factors indicating higher culpability 1. Intimidating behaviour/threats of violence to member(s) of the public 2. Blatant behaviour		

Sexual Offences Act 2003, s 71(1)–(2)

(1) A person commits an offence if—

(a) he is in a lavatory to which the public or a section of the public has or is permitted to have access, whether on payment or otherwise,

(b) he intentionally engages in an activity, and,

(c) the activity is sexual.

(2) For the purposes of this section, an activity is sexual if a reasonable person would, in all the circumstances but regardless of any person's purpose, consider it to be sexual.

SEXUAL PENETRATION OF A CORPSE

Either-way, 6 months/£5,000 (2 years).

Type/nature of activity	Starting point	Range
Repeat offending and/or aggravating factors	26 weeks custody	4 weeks–18 months custody
Basic offence as defined in the act, assuming no aggravating or mitigating factors	Community order	An appropriate non-custodial sentence

Additional aggravating factors: 1. Distress caused to relatives or friends of the deceased 2. Physical damage caused to body of the deceased 3. The corpse was that of a child 4. The offence was committed in a funeral home or mortuary	Additional mitigating factors:

TRAFFICKING FOR SEXUAL EXPLOITATION

Either-way, 6 months/£5,000 (14 years).

Sentence: This offence will rarely if ever be suitable for summary trial. See *R v P* and others [2009] EWCA Crim 2436. **Section 59A:** This section is not currently in force.

Sexual Offences Act 2003, ss 57–60

57 Trafficking into the UK for sexual exploitation

(1) A person commits an offence if he intentionally arranges or facilitates the arrival in, or the entry into, the United Kingdom of another person (B) and either–

   (a) he intends to do anything to or in respect of B, after B's arrival but in any part of the world, which if done will involve the commission of a relevant offence, or

   (b) he believes that another person is likely to do something to or in respect of B, after B's arrival but in any part of the world, which if done will involve the commission of a relevant offence.

58 Trafficking within the UK for sexual exploitation

(1) A person commits an offence if he intentionally arranges or facilitates travel within the United Kingdom by another person (B) and either–

   (a) he intends to do anything to or in respect of B, during or after the journey and in any part of the world, which if done will involve the commission of a relevant offence, or

   (b) he believes that another person is likely to do something to or in respect of B, during or after the journey and in any part of the world, which if done will involve the commission of a relevant offence.

59 Trafficking out of the UK for sexual exploitation

(1) A person commits an offence if he intentionally arranges or facilitates the departure from the United Kingdom of another person (B) and either–

   (a) he intends to do anything to or in respect of B, after B's departure but in any part of the world, which if done will involve the commission of a relevant offence, or

   (b) he believes that another person is likely to do something to or in respect of B, after B's departure but in any part of the world, which if done will involve the commission of a relevant offence.

59A Trafficking people for sexual exploitation

(1) A person ("A") commits an offence if A intentionally arranges or facilitates—

   (a) the arrival in, or entry into, the United Kingdom or another country of another person ("B"),

   (b) the travel of B within the United Kingdom or another country, or

   (c) the departure of B from the United Kingdom or another country,

with a view to the sexual exploitation of B.

(2) For the purposes of subsection (1)(a) and (c) A's arranging or facilitating is with a view to the sexual exploitation of B if, and only if—

   (a) A intends to do anything to or in respect of B, after B's arrival, entry or (as the case may be) departure but in any part of the world, which if done will involve the commission of a relevant offence, or

   (b) A believes that another person is likely to do something to or in respect of B, after B's arrival, entry or (as the case may be) departure but in any part of the world, which if done will involve the commission of a relevant offence.

(3) For the purposes of subsection (1)(b) A's arranging or facilitating is with a view to the sexual exploitation of B if, and only if—

(a) A intends to do anything to or in respect of B, during or after the journey and in any part of the world, which if done will involve the commission of a relevant offence, or

(b) A believes that another person is likely to do something to or in respect of B, during or after the journey and in any part of the world, which if done will involve the commission of a relevant offence.

(4) A person who is a UK national commits an offence under this section regardless of—

    (a) where the arranging or facilitating takes place, or

    (b) which country is the country of arrival, entry, travel or (as the case may be) departure.

(5) A person who is not a UK national commits an offence under this section if—

    (a) any part of the arranging or facilitating takes place in the United Kingdom, or

    (b) the United Kingdom is the country of arrival, entry, travel or (as the case may be) departure.

60 Sections 57 to 59: interpretation and jurisdiction

(1) In sections 57 to 59, "relevant offence" means–

    (a)   an offence under this Part,

    (b)   an offence under section 1(1)(a) of the Protection of Children Act 1978 (c. 37),

    (ba)   an offence under any provision of the Sexual Offences (Northern Ireland) Order 2008,

    (c)   an offence listed in Schedule 1 to the Criminal Justice (Children) (Northern Ireland) Order 1998 (S.I. 1998/1504 (N.I. 9)),

    (d)   an offence under Article 3(1)(a) of the Protection of Children (Northern Ireland) Order 1978 (S.I. 1978/1047 (N.I. 17)), or

    (e)   anything done outside England and Wales and Northern Ireland which is not an offence within any of paragraphs (a) to (d) but would be if done in England and Wales or Northern Ireland.

(2) Sections 57 to 59 apply to anything done whether inside or outside the United Kingdom.

VOYEURISM

Either-way, 6 months/£5,000 (2 years).

Breast: This does not include a man's breast (s 68(1)(a)) (*Bassett* [2009] 1 WLR 1032):

Offence seriousness (culpability and harm)		
A. Identify the appropriate starting point		
Starting points based on first time offender pleading not guilty		
Examples of nature of activity	**Starting point**	**Range**
Basic offence as defined in the Act, assuming no aggravating or mitigating factors, eg the offender spies through a hole he or she has made in a changing room wall	Low level community order	Band B fine to high level community order
Offence with aggravating factors such as recording sexual activity and showing it to others	26 weeks custody	4 weeks custody to Crown Court
Offence with serious aggravating factors such as recording sexual activity and placing it on a website or circulating it for commercial gain	Crown Court	26 weeks to Crown Court

Offence seriousness (culpability and harm)

B. Consider the effect of aggravating and mitigating factors

(other than those within examples above)

The following may be particularly relevant but **these lists are not exhaustive**

Factors indicating higher culpability

1. Threats to prevent the victim reporting an offence
2. Recording activity and circulating pictures/videos
3. Circulating pictures or videos for commercial gain—particularly if victim is vulnerable eg a child or a person with a mental or physical disorder

Factor indicating greater degree of harm

1. Distress to victim eg where the pictures/videos are circulated to people known to the victim

Sexual Offences Act 2003, ss 67(1)–(4), 68

(1) A person commits an offence if—

   (a) for the purpose of obtaining sexual gratification, he observes another person doing a private act, and

   (b) he knows that the other person does not consent to being observed for his sexual gratification.

(2) A person commits an offence if—

   (a) he operates equipment with the intention of enabling another person to observe, for the purpose of obtaining sexual gratification, a third person (B) doing a private act, and

   (b) he knows that B does not consént to his operating equipment with that intention.

(3) A person commits an offence if—

   (a) he records another person (B) doing a private act,

   (b) he does so with the intention that he or a third person will, for the purpose of obtaining sexual gratification, look at an image of B doing the act, and

   (c) he knows that B does not consent to his recording the act with that intention.

(4) A person commits an offence if he installs equipment, or constructs or adapts a structure or part of a structure, with the intention of enabling himself or another person to commit an offence under subsection (1).

68 Voyeurism: interpretation

(1) For the purposes of section 67, a person is doing a private act if the person is in a place which, in the circumstances, would reasonably be expected to provide privacy, and–

   (a) the person's genitals, buttocks or breasts are exposed or covered only with underwear,

   (b) the person is using a lavatory, or

   (c) the person is doing a sexual act that is not of a kind ordinarily done in public.

(2) In section 67, "structure" includes a tent, vehicle or vessel or other temporary or movable structure.

THEFT AND DISHONESTY

ABSTRACTING ELECTRICITY

Either-way, 6 months/£5,000 (5 years).

Theft Act 1968, s 13.

Offence seriousness (culpability and harm)		
A. Identify the appropriate starting point		
Starting points based on first time offender pleading not guilty		
Examples of nature of activity	Starting point	Range
Where the offence results in substantial commercial gain, a custodial sentence may be appropriate		
Offence involving evidence of planning and indication that the offending was intended to be continuing, such as using a device to interfere with the electricity meter or rewiring to bypass the meter	Medium level community order	Band A fine to high level community order

Offence seriousness (culpability and harm)	
B. Consider the effect of aggravating and mitigating factors	
(other than those within examples above)	
The following may be particularly relevant but **these lists are not exhaustive**	
Factor indicating greater degree of harm	
1. Risk of danger caused to property and/or life	

AGGRAVATED VEHICLE-TAKING

Either-way (summary only if damage only and does not exceed £5,000), **Section 12A(2)(a) and (b)**: 6 months/£5,000 (2 years (14 years if accident caused death)). Must endorse and disqualify for at least 12 months. Must disqualify for at least 2 years if offender has had 2 or more disqualifications for periods of 56 days or more in preceding 3 years. **Section 12A(2)(c) and (d)**: 6 months/£5,000 (2 years). Must endorse and disqualify for at least 12 months. Must disqualify for at least 2 years if offender has had 2 or more disqualifications for periods of 56 days or more in preceding 3 years.

Dangerous driving or accident causing injury:

Offence seriousness (culpability and harm)		
A. Identify the appropriate starting point		
Starting points based on first time offender pleading not guilty		
Example of nature of activity	Starting point	Range
Taken vehicle involved in single incident of bad driving where little or no damage or risk of personal injury	High level community order	Medium community order to 12 weeks custody
Taken vehicle involved in incident(s) involving excessive speed or showing off, especially on busy roads or in built-up area	18 weeks custody	12 to 26 weeks custody

Taken vehicle involved in prolonged bad driving involving deliberate disregard for safety of other	Crown Court	Crown Court

Offence seriousness (culpability and harm)
B. Consider the effect of aggravating and mitigating factors
(other than those within examples above)
The following may be particularly relevant but **these lists are not exhaustive**

Factors indicating higher culpability	
1. Disregarding warnings of others 2. Evidence of alcohol or drugs 3. Carrying out other tasks while driving 4. Tiredness 5. Trying to avoid arrest 6. Aggressive driving, such as driving much too close to vehicle in front, inappropriate attempts to overtake, or cutting in after overtaking **Factors indicating greater degree of harm** 1. Injury to others 2. Damage to other vehicle or property	

Damage caused:

Offence seriousness (culpability and harm)		
A. Identify the appropriate starting point		
Starting points based on first time offender pleading not guilty		
Examples of nature of activity	**Starting point**	**Range**
Exceeding authorized use of eg employer's or relative's vehicle; retention of hire car beyond return date; minor damage to taken vehicle	Medium level community order	Low level community order to high level community order
Greater damage to taken vehicle and/or moderate damage to another vehicle and/or moderate damage to another vehicle and/or property	High level community order	Medium level community order to 12 weeks custody
Vehicle taken as part of burglary or from private premises; severe damage	18 weeks custody	12 to 26 week custody (Crown Court if damage over £5,000)

Offence seriousness (culpability and harm)	
B. Consider the effect of aggravating and mitigating factors	
(other than those within examples above)	
The following may be particularly relevant but **these lists are not exhaustive**	

Factors indicating higher culpability	Factors indicating lower culpability
1. Vehicle deliberately damaged/destroyed 2. Offender under influence of alcohol/drugs **Factors indicating greater degree of harm** 1. Passenger(s) carried 2. Vehicle belonging to elderly or disabled person 3. Emergency service vehicle 4. Medium to large goods vehicle 5. Damage caused in moving traffic accident	1. Misunderstanding with owner 2. Damage resulting from actions of another (where this does not provide a defence)

ALCOHOL/TOBACCO, FRAUDULENTLY EVADE DUTY

Either-way, 6 months and/or 3 times the duty evaded or £5,000 fine, whichever is the greater (7 years).

Recklessness: It is not sufficient for the prosecution to show that the defendant was merely reckless (*Panayi* [1989] 1 WLR 187). **Nature of goods:** It is irrelevant that the defendant does not know the precise nature of the goods being imported (*Shivpuri* [1987] AC 1). **Burden of proof:** The burden of proving that duty has been paid falls on the defendant (s 154). **Ancillary order:** The court may make a financial reporting order on conviction. **Appeal:** The prosecution has the right to appeal sentence (*Customs and Excise Commissioners v Brunt* (1998) 163 JP 161).

Sentencing: See Appendix 10: Fraud Guideline.

BURGLARY

Either-way, 6 months/£5,000 (10 years, 14 years if dwelling). Offence is indictable only and must be sent to the Crown Court if:

(1)   D was 18 or over when he committed the offence;
(2)   Offence committed the offence on or after 1 December 1999;
(3)   D had previously been convicted of two other domestic burglary offences in England and Wales; one of those offences has been committed after conviction for the other; and both of the previous domestic burglaries had been committed on or after 1 December 1999.

Or, Any person was subjected to violence or the threat of violence: Magistrates' Courts Act 1980, Sch 1.

Entry: Entry can be partial (*Brown* [1985] Crim LR 212), and can be effected without any part of the body entering the building (for example, cane and hook burglaries). **Building:** 'Building' is a factual not a legal issue and will depend on all of the circumstances (*Brutus v Cozens* [1973] AC 854). **Reckless trespass:** Trespass can be committed knowingly or recklessly (*Collins* [1973] QB 100). **Dwelling:** A communal landing in a block of flats is not a dwelling (Rukwira v *Director of Public Prosecutions* [1993] Crim LR 882, nor is a communal laundry room (*Le Vine* [2010] EWCA Crim 1128). A police cell is not a dwelling *CF* [2006] EWCA Crim 3323.

Non-dwelling:

Step one: Determine the offence category

Category 1: Greater harm and higher culpability

Category 2: Greater harm and lower culpability or lesser harm and higher culpability

Category 3: lesser harm and lower culpability

Factors indicating greater harm	Factors indicating higher culpability
Theft of/damage to property causing a significant degree of loss to the victim (whether economic, commercial or personal value)	Premises or victim deliberately targeted (to include pharmacy or doctor's surgery and targeting due to vulnerability of victim or hostility based on disability, race, sexual orientation and so forth)
Soiling, ransacking or vandalism of property	A significant degree of planning or organisation
Victim on the premises (or returns) while offender present	
Trauma to the victim, beyond the normal inevitable consequence of intrusion and theft	Knife or other weapon carried (where not charged separately)
Violence used or threatened against victim	Equipped for burglary (for example, implements carried and/or use of vehicle)
Context of general public disorder	Member of a group or gang

Factors indicating lesser harm	Factors indicating lower culpability
Nothing stolen or only property of very low value to the victim (whether economic, commercial or personal) Limited damage or disturbance to property	Offence committed on impulse, with limited intrusion into property Offender exploited by others Mental disorder or learning disability, where linked to the commission of the offence

Step 2: Starting point and category range

Offence category	Starting point	Category range
Category 1	Crown court	Crown court
Category 2	18 weeks' custody	Low level community order–crown court (51 weeks' custody)
Category 3	Medium level community order	Band B fine–18 weeks' custody

Factors increasing seriousness	Factors reducing seriousness or reflecting personal mitigation
Statutory aggravating factors: Previous convictions, having regard to a) the nature of the offence to which the conviction relates and its relevance to the current offence; and b) the time that has elapsed since the conviction Offence committed whilst on bail **Other aggravating factors include:** Offence committed at night, particularly where staff present or likely to be present Abuse of a position of trust Gratuitous degradation of the victim Any steps taken to prevent the victim reporting the incident or obtaining assistance and/or from assisting or supporting the prosecution Established evidence of community impact Commission of offence whilst under the influence of alcohol or drugs Failure to comply with current court orders Offence committed whilst on licence Offences Taken Into Consideration (TICs)	Offender has made voluntary reparation to the victim Subordinate role in a group or gang No previous convictions or no relevant/recent convictions Remorse Good character and/or exemplary conduct Determination, and/or demonstration of steps taken to address addiction or offending behaviour Serious medical conditions requiring urgent, intensive or long-term treatment Age and/or lack of maturity where it affects the responsibility of the offender Lapse of time since the offence where this is not the fault of the offender Mental disorder or learning disability, where not linked to the commission of the offence Sole or primary carer for dependent relatives

Additional steps:

Consider any factors which indicate a reduction, such as assistance to the prosecution; reduction for guilty plea; dangerousness; totality principle; compensation and ancillary orders; reasons; consideration for remand time.

Dwelling:

Step one: Determine the offence category

Category 1: Greater harm and higher culpability

Category 2: Greater harm and lower culpability or lesser harm and higher culpability

Category 3: lesser harm and lower culpability

Factors indicating greater harm	Factors indicating higher culpability
Theft of/damage to property causing a significant degree of loss to the victim (whether economic, sentimental or personal value) Soiling, ransacking or vandalism of property Occupier at home (or returns home) while offender present Trauma to the victim, beyond the normal inevitable consequence of intrusion and theft Violence used or threatened against victim Context of general public disorder	Victim or premises deliberately targeted (for example, due to vulnerability or hostility based on disability, race, sexual orientation) A significant degree of planning or organisation Knife or other weapon carried (where not charged separately) Equipped for burglary (for example, implements carried and/or use of vehicle) Member of a group or gang
Factors indicating lesser harm	**Factors indicating lower culpability**
Nothing stolen or only property of very low value to the victim (whether economic, sentimental or personal) Limited damage or disturbance to propert	Offence committed on impulse, with limited intrusion into property Offender exploited by others Mental disorder or learning disability, where linked to the commission of the offence

Step 2: Starting point and category range

Offence category	Starting point	Category range
Category 1	Crown court	Crown court
Category 2	1 year's custody	High level community order–Crown Court (2 years' custody)
Category 3	High level community order	Low level community order–26 weeks' custody

Factors increasing seriousness	Factors reducing seriousness or reflecting personal mitigation
Statutory aggravating factors: Previous convictions, having regard to a) the nature of the offence to which the conviction relates and its relevance to the current offence; and b) the time that has elapsed since the conviction* Offence committed whilst on bail **Other aggravating factors include:** Child at home (or returns home) when offence committed Offence committed at night Gratuitous degradation of the victim Any steps taken to prevent the victim reporting the incident or obtaining assistance and/or from assisting or supporting the prosecution Victim compelled to leave their home (in particular victims of domestic violence)	Offender has made voluntary reparation to the victim Subordinate role in a group or gang No previous convictions or no relevant/recent convictions Remorse Good character and/or exemplary conduct Determination, and/or demonstration of steps taken to address addiction or offending behaviour Serious medical conditions requiring urgent, intensive or long-term treatment Age and/or lack of maturity where it affects the responsibility of the offender Lapse of time since the offence where this is not the fault of the offender Mental disorder or learning disability, where not linked to the commission of the offence

Established evidence of community impact	Sole or primary carer for dependent relatives
Commission of offence whilst under the influence of alcohol or drugs	
Failure to comply with current court orders	
Offence committed whilst on licence	
Offences Taken Into Consideration (TICs)	

* Where sentencing an offender for a qualifying third domestic burglary, the Court must apply Section 111 of the Powers of the Criminal Courts (Sentencing) Act 2000 and impose a custodial term of at least three years, unless it is satisfied that there are particular circumstances which relate to any of the offences or to the offender which would make it unjust to do so.

Additional steps:

Consider any factors which indicate a reduction, such as assistance to the prosecution; reduction for guilty plea; dangerousness; totality principle; compensation and ancillary orders; reasons; consideration for remand time.

Theft Act 1968, s 9(1)–(2)

(1) A person is guilty of burglary if—

    (a) he enters any building or part of a building as a trespasser and with intent to commit any such offence as is mentioned in subsection (2) below; or

    (b) having entered any building or part of a building as a trespasser he steals or attempts to steal anything in the building or that part of it or inflicts or attempts to inflict on any person therein any grievous bodily harm.

(2) The offences referred to in subsection (1) (a) above are offences of stealing anything in the building or part of a building in question, of inflicting on any person therein any grievous bodily harm therein, and of doing unlawful damage to the building or anything therein.

COUNTERFEIT CURRENCY

Either-way, 6 months/£5,000 (10 years (section 15(1) and 16(1); 2 years section 15(2) and 16(2)).

Sentence: Custody is almost inevitable, with sentences of between 3 and 24 months for possession or passing of a low number of notes (eg *Wake* (1992) 13 Cr App R (S) 422, *Dickens* (1993) 14 Cr App R (S) 76, *Luxford* [1996] 1 Cr App R (S) 186, *Howard* (1986) 82 Cr App R 262). Where an offender can demonstrate that the notes were of poor quality and that he did not intend to pass them, a community penalty might be appropriate (*Leslie* [2009] EWCA Crim 884).

Forgery and Counterfeiting Act 1981, ss 15-16

15.— Offences of passing etc. counterfeit notes and coins.

(1) It is an offence for a person—

    (a) to pass or tender as genuine any thing which is, and which he knows or believes to be, a counterfeit of a currency note or of a protected coin; or

    (b) to deliver to another any thing which is, and which he knows or believes to be, such a counterfeit, intending that the person to whom it is delivered or another shall pass or tender it as genuine.

(2) It is an offence for a person to deliver to another, without lawful authority or excuse, any thing which is, and which he knows or believes to be, a counterfeit of a currency note or of a protected coin.

16.— Offences involving the custody or control of counterfeit notes and coins.

(1) It is an offence for a person to have in his custody or under his control any thing which is; and which he knows or believes to be, a counterfeit of a currency note or of a protected coin, intending either to pass or tender it as genuine or to deliver it to another with the intention that he or another shall pass or tender it as genuine.

(2) It is an offence for a person to have in his custody or under his control, without lawful authority or excuse, any thing which is, and which he knows or believes to be, a counterfeit of a currency note or of a protected coin.

(3) It is immaterial for the purposes of subsections (1) and (2) above that a coin or note is not in a fit state to be passed or tendered or that the making or counterfeiting of a coin or note has not been finished or perfected.

DISHONESTLY OBTAINING TELECOMMUNICATIONS SERVICES

Either-way, 6 months/£5,000 (5 years).

Sentence: Using a device to make free calls – *Nadig* (1993) 14 Cr App R (S) 49:

"In our view, it was wrong in principle to sentence each of these first offenders to a prison sentence, suspended or otherwise, for the offence, and in any event to do so without first obtaining social enquiry reports. If the judge relied on the electricity abstraction cases to which we have been referred in the grounds of appeal, he was wrong to do so in the circumstances of this case, which concerned one incident of dishonesty, as distinct from a course of conduct. Those cases may have some relevance to the fraudulent use of the telephone where it has been proved to have taken place over a period of time. But that is not this case. The appellants, all of them in their different ways, but particularly the first and second, have suffered very considerably in the period since conviction and sentence nearly a year ago. It may well be that at the time a fine appropriate to their means could have been properly considered by the court to mark its disapproval of such offences. But time has moved on and the circumstances of the appellants have changed. One additional matter, so far as the first and second appellants are concerned, is that there has been a strain upon the marriage, no doubt contributed to by the inability of the first appellant to work, and the second appellant has returned, temporarily, to Tanzania. The appropriate course now, in our view, is as follows: The prison sentences and the fines should all be quashed, and each appellant should be conditionally discharged for a period of one year and required to pay the order for costs imposed by the learned judge".

At the other end of the scale in *Stephens* [2002] 2 Cr App R (S) 67 a sentence of 12 months was imposed on appeal for an offence which was the precursor to section 126 (Telecommunications Act 1984, s 42A–now repealed), the appellant having 'chipped' telephones so as to enable free calls (Guilty plea; approx. 75 phones, profit of £500 and lost call revenue circa £11,000).

Communications Act 2003, ss 125, 126

125 Dishonestly obtaining electronic communications services

(1) A person who—

(a) dishonestly obtains an electronic communications service, and

(b) does so with intent to avoid payment of a charge applicable to the provision of that service,

is guilty of an offence.

(2) It is not an offence under this section to obtain a service mentioned in section 297(1) of the Copyright, Designs and Patents Act [...].

126 Possession or supply of apparatus etc. for contravening s. 125

(1) A person is guilty of an offence if, with an intention falling within subsection (3), he has in his possession or under his control anything that may be used—

    (a) for obtaining an electronic communications service; or

    (b) in connection with obtaining such a service.

(2) A person is guilty of an offence if—

    (a) he supplies or offers to supply anything which may be used as mentioned in subsection (1); and

    (b) he knows or believes that the intentions in relation to that thing of the person to whom it is supplied or offered fall within subsection (3).

(3) A person's intentions fall within this subsection if he intends—

    (a) to use the thing to obtain an electronic communications service dishonestly;

    (b) to use the thing for a purpose connected with the dishonest obtaining of such a service;

    (c) dishonestly to allow the thing to be used to obtain such a service; or

    (d) to allow the thing to be used for a purpose connected with the dishonest obtaining of such a service.

(4) An intention does not fall within subsection (3) if it relates exclusively to the obtaining of a service mentioned in section 297(1) of the Copyright, Designs and Patents Act 1988.

FALSE ACCOUNTING

Either-way, 6 months/£5,000 (7 years).

Sentencing: See Appendix 10: Fraud Guideline.

Theft Act 1968, s 17(1)

(1) Where a person dishonestly, with a view to gain for himself or another or with intent to cause loss to another, —

    (a) destroys, defaces, conceals or falsifies any account or any record or document made or required for any accounting purpose; or

    (b) in furnishing information for any purpose produces or makes use of any account, or any such record or document as aforesaid, which to his knowledge is or may be misleading, false or deceptive in a material particular.

FOUND ON ENCLOSED PREMISES

Summary only, 3 months/£1,000.

Vagrancy Act 1824, s 4

Enclosed area: A university campus encompassing a large geographic area did not fall within the definition of enclosed area (*Akhurst v Director of Public Prosecutions* [2009] EWHC 806 (Admin)). An office within a building is not an enclosed area as parliament intended it to mean an area in the open air (*Talbot v Oxford City Magistrates' Court* (2009) 173 JP 499).

FRAUD

Either-way, 6 months/£5,000 (10 years).

Sentencing: See Appendix 10: Fraud Guideline.

Fraud Act 2006, ss 1(1)–(2), 2, 3, and 4

1 Fraud

(1) A person is guilty of fraud if he is in breach of any of the sections listed in subsection (2) (which provide for different ways of committing the offence).

(2) The sections are—

(a) section 2 (fraud by false representation),

(b) section 3 (fraud by failing to disclose information), and

(c) section 4 (fraud by abuse of position).

2 Fraud by false representation

(1) A person is in breach of this section if he—

(a) dishonestly makes a false representation, and

(b) intends, by making the representation—

(i) to make a gain for himself or another, or

(ii) to cause loss to another or to expose another to a risk of loss.

(2) A representation is false if—

(a) it is untrue or misleading, and

(b) the person making it knows that it is, or might be, untrue or misleading.

(3) 'Representation' means any representation as to fact or law, including a representation as to the state of mind of—

(a) the person making the representation, or

(b) any other person.

(4) A representation may be express or implied.

(5) For the purposes of this section a representation may be regarded as made if it (or anything implying it) is submitted in any form to any system or device designed to receive, convey or respond to communications (with or without human intervention).

3 Fraud by failing to disclose information

(1) A person is in breach of this section if he—

(a) dishonestly fails to disclose to another person information which he is under a legal duty to disclose, and

(b) intends, by failing to disclose the information—

(i) to make a gain for himself or another, or

(ii) to cause loss to another or to expose another to a risk of loss.

4 Fraud by abuse of position

(1) A person is in breach of this section if he—

(a) occupies a position in which he is expected to safeguard, or not to act against, the financial interests of another person,

(b) dishonestly abuses that position, and

(c) intends, by means of the abuse of that position—

(i) to make a gain for himself or another, or

(ii) to cause loss to another or to expose another to a risk of loss.

(2) A person may be regarded as having abused his position even though his conduct consisted of an omission rather than an act.

FRAUDULENTLY RECEIVING PROGRAMMES

Summary only, Fine £5,000.

It is not an offence for a person to use a decoder card in order to receive from a European broadcaster not based in the UK, satellite broadcasts that the complainant had the exclusive rights to broadcast in the UK (*Murphy v Media Protection* Services [2012] EWHC 466 (Admin)).

Copyright, Designs and Patents Act 1988, s 297

(1) A person who dishonestly receives a programme included in a broadcasting service provided from a place in the United Kingdom with intent to avoid payment of any charge applicable to the reception of the programme commits an offence and is liable on summary conviction to a fine not exceeding level 5 on the standard scale.

(2) Where an offence under this section committed by a body corporate is proved to have been committed with the consent or connivance of a director, manager, secretary or other similar officer of the body, or a person purporting to act in any such capacity, he as well as the body corporate is guilty of the offence and liable to be proceeded against and punished accordingly.

In relation to a body corporate whose affairs are managed by its members "director" means a member of the body corporate.

GOING EQUIPPED FOR THEFT

Either-way, 6 months/£5,000 (3 years).

Offence seriousness (culpability and harm)		
A. Identify the appropriate starting point		
Starting points based on first time offender pleading not guilty		
Examples of nature of activity	**Starting point**	**Range**
Possession of items for theft from shop or of vehicle	Medium level community order	Band C fine to high level community order
Possession of items for burglary, robbery	High level community order	Medium level community order to Crown Court

Offence seriousness (culpability and harm)	
B. Consider the effect of aggravating and mitigating factors	
(other than those within examples above)	
The following may be particularly relevant but **these lists are not exhaustive**	
Factors indicating higher culpability	
1. Circumstances suggest offender equipped for particularly serious offence	
2. Items to conceal identity	

Theft Act 1968, s 25

(1) A person shall be guilty of an offence if, when not at his place of abode, he has with him any article for use in the course of or in connection with any burglary or theft.

(2) A person guilty of an offence under this section shall on conviction on indictment be liable to imprisonment for a term not exceeding three years.

(3) Where a person is charged with an offence under this section, proof that he had with him any article made or adapted for use in committing a burglary or theft shall be evidence that he had it with him for such use.

(4) ...

(5) For purposes of this section an offence under section 12(1) of this Act of taking a conveyance shall be treated as theft.

HANDLING STOLEN GOODS

Either-way, 6 months/£5,000 (14 years).

Suspicion: Mere suspicion that goods are stolen will not suffice. In *Hall* (1985) 81 Cr App R 260, belief was said to be present when someone thought: 'I cannot say for certain that those goods are stolen, but there can be no other reasonable conclusion in the light of all the circumstances of all I have heard and seen'. Similarly, if the person admits that 'my brain is telling me [they are stolen] despite what I have heard'. **Adequate consideration:** If the defendant argues that he has paid an adequate consideration for the goods, it falls upon the prosecution to disprove (*Hogan v Director of Public Prosecutions* [2007] EWHC 978 (Admin)).

Offence seriousness (culpability and harm)
A. Identify the appropriate starting point
Starting points based on first time offender pleading not guilty

Examples of nature of activity	Starting point	Range
Property worth £1,000 or less acquired for offender's own use	Band B fine	Band B fine to low level community order
Property worth £1,000 or less acquired for resale; or Property worth more than £1,000 acquired for offender's own use; or Presence of at least one aggravating factor listed below—regardless of value	Medium level community order	Low level community order to 12 weeks custody Note: the custody threshold is likely to be passed if the offender has a record of dishonesty offences
Sophisticated offending; or Presence of at least two aggravating factors listed below	12 weeks custody	6 weeks custody to Crown Court
Offence committed in context of Offender acts as organizer/distributor of proceeds of crime; or Offender makes self available to other criminals as willing to handle the proceeds of thefts or burglaries; or Offending highly organized, professional; or Particularly serious original offence, such as armed robbery	Crown Court	Crown Court

Offence seriousness (culpability and harm)
B. Consider the effect of aggravating and mitigating factors
(other than those within examples above)
The following may be particularly relevant but **these lists are not exhaustive**

Factors indicating higher culpability	Factors indicating lower culpability
1. Closeness of offender to primary offence Closeness may be geographical, arising from presence at or near the primary offence when it was committed, or temporal, where the handler instigated or encouraged the primary offence beforehand, or, soon after, provided a safe haven or route or disposal 2. High level of profit made or expected by offender	1. Little or no benefit to offender 2. Voluntary restitution to victim **Factor indicating lower degree of harm** 1. Low value of goods

Factors indicating greater degree of harm	
1. Seriousness of the primary offence, including domestic burglary	
2. High value of goods to victim, including sentimental value	
3. Threats of violence or abuse of power by offender over others, such as an adult commissioning criminal activity by children, or a drug dealer pressurizing addicts to steal in order to pay for their habit	

Theft Act 1968, s 22(1)

(1) A person handles stolen goods if (otherwise than in the course of the stealing) knowing or believing them to be stolen goods he dishonestly receives the goods, or dishonestly undertakes or assists in their retention, removal, disposal or realisation by or for the benefit of another person, or if he arranges to do so.

INCOME TAX EVASION

Either-way, 6 months/£5,000 (7 years).

Sentencing: See Appendix 10: Fraud Guideline.

Finance Act 2000, s 144

A person commits an offence if he is knowingly concerned in the fraudulent evasion of income tax by him or any other person.

MAKING, ADAPTING, SUPPLYING, OR OFFERING TO SUPPLY ARTICLES FOR FRAUD

Either-way, 6 months/£5,000 (10 years).

Sentencing: See Appendix 10: Fraud Guideline.

Fraud Act 2006, s 7

(1) A person is guilty of an offence if he makes, adapts, supplies or offers to supply any article—

    (a) knowing that it is designed or adapted for use in the course of or in connection with fraud, or intending it to be used to commit, or assist in the commission of, fraud.

MAKING OFF WITHOUT PAYMENT

Either-way, 6 months/£5,000 (2 years).

Intention: The intention to avoid making payment means a permanent intention not to pay, so a person who genuinely disputes a bill and challenges someone to bring legal action, cannot be said to have committed an offence.

Offence seriousness (culpability and harm)		
A. Identify the appropriate starting point		
Starting points based on first time offender pleading not guilty		
Examples of nature of activity	**Starting point**	**Range**
Single offence committed by an offender acting alone with evidence of little or no planning, goods or services worth less than £200	Band C fine	Band A fine to high level community order
Offence displaying one or more of the following: – offender acting in unison with others – evidence of planning – offence part of a 'spree' – intimidation of victim – goods or services worth £200 or more	Medium level community order	Low level community order to 12 weeks custody

Theft Act 1978, s 3

(1) Subject to subsection (3) below, a person who, knowing that payment on the spot for any goods supplied or service done is required or expected from him, dishonestly makes off without having paid as required or expected and with intent to avoid payment of the amount due shall be guilty of an offence.

(2) For purposes of this section 'payment on the spot' includes payment at the time of collecting goods on which work has been done or in respect of which service has been provided.

(3) Subsection (1) above shall not apply where the supply of the goods or the doing of the service is contrary to law, or where the service done is such that payment is not legally enforceable.

MOTOR VEHICLE INTERFERENCE

Summary only, 3 months/£2,500.

Interference: Looking into cars and touching door handles is insufficient to convict for this offence (*Warren v Metropolitan Police* [1982] Crim LR 831).

Offence seriousness (culpability and harm)		
A. Identify the appropriate starting point		
Starting points based on first time offender pleading not guilty		
Examples of nature of activity	**Starting point**	**Range**
Trying door handles; no entry gained to vehicle; no damage caused	Band C fine	Band A fine to low level community order
Entering vehicle, little or no damage caused	Medium level community order	Band C fine to high level community order
Entering vehicle, with damage caused	High level community order	Medium level community order to 12 weeks custody

Offence seriousness (culpability and harm)
B. Consider the effect of aggravating and mitigating factors
(other than those within examples above)
The following may be particularly relevant but **these lists are not exhaustive**

Factor indicating higher culpability
1. Targeting vehicle in dark/isolated location
Factors indicating greater degree of harm
1. Emergency services vehicle
2. Disabled driver's vehicle
3. Part of series

Criminal Attempts Act 1981, s 9(1)–(2)

(1) A person is guilty of the offence of vehicle interference if he interferes with a motor vehicle or trailer or with anything carried in or on a motor vehicle or trailer with the intention that an offence specified in subsection (2) below shall be committed by himself or some other person.

(2) The offences mentioned in subsection (1) above are—

    (a) theft of the motor vehicle or trailer or part of it;

    (b) theft of anything carried in or on the motor vehicle or trailer; and

    (c) an offence under section 12(1) of the Theft Act 1968 (taking and driving away without consent);

and, if it is shown that a person accused of an offence under this section intended that one of those offences should be committed, it is immaterial that it cannot be shown which it was.

MOBILE PHONE RE-PROGRAMMING

Both offences either-way, 6 months/£5,000 (5 years).

Mobile Telephones (Re-programming) Act 2002, ss 1, 2

1 Re-programming mobile telephone etc.

(1) A person commits an offence if—

    (a) he changes a unique device identifier,

    (b) he interferes with the operation of a unique device identifier,

    (c) he offers or agrees to change, or interfere with the operation of, a unique device identifier, or

    (d) he offers or agrees to arrange for another person to change, or interfere with the operation of, a unique device identifier.

(2) A unique device identifier is an electronic equipment identifier which is unique to a mobile wireless communications device.

(3) But a person does not commit an offence under this section if—

    (a) he is the manufacturer of the device, or

    (b) he does the act mentioned in subsection (1) with the written consent of the manufacturer of the device.

2 Possession or supply of anything for re-programming purposes

(1) A person commits an offence if—

    (a) he has in his custody or under his control anything which may be used for the purpose of changing or interfering with the operation of a unique device identifier, and

    (b) he intends to use the thing unlawfully for that purpose or to allow it to be used unlawfully for that purpose.

(2) A person commits an offence if—

    (a) he supplies anything which may be used for the purpose of changing or interfering with the operation of a unique device identifier, and

(b) he knows or believes that the person to whom the thing is supplied intends to use it unlawfully for that purpose or to allow it to be used unlawfully for that purpose.

(3) A person commits an offence if—

    (a) he offers to supply anything which may be used for the purpose of changing or interfering with the operation of a unique device identifier, and

    (b) he knows or believes that the person to whom the thing is offered intends if it is supplied to him to use it unlawfully for that purpose or to allow it to be used unlawfully for that purpose.

(4) A unique device identifier is an electronic equipment identifier which is unique to a mobile wireless communications device.

(5) A thing is used by a person unlawfully for a purpose if in using it for that purpose he commits an offence under section 1.

OBTAINING SERVICES DISHONESTLY

Either-way, 6 months/£5,000 (5 years).

Sentencing: The offence of obtaining services dishonestly may be committed in circumstances that otherwise could be charged as an offence contrary to section 1 of the Fraud Act 2006 or may be more akin to making of without payment, contrary to section 3 of the Theft Act 1978. For this reason, it has not been included specifically within any of the guidelines for fraud, and one of the following approaches should be used:

- where it involves conduct which can be characterized as a fraud offence (such as obtaining credit through fraud or payment card fraud), the court should apply the guideline for the relevant type of fraud (see Appendix 10); or
- where the conduct could be characterized as *making of without payment* (ie, where an offender, knowing that payment on the spot for any goods supplied or service done is required or expected, dishonestly makes of without having paid and with intent to avoid payment), the guideline for that offence should be used.

Fraud Act 2006, s 11(1)–(2)

(1) A person is guilty of an offence under this section if he obtains services for himself or another—

    (a) by a dishonest act, and

    (b) in breach of subsection (2).

(2) A person obtains services in breach of this subsection if—

    (a) they are made available on the basis that payment has been, is being or will be made for or in respect of them,

    (b) he obtains them without any payment having been made for or in respect of them or without payment having been made in full, and

    (c) when he obtains them, he knows—

        (i) that they are being made available on the basis described in paragraph (a), or

        (ii) that they might be,

but intends that payment will not be made, or will not be made in full.

POSSESSION OF ARTICLES FOR FRAUD

Either-way, 6 months/£5,000 (5 years).

Sentencing: See Appendix 10: Fraud Guideline.

Fraud Act 2006, s 6

A person is guilty of an offence if he has in his possession or under his control any article for use in the course of or in connection with any fraud.

POSSESSION OF FALSE IDENTITY DOCUMENTS

Either-way, 6 months/£5,000 (2 years).

If the document itself is false then it is no defence in a case where the document was being used for establishing a registrable fact, that it bore the correct details of the defendant (*Jamalov* [2010] EWCA Crim 309).

Offence seriousness (culpability and harm)		
A. Identify the appropriate starting point		
Starting points based on first time offender pleading not guilty		
Examples of nature of activity	**Starting point**	**Range**
Single document possessed	Medium level community order	Band C fine to high level community order
Small number of documents, no evidence of dealing	12 weeks custody	6 weeks custody to Crown Court
Considerable number of documents possessed, evidence of involvement in larger operation	Crown Court	Crown Court

Offence seriousness (culpability and harm)	
B. Consider the effect of aggravating and mitigating factors	
(other than those within examples above)	
The following may be particularly relevant but **these lists are not exhaustive**	
Factors indicating higher culpability	**Factors indicating lower culpability**
1. Clear knowledge that documents false	1. Group activity
2. Number of documents possessed (where not in offence descriptions above)	2. Potential impact of use (where not in offence descriptions above)
Factor indicating greater degree of harm	
1. Genuine mistake or ignorance	

Identity Documents Act 2010, ss 6 and 7

Section 6

   (1) It is an offence for a person ("P"), without reasonable excuse, to have in P's possession or under P's control—

      (a) an identity document that is false,

      (b) an identity document that was improperly obtained,

      (c) an identity document that relates to someone else,

      (d) any apparatus which, to P's knowledge, is or has been specially designed or adapted for the making of false identity documents, or

      (e) any article or material which, to P's knowledge, is or has been specially designed or adapted to be used in the making of such documents.

7 Meaning of "identity document"

   (1) For the purposes of sections 4 to 6 "identity document" means any document that is or purports to be—

    (a) an immigration document,

    (b) a United Kingdom passport (within the meaning of the Immigration Act 1971),

    (c) a passport issued by or on behalf of the authorities of a country or territory outside the United Kingdom or by or on behalf of an international organisation,

    (d) a document that can be used (in some or all circumstances) instead of a passport,

    (e) a licence to drive a motor vehicle granted under Part 3 of the Road Traffic Act 1988 or under Part 2 of the Road Traffic (Northern Ireland) Order 1981, or

    (f) a driving licence issued by or on behalf of the authorities of a country or territory outside the United Kingdom.

(2) In subsection (1)(a) "immigration document" means—

    (a) a document used for confirming the right of a person under the EU Treaties in respect of entry or residence in the United Kingdom,

    (b) a document that is given in exercise of immigration functions and records information about leave granted to a person to enter or to remain in the United Kingdom, or

    (c) a registration card (within the meaning of section 26A of the Immigration Act 1971).

(3) In subsection (2)(b) "immigration functions" means functions under the Immigration Acts (within the meaning of the Asylum and Immigration (Treatment of Claimants, etc.) Act 2004).

(4) References in subsection (1) to the issue of a document include its renewal, replacement or re-issue (with or without modifications).

(5) In this section "document" includes a stamp or label.

(6) The Secretary of State may by order amend the definition of "identity document".

PROCEEDS OF CRIME ACT OFFENCES

Either-way, 6 months/£5,000 (14 years).

Criminal Property: In *Anwar* [2009] 1 WLR 980 the court held:

"There are two ways in which the Crown can prove the property derives from crime, a) by showing that it derives from conduct of a specific kind or kinds and that conduct of that kind or those kinds is unlawful, or b) by evidence of the circumstances in which the property is handled which are such as to give rise to the irresistible inference that it can only be derived from crime."

Conduct: In *Keith* [2010] EWCA Crim 477 the court held:

"It is implicit in part 7 of POCA 2002 that the activities which it prohibits will involve some form of concealment or dissipation of the physical proceeds of criminal conduct, and that the intention of the offender and the money launderer is to turn these proceeds into some other physical form that is not readily identifiable. The simplest form of money laundering is obviously exchanging the proceeds of a robbery for bank notes in general circulation. Although the person then in possession of those bank notes is not in possession of the actual notes stolen, they represent the benefit from criminal conduct in the same way as the ones stolen."

Converting: In *Linegar* [2009] EWCA Crim 648 it was held:

"'Converting' involves some kind of action: doing something to something else. Here the appellant converted the cash that he had obtained from his victims into a car and property. These actions were, in common language, laundering the money which was the proceeds of his criminal activity. That process hides those criminal activities. It enables the criminal more easily to escape detection. It provides an apparently innocent cover for the criminal activity."

Legal litigation: See *Bowman v Fels* [2005] EWCA Civ 446 and *Fitzpatrick v Commissoner of Police for the Metropolis* [2012] EWHC 12 (Admin). **Suspect:** In *Da Silva* [2006] EWCA Crim 1654 it was held:

"The essential element in the word "suspect" and its affiliates, in this context, is that the defendant must think that there is a possibility, which is more than fanciful, that the relevant facts exist. A vague feeling of unease would not suffice. But the statute does not require the suspicion to be "clear" or "firmly grounded and targeted on specific facts", or based upon "reasonable grounds".

Identifiable person: Before a person can be found guilty of an offence s.328(1), namely of entering into an arrangement which he knew or suspected facilitated the acquisition of criminal property by or on behalf of another person, that other person had to be identified or at least identifiable at the moment of the arrangement (*Dare v Crown Prosecution Service* [2012] EWHC 2074 (Admin)).

Proceeds of Crime Act 2002, ss 327–329

327 Concealing etc

(1)   A person commits an offence if he—

   (a)   conceals criminal property;
   (b)   disguises criminal property;
   (c)   converts criminal property;
   (d)   transfers criminal property;
   (e)   removes criminal property from England and Wales or from Scotland or from Northern Ireland.

(2)   But a person does not commit such an offence if—

   (a)   he makes an authorised disclosure under section 338 and (if the disclosure is made before he does the act mentioned in subsection (1)) he has the appropriate consent;
   (b)   he intended to make such a disclosure but had a reasonable excuse for not doing so;
   (c)   the act he does is done in carrying out a function he has relating to the enforcement of any provision of this Act or of any other enactment relating to criminal conduct or benefit from criminal conduct.

(2A)   Nor does a person commit an offence under subsection (1) if—

   (a)   he knows, or believes on reasonable grounds, that the relevant criminal conduct occurred in a particular country or territory outside the United Kingdom, and
   (b)   the relevant criminal conduct—
      (i)   was not, at the time it occurred, unlawful under the criminal law then applying in that country or territory, and
      (ii)   is not of a description prescribed by an order made by the Secretary of State.

(2B)   In subsection (2A) "the relevant criminal conduct" is the criminal conduct by reference to which the property concerned is criminal property.

(2C)   A deposit-taking body that does an act mentioned in paragraph (c) or (d) of subsection (1) does not commit an offence under that subsection if—

   (a)   it does the act in operating an account maintained with it, and
   (b)   the value of the criminal property concerned is less than the threshold amount determined under section 339A for the act.

(3)   Concealing or disguising criminal property includes concealing or disguising its nature, source, location, disposition, movement or ownership or any rights with respect to it.

328 Arrangements

(1)   A person commits an offence if he enters into or becomes concerned in an arrangement which he knows or suspects facilitates (by whatever means) the acquisition, retention, use or control of criminal property by or on behalf of another person.

(2)   But a person does not commit such an offence if—

   (a)   he makes an authorised disclosure under section 338 and (if the disclosure is made before he does the act mentioned in subsection (1)) he has the appropriate consent;

(b) he intended to make such a disclosure but had a reasonable excuse for not doing so;

(c) the act he does is done in carrying out a function he has relating to the enforcement of any provision of this Act or of any other enactment relating to criminal conduct or benefit from criminal conduct.

(3) Nor does a person commit an offence under subsection (1) if—

(a) he knows, or believes on reasonable grounds, that the relevant criminal conduct occurred in a particular country or territory outside the United Kingdom, and

(b) the relevant criminal conduct—

(i) was not, at the time it occurred, unlawful under the criminal law then applying in that country or territory, and

(ii) is not of a description prescribed by an order made by the Secretary of State.

(4) In subsection (3) "the relevant criminal conduct" is the criminal conduct by reference to which the property concerned is criminal property.

(5) A deposit-taking body that does an act mentioned in subsection (1) does not commit an offence under that subsection if—

(a) it does the act in operating an account maintained with it, and

(b) the arrangement facilitates the acquisition, retention, use or control of criminal property of a value that is less than the threshold amount determined under section 339A for the act.

329 Acquisition, use and possession

(1) A person commits an offence if he—

(a) acquires criminal property;

(b) uses criminal property;

(c) has possession of criminal property.

(2) But a person does not commit such an offence if—

(a) he makes an authorised disclosure under section 338 and (if the disclosure is made before he does the act mentioned in subsection (1)) he has the appropriate consent;

(b) he intended to make such a disclosure but had a reasonable excuse for not doing so;

(c) he acquired or used or had possession of the property for adequate consideration;

(d) the act he does is done in carrying out a function he has relating to the enforcement of any provision of this Act or of any other enactment relating to criminal conduct or benefit from criminal conduct.

(2A) Nor does a person commit an offence under subsection (1) if—

(a) he knows, or believes on reasonable grounds, that the relevant criminal conduct occurred in a particular country or territory outside the United Kingdom, and

(b) the relevant criminal conduct—

(i) was not, at the time it occurred, unlawful under the criminal law then applying in that country or territory, and

(ii) is not of a description prescribed by an order made by the Secretary of State.

(2B) In subsection (2A) "the relevant criminal conduct" is the criminal conduct by reference to which the property concerned is criminal property.

(2C) A deposit-taking body that does an act mentioned in subsection (1) does not commit an offence under that subsection if—

(a) it does the act in operating an account maintained with it, and

(b) the value of the criminal property concerned is less than the threshold amount determined under section 339A for the act.

(3) For the purposes of this section—

(a) a person acquires property for inadequate consideration if the value of the consideration is significantly less than the value of the property;

(b) a person uses or has possession of property for inadequate consideration if the value of the consideration is significantly less than the value of the use or possession;

(c) the provision by a person of goods or services which he knows or suspects may help another to carry out criminal conduct is not consideration.

RAILWAY FARE EVASION

Summary only, 3months/£1,000 (s 5(3)); £500 fine (s 5(1)).

Offence seriousness (culpability and harm)		
A. Identify the appropriate starting point		
Starting points based on first time offender pleading not guilty		
Examples of nature of activity	**Starting point**	**Range**
Failing to produce ticket or pay fare on request	Band A fine	Conditional discharge to band B fine
Travelling on railway without having paid the fare or knowingly and wilfully travelling beyond the distance paid for, with intent to avoid payment	Band B fine	Band A fine to band C fine

Offence seriousness (culpability and harm)
B. Consider the effect of aggravating and mitigating factors
(other than those within examples above)
The following may be particularly relevant but **these lists are not exhaustive**
Factor indicating higher culpability
1. Offensive or intimidating language or behaviour towards railway staff
Factor indicating greater degree of harm.
1. High level of loss caused or intended to be caused

ROBBERY

Indictable only (Life).

Before or at the time of doing so: Note that theft is a continuing offence, eg *Hale* 68 Cr App R 415 which involved force on a householder after items had been taken. **Force:** Snatching something (in this case a cigarette) from a person's hand, without direct physical contact, did not amount to force (*P v Director of Public Prosecutions* [2012] EWHC 1657 (Admin)). Force does not mean that violence has to be used (*Dawson* (1977) 64 Cr App R 170). **Steals:** It is necessary for the prosecution to establish that a theft has taken place.

Theft Act 1968, s 8

(1) A person is guilty of robbery if he steals, and immediately before or at the time of doing so, and in order to do so, he uses force on any person or puts or seeks to put any person in fear of being then and there subjected to force.

(2) A person guilty of robbery, or of an assault with intent to rob, shall on conviction on indictment be liable to imprisonment for life.

SOCIAL SECURITY BENEFIT, FALSE STATEMENT/REPRESENTATION TO OBTAIN

Either-way (s 111A) 6 months/£5,000 (7 years); Section 112 summary only 3 months/£1,000.

In *Laku*, unreported, 16 July 2008 (Court of Appeal), L made false representations in order to claim benefits and was prosecuted under sections 111A and 111A(1A) of the Social Security Administration Act 1992. On subsequent claims he did not correct the falsehoods. Held: Convictions under section 111A(1A) quashed; he had not failed to notify a change in circumstances as the same false circumstances that founded the convictions under section 111A continued. An offence under section 111A(1B) requires a positive act on the part of the defendant. Sitting back and doing nothing does not amount to (allowing) an offence (*T* [2009] EWCA Crim 1426).

Sentencing: For section 111A see Appendix 10: Fraud Guideline.

Sentencing: Section 112:

Offence seriousness (culpability and harm)		
A. Identify the appropriate starting point		
Starting points based on first time offender pleading not guilty		
Examples of nature of activity	**Starting point**	**Range**
Claim fraudulent from the start, up to £5,000 obtained (s 111A or s 112)	Medium level community order	Band B fine to high level community order
Claim fraudulent from the start, more than £5,000 but less than £20,000 obtained	12 weeks custody	Medium level community order to Crown Court
Claim fraudulent from the start, large-scale, professional offending	Crown Court	Crown Court

Offence seriousness (culpability and harm)	
B. Consider the effect of aggravating and mitigating factors	
(other than those within examples above)	
The following may be particularly relevant but **these lists are not exhaustive**	
Factors indicating higher culpability	**Factors indicating lower culpability**
1. Offending carried out over a long period	1. Pressurized by others
2. Offender acting in unison with one or more others	2. Claim initially legitimate
3. Planning	**Factor indicating lesser degree of harm**
4. Offender motivated by greed or desire to live beyond his/her means	1. Voluntary repayment of amounts overpaid
5. False identities or other personal details used	
6. False or forged documents used	
7. Official documents altered or falsified	

Social Security Administration Act 1992, ss 111A and 112

111A Dishonest representations for obtaining benefit etc

(1) If a person dishonestly—

    (a) makes a false statement or representation; or

    (b) produces or furnishes, or causes or allows to be produced or furnished, any document or information which is false in a material particular;

with a view to obtaining any benefit or other payment or advantage under the relevant social security legislation (whether for himself or for some other person), he shall be guilty of an offence.

(1A) A person shall be guilty of an offence if—

    (a) there has been a change of circumstances affecting any entitlement of his to any benefit or other payment or advantage under any provision of the relevant social security legislation;

    (b) the change is not a change that is excluded by regulations from the changes that are required to be notified;

    (c) he knows that the change affects an entitlement of his to such a benefit or other payment or advantage; and

    (d) he dishonestly fails to give a prompt notification of that change in the prescribed manner to the prescribed person.

(1B) A person shall be guilty of an offence if—

    (a) there has been a change of circumstances affecting any entitlement of another person to any benefit or other payment or advantage under any provision of the relevant social security legislation;

    (b) the change is not a change that is excluded by regulations from the changes that are required to be notified;

    (c) he knows that the change affects an entitlement of that other person to such a benefit or other payment or advantage; and

    (d) he dishonestly causes or allows that other person to fail to give a prompt notification of that change in the prescribed manner to the prescribed person.

(1C) This subsection applies where—

    (a) there has been a change of circumstances affecting any entitlement of a person ('the claimant') to any benefit or other payment or advantage under any provision of the relevant social security legislation;

    (b) the benefit, payment or advantage is one in respect of which there is another person ('the recipient') who for the time being has a right to receive payments to which the claimant has, or (but for the arrangements under which they are payable to the recipient) would have, an entitlement; and

    (c) the change is not a change that is excluded by regulations from the changes that are required to be notified.

(1D) In a case where subsection (1C) above applies, the recipient is guilty of an offence if—

    (a) he knows that the change affects an entitlement of the claimant to a benefit or other payment or advantage under a provision of the relevant social security legislation;

    (b) the entitlement is one in respect of which he has a right to receive payments to which the claimant has, or (but for the arrangements under which they are payable to the recipient) would have, an entitlement; and

    (c) he dishonestly fails to give a prompt notification of that change in the prescribed manner to the prescribed person.

(1E) In a case where that subsection applies, a person other than the recipient is guilty of an offence if—

    (a) he knows that the change affects an entitlement of the claimant to a benefit or other payment or advantage under a provision of the relevant social security legislation;

    (b) the entitlement is one in respect of which the recipient has a right to receive payments to which the claimant has, or (but for the arrangements under which they are payable to the recipient) would have, an entitlement; and

    (c) he dishonestly causes or allows the recipient to fail to give a prompt notification of that change in the prescribed manner to the prescribed person.

(1F) In any case where subsection (1C) above applies but the right of the recipient is confined to a right, by reason of his being a person to whom the claimant is required to make payments in respect of a dwelling, to receive payments of housing benefit—

(a) a person shall not be guilty of an offence under subsection (1D) or (1E) above unless the change is one relating to one or both of the following—

(i)   the claimant's occupation of that dwelling;

(ii) the claimant's liability to make payments in respect of that dwelling; but

(b) subsections (1D)(a) and (1E)(a) above shall each have effect as if after 'knows' there were inserted 'or could reasonably be expected to know'.

(1G) For the purposes of subsections (1A) to (1E) above a notification of a change is prompt if, and only if, it is given as soon as reasonably practicable after the change occurs.

112 False representations for obtaining benefit etc

(1) If a person for the purpose of obtaining any benefit or other payment under the relevant social security legislation whether for himself or some other person, or for any other purpose connected with that legislation—

(a) makes a statement or representation which he knows to be false; or

(b) produces or furnishes, or knowingly causes or knowingly allows to be produced or furnished, any document or information which he knows to be false in a material particular, he shall be guilty of an offence.

(1A) A person shall be guilty of an offence if—

(a) there has been a change of circumstances affecting any entitlement of his to any benefit or other payment or advantage under any provision of the relevant social security legislation;

(b) the change is not a change that is excluded by regulations from the changes that are required to be notified;

(c) he knows that the change affects an entitlement of his to such a benefit or other payment or advantage; and

(d) he fails to give a prompt notification of that change in the prescribed manner to the prescribed person.

(1B) A person is guilty of an offence under this section if—

(a) there has been a change of circumstances affecting any entitlement of another person to any benefit or other payment or advantage under any provision of the relevant social security legislation;

(b) the change is not a change that is excluded by regulations from the changes that are required to be notified;

(c) he knows that the change affects an entitlement of that other person to such a benefit or other payment or advantage; and

(d) he causes or allows that other person to fail to give a prompt notification of that change in the prescribed manner to the prescribed person.

(1C) In a case where subsection (1C) of section 111A above applies, the recipient is guilty of an offence if—

(a) he knows that the change affects an entitlement of the claimant to a benefit or other payment or advantage under a provision of the relevant social security legislation;

(b) the entitlement is one in respect of which he has a right to receive payments to which the claimant has, or (but for the arrangements under which they are payable to the recipient) would have, an entitlement; and

(c) he fails to give a prompt notification of that change in the prescribed manner to the prescribed person.

(1D) In a case where that subsection applies, a person other than the recipient is guilty of an offence if—

    (a) he knows that the change affects an entitlement of the claimant to a benefit or other payment or advantage under a provision of the relevant social security legislation;

    (b) the entitlement is one in respect of which the recipient has a right to receive payments to which the claimant has, or (but for the arrangements under which they are payable to the recipient) would have, an entitlement; and

    (c) he causes or allows the recipient to fail to give a prompt notification of that change in the prescribed manner to the prescribed person.

(1E) Subsection (1F) of section 111A above applies in relation to subsections (1C) and (1D) above as it applies in relation to subsections (1D) and (1E) of that section.

(1F) For the purposes of subsections (1A) to (1D) above a notification of a change is prompt if, and only if, it is given as soon as reasonably practicable after the change occurs.

TAX CREDIT FRAUD

Either-way, 6 months/£5,000 (7 years).

Sentencing: See Appendix 10: Fraud Guideline.

Disposing of monies: Disposing of the proceeds of fraud amounts to a fraudulent activity (*Kolapo* [2009] EWCA Crim 545).

Tax Credits Act 2002, s 35

A person commits an offence if he is knowingly concerned in any fraudulent activity undertaken with a view to obtaining payments of a tax credit by him or any other person.

THEFT

Either-way, 6 months/£5,000 (7 years).

Dishonesty: Dishonesty is a two-part test: Were the accused's actions dishonest according to the ordinary standards of reasonable and honest people? and if so, did the accused know that those actions were dishonest according to those standards?

Breach of trust:

Type/nature of activity	Starting point	Sentencing range
Theft of less than £2,000	Medium level community order	Band B fine to 26 weeks custody
Theft of £2,000 or more but less than £20,000 OR Theft of less than £2,000 in breach of a high degree of trust	18 weeks custody	High level community order to Crown Court
Theft of £20,000 or more OR Theft of £2,000 or more in breach of a high degree of trust	Crown Court	Crown Court

Additional aggravating factors:
1. Long course of offending
2. Suspicion deliberately thrown on others
3. Offender motivated by intention to cause harm or out of revenge

Theft from the person:

Type/nature of activity	Starting point	Sentencing range
Where the effect on the victim is particularly severe, the stolen property is of high value, or substantial consequential loss results, a sentence higher than the range into which the offence would fall may be appropriate.		
Theft from a vulnerable victim involving intimidation or the use or threat of force (falling short of robbery)	18 months custody	12 months–3 years custody
Theft from a vulnerable victim	18 weeks custody	Community order (HIGH) – 12 months custody
Theft from the person not involving vulnerable victim	Community order (MEDIUM)	Fine Band B – 18 weeks custody

Additional aggravating factors:
1. Offender motivated by intention to cause harm or out of revenge
2. Intimidation or face-to-face confrontation with victim [except where this raises offence into the higher sentencing range]
3. Use of force, or threat of force, against victim (not amounting to robbery) [except where this raises the offence into a higher sentencing range]
4. High level of inconvenience caused to victim, eg replacing house keys, credit cards, etc

Theft from shop:

Type/nature of activity	Starting point	Sentencing range
Organized gang/group and Intimidation or the use or threat of force (short of robbery)	12 months custody	36 weeks–4 years custody
Significant intimidation or threats OR Use of force resulting in slight injury OR Very high level of planning OR Significant related damage	6 weeks custody	Community order (HIGH)—36 weeks custody
Low level intimidation or threats OR Some planning eg a session of stealing on the same day or going equipped OR Some related damage	Community order (LOW)	Fine—Community order (MEDIUM)
Little or no planning or sophistication AND Goods stolen of low value	Fine	Conditional discharge—Community order (LOW)

Additional aggravating factors:
1. Child accompanying offender is involved in or aware of theft
2. Offender is subject to a banning order that includes the store targeted
3. Offender motivated by intention to cause harm or out of revenge
4. Professional offending
5. Victim particularly vulnerable (eg small independent shop)
6. Offender targeted high value goods

TWOC (VEHICLE-TAKING WITHOUT CONSENT)

Summary only, 6 months/£5,000. But note this provision in relation to limitation period:

Theft Act 1968, s 12(4A)–(4C)

(4A) Proceedings for an offence under subsection (1) above (but not proceedings of a kind falling within subsection (4) above) in relation to a mechanically propelled vehicle—

    (a) shall not be commenced after the end of the period of three years beginning with the day on which the offence was committed; but

    (b) subject to that, may be commenced at any time within the period of six months beginning with the relevant day.

(4B) In subsection (4A)(b) above 'the relevant day' means—

    (a) in the case of a prosecution for an offence under subsection (1) above by a public prosecutor, the day on which sufficient evidence to justify the proceedings came to the knowledge of any person responsible for deciding whether to commence any such prosecution;

    (b) in the case of a prosecution for an offence under subsection (1) above which is commenced by a person other than a public prosecutor after the discontinuance of a prosecution falling within paragraph (a) above which relates to the same facts, the day on which sufficient evidence to justify the proceedings came to the knowledge of the person who has decided to commence the prosecution or (if later) the discontinuance of the other prosecution;

    (c) in the case of any other prosecution for an offence under subsection (1) above, the day on which sufficient evidence to justify the proceedings came to the knowledge of the person who has decided to commence the prosecution.

(4C) For the purposes of subsection (4A)(b) above a certificate of a person responsible for deciding whether to commence a prosecution of a kind mentioned in subsection (4B)(a) above as to the date on which such evidence as is mentioned in the certificate came to the knowledge of any person responsible for deciding whether to commence any such prosecution shall be conclusive evidence of that fact.

Offence seriousness (culpability and harm)

A. Identify the appropriate starting point

Starting points based on first time offender pleading not guilty

Examples of nature of activity	Starting point	Range
Exceeding authorized use of eg employer's or relative's vehicle; retention of hire car beyond return date	Low level community order	Band B fine to medium level community order
As above with damage caused to lock/ignition; OR Stranger's vehicle involved but no damage caused	Medium level community order	Low level community order to high level community order
Taking vehicle from private premises; OR Causing damage to eg lock/ignition of stranger's vehicle	High level community order	Medium level community order to 26 weeks custody

Offence seriousness (culpability and harm)

B. Consider the effect of aggravating and mitigating factors

(other than those within examples above)

The following may be particularly relevant but **these lists are not exhaustive**

Factors indicating greater degree of harm	Factor indicating lower culpability
1. Vehicle later burnt	1. Misunderstanding with owner
2. Vehicle belonging to elderly/disabled person	**Factor indicating lesser degree of harm**
3. Emergency services vehicle	1. Offender voluntarily returned vehicle to owner
4. Medium to large goods vehicle	
5. Passengers carried	

Theft Act 1968, s 12(1), (5), (6), and (7)

(1) Subject to subsections (5) and (6) below, a person shall be guilty of an offence if, without having the consent of the owner or other lawful authority, he takes any conveyance for his own or another's use or knowing that any conveyance has been taken without such authority, drives it or allows himself to be carried in or on it.

(5) Subsection (1) above shall not apply in relation to pedal cycles; but, subject to subsection (6) below, a person who, without having the consent of the owner or other lawful authority, takes a pedal cycle for his own or another's use, or rides a pedal cycle knowing it to have been taken without such authority, shall on summary conviction be liable to a fine not exceeding level 3 on the standard scale.

(6) A person does not commit an offence under this section by anything done in the belief that he has lawful authority to do it or that he would have the owner's consent if the owner knew of his doing it and the circumstances of it.

(7) For purposes of this section—

   (a) 'conveyance' means any conveyance constructed or adapted for the carriage of a person or persons whether by land, water or air, except that it does not include a conveyance constructed or adapted for use only under the control of a person not carried in or on it, and 'drive' shall be construed accordingly; and

   (b) 'owner', in relation to a conveyance which is the subject of a hiring agreement or hire-purchase agreement, means the person in possession of the conveyance under that agreement.

VAT EVASION

Either-way, 6 months/£5,000 (7 years).

Turning a blind eye is sufficient to establish that a person 'knowingly did one of the prohibited acts (*Ross v Moss* [1965] 2 QB 396). For an evasion there does not need to be any intention permanently to avoid payment (*Dealy* [1995] 1 WLR 658).

Sentencing: See Appendix 10: Fraud Guideline.

Value Added Tax Act 1994, s 72

(1) If any person is knowingly concerned in, or in the taking of steps with a view to, the fraudulent evasion of VAT by him or any other person.

(2) (a) the payment of a VAT credit; or

   (b) a refund under sections 35, 36 or 40 of this Act or section 22 of the 1983 Act; or

   (c) a refund under any regulations made by virtue of section 13(5); or

   (d) a repayment under section 39;

and any reference in those subsections to the amount of the VAT shall be construed—

   (i) in relation to VAT itself or a VAT credit, as a reference to the aggregate of the amount (if any) falsely claimed by way of credit for input tax and the amount (if any) by which output tax was falsely understated, and

(ii)   in relation to a refund or repayment falling within paragraph (b), (c) or (d) above, as a reference to the amount falsely claimed by way of refund or repayment.

VEHICLE INTERFERENCE

Summary only, 3 months/£2,500.

Offence seriousness (culpability and harm)		
A. Identify the appropriate starting point		
Starting points based on first time offender pleading not guilty		
Examples of nature of activity	**Starting point**	**Range**
Trying door handles; no entry gained to vehicle; no damage caused	Band C fine	Band A fine to low level community order
Entering vehicle, little or no damage caused	Medium level community order	Band C fine to high level community order
Entering vehicle, with damage caused	High level community order	Medium level community order to 12 weeks custody

Offence seriousness (culpability and harm)	
B. Consider the effect of aggravating and mitigating factors	
(other than those within examples above)	
The following may be particularly relevant but **these lists are not exhaustive**	
Factor indicating higher culpability	
1. Targeting vehicle in dark/isolated location	
Factors indicating greater degree of harm	
1. Emergency services vehicle	
2. Disabled driver's vehicle	
3. Part of series	

Criminal Attempts Act 1981, s 9(1)–(2)

(1)   A person is guilty of the offence of vehicle interference if he interferes with a motor vehicle or trailer or with anything carried in or on a motor vehicle or trailer with the intention that an offence specified in subsection (2) below shall be committed by himself or some other person.

(2)   The offences mentioned in subsection (1) above are—

(a)   theft of the motor vehicle or trailer or part of it;

(b)   theft of anything carried in or on the motor vehicle or trailer; and

(c)   an offence under section 12(1) of the Theft Act 1968 (taking and driving away without consent);

and, if it is shown that a person accused of an offence under this section intended that one of those offences should be committed, it is immaterial that it cannot be shown which it was.

WEAPONS

COMMON PRINCIPLES

The following principles cover the main offences in this section.

Bladed article: A blade need not be sharp, so a butter knife is capable of being a bladed article (*Brooker v Director of Public Prosecutions* [2005] EWHC 1132 (Admin)), but a screwdriver is not a bladed article (*Davis* [1998] Crim LR 564). **Folding knife**: A folding pocket knife is not a bladed article unless its blade exceeds 3 inches (s 139(3)). A lock knife is not a folding knife, irrespective of blade length; 'To be a folding pocketknife the knife has to be readily and indeed immediately foldable at all times, simply by the folding process. A knife of the type with which these appeals are concerned is not in this category because, in the first place, there is a stage, namely, when it has been opened, when it is not immediately foldable simply by the folding process and, secondly, it requires that further process, namely, the pressing of the button' (*Harris v Director of Public Prosecutions* [1993] 1 WLR 82). **Good reason or lawful authority**: The defendant had a persuasive, not merely evidential burden. Such a reverse burden was proportionate and did not infringe article 6(2) ECHR (*Matthews* [2003] EWCA Crim 813). The offender's state of mind was a relevant consideration. in this case relating to her fear of attack, (*Clancy* [2012] EWCA Crim 8). Forgetfulness combined with other factors could suffice as a good reason, but it could not stand alone as a defence (*Jolie* [2003] EWCA Crim 1543). Forgetfulness combined with the fact that the defendant had the knife with him for work which was casual in nature could amount to a good reason, and a court was wrong to disregard the work element of the defence simply because it was casual (*Chalal v Director of Public Prosecutions* [2010] EWHC 439 (Admin)). Carrying a weapon for the purpose of defending oneself can amount to a good reason provided that the defendant can demonstrate that he was in fear of an imminent attack (*McAuley* [2009] EWCA Crim 2930). The Act was not intended to sanction the permanent or constant carrying of a weapon merely because of some constant or enduring supposed or actual threat or danger to the carrier. The threat must be an imminent particular threat (*Evans v Hughes* (1972) 57 Cr App R 813). If religious reason is cited as a defence then it must be the predominant if not the only motivation for the carrying of the blade (*Wang* [2003] EWCA Crim 3228). It was not a defence that the blade was only part of a multi-function article which was carried out of habit (*Giles* [2003] EWCA Crim 1287). At work also encompassed being at work for oneself (*Manning* [1998] Crim LR 198). **Has with him**: there must be a very close physical link and a degree of immediate control over the weapon by the man alleged to have the weapon with him (*North* [2001] EWCA Crim 544). **Lawful authority**: The reference to lawful authority in the section is a reference to those people who from time to time carry an offensive weapon as a matter of duty, eg the soldier and his rifle and police officer with his truncheon (*Bryan v Mott* (1976) 62 Cr App R 71). Security guards do not have lawful authority to carry weapons (*Spanner* [1973] Crim LR 704), although for a contrary view see *Malnik v Director of Public Prosecutions* [1989] Crim LR 451. **Mens rea**: The prosecution must show that the defendant knew that he was in possession of the weapon (*Cugullere* [1961] 2 All ER 343), even if he did not know what it was (*Densu* [1997] EWCA Crim 2864). **Offensive weapon**: An offensive weapon means any article made (ie offensive per se) or adapted for use for causing injury to the person, or intended by the person having it with him for such use by him, or by some other person (*Simpson* 78 Cr App R 115). An intention to have an item for the causing of injury must be formed before any violence occurred, otherwise any assault involving a weapon would be an offence under this provision also (*C v Director of Public Prosecutions* [2001] EWHC 1093 (Admin)). A butterfly knife is offensive per se (*Director of Public Prosecutions v Hynde* [1998] 1 Cr App R 288). A baseball bat is not offensive per se (*Humphries*, The Independent, 13

April 1987). Other items held to be offensive per se include: a bayonet, a stiletto, a handgun, a flickknife (which includes a flickknife which has a dual use (*Vasili* [2011] EWCA Crim 615). Items which are inherently dangerous but manufactured for a lawful purpose (eg kitchen knife) are not offensive per se. Whether 'sand gloves' are an offensive weapon is one for a jury to decide (*R* [2007] EWCA Crim 3312). It is submitted that items prohibited for sale in England and Wales by virtue of the Criminal Justice Act 1988 (offensive Weapons) (Amendment) Order 1988 are offensive per se. **Public place:** Whether a place is a public place within the meaning of the statute is a question of fact; whether a place is capable of being a public place is a question of law (*Hanrahan* [2004] EWCA Crim 2943). Public place is defined in both the Prevention of Crime Act 1953, s 1(4) as: any highway and any other premises or place to which at the material time the public have or are permitted to have access, whether on payment or otherwise; and in the Criminal Justice Act 1988, s 139(7) to include any place to which at the material time the public have or are permitted access, whether on payment orotherwise. Upper landing of a block of flats held to be a public place (*Knox v Anderton* (1983) 76 Cr App R 156). In *Bates v Director of Public Prosecutions* [1994] 157 JP 1004, the inside of a car, which itself was in a public place, was held to be a public place. A wider challenge to this proposition was rejected in *Ellis* [2010] EWCA Crim 163. **Reasonable excuse:** There is a significant overlap between this defence and good reason (above) so those cases should be considered). The defence is to be viewed objectively, although a defendant's honestly held belief would be relevant to an objective analysis of the defence offered (*N v Director of Public Prosecutions* [2011] EWHC 1807 (Admin)). Reasonable excuse has a wide meaning and the court is not fettered by any restriction on the defence, even where the weapon is offensive per se (*Director of Public Prosecutions v Patterson* [2004] EWHC 2744 (Admin)).Lack of knowledge that the item is an offensive weapon does not go to assisting a defendant establish reasonable excuse (*Densu* [1998] 1 Cr App R 400). The carrying of a police truncheon as part of a fancy dress costume was held in a civil case to be lawful (*Houghton v Chief Constable of Greater Manchester* (1987) 84 Cr App R 319). A Scottish court rejected the conveyance of a nunchuk from a dance to the defendant's home as amounting to a reasonable excuse (*Kincaid v Tudhope*, unreported 23 August 1983). It will be an exceedingly rare case in relation to an object which is an offensive weapon per se that, absent some sort of necessity or some immediate temporal connection between the possession of the object and the innocent purpose for which it is being carried, that the Tribunal of fact will be persuaded that there is a reasonable excuse (*Director of Public Prosecutions v Patterson* [2004] EWHC 2744 (Admin)).

Sentencing guideline

This guideline covers the offences of bladed article and offensive weapon.

Offence seriousness (culpability and harm)		
A. Identify the appropriate starting point		
Starting points based on first time offender pleading not guilty		
Examples of nature of activity	**Starting point**	**Range**
Weapon not used to threaten or cause fear	High level community order	Band C fine to 12 weeks custody
Weapon not used to threaten or cause fear but offence committed in dangerous circumstances	6 weeks custody	High level community order to Crown Court
Weapon used to threaten or cause fear and offence committed in dangerous circumstances	Crown Court	Crown Court

Offence seriousness (culpability and harm)

B. Consider the effect of aggravating and mitigating factors (other than those within examples above)

The following may be particularly relevant but **these lists are not exhaustive**

Factors indicating higher culpability	Factors indicating lower culpability
1. Particularly dangerous weapon	1. Weapon carried only on temporary basis
2. Specifically planned use of weapon to commit violence, threaten violence, or intimidate	2. Original possession legitimate eg in course of trade or business
3. Offence motivated by hostility towards minority individual or group	
4. Offender under influence of drink or drugs	
5. Offender operating in group or gang	
Factors indicating greater degree of harm	
1. Offence committed at school, hospital, or other place where vulnerable persons may be present	
2. Offence committed on premises where people carrying out public services	
3. Offence committed on or outside licensed premises	
4. Offence committed on public transport	
5. Offence committed at large public gathering, especially where there may be risk of disorder	

BLADED ARTICLE

Triable either-way, 6 months/£5,000 (4 years on indictment).

Sentencing guideline

See above (Common Principles).

Criminal Justice Act 1988, s 139(1)–(5)

(1) Subject to subsections (4) and (5) below, any person who has an article to which this section applies with him in a public place shall be guilty of an offence.

(2) Subject to subsection (3) below, this section applies to any article which has a blade or is sharply pointed except a folding pocketknife.

(3) This section applies to a folding pocketknife if the cutting edge of its blade exceeds 3 inches.

(4) It shall be a defence for a person charged with an offence under this section to prove that he had good reason or lawful authority for having the article with him in a public place.

(5) Without prejudice to the generality of subsection (4) above, it shall be a defence for a person charged with an offence under this section to prove that he had the article with him—

    (a) for use at work;

    (b) for religious reasons; or

    (c) as part of any national costume.

BLADED ARTICLE OR OFFENSIVE WEAPON ON SCHOOL PREMISES

Triable either-way, 6 months/£5,000 (4 years on indictment). School (private or state) premises includes surrounding land, playing fields and yards. It is irrelevant whether the school is open or closed.

Sentencing guideline

See above.

Criminal Justice Act 1988, s 139A(1)-(2)

(1) Any person who has an article to which section 139 of this Act applies with him on school premises shall be guilty of an offence.

(2) Any person who has an offensive weapon within the meaning of section 1 of the Prevention of Crime Act 1953 with him on school premises shall be guilty of an offence.

CROSSBOWS ACT 1987

All offences are triable summarily only. Section 1 (Sale) 6 months/£5,000, section 2 (purchase) and section 3 (possession) £1,000 fine. **Exception**: The Act does not apply to crossbows with a draw weight of less than 1.4 kilograms (s 5).

Crossbows Act 1987, s 1, 1A, 2, 3, and 5

Sale and letting on hire, s 1

A person who sells or lets on hire a crossbow or a part of a crossbow to a person under the age of eighteen is guilty of an offence, unless he believes him to be eighteen years of age or older and has reasonable ground for the belief.

Defences, s 1A

(1) It is a defence for a person charged with an offence under section 1 (referred to in this section as "the accused") to show that—

(a) the accused believed the person to whom the crossbow or part was sold or let on hire (referred to in this section as "the purchaser or hirer") to be aged 18 or over, and

(b) either—

    (i) the accused had taken reasonable steps to establish the purchaser or hirer's age, or

    (ii) no reasonable person could have suspected from the purchaser or hirer's appearance that the purchaser or hirer was under the age of 18.

(2) For the purposes of subsection (1)(b)(i), the accused is to be treated as having taken reasonable steps to establish the purchaser or hirer's age if and only if—

(a) the accused was shown any of the documents mentioned in subsection (3), and

(b) the document would have convinced a reasonable person.

(3) Those documents are any document bearing to be—

(a) a passport,

(b) a European Union photocard driving licence, or [...]

Purchase and hiring, s 2

A person under the age of eighteen who buys or hires a crossbow or a part of a crossbow is guilty of an offence.

Possession, s 3

A person under the age of eighteen who has with him—

(a) a crossbow which is capable of discharging a missile, or

(b) parts of a crossbow which together (and without any other parts) can be assembled to form a crossbow capable of discharging a missile,

is guilty of an offence, unless he is under the supervision of a person who is twenty-one years of age or older.

Exception, s 5

This Act does not apply to crossbows with a draw weight of less than 1.4 kilograms.

OFFENSIVE WEAPON

Triable either-way, 6 months/£5,000 (4 years on indictment).

Sentencing guideline

See above (Common Principles).

Prevention of Crime Act 1953, s 1(1)

Any person who without lawful authority or reasonable excuse, the proof whereof shall lie on him, has with him in any public place any offensive weapon shall be guilty of an offence.

THREATENING WITH OFFENSIVE WEAPON IN PUBLIC

Triable either-way, 6 months/£5,000 (4 years on indictment). There is no sentencing guideline applicable to this offence. **Mandatory minimum sentence:** See s 1A(5) below. **Alternative verdict:** See s 1A(10).

Prevention of Crime Act 1953, s 1A

(1) A person is guilty of an offence if that person—

   (a) has an offensive weapon with him or her in a public place,

   (b) unlawfully and intentionally threatens another person with the weapon, and

   (c) does so in such a way that there is an immediate risk of serious physical harm to that other person.

(2) For the purposes of this section physical harm is serious if it amounts to grievous bodily harm for the purposes of the Offences against the Person Act 1861.

(3) In this section "public place" and "offensive weapon" have the same meaning as in section 1.

(4) …

(5) Where a person aged 16 or over is convicted of an offence under this section, the court must impose an appropriate custodial sentence (with or without a fine) unless the court is of the opinion that there are particular circumstances which—

   (a) relate to the offence or to the offender, and

   (b) would make it unjust to do so in all the circumstances.

(6) In this section "appropriate custodial sentence" means—

   (a) in the case of a person who is aged 18 or over when convicted, a sentence of imprisonment for a term of at least 6 months;

   (b) in the case of a person who is aged at least 16 but under 18 when convicted, a detention and training order of at least 4 months.

(7) In considering whether it is of the opinion mentioned in subsection (5) in the case of a person aged under 18, the court must have regard to its duty under section 44 of the Children and Young Persons Act 1933.

(8) In relation to an offence committed before the commencement of section 154(1) of the Criminal Justice Act 2003, the reference in subsection (4)(a) to 12 months is to be read as a reference to 6 months.

(9) In relation to times before the coming into force of paragraph 180 of Schedule 7 to the Criminal Justice and Court Services Act 2000, the reference in subsection (6)(a) to a sentence of imprisonment, in relation to an offender aged under 21 at the time of conviction, is to be read as a reference to a sentence of detention in a young offender institution.

(10) If on a person's trial for an offence under this section (whether on indictment or not) the person is found not guilty of that offence but it is proved that the person committed

an offence under section 1, the person may be convicted of the offence under that section.

THREATENING WITH ARTICLE WITH BLADE OR POINT OR OFFENSIVE WEAPON

Either-way, 6 months/£5,000 (4 years on indictment). There is no sentencing guideline applicable to this offence. **Mandatory minimum sentence:** See s 139AA (7) below. **Alternative verdict:** See s 139AA (12).

Criminal Justice Act 1988, s 139AA

(1) A person is guilty of an offence if that person—

    (a) has an article to which this section applies with him or her in a public place or on school premises,

    (b) unlawfully and intentionally threatens another person with the article, and

    (c) does so in such a way that there is an immediate risk of serious physical harm to that other person.

(2) In relation to a public place this section applies to an article to which section 139 applies.

(3) In relation to school premises this section applies to each of these—

    (a) an article to which section 139 applies;

    (b) an offensive weapon within the meaning of section 1 of the Prevention of Crime Act 1953.

(4) For the purposes of this section physical harm is serious if it amounts to grievous bodily harm for the purposes of the Offences against the Person Act 1861.

(5) In this section—

"public place" has the same meaning as in section 139;

"school premises" has the same meaning as in section 139A.

(6) ...

(7) Where a person aged 16 or over is convicted of an offence under this section, the court must impose an appropriate custodial sentence (with or without a fine) unless the court is of the opinion that there are particular circumstances which—

    (a) relate to the offence or to the offender, and

    (b) would make it unjust to do so in all the circumstances.

(8) In this section "appropriate custodial sentence" means—

    (a) in the case of a person who is aged 18 or over when convicted, a sentence of imprisonment for a term of at least 6 months;

    (b) in the case of a person who is aged at least 16 but under 18 when convicted, a detention and training order of at least 4 months.

(9) In considering whether it is of the opinion mentioned in subsection (7) in the case of a person aged under 18, the court must have regard to its duty under section 44 of the Children and Young Persons Act 1933.

(10) In relation to an offence committed before the commencement of section 154(1) of the Criminal Justice Act 2003, the reference in subsection (6)(a) to 12 months is to be read as a reference to 6 months.

(11) In relation to times before the coming into force of paragraph 180 of Schedule 7 to the Criminal Justice and Court Services Act 2000, the reference in subsection (8)(a) to a sentence of imprisonment, in relation to an offender aged under 21 at the time of conviction, is to be read as a reference to a sentence of detention in a young offender institution.

(12) If on a person's trial for an offence under this section (whether on indictment or not) the person is found not guilty of that offence but it is proved that the person committed an offence under section 139 or 139A, the person may be convicted of the offence under that section.

SALE OF KNIVES AND CERTAIN ARTICLES WITH BLADE OR POINT TO PERSONS UNDER 18

Summary only, 6 months/£5,000.

Statutory defence: It is not sufficient in order to satisfy the defence that the defendant merely proves that he was not negligent, nor was it correct simply to focus on due diligence, which was only one part of the defence that had to be satisfied (*Croydon London Borough Council v Pinch a Pound* [2010] EWHC 3283 (Admin)). **Knife:** A grapefruit knife falls within the definition of knife (*R (Windsor and Maidenhead Royal Borough v East Berkshire Justices* [2010] EWHC 3020 (Admin)).

Sentencing guideline

The guideline above does not apply to this offence.

Criminal Justice Act 1988, s 141A

(1) Any person who sells to a person under the age of eighteen years an article to which this section applies shall be guilty of an offence...

(2) Subject to subsection (3) below, this section applies to—

(a) any knife, knife blade or razor blade,

(b) any axe, and

(c) any other article which has a blade or which is sharply pointed and which is made or adapted for use for causing injury to the person.

(3) This section does not apply to any article described in—

(a) section 1 of the Restriction of Offensive Weapons Act 1959.

(b) an order made under section 141(2) of this Act, or

(c) an order made by the Secretary of State under this section.

(4) It shall be a defence for a person charged with an offence under subsection (1) above to prove that he took all reasonable precautions and exercised all due diligence to avoid the commission of the offence.

PART B SENTENCING

AGE OF OFFENDER

Relevant date: The court should have regard to the offender's age at date of conviction, not date of offence (*Robson* (2007) 1 ALL ER 506). Where a court resentences for a community sentence imposed under the Criminal Justice Act 2003 it must resentence on the basis of the offender's age on the date the original was imposed. When a conditional discharge is activated the relevant age is at the date of the new sentence hearing. Minimum sentences under the Firearms Act 1968, s 51A are determined by reference to the date of the offence.

Offence committed when a child: It is common for a court to have to deal with an adult offender in relation to criminal activity committed when the offender was a child. In *Ghafoor* [2003] 2 Cr App R (S) 89 the court said: 'The approach to be adopted where a defendant crosses a relevant age threshold between the date of the commission of the offence and date of conviction should now be clear. The starting point is the sentence that the defendant would have been likely to receive if he had been sentenced at the date of the commission of the offence. It has been described as a 'powerful factor'. That is for the obvious reason that…the philosophy of restricting sentencing powers in relation to young persons reflects both (a) society's acceptance that young offenders are less responsible for their actions and therefore less culpable than adults, and (b) the recognition that, in consequence, sentencing them should place greater emphasis on rehabilitation and less on retribution and deterrence than in the case of adults. It should be noted that the 'starting point' is not the maximum sentence that could lawfully have been imposed, but the sentence that the offender would have been likely to receive.'

However, in *Bowker* (2008) 1 Cr App R (S) 72 the court said that *Ghafoor* was a powerful starting point, but other factors (such as the need for deterrent sentencing), may justify departing from it.

ALTERATION OF SENTENCE

Magistrates' Courts Act 1980, s 142 allows for the later alteration of sentence, but should be used as a slip rule paying particular regard to the principle of finality of sentence, and should therefore be slow to interfere (*R (Trigger) v Northampton Magistrates Court* [2011] EWHC 149 (Admin)). In exceptional cases, such as were the court has been misled a reopening of sentence may be permissible, provided it is done expeditiously (*R (Holme) v Liverpool Magistrates' Court* [2004] EWHC 3131 (Admin)).

In *Williamson v City of Westminster Magistrates' Court* [2012] EWHC 1444 (Admin) the court stated that 'the power conferred with regard to sentence explicitly refers to replacing a sentence imposed which was invalid. That might be regarded as correcting a classic 'mistake'. It could be contended that it would be in the interests of justice to substitute a new sentence on the grounds that the one originally imposed was manifestly excessive. However, the sentencing provisions, whether in their original or new form in section 142, cannot be read as conferring a power to substitute a new sentence in the same way as an appellate court might do so.'

ANTI-SOCIAL BEHAVIOUR ORDERS

Crime and Disorder Act 1998, s 1C provides for an ASBO to be made following conviction. CrPR 50 applies to the making of such orders.

Crime and Disorder Act 1998, s 1C

(1) This section applies where a person (the 'offender') is convicted of a relevant offence.

(2) If the court considers—

(a) that the offender has acted, at any time since the commencement date, in an anti-social manner, that is to say in a manner that caused or was likely to cause harassment, alarm or distress to one or more persons not of the same household as himself, and

(b) that an order under this section is necessary to protect persons in any place in England and Wales from further anti-social acts by him,

it may make an order which prohibits the offender from doing anything described in the order.

(3) The court may make an order under this section—

(a) if the prosecutor asks it to do so, or

(b) if the court thinks it is appropriate to do so.

(3A) For the purpose of deciding whether to make an order under this section the court may consider evidence led by the prosecution and the defence.

(3B) It is immaterial whether evidence led in pursuance of subsection (3A) would have been admissible in the proceedings in which the offender was convicted.

(4) An order under this section shall not be made except—

(a) in addition to a sentence imposed in respect of the relevant offence; or

(b) in addition to an order discharging him conditionally.

(4A) The court may adjourn any proceedings in relation to an order under this section even after sentencing the offender.

(4B) If the offender does not appear for any adjourned proceedings, the court may further adjourn the proceedings or may issue a warrant for his arrest.

(4C) But the court may not issue a warrant for the offender's arrest unless it is satisfied that he has had adequate notice of the time and place of the adjourned proceedings.

(5) An order under this section takes effect on the day on which it is made, but the court may provide in any such order that such requirements of the order as it may specify shall, during any period when the offender is detained in legal custody, be suspended until his release from that custody.

...

(9) Subsections (7), (10), (10C), (10D), (10E) and (11) of section 1 apply for the purposes of the making and effect of orders made by virtue of this section as they apply for the purposes of the making and effect of anti-social behaviour orders.

(9A) The council for the local government area in which a person in respect of whom an anti-social behaviour order has been made resides or appears to reside may bring proceedings under section 1(10) (as applied by subsection (9) above) for breach of an order under subsection (2) above.

(9AA) Sections 1AA and 1AB apply in relation to orders under this section, with any necessary modifications, as they apply in relation to anti-social behaviour orders.

(9AB) In their application by virtue of subsection (9AA), sections 1AA(1A)(b) and 1AB(6) have effect as if the words 'by complaint' were omitted.

(9AC) In its application by virtue of subsection (9AA), section 1AA(1A)(b) has effect as if the reference to the relevant authority which applied for the anti-social behaviour order were a reference to the chief officer of police, or other relevant authority, responsible under section 1K(2)(a) or (b) for carrying out a review of the order under this section.

(9B) Subsection (9C) applies in relation to proceedings in which an order under subsection (2) is made against a child or young person who is convicted of an offence.

(9C) In so far as the proceedings relate to the making of the order—

    (a) section 49 of the Children and Young Persons Act 1933 (c 12) (restrictions on reports of proceedings in which children and young persons are concerned) does not apply in respect of the child or young person against whom the order is made;

    (b) section 39 of that Act (power to prohibit publication of certain matter) does so apply.

(10)   In this section—

'child' and 'young person' have the same meaning as in the Children and Young Persons Act 1933 (c 12);

'the commencement date' has the same meaning as in section 1 above;

'the court' in relation to an offender means—

    (a) the court by or before which he is convicted of the relevant offence; or

    (b) if he is committed to the Crown Court to be dealt with for that offence, the Crown Court; and

'relevant offence' means an offence committed after the coming into force of section 64 of the Police Reform Act 2002 (c 30).

Post complaint behavior: Admissible both to demonstrate whether a person has acted in an anti-social manner and also as to whether the order is necessary (*Birmingham City Council v Dixon* [2009] EWHC 761 (Admin)). **Relevant case law:** In *Gowan* [2007] EWCA Crim 1360 the court made an ASBO against the defendant's wife. The order was quashed because, the defendant's wife being of the same household as him, there was no power to make it. ASBOs are properly made for the protection of the general public.

In *S v Poole Borough Council* [2002] EWHC 244 (Admin) a youth aged 15 had been engaged in anti-social behaviour for 18 months up to the date of the application. The magistrates' court hearing was concluded five months later and the Crown Court appeal seven and a half months after that. The defendant argued that there was no necessity for an order as there had been no anti-social behaviour for over a year. Describing this argument as hopeless, Simon Brown LJ said:

> It must be expected that, once an application of this sort is made, still more obviously once an ASBO has been made, its effect will be likely to deter future misconduct. That, indeed, is the justification for such orders in the first place ... The conduct on which the magistrates' court, and in turn the Crown Court, should concentrate in determining whether such an order is necessary is that which underlay the authority's application for the order in the first place.

No prohibition may be imposed unless it is *necessary* for the purpose of protecting persons, whether relevant persons or persons elsewhere in England and Wales, from further anti-social acts by the defendant. The leading case is *Boness* [2005] EWCA Crim 2395. From that and other cases (notably *R v P (Shane Tony)* [2004] EWCA Crim 287, *McGrath* [2005] EWCA Crim 353, and *W v Director of Public Prosecutions* [2005] EWCA Civ 1333) the following principles emerge:

(1)   The requirement that a prohibition must be necessary to protect persons from further anti-social acts by the defendant means that the use of an ASBO to punish a defendant is unlawful.

(2)   Each separate prohibition must be targeted at the individual and the specific form of anti-social behaviour it is intended to prevent. The order must be tailored to the defendant and not designed on a word processor for generic use. Therefore the court must ask itself when considering a specific order, 'Is this order necessary to protect persons in any place in England and Wales from further anti-social acts by the defendant?'

(3)   Each prohibition must be precise and capable of being understood by the defendant. Therefore the court should ask itself before making an order: 'Are the terms of this order clear so that the defendant will know precisely what it is that he is prohibited from

doing?' (So that unfamiliar words like 'curtilage' and 'environs' should be avoided, as should vague ones like 'implement' or 'paraphernalia'.) For example, a prohibition should clearly delineate any exclusion zone by reference to a map and clearly identify those whom the defendant must not contact or associate with.

(4) Each prohibition must be prohibitory and not mandatory: this means substantially and not just formally prohibitory.

(5) The terms of the order must be proportionate in the sense that they must be commensurate with the risk to be guarded against. This is particularly important where an order may interfere with an ECHR right protected by the Human Rights Act 1998, eg articles 8, 10, and 11.

(6) There is no requirement that the prohibited acts should by themselves give rise to harassment, alarm, or distress.

(7) An ASBO should not be used merely to increase the sentence of imprisonment which an offender is liable to receive.

(8) Different considerations may apply if the maximum sentence is only a fine, but the court must still go through all the steps to make sure that an ASBO is necessary.

The fact that an order prohibits a defendant from committing a specified criminal offence does not automatically invalidate it. However, the court should not make such an order if the sentence which could be passed following conviction for the offence would be a sufficient deterrent. In addition, the Court of Appeal has indicated that prohibiting behaviour that is in any event a crime does not necessarily address the aim of an ASBO, which is to prevent anti-social behaviour. The better course is to make an anticipatory form of order, namely an order which prevents a defendant from doing an act preparatory to the commission of the offence, thereby helping to prevent the criminal offence from being committed in the first place. For example, an order might prevent a defendant from entering a shopping centre rather than stealing from shops.

In *Boness*, Hooper LJ gave other examples, drawing an analogy with bail conditions designed to prevent a defendant from committing further offences. He said:

If, for example, a court is faced by an offender who causes criminal damage by spraying graffiti then the order should be aimed at facilitating action to be taken to prevent graffiti spraying by him and/or his associates before it takes place. An order in clear and simple terms preventing the offender from being in possession of a can of spray paint in a public place gives the police or others responsible for protecting the property an opportunity to take action in advance of the actual spraying and makes it clear to the offender that he has lost the right to carry such a can for the duration of the order.

If a court wishes to make an order prohibiting a group of youngsters from racing cars or motor bikes on an estate or driving at excessive speed (anti-social behaviour for those living on the estate), then the order should not (normally) prohibit driving whilst disqualified. It should prohibit, for example, the offender whilst on the estate from taking part in, or encouraging, racing or driving at an excessive speed. It might also prevent the group from congregating with named others in a particular area of the estate. Such an order gives those responsible for enforcing order on the estate the opportunity to take action to prevent the anti-social conduct, it is to be hoped, before it takes place.

In *R (Cooke) v Director of Public Prosecutions* [2008] EWHC 2703 (Admin) the court held that an order was not appropriate in relation to an offender who due to mental incapacity was not able to understand its terms, as such an order would fail to protect the public and could therefore not be said to be necessary to protect others.

In *R (McGarrett) v Kingston Crown Court*, unreported, 8 June 2009, the court quashed an indefinite anti-social behaviour order made against a defendant who had been convicted of a single offence of breaching a noise abatement notice. There were no other relevant offences or behaviour that had been considered by the court, and accordingly the test of necessity was not made out.

A condition not to cause harassment, alarm, or distress was too imprecise; conditions to be clear as to what behaviour the order was seeking to discourage (*Heron v Plymouth City Council* [2009] EWHC 3562 (Admin)).

BIND OVER, TO KEEP THE PEACE

Who can be bound over: Any person before the court, as defendant or witness (provided that they have given evidence–a witness statement alone does not suffice (*R v Swindon Crown Court ex p Singh* [1984] 1 WLR 449)), can be bound over. **Consent:** A bind over can only be made by consent, although in obiter comments this requirement was doubted in *R v Lincoln Crown Court, ex p Jude* [1998] 1 WLR 24. It is worth noting however that the court in *Jude* does not appear to have been referred to the earlier case of *Veater v Glennon* [1981] 1 WLR 567 where Lord Lane made clear that consent was a formal requirement; indeed if consent were not required the ability to imprison in the absence of such consent would be rendered otiose. The court should, as a matter of good practice, hear representations (but see *Woking Justices, ex p Gossage* [1973] QB 448 where the court held that there was no duty to hear representations if the court was binding over a person in their own recognizance for a 'just and suitable' sum following acquittal), and *R v North London Magistrate ex p Haywood* [1973] 1 WLR 965 where warning was not necessary when the person's conduct in the courtroom indicates that a breach of the peace is imminent; refusal can result in committal to prison. In respect to an offender under 18 years who refuses to consent the penalty is an attendance centre order (Powers of Criminal Courts (Sentencing) Act 2000, s 60(1)(b)). If following the denial of consent a case is adjourned and the person does not attend court the options are either to proceed in absence or issue a warrant. If the court elects to proceed in absence then it cannot if the case is proved go on to issue a warrant, it must further adjourn the matter to allow the person to attend and indicate whether he now agreed to be bound. If on a further adjournment the person does not attend then a warrant can then be issued over (*R v Liverpool Justices ex p Santos* [1998] 2 Cr App R 108). **Conditions:** The order is to keep the peace and be of good behaviour; further conditions are not permitted. Generally, a binding over to keep the peace is typically only warranted where there is evidence of likely personal danger to others involving violence or the threat of violence (see, for example, *Percy v Director of Public Prosecutions* [1995] 3 All ER 124). The court will set a recognizance to be forfeit on breach. Breach (determined on the civil standard of proof–*R v Marlow Justices ex p O'Sullivan* [1984] QB 381) results solely in surrender of all or part of the recognizance, it is not possible to impose any further penalty (*Gilbert*, unreported, 4 April 1974). If the sum set is more than trivial, enquiry should be made in relation to means; a failure to do so may give rise to a successful challenge (*Lincoln Crown Court, ex p Jude* The Times, 30 April 1997). **Following acquittal:** In *R v Middlesex Crown Court, ex p Khan* (1997) 161 JP 240 the court held: '… if a judge is going to require a man to be bound over in circumstances where he has been acquitted, it is particularly important that he should be satisfied beyond a reasonable doubt that the man poses a potential threat to other persons and that he is a man of violence.' Also see: *Emohare v Thames Magistrates' Court* [2009] EWHC 689 (Admin) where the importance of following the practice direction (below) was emphasised). **Costs:** If an allegation that the person has breached the peace is not well founded costs will lie under Magistrates' Courts act 1980, s 64, not from central funds. Despite the fact that the alleged breach will have been prosecuted by the CPS, costs will fall onto the police, so notice to them must be given before costs can be awarded (*R v Coventry Magistrates' Court, ex p CPS* [1996] Crim LR 723).

The Consolidated Criminal Practice Direction provides:

Consolidated Criminal Practice Direction para III.31.2, III.31.3, III.31.4, and III.31.8

Binding over to keep the peace

III.31.2

Before imposing a binding over order, the court must be satisfied that a breach of the peace involving violence, or an imminent threat of violence, has occurred, or that there is a real risk of violence in the future.

Such violence may be perpetrated by the individual who will be subject to the order, or by a third party as a natural consequence of the individual's conduct.

111.31.3

In light of the judgment in Hashman and Harrup, courts should no longer bind an individual over 'to be of good behaviour'. Rather than binding an individual over to 'keep the peace' in general terms, the court should identify the specific conduct or activity from which the individual must refrain.

Written order

111.31.4

When making an order binding an individual over to refrain from specified types of conduct or activities, the details of that conduct or those activities should be specified by the court in a written order served on all relevant parties. The court should state its reasons for the making of the order, its length and the amount of the recognisance. The length of the order should be proportionate to the harm sought to be avoided and should not generally exceed 12 months.

Burden of proof

III.31.8

The court should be satisfied beyond reasonable doubt of the matters complained of before a binding over order may be imposed. Where the procedure has been commenced on complaint, the burden of proof rests on the complainant. In all other circumstances the burden of proof rests on the prosecution.

BREACH OR REVOCATION OF COMMUNITY ORDER

Breach of the order: Criminal Justice Act 2003, Sch 8 deals with the consequences on breach. A breach must be proved to the criminal standard (*West Yorkshire Probation Board v Boulter* (2005) 169 JP 601).The court has the 3 options detailed in para 9(1). Where the order did not include unpaid work and it is proposed to make the order more onerous by including it, the minimum number of hours is 20 rather than the usual 40. If the breach has occurred due to the offender's ill-health, a court should not resentence (*Bishop* [2004] EWCA Crim 2956). There is no power to commence breach proceedings once the operational period has expired (*West Yorkshire Probation Board v Cruick-shanks* [2010] EWHC 615 (Admin)). **Reasonable excuse for failing to comply with the order**: The burden of proof falls on the defendant, to the civil standard. The fact that a person is appealing against a community order does not give them a reasonable excuse not to comply (*West Midlands Probation Board v Sutton Coldfield Magistrates' Court* [2008] EWHC 15 (Admin)).

Commission of new offence: Sch 8 para 21 and 22 deals with the courts powers when the offender has committed a new offence. The court has three options open to it in respect to the original order: do nothing, and sentence for the new offence; or if the order was made by the Crown Court, commit the offender for sentence; or revoke the order and deal with the offender in any manner in which it could deal with him if he had just been convicted by the court of the offence (having taken into account the offender's level of cooperation with the order).

Revocation: Schedule 8 para 13 details the courts power to revoke a community order, with or without resentencing.

Regard should be had to the definitive Sentencing Council Guideline: New Sentences: Criminal Justice Act 2003), which is binding on all courts:

- Where an offender fails, without reasonable excuse, to comply with one or more requirements, the 'responsible officer' can either give a warning or initiate breach proceedings.

Where the offender fails to comply without reasonable excuse for the second time within a 12-month period, the 'responsible officer' must initiate proceedings.

- In such proceedings the court must either increase the severity of the existing sentence (ie impose more onerous conditions, including requirements aimed at enforcement, such as a curfew or supervision requirement) or revoke the existing sentence and proceed as though sentencing for the original offence. The court is required to take account of the circumstances of the breach, which will inevitably have an impact on its response.
- In certain circumstances (where an offender has wilfully and persistently failed to comply with an order made in respect of an offence that is not itself punishable by imprisonment), the court can impose a maximum of six months custody.
- When increasing the onerousness of requirements, the court must consider the impact on the offender's ability to comply and the possibility of precipitating a custodial sentence for further breach. For that reason, and particularly where the breach occurs towards the end of the sentence, the court should take account of compliance to date and may consider that extending the supervision or operational periods will be more sensible; in other cases it might choose to add punitive or rehabilitative requirements instead. In making these changes the court must be mindful of the legislative restrictions on the overall length of community sentences and on the supervision and operational periods allowed for each type of requirement.
- The court dealing with breach of a community sentence should have as its primary objective ensuring that the requirements of the sentence are finished, and this is important if the court is to have regard to the statutory purposes of sentencing. A court that imposes a custodial sentence for breach without giving adequate consideration to alternatives is in danger of imposing a sentence that is not commensurate with the seriousness of the original offence and is solely a punishment for breach. This risks undermining the purposes it has identified as being important. Nonetheless, courts will need to be vigilant to ensure that there is a realistic prospect of the purposes of the order being achieved.
- A court sentencing for breach must take account of the extent to which the offender has complied with the requirements of the community order, the reasons for breach, and the point at which the breach has occurred. Where a breach takes place towards the end of the operational period and the court is satisfied that the offenders appearance before the court is likely to be sufficient in itself to ensure future compliance, then given that it is not open to the court to make no order, an approach that the court might wish to adopt could be to resentence in a way that enables the original order to be completed properly—for example, a differently constructed community sentence that aims to secure compliance with the purposes of the original sentence.
- If the court decides to make the order more onerous, it must give careful consideration, with advice from the Probation Service, to the offender's ability to comply. A custodial sentence should be the last resort, where all reasonable efforts to ensure that an offender completes a community sentence have failed.

Criminal Justice Act 2003, Sch 8 para 9, 13, 21 and 22

9 Powers of magistrates' court

(1) If it is proved to the satisfaction of a magistrates' court before which an offender appears or is

brought under paragraph 7 that he has failed without reasonable excuse to comply with any of the requirements of the community order, the court must deal with him in respect of the failure in any

one of the following ways—

  (a) by amending the terms of the community order so as to impose more onerous requirements which the court could include if it were then making the order;

(b) where the community order was made by a magistrates' court, by dealing with him, for the offence in respect of which the order was made, in any way in which the court could deal with him if he had just been convicted by it of the offence;

(c) where—

    (i) the community order was made by a magistrates' court,

    (ii) the offence in respect of which the order was made was not an offence punishable by imprisonment,

    (iii) the offender is aged 18 or over, and

    (iv) the offender has wilfully and persistently failed to comply with the requirements of the order, by dealing with him, in respect of that offence, by imposing a sentence of imprisonment or, in the case of a person aged at least 18 but under 21, detention in a young offender institution, for a term not exceeding 6 months.

(2) In dealing with an offender under sub-paragraph (1), a magistrates' court must take into account the extent to which the offender has complied with the requirements of the community order.

(3) In dealing with an offender under sub-paragraph (1)(a), the court may extend the duration of particular requirements (subject to any limit imposed by Chapter 4 of Part 12 of this Act) but may not extend the period specified under section 177(5).

(3A) Where—

(a) the court is dealing with the offender under sub-paragraph (1)(a), and

(b) the community order does not contain an unpaid work requirement, section 199(2)(a) applies in relation to the inclusion of such a requirement as if for "40" there were substituted "20".

(4) In dealing with an offender under sub-paragraph (1)(b), the court may, in the case of an offender who has wilfully and persistently failed to comply with the requirements of the community order, impose a custodial sentence (where the order was made in respect of an offence punishable with such a sentence) notwithstanding anything in section 152(2).

(5) Where a magistrates' court deals with an offender under sub-paragraph (1)(b) or (c), it must revoke the community order if it is still in force.

(5A) Where a magistrates' court dealing with an offender under sub-paragraph (1)(a) would not otherwise have the power to amend the community order under paragraph 16 (amendment by reason of change of residence), that paragraph has effect as if the references to the appropriate court were references to the court dealing with the offender.

(6) Where a community order was made by the Crown Court and a magistrates' court would (apart from this sub-paragraph) be required to deal with the offender under sub-paragraph (1)(a), (b) or (c), it may instead commit him to custody or release him on bail until he can be brought or appear before the Crown Court.

(7) A magistrates' court which deals with an offender's case under subparagraph (6) must send to the Crown Court—

(a) a certificate signed by a justice of the peace certifying that the offender has failed to comply with the requirements of the community order in the respect specified in the certificate, and

(b) such other particulars of the case as may be desirable; and a certificate purporting to be so signed is admissible as evidence of the failure before the Crown Court.

(8) A person sentenced under sub-paragraph (1)(b) or (c) for an offence may appeal to the Crown Court against the sentence.

13 Revocation of order with or without re-sentencing: powers of magistrates' court

(1) This paragraph applies where a community order, other than an order made by the Crown Court and falling within paragraph 14(1)(a), is in force and on the application of

the offender or the responsible officer it appears to the appropriate magistrates' court that, having regard to circumstances which have arisen since the order was made, it would be in the interests of justice—

(a) for the order to be revoked, or

(b) for the offender to be dealt with in some other way for the offence in respect of which the order was made.

(2) The appropriate magistrates' court may—

(a) revoke the order, or

(b) both—

(i) revoke the order, and

(ii) deal with the offender, for the offence in respect of which the order was made, in any way in which it could deal with him if he had just been convicted by the court of the offence.

(3) The circumstances in which a community order may be revoked under subparagraph (2) include the offender's making good progress or his responding satisfactorily to supervision or treatment (as the case requires).

(4) In dealing with an offender under sub-paragraph (2)(b), a magistrates' court must take into account the extent to which the offender has complied with the requirements of the community order.

(5) A person sentenced under sub-paragraph (2)(b) for an offence may appeal to the Crown Court against the sentence.

(6) Where a magistrates' court proposes to exercise its powers under this paragraph otherwise than on the application of the offender, it must summon him to appear before the court and, if he does not appear in answer to the summons, may issue a warrant for his arrest.

(7) In this paragraph "the appropriate magistrates' court" means—

(a) in the case of an order imposing a drug rehabilitation requirement which is subject to review, the magistrates' court responsible for the order, and

(b) in the case of any other community order, a magistrates' court acting in the local justice area concerned.

21 Powers of magistrates' court following subsequent conviction

(1) This paragraph applies where—

(a) an offender in respect of whom a community order made by a magistrates' court is in force is convicted of an offence by a magistrates' court, and

(b) it appears to the court that it would be in the interests of justice to exercise its powers under this paragraph, having regard to circumstances which have arisen since the community order was made.

(2) The magistrates' court may—

(a) revoke the order, or

(b) both—

(i) revoke the order, and

(ii) deal with the offender, for the offence in respect of which the order was made, in any way in which he could have been dealt with for that offence by the court which made the order if the order had not been made.

(3) In dealing with an offender under sub-paragraph (2)(b), a magistrates' court must take into account the extent to which the offender has complied with the requirements of the community order.

(4) A person sentenced under sub-paragraph (2)(b) for an offence may appeal to the Crown Court against the sentence.

(1) Where an offender in respect of whom a community order made by the Crown Court is in force is convicted of an offence by a magistrates' court, the magistrates' court may commit the offender in custody or release him on bail until he can be brought before the Crown Court.

BREACH OF SUPERVISION ORDER

An offence committed during the currency of a supervision order does not put the offender in breach of the order. If an offender breaches any of the terms of the order, the court has the following options (Powers of Criminal Courts (Sentencing) Act 2000, Sch 7):

- If the order was made by a Crown Court it may commit the offender for sentence to the Crown Court that made the order.
- It may impose a fine not exceeding £1,000.
- It may impose an attendance centre order, or curfew order.
- It may revoke the order and deal with the offender in any manner in which it could deal with him if he had just been convicted by the court of the offence (note that this option is not available if the order was made by the Crown Court).

COMMITTAL FOR SENTENCE

See: Allocation, Committal, Sending and Transfer in Part C (for adults) and Part F (youths).

COMMUNITY ORDERS AND SENTENCES: GENERAL PRINCIPLES

Overview:

Age when convicted	10–15 years	16–17 years	18–20 years
Action plan	Yes*	Yes*	No
Attendance centre	Yes*	Yes*	If committed before 4 April 2005
Community orders—CJA 2003	No	No	If committed on or after 4 April 2005
Community punishment	No	Yes*	If committed before 4 April 2005
Community rehabilitation	No	Yes*	If committed before 4 April 2005
Community punishment and rehabilitation	No	Yes*	If committed before 4 April 2005
Curfew	Yes* (maximum 3 months)	Yes* (maximum 3 months)	If committed before 4 April 2005
Drug treatment and testing	No	Yes*	If committed before 4 April 2005
Exclusion order	Yes* (maximum 3 months)	Yes* (maximum 3 months)	If committed before 4 April 2005
Referral order	Yes	Yes	No
Reparation	Yes	Yes	No

Supervision	Yes*	Yes*	No
Youth Rehabilitation Order	Yes	Yes	No

* indicates for an offence prior to 30 November 2009

General criteria: Criminal Justice Act 2003, s 148 provides that a court must not pass a community sentence on an offender unless it is of the opinion that the offence, or the combination of the offence and one or more offences associated with it, was serious enough to warrant such a sentence. Section 148 (5) makes it clear that just because the threshold for a community penalty is crossed, it is not mandatory to impose such a penalty. A community order cannot be imposed for an offence not punishable with imprisonment (Criminal Justice Act 2003, s 150A). When imposing requirements on the offender as part of the community order, a court should balance the requirements, or combination of requirements, with the offender's personal circumstances, and avoid conflict with work, schooling, or religious beliefs. **Following a lengthy remand in custody**: It is arguable that a person held in custody may well have served sufficient punishment and therefore ought not to be sentenced to a community penalty. In *Hemmings* [2008] 1 Cr App R (S) 106 the court held: 'A sentence of a community order, and all the more so one coupled with requirements which have a real impact on the offender's liberty, is a form of punishment. It does not seem to us to be right that the appellant should receive a substantial further punishment in circumstances where he has already received what was in practice the maximum punishment by way of imprisonment which the law could have imposed. That reasoning seems to us to be in line with the reasoning in [earlier cases where] ... the court took the course of imposing a conditional discharge.'

The court went on to impose a conditional discharge that expired immediately upon sentence to ensure that the appellant could not fall foul of the consequences of any breach of the order. In *Rakib* [2011] EWCA Crim 870 the court, considering *Hemmings*, held that time spent in custody was not a determinative factor and the rehabilitative aims of sentencing (s 142(1) of the Criminal Justice Act 2003) may in some cases justify a community penalty even if the offender had served on remand the equivalent of the maximum custodial sentence.

Requirements and length: The Council's guideline provides that the seriousness of the offence should be the initial factor in determining which requirements to include in a community order. It establishes three sentencing ranges within the community order band based on offence seriousness (low, medium, and high), and identifies non-exhaustive examples of requirements that might be appropriate in each. These are set out below. The examples focus on punishment in the community; other requirements of a rehabilitative nature may be more appropriate in some cases.

The particular requirements imposed within the range must be suitable for the individual offender and will be influenced by a wide range of factors, including the stated purpose(s) of the sentence, the risk of reoffending, the ability of the offender to comply, and the availability of the requirements in the local area. Sentencers must ensure that the sentence strikes the right balance between proportionality and suitability. The resulting restriction on liberty must be a proportionate response to the offence that was committed.

Low	Medium	High
Offences only just cross community order threshold, where the seriousness of the offence or the nature of the offender's record means that a discharge or fine is inappropriate.	Offences that obviously fall within the community order band.	Offences only just fall below the custody threshold or the custody threshold is crossed but a community order is more appropriate in the circumstances.

In general, only one requirement will be appropriate and the length may be curtailed if additional requirements are necessary.		More intensive sentences which combine two or more requirements may be appropriate.
Suitable requirements might include: • 40–80 hours unpaid work • curfew requirement within the lowest range (eg up to 12 hours per day for a few weeks) • exclusion requirement, without electronic monitoring, for a few months • prohibited activity requirement • attendance centre requirement (where available).	Suitable requirements might include: • greater number of hours of unpaid work (eg 80–150 hours) • curfew requirement within the middle range (eg up to 12 hours per day for 2–3 months) • exclusion requirement lasting in the region of 6 months • prohibited activity requirement.	Suitable requirements might include: • 150–300 hours unpaid work • activity requirement up to the maximum of 60 days • curfew requirement up to 12 hours per day for 4–6 months • exclusion order lasting in the region of 12 months.

Pre-sentence reports: CJA 2003, s 156 provides:

Criminal Justice Act 2003, s 156

(1) In forming any such opinion as is mentioned in section 148(1) or (2)(b), section 152(2) or section 153(2),or in section 1(4)(b) or (c) of the Criminal Justice and Immigration Act 2008 (youth rehabilitation orders with intensive supervision and surveillance or fostering), a court must take into account all such information as is available to it about the circumstances of the offence or (as the case may be) of the offence and the offence or offences associated with it, including any aggravating or mitigating factors.

(2) In forming any such opinion as is mentioned in section 148(2)(a), the court may take into account any information about the offender which is before it.

(3) Subject to subsection (4), a court must obtain and consider a pre-sentence report before—

    (a) in the case of a custodial sentence, forming any such opinion as is mentioned in section 152(2), section 153(2), section 225(1)(b), section 226(1)(b), section 227(1)(b) or section 228(1)(b)(i), or

    (b) in the case of a community sentence, forming any such opinion as is mentioned in section 148(1) or (2)(b), or in section 1(4)(b) or (c) of the Criminal Justice and Immigration Act 2008, or any opinion as to the suitability for the offender of the particular requirement or requirements to be imposed by the community order or youth rehabilitation order .

(4) Subsection (3) does not apply if, in the circumstances of the case, the court is of the opinion that it is unnecessary to obtain a pre-sentence report.

(5) In a case where the offender is aged under 18, the court must not form the opinion mentioned in subsection (4) unless—

    (a) there exists a previous pre-sentence report obtained in respect of the offender, and

    (b) the court has had regard to the information contained in that report, or, if there is more than one such report, the most recent report.

(6) No custodial sentence or community sentence is invalidated by the failure of a court to obtain and consider a pre-sentence report before forming an opinion referred to in subsection (3), but any court on an appeal against such a sentence—

(a) must, subject to subsection (7), obtain a pre-sentence report if none was obtained by the court below, and

(b) must consider any such report obtained by it or by that court.

(7) Subsection (6)(a) does not apply if the court is of the opinion—

(a) that the court below was justified in forming an opinion that it was unnecessary to obtain a pre-sentence report, or

(b) that, although the court below was not justified in forming that opinion, in the circumstances of the case at the time it is before the court, it is unnecessary to obtain a pre-sentence report.

(8) In a case where the offender is aged under 18, the court must not form the opinion mentioned in subsection (7) unless—

(a) there exists a previous pre-sentence report obtained in respect of the offender, and

(b) the court has had regard to the information contained in that report, or, if there is more than one such report, the most recent report.

COMPENSATION

Magistrates' Court Sentencing Guidelines suggested levels of compensation:

Physical injury		
Type of injury	**Description**	**Starting point**
Graze	Depending on size	Up to £75
Bruise	Depending on size	Up to £100
Cut: no permanent scar	Depending on size and whether stitched	£100–500
Black eye		£125
Eye	Blurred or double vision lasting up to 6 weeks	Up to £1,000
	Blurred or double vision lasting for 6–13 weeks	£1,000
	Blurred or double vision lasting for more than 13 weeks (recovery expected)	£1,750
Brain	Concussion lasting one week	£1,500
Nose	Undisplaced fracture of nasal bone	£1,000
	Displaced fracture requiring manipulation	£2,000
	Deviated nasal septum requiring septoplasty	£2,000
Physical injury		
Type of injury	**Description**	**Starting point**
Loss of non-front tooth	Depending on cosmetic effect	£1,250
Loss of front tooth		£1,750
Facial scar	Minor disfigurement (permanent)	£1,500
Arm	Fractured humerus, radius, ulna (substantial recovery)	£3,300
Shoulder	Dislocated (substantial recovery)	£1,750

Wrist	Dislocated/fractured—including scaphoid fracture (substantial recovery)	£3,300
	Fractured—colles type (substantial recovery)	£4,400
Sprained wrist, ankle	Disabling for up to 6 weeks	Up to £1,000
	Disabling for 6–13 weeks	£1,000
	Disabling for more than 13 weeks	£2,500
Finger	Fractured finger other than index finger (substantial recovery)	£1,000
	Fractured index finger (substantial recovery)	£1,750
	Fractured thumb (substantial recovery)	£2,000
Leg	Fractured fibula (substantial recovery)	£2,500
	Fractured femur, tibia (substantial recovery)	£3,800
Abdomen	Injury requiring laprotomy	£3,800

Mental injury	
Description	Starting point
Temporary mental anxiety (including terror, shock, distress), not medically verified	Up to £1,000
Disabling mental anxiety, lasting more than 6 weeks, medically verified	£1,000
Disability mental illness, lasting up to 28 weeks, confirmed by psychiatric diagnosis	£2,500

Physical and sexual abuse		
Type of abuse	Description	Starting point
Physical abuse of adult	Intermittent physical assaults resulting in accumulation of healed wounds, burns or scalds, but with no appreciable disfigurement	£2,000
Physical abuse of child	Isolated or intermittent assault(s) resulting in weals, hair pulled from scalp etc	£1,000
	Intermittent physical assaults resulting in accumulation of healed wounds, burns, or scalds, but with no appreciable disfigurement	£2,000
Sexual abuse of adult	Non-penetrative indecent physical acts over clothing	£1,000
	Non-penetrative indecent act(s) under clothing	£2,000
Sexual abuse of child (under 18)	Non-penetrative indecent physical act(s) over clothing	£1,000
	Non-penetrative frequent assaults over clothing or non-penetrative indecent act under clothing	£2,000
	Repetitive indecent acts under clothing	£3,300

General principles: A court can award compensation in respect to both offences charged and those taken into consideration when sentencing provided that the overall total compensation does not exceed £5,000 in relation to any one offence and an aggregate total of offences charged multiplied by £5,000. **Motor vehicle damage:** In relation to motor vehicle damage the maximum payable will generally be the excess not paid by the Motor Insurer's Bureau (currently £300), save where it is in respect to a vehicle stolen or taken without consent and there is damage to that vehicle, or the claim is not covered by the MIB. In relation to offences involving vehicles under the Theft Act, damage to vehicles other than the one taken cannot be the subject of a claim for compensation (*Divers* [2006] EWCA Crim 169), nor can damage to other property be included (e.g. *Mayor v Oxford* (1980) 2 Cr App R (S) 80); note that earlier cases refer to now repealed sections, but these have been largely replicated in section 130 of the Act–for which see *Stapylton* [2012] EWCA Crim 728). If loss is not agreed then the prosecution must be in a position to prove loss, but it will rarely be appropriate for the court to hear evidence from a third-party (*Bewick* [2007] EWCA Crim 3297) and in most cases will be able to draw common sense inferences from the admitted or proven facts that support the conviction. A court should not entertain complex arguments in relation to loss, it being better to have such issues decided by the civil courts (*Horsham Justices, ex p Richards* [1985] 2 All ER 1114), but in *Pola* [2009] EWCA Crim 655 the court upheld an award of compensation in the sum of £90,000 for serious head injury where the judge was in possession of cogent evidence and had properly applied the statutory framework. **Means**: A means enquiry should be carried out in order to assess the offender's ability to pay (*Gray* [2011] EWCA 225). If counsel puts before the court information relating to the means of the offender with the view to the making of a compensation order, particularly where the making of a compensation order is expected to affect the decision whether to impose a custodial sentence on the offender, or the length of such sentence, it is the responsibility of counsel to satisfy himself or herself of the accuracy of the information. It is not sufficient to rely on instructions without further inquiry or supporting documentation (*Hobden* [2009] EWCA Crim 1584). **Compensation, fines and imprisonment**: if there are insufficient resources to pay both a compensation order must take priority. There is nothing in principle wrong, in an appropriate case imposing both imprisonment and compensation.

Powers of Criminal Courts (Sentencing) Act 2000, s 130(1)–(10)

(1) A court by or before which a person is convicted of an offence, instead of or in addition to dealing with him in any other way, may, on application or otherwise, make an order (in this Act referred to as a 'compensation order') requiring him—

   (a) to pay compensation for any personal injury, loss or damage resulting from that offence or any other offence which is taken into consideration by the court in determining sentence; or

   (b) to make payments for funeral expenses or bereavement in respect of a death resulting from any such offence, other than a death due to an accident arising out of the presence of a motor vehicle on a road; but this is subject to the following provisions of this section and to section 131 below.

(2) Where the person is convicted of an offence the sentence for which is fixed by law or falls to be imposed under 110(2) or 111(2) above, section 51A(2) of the Firearms Act 1968, section 225, 226, 227 or 228 of the Criminal Justice Act 2003 or section 29(4) or (6) of the Violent Crime Reduction Act 2006, subsection (1) above shall have effect as if the words 'instead of or' were omitted.

(3) A court shall give reasons, on passing sentence, if it does not make a compensation order in a case where this section empowers it to do so.

(4) Compensation under subsection (1) above shall be of such amount as the court considers appropriate, having regard to any evidence and to any representations that are made by or on behalf of the accused or the prosecutor.

(5) In the case of an offence under the Theft Act 1968 or Fraud Act 2006, where the property in question is recovered, any damage to the property occurring while it was out of the owner's possession shall be treated for the purposes of subsection (1) above as having resulted from the offence, however and by whomever the damage was caused.

(6) A compensation order may only be made in respect of injury, loss or damage (other than

loss suffered by a person's dependants in consequence of his death) which was due to an accident arising out of the presence of a motor vehicle on a road, if—

    (a) it is in respect of damage which is treated by subsection (5) above as resulting from an offence under the Theft Act 1968 or Fraud Act 2006; or

    (b) it is in respect of injury, loss or damage as respects which—

        (i) the offender is uninsured in relation to the use of the vehicle; and

        (ii) compensation is not payable under any arrangements to which the Secretary of State is a party.

(7) Where a compensation order is made in respect of injury, loss or damage due to an accident arising out of the presence of a motor vehicle on a road, the amount to be paid may include an amount representing the whole or part of any loss of or reduction in preferential rates of insurance attributable to the accident.

(8) A vehicle the use of which is exempted from insurance by section 144 of the Road Traffic Act 1988 is not uninsured for the purposes of subsection (6) above.

(9) A compensation order in respect of funeral expenses may be made for the benefit of any one who incurred the expenses.

(10) A compensation order in respect of bereavement may be made only for the benefit of a person for whose benefit a claim for damages for bereavement could be made under section 1A of the Fatal Accidents Act 1976; and the amount of compensation in respect of bereavement shall not exceed the amount for the time being specified in section 1A (3) of that Act.

CONCURRENT AND CONSECUTIVE SENTENCES

Concurrent Sentences:

Criminal Justice Act 2003, s 263

(1) This section applies where—

    (a) a person ("the offender") has been sentenced to two or more terms of imprisonment which are wholly or partly concurrent, and

    (b) the sentences were passed on the same occasion or, where they were passed on different occasions, the person has not been released under this Chapter at any time during the period beginning with the first and ending with the last of those occasions.

(2) Where this section applies—

    (a) nothing in this Chapter requires the Secretary of State to release the offender in respect of any of the terms unless and until he is required to release him in respect of each of the others,

    (b) section 244 does not authorise the Secretary of State to release him on licence under that section in respect of any of the terms unless and until that section authorises the Secretary of State to do so in respect of each of the others,

    (c) on and after his release under this Chapter the offender is to be on licence for so long, and subject to such conditions, as is required by this Chapter in respect of any of the sentences.

(3) Where the sentences include one or more sentences of twelve months or more and one or more sentences of less than twelve months, the terms of the licence may be determined by the Secretary of State in accordance with section 250(4)(b), without regard to the requirements of any custody plus order or intermittent custody order.

(4) In this section "term of imprisonment" includes a determinate sentence of detention under section 91 of the Sentencing Act or under section 228 of this Act or a sentence of detention in a young offender institution under section 96 of the Sentencing Act or section 227 of this Act.

Consecutive Sentences:

Magistrates Courts Act 1980, s 133

(1)   Subject to section 265 of the Criminal Justice Act 2003, a magistrates' court imposing imprisonment or youth custody on any person may order that the term of imprisonment or youth custody shall commence on the expiration of any other term of imprisonment or youth custody imposed by that or any other court; but where a magistrates' court imposes two or more terms of imprisonment or youth custody to run consecutively the aggregate of such terms shall not, subject to the provisions of this section, exceed 6 months.

(2)   If two or more of the terms imposed by the court are imposed in respect of an offence triable either way which was tried summarily otherwise than in pursuance of section 22(2) above, the aggregate of the terms so imposed and any other terms imposed by the court may exceed 6 months but shall not, subject to the following provisions of this section, exceed 12 months.

(2A)   In relation to the imposition of terms of detention in a young offender institution subsection (2) above shall have effect as if the reference to an offence triable either way were a reference to such an offence or an offence triable only on indictment.

(3)   The limitations imposed by the preceding subsections shall not operate to reduce the aggregate of the terms that the court may impose in respect of any offences below the term which the court has power to impose in respect of any one of those offences.

(4)   Where a person has been sentenced by a magistrates' court to imprisonment and a fine for the same offence, a period of imprisonment imposed for non-payment of the fine, or for want of sufficient distress to satisfy the fine, shall not be subject to the limitations imposed by the preceding subsections.

(5)   For the purposes of this section a term of imprisonment shall be deemed to be imposed in respect of an offence if it is imposed as a sentence or in default of payment of a sum adjudged to be paid by the conviction or for want of sufficient distress to satisfy such a sum.

Restriction: The statutory restriction on consecutive sentences applies only to sentences imposed on the same occasion (*Prime* (1983) 5 Cr App R (S) 127). **General Principle**: In *Ralphs* [2009] EWCA 2555 Crim the court summarised the main principles:

"Consecutive terms should not normally be imposed for offences which arise out of the same incident or transaction. R v Noble [2003] 1CAR(S) 312 provides a clear example: consecutive sentences for causing several deaths by dangerous driving were quashed. Notwithstanding the numerous deaths there was a single act of dangerous driving. However there is sometimes a difficulty in deciding whether criminality under consideration may or may not be regarded as a single incident. The fact that offences are committed simultaneously is not necessarily conclusive. Thus R v Fletcher [2002] 2 CAR (S) 127 exemplifies orders for consecutive sentences in the context of indecent assault and threats to kill which arose out of the same incident. Examples abound of occasions when consecutive sentences are justifiably imposed. Obvious examples include a robbery committed with the use of a firearm, or violent resistance of arrest, or offences committed on bail: in all these examples however distinct offences are committed in circumstances where the offences, although distinct, can properly be said to increase the relevant criminality. A further principle, identified [...] is that a court "may impose consecutive sentences for offences committed on the same occasion when there are exceptional circumstances which justify a departure from the usual practice". (See R v Wheatley [1983] 5CAR (S) 417 (a case of a driver driving without insurance but after consuming excess alcohol) applied in R v Dillon [1983] 5CAR (S) 439, R v Lawrence [1989] 11 CAR (S) 580 and R v Hardy [2006] 2CAR (S) 4). Our attention was also drawn to R v Jameson and Jameson [2009] 2 CAR (S) 26 [...] where it was stated that: "...A sentencing judge should pass a total sentence which properly reflects the overall criminality of the defendant and the course and nature of the criminal conduct disclosed by the offences for which he stands to be sentenced, while always having regard to the principle of totality. However, the imposition of concurrent sentences for like offences may not be appropriate where, as here, the statutory maximum sentence for an offence prevents the proper reflection of these matters".".

Criminal Justice Act 2003, s 264

(1) This section applies where—

   (a) a person ("the offender") has been sentenced to two or more terms of imprisonment which are to be served consecutively on each other, and

   (b) the sentences were passed on the same occasion or, where they were passed on different occasions, the person has not been released under this Chapter at any time during the period beginning with the first and ending with the last of those occasions, and

   (c) none of those terms is a term to which an intermittent custody order relates.

(2) Nothing in this Chapter requires the Secretary of State to release the offender on licence until he has served a period equal in length to the aggregate of the length of the custodial periods in relation to each of the terms of imprisonment.

(3) Where any of the terms of imprisonment is a term of twelve months or more, the offender is, on and after his release under this Chapter, to be on licence—

   (a) until he would, but for his release, have served a term equal in length to the aggregate length of the terms of imprisonment, and

   (b) subject to such conditions as are required by this Chapter in respect of each of those terms of imprisonment.

(4) Where each of the terms of imprisonment is a term of less than twelve months, the offender is, on and after his release under this Chapter, to be on licence until the relevant time, and subject to such conditions as are required by this Chapter in respect of any of the terms of imprisonment, and none of the terms is to be regarded for any purpose as continuing after the relevant time.

(5) In subsection (4) "the relevant time" means the time when the offender would, but for his release, have served a term equal in length to the aggregate of—

   (a) all the custodial periods in relation to the terms of imprisonment, and

   (b) the longest of the licence periods in relation to those terms.

(6) In this section—

   (a) "custodial period"—

      (i) in relation to an extended sentence imposed under section 227 or 228 , means one-half of the appropriate custodial term determined under that section,

      (ii) in relation to a term of twelve months or more, means one—half of the term, and

      (iii) in relation to a term of less than twelve months complying with section 181, means the custodial period as defined by subsection (3)(a) of that section;

   (b) "licence period", in relation to a term of less than twelve months complying with section 181, has the meaning given by subsection (3)(b) of that section.

(7) This section applies to a determinate sentence of detention under section 91 of the Sentencing Act or under section 228 of this Act or a sentence of detention in a young offender institution under section 96 of the Sentencing Act or section 227 of this Act as it applies to a term of imprisonment of 12 months or more.

In *R (Elam) v Secretary of State for Justice* [2012] EWCA Civ 29 it was held that: "The s.264 regime thus applies (for the purpose of ascertaining licence expiry dates) in every case save one

— namely where all the sentences in question are passed for pre-4 April 2005 offences. In that case, but no other, s.37(1) of the 1991 Act (preserved for this purpose by paragraph 19) has effect to determine the licence expiry date. S.37(1) cannot apply to pre-4 April 2005 offences sentenced alongside later offences because all the sentences passed could not and would not then be aggregated under s.264(3)(a); and, as I have stated, the resulting licence expiry date would not be as prescribed by s.264."

CONDITIONAL AND ABSOLUTE DISCHARGE

Reason for imposition: When not expedient to inflict any punishment having regard to the circumstances including the nature of the offence and the character of the offender (PCC(S)A 2000, s 12). **Prohibition on imposing**: On an offender convicted of an offence within 2 years of being warned under Crime and Disorder Act 1998, s 65 (unless there are exceptional circumstances). If the defendant is subject to a suspended sentence of imprisonment imposed by the crown court, it will not be appropriate to impose a discharge. The court should instead commit the offender to the crown court in order that both matters be dealt with at the same time (*Moore* [1995] QB 353). In *Lynch* [2007] EWCA Crim 2624 the court quashed a discharge made following the defendant having been on remand for the maximum period for which custody could have been imposed. **Duration**: 3 years maximum for a conditional discharge. **Additional orders**: The following orders can be made alongside a discharge: costs, disqualification, endorsement, deportation, compensation, deprivation and restitution orders, serious crime prevention orders, drinking exclusion and banning orders, notification requirements (in respect only to a defendant conditionally discharged) (see Powers of• Criminal Courts (Sentencing) Act 2000, s 12(7); other provisions are contained across various acts). It is not permissible to make a confiscation order and therefore an offender pleading guilty before a magistrates' court should not be committed for sentence for that sole purpose (*Clarke* [2009] EWCA Crim 1074). **Activation**: There is no obligation on a court to resentence. Where an offence is committed during the currency of the discharge, irrespective of whether the order has expired at the time of sentence. The offender will be sentenced according to his age at the date of (new) sentence, not at the age at which the offence was committed. A magistrates' court can commit an offender for sentence to the crown court if the order was imposed by that court (it has no obligation to do so, but is unable to deal with the matter itself). Status: An offence that results in discharge is not to be regarded as a conviction (Powers of Criminal Courts (Sentencing) Act 2000, s14(1)).

CONFISCATION–PROCEEDS OF CRIME ACT 2002

A magistrates' court has no power to conduct a proceeds of crime inquiry following conviction (save for a limited number of offences committed prior to 24 March 2003 (Criminal Justice Act 1988, Sch 4)). A power to commit for sentence does however exist and a court exercising that power should indicate (s 70(5)) whether it would have exercised that power but for the issue of confiscation, and a full contemporaneous note of that decision ought to be taken (*Blakeburn* [2007] EWCA Crim 1803). A court has no discretion but to commit if the prosecution makes an application under section 70, however late in the proceedings it is made, unless to grant such an application would amount to an abuse of process (*Bagley v Blackpool and Fleetwood Magistrates' Court* [2009] EWHC 3652 (Admin)) . Given that powers under the 2002 Act cannot be exercised following the imposition of a discharge, courts should not commit for sentence under this provision in such instances.

Proceeds of Crime Act 2002, s 70

(1) This section applies if—

  (a) a defendant is convicted of an offence by a magistrates' court, and

  (b) the prosecutor asks the court to commit the defendant to the Crown Court with a view to a confiscation order being considered under section 6.

(2) In such a case the magistrates' court—

   (a) must commit the defendant to the Crown Court in respect of the offence, and

   (b) may commit him to the Crown Court in respect of any other offence falling within subsection (3).

(3) An offence falls within this subsection if—

   (a) the defendant has been convicted of it by the magistrates' court or any other court, and

   (b) the magistrates' court has power to deal with him in respect of it.

(4) If a committal is made under this section in respect of an offence or offences—

   (a) section 6 applies accordingly, and

   (b) the committal operates as a committal of the defendant to be dealt with by the Crown Court in accordance with section 71.

(5) If a committal is made under this section in respect of an offence for which (apart from this section) the magistrates' court could have committed the defendant for sentence under section 3(2) of the Sentencing Act (offences triable either way) or under section 3B(2) of that Act (committal of child or young person) the court must state whether it would have done so.

(6) A committal under this section may be in custody or on bail.

CUSTODIAL SENTENCES

Type of Sentence	10–12 years	12–14 years	15–17 years	18–20 years	21 years+	Additional information
Detention and training order	n/a	Yes, if offender is a persistent offender	Yes	n/a	n/a	Maximum length 24 months, or note exceeding statutory maximum for the offence
Young Offender Institution	n/a	n/a	n/a	Yes	n/a	Minimum sentence of 21 days, maximum sentence of 6 months for any single offence, 12 months in respect to two or more either-way offences (subject to any statutory maximum)
Imprisonment	n/a	n/a	n/a	n/a	Yes	Minimum 5 days (except where Magistrates' Courts Act 1980, ss 135, 136 applies. Maximum sentence of 6 months for any single offence, 12 months in respect to two or more either-way offences (subject to any statutory maximum)

Threshold: The court must not pass a custodial sentence unless it is of the opinion that the offence, or the combination of the offence and one or more offences associated with it, was so serious that neither a fine alone nor a community sentence can be justified for the offence. Nothing prevents the court from passing a custodial sentence on the offender if (a) he fails to express his willingness to comply with a requirement which is proposed by the court to be included in a community order and which requires an expression of such willingness, or (b) he fails to comply with an order under section 161(2) (pre-sentence drug testing) (Criminal Justice Act 2003, s 152).

In *Howells* [1999] 1 Cr App R (S) 335 the court made the following observations in relation to the assessment of seriousness: "There is no bright line which separates offences which are so serious that only a custodial sentence can be justified from offences which are not so serious as to require the passing of a custodial sentence. But it cannot be said that the "right-thinking members of the public" test is very helpful, since the sentencing court has no means of ascertaining the views of right-thinking members of the public and inevitably attributes to such right-thinking members its own views. So, when applying this test, the sentencing court is doing little more than reflect its own opinion whether justice would or would not be done and be seen to be done by the passing of a non-custodial sentence. In the end, the sentencing court is bound to give effect to its own subjective judgment of what justice requires on the peculiar facts of the case before it. It would be dangerous and wrong for this court to lay down prescriptive rules governing the exercise of that judgment, and any guidance we give, however general, will be subject to exceptions and qualifications in some cases. We do however think that in approaching cases which are on or near the custody threshold courts will usually find it helpful to begin by considering the nature and extent of the defendant's criminal intention and the nature and extent of any injury or damage caused to the victim. Other things being equal, an offence which is deliberate and premeditated will usually be more serious than one which is spontaneous and unpremeditated or which involves an excessive response to provocation; an offence which inflicts personal injury or mental trauma, particularly if permanent, will usually be more serious than one which inflicts financial loss only. In considering the seriousness of any offence the court may take into account any previous convictions of the offender or any failure to respond to previous sentences [...] and must treat it as an aggravating factor if the offence was committed while the offender was on bail [...]. In deciding whether to impose a custodial sentence in borderline cases the sentencing court will ordinarily take account of matters relating to the offender: The court will have regard to an offender's admission of responsibility for the offence, particularly if reflected in a plea of guilty tendered at the earliest opportunity and accompanied by hard evidence of genuine remorse, as shown (for example) by an expression of regret to the victim and an offer of compensation. Attention is drawn to section 48 of the Criminal Justice and Public Order Act 1994. Where offending has been fuelled by addiction to drink or drugs, the court will be inclined to look more favourably on an offender who has already demonstrated (by taking practical steps to that end) a genuine, self-motivated determination to address his addiction. Youth and immaturity, while affording no defence, will often justify a less rigorous penalty than would be appropriate for an adult. Some measure of leniency will ordinarily be extended to offenders of previous good character, the more so if there is evidence of positive good character (such as a solid employment record or faithful discharge of family duties) as opposed to a mere absence of previous convictions. It will sometimes be appropriate to take account of family responsibilities, or physical or mental disability. While the court will never impose a custodial sentence unless satisfied that it is necessary to do so, there will be even greater reluctance to impose a custodial sentence on an offender who has never before served such a sentence. Courts should always bear in mind that criminal sentences are in almost every case intended to protect the public, whether by punishing the offender or reforming him, or deterring him and others, or all of these things. Courts cannot and should not be unmindful of the important public dimension of criminal sentencing and the importance of maintaining public confidence in the sentencing system. Where the court is of the opinion that an offence, or the combination of an offence and one or more offences associated with it, is so serious that only a custodial sentence can be justified and that such a sentence should be passed, the sentence imposed should be no longer than is necessary to meet the penal purpose which the court has in mind. We draw attention to the important observations of the Vice-President (Rose LJ) giving the judgment of the court in R v Ollerenshaw, unreported, 23 April 1998, where he said:

> "When a court is considering imposing a comparatively short period of custody, that is of about 12 months or less, it should generally ask itself, particularly where the defendant has not previously been sentenced to custody, whether an even shorter period might be equally

effective in protecting the interests of the public, and punishing and deterring the criminal. For example, there will be cases where, for these purposes, 6 months may be just as effective as 9, or 2 months may be just as effective as 4. Such an approach is no less valid, in the light of today's prison overcrowding, than it was at the time of R v Bibi (1980) 71 Cr. App. R 360." "

It should be noted that there is a plethora of case law dealing with the issue of seriousness that pre-dates the binding sentencing guideline (Overarching Principles: Seriousness). It is to be doubted whether these cases (for example *Kefford* [2002] EWCA Crim 519) now enjoy the force of law that they once did.

DEFERMENT OF SENTENCE

Generally: In *George* (79) Cr App R 26 the court held:

"The purpose of deferment is therefore to enable the court to take into account the defendant's conduct after conviction or any change in circumstances and then only if it is in the interests of justice to exercise the power. It will, one imagines, seldom be in the interests of justice to stipulate that the conduct required is reparation by the defendant. The power is not to be used as an easy way out for a court which is unable to make up its mind about the correct sentence (see Burgess (July 18, 1974 unreported)). Experience has shown that great care should be exercised by the court when using this power. The court should make it clear to the defendant what the particular purposes are which the court has in mind [...] and what conduct is expected of him during deferment. The failure to do so, or more often the failure on the part of the defendant or his representatives to appreciate what those purposes are or that conduct is, has been a fruitful source of appeals to this Court. It is essential that the deferring court should make a careful note of the purposes for which the sentence is being deferred and what steps, if any, it expects the defendant to take during the period of deferment. Ideally the defendant himself should be given notice in writing of what he is expected to do or refrain from doing, so that there can be no doubt in his mind what is expected of him. Thus the task of the court which comes to deal with the offender at the expiration of the period of deferment is as follows: First the purpose of the deferment and any requirement imposed by the deferring court must be ascertained. Secondly the court must determine if the defendant has substantially conformed or attempted to conform with the proper expectations of the deferring court, whether with regard to finding a job or as the case may be. If he has, then the defendant may legitimately expect that an immediate custodial sentence will not be imposed. If he has not, then the court should be careful to state with precision in what respects he has failed. If the court does not set out its reasons in this way, there is a danger, particularly where the sentencing court is differently constituted from the deferring court, that it may appear that the former is disregarding the deferment and is saying in effect that the sentence should never have been deferred and that the defendant should have been sentenced to immediate imprisonment by the latter (see Glossop (1981) 3 Cr.App.R.(S.) 347). In many cases a short probation order may be preferable to a deferment of sentence. Such an order enables the defendant's behaviour to be monitored by the probation officer; it ensures that formal notice of the requirements of the court are given to the defendant. On the other hand a deferment of sentence will be more appropriate where the conduct required of the defendant is not sufficiently specific to be made the subject of a condition imposed as part of a probation order without creating uncertainty in the mind of the probation officer and the defendant as to whether there has been a breach of the order; for example, where the defendant is to make a real effort to find work, or where the sentencer wishes to see whether a change in the defendant's attitude and circumstances, which appears to be a possibility at the time of deferment, does in fact come about. Again, deferment may be the appropriate course where the steps to be taken by the defendant could not of their nature be the subject of a condition, for example where he is to make reparation, or at least demonstrate a real intention and capacity to do so. These are only examples. It is unnecessary and undesirable to attempt an exhaustive definition of the circumstances in which the procedure should be employed. It is sufficient to say that it should not be adopted without careful consideration of whether the sentencer's intentions could not best be achieved by other means, and that if deferment is decided upon, care must be taken to avoid the risk of misunderstanding and a sense of injustice when the defendant returns before the court."

Sentencing Guideline:

Under the new framework, there is a wider range of sentencing options open to the courts, including the increased availability of suspended sentences, and deferred sentences are likely to be used in very limited circumstances. A deferred sentence enables the court to review the conduct of the defendant before passing sentence, having first prescribed certain requirements. It also provides several opportunities for an offender to have some influence as to the sentence passed—

    a)   it tests the commitment of the offender not to re-offend;

    b)   it gives the offender an opportunity to do something where progress can be shown within a short period;

    c)   it provides the offender with an opportunity to behave or refrain from behaving in a particular way that will be relevant to sentence.

Given the new power to require undertakings and the ability to enforce those undertakings before the end of the period of deferral, the decision to defer sentence should be predominantly for a small group of cases at either the custody threshold or the community sentence threshold where the sentencer feels that there would be particular value in giving the offender the opportunities listed because, if the offender complies with the requirements, a different sentence will be justified at the end of the deferment period.

This could be a community sentence instead of a custodial sentence or a fine or discharge instead of a community sentence. It may, rarely, enable a custodial sentence to be suspended rather than imposed immediately.

> The use of deferred sentences should be predominantly for a small group of cases close to a significant threshold where, should the defendant be prepared to adapt his behaviour in a way clearly specified by the sentencer, the court may be prepared to impose a lesser sentence.

A court may impose any conditions during the period of deferment that it considers appropriate. These could be specific requirements as set out in the provisions for community sentences, or requirements that are drawn more widely. These should be specific, measurable conditions so that the offender knows exactly what is required and the court can assess compliance; the restriction on liberty should be limited to ensure that the offender has a reasonable expectation of being able to comply whilst maintaining his or her social responsibilities.

Given the need for clarity in the mind of the offender and the possibility of sentence by another court, the court should give a clear indication (and make a written record) of the type of sentence it would be minded to impose if it had not decided to defer and ensure that the offender understands the consequences of failure to comply with the court's wishes during the deferral period.

> When deferring sentence, the sentencer must make clear the consequence of not complying with any requirements and should indicate the type of sentence it would be minded to impose. Sentencers should impose specific, measurable conditions that do not involve a serious restriction on liberty.

Powers of Criminal Courts (Sentencing) Act 2000, ss 1, 1A(1)–(2), 1B, 1C, and 1D

1 Deferment of sentence

    (1)   The Crown Court or a magistrates' court may defer passing sentence on an offender for the purpose of enabling the court, or any other court to which it falls to deal with him, to have regard in dealing with him to—

    (a) his conduct after conviction (including, where appropriate, the making by him of reparation for his offence); or

    (b) any change in his circumstances;

but this is subject to subsections (3) and (4) below.

(2) Without prejudice to the generality of subsection (1) above, the matters to which the court to which it falls to deal with the offender may have regard by virtue of paragraph (a) of that subsection include the extent to which the offender has complied with any requirements imposed under subsection (3)(b) below.

(3) The power conferred by subsection (1) above shall be exercisable only if—

    (a) the offender consents;

    (b) the offender undertakes to comply with any requirements as to his conduct during the period of the deferment that the court considers it appropriate to impose; and

    (c) the court is satisfied, having regard to the nature of the offence and the character and circumstances of the offender, that it would be in the interests of justice to exercise the power.

(4) Any deferment under this section shall be until such date as may be specified by the court, not being more than six months after the date on which the deferment is announced by the court; and, subject to section 1D(3) below, where the passing of sentence has been deferred under this section it shall not be further so deferred.

(5) Where a court has under this section deferred passing sentence on an offender, it shall forthwith give a copy of the order deferring the passing of sentence and setting out any requirements imposed under subsection (3) (b) above—

    (a) to the offender,

    (b) ...

(6) Notwithstanding any enactment, a court which under this section defers passing sentence on an offender shall not on the same occasion remand him.

(7) Where—

    (a) a court which under this section has deferred passing sentence on an offender proposes to deal with him on the date originally specified by the court, or

    (b) the offender does not appear on the day so specified, the court may issue a summons requiring him to appear before the court at a time and place specified in the summons, or may issue a warrant to arrest him and bring him before the court at a time and place specified in the warrant.

(8) Nothing in this section or sections 1A to 1D below shall affect—

    (a) the power of the Crown Court to bind over an offender to come up for judgment when called upon; or

    (b) the power of any court to defer passing sentence for any purpose for which it may lawfully do so apart from this section.

1A Further provision about undertakings

(1) Without prejudice to the generality of paragraph (b) of section 1(3) above, the requirements that may be imposed by virtue of that paragraph include requirements as to the residence of the offender during the whole or any part of the period of deferment.

(2) Where an offender has undertaken to comply with any requirements imposed under section 1(3)(b) above the court may appoint—

    (a) an officer of a local probation board or an officer of a provider of probation services, or

    (b) any other person whom the court thinks appropriate, to act as a supervisor in relation to him.

1B Breach of undertakings

(1) A court which under section 1 above has deferred passing sentence on an offender may deal with him before the end of the period of deferment if—

    (a) he appears or is brought before the court under subsection (3) below; and

    (b) the court is satisfied that he has failed to comply with one or more requirements imposed under section 1(3)(b) above in connection with the deferment.

(2) Subsection (3) below applies where—

    (a) a court has under section 1 above deferred passing sentence on an offender;

    (b) the offender undertook to comply with one or more requirements imposed under section 1(3)(b) above in connection with the deferment; and

    (c) a person appointed under section 1A(2) above to act as a supervisor in relation to the offender has reported to the court that the offender has failed to comply with one or more of those requirements.

(3) Where this subsection applies, the court may issue—

    (a) a summons requiring the offender to appear before the court at a time and place specified in the summons; or

    (b) a warrant to arrest him and bring him before the court at a time and place specified in the warrant.

1C Conviction of offence during period of deferment

(1) A court which under section 1 above has deferred passing sentence on an offender may deal with him before the end of the period of deferment if during that period he is convicted in Great Britain of any offence.

(2) Subsection (3) below applies where a court has under section 1 above deferred passing sentence on an offender in respect of one or more offences and during the period of deferment the offender is convicted in England and Wales of any offence ('the later offence').

(3) Where this subsection applies, then (without prejudice to subsection (1) above and whether or not the offender is sentenced for the later offence during the period of deferment), the court which passes sentence on him for the later offence may also, if this has not already been done, deal with him for the offence or offences for which passing of sentence has been deferred, except that—

    (a) the power conferred by this subsection shall not be exercised by a magistrates' court if the court which deferred passing sentence was the Crown Court; and

    (b) the Crown Court, in exercising that power in a case in which the court which deferred passing sentence was a magistrates' court, shall not pass any sentence which could not have been passed by a magistrates' court in exercising that power.

(4) Where a court which under section 1 above has deferred passing sentence on an offender proposes to deal with him by virtue of subsection (1) above before the end of the period of deferment, the court may issue—

    (a) a summons requiring him to appear before the court at a time and place specified in the summons; or

    (b) a warrant to arrest him and bring him before the court at a time and place specified in the warrant.

1D Deferment of sentence: supplementary

(1) In deferring the passing of sentence under section 1 above a magistrates' court shall be regarded as exercising the power of adjourning the trial conferred by section 10(1) of the Magistrates' Courts Act 1980, and accordingly sections 11(1) and 13(1) to (3A) and (5) of that Act (non-appearance of the accused) apply (without prejudice to section 1(7) above) if the offender does not appear on the date specified under section 1(4) above.

(2) Where the passing of sentence on an offender has been deferred by a court ('the original court') under section 1 above, the power of that court under that section to deal with the offender at the end of the period of deferment and any power of that court under section 1B(1) or 1C(1) above, or of any court under section 1C(3) above, to deal with the offender—

(a) is power to deal with him, in respect of the offence for which passing of sentence has been deferred, in any way in which the original court could have dealt with him if it had not deferred passing sentence; and

(b) without prejudice to the generality of paragraph (a) above, in the case of a magistrates' court, includes the power conferred by section 3 below to commit him to the Crown Court for sentence.

(3) Where—

(a) the passing of sentence on an offender in respect of one or more offences has been deferred under section 1 above, and

(b) a magistrates' court deals with him in respect of the offence or any of the offences by committing him to the Crown Court under section 3 below, the power of the Crown Court to deal with him includes the same power to defer passing sentence on him as if he had just been convicted of the offence or offences on indictment before the court.

(4) Subsection (5) below applies where—

(a) the passing of sentence on an offender in respect of one or more offences has been deferred under section 1 above;

(b) it falls to a magistrates' court to determine a relevant matter; and

(c) a justice of the peace is satisfied—

(i) that a person appointed under section 1A(2)(b) above to act as a supervisor in relation to the offender is likely to be able to give evidence that may assist the court in determining that matter; and

(ii) that that person will not voluntarily attend as a witness.

(5) The justice may issue a summons directed to that person requiring him to attend before the court at the time and place appointed in the summons to give evidence.

(6) For the purposes of subsection (4) above a court determines a relevant matter if it—

(a) deals with the offender in respect of the offence, or any of the offences, for which the passing of sentence has been deferred; or

(b) determines, for the purposes of section 1B(1)(b) above, whether the offender has failed to comply with any requirements imposed under section 1(3)(b) above.

DEPORTATION

Automatic: UK Borders Act 2007, section 32, provides for the automatic deportation of some offenders sentenced to imprisonment for a period of at least 12 months. The 12 months must be for a single offence, and the Act only applies to those aged 18 or over. Accordingly, this power is not available to a magistrates' court until such time as sentencing powers are increased.

Recommendation for: It is extremely unlikely that the magistrates' court will be seized of cases where an order for deportation might be appropriate, and generally speaking it will only be in an exceptional case that deportation falling outside the automatic scheme (above) will be appropriate (*Kluxen* [2010] EWCA Crim 1081). However the court observed as follows: "In our view it will rarely be that [the test] is satisfied in the case of an offender none of whose offences merits a custodial sentence of 12 months or more. An offender who repeatedly commits minor offences could conceivably do so, as could a person who commits a single offence involving for example the possession or use of false identity documents for which he receives a custodial sentence of less than 12 months. Age: A recommendation can only be made in relation to an offender aged 17 years or over (Immigration Act 1971, s 3(6)) who is not a British Citizen. If the offender asserts that he is not a British Citizen then the burden of proving it falls on him (Immigration Act 1971, s 3(8)). The Secretary of State is not obliged to act on the recommendation, and will have to also ensure that ECHR protections are observed (*AA v UK* [2011] ECHR 1345). **Test for deportation**: The Court must consider whether the accused's continued presence in the United Kingdom is to its detriment. This country has no use for criminals of other nationalities, particularly if they have committed serious crimes or have long criminal records. The more serious the crime and the longer the record the more obvious it is that there should be an order recommending deportation. On the other hand, a minor offence would not merit an order recommending deportation (*Nazari* (1980) 71 Cr App R 87). General guidelines were issued in *Nazari*:

> "First, the court must consider, as was said by Sachs L.J., in Caird's case (supra), whether the accused's continued presence in the United Kingdom is to its detriment. This country has no use for criminals of other nationalities, particularly if they have committed serious crimes or have long criminal records. That is self-evident. The more serious the crime and the longer the record the more obvious it is that there should be an order recommending deportation. On the other hand, a minor offence would not merit an order recommending deportation. In the Greater London area, for example, shoplifting is an offence which is frequently committed by visitors to this country. Normally an arrest for shoplifting followed by conviction, even if there were more than one offence being dealt with, would not merit a recommendation for deportation. But a series of shoplifting offences on different occasions may justify a recommendation for deportation. Even a first offence of shoplifting might merit a recommendation if the offender were a member of a gang carrying out a planned raid on a departmental store.

> Secondly, the courts are not concerned with the political systems which operate in other countries. They may be harsh; they may be soft; they may be oppressive; they may be the quintessence of democracy. The court has no knowledge of those matters over and above that which is common knowledge; and that may be wrong. In our judgment it would be undesirable for this Court or any other court to express views about regimes which exist outside the United Kingdom of Great Britain and Northern Ireland. It is for the Home Secretary to decide in each case whether an offender's return to his country of origin would have consequences which would make his compulsory return unduly harsh. The Home Secretary has opportunities of informing himself about what is happening in other countries which the courts do not have. The sort of argument which was put up in this case is one which we did not find attractive. It may well be that the regime in Iran at the present time is likely to be unfavourable from the point of view of the applicant. Whether and how long it will continue to be so we do not know. Whether it will be so by the end of this man's sentence of imprisonment must be a matter of speculation. When the time comes for him to be released from prison the Home Secretary, we are sure, will bear in mind the very matters which we have been urged to consider, namely, whether it would be unduly harsh to send him back to his country of origin. The next matter to which we invite attention by way of guidelines is the effect that an order recommending deportation will have upon others who are not before the court and who are innocent persons. This Court and all other courts would have no wish to break up families or impose hardship on innocent people. The case of Fernandez illustrates this very clearly indeed. Mrs. Fernandez is an admirable person, a good wife and mother, and a credit to herself and someone whom most of us would want to have in this country. As we have already indicated, if her husband is deported she will have a heartrending choice to make; whether she should go with her husband or leave him and look after the interests of the children. That is the kind of situation which should be considered very carefully before a recommendation for deportation is made."

In subsequent cases, in which the court was dealing only with EU citizens, it was said that the court must consider whether the offender's conduct (including the instant offence and any earlier ones) constituted

"...a genuine and sufficiently serious threat to the requirements of public policy affecting one of the fundamental interests of society".

These were the cases of *Kraus* (1982) 4 Crim. App. R. (S.) 113; *Compassi* (1987) 9 Crim. App. R. (S.) 270; *Escauriaza* (1988) 87 Crim. App. R. 344; and *Spura* (1988) 10 Crim. App. R. (S.) 376. In all of these cases the Court adopted the reasoning of the European Court of Justice in *Bouchereau* [1987] QB 732. In *Kluxen* [2010] EWCA Crim 1081 the court summarised the position thus:

i) In cases to which the 2007 Act applies, it is no longer necessary or appropriate to recommend the deportation of the offender concerned. ii) In cases to which the 2007 Act does not apply, it will rarely be appropriate to recommend the deportation of the offender concerned, whether or not the offender is a citizen of the EU. iii) If in a case to which the 2007 Act does not apply a Court is, exceptionally, considering recommending the deportation of the offender concerned, it should apply the *Nazari* test in tandem with the *Bouchereau* test, there being no practical difference between the two. This is so whether the offender is or is not a citizen of the EU.

iv) However, the Court should not take into account the Convention Rights of the offender; the political situation in the country to which the offender may be deported; the effect that a recommendation might have on innocent persons not before the Court; the provisions of Article 28 of Directive 2004/38; or the 2006 Regulations.

Avoiding deportation: It is wrong for a court not to pass a sentence that would otherwise be appropriate in order to avoid the effects of deportation (*Rahimi* [2011] EWCA Crim 2268).

DEPRIVATION ORDER

Also known as: Forfeiture and destruction orders. **Warning by court**: Failure to warn that an order is being proposed, and inviting representations may result in the order being quashed (*Ball* [2002] EWCA Crim 2777). **Any property**: Property intended to be used for any offence can be made the subject of an order, not just property in relation to the offence for which the offender is before the court (*O'Farrell* [1988] Crim LR 387). **Straightforward cases**: Orders should only be made in straightforward cases involving unencumbered property (*Troth* [1980] Crim LR 249); where the property is funded by outstanding finance (*Thomas* [2012] EWCA Crim 1159) or is owned by a third-party (for example an employer), or where it would generally be disproportionate to deprive the owner of the property, it may not be appropriate to make a deprivation order as such property is likely to be returned as a result of civil proceedings (*Kearney* [2011] EWCA Crim 826; *O'leary International Limited v Chief Constable of North Wales Police* [2012] EWHC 1516 (Admin); *Trans Berckx BVBA v North Avon Magistrates' Court* [2011] EWHC 2605 (Admin)). **Proportionality**: An order should not be made if to do so would cause the offender undue hardship (*Tavenor* (Unreported) 4 April 1974) nor where the total sentence would offend the principle of totality (*Scully* (1985) 7 Cr App R (S) 119).

Powers of Criminal Courts (Sentencing) Act 2000, s 143

(1) Where a person is convicted of an offence and the court by or before which he is convicted is satisfied that any property which has been lawfully seized from him, or which was in his possession or under his control at the time when he was apprehended for the offence or when a summons in respect of it was issued—

(a) has been used for the purpose of committing, or facilitating the commission of, any offence, or

(b) was intended by him to be used for that purpose, the court may (subject to subsection (5) below) make an order under this section in respect of that property.

(2) Where a person is convicted of an offence and the offence, or an offence which the court has taken into consideration in determining his sentence, consists of unlawful possession of property which—

(a) has been lawfully seized from him, or

(b) was in his possession or under his control at the time when he was apprehended for the offence of which he has been convicted or when a summons in respect of that offence was issued,

the court may (subject to subsection (5) below) make an order under this section in respect of that property.

(3) An order under this section shall operate to deprive the offender of his rights, if any, in the property to which it relates, and the property shall (if not already in their possession) be taken into the possession of the police.

(4) Any power conferred on a court by subsection (1) or (2) above may be exercised—

(a) whether or not the court also deals with the offender in any other way in respect of the offence of which he has been convicted; and

(b) without regard to any restrictions on forfeiture in any enactment contained in an Act passed before 29th July 1988.

(5) In considering whether to make an order under this section in respect of any property, a court shall have regard—

(a) to the value of the property; and

(b) to the likely financial and other effects on the offender of the making of the order (taken together with any other order that the court contemplates making).

(6) Where a person commits an offence to which this subsection applies by—

(a) driving, attempting to drive, or being in charge of a vehicle, or

(b) failing to comply with a requirement made under section 7 or 7A of the Road Traffic Act 1988 (failure to provide specimen for analysis or laboratory test or to give permission for such a test) in the course of an investigation into whether the offender had committed an offence while driving, attempting to drive or being in charge of a vehicle, or

(c) failing, as the driver of a vehicle, to comply with subsection (2) or (3) of section 170 of the Road Traffic Act 1988 (duty to stop and give information or report accident),

the vehicle shall be regarded for the purposes of subsection (1) above (and section 144(1)(b) below) as used for the purpose of committing the offence (and for the purpose of committing any offence of aiding, abetting, counselling or procuring the commission of the offence).

(7) Subsection (6) above applies to—

(a) an offence under the Road Traffic Act 1988 which is punishable with imprisonment;

(b) an offence of manslaughter; and

(c) an offence under section 35 of the Offences Against the Person Act 1861 (wanton and furious driving).

(8) Facilitating the commission of an offence shall be taken for the purposes of subsection (1) above to include the taking of any steps after it has been committed for the purpose of disposing of any property to which it relates or of avoiding apprehension or detection.

DETENTION AND TRAINING ORDER

Detention and training is the custodial option (Powers of Criminal Courts (Sentencing) Act 2000, s 100) for those aged between 10 and 17 years not sentenced to detention under PCC(S)A 2000, s 91. **Eligibility:** The order is not currently available to those aged under 12 years, not to those aged between 12 and 14 years of age unless they are deemed to be a 'persistent offender'. The offence must be 'so serious' that only a custodial sentence is appropriate. **Persistent Offender**: The Definitive Youth Sentencing Guidelines states the following: "'Persistent offender' is not defined in legislation but has been considered by the Court of Appeal on a number of occasions. However, following the implementation of the 2008 Act, the sentencing framework is different from that when the definition was judicially developed, particularly the greater emphasis on the requirement to use a custodial sentence as 'a measure of last resort'. A dictionary definition of 'persistent offender' is 'persisting or having a tendency to persist'; 'persist' is defined as 'to continue firmly or obstinately in a course of action in spite of difficulty or opposition'. In determining whether an offender is a persistent offender for these purposes, a court should consider the simple test of whether the young person is one who persists in offending:

i) in most circumstances, the normal expectation is that the offender will have had some contact with authority in which the offending conduct was challenged before being classed as 'persistent'; a finding of persistence in offending may be derived from information about previous convictions but may also arise from orders which require an admission or finding of guilt–these include reprimands, final warnings, restorative justice disposals and conditional cautions; since they do not require such an admission, penalty notices for disorder are unlikely to be sufficiently reliable;

ii) a young offender is certainly likely to be found to be persistent (and, in relation to a custodial sentence, the test of being a measure of last resort is most likely to be satisfied) where the offender has been convicted of, or made subject to a pre-court disposal that involves an admission or finding of guilt in relation to, imprisonable offences on at least 3 occasions in the past 12 months.

Even where a young person is found to be a persistent offender, a court is not obliged to impose the custodial sentence or youth rehabilitation order with intensive supervision and surveillance or fostering that becomes available as a result of that finding. The other tests continue to apply and it is clear that Parliament expects custodial sentences to be imposed only rarely on those aged 14 or less." **Relevant date**: The relevant age is at the date of offence and is therefore available for adult offenders who committed the offence whilst a young offender (*A v Director of Public Prosecutions* [2002] 2 Cr App R (S) 88). **Duration**: For a maximum of 2 years provided the order does not exceed the maximum available for the offence(s). However, the order must be made to correspond to one of the following lengths: 4, 6, 8, 10, 12, 18 or 24 months. It will be seen therefore that the order is not available for all offences that carry a custodial penalty (eg obstructing a police constable as that offence carries a maximum penalty of 3 months and the minimum order is for 4 months detention and training). Aggregate terms: Consecutive terms can be ordered with recourse to any limitation on length (*Norris* (2000) 164 JP 689) (subject to not exceeding 2 years), for example it is permissible to impose 8 months on offence 1 and 8 months on offence 2, making a total of 16 months. It would not be permissible simply to have imposed 16 months on offence 1 (as that length is not permissible for a single sentence) and no separate penalty on offence 2. **Time on remand or qualifying curfew**: Time on remand and on qualifying curfew must generally be allowed for (Powers of Criminal Courts (Sentencing) Act 2000, s 101) but it need not correspond accurately to the actual time served In *Fieldhouse* [2000] Crim LR 1020 the court held:

"[It is not] appropriate or desirable that any precise reflection should be sought to be given, in making detention and training orders, of a day or two spent in custody. Of course if a significant time has been spent in custody, a matter of weeks or months, the proper approach of the court, taking such a period into account, is to reduce, if possible, the sentence otherwise appropriate to reflect that period. But, in my judgment, it is impossible for courts to fine tune, by reference to a few days in custody, the sentence which is appropriate in making detention and training orders."

And further went on to say:

"As to longer periods spent in custody on remand, the way in which the courts are able to reflect these will depend on all the circumstances of the particular case including the apparent impact, if any, of the period in custody on the offender, the length of time spent in custody and the relationship between that period and the period of detention and training order otherwise contemplated. Parliament has chosen to confer on the courts…the power to make detention and training orders only in steps of four, six, eight, 10, 12, 18 or 24 months, and periods spent in custody may range from days to months. Therefore, in our judgment, no rule of general application can be devised to cover the infinitely various situations which may arise. However, the proper approach can perhaps best be illustrated by taking by way of example, a defendant who has spent four weeks in custody on remand – that is the equivalent of a two month term. The court is likely to take such a period into account in different ways according to the length of the detention and training order which initially seems appropriate for the particular offence and offender. If that period is four months, the court may conclude that a non-custodial sentence is appropriate. If that period is six, eight, 10 or 12 months, the court is likely to impose a period of four, six, eight or 10 months respectively. If that period is 18 or 24 months, the court may well conclude that no reduction can properly be made from 18 or 24 months, although the court will of course bear in mind in such a case, as in all others involving juveniles, the continuing importance of limiting the period of custody to the minimum necessary. The observations to this effect in Mills (1998) 2 Cr.App.R (S) 128 at 131 still hold good. In relation to those offenders for whom long-term detention…may otherwise be appropriate, a detention and training order of 24 months may be a proper sentence even on a plea of guilty and even when a significant period has been spent in custody."

See: *March* [2002] 2 Cr App R (S) 98 cited in Reduction in Sentence for Early Plea for other examples of when it is appropriate to withhold the discount for guilty plea.

Breach of supervision: The return period specified in section 104(3) (below) is the period between the date on which the breach was proved and the expiry of the order (*H v Doncaster Youth Court* [2009] EWHC 3463 (Admin)) note that a different term applies under section 105 when an offender commits a new offence. **Early release**: Release is normally at the half-way point of the sentence but can be granted 1 month earlier for sentences of less than 18 months, and 1 or 2 months earlier in respect to other orders (Powers of Criminal Courts (Sentencing) Act 2000, s 102). **Breach**: The courts powers on breach are set out in section 104(3) of the 2000 Act. If supervision period has expired the penalty on breach is limited to a fine.

Powers of Criminal Courts (Sentencing) Act 2000, s 101, 104 and 105

101 Term of order, consecutive terms and taking account of remands.

(1) Subject to subsection (2) below, the term of a detention and training order made in respect of an offence (whether by a magistrates' court or otherwise) shall be 4, 6, 8, 10, 12, 18 or 24 months.

(2) The term of a detention and training order may not exceed the maximum term of imprisonment that the Crown Court could (in the case of an offender aged 21 or over) impose for the offence.

(3) Subject to subsections (4) and (6) below, a court making a detention and training order may order that its term shall commence on the expiry of the term of any other detention and training order made by that or any other court.

(4) A court shall not make in respect of an offender a detention and training order the effect of which would be that he would be subject to detention and training orders for a term which exceeds 24 months.

(5) Where the term of the detention and training orders to which an offender would otherwise be subject exceeds 24 months, the excess shall be treated as remitted.

(6) A court making a detention and training order shall not order that its term shall commence on the expiry of the term of a detention and training order under which the period of supervision has already begun (under section 103(1) below).

(7) Where a detention and training order ("the new order") is made in respect of an offender who is subject to a detention and training order under which the period of supervision has begun ("the old order"), the old order shall be disregarded in determining—

(a) for the purposes of subsection (4) above whether the effect of the new order would be that the offender would be subject to detention and training orders for a term which exceeds 24 months; and

(b) for the purposes of subsection (5) above whether the term of the detention and training orders to which the offender would (apart from that subsection) be subject exceeds 24 months.

(8) In determining the term of a detention and training order for an offence, the court shall take account of any period for which the offender has been remanded —

(a) in custody, or

(b) on bail subject to a qualifying curfew condition and an electronic monitoring condition (within the meaning of section 240A of the Criminal Justice Act 2003),

in connection with the offence, or any other offence the charge for which was founded on the same facts or evidence.

(9) Where a court proposes to make detention and training orders in respect of an offender for two or more offences—

(a) subsection (8) above shall not apply; but

(b) in determining the total term of the detention and training orders it proposes to make in respect of the offender, the court shall take account of the total period (if any) for which he has been remanded as mentioned in that subsection in connection with any of those offences, or any other offence the charge for which was founded on the same facts or evidence.

(10) Once a period of remand has, under subsection (8) or (9) above, been taken account of in relation to a detention and training order made in respect of an offender for any offence or offences, it shall not subsequently be taken account of (under either of those subsections) in relation to such an order made in respect of the offender for any other offence or offences.

(11) Any reference in subsection (8) or (9) above to an offender's being remanded in custody is a reference to his being—

(a) held in police detention;

(b) remanded in or committed to custody by an order of a court;

(c) remanded or committed to local authority accommodation under section 23 of the Children and Young Persons Act 1969 and placed and kept in secure accommodation or detained in a secure training centre pursuant to arrangements under subsection (7A) of that section; or

(d) remanded, admitted or removed to hospital under section 35, 36, 38 or 48 of the Mental Health Act 1983.

(12) A person is in police detention for the purposes of subsection (11) above—

(a) at any time when he is in police detention for the purposes of the Police and Criminal Evidence Act 1984; and

(b) at any time when he is detained under section 41 of the Terrorism Act 2000;

and in that subsection "secure accommodation" has the same meaning as in section 23 of the Children and Young Persons Act 1969.

(12A) Section 243 of the Criminal Justice Act 2003 (persons extradited to the United Kingdom) applies in relation to a person sentenced to a detention and training order as it applies in relation to a fixed-term prisoner, with the reference in subsection (2) of that section to section 240 being read as a reference to subsection (8) above.

(13) For the purpose of any reference in sections 102 to 105 below to the term of a detention and training order, consecutive terms of such orders and terms of such orders which are wholly or partly concurrent shall be treated as a single term if—

   (a) the orders were made on the same occasion; or

   (b) where they were made on different occasions, the offender has not been released (by virtue of subsection (2), (3), (4) or (5) of section 102 below) at any time during the period beginning with the first and ending with the last of those occasions.

104 Breach of supervision requirements.

(1) Where a detention and training order is in force in respect of an offender and it appears on information to a justice of the peace that the offender has failed to comply with requirements under section 103(6)(b) above, the justice—

   (a) may issue a summons requiring the offender to appear at the place and time specified in the summons; or

   (b) if the information is in writing and on oath, may issue a warrant for the offender's arrest.

(2) Any summons or warrant issued under this section shall direct the offender to appear or be brought–

   (a) before a youth court [acting in the local justice in which the offender resides; or

   (b) if it is not known where the offender resides, before a youth court acting in the same local justice area as the justice who issued the summons or warrant.

(3) If it is proved to the satisfaction of the youth court before which an offender appears or is brought under this section that he has failed to comply with requirements under section 103(6)(b) above, that court may—

   (a) order the offender to be detained, in such youth detention accommodation as the Secretary of State may determine, for such period, not exceeding the shorter of three months or the remainder of the term of the detention and training order, as the court may specify; or

   (b) impose on the offender a fine not exceeding level 3 on the standard scale.

(4) An offender detained in pursuance of an order under subsection (3)(a) above shall be deemed to be in legal custody.

(5) A fine imposed under subsection (3)(b) above shall be deemed, for the purposes of any enactment, to be a sum adjudged to be paid by a conviction.

(6) An offender may appeal to the Crown Court against any order made under subsection (3) (a) or (b) above.

105 Offences during currency of order.

(1) This section applies to a person subject to a detention and training order if—

   (a) after his release and before the date on which the term of the order ends, he commits an offence punishable with imprisonment in the case of a person aged 21 or over ("the new offence"); and

   (b) whether before or after that date, he is convicted of the new offence.

(2) Subject to section 8(6) above (duty of adult magistrates' court to remit young offenders to youth court for sentence), the court by or before which a person to whom this section applies is convicted of the new offence may, whether or not it passes any other sentence on him, order him to be detained in such [youth detention] 1 accommodation as the Secretary of State may determine for the whole or any part of the period which—

   (a) begins with the date of the court's order; and

   (b) is equal in length to the period between the date on which the new offence was committed and the date mentioned in subsection (1) above.

(3) The period for which a person to whom this section applies is ordered under subsection (2) above to be detained in youth detention accommodation—

    (a) shall, as the court may direct, either be served before and be followed by, or be served concurrently with, any sentence imposed for the new offence; and

    (b) in either case, shall be disregarded in determining the appropriate length of that sentence.

(4) Where the new offence is found to have been committed over a period of two or more days, or at some time during a period of two or more days, it shall be taken for the purposes of this section to have been committed on the last of those days.

(5) A person detained in pursuance of an order under subsection (2) above shall be deemed to be in legal custody.

DETENTION IN A YOUNG OFFENDER INSTITUTION

Detention in a young offender institution (Powers of Criminal Courts (Sentencing) Act 2000, s 96) is the custodial option for those aged between 18 and 20 years. **Eligibility**: The offence must be 'so serious' that only a custodial sentence is appropriate. *Duration:* Detention must be for a period not less than 21 days and not exceeding the maximum penalty available to the court for the offence(s) in question. **Suspension**: The court has the power to impose a suspended sentence order.

DETENTION UNDER SECTION 91 PCC(S)A 2000

Eligibility: The offender must be aged between 10 and 17 years. The offence must be 'so serious' that only a custodial sentence is appropriate, and such sentences can only be imposed by a crown court once a youth court has declined jurisdiction (the so-called 'grave crime' procedure). In respect to offenders aged 16 or 17 years the offence must be one falling within section 91(1), (1A), (1B) or (1C). In respect to offenders aged between 10 and 15 years the offence must be one falling within section 91(1). The distinction between the provisions is that certain firearms offences fall to be sentenced under this power due to mandatory minimum terms. Where a court is of the view that a sentence under this provision ought to be imposed (ie a sentence in excess of 2 years) jurisdiction should be declined (Magistrates' Court Act 1980, s 24(1)). **Sentence in excess of 2 years**: In *R (H and others) v Southampton Youth Court* [2005] 2 Cr App R 30, the court laid down the following general guidance:

> "The general policy of the legislature is that those who are under 18 years of age and in particular children of under 15 years of age should, wherever possible, be tried in the youth court. It is that court which is best designed to meet their specific needs. A trial in the Crown Court with the inevitably greater formality and greatly increased number of people involved (including a jury and the public) should be reserved for the most serious cases...It is a further policy of the legislature that, generally speaking, first-time offenders aged 12 to 14 and all offenders under 12 should not be detained in custody and decisions as to jurisdiction should have regard to the fact that the exceptional power to detain for grave offences should not be used to water down the general principle. Those under 15 will rarely attract a period of detention and, even more rarely, those who are under 12...In each case the court should ask itself whether there is a real prospect, having regard to his or her age, that this defendant whose case they are considering might require a sentence of, or in excess of, two years or, alternatively, whether although the sentence might be less than two years, there is some unusual feature of the case which justifies declining jurisdiction ..."

The decision maker should not decide what sentence he or she would consider appropriate, nor predict the actual sentence which would be passed, but to ask whether there is a real prospect that the case may attract a sentence to which section 91 would apply. Thus, what the court should have in mind is what is within the available range of sentences which are not manifestly excessive, not attempting to establish where within the range a sentence will necessarily be. Plainly, regard must be had to the particular facts of a case in forming an appropriate assessment of what the sentencing range might be (*Crown Prosecution Service v Newcastle Upon Tyne Youth Court* [2010] EWHC 2773 (Admin)).

Powers of Criminal Courts (Sentencing) Act 2000, s 91

(1) Subsection (3) below applies where a person aged under 18 is convicted on indictment of—

 (a) an offence punishable in the case of a person aged 21 or over with imprisonment for 14 years or more, not being an offence the sentence for which is fixed by law; or

 (b) an offence under section 3 of the Sexual Offences Act 2003 (in this section, 'the 2003 Act') (sexual assault); or

 (c) an offence under section 13 of the 2003 Act (child sex offences committed by children or young persons); or

 (d) an offence under section 25 of the 2003 Act (sexual activity with a child family member); or

 (e) an offence under section 26 of the 2003 Act (inciting a child family member to engage in sexual activity).

(1A) Subsection (3) below also applies where—

 (a) a person aged under 18 is convicted on indictment of an offence—

  (i) under subsection (1)(a), (ab), (aba), (ac), (ad), (ae), (af) or (c) of section 5 of the Firearms Act 1968 (prohibited weapons), or

  (ii) under subsection (1A)(a) of that section,

 (b) the offence was committed after the commencement of section 51A of that Act and for the purposes of subsection (3) of that section at a time when he was aged 16 or over, and

 (c) the court is of the opinion mentioned in section 51A(2) of that Act (exceptional circumstances which justify its not imposing required custodial sentence).

(1B) Subsection (3) below also applies where—

 (a) a person aged under 18 is convicted on indictment of an offence under the Firearms Act 1968 that is listed in section 51A(1A)(b), (e) or (f) of that Act and was committed in respect of a firearm or ammunition specified in section 5(1)(a), (ab), (aba), (ac), (ad), (ae), (af) or (c) or section 5(1A)(a) of that Act;

 (b) the offence was committed after the commencement of section 30 of the Violent Crime Reduction Act 2006 and for the purposes of section 51A(3) of the Firearms Act 1968 at a time when he was aged 16 or over; and

 (c) the court is of the opinion mentioned in section 51A(2) of the Firearms Act 1968.

(1C) Subsection (3) below also applies where—

 (a) a person aged under 18 is convicted of an offence under section 28 of the Violent Crime Reduction Act 2006 (using someone to mind a weapon);

 (b) section 29(3) of that Act applies (minimum sentences in certain cases); and

 (c) the court is of the opinion mentioned in section 29(6) of that Act (exceptional circumstances which justify not imposing the minimum sentence).

(3) If the court is of the opinion that neither a community sentence nor a detention and training order is suitable, the court may sentence the offender to be detained for such period, not exceeding the maximum term of imprisonment with which the offence is punishable in the case of a person aged 21 or over, as may be specified in the sentence.

(4) Subsection (3) above is subject to (in particular) section 152 and 153 of the Criminal Justice Act 2003.

(5) Where—

    (a) subsection (2) of section 51A of the Firearms Act 1968, or

    (b) subsection (6) of section 29 of the Violent Crime Reduction Act 2006, requires the imposition of a sentence of detention under this section for a term of at least the term provided for in that section, the court shall sentence the offender to be detained for such period, of at least the term so provided for but not exceeding the maximum term of imprisonment with which the offence is punishable in the case of a person aged 18 or over, as may be specified in the sentence.

DETERMINING SERIOUSNESS

Criminal Justice Act 2003, s 143

(1) In considering the seriousness of any offence, the court must consider the offender's culpability in committing the offence and any harm which the offence caused, was intended to cause or might foreseeably have caused.

(2) In considering the seriousness of an offence ("the current offence") committed by an offender who has one or more previous convictions, the court must treat each previous conviction as an aggravating factor if (in the case of that conviction) the court considers that it can reasonably be so treated having regard, in particular, to—

    (a) the nature of the offence to which the conviction relates and its relevance to the current offence, and

    (b) the time that has elapsed since the conviction.

(3) In considering the seriousness of any offence committed while the offender was on bail, the court must treat the fact that it was committed in those circumstances as an aggravating factor.

(4) Any reference in subsection (2) to a previous conviction is to be read as a reference to—

    (a) a previous conviction by a court in the United Kingdom,

    (aa) a previous conviction by a court in another member State of a relevant offence under the law of that State,

    (b) a previous conviction of a service offence within the meaning of the Armed Forces Act 2006 ("conviction" here including anything that under section 376(1) and (2) of that Act is to be treated as a conviction), or

    (c) a finding of guilt in respect of a member State service offence.

(5) Subsections (2) and (4) do not prevent the court from treating—

    (a) a previous conviction by a court outside both the United Kingdom and any other member State, or

    (b) a previous conviction by a court in any member State (other than the United Kingdom) of an offence which is not a relevant offence,

as an aggravating factor in any case where the court considers it appropriate to do so.

(6) For the purposes of this section—

    (a) an offence is "relevant" if the offence would constitute an offence under the law of any part of the United Kingdom if it were done in that part at the time of the conviction of the defendant for the current offence,

    (b) "member State service offence" means an offence which—

        (i) was the subject of proceedings under the service law of a member State other than the United Kingdom, and

        (ii) would constitute an offence under the law of any part of the United Kingdom, or a service offence (within the meaning of the Armed Forces Act 2006), if it were done in any part of the United Kingdom, by a member of Her Majesty's forces, at the time of the conviction of the defendant for the current offence, [...]

DISQUALIFICATION FROM DRIVING

Disqualification (Road Traffic Offenders Act 1988, s 34) occurs as a result of: Obligatory disqualification, discretionary disqualification, accumulation of 12 or more penalty points (so called 'totting up'), as an ancillary penalty under PCC(S)A 2000, ss 146, 147, fine default, non-payment of child support and in relation to new drivers accumulating 6 or more points within the first 2 years of having passed a driving test. There is also provision for interim disqualification. **Disqualification in absence**: This is prohibited unless the court has previously adjourned proceedings and sent a notice detailing the reason for adjournment (Magistrates' Courts Act 1980, s 11(4)). **Warning**: A discretionary disqualification should not be imposed without first warning the defendant and giving an opportunity for representations (*Ireland* [1989] Crim LR 458). **Aiders and abetters**: Any mandatory disqualification is treated as if it were a discretionary one—this concession does not however affect in any way the courts power to disqualify under the totting up provisions (see s 34(5) and *Ullah v Luckhurst* [1977] Crim LR 295). **Hospital orders**: Where an order is made under the Mental Health Act 1983, s 37(3) the court may not order disqualification. **Defence available for certain offences**: Following conviction for an offence under the Road Traffic Act 1988, ss 40A, 41A the court shall not order disqualification if the defendant did not know or have reasonable cause to believe that the facts giving rise to the offence were present. Discharge: The imposition of an absolute or conditional discharge does not affect the imposition of a disqualification (Road Traffic Offenders Act 1988, s 46(1)). **Length**: Disqualification for life may be imposed if the defendant poses a danger to the public which will persist for an indefinite period, the court having ordinarily heard expert evidence to that effect (*King* [1993] RTR 345). An indefinite period of disqualification cannot be imposed (*Fowler* [1937] 2 All ER 380). Whilst disqualification is in itself a punishment, it should not interfere with the rehabilitative purposes of sentence, and unless justified should not be extended long after the primary sentence has concluded (*Lee* [1991] RTR 30). Repeat offenders will not however be so fortunate as was emphasized in *Thomas* [1983] 1 WLR 1490: "a culpable offender like the appellant cannot expect that his period of disqualification will be no longer than the period which he is likely to spend in prison: see R v Hansel (Note) [1983] RTR 445, 447B, decided by this court on 17 November 1982. The period of disqualification must depend on all the facts of the particular case". In *Cully* [2006] RTR 32 the court dealt with drivers who require a licence in order to earn a living:

> "where an appellant has a job which involves driving, where there is no apparent risk indicated by the circumstances of the particular offence to the public from his continuing to drive, and where a lengthy period of disqualification would impose financial strains upon him, it would be too punitive to impose a lengthy period of disqualification. It might defeat the purpose of the sentence, which is to mark the seriousness of the offence by a period of imprisonment, if it were to deprive the offender of his livelihood and in the present case put at risk the continued livelihood of those whom he employed. We consider that the purpose of a disqualification from driving is so far as possible to protect the public. Often it may be that drivers come before the sentencing court with an appalling driving record. In such cases an extended period of disqualification may be appropriate since the offence indicates the risk to the public in the individual continuing to drive. Where circumstances do not suggest that there is any such risk, a period of disqualification, though inevitable as it is in a case of dangerous driving, can, and should in our view, be kept to the minimum."

Disqualification until re-test passed: A court must order the defendant to undertake a re-test before a licence can be obtained if convicted of any of these offences (Road Traffic Offenders Act 1988, s 36): (a) manslaughter (motor), (b) causing death by dangerous driving and (c) dangerous driving. It should be noted that in addition to the offences mentioned in section 36(2), the following offence has been prescribed under s 36(3) (SI 2001/4051): causing death by careless driving while under the influence of drink or drugs.

Obligatory Minimum Period of Disqualification: An obligatory disqualification does not remove any penalty points endorsed on the driving licence at the time of disqualification. The driving licence must be endorsed but points will not be added (Road Traffic Offenders Act 1988, s 29(1)(a)).

Offences carrying disqualification will result in the following disqualification periods (subject to special reasons being successfully argued):

Minimum 6 months disqualification	Minimum 12 months disqualification	Minimum 2 years disqualification	Minimum 3 years disqualification
An offence under Road Traffic Act 1988, s 40A if the driver has within the three years immediately preceding the commission of the offence been convicted of any such offence.	All other offences involving obligatory disqualification.	(1) Where more than one disqualification for a fixed period of 56 days or more has been imposed within the 3 years preceding the commission of the offence (there shall be disregarded any disqualification imposed under section 26 of the 1988 Act or section 147 of the Powers of Criminal Courts (Sentencing) Act 2000 or section 223A or 436A of the Criminal Procedure (Scotland) Act 1975 and any disqualification imposed in respect of an offence of stealing a motor vehicle, an offence under section 12 or 25 of the Theft Act 1968, an offence under section 178 of the Road Traffic Act 1988, or an attempt to commit such an offence). (2) Where the offence is manslaughter, causing death by dangerous driving, causing death by careless driving while under the influence of drink or drugs	An offence under the Road Traffic Act 1988, sections: 3A, 4(1), 5(1)(a), 7(6), 7A(6) if the driver has within the 10 years immediately preceding the commission of the offence been convicted of any such offence. This rule applies even where the offender was not disqualified for the original offence due to special reasons having been found (*Boliston v Gibbons* [1985] RTR 176), and also where the the offender was a secondary participant in the offence (*Makeham v Donaldson* [1981] RTR 511).

Drink drive rehabilitation scheme: A court may order a reduction in the period of disqualification (not less than 3 months, not more than ¼ of the total disqualification) if the offender (who must be aged at least 17 years) successfully completes a rehabilitation course (Road Traffic Offenders Act 1988, s 34A). This course is available only where a disqualification of 12 months or more is imposed for any of the following offences: Road Traffic Act 1988, ss 3A, 4, 5 and 7. The legislation does not dictate anything other than general criteria to be met for the making of such orders and it therefore should be made available in most cases before the court. The Road Safety Act 2006, s 35 extends the scheme to the following offences, but is not yet in force: ss 3, 7A(6), 17(4) and 36. **Alcohol ignition locks**: This procedure is provided for under the Road Safety Act 2006, s 15, but is not currently in force. **Special Reasons**: See later section under that name.

Discretionary Disqualification

Ordinarily, discretionary disqualification (Road Traffic Offenders Act 1988, s 34(2)) ought to be considered before consideration of penalty points. In the event that an offender would fall to be disqualified as a result of accumulating 12 or more penalty points if points were to be endorsed (Road Traffic Offenders Act, s 35), the issue arises as to whether that person should be disqualified under those provisions, or under the discretionary provisions. The correct approach is to consider the defendant's driving record as a whole. If disqualification in excess of that to be imposed as a result of totting up is required then discretionary disqualification should not be imposed under s 34(2), instead the defendant should be disqualified under the normal totting up provisions (*Jones v Director of Public Prosecutions* [2001] RTR 8).

Penalty Points Disqualification ('Totting Up')

Where the total points that are required to be taken into account (see s 29 below) exceed 12, disqualification must be ordered unless mitigating circumstances are found (Road Traffic Offenders Act 1988, s 35). **Effect**: As well as having the effect of disqualifying the driver from driving, all penalty points are cleared from the licence (s 29(1)(b)), it is important to note that conviction within the context of section 29 means the date on which the defendant is sentenced, not the date on which he was actually convicted of the offence, a distinction which is often critical when offences are sentenced out of sequence, which is so often the case (*Brentwood Justices, ex p Richardson* [1993] RTR 374). **Offences not on same occasion**: Where offences are before the court and were not committed on the same occasion, points in relation to all offences must be taken into account, but note that in all cases only one penalty point disqualification can be imposed. **Offences on same occasion**: The starting point is section 28(4) which states that: "where a person is convicted (whether on the same occasion or not) of two or more offences committed on the same occasion and involving obligatory endorsement, the total number of penalty points to be attributed to them is the number or highest number that would be attributed on a conviction of one of them (so that if the convictions are on different occasions the number of penalty points to be attributed to the offences on the later occasion or occasions shall be restricted accordingly)". However, a court, 'if it thinks fit' may impose points for each offence. **Same occasion**: This is a paucity of English case law on this topic, and a significant difference of approach between the English and Scottish courts. Failing to stop and then failing to report arise out of the same incident and therefore are offences on the same occasion (*Johnson v Finbow* [1983] 1 WLR 879). A decision of the Scottish High Court, *McKeever v Walkingshaw* (1995) 1996 SLT 1228 decided that a single course of driving may give rise to offences having occurred on more than one occasion (speeding and then less than 2 miles later committing a further offence). Similarly a moving traffic offence which resulted in the driver being stopped and asked to give a specimen of breath (which he declined) was similarly held to be separate occasions (*Cameron v Brown* (1996) 1997 SLT 914). Whether offences occur on the same occasion is primarily a matter of fact. **Mitigating circumstances (commonly known as 'Exceptional hardship')**: The Road Traffic Act 1988, s 35(1) permits a court not to disqualify (at all) or to disqualify for a period of less than the mandatory 6 months if satisfied, having regard to all the circumstances, that there are grounds for mitigating the normal consequences of the conviction. It has been held to be a mitigating circumstance that a disqualification would offend a rehabilitative purpose of sentencing (*Preston* [1986] RTR 136), and also if such a disqualification would offend general sentencing policy (*Thomas* [1984] Crim LR 49, affirming the general principle that lengthy disqualification ought not to be imposed alongside imprisonment). **Proof**: It is for the defendant to establish that mitigating circumstances exist (*Owen v Jones* [1988] RTR 102); ordinarily this will require evidence on oath, unless the magistrates' are otherwise satisfied (which will only be in exceptional cases). **Excluded factors**: Section 35(4) excludes consideration of the following factors: (1) Any circumstances which, within the three years immediately preceding the conviction, have been taken into account under that subsection in ordering the offender to be disqualified for a shorter period or not ordering him to be disqualified. The burden is on the defendant to prove that the circumstances now being advanced are different (*Sandbach Justices, ex p Pescud* (1984) 5 Cr App R (S) 177), he may do this by producing the court register or advancing oral evidence on oath. (2) Hardship, other than exceptional hardship. It will be a matter of fact to be decided on a case by case basis, but should amount to hardship which is 'out of the ordinary' (*Fay v Fay* [1982] 2 All ER 922). It should not be assumed that loss of job in itself will suffice (*Brennan v McKay* (1996) 1997 SLT 603). Hardship is not confined to the offender and may extend to employees, family etc. (*Cornwall v Coke* [1976] Crim LR 519). (3) Any circumstances that are alleged to make the offence or any of the offences not a serious one. This does not preclude, in an appropriate case, the defendant being able to advance special reasons.

Road Traffic Offenders Act 1998, s 29

(1) Where a person is convicted of an offence involving obligatory endorsement, the penalty points to be taken into account on that occasion are (subject to subsection (2) below)—

    (a) any that are to be attributed to the offence or offences of which he is convicted, disregarding any offence in respect of which an order under section 34 of this Act is made, and

    (b) any that were on a previous occasion ordered to be endorsed on the counterpart of any licence held by him or on his driving record, unless the offender has since that occasion and before the conviction been disqualified under section 35 of this Act.

(2) If any of the offences was committed more than three years before another, the penalty points in respect of that offence shall not be added to those in respect of the other.

(3) In relation to licences which came into force before 1st June 1990, the reference in subsection (1) above to the counterpart of a licence shall be construed as a reference to the licence itself.

Disqualification where vehicle used for crime

Powers are contained in Powers of Criminal Courts (Sentencing) Act 2000, s 146, 147 to disqualify when a vehicle is used for the purpose of criminal activity. Note that as far as section 147 is concerned, only s 147(2), (4) applies to the magistrates' court. Section 146 is much wider in scope than section 147, and need not even involve a motoring related offence (*Sofekun* [2008] EWCW Crim 2035) and its use is now preferred in the magistrates' court. In cases where a longer period of disqualification is being considered due to the vehicle having been used in the commission of the offence it is submitted that committal for sentence will normally take place in any event, so consideration of the detailed body of case law relating to section 147 is not necessary here. A novel use of section 146 was in *Waring* [2005] EWCA Crim 1080 where an 18 months period of disqualification was imposed on a defendant who had escaped being breathalysed. In *Sofekun* the court rejected a submission that the earlier case of *Cliff* [2005] 2 Cr App R (S) 118 "should be taken to have created any restrictions on the exercise of the power" observing that such a restriction "cannot otherwise be found in the statutory provision itself. Section 146 makes disqualification from driving available to a sentencing court as part of the overall punitive element of a sentence". **Passengers:** A disqualification can be imposed on a passenger (*Gilder* [2011] EWCA Crim 1159). **Period:** In *Bowling* [2008] EWCA Crim 1148 the court held: "The general rule is that if a defendant is given custodial sentence, then if the court imposes a period of disqualification from driving under section 147, it will do so for a period equal to or slightly in excess of the period of custody. The policy behind this general rule is that the court should not impose a period of disqualification that will inhibit the offender from rehabilitating himself. This is particularly so in cases where the offender is dependent on the ability to drive for his livelihood. The question that arises in this case, is whether the nature of the offence is such that it is in the public interest that those general principles should not apply. If those general principles do apply, then it is arguable that the period of disqualification was excessive. If they do not, then that might not be so". In *Harkins* [2011] EWCA Crim 2227 the court observed: "The point of disqualification under the Powers of Criminal Courts (Sentencing) Act 2000 s.147 was to punish and to deter, by removing access to a lawful use of a vehicle that had been used in commission of the offences for which the sentences were passed. For the disqualification to be effective, it was implicit that it had to apply after release from custody and that would be proportionate provided rehabilitation would not be seriously impaired by the period of disqualification. Proportionality was preserved by the general practice of keeping the period of disqualification broadly commensurate with the custodial sentence, Bowling considered. The sentencing judge was not required to fine tune the period of disqualification in line with the precise calculation of release dates and periods spent on licence, nor was he required to have regard to any direction for credit for time spent on remand, unless there would be a gross disparity between the sentence passed and the disqualification (see para.16 of judgment). Where the disqualification fell to be imposed for only one or some of the counts making up the total sentence, it was not wrong in principle to match the period of disqualification to the total sentence, provided the result was not a period of disqualification which was disproportionate to the custodial sentence passed (para.17)." But see for example *Stokes* [2012] EWCA Crim 1364 for a case where the general rule was not followed.

Powers of Criminal Courts (Sentencing) Act 2000, s 146, 147

146.— Driving disqualification for any offence.

(1) The court by or before which a person is convicted of an offence committed after 31st December 1997 may, instead of or in addition to dealing with him in any other way, order him to be disqualified, for such period as it thinks fit, for holding or obtaining a driving licence.

(2) Where the person is convicted of an offence the sentence for which is fixed by law or falls to be imposed under section 110(2) or 111(2) above, section 51A(2) of the Firearms Act 1968, section 225(2) or 226(2) of the Criminal Justice Act 2003 or section 29(4) or (6) of the Violent Crime Reduction Act 2006, subsection (1) above shall have effect as if the words "instead of or" were omitted.

147.— Driving disqualification where vehicle used for purposes of crime.

(1) [...]

(2) This section also applies where a person is convicted by or before any court of common assault or of any other offence involving an assault (including an offence of aiding, abetting, counselling or procuring, or inciting to the commission of, an offence).

(3) [...]

(4) If, in a case to which this section applies by virtue of subsection (2) above, the court is satisfied that the assault was committed by driving a motor vehicle, the court may order the person convicted to be disqualified, for such period as the court thinks fit, for holding or obtaining a driving licence.

Fine defaulters: Driving disqualification

This provision is not currently in force.

Criminal Justice Act 2003, s 301

(1) Subsection (2) applies in any case where a magistrates' court—

(a) has power under Part 3 of the Magistrates' Courts Act 1980 (c. 43) to issue a warrant of commitment for default in paying a sum adjudged to be paid by a conviction (other than a sum ordered to be paid under section 6 of the Proceeds of Crime Act 2002 (c. 29)), or

(b) would, but for section 89 of the Sentencing Act (restrictions on custodial sentences for persons under 18), have power to issue such a warrant for such default.

(2) The magistrates' court may, instead of issuing a warrant of commitment or, as the case may be, proceeding under section 81 of the Magistrates' Courts Act 1980 (enforcement

of fines imposed on young offenders), order the person in default to be disqualified, for such period not exceeding twelve months as it thinks fit, for holding or obtaining a driving licence.

(3) Where an order has been made under subsection (2) for default in paying any sum—

(a) on payment of the whole sum to any person authorised to receive it, the order shall cease to have effect, and

(b) on payment of part of the sum to any such person, the total number of weeks or months to which the order relates is to be taken to be reduced by a proportion corresponding to that which the part paid bears to the whole sum.

(4) In calculating any reduction required by subsection (3)(b) any fraction of a week or month is to be disregarded.

Non-payment of child support: Disqualification

Child Support Act 1991, ss 39A, 40B

39A.— Commitment to prison and disqualification from driving.

(1) Where the Commission has sought—

(a) in England and Wales to levy an amount by distress under this Act; or

(b) to recover an amount by virtue of section 36 or 38,

and that amount, or any portion of it, remains unpaid it may apply to the court under this section.

(2) An application under this section is for whichever the court considers appropriate in all the circumstances of—

(a) the issue of a warrant committing the liable person to prison; or

(b) an order for him to be disqualified from holding or obtaining a driving licence.

(3) On any such application the court shall (in the presence of the liable person) inquire as to—

(a) whether he needs a driving licence to earn his living;

(b) his means; and

(c) whether there has been wilful refusal or culpable neglect on his part.

(4) The Commission may make representations to the court as to whether it thinks it more appropriate to commit the liable person to prison or to disqualify him from holding or obtaining a driving licence; and the liable person may reply to those representations.

40B.— Disqualification from driving: further provision.

(1) If, but only if, the court is of the opinion that there has been wilful refusal or culpable neglect on the part of the liable person, it may—

(a) order him to be disqualified, for such period specified in the order but not exceeding two years as it thinks fit, from holding or obtaining a driving licence (a "disqualification order"); or

(b) make a disqualification order but suspend its operation until such time and on such conditions (if any) as it thinks just.

(2) The court may not take action under both section 40 and this section.

(3) A disqualification order must state the amount in respect of which it is made, which is to be the aggregate of—

(a) the amount mentioned in section 35(1), or so much of it as remains outstanding; and

(b) an amount (determined in accordance with regulations made by the Secretary of State) in respect of the costs of the application under section 39A.

(4) A court which makes a disqualification order shall require the person to whom it relates to produce any driving licence held by him, and its counterpart (within the meaning of section 108(1) of the Road Traffic Act 1988).

(5) On an application by the Commission or the liable person, the court–

   (a) may make an order substituting a shorter period of disqualification, or make an order revoking the disqualification order, if part of the amount referred to in subsection (3) (the "amount due") is paid to any person authorised to receive it; and

   (b) must make an order revoking the disqualification order if all of the amount due is so paid.

(6) The Commission may make representations to the court as to the amount which should be paid before it would be appropriate to make an order revoking the disqualification order under subsection (5)(a), and the person liable may reply to those representations.

(7) The Commission may make a further application under section 39A if the amount due has not been paid in full when the period of disqualification specified in the disqualification order expires.

(8) Where a court–

   (a) makes a disqualification order;

   (b) makes an order under subsection (5); or

   (c) allows an appeal against a disqualification order,

it shall send notice of that fact to the Commission; and the notice shall contain such particulars and be sent in such manner and to such address as the Commission may determine.

(9) Where a court makes a disqualification order, it shall also send any driving licence and its counterpart, on their being produced to the court, to the Commission at such address as it may determine.

New drivers: Accumulation of 6 or more penalty points

New drivers are subject to a two-year probationary period. If at any time during that period points are imposed on a driving licence, and the points on the licence total 6 or more, the licence will be sent to the secretary of State for revocation (Road Traffic (New Drivers) Act 1995). The relevant date is the date of offence, not conviction, so a defendant cannot escape the provision by delaying conviction. The defendant will need to re-pass his driving test in order to obtain a new licence. Any new licence will not be subject to a new probationary period (nor any part of the period remaining from the point of first passing his driving test). Points which were imposed prior to the defendant obtaining his full driving licence are not to be disregarded (*Adebowale v Bradford Crown Court* [2004] EWHC 1741 (Admin)). If an appeal is lodged the defendant remains entitled to drive (s 5 of the 1995 Act).

Deception

If an offender escapes the proper consequences of a driving conviction due to a deception of any nature then he can, on conviction for that offence, be disqualified for the original offence, the sentencing court having the same powers as the original court (Road Traffic Offenders Act 1988, s 49).

Interim disqualification

An interim order for disqualification can be made on one occasion only, for a maximum period of 6 months, such disqualification being credited against any final order imposed. In an appropriate case a court can order a person not drive a motor vehicle as a condition of bail provided that the principles under the Bail Act 1976 are adhered to.

Road Traffic Offenders Act 1988, s 26

(1) Where a magistrates' court—

(a) commits an offender to the Crown Court under section 6 of the Powers of Criminal Courts (Sentencing) Act 2000 or any enactment mentioned in subsection (4) of that section applies, or

(b) remits an offender to another magistrates' court under section 10 of that Act,

to be dealt with for an offence involving obligatory or discretionary disqualification, it may order him to be disqualified until he has been dealt with in respect of the offence.

(2) Where a court in England and Wales—

(a) defers passing sentence on an offender under section 1 of that Act in respect of an offence involving obligatory or discretionary disqualification, or

(b) adjourns after convicting an offender of such an offence but before dealing with him for the offence,

it may order the offender to be disqualified until he has been dealt with in respect of the offence.

Suspension of disqualification pending appeal

The fact that an appeal is pending does not of itself remove any disqualification or endorsement imposed by the sentencing court (*R v Thames Magistrates' Court, ex p Levy*, The Times 17 July 1997; *Singh v Director of Public Prosecutions*[1999] Crim LR 914), and it is therefore important to consider the lifting of any disqualification pending an appeal to the Crown or High Court. A notice of appeal must be lodged, but that of itself does not suspend the disqualification (*Kidner v Daniels* (1910) 74 JP 127), nor should a court ordinarily suspend a disqualification in the absence of an application from the defendant (*Taylor v Commissioner of Police for the Metropolis* [1987] RTR 118); an application must be made to the Magistrates' Court (Road Traffic Offenders Act 1988, s 39), Crown Court or High Court as appropriate. **Criteria**: In *Grant v Director of Public Prosecutions* [2002] EWHC 3081 (Admin) the court held: "It is inevitable that an order or decision is regarded as binding and effective unless and until it is set aside. This must mean that a stay of order, pending appeal, is only granted in exceptional circumstances".

Return of driving licence

For disqualifications of at least 2 years duration an offender can apply for the return of his driving licence after the expiry of a minimum period. There is no power to remove the requirement that a person pass a new driving test, but the power to return the licence early can nonetheless be used to bring the disqualification period to an end earlier than it otherwise would have been (*Nuttall* [1971] RTR 279). The provision also applies to those disqualified for a minimum 3 year period due to a second specified offence having been committed in a 10 year period (*Damer v Davison* [1976] RTR 44). **Procedure**: CrPR 55 applies and the application must be made in writing. The application should be made to the same court that imposed the disqualification. Where a disqualification made by a magistrates' court is appealed to the crown court and varied, the application for removal should be made to the original magistrates' court (Magistrates Courts Act 1980, s 110). There is no power to remove only part of the remaining disqualification, the court must either grant or reject the application (*Cottrell* [1956] 1 All ER 751). **Renewal**: If an application is unsuccessful a further application cannot be made until 3 months have elapsed. **Costs**: An application for removal of disqualification falls within the definition of criminal proceedings and an eligible defendant is entitled to apply for a representation order to fund the application (*R v Liverpool Crown Court, ex p McCann* [1995] RTR 23). Section 42(5) states that an applicant may be ordered to pay the costs of the opposing party, even if successful. It is doubted, in the light of *McCann* whether this provision is compatible with ECHR Art 6.

Road Traffic Offenders Act 1988, s 42

(1) Subject to the provisions of this section, a person who by an order of a court is disqualified may apply to the court by which the order was made to remove the disqualification.

(2) On any such application the court may, as it thinks proper having regard to—

(a) the character of the person disqualified and his conduct subsequent to the order,

(b) the nature of the offence, and

(c) any other circumstances of the case,

either by order remove the disqualification as from such date as may be specified in the order or refuse the application.

(3) No application shall be made under subsection (1) above for the removal of a disqualification before the expiration of whichever is relevant of the following periods from the date of the order by which the disqualification was imposed, that is—

(a) two years, if the disqualification is for less than four years,

(b) one half of the period of disqualification, if it is for less than ten years but not less than four years,

(c) five years in any other case;

and in determining the expiration of the period after which under this subsection a person may apply for the removal of a disqualification, any time after the conviction during which the disqualification was suspended or he was not disqualified shall be disregarded.

(4) Where an application under subsection (1) above is refused, a further application under that subsection shall not be entertained if made within three months after the date of the refusal.

[…]

(6) The preceding provisions of this section shall not apply where the disqualification was imposed by order under section 36(1) of this Act.

DISQUALIFICATION OF COMPANY DIRECTORS

Both the internal and external management of the company are relevant to section 2(1) of the 1986 Act (*Corbin* (1984) 6 Cr App R (S) 17). It may be inappropriate for a court to order compensation to be paid by a director who by virtue of the making of this order will be deprived of the ability to earn a living (*Holmes* (1992) 13 Cr App R (S) 29).

Company Directors Disqualification Act 1986, ss 2, 5

2.— Disqualification on conviction of indictable offence.

(1) The court may make a disqualification order against a person where he is convicted of an indictable offence (whether on indictment or summarily) in connection with the promotion, formation, management, liquidation or striking off of a company with the receivership of a company's property or with his being an administrative receiver of a company.

(2) "The court" for this purpose means—

(a) any court having jurisdiction to wind up the company in relation to which the offence was committed, or

(b) the court by or before which the person is convicted of the offence, or

(c) in the case of a summary conviction in England and Wales, any other magistrates' court acting in the same local justice area;

and for the purposes of this section the definition of "indictable offence" in Schedule 1 to the Interpretation Act 1978 applies for Scotland as it does for England and Wales.

(3) The maximum period of disqualification under this section is—

(a) where the disqualification order is made by a court of summary jurisdiction, 5 years, and

(b) in any other case, 15 years.

5.— Disqualification on summary conviction.

(1) An offence counting for the purposes of this section is one of which a person is convicted (either on indictment or summarily) in consequence of a contravention of, or failure to

comply with, any provision of the companies legislation requiring a return, account or other document to be filed with, delivered or sent, or notice of any matter to be given, to the registrar of companies (whether the contravention or failure is on the person's own part or on the part of any company).

(2)   Where a person is convicted of a summary offence counting for those purposes, the court by which he is convicted (or, in England and Wales, any other magistrates' court acting in the same local justice area) may make a disqualification order against him if the circumstances specified in the next subsection are present.

(3)   Those circumstances are that, during the 5 years ending with the date of the conviction, the person has had made against him, or has been convicted of, in total not less than 3 default orders and offences counting for the purposes of this section; and those offences may include that of which he is convicted as mentioned in subsection (2) and any other offence of which he is convicted on the same occasion.

(4)   For the purposes of this section—

(a) the definition of "summary offence" in Schedule 1 to the Interpretation Act 1978 applies for Scotland as for England and Wales, and

(b) "default order" means the same as in section 3(3)(b).

(4A)   In this section "the companies legislation" means the Companies Acts and Parts 1 to 7 of the Insolvency Act 1986 (company insolvency and winding up).

(5)   The maximum period of disqualification under this section is 5 years.

DRINKING BANNING ORDER

Where a defendant (aged 16 or over) is convicted of an offence, and at the time of the that offence being committed he was under the influence of alcohol (Violence Crime Reduction Act 2006, s 6) the court must consider whether that defendant has engaged in criminal or disorderly conduct while under the influence of alcohol and whether such an order is necessary to protect other persons from further conduct by him of that kind while he is under the influence of alcohol (VCRA 2006, s 3(2)). **Duration**: not less than 2 months, not more than 2 years. **Prohibitions**: Any that is necessary to prevent criminal or disorderly conduct while under the influence of alcohol, and must include prohibitions as the court considers necessary on the offender's entering licensed premises. **Breach**: Fine level 4. **Variation/discharge**: See s 8. **Availability of order**: As of 1 November 2010 the orders can be made in the following Local Justice Areas: Birmingham; Bristol; Burnley, Pendle and Rossendale; Cardiff Central and South West Staffordshire; City of London; City of Salford; City of Westminster; Corby; Coventry District; Denbighshire; Doncaster; East Berkshire; East Dorset; East Kent; Fenland; Fylde Coast; Grimsby and Cleethorpes; Gwent; Hackney and Tower Hamlets; Halton; Hull and Holderness; Hammersmith and Fulham, and Kensington and Chelsea; Hartlepool; Lambeth and Southwark; Leicester; Lincoln District; Manchester City; Mansfield; Merthyr Tydfil; Newcastle Upon Tyne District; North East Derbyshire and Dales; North East Suffolk; North Kent; North Staffordshire; North Tyneside District; Northampton; Nottingham; Plymouth District; Reading; Sedgemoor; South Devon; South East Hampshire; Southampton; Southern Derbyshire; Sussex (Central); Teesside; Wakefield; West Cornwall; West Hertfordshire. **Criminal Procedure Rules**: The prosecution should comply with CrPR 50.

Violent Crime Reduction Act 2006, ss 6, 7, 8

6 Orders on conviction in criminal proceedings

(1)   This section applies where–

(a) an individual aged 16 or over is convicted of an offence (the "offender"); and

(b) at the time he committed the offence, he was under the influence of alcohol.

(2) The court must consider whether the conditions in section 3(2) are satisfied in relation to the offender.

(3) If the court decides that the conditions are satisfied in relation to the offender, it may make a drinking banning order against him.

(4) If the court–

   (a) decides that the conditions are satisfied in relation to the offender, but

   (b) does not make a drinking banning order,

it must give its reasons for not doing so in open court.

(5) If the court decides that the conditions are not satisfied in relation to the offender, it must state that fact in open court and give its reasons.

7 Supplementary provision about orders on conviction

(1) For the purpose of deciding whether to make a drinking banning order under section 6 the court may consider evidence led by the prosecution and evidence led by the defence.

(2) It is immaterial whether the evidence would have been admissible in the proceedings in which the offender was convicted.

(3) A drinking banning order under section 6 must not be made except–

   (a) in addition to a sentence imposed in respect of the offence; or

   (b) in addition to an order discharging the offender conditionally.

(4) The court may adjourn any proceedings in relation to a drinking banning order under section 6 even after sentencing the offender.

(5) If the offender does not appear for any adjourned proceedings, the court may further adjourn the proceedings or may issue a warrant for his arrest.

(6) But the court may not issue a warrant for the offender's arrest unless it is satisfied that he has had adequate notice of the time and place of the adjourned proceedings.

(7) A drinking banning order under section 6 takes effect on–

   (a) the day on which it is made; or

   (b) if on that day the offender is detained in legal custody, the day on which he is released from that custody.

(8) Subsection (9) applies in relation to proceedings in which a drinking banning order is made under section 6 against a young person.

(9) In so far as the proceedings relate to the making of the order–

   (a) section 49 of the Children and Young Persons Act 1933 (c. 12) (restrictions on reports of proceedings in which children and young persons are concerned) does not apply in respect of the young person against whom the order is made; and

   (b) section 39 of that Act (power to prohibit publication of certain matters) does so apply.

8 Variation or discharge of orders under s. 6

(1) The following persons may apply to the court which made a drinking banning order under section 6 for the order to be varied or discharged by a further order–

   (a) the subject;

   (b) the Director of Public Prosecutions ; or

   (c) a relevant authority.

(2) If the subject makes an application under subsection (1), he must also send notice of his application to the Director of Public Prosecutions .

(3) If the Director of Public Prosecutions or a relevant authority makes an application under subsection (1), he or it must also send notice of the application to the subject.

(4) In the case of an order under section 6 made by a magistrates' court, the reference in subsection (1) to the court which made the order includes a reference to a relevant local court.

(5) An order under section 6 may not be varied so as to extend the specified period to more than two years.

(6) No order under section 6 is to be discharged on an application under subsection (1)(a) unless–

    (a) it is discharged from a time after the end of the period that is half the duration of the specified period; or

    (b) the Director of Public Prosecutions has consented to its earlier discharge.

EXCLUSION FROM LICENSED PREMISES

A court should specify which premises the defendant is to be excluded from by reference to name and address, otherwise an order may be quashed for uncertainty (*Lomas* [2007] EWCA Crim 1792); although it is permissible to exclude from all premises within a clearly defined geographic area (*Arrowsmith* [2003] Crim App R (S) 46). An order banning a person from all licensed premises in a particular County was quashed in relation to an offender who had committed only their first offence (*Grady* [1990] Crim LR 608).

Licensed Premises (Exclusion of Certain Persons) Act 1980, s1

(1) Where a court by or before which a person is convicted of an offence committed on licensed premises is satisfied that in committing that offence he resorted to violence or offered or threatened to resort to violence, the court may, subject to subsection (2) below, make an order (in this Act referred to as an "exclusion order") prohibiting him from entering those premises or any other specified premises, without the express consent of the licensee of the premises or his servant or agent.

(2) An exclusion order may be made either—

    (a) in addition to any sentence which is imposed in respect of the offence of which the person is convicted; or

    (b) where the offence was committed in England and Wales, notwithstanding the provisions of section 12 and 14 of the Powers of Criminal Courts (Sentencing) Act 2000 (cases in which absolute and conditional discharges may be made, and their effect), in addition to an order discharging him absolutely or conditionally;

    (c) [...]

(3) An exclusion order shall have effect for such period, not less than three months or more than two years, as is specified in the order, unless it is terminated under section 2(2) below.

FINANCIAL CIRCUMSTANCES ORDER

In *Hobden* [2009] EWCA Crim 1584 the court disapproved of financial information being communicated from the defendant to her solicitor, for the purposes of it being advanced before a court, suggesting that were there is any doubt as to a defendant's honesty in relation to financial matters the better course is to make a formal order.

Criminal Justice Act 2003, s 162

(1) Where an individual has been convicted of an offence, the court may, before sentencing him, make a financial circumstances order with respect to him.

(2) Where a magistrates' court has been notified in accordance with section 12(4 of the Magistrates' Courts Act 1980 (c. 43) that an individual desires to plead guilty without appearing before the court, the court may make a financial circumstances order with respect to him.

(3) In this section "a financial circumstances order" means, in relation to any individual, an order requiring him to give to the court, within such period as may be specified in the order, such a statement of his financial circumstances as the court may require.

(4) An individual who without reasonable excuse fails to comply with a financial circumstances order is liable on summary conviction to a fine not exceeding level 3 on the standard scale.

(5) If an individual, in furnishing any statement in pursuance of a financial circumstances order—

   (a) makes a statement which he knows to be false in a material particular,
   (b) recklessly furnishes a statement which is false in a material particular, or
   (c) knowingly fails to disclose any material fact,

he is liable on summary conviction to a fine not exceeding level 4 on the standard scale.

(6) Proceedings in respect of an offence under subsection (5) may, notwithstanding anything in section 127(1) of the Magistrates' Courts Act 1980 (c. 43) (limitation of time), be commenced at any time within two years from the date of the commission of the offence or within six months from its first discovery by the prosecutor, whichever period expires the earlier.

Criminal Justice Act 1991, s 20A

(1) A person who is charged with an offence who, in furnishing a statement of his financial circumstances in response to an official request—

   (a) makes a statement which he knows to be false in a material particular;
   (b) recklessly furnishes a statement which is false in a material particular; or
   (c) knowingly fails to disclose any material fact,

shall be liable on summary conviction to imprisonment for a term not exceeding three months or a fine not exceeding level 4 on the standard scale or both.

(1A) A person who is charged with an offence who fails to furnish a statement of his financial circumstances in response to an official request shall be liable on summary conviction to a fine not exceeding level 2 on the standard scale.

(2) For the purposes of this section an official request is a request which—

   (a) is made by the designated officer for the magistrates' court or the appropriate officer of the Crown Court, as the case may be; and
   (b) is expressed to be made for informing the court, in the event of his being convicted, of his financial circumstances for the purpose of determining the amount of any fine the court may impose and how it should be paid.

(3) Proceedings in respect of an offence under this section may, notwithstanding anything in section 127(1) of the 1980 Act (limitation of time), be commenced at any time within two years from the date of the commission of the offence or within six months from its first discovery by the prosecutor, whichever period expires the earlier.

FINANCIAL REPORTING ORDER

Compatibility: These orders do not infringe Art 7 ECHR (*Adams* [2008] EWCA Crim 914). **Criteria**: In *Wright* [2008] EWCA Crim 3207 the court held: "Financial reporting order may be made if, but only if, two conditions are met. The first condition is conviction of a specified offence. The second is that the judge is satisfied that the risk of the person committing another (not necessarily the same) specified offence is sufficiently high to justify the making of a financial reporting order... We should say that whilst this form of order is newly created it ought not to be thought that it is routinely to be made without proper thought. We do not seek to set out any general rules for when it will be appropriate or not. This is not the right place in which to do that. No doubt the paradigm case for such an order is the defendant with a history of unsatisfactory business or financial dealing who at some stage at least is likely to be at large and engaged in business, commercial or financial activity which would otherwise be unsupervised or unmonitored.

But it is perfectly clear that the section embraces also the appellant who is going to be a prisoner and, at least in the case of the very exceptional facts of this prisoner, we have no doubt that an order can be appropriate... We are quite sure that judges who are asked to make financial reporting orders should give careful consideration to whether it would actually achieve anything. They should certainly look at alternative powers which are available to financial investigators if they would have much the same effect."

Serious Organised Crime and Police Act 2005, ss 76, 79

76 Financial reporting orders: making

(1) A court sentencing or otherwise dealing with a person convicted of an offence mentioned in subsection (3) may also make a financial reporting order in respect of him.

(2) But it may do so only if it is satisfied that the risk of the person's committing another offence mentioned in subsection (3) is sufficiently high to justify the making of a financial reporting order.

(3) The offences are—

(aa) an offence under either of the following provisions of the Fraud Act 2006–
  (i) section 1 (fraud),
  (ii) section 11 (obtaining services dishonestly),
(ab) a common law offence of conspiracy to defraud,
(ac) an offence under section 17 of the Theft Act 1968 (c. 60) (false accounting),
(c) any offence specified in Schedule 2 to the Proceeds of Crime Act 2002 (c. 29) ("lifestyle offences").
(da) an offence under any of the following provisions of the Bribery Act 2010—

section 1 (offences of bribing another person),

section 2 (offences relating to being bribed),

section 6 (bribery of foreign public officials),

(g) an offence under any of the following provisions of the Criminal Justice Act 1988 (c. 33)–

section 93A (assisting another to retain the benefit of criminal conduct),

section 93B (acquisition, possession or use of proceeds of criminal conduct),

section 93C (concealing or transferring proceeds of criminal conduct),

(h) an offence under any of the following provisions of the Drug Trafficking Act 1994 (c. 37) 6–

section 49 (concealing or transferring proceeds of drug trafficking),

section 50 (assisting another person to retain the benefit of drug trafficking),

section 51 (acquisition, possession or use of proceeds of drug trafficking),

(i) an offence under any of the following provisions of the Terrorism Act 2000 (c. 11)–

section 15 (fund-raising for purposes of terrorism),

section 16 (use and possession of money etc. for purposes of terrorism),

section 17 (funding arrangements for purposes of terrorism),

section 18 (money laundering in connection with terrorism),

(j) an offence under section 329 of the Proceeds of Crime Act 2002 (c. 29) 7 (acquisition, use and possession of criminal property),
(k) a common law offence of cheating in relation to the public revenue,
(l) an offence under section 170 of the Customs and Excise Management Act 1979 (c. 2) 8 (fraudulent evasion of duty),

(m) an offence under section 72 of the Value Added Tax Act 1994 (c. 23) 9 (offences relating to VAT),

(n) an offence under section 106A of the Taxes Management Act 1970 (fraudulent evasion of income tax),

(o) an offence under section 35 of the Tax Credits Act 2002 (c. 21) (tax credit fraud),

(p) an offence of attempting, conspiring in or inciting the commission of an offence mentioned in paragraphs (aa), (ac) or (d) to (o),

(q) an offence of aiding, abetting, counselling or procuring the commission of an offence mentioned in paragraphs (aa), (ac) or (d) to (o).

(4) The Secretary of State may by order amend subsection (3) so as to remove an offence from it or add an offence to it.

(5) A financial reporting order—

(a) comes into force when it is made, and

(b) has effect for the period specified in the order, beginning with the date on which it is made.

(6) If the order is made by a magistrates' court, the period referred to in subsection (5)(b) must not exceed 5 years.

(7) Otherwise, that period must not exceed—

(a) if the person is sentenced to imprisonment for life, 20 years,

(b) otherwise, 15 years.

79 Financial reporting orders: effect

(1) A person in relation to whom a financial reporting order has effect must do the following.
(2) He must make a report, in respect of—

(a) the period of a specified length beginning with the date on which the order comes into force, and

(b) subsequent periods of specified lengths, each period beginning immediately after the end of the previous one.

(3) He must set out in each report, in the specified manner, such particulars of his financial affairs relating to the period in question as may be specified.

(4) He must include any specified documents with each report.

(5) He must make each report within the specified number of days after the end of the period in question.

(6) He must make each report to the specified person.

(7) Rules of court may provide for the maximum length of the periods which may be specified under subsection (2).

(8) In this section, "specified" means specified by the court in the order.

(9) [...]

(10) A person who without reasonable excuse includes false or misleading information in a report, or otherwise fails to comply with any requirement of this section, is guilty of an offence and is liable on summary conviction to—

(a) imprisonment for a term not exceeding—

(i) in England and Wales, 6 months,

[...], or

(b) a fine not exceeding level 5 on the standard scale, or to both.

FINES

Scale: Level 1 (£200), level 2 (£500), level 3 (£1,000), level 4 (£2,500), level 5 (£5,000) (Criminal Justice Act 1982, s 37). A fine may not exceed £250 for an offender aged under 14, nor exceed

£1,000 for an offender aged under 18 (Powers of Criminal Courts (Sentencing) Act 2000, s 135). **Periodical payment**: Payment may be ordered in full immediately or by instalment, and the court has power to allow further time for payment (Magistrates' Courts Act 1980, s 75). When fining foreign offenders (eg lorry drivers) regard should be had to Home Office Circular 1/1987). **Period**: There is no principle requiring a financial penalty payable by instalments to run for no more than a year, provided it was not an undue burden and so too severe a punishment (Olliver and Olliver (1989) 11 Cr App R (S) 10). **Fixing of fines**: A fine must be commensurate with the seriousness of the offence and the financial circumstances of the offender (CJA 2003, s 164). If an offender refuses to disclose his finances then the court may presume his to have the ability to discharge the fine proposes (however note that it may be a criminal offence to refuse to disclose) (*Higgins* (1988) 10 Cr App R (S) 144). The Magistrates' Court Sentencing Guideline (Appendix 2) details the general approach to fines in relation to individuals. **Credit for custody**: A court should give credit when fixing a fine for any time spent in custody, how much credit can be given, and in what manner, depends very much on the circumstances of the cases and is in the discretion of the sentencing judge. (*Warden* [1996] 2 Cr App R (S) 269). **Discharge**: Unless the defendant is being sentenced for more than one offence a fine cannot be imposed alongside a discharge (*McClelland* (1951) 35 Cr App R 22; *Sanck* (1990) 12 Cr App R (S) 155). **Imprisonment**: There is no objection in principle to a fine being imposed in addition to a custodial sentence, but the circumstances in which it is proper to do so will be rare. **Public bodies**: Care should be taken when fining public bodies as they cannot simply recoup the monies by increasing fees or charges (*Southampton University Hospital NHS Trust* [2006] EWCA Crim 2971). **Companies**: In *Thames Water Utilities Ltd* [2010] EWCA Crim 202 the court set out the general approach to fines: i) First assess the seriousness of the offence by reference to its facts. This assessment should include consideration of all aggravating and mitigating features relating to the offence itself. ii) Given the resultant assessment of seriousness, and consideration thereafter of the offender's means, the Court should then identify the amount of a notional fine after a trial. The notional fine should combine both the punishment and deterrent elements of the sentence. The deterrent element should be the amount, over and above the amount of the punishment element, that is required to reach a total figure that brings the necessary message home to the offender's managers and shareholders (and thereby to others). iii) The Court should then consider the making of any appropriate compensation order(s), and (if made) the extent to which the amount of any such order(s) should be imposed in addition to, or deducted from, the amount of the notional fine identified thus far. In addition to the requisite consideration of the means of the offender, the fact of a prompt offer by the offender to submit to such an order or orders may be a significant feature in such a decision. iv) The Court should then go on to consider the question of the extent to which (in addition, if it be the case, to the acceptance of any compensation order or orders) the offender has brought the message home to itself, and then the extent (if any) to which that should be reflected in a deduction from the amount of the notional fine thus far identified as appropriate. The cost of putting right the failures that led to the offence, and of ensuring lack of repetition, should not be taken into account in this regard. Such corrective action should be regarded, save in the most exceptional case, as the minimum response to an offence, with failure to carry it out being regarded as a significant aggravating feature. In contrast, the making of substantial voluntary reparation should, depending on its nature and amount, generally be regarded as a significant mitigating feature in this respect, typically requiring at least some reduction in the level of the deterrent element of the notional fine thus far identified. It may, in an appropriate case, result in a very significant reduction. In an exceptional case it may even reduce the deterrent element of the notional fine to a nil amount. However, a deduction for voluntary reparation should not generally reduce the level of the notional fine below the amount already identified as representing the punishment element of the sentence. There may, nevertheless, be very exceptional cases in which justice requires that the extent and amount of voluntary reparation should, at this stage of the process, be reflected in a reduction of the notional fine to an amount below that hitherto identified as representing the punishment element of the sentence. This will all depend upon the particular facts of each case. v) Having made any reduction for the extent to which the offender has brought the necessary deterrent message home to itself, the Court (which will have considered the mitigating features of the offence itself when assessing seriousness) should then consider whether there are any other mitigating features requiring any further reduction in the amount, thus far reached, of the notional fine. vi) The Court should deduct the appropriate percentage of discount for the plea, thereby arriving at the final amount of the actual fine to be imposed (together with any compensation order/orders).

Criminal Justice Act 2003, s 164

(1) Before fixing the amount of any fine to be imposed on an offender who is an individual, a court must inquire into his financial circumstances.

(2) The amount of any fine fixed by a court must be such as, in the opinion of the court, reflects the seriousness of the offence.

(3) In fixing the amount of any fine to be imposed on an offender (whether an individual or other person), a court must take into account the circumstances of the case including, among other things, the financial circumstances of the offender so far as they are known, or appear, to the court.

(4) Subsection (3) applies whether taking into account the financial circumstances of the offender has the effect of increasing or reducing the amount of the fine.

(4A) In applying subsection (3), a court must not reduce the amount of a fine on account of any surcharge it orders the offender to pay under section 161A, except to the extent that he has insufficient means to pay both.

(5) Where—

    (a) an offender has been convicted in his absence in pursuance of section 11 or 12 of the Magistrates' Courts Act 1980 (c. 43) (non-appearance of accused), or

    (b) an offender—

        (i) has failed to furnish a statement of his financial circumstances in response to a request which is an official request for the purposes of section 20A of the Criminal Justice Act 1991 (c.53) (offence of making false statement as to financial circumstances),

        (ii) has failed to comply with an order under section 162(1), or

        (iii) has otherwise failed to co-operate with the court in its inquiry into his financial circumstances,

and the court considers that it has insufficient information to make a proper determination of the financial circumstances of the offender, it may make such determination as it thinks fit.

Magistrates' Courts Act 1980, ss 32, 82(1), (6), 88, 89

32.— Penalties on summary conviction for offences triable either way.

(1) On summary conviction of any of the offences triable either way listed in Schedule 1 to this Act a person shall be liable to imprisonment for a term not exceeding 6 months or to a fine not exceeding the prescribed sum or both, except that—

    (a) a magistrates' court shall not have power to impose imprisonment for an offence so listed if the Crown Court would not have that power in the case of an adult convicted of it on indictment .

    [...]

(2) For any offence triable either way which is not listed in Schedule 1 to this Act, being an offence under a relevant enactment, the maximum fine which may be imposed on summary conviction shall by virtue of this subsection be the prescribed sum unless the offence is one for which by virtue of an enactment other than this subsection a larger fine may be imposed on summary conviction.

(3) Where, by virtue of any relevant enactment, a person summarily convicted of an offence triable either way would, apart from this section, be liable to a maximum fine of one amount in the case of a first conviction and of a different amount in the case of a second

or subsequent conviction, subsection (2) above shall apply irrespective of whether the conviction is a first, second or subsequent one.

(4) Subsection (2) above shall not affect so much of any enactment as (in whatever words) makes a person liable on summary conviction to a fine not exceeding a specified amount for each day on which a continuing offence is continued after conviction or the occurrence of any other specified event.

(5) Subsection (2) above shall not apply on summary conviction of any of the following offences:—

(a) offences under section 5(2) of the Misuse of Drugs Act 1971 (having possession of a controlled drug) where the controlled drug in relation to which the offence was committed was a Class B or Class C drug;

(b) offences under the following provisions of that Act, where the controlled drug in relation to which the offence was committed was a Class C drug, namely—

    (i) section 4(2) (production, or being concerned in the production, of a controlled drug);

    (ii) section 4(3) (supplying or offering a controlled drug or being concerned in the doing of either activity by another);

    (iii) section 5(3) (having possession of a controlled drug with intent to supply it to another);

    (iv) section 8 (being the occupier, or concerned in the management, of premises and permitting or suffering certain activities to take place there);

    (v) section 12(6) (contravention of direction prohibiting practitioner etc. from possessing, supplying etc. controlled drugs); or

    (vi) section 13(3) (contravention of direction prohibiting practitioner etc. from prescribing, supplying etc. controlled drugs).

(6) Where, as regards any offence triable either way, there is under any enactment (however framed or worded) a power by subordinate instrument to restrict the amount of the fine which on summary conviction can be imposed in respect of that offence—

(a) subsection (2) above shall not affect that power or override any restriction imposed in the exercise of that power; and

(b) the amount to which that fine may be restricted in the exercise of that power shall be any amount less than the maximum fine which could be imposed on summary conviction in respect of the offence apart from any restriction so imposed.

[...]

(8) In subsection (5) above "controlled drug", "Class B drug" and "Class C drug" have the same meaning as in the Misuse of Drugs Act 1971.

(9) In this section—

"fine" includes a pecuniary penalty but does not include a pecuniary forfeiture or pecuniary compensation;

"the prescribed sum" means £5,000 or such sum as is for the time being substituted in this definition by an order in force under section 143(1) below;

"relevant enactment" means an enactment contained in the Criminal Law Act 1977 or in any Act passed before, or in the same Session as, that Act.

82.— Restriction on power to impose imprisonment for default.

(1) A magistrates' court shall not on the occasion of convicting an offender of an offence issue a warrant of commitment for a default in paying any sum adjudged to be paid by the conviction unless—

(a) in the case of an offence punishable with imprisonment, he appears to the court to have sufficient means to pay the sum forthwith;

(b) it appears to the court that he is unlikely to remain long enough at a place of abode in the United Kingdom to enable payment of the sum to be enforced by other methods; or

(c) on the occasion of that conviction the court sentences him to immediate imprisonment, youth custody or detention in a detention centre for that or another offence or he is already serving a sentence of custody for life, or a term of imprisonment, youth custody, detention under section 9 of the Criminal Justice Act 1982 or detention in a detention centre.

(6) Where a magistrates' court issues a warrant of commitment on the ground that one of the conditions mentioned in subsection (1) or (4) above is satisfied, it shall state that fact, specifying the ground, in the warrant.

88.— Supervision pending payment.

(1) Where any person is adjudged to pay a sum by a summary conviction and the convicting court does not commit him to prison forthwith in default of payment, the court may, either on the occasion of the conviction or on a subsequent occasion, order him to be placed under the supervision of such person as the court may from time to time appoint.

(2) An order placing a person under supervision in respect of any sum shall remain in force so long as he remains liable to pay the sum or any part of it unless the order ceases to have effect or is discharged under subsection (3) below.

(3) An order under this section shall cease to have effect on the making of a transfer of fine order under section 89 below with respect to the sum adjudged to be paid and may be discharged by the court that made it, without prejudice in either case to the making of a new order.

(4) Where a person under 21 years old has been adjudged to pay a sum by a summary conviction and the convicting court does not commit him to detention under section 108 of the Powers of Criminal Courts (Sentencing) Act 2000 forthwith in default of payment, the court shall not commit him to to such detention in default of payment of the sum, or for want of sufficient distress to satisfy the sum, unless he has been placed under supervision in respect of the sum or the court is satisfied that it is undesirable or impracticable to place him under supervision.

(5) Where a court, being satisfied as aforesaid, commits a person under 21 years old to such detention without an order under this section having been made, the court shall state the grounds on which it is so satisfied in the warrant of commitment.

(6) Where an order placing a person under supervision with respect to a sum is in force, a magistrates' court shall not commit him to prison in default of payment of the sum, or for want of sufficient distress to satisfy the sum, unless the court has before committing him taken such steps as may be reasonably practicable to obtain from the person appointed for his supervision an oral or written report on the offender's conduct and means and has considered any report so obtained, in addition, in a case where an inquiry is required by section 82 above, to that inquiry.

89.— Transfer of fine order.

(1) Where a magistrates' court in a local justice area has, or is treated by any enactment as having, adjudged a person by a conviction to pay a sum and it appears to the court, or where that sum is the subject of a collection order, it appears to the court or the fines officer as the case may be, that the person is residing in England and Wales, the court or the fines officer, as the case may be, may make a transfer of fine order, that is to say, an order making payment enforceable in [another local justice area and that area shall be specified in the order.

(2) As from the date on which a transfer of fine order is made with respect to any sum, all functions under this Part of this Act or under Schedule 5 to the Courts Act 2003 relating to that sum which, if no order had been made, would have been exercisable by any court

or person mentioned in column 1 of the Table below shall be exercisable by the court or person mentioned in the corresponding entry in column 2, and not otherwise.

Column 1	Column 2
(A) The court which made the order.	
(B) A court acting in the same local justice area as was the fines officer who made the order.	In either case, a court acting in the local justice area specified in the order.
The designated officer for the court mentioned in the row above.	The designated officer for the court mentioned in the row above.
(A) The fines officer who made the order.	
(B) A fines officer acting in the same local justice area as was the court which made the order.	In either case, a fines officer acting in the local justice area specified in the order.

(2A) The functions of the court under this Part of this Act to which subsection (2) above relates shall be deemed to include the court's power to apply to the Secretary of State under any regulations made by him under section 24(1)(a) of the Criminal Justice Act 1991 (power to deduct fines etc. from income support)..

(3) A court or a fines officer, as the case may be, by which or whom functions in relation to any sum are for the time being exercisable by virtue of a transfer of fine order may make a further transfer of fine order with respect to that sum.

(4) In this section and sections 90 and 91 below, references to this Part of this Act do not include references to section 81(1) above.

FOOTBALL BANNING ORDER

Banning orders (Football Spectators Act 1989) can be imposed when an offender is convicted of a relevant offence (see Sch 1 of the Act below) and if the court is satisfied that there are reasonable grounds to believe that making a banning order would help to prevent violence or disorder at or in connection with any regulated football matches, it must make such an order in respect of the offender.

The court made the following observation in *Boggild* [2011] EWCA Crim 1928:

"...it is palpably not the scheme of the Act to make a football banning order the inevitable consequence of a football related conviction. By contrast, what the Act does is to pose a test for the judge to address and require an order only if that test is met... The fact that deterrence of others may be a relevant consideration enables the judge to take it into account when deciding whether making an order would help to prevent violence or disorder and thus that the statutory test is met. It is however a matter for the judge to reach a conclusion in each case. The more serious and prolonged the football related violence, or the more prominent the role of the offender, no doubt the greater the scope for the satisfaction of the statutory test on reasonable grounds... It is important that judges who are considering the rather complex provisions of the Football Spectators Act 1989 should have in mind the nature of the regime for which it provides. They ought also to address their minds to the differences between the consequences of a football banning order on the one hand and a prohibited activities requirement attached either to a suspended sentence or a community order on the other. They are not to be treated as equivalents... There is some difference between the two kinds of order as to sanction. That, as it seems to me, is not a large difference. Disobedience to a football banning order is itself an offence, whereas disobedience to a prohibited activity requirement is not. But there is ample sanction for

298

disobedience to a prohibited activity requirement because if it is attached to a suspended sentence the suspended sentence can be activated for breach, and if it is attached to a community order then on breach the court can re-sentence for the original offence and that may well involve loss of liberty. The principal difference between the two forms of order lies in the regime which exists. It is apparent, from the description that I have endeavoured to give at the outset of this judgment, that there is quite a sophisticated regime for the co-ordination of intelligence relating to those who are subject to football banning orders. Where such an order is in contemplation, judges who are addressing the test of whether making an order would help to prevent violence or disorder ought, as it seems to me, to have in mind the extent of the regime as well of course as its potentially draconian effect."

In *Doyle and Others* [2012] EWCA Crim 995 the court made the following observations:

"Relevant offences"

i)   There are some offences listed in para (a) and (p) which are ipso facto relevant. Those are, in essence, offences which of their nature are concerned with football.

ii) Offences listed under paragraph (b) must have been committed whilst entering or trying to enter the ground.

iii) Offences listed under paragraphs (c) to (f) must have been committed during the period relevant to a football match (which means 24 hours either side of the match–see paragraph 4(2)(b)) and when D was at, or entering or leaving, premises, although it would seem that the premises can be any premises and are not confined to football grounds; they might well, for example, be a public house.

iv) Offences listed under paragraphs (g) to (o) and (q) will be relevant if they are "related to football matches"; this calls for a judgment of the court declaring this to be so. The decision is called in the Act a "declaration of relevance"; see s 23.

"Related to football matches"

The judgment which is required in relation to offences listed under (g) to (o) & (q) is therefore not an assessment of the legal character of the offence. It is a determination whether on the particular facts of the offence as it was committed on the occasion in question, the offence was "related to football matches".

Although the test is expressed in terms of "matches" in the plural, it would appear that it would suffice if the behaviour was, on the particular facts, related to a single match. But it is clear that what the Act is targeting is those offences which have a connection with football, generally with the defendant's following of the game.

Paragraphs (g) to (o), although not (q), are all concerned with offences committed when the defendant was on a journey to or from a football match at the stipulated level (essentially Blue Square North or South or above). It is obvious that football disorder and violence can often occur on such journeys. Equally, because the Act requires the judgment of the court whether the particular offence was "related to football matches" it is clear that the *mere* fact that defendant was on a journey to or from a match is not enough. There must be another connection. The offence must be 'related to football matches'.

The Act offers no definition of when this condition will be met. It is (no doubt deliberately) left to the judgment of the judge on the particular facts before him. It would be wrong to attempt to define when the condition will be met. The facts which may occur will vary too much. It is not difficult to say that a pitched battle between opposing fans as they walk away from the ground is 'related', or that a defendant who, when on his own twenty miles away from the ground on his journey home meets a rival for a woman's affections and hits him, is not committing an offence related to football matches. But in between there will be infinite graduations of conduct, and they must be left to the judge in each case. In one or two reported cases the court has taken into account whether what was described as the "spark" for an offence of violence was a football factor, such a dispute with opposing fans, but this is only an example of the kind of matter which may be relevant and must not be taken as a substitute test. If a football-related 'spark' is present that will no doubt be likely to lead to the conclusion that the offence was related to football matches. But it is all too notorious that the 'spark' for offences of violence may sometimes be illusory, or minimal, or simply irrelevant. If the offence be one committed by a group of football fans clearly acting as such, in a group whose identity is clearly football-oriented, their violence may well justify the expression "related to football matches" even if the particular *casus belli* is that exception is taken to another person for no particular reason. We offer only the observation that it will not by itself be enough, to make an offence "related to football matches" that it would not have occurred "but for" the fact that D was en route to or from a match. If that by itself were enough, then every offence of the listed kind which was committed on a journey to or from a match would automatically qualify and the additional test of relation to football matches would be unnecessary and meaningless.

<u>The condition in s 14A(2)</u>

Whether this condition is met will in some cases be the key question. No doubt the more the offence is linked to football grievances or the group "culture" of a set of fans linked by their support for a team, the more likely it will be that an FBO will help prevent violence or disorder. The more there is a history of football related offending, the greater will be the likelihood that the condition will be met. However, it is clear that it is possible for this condition to be met by the commission of a single offence, of which the defendant has just been convicted. What it is important to remember is that this condition clearly contemplates that there must be a risk of repetition of violence or disorder at a match before it is met. The test of reasonable grounds to believe that a FBO will help prevent violence or disorder at regulated matches does not set a high hurdle, but it is clear that it is not automatically satisfied just because the instant offence was football-related. If that were so, the condition would add nothing and would not be needed. Many football-related offences will give rise to exactly this risk, but not all will. Boggild was an example of one which the judge determined did not.

Declaration of relevance: In relation to some offences listed in Sch 1, the court must make a declaration of relevant before being able to make a banning order. Five days' notice must be given by the prosecution, which can be waived by the defence or by the court if the interests of justice do not require such a period of notice to be given. The declaration is that the offence related to that match or to that match and any other football match which took place during that period. The relevant periods are:

(a) in the case of a match which takes place on the day on which it is advertised to take place, the period:
(i) beginning 24 hours before whichever is the earlier of the start of the match and the time at which it was advertised to start; and
(ii) ending 24 hours after it ends;
(b) in the case of a match which does not take place on the day on which it was advertised to take place, the period:
(i) beginning 24 hours before the time at which it was advertised to start on that day; and
(ii) ending 24 hours after that time.

In *Arbery* [2008] EWCA Crim 702 the offenders were drinking in a public house following a football match, waiting for their train home when violence broke out with rival supporters. A football banning order was quashed on appeal as the court held that the offence arose out of a disagreement in the pub, completely unrelated to football.

In *Eliot* [2007] EWCA Crim 1002 the court gave a helpful insight into how the issue of 'relevance' might be approached:

"Did the offences committed in the present case relate to the match? Clearly, the presence of the applicants in London and indeed at Leicester Square related to the match. But it is not their presence, or their allegiance, which is the touchstone of the declaration; it is the relationship between the offence and the match. Here, the offences were sparked by the presence of a group of football supporters in London. The spark, however, had nothing to do with the match itself on the facts as found by the judge. The violence took place, not because of anything that had happened at the football match, or between supporters but because of disparaging remarks made to a lady who had nothing to do with the football match and remarks which had nothing to do with the football match. In those circumstances, we do not consider that, in this case, the statutory requirement was satisfied."

In *Director of Public Prosecutions v Beaumont* [2008] EWHC 523 (Admin) the court rejected an argument that there was a temporal limit to the making of a banning order. In that case the violence erupted more than one hour after the end of the match.

Prohibition: The core requirements of such an order are to prohibit the offender from attending regulated football matches in England and Wales. When matches are being played abroad, the order will require the offender to report to a police station and surrender his passport (unless there are exceptional circumstances certified by the court as to why this should not be done). Other requirements can be imposed, eg not to go within a certain distance of a football ground. A travel restriction, imposed as part of a banning order, does not infringe European Community Law, or the European Convention on Human Rights (*Gough v Chief Constable of Derbyshire* [2002] EWCA Civ 351).

Duration: The order must be for a period of between three and five years, or six and ten years if a custodial sentence (which includes a sentence of detention) is imposed for the original offence.

Disclosure: In *Newman v Commissioner of Police for the Metropolis*, [2009] EWHC 1642 (Admin), the court held that police were entitled to rely upon compilation witness statements and compilation video footage, and had no duty to disclose the underlying material from which it was drawn. There is no statutory disclosure regime applicable to the making of banning orders and a court should apply normal principles of 'fairness'. Advocates seeking disclosure should be careful to specify the material that they wish to view and the reasons why. An application that amounts to nothing more than a 'fishing expedition' ought to be refused. **Appeals**: An appeal lies to the Crown Court in respect to the making of a banning order, or dismissal of prosecution application (Football Spectators Act 1989, s 14D). **Termination**: A court may terminate an order once two-thirds of the period has elapsed (Football Spectators Act 1989, s 14H).

Football Spectators Act 1989, Sch 1

This Schedule applies to the following offences:

    (a) any offence under 14J(1), 19(6), 20(10) or 21C(2) of this Act or section 68(1) or (5) of the Police, Public Order and Criminal Justice (Scotland) Act 2006 by virtue of section 106 of the Policing and Crime Act 2009,

    (b) any offence under section 2 or 2A of the Sporting Events (Control of Alcohol etc.) Act 1985 (alcohol, containers, and fireworks) committed by the accused at any football match to which this Schedule applies or while entering or trying to enter the ground,

    (c) any offence under section 4A or 5 of the Public Order Act 1986 (harassment, alarm, or distress) or any provision of Part III of that Act (racial hatred) committed during a period relevant to a football match to which this Schedule applies at any premises while the accused was at, or was entering or leaving or trying to enter or leave, the premises,

    (d) any offence involving the use or threat of violence by the accused towards another person committed during a period relevant to a football match to which this Schedule applies at any premises while the accused was at, or was entering or leaving or trying to enter or leave, the premises,

(e) any offence involving the use or threat of violence towards property committed during a period relevant to a football match to which this Schedule applies at any premises while the accused was at, or was entering or leaving or trying to enter or leave, the premises,

(f) any offence involving the use, carrying or possession of an offensive weapon or a firearm committed during a period relevant to a football match to which this Schedule applies at any premises while the accused was at, or was entering or leaving or trying to enter or leave, the premises,

(g) any offence under section 12 of the Licensing Act 1872 (persons found drunk in public places, etc) of being found drunk in a highway or other public place committed while the accused was on a journey to or from a football match to which this Schedule applies being an offence as respects which the court makes a declaration that the offence related to football matches,

(h) any offence under section 91(1) of the Criminal Justice Act 1967 (disorderly behaviour while drunk in a public place) committed in a highway or other public place while the accused was on a journey to or from a football match to which this Schedule applies being an offence as respects which the court makes a declaration that the offence related to football matches,

(j) any offence under section 1 of the Sporting Events (Control of Alcohol etc.) Act 1985 (alcohol on coaches or trains to or from sporting events) committed while the accused was on a journey to or from a football match to which this Schedule applies being an offence as respects which the court makes a declaration that the offence related to football matches,

(k) any offence under section 4A or 5 of the Public Order Act 1986 (harassment, alarm, or distress) or any provision of Part III of that Act (racial hatred) committed while the accused was on a journey to or from a football match to which this Schedule applies being an offence as respects which the court makes a declaration that the offence related to football matches,

(l) any offence under section 4 or 5 of the Road Traffic Act 1988 (driving etc when under the influence of drink or drugs or with an alcohol concentration above the prescribed limit) committed while the accused was on a journey to or from a football match to which this Schedule applies being an offence as respects which the court makes a declaration that the offence related to football matches,

(m) any offence involving the use or threat of violence by the accused towards another person committed while one or each of them was on a journey to or from a football match to which this Schedule applies being an offence as respects which the court makes a declaration that the offence related to football matches,

(n) any offence involving the use or threat of violence towards property committed while the accused was on a journey to or from a football match to which this Schedule applies being an offence as respects which the court makes a declaration that the offence related to football matches,

(o) any offence involving the use, carrying or possession of an offensive weapon or a firearm committed while the accused was on a journey to or from a football match to which this Schedule applies being an offence as respects which the court makes a declaration that the offence related to football matches,

(p) any offence under the Football (Offences) Act 1991,

(q) any offence under section 4A or 5 of the Public Order Act 1986 (harassment, alarm, or distress) or any provision of Part 3 or 3A of that Act (hatred by reference to race etc)—

(i) which does not fall within paragraph (c) or (k) above,

(ii) which was committed during a period relevant to a football match to which this Schedule applies, and

(iii) as respects which the court makes a declaration that the offence related to that match or to that match and any other football match which took place during that period,

(r) any offence involving the use or threat of violence by the accused towards another person—

    (i) which does not fall within paragraph (d) or (m) above,

    (ii) which was committed during a period relevant to a football match to which this Schedule applies, and

    (iii) as respects which the court makes a declaration that the offence related to that match or to that match and any other football match which took place during that period,

(s) any offence involving the use or threat of violence towards property—

    (i) which does not fall within paragraph (e) or (n) above,

    (ii) which was committed during a period relevant to a football match to which this Schedule applies, and

    (iii) as respects which the court makes a declaration that the offence related to that match or to that match and any other football match which took place during that period,

(t) any offence involving the use, carrying or possession of an offensive weapon or a firearm—

    (i) which does not fall within paragraph (f) or (o) above,

    (ii) which was committed during a period relevant to a football match to which this Schedule applies, and

    (iii) as respects which the court makes a declaration that the offence related to that match or to that match and any other football match which took place during that period.

(u) any offence under section 166 of the Criminal Justice and Public Order Act 1994 (sale of tickets by unauthorised persons) which relates to tickets for a football match.

FOREIGN TRAVEL ORDER

These orders are applied for on a freestanding basis.

Sexual Offences Act 2003, ss 114-119, 122

114 Foreign travel orders: applications and grounds

(1) A chief officer of police may by complaint to a magistrates' court apply for an order under this section (a "foreign travel order") in respect of a person ("the defendant") who resides in his police area or who the chief officer believes is in or is intending to come to his police area if it appears to the chief officer that–

    (a) the defendant is a qualifying offender, and

    (b) the defendant has since the appropriate date acted in such a way as to give reasonable cause to believe that it is necessary for such an order to be made.

(2) An application under subsection (1) may be made to any magistrates' court whose commission area includes any part of the applicant's police area.

(3) On the application, the court may make a foreign travel order if it is satisfied that–

    (a) the defendant is a qualifying offender, and

    (b) the defendant's behaviour since the appropriate date makes it necessary to make such an order, for the purpose of protecting children generally or any child from serious sexual harm from the defendant outside the United Kingdom.

115 Section 114: interpretation

(1) Subsections (2) to (5) apply for the purposes of section 114.

(2) "Protecting children generally or any child from serious sexual harm from the defendant outside the United Kingdom" means protecting persons under 16 generally or any particular person under 18 from serious physical or psychological harm caused by the defendant doing, outside the United Kingdom, anything which would constitute an offence listed in Schedule 3 if done in any part of the United Kingdom.

(3) Acts and behaviour include those occurring before the commencement of this Part.

(4) "Qualifying offender" has the meaning given by section 116.

(5) "Appropriate date", in relation to a qualifying offender, means the date or (as the case may be) the first date on which he was convicted, found or cautioned as mentioned in subsection (1) or (3) of section 116.

116 Section 114: qualifying offenders

(1) A person is a qualifying offender for the purposes of section 114 if, whether before or after the commencement of this Part, he–

    (a) has been convicted of an offence within subsection (2),

    (b) has been found not guilty of such an offence by reason of insanity,

    (c) has been found to be under a disability and to have done the act charged against him in respect of such an offence, or

    (d) in England and Wales or Northern Ireland, has been cautioned in respect of such an offence.

(2) The offences are–

    (a) an offence within any of paragraphs 13 to 15, 44 to 46, 77, 78 and 82 of Schedule 3;

    (b) an offence within paragraph 31 of that Schedule, if the intended offence was an offence against a person under 18;

    (c) an offence within paragraph 93 or 93A of that Schedule, if–

        (i) the corresponding civil offence is an offence within any of paragraphs 13 to 15 of that Schedule;

        (ii) the corresponding civil offence is an offence within paragraph 31 of that Schedule, and the intended offence was an offence against a person under 18; or

        (iii) the corresponding civil offence is an offence within any of paragraphs 1 to 12, 16 to 30 and 32 to 35 of that Schedule, and the victim of the offence was under 18 at the time of the offence.

    (d) an offence within any other paragraph of that Schedule, if the victim of the offence was under 18 at the time of the offence.

(2A) In subsection (2)(c) references to the corresponding civil offence are to be read, in relation to an offence within paragraph 93A of Schedule 3, as references to the corresponding offence under the law of England and Wales.

(3) A person is also a qualifying offender for the purposes of section 114 if, under the law in force in a country outside the United Kingdom and whether before or after the commencement of this Part–

    (a) he has been convicted of a relevant offence (whether or not he has been punished for it),

    (b) a court exercising jurisdiction under that law has made in respect of a relevant offence a finding equivalent to a finding that he is not guilty by reason of insanity,

    (c) such a court has made in respect of a relevant offence a finding equivalent to a finding that he is under a disability and did the act charged against him in respect of the offence, or

    (d) he has been cautioned in respect of a relevant offence.

(4) In subsection (3), "relevant offence" means an act which–

    (a) constituted an offence under the law in force in the country concerned, and

(b) would have constituted an offence within subsection (2) if it had been done in any part of the United Kingdom.

(5) An act punishable under the law in force in a country outside the United Kingdom constitutes an offence under that law for the purposes of subsection (4), however it is described in that law.

(6) Subject to subsection (7), on an application under section 114 the condition in subsection (4)(b) above (where relevant) is to be taken as met unless, not later than rules of court may provide, the defendant serves on the applicant a notice–

(a) stating that, on the facts as alleged with respect to the act concerned, the condition is not in his opinion met,

(b) showing his grounds for that opinion, and

(c) requiring the applicant to prove that the condition is met.

(7) The court, if it thinks fit, may permit the defendant to require the applicant to prove that the condition is met without service of a notice under subsection (6).

117 Foreign travel orders: effect

(1) A foreign travel order has effect for a fixed period of not more than 5 years, specified in the order.

(2) The order prohibits the defendant from doing whichever of the following is specified in the order–

(a) travelling to any country outside the United Kingdom named or described in the order,

(b) travelling to any country outside the United Kingdom other than a country named or described in the order, or

(c) travelling to any country outside the United Kingdom.

(3) The only prohibitions that may be included in the order are those necessary for the purpose of protecting children generally or any child from serious sexual harm from the defendant outside the United Kingdom.

(4) If at any time while an order (as renewed from time to time) has effect a defendant is not a relevant offender, the order causes him to be subject to the requirements imposed by regulations made under section 86(1) (and for these purposes the defendant is to be treated as if he were a relevant offender).

(5) Where a court makes a foreign travel order in relation to a person already subject to such an order (whether made by that court or another), the earlier order ceases to have effect.

(6) Section 115(2) applies for the purposes of this section and section 118.

117A Foreign travel orders: surrender of passports

(1) This section applies in relation to a foreign travel order which contains a prohibition within section 117(2)(c).

(2) The order must require the defendant to surrender all of the defendant's passports, at a police station specified in the order—

(a) on or before the date when the prohibition takes effect, or

(b) within a period specified in the order.

(3) Any passports surrendered must be returned as soon as reasonably practicable after the person ceases to be subject to a foreign travel order containing a prohibition within section 117(2)(c).

(4) Subsection (3) does not apply in relation to—

(a) a passport issued by or on behalf of the authorities of a country outside the United Kingdom if the passport has been returned to those authorities;

(b) a passport issued by or on behalf of an international organisation if the passport has been returned to that organisation.

(5) In this section "passport" means—

    (a) a United Kingdom passport within the meaning of the Immigration Act 1971;

    (b) a passport issued by or on behalf of the authorities of a country outside the United Kingdom, or by or on behalf of an international organisation;

    (c) a document that can be used (in some or all circumstances) instead of a passport.

118 Foreign travel orders: variations, renewals and discharges

(1) A person within subsection (2) may by complaint to the appropriate court apply for an order varying, renewing or discharging a foreign travel order.

(2) The persons are–

    (a) the defendant;

    (b) the chief officer of police on whose application the foreign travel order was made;

    (c) the chief officer of police for the area in which the defendant resides;

    (d) a chief officer of police who believes that the defendant is in, or is intending to come to, his police area.

(3) Subject to subsection (4), on the application the court, after hearing the person making the application and (if they wish to be heard) the other persons mentioned in subsection (2), may make any order, varying, renewing or discharging the foreign travel order, that the court considers appropriate.

(4) An order may be renewed, or varied so as to impose additional prohibitions on the defendant, only if it is necessary to do so for the purpose of protecting children generally or any child from serious sexual harm from the defendant outside the United Kingdom (and any renewed or varied order may contain only such prohibitions as are necessary for this purpose).

(5) In this section "the appropriate court" means–

    (a) the court which made the foreign travel order;

    (b) a magistrates' court for the area in which the defendant resides; or

    (c) where the application is made by a chief officer of police, any magistrates' court whose commission area includes any part of his police area.

119 Foreign travel orders: appeals

(1) A defendant may appeal to the Crown Court–

    (a) against the making of a foreign travel order;

    (b) against the making of an order under section 118, or the refusal to make such an order.

(2) On any such appeal, the Crown Court may make such orders as may be necessary to give effect to its determination of the appeal, and may also make such incidental or consequential orders as appear to it to be just.

(3) Any order made by the Crown Court on an appeal under subsection (1)(a) (other than an order directing that an application be re-heard by a magistrates' court) is for the purposes of section 118(5) to be treated as if it were an order of the court from which the appeal was brought (and not an order of the Crown Court).

122 Offence: breach of foreign travel order

(1) A person commits an offence if, without reasonable excuse, he does anything which he is prohibited from doing by a foreign travel order.

(1A) A person commits an offence if, without reasonable excuse, the person fails to comply with a requirement under section 117A(2).

(2) A person guilty of an offence under this section is liable–

    (a) on summary conviction, to imprisonment for a term not exceeding 6 months or a fine not exceeding the statutory maximum or both;

(b) on conviction on indictment, to imprisonment for a term not exceeding 5 years.

(3) Where a person is convicted of an offence under this section, it is not open to the court by or before which he is convicted to make, in respect of the offence, an order for conditional discharge [...]

FORFEITURE ORDER

Misuse of Drugs Act 1971, s 27

(1) Subject to subsection (2) below, the court by or before which a person is convicted of an offence under this Act or an offence falling within subsection (3) below or an offence to which section 1 of the Criminal Justice (Scotland) Act 1987 relates may order anything shown to the satisfaction of the court to relate to the offence, to be forfeited and either destroyed or dealt with in such other manner as the court may order.

(2) The court shall not order anything to be forfeited under this section, where a person claiming to be the owner of or otherwise interested in it applies to be heard by the court, unless an opportunity has been given to him to show cause why the order should not be made.

(3) An offence falls within this subsection if it is an offence which is specified in—

(a) paragraph 1 of Schedule 2 to the Proceeds of Crime Act 2002 (drug trafficking offences), or

(b) so far as it relates to that paragraph, paragraph 10 of that Schedule.

GUARDIANSHIP AND HOSPITAL ORDERS

Purpose: Treatment that will militate against future offending (*Birch* (1989) 11 Cr App R (S) 202). **Approach:** First, [the court] should decide whether a period of compulsory detention is apposite. If the answer is that it is not, or may not be, the possibility of a probation order with a condition of in or outpatient treatment should be considered. Secondly, the judge will ask himself whether the conditions contained in section 37(2)(a) for the making of a hospital order are satisfied. Here the judge acts on the evidence of the doctors. If left in doubt, he may wish to avail himself of the valuable provisions of sections 38 and 39 (which are not used as often as they might be) to make an interim hospital order, giving the court and the doctors further time to decide between hospital with or without restrictions and some other disposal, and to require the Regional Health Authority to furnish information on arrangements for the admission of the offender. If the judge concludes that the conditions empowering him to make an order are satisfied, he will consider whether to make such an order, or whether "the most suitable method of disposing of the case" (s.37(2)(b)) is to impose a sentence of imprisonment (*Birch* (1989) 11 Cr App R (S) 202). **Restriction orders:** A court has power to commit an offender to the crown court for the purposes of a restriction order if the conditions are thought to be met, and may order hospital detention prior to the case being dealt with by the crown court (Mental Health Act 1983, ss 43, 44).

Mental Health Act 1983, ss 37, 38

37.— Powers of courts to order hospital admission or guardianship.

(1) Where a person is convicted before the Crown Court of an offence punishable with imprisonment other than an offence the sentence for which is fixed by law , or is convicted by a magistrates' court of an offence punishable on summary conviction with imprisonment, and the conditions mentioned in subsection (2) below are satisfied, the court may by order authorise his admission to and detention in such hospital as may be specified in the order or, as the case may be, place him under the guardianship of a local social services authority or of such other person approved by a local social services authority as may be so specified.

(1A)   In the case of an offence the sentence for which would otherwise fall to be imposed—

    (a) under section 51A(2) of the Firearms Act 1968,

    (b) under section 110(2) or 111(2) of the Powers of Criminal Courts (Sentencing) Act 2000,

    (c) under [section 225(2) or 226(2) of the Criminal Justice Act 2003, or 5

    (d) under section 29(4) or (6) of the Violent Crime Reduction Act 2006 (minimum sentences in certain cases of using someone to mind a weapon).

nothing in those provisions shall prevent a court from making an order under subsection (1) above for the admission of the offender to a hospital.

(1B)   References in subsection (1A) above to a sentence falling to be imposed under any of the provisions mentioned in that subsection are to be read in accordance with section 305(4) of the Criminal Justice Act 2003.

(2)   The conditions referred to in subsection (1) above are that—

    (a) the court is satisfied, on the written or oral evidence of two registered medical practitioners, that the offender is suffering from mental disorder and that either—

        (i)   the mental disorder from which the offender is suffering is of a nature or degree which makes it appropriate for him to be detained in a hospital for medical treatment and appropriate medical treatment is available for him; or

        (ii) in the case of an offender who has attained the age of 16 years, the mental disorder is of a nature or degree which warrants his reception into guardianship under this Act; and

    (b) the court is of the opinion, having regard to all the circumstances including the nature of the offence and the character and antecedents of the offender, and to the other available methods of dealing with him, that the most suitable method of disposing of the case is by means of an order under this section.

(3)   Where a person is charged before a magistrates' court with any act or omission as an offence and the court would have power, on convicting him of that offence, to make an order under subsection (1) above in his case, then, if the court is satisfied that the accused did the act or made the omission charged, the court may, if it thinks fit, make such an order without convicting him.

(4)   An order for the admission of an offender to a hospital (in this Act referred to as "a hospital order") shall not be made under this section unless the court is satisfied on the written or oral evidence of the approved clinician who would have overall responsibility for his case or of some other person representing the managers of the hospital that arrangements have been made for his admission to that hospital, and for his admission to it within the period of 28 days beginning with the date of the making of such an order; and the court may, pending his admission within that period, given such directions as it thinks fit for his conveyance to and detention in a place of safety.

(5)   If within the said period of 28 days it appears to the Secretary of State that by reason of an emergency or other special circumstances it is not practicable for the patient to be received into the hospital specified in the order, he may give directions for the admission of the patient to such other hospital as appears to be appropriate instead of the hospital so specified; and where such directions are given—

    (a) the Secretary of State shall cause the person having the custody of the patient to be informed, and

    (b) the hospital order shall have effect as if the hospital specified in the directions were substituted for the hospital specified in the order.

(6)   An order placing an offender under the guardianship of a local social services authority or of any other person (in this Act referred to as "a guardianship order") shall not be

made under this section unless the court is satisfied that that authority or person is willing to receive the offender into guardianship.

[...]

(8) Where an order is made under this section, the court shall not—

(a) pass sentence of imprisonment or impose a fine or make a community order (within the meaning of Part 12 of the Criminal Justice Act 2003 or a youth rehabilitation order (within the meaning of Part 1 of the Criminal Justice and Immigration Act 2008) in respect of the offence,

(b) if the order under this section is a hospital order, make a referral order (within the meaning of the Powers of Criminal Courts (Sentencing) Act 2000) in respect of the offence, or

(c) make in respect of the offender an order under section 150 of that Act (binding over of parent or guardian),

but the court may make any other order which it has power to make apart from this section; and for the purposes of this subsection "sentence of imprisonment" includes any sentence or order for detention.

38.— Interim hospital orders.

(1) Where a person is convicted before the Crown Court of an offence punishable with imprisonment (other than an offence the sentence for which is fixed by law) or is convicted by a magistrates' court of an offence punishable on summary conviction with imprisonment and the court before or by which he is convicted is satisfied, on the written or oral evidence of two registered medical practitioners—

(a) that the offender is suffering from mental disorder; and

(b) that there is reason to suppose that the mental disorder from which the offender is suffering is such that it may be appropriate for a hospital order to be made in his case,

the court may, before making a hospital order or dealing with him in some other way, make an order (in this Act referred to as "an interim hospital order") authorising his admission to such hospital as may be specified in the order and his detention there in accordance with this section.

(2) In the case of an offender who is subject to an interim hospital order the court may make a hospital order without his being brought before the court if he is represented by an authorised person who is given an opportunity of being heard.

(3) At least one of the registered medical practitioners whose evidence is taken into account under subsection (1) above shall be employed at the hospital which is to be specified in the order.

(4) An interim hospital order shall not be made for the admission of an offender to a hospital unless the court is satisfied, on the written or oral evidence of the approved clinician who would have overall responsibility for his case or of some other person representing the managers of the hospital, that arrangements have been made for his admission to that hospital and for his admission to it within the period of 28 days beginning with the date of the order; and if the court is so satisfied the court may, pending his admission, given directions for his conveyance to and detention in a place of safety.

(5) An interim hospital order—

(a) shall be in force for such period, not exceeding 12 weeks, as the court may specify when making the order; but

(b) may be renewed for further periods of not more than 28 days at a time if it appears to the court, on the written or oral evidence of the responsible clinician, that the continuation of the order is warranted;

but no such order shall continue in force for more than twelve months in all and the court shall terminate the order if it makes a hospital order in respect of the offender or decides after considering the written or oral evidence of the responsible clinician to deal with the offender in some other way.

(6) The power of renewing an interim hospital order may be exercised without the offender being brought before the court if he is represented by counsel or a solicitor and his counsel or solicitor is given an opportunity of being heard.

(7) If an offender absconds from a hospital in which he is detained in pursuance of an interim hospital order, or while being conveyed to or from such a hospital, he may be arrested without warrant by a constable and shall, after being arrested, be brought as soon as practicable before the court that made the order; and the court may thereupon terminate the order and deal with him in any way in which it could have dealt with him if no such order had been made.

NEWTON HEARING

In *Newton* (1983) 77 Cr App R 13 the court set out the procedure to be adopted in order to resolve any differences between prosecution and defence so far as the factual basis of sentence is concerned. A court can reject a basis of plea that is manifestly untenable or absurd (*Taylor* [2007] Crim LR 491). In *Underwood* [2004] EWCA Crim 2256, the court offered this additional guidance:

"(1) The starting point has to be the defendant's instructions. His advocate will appreciate whether any significant facts about the prosecution evidence are disputed and the factual basis on which the defendant intends to plead guilty. Responsibility for taking initiative and alerting the prosecutor to the disputed areas rests with the defence. (2) Where the Crown accepts the defendant's account of the disputed facts, the agreement should be written down and signed by both advocates. It should then be made available to the judge. If pleas have already been accepted and approved then it should be available before the sentencing hearing begins. If the agreed basis of plea is not signed by both advocates, the judge is entitled to ignore it. The Crown might reject the defendant's version. If so, the areas of dispute should be identified in writing, focusing the court's attention on the precise facts in dispute. (3) The prosecution's position might be that they have no evidence to contradict the defence's assertions. In those circumstances, particularly if the facts relied on by the defendant arise from his personal knowledge and depend on his own account of the facts, the Crown should not normally agree the defendant's account unless supported by other material. The court should be notified at the outset in writing of the points in issue and the Crown's responses. (4) After submissions, the judge will decide how to proceed. If not already decided, he would address the question of whether he should approve the Crown's acceptance of pleas. Then he would address the proposed basis of plea. It should be emphasized that whether or not the basis of plea is agreed, the judge is not bound by any such agreement and is entitled of his own motion to insist that any evidence relevant to the facts in dispute should be called before him, paying appropriate regard to any agreement reached by the advocates and any reasons which the Crown, in particular, might advance to justify him proceeding immediately to sentence. The judge is responsible for the sentencing decision and may order a Newton hearing to ascertain the truth about disputed facts. (5) Relevant evidence should be called by prosecution and defence, particularly where the issue arises from facts which are within the exclusive knowledge of the defendant. If the defendant is willing to give evidence he should be called and, if not, subject to any explanation offered, the judge may draw such inference as he sees fit. The judge can reject the evidence called by the prosecution or by the defendant or his witnesses even if the Crown has not called contradictory evidence. The judge's conclusions should be explained in the judgment. (6) There are occasions when a Newton hearing would be inappropriate. Some issues require a jury's verdict; if a defendant denies that a specific criminal offence has been committed, the tribunal for deciding whether the offence has been proved is the jury. At the end of a Newton hearing the judge cannot make findings of fact and sentence on a basis which is inconsistent with the pleas to counts which have already been accepted and approved by the court. Particular care is needed in relation to a multi-count indictment involving one defendant or, an indictment involving a number of defendants. Where there are a number of defendants to a joint enterprise, the judge, while reflecting on the individual basis of pleas, should bear in mind the relative seriousness of the joint enterprise on which the defendants were involved. (7) Normally, matters of mitigation are not dealt with by way of a Newton hearing but it is always open to the court to allow a defendant to give evidence on matters of mitigation which are within his own knowledge. The judge is entitled to decline to hear evidence about disputed facts if the case advanced is, for good reason, to be regarded as absurd or obviously untenable. (8) If the issues at the Newton hearing are wholly resolved in the defendant's favour, mitigation for guilty pleas should not be reduced. If the defendant is disbelieved or obliges the prosecution to call evidence from the victim, who is then subjected to cross-examination which, because it is entirely unfounded, causes unnecessary and inappropriate distress, or if the defendant conveys that he has no insight into the consequences of his offence, and no genuine remorse, the judge might reduce the discount for the guilty pleas. There may be a few exceptional cases in which the normal entitlement to credit for a plea of guilty is wholly dissipated by the Newton hearing, and, in such cases, the judge should explain his reasons."

OFFENCES TAKEN INTO CONSIDERATION

The Sentencing Council has produced a definitive guideline which is part of the Magistrates' Court Sentencing Guidelines. In *Miles* [2006] EWCA Crim 256 the court held: "...the sentence is intended to reflect a defendant's overall criminality. Offences cannot be taken into consideration without the express agreement of the offender. That is an essential prerequisite. The offender is pleading guilty to the offences. If they are to be taken into account (and the court is not obliged to take them into account) they have relevance to the overall criminality. When assessing the significance of TICs, as they are often called, of course the court is likely to attach weight to the demonstrable fact that the offender has assisted the police, particularly if they are enabled to clear up offences which might not otherwise be brought to justice. It is also true that cooperative behaviour of that kind will often provide its own very early indication of guilt, and usually means that no further proceedings at all need be started. They may also serve to demonstrate a genuine determination by the offender (and we deliberately use the colloquialism) to wipe the slate clean, so that when he emerges from whatever sentence is imposed on him, he can put his past completely behind him, without having worry or concern that offences may be revealed and that he is then returned to court. As in so many aspects of sentencing, of course, the way in which the court deals with offences to be taken into consideration depends on context. In some cases the offences taken into consideration will end up by adding nothing or nothing very much to the sentence which the court would otherwise impose. On the other hand, offences taken into consideration may aggravate the sentence and lead to a substantial increase in it. For example, the offences may show a pattern of criminal activity which suggests careful planning or deliberate rather than casual involvement in a crime. They may show an offence or offences committed on bail, after an earlier arrest. They may show a return to crime immediately after the offender has been before the court and given a chance that, by committing the crime, he has immediately rejected. There are many situations where similar issues may arise. One advantage to the defendant, of course, is that if once an offence is taken into consideration, there is no likely risk of any further prosecution for it. If, on the other hand, it is not, that risk remains. In short, offences taken into consideration are indeed taken into consideration. They are not ignored or expunged or disregarded."

PARENTS AND GUARDIANS

Fines etc: In relation to those under 16 years the order must be made against a parent/guardian unless it is unreasonable to do so (for example where the parent could have done no more to prevent offending, *Sheffield Crown Court, ex p Clarkson* (1986) 8 Cr App R (S) 454). In relation to those aged 16 or 17 years the order can be made against a parent or guardian (Powers of Criminal Courts (Sentencing) Act 2000, s 137). The means of the parent or guardian must be considered (*Lenihan v West Yorkshire Police* (1981) Cr App R (S) 42). Orders should not be made against local authorities unless the authority failed in its duty toward the child and that failure was causative of the offending (*Bedfordshire County Council v Director of Public Prosecutions* (1996) 1 Cr App R (S) 322). **Bind over:** A court must bind over a parent or guardian when an offender aged under 16 years is convicted of an offence, and may do so if the offender is aged 16 or 17 years. Failure to consent to being bound over can result in a fine not exceeding £1,000. **Parenting orders:** See CDA 1998, s 8. A parenting order can be made alongside a referral order (Criminal Justice Act 2003, s 324 and Sch 34). **Commencement:** Section 8A was not in force at the time of writing.

Crime and Disorder Act 1998, ss 8, 8A, 9, 10

8.— Parenting orders.

(1)   This section applies where, in any court proceedings—

  (a)   a child safety order is made in respect of a child or the court determines on an application under section 12(6) below that a child has failed to comply with any requirement included in such an order;

  (aa) a parental compensation order is made in relation to a child's behaviour;

  (b)   an anti-social behaviour order or sex offender order is made in respect of a child or young person;

  (c)   a child or young person is convicted of an offence; or

  (d)   a person is convicted of an offence under section 443 (failure to comply with school attendance order) or section 444 (failure to secure regular attendance at school of registered pupil) of the Education Act 1996.

(2)   Subject to subsection (3) and section 9(1) below, if in the proceedings the court is satisfied that the relevant condition is fulfilled, it may make a parenting order in respect of a person who is a parent or guardian of the child or young person or, as the case may be, the person convicted of the offence under section 443 or 444 ("the parent").

(3)   A court shall not make a parenting order unless it has been notified by the Secretary of State that arrangements for implementing such orders are available in the are in which it appears to the court that the parent resides or will reside and the notice has not been withdrawn.

(4)   A parenting order is an order which requires the parent–

  (a)   to comply, for a period not exceeding twelve months, with such requirements as are specified in the order, and

  (b)   subject to subsection (5) below, to attend, for a concurrent period not exceeding three months, such counselling or guidance programme as may be specified in directions given by the responsible officer.

(5)   A parenting order may, but need not, include such a requirement as is mentioned in subsection (4)(b) above in any case where a parenting order under this section or any other enactment has been made in respect of the parent on a previous occasion.

(6)   The relevant condition is that the parenting order would be desirable in the interests of preventing—

  (a)   in a case falling within paragraph (a), (aa) or (b) of subsection (1) above, any repetition of the kind of behaviour which led to the child safety order, parental compensation order, anti-social behaviour order or sex offender order being made;

(b) in a case falling within paragraph (c) of that subsection, the commission of any further offence by the child or young person;

(c) in a case falling within paragraph (d) of that subsection, the commission of any further offence under section 443 or 444 of the Education Act 1996.

(7) The requirements that may be specified under subsection (4)(a) above are those which the court considers desirable in the interests of preventing any such repetition or, as the case may be, the commission of any such further offence.

(7A) A counselling or guidance programme which a parent is required to attend by virtue of subsection (4)(b) above may be or include a residential course but only if the court is satisfied–

(a) that the attendance of the parent at a residential course is likely to be more effective than his attendance at a non-residential course in preventing any such repetition or, as the case may be, the commission of any such further offence, and

(b) that any interference with family life which is likely to result from the attendance of the parent at a residential course is proportionate in all the circumstances.

(8) In this section and section 9 below "responsible officer", in relation to a parenting order, means one of the following who is specified in the order, namely—

(a) an officer of a local probation board or an officer of a provider of probation services;

(b) a social worker of a local authority; and

(bb) a person nominated by a person appointed as director of children's services under section 18 of the Children Act 2004 or by a person appointed as chief education officer under section 532 of the Education Act 1996.

(c) a member of a youth offending team.

8A Parenting order on breach of anti-social behaviour order

(1) This section applies where a person under the age of 16 is convicted of an offence under section 1(10) above in respect of an anti-social behaviour order.

(2) The court by or before which the person is so convicted must make a parenting order in respect of a person who is a parent or guardian of the person convicted, unless it is of the opinion that there are exceptional circumstances that would make a parenting order inappropriate.

(3) The parenting order must specify such requirements as the court considers would be desirable in the interests of preventing—

(a) any repetition of the kind of behaviour which led to the antisocial behaviour order being made; or

(b) the commission of any further offence by the person convicted.

(4) If the court does not make a parenting order because it is of the opinion that there are exceptional circumstances that would make it inappropriate, it must state in open court that it is of that opinion and what those circumstances are.

(5) The following subsections of section 8 above apply to parenting orders made under this section—

(a) subsection (3) (court not to make parenting order unless arrangements available in local area);

(b) subsection (4) (definition of parenting order);

(c) subsection (5) (counselling or guidance programme not necessary if previous parenting order);

(d) subsection (7A) (residential courses).

(6) The following subsections of section 9 below apply to parenting orders made under this section—

(a) subsection (3) (court to explain effect of parenting order);

(b) subsection (4) (parenting order not to conflict with religious beliefs, work or education);

(c) subsections (5) and (6) (applications to vary or discharge parenting order);

(d) subsection (7) (failure to comply with parenting order).

9.— Parenting orders: supplemental.

(1) Where a person under the age of 16 is convicted of an offence, the court by or before which he is so convicted—

(a) if it is satisfied that the relevant condition is fulfilled, shall make a parenting order; and

(b) if it is not so satisfied, shall state in open court that it is not and why it is not.

(1A) The requirements of subsection (1) do not apply where the court makes a referral order in respect of the offence.

(1B) If an anti-social behaviour order is made in respect of a person under the age of 16 the court which makes the order–

(a) must make a parenting order if it is satisfied that the relevant condition is fulfilled;

(b) if it is not so satisfied, must state in open court that it is not and why it is not.

(2) Before making a parenting order—

(a) in a case falling within paragraph (a) of subsection (1) of section 8 above;

(b) in a case falling within paragraph (b) or (c) of that subsection, where the person concerned is under the age of 16; or

(c) in a case falling within paragraph (d) of that subsection, where the person to whom the offence related is under that age,

a court shall obtain and consider information about the person's family circumstances and the likely effect of the order on those circumstances.

(2A) In a case where a court proposes to make both a referral order in respect of a child or young person convicted of an offence and a parenting order, before making the parenting order the court shall obtain and consider a report by an appropriate officer—

(a) indicating the requirements proposed by that officer to be included in the parenting order;

(b) indicating the reasons why he considers those requirements would be desirable in the interests of preventing the commission of any further offence by the child or young person; and

(c) if the child or young person is aged under 16, containing the information required by subsection (2) above.

(2B) In subsection (2A) above "an appropriate officer" means—

(a) an officer of a local probation board or an officer of a provider of probation services;

(b) a social worker of a local authority [...]; or

(c) a member of a youth offending team.

(3) Before making a parenting order, a court shall explain to the parent in ordinary language—

(a) the effect of the order and of the requirements proposed to be included in it;

(b) the consequences which may follow (under subsection (7) below) if he fails to comply with any of those requirements; and

(c) that the court has power (under subsection (5) below) to review the order on the application either of the parent or of the responsible officer.

(4) Requirements specified in, and directions given under, a parenting order shall, as far as practicable, be such as to avoid—

(a) any conflict with the parent's religious beliefs; and

(b) any interference with the times, if any, at which he normally works or attends an educational establishment.

(5) If while a parenting order is in force it appears to the court which made it, on the application of the responsible officer or the parent, that it is appropriate to make an order under this subsection, the court may make an order discharging the parenting order or varying it—

(a) by cancelling any provision included in it; or

(b) by inserting in it (either in addition to or in substitution for any of its provisions) any provision that could have been included in the order if the court had then had power to make it and were exercising the power.

(6) Where an application under subsection (5) above for the discharge of a parenting order is dismissed, no further application for its discharge shall be made under that subsection by any person except with the consent of the court which made the order.

(7) If while a parenting order is in force the parent without reasonable excuse fails to comply with any requirement included in the order, or specified in directions given by the responsible officer, he shall be liable on summary conviction to a fine not exceeding level 3 on the standard scale.

(7A) In this section "referral order" means an order under section 16(2) or (3) of the Powers of Criminal Courts (Sentencing) Act 2000 (referral of offender to youth offender panel).

10.— Appeals against parenting orders.

(1) An appeal shall lie—

(a) to a county court against the making of a parenting order by virtue of paragraph (a) of subsection (1) of section 8 above; and

(b) to the Crown Court against the making of a parenting order by virtue of paragraph (b) of that subsection.

(2) On an appeal under subsection (1) above a county court or the Crown Court—

(a) may make such orders as may be necessary to give effect to its determination of the appeals; and

(b) may also make such incidental or consequential orders as appear to it to be just.

(3) Any order of a county court or the Crown Court made on an appeal under subsection (1) above (other than one directing that an application be re-heard by a magistrates' court) shall, for the purposes of subsections (5) to (7) of section 9 above, be treated as if it were an order of the court from which the appeal was brought and not an order of a county court or the Crown Court.

(4) A person in respect of whom a parenting order is made by virtue of section 8(1)(c) above shall have the same right of appeal against the making of the order as if—

(a) the offence that led to the making of the order were an offence committed by him; and

(b) the order were a sentence passed on him for the offence.

(5) A person in respect of whom a parenting order is made by virtue of section 8(1)(d) above shall have the same right of appeal against the making of the order as if the order were a sentence passed on him for the offence that led to the making of the order.

[...]

PENALTY POINTS

Where an offence carries endorsement of penalty points, such points will be endorsed (Road Traffic Offenders Act 1988, s 44) unless there are special reasons found, the provisions of the Mental Health Act 1983, s 37(3) apply, or the defendant has a specific defence under Road Traffic Act 1988, ss 40A, 41A. **Attempts:** The Road Traffic Act 1988 specifies a number of summary offences which may be attempted; endorsement follows in the usual manner. The Criminal Attempts Act 1981, s 4(1)(c) deals similarly with either-way offences that are tried summarily. **Aiding and abetting:** A secondary party can be sentenced as if he were a principal offender (Magistrates' Courts Act 1980, s 44). Where an offence carries obligatory disqualification for a principal offender an aider or abettor will not fall to be disqualified, but instead the offence will attract 10 penalty points. **Offences on same occasion:** The starting point is section 28(4) which states that: "where a person is convicted (whether on the same occasion or not) of two or more offences committed on the same occasion and involving obligatory endorsement, the total number of penalty points to be attributed to them is the number or highest number that would be attributed on a conviction of one of them (so that if the convictions are on different occasions the number of penalty points to be attributed to the offences on the later occasion or occasions shall be restricted accordingly)". However, a court, 'if it thinks fit' may impose points for each offence. **Same occasion:** This is a paucity of English case law on this topic, and a significant difference of approach between the English and Scottish courts. Failing to stop and then failing to report arise out of the same incident and therefore are offences on the same occasion (*Johnson v Finbow* [1983] 1 WLR 879). A decision of the Scottish High Court, *McKeever v Walkingshaw* (1995) 1996 SLT 1228 decided that a single course of driving may give rise to offences having occurred on more than one occasion (speeding and then less than 2 miles later committing a further offence). Similarly a moving traffic offence which resulted in the driver being stopped and asked to give a specimen of breath (which he declined) was similarly held to be separate occasions (*Cameron v Brown* (1996) 1997 SLT 914). Whether offences occur on the same occasion is primarily a matter of fact. **Special reasons:** If special reasons are established (see later) the court has the option either to endorse with the appropriate points, or not endorse at all. **Disqualification:** If the court disqualifies for any offence then no points can be endorsed (in respect to that or any other offence for which he was convicted of on that occasion) (*Martin v Director of Public Prosecutions* [2000] RTR 188).

PRE-SENTENCE REPORTS

Generally:

Criminal Justice Act 2003, s 156

(1) In forming any such opinion as is mentioned in section 148(1) or (2)(b), section 152(2) or section 153(2), or in section 1(4)(b) or (c) of the Criminal Justice and Immigration Act 2008 (youth rehabilitation orders with intensive supervision and surveillance or fostering), a court must take into account all such information as is available to it about the circumstances of the offence or (as the case may be) of the offence and the offence or offences associated with it, including any aggravating or mitigating factors.

(2) In forming any such opinion as is mentioned in section 148(2)(a), the court may take into account any information about the offender which is before it.

(3) Subject to subsection (4), a court must obtain and consider a pre-sentence report before—

(a) in the case of a custodial sentence, forming any such opinion as is mentioned in section 152(2), section 153(2), section 225(1)(b), section 226(1)(b), section 227(1)(b) or section 228(1)(b)(i), or

(b) in the case of a community sentence, forming any such opinion as is mentioned in section 148(1) or (2)(b), or in section 1(4)(b) or (c) of the Criminal Justice and Immigration Act 2008, or any opinion as to the suitability for the offender of the particular requirement or requirements to be imposed by the community order or youth rehabilitation order.

(4) Subsection (3) does not apply if, in the circumstances of the case, the court is of the opinion that it is unnecessary to obtain a pre-sentence report.

(5) In a case where the offender is aged under 18, the court must not form the opinion mentioned in subsection (4) unless—

    (a) there exists a previous pre-sentence report obtained in respect of the offender, and

    (b) the court has had regard to the information contained in that report, or, if there is more than one such report, the most recent report.

(6) No custodial sentence or community sentence is invalidated by the failure of a court to obtain and consider a pre-sentence report before forming an opinion referred to in subsection (3), but any court on an appeal against such a sentence—

    (a) must, subject to subsection (7), obtain a pre-sentence report if none was obtained by the court below, and

    (b) must consider any such report obtained by it or by that court.

(7) Subsection (6)(a) does not apply if the court is of the opinion—

    (a) that the court below was justified in forming an opinion that it was unnecessary to obtain a pre-sentence report, or

    (b) that, although the court below was not justified in forming that opinion, in the circumstances of the case at the time it is before the court, it is unnecessary to obtain a pre-sentence report.

(8) In a case where the offender is aged under 18, the court must not form the opinion mentioned in subsection (7) unless—

    (a) there exists a previous pre-sentence report obtained in respect of the offender, and

    (b) the court has had regard to the information contained in that report, or, if there is more than one such report, the most recent report.

Mentally disordered offenders:

Criminal Justice Act 2003, s 157

(1) Subject to subsection (2), in any case where the offender is or appears to be mentally disordered, the court must obtain and consider a medical report before passing a custodial sentence other than one fixed by law.

(2) Subsection (1) does not apply if, in the circumstances of the case, the court is of the opinion that it is unnecessary to obtain a medical report.

(3) Before passing a custodial sentence other than one fixed by law on an offender who is or appears to be mentally disordered, a court must consider—

    (a) any information before it which relates to his mental condition (whether given in a medical report, a pre-sentence report or otherwise), and

    (b) the likely effect of such a sentence on that condition and on any treatment which may be available for it.

(4) No custodial sentence which is passed in a case to which subsection (1) applies is invalidated by the failure of a court to comply with that subsection, but any court on an appeal against such a sentence—

    (a) must obtain a medical report if none was obtained by the court below, and

    (b) must consider any such report obtained by it or by that court.

(5) In this section "mentally disordered", in relation to any person, means suffering from a mental disorder within the meaning of the Mental Health Act 1983 (c. 20).

(6) In this section "medical report" means a report as to an offender's mental condition made or submitted orally or in writing by a registered medical practitioner who is

approved for the purposes of section 12 of the Mental Health Act 1983 by the Secretary of State as having special experience in the diagnosis or treatment of mental disorder.

(7) Nothing in this section is to be taken to limit the generality of section 156.

PREVIOUS CONVICTIONS

Criminal Justice Act 2003, s 143

(1) In considering the seriousness of any offence, the court must consider the offender's culpability in committing the offence and any harm which the offence caused, was intended to cause or might forseeably have caused.

(2) In considering the seriousness of an offence ("the current offence") committed by an offender who has one or more previous convictions, the court must treat each previous conviction as an aggravating factor if (in the case of that conviction) the court considers that it can reasonably be so treated having regard, in particular, to—

(a) the nature of the offence to which the conviction relates and its relevance to the current offence, and

(b) the time that has elapsed since the conviction.

(3) In considering the seriousness of any offence committed while the offender was on bail, the court must treat the fact that it was committed in those circumstances as an aggravating factor.

(4) Any reference in subsection (2) to a previous conviction is to be read as a reference to—

(a) a previous conviction by a court in the United Kingdom,

(aa) a previous conviction by a court in another member State of a relevant offence under the law of that State,

(b) a previous conviction of a service offence within the meaning of the Armed Forces Act 2006 ("conviction" here including anything that under section 376(1) and (2) of that Act is to be treated as a conviction), or

(c) a finding of guilt in respect of a member State service offence.

(5) Subsections (2) and (4) do not prevent the court from treating—

(a) a previous conviction by a court outside both the United Kingdom and any other member State, or

(b) a previous conviction by a court in any member State (other than the United Kingdom) of an offence which is not a relevant offence,

as an aggravating factor in any case where the court considers it appropriate to do so.

(6) For the purposes of this section—

(a) an offence is "relevant" if the offence would constitute an offence under the law of any part of the United Kingdom if it were done in that part at the time of the conviction of the defendant for the current offence,

(b) "member State service offence" means an offence which—

(i) was the subject of proceedings under the service law of a member State other than the United Kingdom, and

(ii) would constitute an offence under the law of any part of the United Kingdom, or a service offence (within the meaning of the Armed Forces Act 2006), if it were done in any part of the United Kingdom, by a member of Her Majesty's forces, at the time of the conviction of the defendant for the current offence,

(c) "Her Majesty's forces" has the same meaning as in the Armed Forces Act 2006, and

(d) "service law", in relation to a member State other than the United Kingdom, means the law governing all or any of the naval, military or air forces of that State.

PROSECUTION COSTS

The following principles can be derived from *Northallerton Magistrates' Court, ex p Dove* [2000] 1 Cr App R (S) 136: An order to pay costs to the prosecutor should never exceed the sum which, having regard to the defendant's means and any other financial order imposed upon him, the defendant was able to pay and which it was reasonable to order the defendant to pay. Such an order should never exceed the sum that the prosecutor had actually and reasonably incurred (or was liable to a third-party to pay, for example, when that third-party commissions a report on behalf of the prosecution). The purpose of such an order was to compensate the prosecutor and not punish the defendant. Where the defendant had by his conduct put the prosecutor to avoidable expense he might, subject to his means, be ordered to pay some or all of that sum to the prosecutor. However, he was not to be punished for exercising his constitutional right to defend himself. Whilst there was no requirement that any sum ordered by justices to be paid to a prosecutor by way of costs should stand in any arithmetical relationship to any fine imposed, the costs ordered to be paid should not in any ordinary way be grossly disproportionate to the fine. Justices should ordinarily begin by deciding on the appropriate fine to reflect the criminality of the defendant's offence, always bearing in mind his means and ability to pay, and then consider what, if any, costs he should be ordered to pay to the prosecutor. If, when the costs sought by the prosecutor were added to the proposed fine, the total exceeded the sum which in the light of the defendant's means and all other relevant circumstances the defendant could reasonably be ordered to pay, it was preferable to achieve an acceptable total by reducing the sum of costs which the defendant was ordered to pay rather than by reducing the fine. If the offender fails to disclose properly his means to the court, reasonable inferences can be drawn as to his means from evidence they had heard and all the circumstances of the case.

In rare cases where a criminal prosecution is brought to establish commercial rights and interests (eg television broadcast rights) a court can order that the civil as opposed to criminal costs regime ought to apply (*Murphy v Media Protection Services Ltd* [2012] EWHC 529 (Admin)).

CPS costs scale: In *Dickinson* [2010] EWCA Crim 2143 the CPS costs scale was deemed to be fair and reasonable. The policy of CPS is to apply for costs against convicted defendants unless the particular circumstances of a case mean that such an application would lack merit or an order for costs would be impractical. The following scales provide guidance on the level of costs incurred by the CPS in various types of proceedings. The scales represent the average costs incurred in a wide range of cases and provide a benchmark to estimate the costs in individual cases (excluding very high-cost cases). The scales are indicative of single-defendant cases only and the figure should be increased by 20 per cent for each additional defendant. More complex cases should attract the higher range of costs and relatively straightforward cases the lower range. The figures include all staff preparation costs, including advocacy in magistrates' courts and time spent in the Crown Court by paralegal officers/assistants. Add to these figures witness expenses, counsel fees or Crown Advocate's advocacy costs (for Crown Court cases), and other specific costs, where appropriate. When seeking a costs order, prosecutors should inform the court of all costs incurred and invite the court to consider what should be paid. Discretion should be exercised in putting forward a reasonable estimate of the costs incurred in the individual case.

The average hourly rates appropriate to CPS staff are:

Lawyers £69 per hour; Paralegals £51 per hour; Support staff £44 per hour.

Types of Proceedings

Magistrates' Court	Lower	Average	Higher
Proof in Absence		£85 (set amount)	
Early Guilty Plea (EFH)		£85	£100
Summary Guilty Plea	£105	£135	£160
Summary Trial	£620	£775	£930
Either way Guilty Plea	£145	£185	£220
Either way Trial	£770	£965	£1,150

RACIALLY AND RELIGIOUSLY AGGRAVATED CRIMES

There are a number of aggravated offences created under sections 29 to 32 CDA 1998. The CJA 2003, s 145 allows for an uplift to be imposed in relation to other offences where there is racial or religious aggravation. The court should first state what sentence it would pass but for the aggravating feature and then add an uplift to reflect the racial or religious aggravation (*Kelly; Donnelly* [2001] EWCA Crim 170). Racially or religiously aggravated: An offence is racially or religiously aggravated if (a) at the time of committing the offence, or immediately before or after doing so, the offender demonstrates towards the victim of the offence hostility based on the victim's membership (or presumed membership) of a racial or religious group; or (b) the offence is motivated (wholly or partly) by hostility towards members of a racial or religious group based on their membership of that group.

Criminal Justice Act 2003, s 145

(1) This section applies where a court is considering the seriousness of an offence other than one under sections 29 to 32 of the Crime and Disorder Act 1998 (c. 37) (racially or religiously aggravated assaults, criminal damage, public order offences and harassment etc).

(2) If the offence was racially or religiously aggravated, the court—

(a) must treat that fact as an aggravating factor, and
(b) must state in open court that the offence was so aggravated.

(3) Section 28 of the Crime and Disorder Act 1998 (meaning of "racially or religiously aggravated") applies for the purposes of this section as it applies for the purposes of sections 29 to 32 of that Act.

REDUCTION IN SENTENCE FOR EARLY PLEA

A court when sentencing must take into account the stage at which any guilty plea was indicated and the circumstances in which the indication was given (Criminal Justice Act 2003, s 144). The reduction has no impact on sentencing decisions in relation to ancillary orders, including disqualification. Where the prosecution case is overwhelming, it may not be appropriate to give the full reduction that would otherwise be given (*Wilson* [2012] EWCA Crim 386). In *March* [2002] 2 Cr App R (S) 98 the court gave the following as examples of cases which may justify the refusal of credit following a guilty plea:

Guilty pleas should, in general, attract lower sentences, is in the public interest; they save time and expense and may be taken as an indication of remorse. If anything, guilty pleas are all the more important in cases which, if fought, will require vulnerable witnesses to give evidence. The principle, however, is only a general principle; for instance, there is no invariable rule to the effect that a maximum sentence cannot be given in the case of a guilty plea. There are a number of well-established exceptions to the general rule and their list is not closed. When such an exception applies, a maximum sentence may be imposed, even in the event of a guilty plea. That said, given the general principle, it will rarely be appropriate to impose a maximum sentence where there has been a guilty plea. The exceptions to the general rule include at least the following: (i) where the imposition of the maximum term is necessary for the protection of the public; (ii) where the plea was of a tactical nature; (iii) cases where a plea is practically speaking inevitable; (iv) where the count is a specimen count. As to the effect of these exceptions, we incline to the view that the existence of an exception does not automatically mean that the maximum sentence is to be imposed regardless of a plea of guilty; all the circumstances fall to be considered. On the authority of Reay (supra), at p.535, it would appear that a further exception to the general principle arises in cases where the offence is of such seriousness that the public interest requires the imposition of a maximum sentence. If seriousness of the offence, by itself, meant that the maximum sentence was to be imposed despite a plea of guilty, then reconciling this suggested exception and the authorities would not be straightforward; see, for example, Sharkey and Daniels (supra), where a guilty plea in respect of an appalling offence with grave consequences attracted a discount. In our judgment, the answer to this concern lies in the analysis set out in (3) above. Seriousness of the offence is a factor to be considered with all the other circumstances of the case in coming to the sentencing decision; in an exceptionally serious case, the court may (not must) impose the maximum sentence despite a plea of guilty. On this footing all the authorities can be reconciled; the rationale of the general principle is preserved (it would lack content if it could never operate in a serious case); finally, the court is not deprived of the power to refuse a discount on commonsense grounds in an exceptionally serious case. Turning to the framework for young offenders (ie. any persons aged under 18), Parliament has legislated for a maximum 24 month term for Detention and Training Orders: ss. 100 and 101 of the Act. Here, as elsewhere, Judges are bound by legislation; that maximum must be respected. If it is too low, the remedy lies with others – not with the courts.

In certain, limited, circumstances, set out in s.91 of the Act, to which s.100 is subject, a person aged under 18 may be detained for longer than 24 months ... In a case where it is open to a Judge to sentence a young offender to a term of detention in excess of 24 months, pursuant to s.91, the discount for a plea of guilty may (depending on all the circumstances) properly be reflected by the Judge sentencing the offender to the maximum 24 months Detention and Training Order. In such a case, the offender cannot complain of not receiving a further discount; he has benefited from his plea of guilty by the Judge confining the sentence to the maximum Detention and Training period rather than imposing a longer sentence under s.91."

Overwhelming evidence: Whilst there is a presumption in favour of the full reduction being given where a plea has been indicated at the first reasonable opportunity, the fact that the prosecution case is overwhelming without relying on admissions from the defendant may be a reason justifying departure from the guideline. **Maximum sentence in lieu of committal**: Despite a guilty plea being entered which would normally attract a reduction in sentence, a magistrates' court may impose a sentence of imprisonment of 6 months for a single either-way offence where, but for the plea, that offence would have been committed to the Crown Court for sentence. Similarly, a detention and training order of 24 months may be imposed on an offender aged under 18 if the offence is one which would but for the plea have attracted a sentence of long-term detention in excess of 24 months under the Powers of Criminal Courts (Sentencing) Act 2000, section 91. Where an offence triable either way is committed to the Crown Court for trial and the defendant pleads guilty at the first hearing in that Court, the reduction will be less than if there had been an indication of a guilty plea given to the magistrates' court (recommended reduction of one third) but more than if the plea had been entered after a trial date had been set (recommended reduction of one quarter), and is likely to be in the region of 30%. **First reasonable opportunity**: This will depend on the facts of the case, but in some instances it will have been the opportunity to admit guilt when interviewed by the police (*Cundell* [2008] EWCA Crim 1420).

The Sentencing Council prescribes the following discount in relation to early plea:

In each category, there is a presumption that the recommended reduction will be given unless there are good reasons for a lower amount		
First reasonable opportunity	After a trial date is set	Door of the court/after trial has begun
recommended 1/3	recommended 1/4	recommended 1/10

REFERRAL ORDER

Mandatory: A referral order must be made where the offence is punishable with imprisonment, the offender has pleaded guilty to the offence (or offences), the court is not imposing an absolute discharge, hospital order or custodial sentence, and the defendant has not previously been convicted of an offence or been bound over. **Discretionary**: The court may make an order where: the defendant pleads guilty to a non-imprisonable offence; or, the defendant has never previously been convicted (in the United Kingdom) of an offence and enters a guilty plea to the offence, or if there is more than one, at least one of the offences; or the defendant has been dealt with by a UK court for any offence other than the offence and any connected offence on only one previous occasion, but was not referred to a youth offender panel on that occasion; or the defendant has been dealt with by a UK court for any offence other than the offence and any connected offence on only one previous occasion, and was referred to a youth offender panel on that occasion, and an appropriate officer recommends that the defendant is suitable for a further referral order, and the court considers that there are exceptional circumstances justifying the defendant to be so referred. **Where the offender pleads not guilty to all offences**: The order is not available on conviction. **Compliance period**: Not less than 3 and not more than 12 months. **Concurrent orders**: More than one order may be in force at the same time. **Other orders**: The court is permitted to order costs, compensation and make a parenting order at the same time as imposing a referral order.

REMAND TO HOSPITAL FOR REPORTS

Mental Health Act 1983, s 35

(1) Subject to the provisions of this section, the Crown Court or a magistrates' court may remand an accused person to a hospital specified by the court for a report on his mental condition.

(2) For the purposes of this section an accused person is—

    (a) in relation to the Crown Court, any person who is awaiting trial before the court for an offence punishable with imprisonment or who has been arraigned before the court for such an offence and has not yet been sentenced or otherwise dealt with for the offence on which he has been arraigned;

    (b) in relation to a magistrates' court, any person who has been convicted by the court of an offence punishable on summary conviction with imprisonment and any person charged with such an offence if the court is satisfied that he did the act or made the omission charged or he has consented to the exercise by the court of the powers conferred by this section.

(3) Subject to subsection (4) below, the powers conferred by this section may be exercised if—

    (a) the court is satisfied, on the written or oral evidence of a registered medical practitioner, that there is reason to suspect that the accused person is suffering from mental disorder; and

    (b) the court is of the opinion that it would be impracticable for a report on his mental condition to be made if he were remanded on bail;

but those powers shall not be exercised by the Crown Court in respect of a person who has been convicted before the court if the sentence for the offence of which he has been convicted is fixed by law.

(4) The court shall not remand an accused person to a hospital under this section unless satisfied, on the written or oral evidence of the approved clinician who would be responsible for making the report or of some other person representing the managers of the hospital, that arrangements have been made for his admission to that hospital and for his admission to it within the period of seven days beginning with the date of the remand; and if the court is so satisfied it may, pending his admission, give directions for his conveyance to and detention in a place of safety.

(5) Where a court has remanded an accused person under this section it may further remand him if it appears to the court, on the written or oral evidence of the approved clinician

responsible for making the report, that a further remand is necessary for completing the assessment of the accused person's mental condition.

(6) The power of further remanding an accused person under this section may be exercised by the court without his being brought before the court if he is represented by an authorised person who is given an opportunity of being heard.

(7) An accused person shall not be remanded or further remanded under this section for more than 28 days at a time or for more than 12 weeks in all; and the court may at any time terminate the remand if it appears to the court that it is appropriate to do so.

(8) An accused person remanded to hospital under this section shall be entitled to obtain at his own expense an independent report on his mental condition from a registered medical practitioner or approved clinician chosen by him and to apply to the court on the basis of it for his remand to be terminated under subsection (7) above.

(9) Where an accused person is remanded under this section—

(a) a constable or any other person directed to do so by the court shall convey the accused person to the hospital specified by the court within the period mentioned in subsection (4) above; and

(b) the managers of the hospital shall admit him within that period and thereafter detain him in accordance with the provisions of this section.

(10) If an accused person absconds from a hospital to which he has been remanded under this section, or while being conveyed to or from that hospital, he may be arrested without warrant by any constable and shall, after being arrested, be brought as soon as practicable before the court that remanded him; and the court may thereupon terminate the remand and deal with him in any way in which it could have dealt with him if he had not been remanded under this section.

REMITTING A JUVENILE

If a youth is convicted before a magistrates' court, that court must remit the case to a youth court for sentence unless it proposes to deal with him by way of discharge, fine, or parental bind over. An offender who was a youth at the start of the proceedings and falls to be sentenced when an adult should be remitted to the youth court in the same manner (Powers of Criminal Courts (Sentencing) Act 2000, s 8).

REPARATION ORDER

Powers of Criminal Courts (Sentencing) Act 2000, s 73

(1) Where a child or young person (that is to say, any person aged under 18) is convicted of an offence other than one for which the sentence is fixed by law, the court by or before which he is convicted may make an order requiring him to make reparation specified in the order—

(a) to a person or persons so specified; or

(b) to the community at large;

and any person so specified must be a person identified by the court as a victim of the offence or a person otherwise affected by it.

(2) An order under subsection (1) above is in this Act referred to as a "reparation order".

(3) In this section and section 74 below "make reparation", in relation to an offender, means make reparation for the offence otherwise than by the payment of compensation; and the requirements that may be specified in a reparation order are subject to section 74(1) to (3).

(4) The court shall not make a reparation order in respect of the offender if it proposes—

(a) to pass on him a custodial sentence; or

(b) to make in respect of him a youth rehabilitation order or a referral order.

(4A) The court shall not make a reparation order in respect of the offender at a time when a youth rehabilitation order is in force in respect of him unless when it makes the reparation order it revokes the youth rehabilitation order.

(4B) Where a youth rehabilitation order is revoked under subsection (4A), paragraph 24 of Schedule 2 to the Criminal Justice and Immigration Act 2008 (breach, revocation or amendment of youth rehabilitation order) applies to the revocation.

(5) Before making a reparation order, a court shall obtain and consider a written report by [an officer of a local probation board, an officer of a provider of probation services, a social worker of a local authority or a member of a youth offending team indicating—

(a) the type of work that is suitable for the offender; and

(b) the attitude of the victim or victims to the requirements proposed to be included in the order.

(6) The court shall not make a reparation order unless it has been notified by the Secretary of State that arrangements for implementing such orders are available in the area proposed to be named in the order under section 74(4) below and the notice has not been withdrawn.

[...]

(8) The court shall give reasons if it does not make a reparation order in a case where it has power to do so.

RESTITUTION ORDER

In *Webbe* [2001] EWCA Crim 1217 the court stated: "a court passing sentence in handling cases should always have in mind the power to make restitution orders."

Powers of Criminal Courts (Sentencing) Act 2000, s 148

(1) This section applies where goods have been stolen, and either—

(a) a person is convicted of any offence with reference to the theft (whether or not the stealing is the gist of his offence); or

(b) a person is convicted of any other offence, but such an offence as is mentioned in paragraph (a) above is taken into consideration in determining his sentence.

(2) Where this section applies, the court by or before which the offender is convicted may on the conviction (whether or not the passing of sentence is in other respects deferred) exercise any of the following powers—

(a) the court may order anyone having possession or control of the stolen goods to restore them to any person entitled to recover them from him; or

(b) on the application of a person entitled to recover from the person convicted any other goods directly or indirectly representing the stolen goods (as being the proceeds of any disposal or realisation of the whole or part of them or of goods so representing them), the court may order those other goods to be delivered or transferred to the applicant; or

(c) the court may order that a sum not exceeding the value of the stolen goods shall be paid, out of any money of the person convicted which was taken out of his possession on his apprehension, to any person who, if those goods were in the possession of the person convicted, would be entitled to recover them from him; and in this subsection "the stolen goods" means the goods referred to in subsection (1) above.

(3) Where the court has power on a person's conviction to make an order against him both under paragraph (b) and under paragraph (c) of subsection (2) above with reference to the stealing of the same goods, the court may make orders under both paragraphs provided that the person in whose favour the orders are made does not thereby recover more than the value of those goods.

(4) Where the court on a person's conviction makes an order under subsection (2)(a) above for the restoration of any goods, and it appears to the court that the person convicted—

(a) has sold the goods to a person acting in good faith, or
(b) has borrowed money on the security of them from a person so acting,

the court may order that there shall be paid to the purchaser or lender, out of any money of the person convicted which was taken out of his possession on his apprehension, a sum not exceeding the amount paid for the purchase by the purchaser or, as the case may be, the amount owed to the lender in respect of the loan.

(5) The court shall not exercise the powers conferred by this section unless in the opinion of the court the relevant facts sufficiently appear from evidence given at the trial or the available documents, together with admissions made by or on behalf of any person in connection with any proposed exercise of the powers.

(6) In subsection (5) above "the available documents" means—

(a) any written statements or admissions which were made for use, and would have been admissible, as evidence at the trial; and
(b) such documents as were served on the offender in pursuance of regulations made under paragraph 1 of Schedule 3 to the Crime and Disorder Act 1998.

(7) Any order under this section shall be treated as an order for the restitution of property within the meaning of section 30 of the Criminal Appeal Act 1968 (which relates to the effect on such orders of appeals).

(8) Subject to subsection (9) below, references in this section to stealing shall be construed in accordance with section 1(1) of the Theft Act 1968 (read with the provisions of that Act relating to the construction of section 1(1)).

(9) Subsections (1) and (4) of section 24 of that Act (interpretation of certain provisions) shall also apply in relation to this section as they apply in relation to the provisions of that Act relating to goods which have been stolen.

(10) In this section and section 149 below, "goods", except in so far as the context otherwise requires, includes money and every other description of property (within the meaning of the Theft Act 1968) except land, and includes things severed from the land by stealing.

(11) An order may be made under this section in respect of money owed by the Crown.

RESTRAINING ORDER

A restraining order may be imposed either on conviction (s 5) or acquittal (s 5A). **Victim:** An order should identify the person(s) that it is seeking to protect (*Mann*, The Times, 11 April 2000); An order can be made protecting a group or a corporate person (*Buxton* [2010] EWCA Crim 2923). **Acquittal:** Acquittal includes where the prosecution offers no evidence, but not where proceedings are discontinued or adjourned sine die. **Evidence:** A court "[Has] to bear in mind the fundamental principle underlying these rules namely that any person faced with the possible imposition of a restraining order should be given proper notice of what is sought, the evidential basis for the application and, in addition, be allowed a proper opportunity to address the evidence and make informed representations as to the appropriateness of such an order. Thus, if the trial judge contemplates making such an order in relation to a defendant immediately following a trial (whatever the result of that trial), provided his or her representative has had the opportunity specifically to address all relevant issues, then consideration can properly be given to exercising the discretion contained in Rule 50.9" (*Brough* [2011] EWCA Crim 1843). In *Major* [2010] EWCA Crim 3016 the court held: "We cannot accept that an order may only be made on uncontested facts or used only rarely... The fact that a jury was not sure that the conduct alleged amounted to harassment is not necessarily a ground for concluding that there is no risk of harassment in the future. The section is silent as to the standard of proof which must be satisfied before an order may be made, but the order is a civil order and so the ordinary civil standard of proof applies. Applying that standard a court may well conclude that whereas the conduct alleged has not been proved to the required criminal standard, it has been proved on the balance of probabilities and such a conclusion would not contradict the verdict of a jury or implicitly suggest that the defendant was in fact guilty. Section 5A addresses a future risk, the evidential basis for such an assessment being the conduct of the defendant. The evidence as to that will usually be the evidence given at trial, but it can be further evidence (see above). The evidence does not have to establish on the balance of probabilities that there has been harassment. It is enough if the evidence establishes conduct which falls short of harassment but which may well in the judgment of the sentencing judge, if repeated, amount to harassment, so making an order necessary. Compliance by a defendant with bail conditions which prohibited conduct with the victim, while a consideration, may not be a ground for not making an order. A court may conclude that compliance with the bail conditions was explained by the defendant's concerns that he or she may be remanded in custody and that without such a sanction the victim would be at risk... Is a judge required to identify the factual basis for imposing an order? In short, yes. These proceedings are no different to any other proceedings leading to sentence where the factual basis has to be established and the sentencing judge has to exercise a judgment on the facts. It must not be overlooked that absent a conviction it may not be possible to determine the factual basis for the order". See also: *Kapotra* [2011] EWCA Crim 1843. **Views of victim**: In *Picken* [2006] EWCA Crim 2194 the court held: " ...the judge should not have made an order without finding out what [the complainant's] position was. If he had been satisfied that she wished to continue relations with the applicant, then it would have been inappropriate for him to have made the order". It should be noted however than an order might be considered appropriate in order to protect children, even in circumstances where the complainant refuses protection, such instances will however be rare. The principle in *Picken* has been recently reaffirmed (*Brown* [2012] EWCA Crim 1152). **Variation**: A variation under section 5(4) includes an application to extend the order beyond the original expiry date (*Hall* [2005] EWHC 2612 (Admin)). Unless something had demonstrably changed so as to justify the discharge or amendment of the order, an application ought to be refused (*Shaw v Director of Public Prosecutions* [2005] 7 Archbold News 2, DC). If an order is varied a new revised order should be drawn up (*Liddle* [2002] 1 Archbold News 2, CA). **Terms**: An order can be made restraining someone from publishing true statements if to so publish would amount to harassment (*Debnath* [2006] 2 Cr App R (S) 25). **CrPR**: Rule 50 applies.

Protection From Harassment Act 1997, ss 5, 5A

5.— Restraining orders on conviction.

(1) A court sentencing or otherwise dealing with a person ("the defendant") convicted of an offence may (as well as sentencing him or dealing with him in any other way) make an order under this section.

(2) The order may, for the purpose of protecting the victim or victims of the offence, or any other person mentioned in the order, from conduct which—

(a) amounts to harassment, or

(b) will cause a fear of violence,

prohibit the defendant from doing anything described in the order.

(3) The order may have effect for a specified period or until further order.

(3A) In proceedings under this section both the prosecution and the defence may lead, as further evidence, any evidence that would be admissible in proceedings for an injunction under section 3.

(4)   The prosecutor, the defendant or any other person mentioned in the order may apply to the court which made the order for it to be varied or discharged by a further order.

(4A)   Any person mentioned in the order is entitled to be heard on the hearing of an application under subsection (4).

(5)   If without reasonable excuse the defendant does anything which he is prohibited from doing by an order under this section, he is guilty of an offence.

(6)   A person guilty of an offence under this section is liable—

(a) on conviction on indictment, to imprisonment for a term not exceeding five years, or a fine, or both, or

(b) on summary conviction, to imprisonment for a term not exceeding six months, or a fine not exceeding the statutory maximum, or both.

(7)   A court dealing with a person for an offence under this section may vary or discharge the order in question by a further order.

5A Restraining orders on acquittal

(1)   A court before which a person ("the defendant") is acquitted of an offence may, if it considers it necessary to do so to protect a person from harassment by the defendant, make an order prohibiting the defendant from doing anything described in the order.

(2)   Subsections (3) to (7) of section 5 apply to an order under this section as they apply to an order under that one.

(3)   Where the Court of Appeal allow an appeal against conviction they may remit the case to the Crown Court to consider whether to proceed under this section.

(4)   Where—

(a) the Crown Court allows an appeal against conviction, or

(b) a case is remitted to the Crown Court under subsection (3),

the reference in subsection (1) to a court before which a person is acquitted of an offence is to be read as referring to that court.

(5)   A person made subject to an order under this section has the same right of appeal against the order as if—

(a) he had been convicted of the offence in question before the court which made the order, and

(b) the order had been made under section 5.

RETURN TO CUSTODY

This provision applies to those sentenced prior to 4 April 2005, and to all offenders sentenced after that date to a term of imprisonment not exceeding 12 months. In *Pick* [2005] EWCA Crim 1853 the court held: "Section 116 is punitive in nature. Parliament intended that a defendant should remain liable to be returned to prison for all or any part of the sentence still unserved at the time of the commission of a further offence. The fact that a court has already imposed a return to prison upon conviction of a further offence will not prevent another court from exercising the same power in respect of any later offending taking place before the defendant has served the original sentence, in respect of which he is on licence, in full."

Powers of Criminal Courts (Sentencing) Act 2000, s 116

(1)   This section applies to a person if—

(a) he has been serving a determinate sentence of imprisonment which he began serving on or after 1st October 1992;

(b) he is released under any provision of Part 2 of the Criminal Justice Act 1991 (early release of prisoners) other than section 33(1A);

      (c) before the date on which he would (but for his release) have served his sentence in full, he commits an offence punishable with imprisonment ("the new offence"); and

      (d) whether before or after that date, he is convicted of the new offence.

(2)   Subject to subsection (3) below, the court by or before which a person to whom this section applies is convicted of the new offence may, whether or not it passes any other sentence on him, order him to be returned to prison for the whole or any part of the period which—

      (a) begins with the date of the order; and

      (b) is equal in length to the period between the date on which the new offence was committed and the date mentioned in subsection (1)(c) above.

(3)   A magistrates' court—

      (a) shall not have power to order a person to whom this section applies to be returned to prison for a period of more than six months; but

      (b) subject to section 25 of the Criminal Justice and Public Order Act 1994 (restrictions on granting bail), may commit him in custody or on bail to the Crown Court to be dealt with under subsection (4) below.

(4)   [...]

(5)   Subsection (3)(b) above shall not be taken to confer on the magistrates' court a power to commit the person to the Crown Court for sentence for the new offence, but this is without prejudice to any such power conferred on the magistrates' court by any other provision of this Act.

(6)   The period for which a person to whom this section applies is ordered under subsection (2) or (4) above to be returned to prison—

      (a) shall be taken to be a sentence of imprisonment for the purposes of Part II of the Criminal Justice Act 1991 and this section;

      (b) shall, as the court may direct, either be served before and be followed by, or be served concurrently with, the sentence imposed for the new offence; and

      (c) in either case, shall be disregarded in determining the appropriate length of that sentence.

(7)   As a consequence of subsection (6)(a) above, the court shall not be prevented by section 265 of the Criminal Justice Act 2003 (restriction on consecutive sentences for released prisoners) from making any direction authorised by subsection (6)(b) above.

(8)   Where the new offence is found to have been committed over a period of two or more days, or at some time during a period of two or more days, it shall be taken for the purposes of this section to have been committed on the last of those days.

(9)   [...]

(10) This section and section 117 below apply to persons serving—

      (a) determinate sentences of detention under section 91 above, or

      (b) sentences of detention in a young offender institution,

as they apply to persons serving equivalent sentences of imprisonment; and references in this section and section 117 to imprisonment or prison shall be construed accordingly.

(11) In this section "sentence of imprisonment" does not include a committal for contempt of court or any kindred offence.

RISK OF SEXUAL HARM ORDER

These orders are applied for on a freestanding basis.

Sexual Offences Act 2003, ss 123-128

123 Risk of sexual harm orders: applications, grounds and effect

(1) A chief officer of police may by complaint to a magistrates' court apply for an order under this section (a "risk of sexual harm order") in respect of a person aged 18 or over ("the defendant") who resides in his police area or who the chief officer believes is in, or is intending to come to, his police area if it appears to the chief officer that–

    (a) the defendant has on at least two occasions, whether before or after the commencement of this Part, done an act within subsection (3), and

    (b) as a result of those acts, there is reasonable cause to believe that it is necessary for such an order to be made.

(2) An application under subsection (1) may be made to any magistrates' court whose commission area includes–

    (a) any part of the applicant's police area, or

    (b) any place where it is alleged that the defendant acted in a way mentioned in subsection (1)(a).

(3) The acts are–

    (a) engaging in sexual activity involving a child or in the presence of a child;

    (b) causing or inciting a child to watch a person engaging in sexual activity or to look at a moving or still image that is sexual;

    (c) giving a child anything that relates to sexual activity or contains a reference to such activity;

    (d) communicating with a child, where any part of the communication is sexual.

(4) On the application, the court may make a risk of sexual harm order if it is satisfied that–

    (a) the defendant has on at least two occasions, whether before or after the commencement of this section, done an act within subsection (3); and

    (b) it is necessary to make such an order, for the purpose of protecting children generally or any child from harm from the defendant.

(5) Such an order–

    (a) prohibits the defendant from doing anything described in the order;

    (b) has effect for a fixed period (not less than 2 years) specified in the order or until further order.

(6) The only prohibitions that may be imposed are those necessary for the purpose of protecting children generally or any child from harm from the defendant.

(7) Where a court makes a risk of sexual harm order in relation to a person already subject to such an order (whether made by that court or another), the earlier order ceases to have effect.

124 Section 123: interpretation

(1) Subsections (2) to (7) apply for the purposes of section 123.

(2) "Protecting children generally or any child from harm from the defendant" means protecting children generally or any child from physical or psychological harm, caused by the defendant doing acts within section 123(3).

(3) "Child" means a person under 16.

(4) "Image" means an image produced by any means, whether of a real or imaginary subject.

(5) "Sexual activity" means an activity that a reasonable person would, in all the circumstances but regardless of any person's purpose, consider to be sexual.

(6) A communication is sexual if–

    (a) any part of it relates to sexual activity, or

(b) a reasonable person would, in all the circumstances but regardless of any person's purpose, consider that any part of the communication is sexual.

(7) An image is sexual if–

(a) any part of it relates to sexual activity, or

(b) a reasonable person would, in all the circumstances but regardless of any person's purpose, consider that any part of the image is sexual.

125 RSHOs: variations, renewals and discharges

(1) A person within subsection (2) may by complaint to the appropriate court apply for an order varying, renewing or discharging a risk of sexual harm order.

(2) The persons are–

(a) the defendant;

(b) the chief officer of police on whose application the risk of sexual harm order was made;

(c) the chief officer of police for the area in which the defendant resides;

(d) a chief officer of police who believes that the defendant is in, or is intending to come to, his police area.

(3) Subject to subsections (4) and (5), on the application the court, after hearing the person making the application and (if they wish to be heard) the other persons mentioned in subsection (2), may make any order, varying, renewing or discharging the risk of sexual harm order, that the court considers appropriate.

(4) An order may be renewed, or varied so as to impose additional prohibitions on the defendant, only if it is necessary to do so for the purpose of protecting children generally or any child from harm from the defendant (and any renewed or varied order may contain only such prohibitions as are necessary for this purpose).

(5) The court must not discharge an order before the end of 2 years beginning with the day on which the order was made, without the consent of the defendant and–

(a) where the application is made by a chief officer of police, that chief officer, or

(b) in any other case, the chief officer of police for the area in which the defendant resides.

(6) Section 124(2) applies for the purposes of this section.

(7) In this section "the appropriate court" means–

(a) the court which made the risk of sexual harm order;

(b) a magistrates' court for the area in which the defendant resides; or

(c) where the application is made by a chief officer of police, any magistrates' court whose commission area includes any part of his police area.

126 Interim RSHOs

(1) This section applies where an application for a risk of sexual harm order ("the main application") has not been determined.

(2) An application for an order under this section ("an interim risk of sexual harm order")–

(a) may be made by the complaint by which the main application is made, or

(b) if the main application has been made, may be made by the person who has made that application, by complaint to the court to which that application has been made.

(3) The court may, if it considers it just to do so, make an interim risk of sexual harm order, prohibiting the defendant from doing anything described in the order.

(4) Such an order–

(a) has effect only for a fixed period, specified in the order;

(b) ceases to have effect, if it has not already done so, on the determination of the main application.

(5) The applicant or the defendant may by complaint apply to the court that made the interim risk of sexual harm order for the order to be varied, renewed or discharged.

127 RSHOs and interim RSHOs: appeals

(1) A defendant may appeal to the Crown Court–

(a) against the making of a risk of sexual harm order;

(b) against the making of an interim risk of sexual harm order; or

(c) against the making of an order under section 125, or the refusal to make such an order.

(2) On any such appeal, the Crown Court may make such orders as may be necessary to give effect to its determination of the appeal, and may also make such incidental or consequential orders as appear to it to be just.

(3) Any order made by the Crown Court on an appeal under subsection (1)(a) or (b) (other than an order directing that an application be re-heard by a magistrates' court) is for the purpose of section 125(7) or 126(5) (respectively) to be treated as if it were an order of the court from which the appeal was brought (and not an order of the Crown Court).

128 Offence: breach of RSHO or interim RSHO

(1) A person commits an offence if, without reasonable excuse, he does anything which he is prohibited from doing by–

(a) a risk of sexual harm order; or

(b) an interim risk of sexual harm order.

(1A) In subsection (1) and, accordingly, in section 129(5) the references to a risk of sexual harm order and to an interim risk of sexual harm order include references, respectively–

(a) to an order under section 2 of the Protection of Children and Prevention of Sexual Offences (Scotland) Act 2005 (RSHOs in Scotland); and

(b) to an order under section 5 of that Act (interim RSHOs in Scotland);

and, for the purposes of this section, prohibitions imposed by an order made in one part of the United Kingdom apply (unless expressly confined to particular localities) throughout that and every other part of the United Kingdom.

(2) A person guilty of an offence under this section is liable–

(a) on summary conviction, to imprisonment for a term not exceeding 6 months or a fine not exceeding the statutory maximum or both;

(b) on conviction on indictment, to imprisonment for a term not exceeding 5 years.

(3) Where a person is convicted of an offence under this section, it is not open to the court by or before which he is convicted to make, in respect of the offence, an order for conditional discharge.

SENTENCING GUIDELINES

Guidelines issued by the Sentencing Guidelines Council are to be treated as if they were guidelines issued by the Sentencing Council (SI 816/2010).

Criminal Justice Act 2003, s 174(2)

(2) In complying with subsection (1)(a), the court must—

(a) identify any definitive sentencing guidelines relevant to the offender's case and explain how the court discharged any duty imposed on it by section 125 of the Coroners and Justice Act 2009,

(aa) where the court did not follow any such guidelines because it was of the opinion that it would be contrary to the interests of justice to do so, state why it was of that opinion...

SEXUAL OFFENCES NOTIFICATION

Notification requirements follow as an automatic consequence of a conviction for an offence listed in SOA 2003, Sch 3 and are not dependent on any order of the court. Some offences listed in Sch 3 are conditional and care should be taken to understand the consequences of plea (eg for an offence of gross indecency to trigger notification the defendant must be aged 20 years or over, and the victim be aged under 18 years). Sch3 is reproduced in Appendix 3. The notification requirements, which are notified to the defendant at time of conviction are onerous (for the most recent amendments to those requirements see: The Sexual Offences Act 2003 (Notification Requirements) (England and Wales) Regulations 2012). **Community orders**: A community order solely to complete unpaid work within a period of 12 months is a qualifying order even if the work is completed earlier (D [2008] EWCA Crim 2795). **Young offenders**: If the defendant is aged under 18 years the court has the option to impose the notification requirements onto a person with parental responsibility for the child (Sexual Offences Act 2003, s 89). **Period**: SOA, s 82 applies (see table below). Indefinite notification was ruled incompatible with the ECHR by the Supreme Court (F [2011] 1 AC 331; The Sexual Offences Act 2003 (Remedial Order) 2012 came in to force on 30 July 2012 and provides for the removal of notification requirements in certain cases. **Mitigation**: The imposition of notification requirements does not mitigate an otherwise proper sentence as it is not a form of punishment in itself (*Attorney General's Reference (No 50 of 1997)* [1998] 2 Cr App R (S) 155).

Penalty	Notification period for an adult	Notification period for an offender aged under 18 years
Caution	2 years	1 year
Conditional discharge	Period of discharge	Period of discharge
A person of any other description (sentenced to a community penalty or fine)	5 years	2 ½ years
Imprisonment for a term of 6 months or less (or admitted to hospital without a restriction order)	7 years	3 ½ years
Imprisonment for a minimum term of 6 months but less than 30 months	10 years	5 years
Sentence of imprisonment for life, or a term of 30 months or more, or hospital order with restriction	Indefinite	Indefinite

SEXUAL OFFENCES PREVENTION ORDER

Trigger: Following conviction for an offence specified in Schedule 3 (other than paragraph 60) or 5 to the Sexual offences Act 2003, the court may go on to consider whether or not to make a sexual offences prevention order (Sexual offences Act 2003, s 104). A freestanding application can also be made by the police. Schedule 5 contains a wide range of non-sexual offences. **Test**: A court may make such an order if satisfied that it is necessary to make such an order, for the purpose of protecting the public or any particular members of the public from serious sexual harm from the defendant. The offence in question may predate 1 May 2004. It is important to note that there is nothing in section 104 to indicate that a court must believe a defendant to be 'dangerous' (within the meaning of the public protection sentencing regime) before it can make such an order (*Richards* [2006] EWCA Crim 2519). In *Smith* [2011] EWCA Crim 1772 the court offered detailed guidance in relation to the drafting of such orders (see Appendix 5). **Effect**: A sexual offences prevention order: prohibits the defendant from doing anything described in the order; and has effect for a fixed period (not less than five years) specified in the order or until further order. The only prohibitions that may be included in the order are those necessary for the purpose of protecting the public or any particular members of the public from serious sexual harm from the defendant. **Alternative**: An order may not be appropriate if the same condition could be imposed as part of a community order (*AM* [2012] EWCA Crim 880). **Duration**: An order must be made for a period not less than five years, and may be indefinite. **CrPR**: Rule 50 applies.

Sexual Offences Act 2003, s 104

(1) A court may make an order under this section in respect of a person ("the defendant") where any of subsections (2) to (4) applies to the defendant and–

    (a) where subsection (4) applies, it is satisfied that the defendant's behaviour since the appropriate date makes it necessary to make such an order, for the purpose of protecting the public or any particular members of the public from serious sexual harm from the defendant;

    (b) in any other case, it is satisfied that it is necessary to make such an order, for the purpose of protecting the public or any particular members of the public from serious sexual harm from the defendant.

(2) This subsection applies to the defendant where the court deals with him in respect of an offence listed in Schedule 3 or 5.

(3) This subsection applies to the defendant where the court deals with him in respect of a finding–

    (a) that he is not guilty of an offence listed in Schedule 3 or 5 by reason of insanity, or

    (b) that he is under a disability and has done the act charged against him in respect of such an offence.

(4) This subsection applies to the defendant where–

    (a) an application under subsection (5) has been made to the court in respect of him, and

    (b) on the application, it is proved that he is a qualifying offender.

(5) A chief officer of police may by complaint to a magistrates' court apply for an order under this section in respect of a person who resides in his police area or who the chief officer believes is in, or is intending to come to, his police area if it appears to the chief officer that–

    (a) the person is a qualifying offender, and

    (b) the person has since the appropriate date acted in such a way as to give reasonable cause to believe that it is necessary for such an order to be made.

(6) An application under subsection (5) may be made to any magistrates' court whose commission area includes–

    (a) any part of the applicant's police area, or

    (b) any place where it is alleged that the person acted in a way mentioned in subsection (5)(b).

SEXUAL ORIENTATION [OR TRANSGENDER IDENTITY] OR DISABILITY

The court should first state what sentence it would pass but for the aggravating feature and then add an uplift to reflect the hostility (*Kelly; Donnelly* [2001] EWCA Crim 170). The Legal Aid, Sentencing and Punishment of Offenders Act 2012, s 65 will extend section 146 to cover transgender identity (not yet in force).

Criminal Justice Act 2003, s 146

(1) This section applies where the court is considering the seriousness of an offence committed in any of the circumstances mentioned in subsection (2).

(2) Those circumstances are—

    (a) that, at the time of committing the offence, or immediately before or after doing so, the offender demonstrated towards the victim of the offence hostility based on—

        (i) the sexual orientation (or presumed sexual orientation) of the victim, or

        (ii) a disability (or presumed disability) of the victim, or

    (b) that the offence is motivated (wholly or partly)—

        (i) by hostility towards persons who are of a particular sexual orientation, or

        (ii) by hostility towards persons who have a disability or a particular disability.

(3) The court—

    (a) must treat the fact that the offence was committed in any of those circumstances as an aggravating factor, and

    (b) must state in open court that the offence was committed in such circumstances.

(4) It is immaterial for the purposes of paragraph (a) or (b) of subsection (2) whether or not the offender's hostility is also based, to any extent, on any other factor not mentioned in that paragraph.

(5) In this section "disability" means any physical or mental impairment.

SPECIAL REASONS

If special reasons are established a court may exercise its discretion not to endorse penalty points on a licence. A court does not have the power to endorse a lesser number of points. Similarly, special reasons may also justify a court in not imposing a mandatory period of disqualification or in reducing the period of disqualification to be served. **Proof**: The burden of proof rests on the defendant who must call evidence to the fact rather than merely assert it (*Jones v English* [1951] 2 All ER 853) and satisfy the court to the civil standard (*Pugsley v Hunter* [1973] RTR 284). A failure to notify the prosecution of the intention to plead special reasons may form the basis of questions from the prosecution and proper comment as to the bona fides of that approach (*Director of Public Prosecutions* v *O'Connor* [1992] RTR 66); given the greater emphasis on case management since that decision a prosecutor is likely to succeed in securing an adjournment in an appropriate case. In a number of earlier cases the court has rejected hearsay evidence being advanced by the defendant (which in cases such as spiked drinks allegations may be the best a defendant can do), these authorities should however be revisited in light of the Criminal Evidence Act 2003. **What is a special reason?** *Crossen* [1939] 1 NI 106: A special reason is something special to the facts of the offence, a mitigating or extenuating circumstance, not amounting in law to a defence to the charge, yet directly connected with the commission of the offence and one which the court ought properly to take into consideration. A circumstance peculiar to the offender as distinguished from the offence is not a 'special reason' within the exception. **Minor offending**: In *Nicholson v Brown* [1974] RTR 177 the court held: "I would not accept the proposition that if a man is guilty of driving without due care and attention, he can be excused endorsement of his licence on the basis of special reasons merely because it was not a bad case, or merely because the degree of blameworthiness was slight. I think that the line must be drawn firmly at guilt or innocence in those cases. If the defendant is guilty, then the consequences of endorsement of the licence must follow, unless there is some special reason properly to be treated as such, not such a matter as that the offence was not a serious one". **What does not amount to a special reason?** Allowance for fact that defendant prohibited from driving as a condition of bail (*Kwame* [1975] RTR 106). Good character, hardship to self or others (*Whittall v Kirby* [1946] 2 All ER 552); Public servant and necessity to have a licence to discharge that role, eg doctor (*Holroyd v Berry* [1973] RTR 145 where it was held: "it would be enlarging an escape route which is intentionally narrow if this court were now to hold in a case such as the present that the reasons advanced were special reasons. In my view it would be opening the door dangerously wide if this appeal were to be allowed"). A belief that the effect of any alcohol would have worn off by the morning is not a special reason (*Director of Public Prosecutions v O'Meara* [1989] RTR 84). **Drunk drivers**: Special considerations arise where the driver is drunk and the driver is met with an emergency situation. In *Director of Public Prosecutions v Bristow* [1998] RTR 100 the court held that a court should ask:

> "what would a sober, reasonable and responsible friend of the defendant present at the time, but himself a non-driver and thus unable to help, have advised in the circumstances: drive or do not drive? The justices could only properly find special reasons and exercise their discretion not to disqualify if they thought it a real possibility rather than merely an off-chance that such a person would have advised the defendant to drive. Amongst the most critical circumstances influencing that advice would, of course, be these: (1) How much has the defendant had to drink? (2) Having regard to that, what threat would he pose to others when driving in that condition, given the distance he was proposing to drive, the likely state of the roads and the condition of his vehicle? (3) How acute a problem is there? (4) What, if any, alternatives are open to the defendant to solve that problem?"

Mistake as to drink: A mistake as to the quantity drunk cannot be a special reason, although if a defendant did not know that he was drinking alcohol at all it might (*Newnham v Trigg* [1970] RTR 107), nor can a belief that a drink is not alcoholic, unless the defendant made specific enquiry and was misled (*Robinson v Director of Public Prosecutions*[2007] EWHC 2718 (Admin)).

Examples of special reasons: The following are all examples of special reasons upheld by the courts: **Shortness of distance driven**: This may amount to a special reason provided that there is unlikely to be contact with other vehicles or a danger caused. In *Chatters v Burke* [1986] 3 All ER 168 the court set out 7 matters that ought to be considered by a court: distance driven, manner of driving, state of the vehicle, whether there was an intention to drive further, road and traffic conditions, possibility of danger to other road users (the most important factor to be considered), and reason for the driving. What a defendant intended to do can be as important a factor as what he in fact did do (see for example *Director of Public Prosecutionsv Humphries* [2000] RTR 52 a case where the defendant would have driven a stolen car whilst drunk). **Spiked/laced drinks**: A high reading may well be a reason not to exercise discretion not to disqualify even where the defendant is not culpable (*Robinson v Director of Public Prosecutions* [2007] EWHC 2718 (Admin)). It follows as a matter of common sense that the higher the reading the less likely a defendant is to be able to establish the defence. In order to succeed with a laced drink defence it must be evidenced that (1) the drink was in fact laced, (2) the defendant did not know or suspect that the drink was laced, and (3) that but for the drink being laced his alcohol level would have been below the prescribed limit, which is normally to be demonstrated by expert evidence unless the conclusion is obvious (*Pugsley v Hunter* [1973] RTR 284). **Defendant misled**: This scenario often arises in no insurance cases. The defendant must evidence that he was misled (whether by act or omission of another). An honest but mistaken belief, absent being misled will not suffice (*Rennison v Knowler* [1947] 1 All ER 302). **Emergency cases**: In *R v Mander*, unreported, 13 May 2008, CA, the court found special reasons where a taxi driver, upon three of five passengers alighting without paying, drove dangerously for approximately nine-tenths of a mile. The court declined, however, to exercise its discretion to reduce the period of disqualification on the grounds that the defendant had overreacted to the circumstances. In *Warring-Davies v Director of Public Prosecutions* [2009] EWHC 1172 (Admin) the court emphasized the need to find a causal link between any alleged medical condition and the driving in question. In *Director of Public Prosecutions v Harrison* [2007] EWHC 556 (Admin) the court held it wrong to find special reasons where a drunken person drove 446 yards in order to find youths who had harassed him earlier. In *Director of Public Prosecutions v Oram* [2005] EWHC 964 (Admin) the court held that special reasons would not be arguable to a drunk driver who relied upon shortness of distance driven alone.

Taylor v Rajan [1974] RTR 304 deals with the principles involved in 'emergency' cases: "This is not the first case in which the court has had to consider whether driving in an emergency could justify a conclusion that there are special reasons for not disqualifying the driver. If a man, in the well-founded belief that he will not drive again, puts his car in the garage, goes into his house and has a certain amount to drink in the belief that he is not going to drive again, and if thereafter is an emergency which requires him in order to deal with it to take his car out despite his intention to leave it in the garage, then that is a situation which can in law amount to a special reason for not disqualifying a driver. On the other hand, Justices who are primarily concerned with dealing with this legislation should approach the exercise of the resulting discretion with great care. The mere fact that the facts disclose a special reason does not mean that the driver is to escape disqualification as a matter of course. There is a very serious burden upon the Justices, even when a special reason has been disclosed, to decide whether in their discretion they should decline to disqualify a particular case. The Justices should have very much in mind that if a man deliberately drives when he knows he has consumed a considerable quantity of drink, he presents a potential source of danger to the public which no private crisis can likely excuse. One of the most important matters which Justices have to consider in the exercise of this discretion is whether the emergency (and I call it such for want of a more convenient word) was sufficiently acute to justify the driver taking his car out. The Justices should only exercise a discretion in favour of the driver in clear and compelling circumstances... The Justices therefore must consider the whole of the circumstances. They must consider the nature and degree of the crisis or emergency which has caused the defendant to take the car out. They must consider with particular care whether there were alternative means of transport or methods of dealing with the crisis other than and alternative to the use by the defendant of his own car. They should have regard to the manner in which the defendant drove ... and they should generally have regard to whether the defendant acted responsibly or otherwise... The matter must be considered objectively and the quality and gravity of the crisis must be assessed in that way. Last, but by no means least, if the alcohol content in the defendant's blood and body is very high, that is a powerful reason for saying that the discretion should not be exercised in his favour. Indeed, if the alcohol content exceeds 100 milligrammes per hundred millilitres of blood, the Justices should rarely, if ever, exercise this discretion in favour of the defendant driver".

SUSPENDED SENTENCE ORDER

A suspended sentence order can be made in respect of a minimum custodial sentence of 14 days and not more than 6 months (made up of single or consecutive periods). It is not appropriate to make such an order when a defendant has served on remand a period equivalent to the appropriate sentence for the offence (*Peppard* (1990) 12 Cr App R (S) 88). A court must impose: An operational period (which is the length of time the order is in force) of between 6 and 24months, a supervision period (which is the time in which all of the community requirements should be completed) of between 6 and 24 months (which must not extend beyond the operational period) and at least one community requirement (*Lees-Wolfenden* [2007] 1 Cr App R (S) 119). An unpaid work requirement continues until the work is completed or until the expiry of the operational period, whichever is sooner. **Presumption**: On breach the presumption is that the order will be activated. In *Sheppard* [2008] EWCA Crim 799 the court held:

"It seems to us that the statutory provisions envisage a two stage test. First, where there has been a breach, the court must order that the suspended sentence take effect either in whole or in part unless it would be unjust to do so. The extent of compliance with the original order is relevant to that decision. So, for example, if 95 per cent of the order had been complied with, a court might conclude that it was unjust to order that any part of the custodial term take effect. Secondly, if it is not unjust to activate the suspended sentence, then the court must decide whether or not to impose the original sentence or modify the term. It seems clear from the Schedule that either of those options are available to the court and therefore either of them are available in circumstances where there has been part compliance. Part compliance is, of course, relevant again at this stage, because if there had been substantial and prompt compliance with the order then, even if a suspended sentence is to be activated, the court may be minded to impose a lesser term than that originally specified. Applying, therefore, the two stage test, it is plain that in this case it was not unjust to impose a custodial sentence following the breaches of the order. Indeed, [counsel] does not suggest otherwise. As to the second stage, it is clear to us that such compliance as there has been on the part of the applicant has been dilatory, spasmodic and, to use the judge's word, grudging. The applicant has been repeatedly in breach of the terms of the order. In those circumstances, although we consider that his part compliance is a factor which should be taken into account in the exercise of the court's discretion, we have concluded that it should not, on the facts of this case, lead to any reduction in the 12 month term. [Counsel] made extremely attractive submissions to us to the effect that, if there had been any compliance with the terms of a suspended sentence order, then some credit ought to be given almost as an automatic consequence. However, it seems to us that it is not appropriate for a sentencing court always to give credit and to reduce the suspended sentence in such circumstances. Community orders and suspended sentences are seen by some sections of the public as a soft alternative to prison. For the public to have confidence in them, they must be properly enforced by the courts. If there are repeated breaches, as there were in this case, then defendants must know that they will face the probability that the full sentence originally imposed will be reactivated. It is also right for us to note that the probation service spend a good deal of time and effort providing the services in respect of which community orders depend. It is important that the courts ensure that such time and resources are not wasted on those defendants who only comply with the terms of the orders when they feel like it. It is also important that the probation service knows that courts may well impose full terms when community service orders and suspended sentence orders are breached; they can then give a clear message to those who are subject to such orders".

Legislation: CJA 2003, Sch 12 deals with breach (See Appendix 4). **Breach of requirements:** The court may order the offender to serve the whole of the custodial period that has been suspended, a shorter period. If it is unjust to order a return to custody a court may impose more onerous community requirements, extend the operational period (maximum 2 years) or extend the supervision period (maximum 2 years, but cannot extend beyond the operational period). There is no power to revoke the order and simply re-sentence (*Phipps* (2008) Crim LR 398). Where the operational period has expired the only course of action open to the court is to activate all or part of the custodial period. **Breach following conviction for a new offence:** Activation of a SSO might be appropriate even if the new offence does not warrant custody (*Nobbs v Director of Public Prosecutions [2008] EWHC 1653*). **Forthcoming changes:** When the Legal Aid, Sentencing and Punishment of Offenders Act 2012, s 69 is in force there will be a power , on breach, to fine the offender (up to £2,500). **Crown court orders:** A magistrates' court may deal with an order imposed by a crown court if the crown court has stipulated as such when making the order, but only in so far as a breach of requirements is concerned. If the breach is as a result of re-offending a magistrates' court has no jurisdiction to deal with a crown court suspended sentence order (*Burbridge* [2007] EWCA Crim 2968). **Aggravating new offence:** A new offence is not aggravated by the mere fact that it was committed whilst the defendant was subject to a suspended sentence order in circumstances where the SSO is to be activated in full (*Levesconte* [2011] EWCA Crim 2754). The court in *Levesconte* left open the question of aggravation where the sentence is not activated in full.

Criminal Justice Act 2003, ss 189–192

89 Suspended sentences of imprisonment

(1) A court which passes a sentence of imprisonment or, in the case of a person aged at least 18 but under 21, detention in a young offender institution for a term of at least 14 days but not more than twelve months, or in the case of a magistrates' court, at least 14 days but not more than six months may—

(a) order the offender to comply during a period specified for the purposes of this paragraph in the order (in this Chapter referred to as "the supervision period") with one or more requirements falling within section 190(1) and specified in the order, and

(b) order that the sentence of imprisonment or detention in a young offender institution] is not to take effect unless either—

    (i)   during the supervision period the offender fails to comply with a requirement imposed under paragraph (a), or

    (ii) during a period specified in the order for the purposes of this sub-paragraph (in this Chapter referred to as "the operational period") the offender commits in the United Kingdom another offence (whether or not punishable with imprisonment),

and (in either case) a court having power to do so subsequently orders under paragraph 8 of Schedule 12 that the original sentence is to take effect.

(2) Where two or more sentences imposed on the same occasion are to be served consecutively, the power conferred by subsection (1) is not exercisable in relation to any of them unless the aggregate of the terms of the sentences does not exceed twelve months, or in the case of a magistrates' court, six months.

(3) The supervision period and the operational period must each be a period of not less than six months and not more than two years beginning with the date of the order.

(4) The supervision period must not end later than the operational period.

(5) A court which passes a suspended sentence on any person for an offence may not impose a community sentence in his case in respect of that offence or any other offence of which he is convicted by or before the court or for which he is dealt with by the court.

(6) Subject to any provision to the contrary contained in the Criminal Justice Act 1967 (c. 80), the Sentencing Act or any other enactment passed or instrument made under any enactment after 31st December 1967, a suspended sentence which has not taken effect under paragraph 8 of Schedule 12 is to be treated as a sentence of imprisonment or in the case of a person aged at least 18 but under 21, a sentence of detention in a young offender institution for the purposes of all enactments and instruments made under enactments.

(7) In this Part—

(a) "suspended sentence order" means an order under subsection (1),

(b) "suspended sentence" means a sentence to which a suspended sentence order relates, and

(c) "community requirement", in relation to a suspended sentence order, means a requirement imposed under subsection (1)(a).

190 Imposition of requirements by suspended sentence order

(1) The requirements falling within this subsection are—

(a) an unpaid work requirement (as defined by section 199),

(b) an activity requirement (as defined by section 201),

(c) a programme requirement (as defined by section 202),

(d) a prohibited activity requirement (as defined by section 203),

(e) a curfew requirement (as defined by section 204),

(f) an exclusion requirement (as defined by section 205),

(g) a residence requirement (as defined by section 206),

(h) a mental health treatment requirement (as defined by section 207),

(i) a drug rehabilitation requirement (as defined by section 209),

(j) an alcohol treatment requirement (as defined by section 212),

(k) a supervision requirement (as defined by section 213), and

(l) in a case where the offender is aged under 25, an attendance centre requirement (as defined by section 214).

(2) Section 189(1)(a) has effect subject to section 218 and to the following provisions of Chapter 4 relating to particular requirements—

    (a) section 199(3) (unpaid work requirement),
    (b) section 201(3) and (4) (activity requirement),
    (c) section 202(4) and (5) (programme requirement),
    (d) section 203(2) (prohibited activity requirement),
    (e) section 207(3) (mental health treatment requirement),
    (f) section 209(2) (drug rehabilitation requirement), and
    (g) section 212(2) and (3) (alcohol treatment requirement).

(3) Where the court makes a suspended sentence order imposing a curfew requirement or an exclusion requirement, it must also impose an electronic monitoring requirement (as defined by section 215) unless—

    (a) the court is prevented from doing so by section 215(2) or 218(4), or
    (b) in the particular circumstances of the case, it considers it inappropriate to do so.

(4) Where the court makes a suspended sentence order imposing an unpaid work requirement, an activity requirement, a programme requirement, a prohibited activity requirement, a residence requirement, a mental health treatment requirement, a drug rehabilitation requirement, an alcohol treatment requirement, a supervision requirement or an attendance centre requirement, the court may also impose an electronic monitoring requirement unless the court is prevented from doing so by section 215(2) or 218(4).

(5) Before making a suspended sentence order imposing two or more different requirements falling within subsection (1), the court must consider whether, in the circumstances of the case, the requirements are compatible with each other.

191 Power to provide for review of suspended sentence order

(1) A suspended sentence order may—

    (a) provide for the order to be reviewed periodically at specified intervals,
    (b) provide for each review to be made, subject to section 192(4), at a hearing held for the purpose by the court responsible for the order (a "review hearing"),
    (c) require the offender to attend each review hearing, and
    (d) provide for the responsible officer to make to the court responsible for the order, before each review, a report on the offender's progress in complying with the community requirements of the order.

(2) Subsection (1) does not apply in the case of an order imposing a drug rehabilitation requirement (provision for such a requirement to be subject to review being made by section 210).

(3) In this section references to the court responsible for a suspended sentence order are references—

    (a) where a court is specified in the order in accordance with subsection (4), to that court;
    (b) in any other case, to the court by which the order is made.

(4) Where the area specified in a suspended sentence order made by a magistrates' court is not the area for which the court acts, the court may, if it thinks fit, include in the order provision specifying for the purpose of subsection (3) a magistrates' court which acts for the area specified in the order.

(5) Where a suspended sentence order has been made on an appeal brought from the Crown Court or from the criminal division of the Court of Appeal, it is to be taken for the purposes of subsection (3)(b) to have been made by the Crown Court.

192 Periodic reviews of suspended sentence order

(1) At a review hearing (within the meaning of subsection (1) of section 191) the court may, after considering the responsible officer's report referred to in that subsection, amend the

community requirements of the suspended sentence order, or any provision of the order which relates to those requirements.

(2) The court—

    (a) may not amend the community requirements of the order so as to impose a requirement of a different kind unless the offender expresses his willingness to comply with that requirement,

    (b) may not amend a mental health treatment requirement, a drug rehabilitation requirement or an alcohol treatment requirement unless the offender expresses his willingness to comply with the requirement as amended,

    (c) may amend the supervision period only if the period as amended complies with section 189(3) and (4),

    (d) may not amend the operational period of the suspended sentence, and

    (e) except with the consent of the offender, may not amend the order while an appeal against the order is pending.

(3) For the purposes of subsection (2)(a)—

    (a) a community requirement falling within any paragraph of section 190(1) is of the same kind as any other community requirement falling within that paragraph, and

    (b) an electronic monitoring requirement is a community requirement of the same kind as any requirement falling within section 190(1) to which it relates.

(4) If before a review hearing is held at any review the court, after considering the responsible officer's report, is of the opinion that the offender's progress in complying with the community requirements of the order is satisfactory, it may order that no review hearing is to be held at that review; and if before a review hearing is held at any review, or at a review hearing, the court, after considering that report, is of that opinion, it may amend the suspended sentence order so as to provide for each subsequent review to be held without a hearing.

(5) If at a review held without a hearing the court, after considering the responsible officer's report, is of the opinion that the offender's progress under the order is no longer satisfactory, the court may require the offender to attend a hearing of the court at a specified time and place.

(6) If at a review hearing the court is of the opinion that the offender has without reasonable excuse failed to comply with any of the community requirements of the order, the court may adjourn the hearing for the purpose of dealing with the case under paragraph 8 of Schedule 12.

(7) At a review hearing the court may amend the suspended sentence order so as to vary the intervals specified under section 191(1).

(8) In this section any reference to the court, in relation to a review without a hearing, is to be read—

    (a) in the case of the Crown Court, as a reference to a judge of the court, and

    (b) in the case of a magistrates' court, as a reference to a justice of the peace.

TIME SERVED ON REMAND

Curfew: Credit could only be given for an electronically monitored curfew, to do otherwise would be an attempt to rewrite the legislation (*Barrett* [2009] EWCA Crim 2213). **Procedure:** In *Irving* [2010] EWCA Crim 189 the court held: "The net effect is that the court is required to make when passing sentence a specific order as to the number of days for which credit is to be given. That number is one-half of the days on which the defendant was subject to a court order for bail containing a condition imposing a curfew for at least nine hours per day and requiring electronic tagging. The first day of such conditions is counted, however long the curfew lasted that day; the last day is not. If the process of halving the number produces a half, that half number is rounded up". In *Monaghan* [2009] EWCA Crim 2699 the court set out the principles to be applied in some considerable detail and regard should be had to that case if more complex scenarios should arise.

Criminal Justice Act 2003, ss 240, 240A

240 Crediting of periods of remand in custody: terms of imprisonment and detention

(1) This section applies where—

    (a) a court sentences an offender to imprisonment for a term in respect of an offence committed after the commencement of this section, and

    (b) the offender has been remanded in custody (within the meaning given by section 242) in connection with the offence or a related offence, that is to say, any other offence the charge for which was founded on the same facts or evidence.

(2) It is immaterial for that purpose whether the offender—

    (a) has also been remanded in custody in connection with other offences; or

    (b) has also been detained in connection with other matters.

(3) Subject to subsection (4), the court must direct that the number of days for which the offender was remanded in custody in connection with the offence or a related offence is to count as time served by him as part of the sentence.

(4) Subsection (3) does not apply if and to the extent that—

    (a) rules made by the Secretary of State so provide in the case of—

        (i) a remand in custody which is wholly or partly concurrent with a sentence of imprisonment, or

        (ii) sentences of imprisonment for consecutive terms or for terms which are wholly or partly concurrent, or

    (b) it is in the opinion of the court just in all the circumstances not to give a direction under that subsection.

(5) Where the court gives a direction under subsection (3), it shall state in open court—

    (a) the number of days for which the offender was remanded in custody, and

    (b) the number of days in relation to which the direction is given.

(6) Where the court does not give a direction under subsection (3), or gives such a direction in relation to a number of days less than that for which the offender was remanded in custody, it shall state in open court—

    (a) that its decision is in accordance with rules made under paragraph (a) of subsection (4), or

    (b) that it is of the opinion mentioned in paragraph (b) of that subsection and what the circumstances are.

(7) For the purposes of this section a suspended sentence—

    (a) is to be treated as a sentence of imprisonment when it takes effect under paragraph 8(2)(a) or (b) of Schedule 12, and

    (b) is to be treated as being imposed by the order under which it takes effect.

(8) For the purposes of the reference in subsection (3) to the term of imprisonment to which a person has been sentenced (that is to say, the reference to his "sentence"), consecutive terms and terms which are wholly or partly concurrent are to be treated as a single term if—

    (a) the sentences were passed on the same occasion, or

    (b) where they were passed on different occasions, the person has not been released under this Chapter at any time during the period beginning with the first and ending with the last of those occasions.

(9) Where an offence is found to have been committed over a period of two or more days, or at some time during a period of two or more days, it shall be taken for the purposes of subsection (1) to have been committed on the last of those days.

(10) This section applies to a determinate sentence of detention under section 91 of the Sentencing Act or section 228 of this Act or a sentence of detention in a young offender institution under section 96 of the Sentencing Act or section 227 of this Act as it applies to an equivalent sentence of imprisonment.

240A Crediting periods of remand on bail: terms of imprisonment and detention

(1) This section applies where—

   (a) a court sentences an offender to imprisonment for a term in respect of an offence committed on or after 4th April 2005,

   (b) the offender was remanded on bail by a court in course of or in connection with proceedings for the offence, or any related offence, after the coming into force of section 21 of the Criminal Justice and Immigration Act 2008, and

   (c) the offender's bail was subject to a qualifying curfew condition and an electronic monitoring condition ("the relevant conditions").

(2) Subject to subsection (4), the court must direct that the credit period is to count as time served by the offender as part of the sentence.

(3) The "credit period" is the number of days represented by half of the sum of—

   (a) the day on which the offender's bail was first subject to conditions that, had they applied throughout the day in question, would have been relevant conditions, and

   (b) the number of other days on which the offender's bail was subject to those conditions (excluding the last day on which it was so subject), rounded up to the nearest whole number.

(4) Subsection (2) does not apply if and to the extent that—

   (a) rules made by the Secretary of State so provide, or

   (b) it is in the opinion of the court just in all the circumstances not to give a direction under that subsection.

(5) Where as a result of paragraph (a) or (b) of subsection (4) the court does not give a direction under subsection (2), it may give a direction in accordance with either of those paragraphs to the effect that a period of days which is less than the credit period is to count as time served by the offender as part of the sentence.

(6) Rules made under subsection (4)(a) may, in particular, make provision in relation to—

   (a) sentences of imprisonment for consecutive terms;

   (b) sentences of imprisonment for terms which are wholly or partly concurrent;

   (c) periods during which a person granted bail subject to the relevant conditions is also subject to electronic monitoring required by an order made by a court or the Secretary of State.

(7) In considering whether it is of the opinion mentioned in subsection (4)(b) the court must, in particular, take into account whether or not the offender has, at any time whilst on bail subject to the relevant conditions, broken either or both of them.

(8) Where the court gives a direction under subsection (2) or (5) it shall state in open court—

   (a) the number of days on which the offender was subject to the relevant conditions, and

   (b) the number of days in relation to which the direction is given.

(9) Subsection (10) applies where the court—

   (a) does not give a direction under subsection (2) but gives a direction under subsection (5), or

   (b) decides not to give a direction under this section.

(10)   The court shall state in open court—

   (a) that its decision is in accordance with rules made under paragraph (a) of subsection (4), or

   (b) that it is of the opinion mentioned in paragraph (b) of that subsection and what the circumstances are.

(11)   Subsections (7) to (10) of section 240 apply for the purposes of this section as they apply for the purposes of that section but as if—

   (a) in subsection (7)—

      (i)   the reference to a suspended sentence is to be read as including a reference to a sentence to which an order under section 118(1) of the Sentencing Act relates;

      (ii) in paragraph (a) after "Schedule 12" there were inserted "or section 119(1)(a) or (b) of the Sentencing Act"; and

   (b) in subsection (8) the reference to subsection (3) of section 240 is to be read as a reference to subsection (2) of this section and, in paragraph (b), after "Chapter" there were inserted "or Part 2 of the Criminal Justice Act 1991".

(12)   In this section—

"electronic monitoring condition" means any electronic monitoring requirements imposed under section 3(6ZAA) of the Bail Act 1976 for the purpose of securing the electronic monitoring of a person's compliance with a qualifying curfew condition;

"qualifying curfew condition" means a condition of bail which requires the person granted bail to remain at one or more specified places for a total of not less than 9 hours in any given day; and

"related offence" means an offence, other than the offence for which the sentence is imposed ("offence A"), with which the offender was charged and the charge for which was founded on the same facts or evidence as offence A.

VICTIM IMPACT (PERSONAL) STATEMENTS

In *Perks* [2001] Cr App R (S) 19 the court held:

1. A sentencer must not make assumptions, unsupported by evidence, about the effects of an offence on the victim.

2. If an offence has had a particularly damaging or distressing effect upon a victim, this should be known to and taken into account by the court when passing sentence.

3. Evidence of the effects of an offence on the victim must be in proper form, a Section 9 witness statement, an expert's report or otherwise, duly served upon the defendant or his representatives prior to sentence.

4. Evidence of the victim alone should be approached with care, the more so if it relates to matters which the Defence cannot realistically be expected to investigate.

5. The opinions of the victim and the victim's close relatives on the appropriate level of sentence should not be taken into account. The court must pass what it judges to be the appropriate sentence having regard to the circumstances of the offence and of the offender subject to two exceptions:–

   (i)   Where the sentence passed on the offender is aggravating the victim's distress, the sentence may be moderated to some degree.

   (ii) Where the victim's forgiveness or unwillingness to press charges provide evidence that his or her psychological or mental suffering must be very much less than would normally be the case.

VICTIM SURCHARGE

A court must ordinarily impose a victim surcharge, currently set at £15, when fining an adult offender for an offence committed on or after 1 April 2007 (Criminal Justice Act 2003, s 161A, and SI 2007/1079). If the offender has insufficient resources the fine should be reduced in order to accommodate payment of the surcharge. If the offender's resources are insufficient to pay both the surcharge and compensation, compensation takes precedence and the surcharge can be reduced or removed entirely.

As of 1 October 2012 the following provisions will apply (SI 2012/1696):

Offenders aged 18 or over	Offenders aged under 18 years	Companies etc
a) a conditional discharge at a flat rate of £15; b) a fine at 10% of the fine value, with a minimum amount of £20 and a maximum amount of £120; c) a community sentence at a flat rate of £60; d) a suspended sentence of imprisonment or detention in a young offenders' institution at– 　i) £80 for a sentence of 6 months and below; and 　ii) £100 for a sentence of over six months but not more than 12 months; e) an immediate sentence of imprisonment or detention in a young offenders' institution (initially imposed only by a Crown Court) at- 　i) £80 for a sentence of 6 months and below 　ii) £100 for a sentence of over 6 months and up to 2 years; and 　iii) £120 for a sentence over 2 years.	a) a conditional discharge at £10; b) a fine, a Youth Rehabilitation Order or Referral Order at £15; and c) a custodial sentence of any length (initially imposed only by a Crown Court) at £20.	a) a conditional discharge at a flat rate of £15; and b) a fine at 10% of the fine value, with a minimum amount of £20 and a maximum amount of £120.

Mixed disposal: Where the defendant is dealt with in different ways (so for example a fine in relation to one offence and custody in relation to another) only one surcharge (whichever is the higher) will be paid. **Transitional provision:** A) an offender is dealt with by a court for more than one offence, and at least one of these was committed either side of the 1 October 2012 implementation date. In such cases, the surcharge will be payable if the person is fined, at a rate of £15 as specified by the 2007 Order. B) a court deals with an adult offender for more than one offence, and at least one of those offences was committed when under 18, the surcharge will be payable at the rate for under 18s.

YOUTH REHABILITATION ORDER

The Youth Rehabilitation Order (Criminal Justice and Immigration Act 2008, s 1) is the only community order available for young offenders. **Components:** An order must be made up of one or more of the following requirements (along with the options of electronic monitoring, intensive supervision and surveillance or fostering): An activity requirement (maximum 90 days, or 180 if ISSR imposed); a supervision requirement; in a case where the offender is aged 16 or 17 at the time of the conviction, an unpaid work requirement (40–240 hours); a programme requirement; an attendance centre requirement (Age 14: maximum 12 hours; 14–15: 12–24 hours; 16–17: 12–36 hours); a prohibited activity requirement; a curfew requirement (2–12 hours daily for maximum of 6 months); an exclusion requirement (maximum three months); a residence requirement; a local authority residence requirement (maximum six months or until offender aged 18 years if sooner); a mental health treatment requirement; a drug treatment requirement; a drug testing requirement; an intoxicating substance treatment requirement; an education requirement. **ISSR/ Intensive fostering**: Intensive supervision and surveillance is only for those aged 15 years and over, unless a persistent offender. Fostering is for a maximum period of 12 months or until offender aged 18 years if sooner. These requirements can only be imposed for imprisonable offences in relation to offences that are so serious that but for the imposition of such an order, custody would be the only appropriate option. **Breach**: In a YRO case a warning is required if the supervising officer finds there is a failure to comply without reasonable excuse. If following a further second warning, within the 12-month 'warned period', there is then a third failure to comply without reasonable excuse, the officer must refer the case to court for breach proceedings, although YOTs will have additional discretion in exceptional circumstances following a third failure to comply. The officer also has the discretion to refer the case to court at an earlier warning stage. When dealing with the breach of a YRO, the court has the following options: no action; fine; amend the YRO, but not with ISSR or Intensive Fostering unless that already applies; revoke the YRO and resentence. Custody is an option for breach of a YRO only if the original offence is imprisonable or in the case of a non-imprisonable offence if, following 'wilful and persistent' non-compliance, a YRO with an ISSR or Intensive Fostering provision is made and that further YRO is then also subject to non-compliance (in this instance a maximum 4 month detention and training order can be imposed). Persistent breach is where there have been 3 breaches resulting in an appearance before the court. The court, if passing a custodial sentence, must state that a YRO with an ISSR or Intensive Fostering provision is not appropriate and the reasons why. This is in addition to meeting the existing criteria, ie the court forming the opinion that the offence(s) is so serious that a community sentence cannot be justified. **Expiry**: A court can only take action in relation to an order that was in force at the time the complaint (of breach) was laid. **New offence**: The commission of a new offence does not put the defendant in breach of this order, but revocation and re-sentence may be appropriate depending on how the new matter is disposed of.

Criminal Justice and Immigration Act 2008, Sch 2, para 6

(1) This paragraph applies where—

    (a) an offender appears or is brought before a youth court or other magistrates' court under paragraph 5, and

    (b) it is proved to the satisfaction of the court that the offender has failed without reasonable excuse to comply with the youth rehabilitation order.

(2) The court may deal with the offender in respect of that failure in any one of the following ways—

    (a) by ordering the offender to pay a fine of an amount not exceeding—

        (i) £250, if the offender is aged under 14, or

        (ii) £1,000, in any other case;

    (b) by amending the terms of the youth rehabilitation order so as to impose any requirement which could have been included in the order when it was made—

        (i) in addition to, or

        (ii) in substitution for,

any requirement or requirements already imposed by the order;

    (c) by dealing with the offender, for the offence in respect of which the order was made, in any way in which the court could have dealt with the offender for that offence (had the offender been before that court to be dealt with for it).

(3) Sub-paragraph (2)(b) is subject to sub-paragraphs (6) to (9).

(4) In dealing with the offender under sub-paragraph (2), the court must take into account the extent to which the offender has complied with the youth rehabilitation order.

(5) A fine imposed under sub-paragraph (2)(a) is to be treated, for the purposes of any enactment, as being a sum adjudged to be paid by a conviction.

(6) Any requirement imposed under sub-paragraph (2)(b) must be capable of being complied with before the date specified under paragraph 32(1) of Schedule 1.

(7) Where—

    (a) the court is dealing with the offender under sub-paragraph (2)(b), and

    (b) the youth rehabilitation order does not contain an unpaid work requirement,

paragraph 10(2) of Schedule 1 applies in relation to the inclusion of such a requirement as if for '40' there were substituted '20'.

(8) The court may not under sub-paragraph (2)(b) impose—

    (a) an extended activity requirement, or

    (b) a fostering requirement,

if the order does not already impose such a requirement.

(9) Where—

    (a) the order imposes a fostering requirement (the 'original requirement'), and

    (b) under sub-paragraph (2)(b) the court proposes to substitute a new fostering requirement ('the substitute requirement') for the original requirement,

paragraph 18(2) of Schedule 1 applies in relation to the substitute requirement as if the reference to the period of 12 months beginning with the date on which the original requirement first had effect were a reference to the period of 18 months beginning with that date.

PART C PRE-TRIAL

ABUSE OF PROCESS

Burden of proof: The burden of proof falls upon the defendant, decided at the civil standard (*R v Telford Justices ex p Badhan* (1991) 93 Cr App R 171), although it is a power to be exercised only sparingly.

Delay: It is almost inconceivable that delay will found a proper basis to say proceedings in the magistrates' court. In *Attorney-General's Reference (No 1 of 1990)* [1992] QB 630 the court held:

> "Firstly, it is for the defence to prove, on the balance of probabilities, that the continuation of the proceedings would amount to an abuse of the process of the Court and should therefore be stayed.
>
> Secondly, stays of proceedings in such circumstances should be the exception rather than the rule, and where the application for a stay is based on delay a stay should be an exception rather than the rule even if the stay could be said to be unjustifiable. Still more rarely should a stay be imposed in the absence of any fault on the part of the complainant. No stay should be imposed unless the defendant shows, on the balance of probabilities, that because of the delay he will suffer serious prejudice to the extent that no fair trial can be held.
>
> The third proposition of law that seems to me to arise from the authorities is that the judge considering an application to stay of this kind may have regard to his powers to exclude evidence, to give appropriate directions to the jury about the delay, and in particular to give directions to the jury about the difficulties which the delay has presented to the defence.
>
> The fourth relevant proposition of law, as it seems to me, is that the judge may also take into account the extent to which a prosecution case depends on contemporaneous documents. The more it does so, the more difficult it will be for a defendant to establish that an indictment will be stayed.
>
> Fifthly, where delay results from the reticence of an alleged victim in reporting an allegation of sexual abuse, one is entitled to adopt an understanding attitude towards the difficulties that can be encountered by such witnesses in making complaints about sexual abuse."

A seemingly more liberal approach was taken in *R (Flaherty) v City of Westminster Magistrates' Court* [2008] EWHC 2589 (Admin) where a delay of 2 years (effectively inactivity of the prosecution) during enforcement proceedings was held to amount to an abuse of process, and in *Ali v CPS* [2007] EWCA Crim 691 where a delay of 7 years was sufficient to support a stay for abuse where documentary evidence pertinent to the complainant's credibility had been lost.

Failure to preserve evidence: In *R (Ebrahim) v Feltham Magistrates' Court* [2001] EWHC 130 (Admin) the court held:

"We would suggest that in similar cases in future, a court should structure its inquiries in the following way:

(1) In the circumstances of the particular case, what was the nature and extent of the investigating authorities' and the prosecutors' duty, if any, to obtain and/or retain the videotape evidence in question? Recourse should be had in this context to the contents of the 1997 code and the Attorney-General's guidelines.

(2) If in all the circumstances there was no duty to obtain and/or retain that videotape evidence before the defence first sought its retention, then there can be no question of the subsequent trial being unfair on this ground.

(3) If such evidence is not obtained and/or retained in breach of the obligations set out in the code and/or the guidelines, then the principles set out in paragraphs 25 and 28 of this judgment should generally be applied.

(4) If the behaviour of the prosecution has been so very bad that it is not fair that the defendant should be tried, then the proceedings should be stayed on that ground. The test in paragraph 23 of this judgment is a useful one.

We would add the following two matters by way of procedural guidance:

(5) If a complaint of this type is raised on an appeal by a defendant from his conviction on the magistrates' court, he should not apply for the proceedings to be stayed. He should apply for an order allowing his appeal and quashing his conviction on the grounds that the original trial was unfair and the unfairness was of such a nature that it cannot now be remedied on appeal.

(6) If a ruling on a stay application is made in a lower court, the court should give its reasons, however briefly, and it is the professional duty of the advocates for the parties to take a note of these. If the decision is to be challenged on judicial review, this court will expect to see a note of the lower court's reasons before deciding whether to grant permission for the application to proceed. If any relevant oral evidence was given, this court will hope that an agreed note can be prepared, summarising its effect."

Manipulation, abuse or misuse of court process: A magistrates' court has no power to adjudicate on this issue, proceedings should be stayed (if necessary) pending judicial review.

Promise not to prosecute: An offer of a caution is not a bar to future prosecution (*Hayter v L* [1998] 1 WLR 854), unless accompanied by a clear assurance that no prosecution will follow (eg *Jones v Whalley* [2006] UKHL 41; *R (H) v Guildford Youth Court* [2008] EWHC 506 (Admin)). A decision of counsel, communicated to the defendant, that a charge would be dropped, could not lawfully be reversed by the CPS at a later time, even where the initial decision was made without authority (*Bloomfield* [1997] 1 Cr App R 135). **Vexatious or hopelessly misconceived prosecution:** eg *R (Craik) v Newcastle Upon Tyne Magistrates' Court* [2010] EWHC 935 (Admin).

General principles: An abuse of process arises when (*Maxwell* [2010] UKSC 48):

"It is well established that the court has the power to stay proceedings in two categories of case, namely (i) where it will be impossible to give the accused a fair trial, and (ii) where it offends the court's sense of justice and propriety to be asked to try the accused in the particular circumstances of the case. In the first category of case, if the court concludes that an accused cannot receive a fair trial, it will stay the proceedings without more. No question of the balancing of competing interests arises. In the second category of case, the court is concerned to protect the integrity of the criminal justice system. Here a stay will be granted where the court concludes that in all the circumstances a trial will "offend the court's sense of justice and propriety" (per Lord Lowry in R v Horseferry Road Magistrates' Court, Ex p Bennett [1994] 1 AC 42, 74G) or will "undermine public confidence in the criminal justice system and bring it into disrepute" (per Lord Steyn in R v Latif and Shahzad [1996] 1 WLR 104, 112F).

In Latif at page 112H, Lord Steyn said that the law in relation to the second category of case was "settled". As he put it:

"The law is settled. Weighing countervailing considerations of policy and justice, it is for the judge in the exercise of his discretion to decide whether there has been an abuse of process, which amounts to an affront to the public conscience and requires the criminal proceedings to be stayed: R v. Horseferry Road Magistrates' Court, Ex p Bennett [1994] 1 A.C. 42 Ex p Bennett was a case where a stay was appropriate because a defendant had been forcibly abducted and brought to this country to face trial in disregard of extradition laws. The speeches in Ex p Bennett conclusively establish that proceedings may be stayed in the exercise of the judge's discretion not only where a fair trial is impossible but also where it would be contrary to the public interest in the integrity of the criminal justice system that a trial should take place. An infinite variety of cases could arise. General guidance as to how the discretion should be exercised in particular circumstances will not be useful. But it is possible to say that in a case such as the present the judge must weigh in the balance the public interest in ensuring that those that are charged with grave crimes should be tried and the competing public interest in not conveying the impression that the court will adopt the approach that the end justifies any means." "

Procedure: A magistrates' court may determine the first category of abuse only, if an argument arises in relation to the second category, the matter must be litigated by way of judicial review (*R v Horseferry Road Magistrates' Court ex p Bennett* (1994) 98 Cr App R 114).

ADJOURNMENTS

General approach: In *Crown Prosecution Service v Picton* [2006] EWHC 1108 (Admin) the court laid down the following general approach:

(1) A decision whether to adjourn is a decision within the discretion of the trial court. An appellate court will interfere only if very clear grounds for doing so are shown.

(2) Magistrates should pay great attention to the need for expedition in the prosecution of criminal proceedings; delays are scandalous; they bring the law into disrepute; summary justice should be speedy justice; an application for an adjournment should be rigorously scrutinized.

(3) Where an adjournment is sought by the prosecution, magistrates must consider both the interest of the defendant in getting the matter dealt with, and the interest of the public that criminal charges should be adjudicated upon: the guilty convicted as well as the innocent acquitted. With a more serious charge, the public interest that there be a trial will carry greater weight.

(4) Where an adjournment is sought by the accused, the magistrates must consider whether, if it is not granted, the accused will be able fully to present his defence and, if he will not be able to do so, the degree to which his ability to do so is compromised.

(5) In considering the competing interests of the parties, the magistrates should examine the likely consequences of the proposed adjournment, in particular, its likely length, and the need to decide the facts while recollections are fresh.

(6) The reason that the adjournment is required should be examined and, if it arises through the fault of the party asking for the adjournment, that is a factor against granting the adjournment, carrying weight in accordance with the gravity of the fault. If that party was not at fault, then that may favour an adjournment. Likewise, if the party opposing the adjournment has been at fault, then that will favour an adjournment.

(7) The magistrates should take appropriate account of the history of the case, and whether there have been earlier adjournments and at whose request and why.

(8) Lastly, of course, the factors to be considered cannot be comprehensively stated but depend upon the particular circumstances of each case, and they will often overlap. The court's duty is to do justice between the parties in the circumstances as they have arisen.

Entitlement to adjourn?: In *Aravinthan Visvaratnam v Brent Magistrates' Court* [2009] EWHC 3017 (Admin) the court made these observations:

"The prosecution must not think that they are always allowed at least one application to adjourn the case. If that idea were to gain currency, no trial would ever start on the first date set for trial.

So these are the competing considerations. I have no doubt that there is a high public interest in trials taking place on the date set for trial, and that trials should not be adjourned unless there is a good and compelling reason to do so. The sooner the prosecution understand this—that they cannot rely on their own serious failures properly to warn witnesses—the sooner the efficiency in the Magistrates' Court system improves. An improvement in timeliness and the achievement of a more effective and efficient system of criminal justice in the Magistrates' Court will bring about great benefits to victims and to witnesses and huge savings in time and money."

Adequate time to prepare case: In *Thames Magistrates' Court ex p Polemis* [1974] 1 WLR 1371 the court held:

"...the opportunity to present a case to the court is not confined to being given an opportunity to stand up and say what you want to say; it necessarily extends to a reasonable opportunity to prepare your case before you are called upon to present it. A mere allocation of court time is of no value if the party in question is deprived of the opportunity of getting his tackle in order and being able to present his case in the fullest sense."

Case management principles: Where a defendant was unable, through no fault of his own, to call an important witness, an adjournment should be granted to give an opportunity for that witness to be traced and steps taken to secure attendance (*Khurshied v Peterborough Magistrates' Court* [2009] EWHC 1136 (Admin)). In *Essen v Director of Public Prosecutions* [2005] EWHC 1077 (Admin), the court was concerned with a failure of the CPS, due to administrative error, to warn its witnesses for trial. The court held that in the absence of some other counterprevailing factor an adjournment ought not to be granted. The fact that a crime may go unpunished is not sufficient as:

"In that case no prosecutor, however dilatory, need attend to the requirement to be ready for trial on the set date ... The prejudice to the defendant [of an adjournment in those circumstances] was manifest. The CPS had no ground for seeking clemency. It was the sole author of its own misfortune."

A prosecutor should always be given some time to make inquiries as to why a witness is not present (*R v Swansea Justices, ex p Director of Public Prosecutions* The Times, 30 March 1990). If the prosecution has failed to carry out its statutory duties in relation to disclosure under the Criminal Procedure and Investigations Act 1996, an adjournment should be granted to the defence (*Swash v Director of Public Prosecutions* [2009] EWHC 803 (Admin)). A failure to make proper inquiry into a defendant's absence, which had it been carried out would have led to the adjournment of the matter, will result in any resulting conviction following trial in absence being quashed (*R (James) v Tower Bridge Magistrates' Court*, unreported, 9 June 2009, DC).

Where a defendant provides a medical note in relation to non-attendance, a court should give reasons for finding such medical excuses spurious, it being rarely if ever appropriate to reject a medical certificate (even if not meeting the normal requirements as to information required) without first giving the defendant an opportunity to respond (*Evans v East Lancashire Magistrates' Court* [2010] EWHC 2108 (Admin)).

In *R v Bolton Magistrates' Court, ex p Merna* [1991] Crim LR 848 the court said:

"If the court suspects the [medical] grounds to be spurious or believes them to be inadequate, the court should ordinarily express its doubts and thereby give the defendant an opportunity to seek to resolve the doubts. It may call for better evidence, require further inquiries to be made or adopt any other expedient fair to both parties. The ultimate test must always be one of fairness and if a defendant claims to be ill with apparently responsible professional support for his claim, the court should not reject that claim and proceed to hear the case in a defendant's absence without satisfying itself that the claim may properly be rejected and that no unfairness will thereby be done."

If a defendant raises matters for the first time in the proceedings (so-called 'ambush defences'), the court is fully justified in adjourning the matter in order to allow the prosecution to properly deal with them (eg *R (Lawson) v Stratford Magistrates' Court* [2007] EWHC 2490 (Admin) where compliance with signage regulations in relation to a prosecution for speeding were raised for the first time in cross-examination). In *R (Taylor) v Southampton Magistrates' Court*, unreported, 18 November 2008 it was held that during a trial for failing to comply with a notice under section 172 of the Road Traffic Act 1988, a District Judge was right to adjourn the case in order for the prosecution to be able to gather evidence (if such evidence existed) to prove service of the notice. There was no question of bias even though the court acted of its own motion. What is interesting about this case is that there was no issue of 'ambush', the prosecution having not only been put to proof of all issues, but the specific issue having been raised. That was not enough for the court in this instance, in the absence of a positive defence case that the notice had not in fact been served.

ALLOCATION, COMMITTAL, SENDING AND TRANSFER–OLD PROVISIONS

Note: On 18 June 2012 substantial changes to these provisions took effect in 12 criminal justices areas. See the next section for those revisions.

Youths: See Part F Allocation, Committal, Sending and Transfer.

Overview: In the following instances the court may decline or be deprived of jurisdiction to try a matter:

- indictable only matters—sent to the Crown Court;
- either-way matters where jurisdiction is declined or the defendant has elected Crown Court trial (plea before venue procedure) —committed to the Crown Court;
- transfer cases—transferred to the Crown Court;
- voluntary bill of indictment (not covered in this book).

Method:	Notes:
Committal proceedings. Section 6 of the Magistrates' Courts Act 1980	Committal can be by consent if a prima facie case (s 6(2)), or via contested hearing (s 6(1)). No right to require oral evidence and no defence evidence allowed. Court has no discretion to exclude evidence under Police and Criminal Evidence Act 1984, ss 76, 78. The court may commit on any indictable offence (although if different from the one charged it may proceed if it wishes to try the matter summarily: *R v Cambridge Justices, ex p Fraser* [1985] 1 All ER 668). Court can also commit summary offences to be tried on the indictment, eg common assault (Criminal Justice Act 1988, s 40).
	Court can commit other summary offences if they are imprisonable or carry discretionary or obligatory disqualification from driving (Criminal Justice Act 1988, s 41). Provided the defendant is represented the case can be committed in his absence (*R v Liverpool Magistrates' Court, ex p Quantrell* [1999] Crim LR 734).
Sending. Section 51, 51A of the Crime and Disorder Act 1998	The court will send the indictable only matter, along with any related either-way matters. This may involve sending one or more co-defendants. Note: A sending is not a remand within the meaning of ss 128, 128A MCA 1980, and therefore the initial 8 day limitation on a remand in custody does not apply.
	An either-way offence is related to an indictable offence if the charge for the either-way offence could be joined in the same indictment as the charge for the indictable offence. A summary offence is related to an indictable offence if it arises out of circumstances which are the same as or connected with those giving rise to the indictable offence. The court can also send related summary offences if they are imprisonable or carry discretionary or obligatory disqualification from driving. It does not

	matter that all matters are not sent on the same occasion. In the case of a youth charged with an adult (not necessarily on the same occasion), the youth will be sent if it is in the interests of justice to try him with the adult. There is no power to send a case to the Crown Court in the absence of a defendant, even if that person is legally represented.
Transfer cases.	Applicable to fraud cases (Criminal Justice Act 1987, s 4) and child cases (Criminal Justice Act 1991, s 53).

Plea before venue:

Magistrates' Courts Act 1980, ss 17A, 17B, 17D

17A.— Initial procedure: accused to indicate intention as to plea.

(1) This section shall have effect where a person who has attained the age of 18 years appears or is brought before a magistrates' court on an information charging him with an offence triable either way.

(2) Everything that the court is required to do under the following provisions of this section must be done with the accused present in court.

(3) The court shall cause the charge to be written down, if this has not already been done, and to be read to the accused.

(4) The court shall then explain to the accused in ordinary language that he may indicate whether (if the offence were to proceed to trial) he would plead guilty or not guilty, and that if he indicates that he would plead guilty—

    (a) the court must proceed as mentioned in subsection (6) below; and

    (b) he may be committed for sentence to the Crown Court under section 3 of the Powers of Criminal Courts (Sentencing) Act 2000 below if the court is of such opinion as is mentioned in subsection (2) of that section.

(5) The court shall then ask the accused whether (if the offence were to proceed to trial) he would plead guilty or not guilty.

(6) If the accused indicates that he would plead guilty the court shall proceed as if—

    (a) the proceedings constituted from the beginning the summary trial of the information; and

    (b) section 9(1) above was complied with and he pleaded guilty under it.

(7) If the accused indicates that he would plead not guilty section 18(1) below shall apply.

(8) If the accused in fact fails to indicate how he would plead, for the purposes of this section and section 18(1) below he shall be taken to indicate that he would plead not guilty.

(9) Subject to subsection (6) above, the following shall not for any purpose be taken to constitute the taking of a plea—

    (a) asking the accused under this section whether (if the offence were to proceed to trial) he would plead guilty or not guilty;

    (b) an indication by the accused under this section of how he would plead.

17B.— Intention as to plea: absence of accused.

(1) This section shall have effect where—

    (a) a person who has attained the age of 18 years appears or is brought before a magistrates' court on an information charging him with an offence triable either way.

    (b) the accused is represented by a legal representative,

    (c) the court considers that by reason of the accused's disorderly conduct before the court it is not practicable for proceedings under section 17A above to be conducted in his presence, and

    (d) the court considers that it should proceed in the absence of the accused.

(2) In such a case—

(a) the court shall cause the charge to be written down, if this has not already been done, and to be read to the representative;

(b) the court shall ask the representative whether (if the offence were to proceed to trial) the accused would plead guilty or not guilty;

(c) if the representative indicates that the accused would plead guilty the court shall proceed as if the proceedings constituted from the beginning the summary trial of the information, and as if section 9(1) above was complied with and the accused pleaded guilty under it;

(d) if the representative indicates that the accused would plead not guilty section 18(1) below shall apply.

(3) If the representative in fact fails to indicate how the accused would plead, for the purposes of this section and section 18(1) below he shall be taken to indicate that the accused would plead not guilty.

(4) Subject to subsection (2)(c) above, the following shall not for any purpose be taken to constitute the taking of a plea—

(a) asking the representative under this section whether (if the offence were to proceed to trial) the accused would plead guilty or not guilty;

(b) an indication by the representative under this section of how the accused would plead.

17D Maximum penalty under section 17A(6) or 17B(2)(c) for certain offences

(1) If—

(a) the offence is a scheduled offence (as defined in section 22(1) below);

(b) the court proceeds in relation to the offence in accordance with section 17A(6) or 17B(2)(c) above; and

(c) the court convicts the accused of the offence,

the court shall consider whether, having regard to any representations made by him or by the prosecutor, the value involved (as defined in section 22(10) below) appears to the court to exceed the relevant sum (as specified for the purposes of section 22 below).

(2) If it appears to the court clear that the value involved does not exceed the relevant sum, or it appears to the court for any reason not clear whether the value involved does or does not exceed the relevant sum—

(a) subject to subsection (4) below, the court shall not have power to impose on the accused in respect of the offence a sentence in excess of the limits mentioned in section 33(1)(a) below; and

(b) sections 3 and 4 of the Powers of Criminal Courts (Sentencing) Act 2000 shall not apply as regards that offence.

(3) Subsections (9) to (12) of section 22 below shall apply for the purposes of this section as they apply for the purposes of that section (reading the reference to subsection (1) in section 22(9) as a reference to subsection (1) of this section).

(4) Subsection (2)(a) above does not apply to an offence under section 12A of the Theft Act 1968 (aggravated vehicle-taking).

Plea before venue: following an indication of not guilty:

Magistrates' Courts Act 1980, ss 18-20

18.— Initial procedure on information against adult for offence triable either way.

(1) Sections 19 to 23 below shall have effect where a person who has attained the age of 18 years appears or is brought before a magistrates' court on an information charging him with an offence triable either way and—

355

    (a) he indicates under section 17A above that (if the offence were to proceed to trial) he would plead not guilty, or

    (b) his representative indicates under section 17B above that (if the offence were to proceed to trial) he would plead not guilty.

(2) Without prejudice to section 11(1) above, everything that the court is required to do under sections 19 to 22 below must be done before any evidence is called and, subject to subsection (3) below and section 23 below, with the accused present in court.

(3) The court may proceed in the absence of the accused in accordance with such of the provisions of sections 19 to 22 below as are applicable in the circumstances if the court considers that by reason of his disorderly conduct before the court it is not practicable for the proceedings to be conducted in his presence; and subsections (3) to (5) of section 23 below, so far as applicable, shall have effect in relation to proceedings conducted in the absence of the accused by virtue of this subsection (references in those subsections to the person representing the accused being for this purpose read as references to the person, if any, representing him).

(4) A magistrates' court proceeding under sections 19 to 23 below may adjourn the proceedings at any time, and on doing so on any occasion when the accused is present may remand the accused, and shall remand him if—

    (a) on the occasion on which he first appeared, or was brought, before the court to answer to the information he was in custody or, having been released on bail, surrendered to the custody of the court; or

    (b) he has been remanded at any time in the course of proceedings on the information;

and where the court remands the accused, the time fixed for the resumption of the proceedings shall be that at which he is required to appear or be brought before the court in pursuance of the remand or would be required to be brought before the court but for section 128(3A) below.

(5) The functions of a magistrates' court under sections 19 to 23 below may be discharged by a single justice, but the foregoing provision shall not be taken to authorise the summary trial of an information by a magistrates' court composed of less than two justices.

19.— Court to begin by considering which mode of trial appears more suitable.

(1) The court shall consider whether, having regard to the matters mentioned in subsection (3) below and any representations made by the prosecutor or the accused, the offence appears to the court more suitable for summary trial or for trial on indictment.

(2) Before so considering, the court—

[...]

    (b) shall afford first the prosecutor and then the accused an opportunity to make representations as to which mode of trial would be more suitable.

(3) The matters to which the court is to have regard under subsection (1) above are the nature of the case; whether the circumstances make the offence one of serious character; whether the punishment which a magistrates' court would have power to inflict for it would be adequate; and any other circumstances which appear to the court to make it more suitable for the offence to be tried in one way rather than the other.

(4) If the prosecution is being carried on by the Attorney General, the Solicitor General or the Director of Public Prosecutions and he applies for the offence to be tried on indictment, the preceding provisions of this section and sections 20 and 21 below shall not apply, and the court shall proceed to inquire into the information as examining justices.

(5) The power of the Director of Public Prosecutions under subsection (4) above to apply for an offence to be tried on indictment shall not be exercised except with the consent of the Attorney General.

20.— Procedure where summary trial appears more suitable.

(1) If, where the court has considered as required by section 19(1) above, it appears to the court that the offence is more suitable for summary trial, the following provisions of this section shall apply (unless excluded by section 23 below).

(2) The court shall explain to the accused in ordinary language—

   (a) that it appears to the court more suitable for him to be tried summarily for the offence, and that he can either consent to be so tried or, if he wishes, be tried by a jury; and

   (b) that if he is tried summarily and is convicted by the court, he may be committed for sentence to the Crown Court under section 3 of the Powers of Criminal Courts (Sentencing) Act 2000 if the convicting court, is of such opinion as is mentioned in subsection (2) of that section.

(3) After explaining to the accused as provided by subsection (2) above the court shall ask him whether he consents to be tried summarily or wishes to be tried by a jury, and—

   (a) if he consents to be tried summarily, shall proceed to the summary trial of the information;

   (b) if he does not so consent, shall proceed to inquire into the information as examining justices.

21. Procedure where trial on indictment appears more suitable.

If, where the court has considered as required by section 19(1) above, it appears to the court that the offence is more suitable for trial on indictment, the court shall tell the accused that the court has decided that it is more suitable for him to be tried for the offence by a jury, and shall proceed to inquire into the information as examining justices.

Crime and Disorder Act 1998, s 51

(1) Where an adult appears or is brought before a magistrates' court ("the court") charged with an offence triable only on indictment ("the indictable-only offence"), the court shall send him forthwith to the Crown Court for trial—

   (a) for that offence, and

   (b) for any either-way or summary offence with which he is charged which fulfils the requisite conditions (as set out in subsection (11) below).

(2) Where an adult who has been sent for trial under subsection (1) above subsequently appears or is brought before a magistrates' court charged with an either-way or summary offence which fulfils the requisite conditions, the court may send him forthwith to the Crown Court for trial for the either-way or summary offence.

(3) Where—

   (a) the court sends an adult for trial under subsection (1) above;

   (b) another adult appears or is brought before the court on the same or a subsequent occasion charged jointly with him with an either-way offence; and

   (c) that offence appears to the court to be related to the indictable-only offence,

the court shall where it is the same occasion, and may where it is a subsequent occasion, send the other adult forthwith to the Crown Court for trial for the either-way offence.

(4) Where a court sends an adult for trial under subsection (3) above, it shall at the same time send him to the Crown Court for trial for any either-way or summary offence with which he is charged which fulfils the requisite conditions.

(5) Where—

   (a) the court sends an adult for trial under subsection (1) or (3) above; and

   (b) a child or young person appears or is brought before the court on the same or a subsequent occasion charged jointly with the adult with an indictable offence for which the adult is sent for trial, the court shall, if it considers it necessary in the interests of justice to do so, send the child or young person forthwith to the Crown Court for trial for the indictable offence.

(6) Where a court sends a child or young person for trial under subsection (5) above, it may at the same time send him to the Crown Court for trial for any either-way or summary offence with which he is charged which fulfils the requisite conditions.

(7) The court shall specify in a notice the offence or offences for which a person is sent for trial under this section and the place at which he is to be tried; and a copy of the notice shall be served on the accused and given to the Crown Court sitting at that place.

(8) In a case where there is more than one indictable-only offence and the court includes an either-way or a summary offence in the notice under subsection (7) above, the court shall specify in that notice the indictable-only offence to which the either-way offence or, as the case may be, the summary offence appears to the court to be related.

(9) The trial of the information charging any summary offence for which a person is sent for trial under this section shall be treated as if the court had adjourned it under section 10 of the 1980 Act and had not fixed the time and place for its resumption.

(10) In selecting the place of trial for the purpose of subsection (7) above, the court shall have regard to—

(a) the convenience of the defence, the prosecution and the witnesses;

(b) the desirability of expediting the trial; and

(c) any direction given by or on behalf of the Lord Chief Justice with the concurrence of the Lord Chancellor under section 75(1) of the Supreme Court Act 1981.

(11) An offence fulfils the requisite conditions if—

(a) if appears to the court to be related to the indictable-only offence; and

(b) in the case of a summary offence, it is punishable with imprisonment or involves obligatory or discretionary disqualification from driving.

(12) For the purposes of this section—

(a) "adult" means a person aged 18 or over, and references to an adult include references to a corporation;

(b) "either-way offence" means an offence which, if committed by an adult, is triable either on indictment or summarily;

(c) an either-way offence is related to an indictable-only offence if the charge for the either-way offence could be joined in the same indictment as the charge for the indictable-only offence;

(d) a summary offence is related to an indictable-only offence if it arises out of circumstances which are the same as or connected with those giving rise to the indictable-only offence.

Magistrates' Courts Act 1980, s 6

(1) A magistrates' court inquiring into an offence as examining justices shall on consideration of the evidence—

(a) commit the accused for trial if it is of opinion that there is sufficient evidence to put him on trial by jury for any indictable offence;

(b) discharge him if it is not of that opinion and he is in custody for no other cause than the offence under inquiry;

but the preceding provisions of this subsection have effect subject to the provisions of this and any other Act relating to the summary trial of indictable offences.

(2) If a magistrates' court inquiring into an offence as examining justices is satisfied that all the evidence tendered by or on behalf of the prosecutor falls within section 5A(3) above, it may commit the accused for trial for the offence without consideration of the contents of any statements, depositions or other documents, and without consideration of any exhibits which are not documents, unless—

(a) the accused or one of the accused has no legal representative acting for him in the case, or

(b) a legal representative for the accused or one of the accused, as the case may be, has requested the court to consider a submission that there is insufficient evidence to put that accused on trial by jury for the offence;

and subsection (1) above shall not apply to a committal for trial under this subsection.

(3) Subject to section 4 of the Bail Act 1976 and section 41 below, the court may commit a person for trial—

(a) in custody, that is to say, by committing him to custody there to be safety kept until delivered in due course of law, or

(b) on bail in accordance with the Bail Act 1976, that is to say, by directing him to appear before the Crown Court for trial;

and where his release on bail is conditional on his providing one or more surety or sureties and, in accordance with section 8(3) of the Bail Act 1976, the court fixes the amount in which the surety is to be bound with a view to his entering into his recognizance subsequently in accordance with subsections (4) and (5) or (6) of that section the court shall in the meantime commit the accused to custody in accordance with paragraph (a) of this subsection.

(4) Where the court has committed a person to custody in accordance with paragraph (a) of subsection (3) above, then, if that person is in custody for no other cause, the court may, at any time before his first appearance before the Crown Court, grant him bail in accordance with the Bail Act 1976 subject to a duty to appear before the Crown Court for trial.

(5) Where a magistrates' court acting as examining justices commits any person for trial or determines to discharge him, the designated officer for the court shall, on the day on which the committal proceedings are concluded or the next day, cause to be displayed in a part of the court house to which the public have access a notice—

(a) in either case giving that person's name, address, and age (if known);

(b) in a case where the court so commits him, stating the charge or charges on which he is committed and the court to which he is committed;

(c) in a case where the court determines to discharge him, describing the offence charged and stating that it has so determined;

but this subsection shall have effect subject to section 4 of the Sexual Offences (Amendment) Act 1976 (anonymity of complainant in rape etc. cases).

(6) A notice displayed in pursuance of subsection (5) above shall not contain the name or address of any person under the age of 18 years unless the justices in question have stated that in their opinion he would be mentioned in the notice apart from the preceding provisions of this subsection and should be mentioned in it for the purpose of avoiding injustice to him.

ALLOCATION, COMMITTAL, SENDING AND TRANSFER–NEW PROVISIONS

Note: The provisions in this section apply only in these criminal justice areas as of 18 June 2012 (see section above for provisions operating in all other areas). The guidance in this section is largely drawn from training materials issued to justices clerks (© Copyright):

Bath and Wansdyke; Berkshire; Bristol; Liverpool and Knowsley; North Avon; North Hampshire; North Somerset; Ormskirk; Sefton; St Helens; Wigan and Leigh; and Wirral.

Youths: See Part F Allocation, Committal, Sending and Transfer.

Overview: See the end of this section for an overview flowchart.

Cases that must be sent forthwith:

The following offences must be sent for trial to the crown court forthwith. There is no plea before venue procedure to be undertaken.

(1)   Indictable only offences (Crime and Disorder Act 1998, s 51(2)(a)).

(2)   Offences for which a notice is served–serious or complex fraud cases (Crime and Disorder Act 1998, s 51B), or certain cases involving children (Crime and Disorder Act 1998, s 51C).

(3)   Either-way offences related to an indictable-only offence, or one covered by a notice under section 51B or 51C CDA 1998, in respect to the same defendant is being sent to the crown court (Crime and Disorder Act 1998, s 50A(3)(a)). Where a defendant is sent to the Crown Court for trial for an indictable-only offence, or for an offence in respect of which notice has been given under ss.51B or 51C CDA 1998, the court must at the same time send them for trial for any either-way offence which appears to the court to be related. However, where the defendant appears on the related either-way charge on a subsequent occasion, the court may send them for trial.

Note: Related summary offences must likewise be sent in such circumstances if the offence "is punishable with imprisonment or involves obligatory or discretionary disqualification from driving". This raises the question as to whether all offences are now punishable with discretionary disqualification. Compare this with s.6 PCC(S)A 2000 which specifically refers to disqualification imposed under the Road Traffic Offenders Act 1988.

(4)   Either-way offence related to an indictable-only offence, or one covered by a notice under s.51B or s.51C CDA 1998, in respect of which another defendant is being sent to the Crown Court–s.50A(3)(a) CDA 1998 and r.9.7 CrimPR 2011. Where an adult defendant A is sent to the Crown Court for trial under s.51(2)(a) or (c) CDA 1998, and defendant B is jointly charged with an either-way offence which is related to the indictable-only or 'notice' offence for which A is sent, the court must at the same time send B for trial for the either-way offence. Related summary offences must likewise be sent in such circumstances if the offence "is punishable with imprisonment or involves obligatory or discretionary disqualification from driving" (see note at (3) above). However, if adult B appears before the court on a subsequent occasion to A, the court may send B to the Crown Court for trial.

Plea before venue for either-way offences

With the exception of (2)–(4) above, all other either-way offences are dealt with by way of the plea before venue procedure. If the case is to be tried at the crown court, the case will be sent for trial as all committal proceedings are abolished in the 12 pilot areas.

(a)   *Plea before venue under s.17A MCA 1980–s.50A(3)(b) CDA 1998*

The allegation should be put to the defendant, who should be informed of the plea before venue procedure, warned of the possibility of committal for sentence and asked whether they intend to plead guilty. This will be under s.3 PCC(S)A 2000 on the basis that the Crown Court should, in the court's opinion, have the power to deal with the offender in any way it could deal with them if they had been convicted on indictment. It could also be under s.3A PCC(S)A 2000 where applicable (defendant convicted of a specified offence and the court considers that the defendant qualifies for a sentence of imprisonment for public protection or an extended sentence because of the significant risk to the public of serious harm from the commission of further specified offences by the defendant).

If the defendant indicates a guilty plea, they are treated as having been tried summarily and convicted. The court may then commit for sentence under s.3 or (where applicable) must commit under s.3A PCC(S)A 2000.

However, where the defendant is charged with offences relating to criminal damage the court must consider whether the value of the damage exceeds the relevant sum (£5,000). If it appears that the value involved does not exceed the relevant sum, or it is not clear whether the value involved exceeds the relevant sum, the court cannot commit for sentence under ss.3 or 4 PCC(S) A 2000, and is restricted to the maximum sentence specified in s.33 MCA 1980. The provisions under s.17D MCA 1980 do not apply to offences of aggravated vehicle-taking (s.17D(4)).

Section 17B MCA 1980 provides that the plea before venue procedure may take place in the absence of a legally represented defendant, if it is not practicable for the proceedings to be conducted in the defendant's presence by reason of their disorderly conduct. The matters will be put to, and pleas taken from, the legal representative.

(b) Indication of a not guilty plea in certain circumstances–s.50A(3)(b) CDA 1998

Where there is an indication of a not guilty plea in the following circumstances:

- the defendant is sent to the Crown Court for trial for a related offence;
- the defendant is charged jointly with another adult defendant who is sent to the Crown Court for trial for a related offence (see s.50A(3)(b)(iii)(a) and s. 51(5) CDA 1998). This changes the current position and reverse the decision in *Nicholls v Brentwoood Justices'* (1992) 1 AC that a defendant who consents to summary trial should be so tried even where a co-defendant has elected Crown Court trial. The court will now send to the Crown Court for trial all co-defendants appearing on the same occasion and pleading not guilty if any one of them elects trial on indictment. In a multi-handed case which appears suitable for summary trial, the procedure is to ask all the defendants in turn whether they consent; if one refuses, all should be sent.
- the defendant is charged jointly, or charged with a related either-way offence, with a youth defendant who is sent to the Crown Court for trial,

the court shall send the defendant to the Crown Court for trial if they appear on the same occasion, and may send the defendant to the Crown Court for trial if the defendant appears on a subsequent occasion.

(c) Decision as to allocation–s.19 MCA 1980

In all other cases where a not guilty plea is indicated or the court has declined to exercise its discretion to send to the Crown Court as in the circumstances described above, the court must determine whether the offence appears more suitable for summary trial or trial on indictment.

The court shall give the prosecution the opportunity to inform the court of the defendant's previous convictions (if any) and allow representations from both prosecution and defence. Previous convictions are defined in s.19(5).

The court shall consider:

- whether its powers of sentence would be adequate;
- any representations made by the prosecution or defence;

and shall have regard to the allocation guideline issued by the Sentencing Council.

The allocation guideline (effective from 11 June 2012) states that, in general, either-way offences should be tried summarily unless it is likely that the court's sentencing powers will be insufficient. It adds that 'the court should assess the likely sentence in the light of the facts alleged by the prosecution case, taking into account all aspects of the case including those advanced by the defence', echoing the new s.19 MCA 1980.

The *Magistrates' Court Sentencing Guidelines* for the relevant offences should be referred to when allocation decisions are being made.

(However, note that where the guideline sets out the relevant statutory provisions it refers specifically to the unamended version of s.19 MCA 1980 and to the old committal for sentence powers.)

In considering the adequacy of its sentencing powers when dealing with two or more offences, the court should consider its potential sentencing powers in the light of the maximum aggregate sentence the magistrates could impose for all the offences taken together, if the charges could be joined in the same indictment or arise out of the same or connected circumstances.

Note: the restriction under s.42 MCA 1980 on magistrates dealing with summary trial having become aware of a defendant's previous convictions during a bail hearing is abolished.

(d)   *Decision that trial on indictment appears more suitable–s.21 MCA 1980*

If the court decides that the offence appears more suitable for trial on indictment, the defendant is sent forthwith to the Crown Court.

(e)   *Decision that summary trial appears more suitable–s.20(1) and (2) MCA 1980*

If the court decides that the case is more suitable for summary trial, it must explain to the defendant that:

- the case appears suitable for summary trial;
- they can consent to be tried summarily or choose to be tried on indictment; and
- if they consent to be tried summarily and are convicted, they may be committed to the Crown Court for sentence (on the basis that the Crown Court should have the power to deal with the defendant in any way it could have done if there had been a conviction on indictment or if, in the case of a specified offence, they qualify for a sentence of imprisonment for public protection or an extended sentence).

(f)   *Indication of sentence–ss.20(3)–(7), 20A MCA 1980*

At this stage, the defendant may request an indication of sentence, i.e. an indication of whether a custodial or non-custodial sentence would be more likely if they were to be tried summarily and plead guilty. It should be no more specific.

The court may, but need not, give an indication of sentence. It would appear that the court cannot give an indication of sentence unless the defendant requests one.

If the court gives an indication of sentence, the court should ask the defendant whether they wish to reconsider the earlier indication of plea which was given.

If the defendant indicates that they wish to plead guilty, they are treated as if they had been tried summarily and pleaded guilty. In these circumstances, an indication of sentence prevents a court from imposing a custodial sentence for the offence unless either:

- the court indicated that a custodial sentence would be given;
- the defendant is committed to the Crown Court as a dangerous offender under s.3A PCC(S) A 2000; or
- the defendant is committed to the Crown Court for sentence under s.4 PCC(S)A 2000, having been committed for trial for related offences.

If the defendant does not change their plea to guilty, the indication of sentence shall not be binding on any court (whether a magistrates' court or not), and in these circumstances no sentence may be challenged or be the subject of appeal in any court because it is not consistent with an indication of sentence. Equally, an indication of a custodial sentence does not prevent the court from imposing a non-custodial sentence. Any indication as to sentence must be entered in the court register.

(g)   *No indication requested from or given by the court–s.20(8) and (9) MCA 1980*

Where the court does not give an indication of sentence, whether requested to do so or not, or the defendant does not indicate that they wish to reconsider the indication of plea or does not indicate that they would plead guilty, the court must ask the defendant whether they consent to summary trial or wish to be tried on indictment.

(h) *Defendant consents to summary trial–s.20(9)(a) MCA 1980*

If the defendant consents to summary trial, the court shall proceed to summary trial of the information.

The court's power under s.25 MCA 1980 to change from summary trial to committal proceedings and vice versa is abolished. Instead, s.25 is amended to allow the prosecution (not the defence) to make an application, before summary trial begins and before any other application or issue in relation to the summary trial is dealt with, for an either-way offence allocated for summary trial to be sent to the Crown Court for trial. This would suggest that, for example, once an application for special measures has been determined, or there has been a pre-trial binding ruling in respect of evidence of bad character, the court is precluded from hearing such an application. The court may grant the application "only if it is satisfied that the sentence which a magistrates' court would have power to impose for the offence would be inadequate." This suggests that the provision will be used where the prosecution becomes aware of information making the offence more serious than was first realised. Where there is a successful application by the prosecution for the offence to be tried on indictment, the case will be sent forthwith to the Crown Court for trial.

(i) *Defendant does not consent to summary trial–s.20(9)(b) MCA 1980*

If the defendant does not consent to summary trial, they must be sent forthwith to the Crown Court for trial.

Magistrates' Courts Act 1980, ss 17A, 17B, 17D, 18–21, 25

17A.— Initial procedure: accused to indicate intention as to plea.

(1) This section shall have effect where a person who has attained the age of 18 years appears or is brought before a magistrates' court on an information charging him with an offence triable either way.

(2) Everything that the court is required to do under the following provisions of this section must be done with the accused present in court.

(3) The court shall cause the charge to be written down, if this has not already been done, and to be read to the accused.

(4) The court shall then explain to the accused in ordinary language that he may indicate whether (if the offence were to proceed to trial) he would plead guilty or not guilty, and that if he indicates that he would plead guilty—

(a) the court must proceed as mentioned in subsection (6) below; and

(b) he may (unless section 17D(2) below were to apply) be committed for sentence to the Crown Court under section 3 or (if applicable) 3A of the Powers of Criminal Courts (Sentencing) Act 2000 if the court is of such opinion as is mentioned in subsection (2) of the applicable section.

(5) The court shall then ask the accused whether (if the offence were to proceed to trial) he would plead guilty or not guilty.

(6) If the accused indicates that he would plead guilty the court shall proceed as if—

(a) the proceedings constituted from the beginning the summary trial of the information; and

(b) section 9(1) above was complied with and he pleaded guilty under it.

(7) If the accused indicates that he would plead not guilty section 18(1) below shall apply.

(8) If the accused in fact fails to indicate how he would plead, for the purposes of this section and section 18(1) below he shall be taken to indicate that he would plead not guilty.

(9) Subject to subsection (6) above, the following shall not for any purpose be taken to constitute the taking of a plea—

(a) asking the accused under this section whether (if the offence were to proceed to trial) he would plead guilty or not guilty;

(b) an indication by the accused under this section of how he would plead.

(10) If in respect of the offence the court receives a notice under section 51B or 51C of the Crime and Disorder Act 1998 (which relate to serious or complex fraud cases and to certain cases involving children respectively), the preceding provisions of this section and the provisions of section 17B below shall not apply, and the court shall proceed in relation to the offence in accordance with section 51 or, as the case may be, section 51A of that Act.

17B.— Intention as to plea: absence of accused.

(1) This section shall have effect where—

(a) a person who has attained the age of 18 years appears or is brought before a magistrates' court on an information charging him with an offence triable either way.

(b) the accused is represented by a legal representative,

(c) the court considers that by reason of the accused's disorderly conduct before the court it is not practicable for proceedings under section 17A above to be conducted in his presence, and

(d) the court considers that it should proceed in the absence of the accused.

(2) In such a case—

(a) the court shall cause the charge to be written down, if this has not already been done, and to be read to the representative;

(b) the court shall ask the representative whether (if the offence were to proceed to trial) the accused would plead guilty or not guilty;

(c) if the representative indicates that the accused would plead guilty the court shall proceed as if the proceedings constituted from the beginning the summary trial of the information, and as if section 9(1) above was complied with and the accused pleaded guilty under it;

(d) if the representative indicates that the accused would plead not guilty section 18(1) below shall apply.

(3) If the representative in fact fails to indicate how the accused would plead, for the purposes of this section and section 18(1) below he shall be taken to indicate that the accused would plead not guilty.

(4) Subject to subsection (2)(c) above, the following shall not for any purpose be taken to constitute the taking of a plea—

(a) asking the representative under this section whether (if the offence were to proceed to trial) the accused would plead guilty or not guilty;

(b) an indication by the representative under this section of how the accused would plead.

17D Maximum penalty under section 17A(6) or 17B(2)(c) for certain offences

(1) If—

(a) the offence is a scheduled offence (as defined in section 22(1) below);

(b) the court proceeds in relation to the offence in accordance with section 17A(6) or 17B(2)(c) above; and

(c) the court convicts the accused of the offence,

the court shall consider whether, having regard to any representations made by him or by the prosecutor, the value involved (as defined in section 22(10) below) appears to the court to exceed the relevant sum (as specified for the purposes of section 22 below).

(2) If it appears to the court clear that the value involved does not exceed the relevant sum, or it appears to the court for any reason not clear whether the value involved does or does not exceed the relevant sum—

(a) subject to subsection (4) below, the court shall not have power to impose on the accused in respect of the offence a sentence in excess of the limits mentioned in section 33(1)(a) below; and

(b) sections 3 and 4 of the Powers of Criminal Courts (Sentencing) Act 2000 shall not apply as regards that offence.

(3) Subsections (9) to (12) of section 22 below shall apply for the purposes of this section as they apply for the purposes of that section (reading the reference to subsection (1) in section 22(9) as a reference to subsection (1) of this section).

(4) Subsection (2)(a) above does not apply to an offence under section 12A of the Theft Act 1968 (aggravated vehicle-taking).

8.— Initial procedure on information against adult for offence triable either way.

(1) Sections 19 to 23 below shall have effect where a person who has attained the age of 18 years appears or is brought before a magistrates' court on an information charging him with an offence triable either way and—

(a) he indicates under section 17A above that (if the offence were to proceed to trial) he would plead not guilty, or

(b) his representative indicates under section 17B above that (if the offence were to proceed to trial) he would plead not guilty.

(2) Without prejudice to section 11(1) above, everything that the court is required to do under sections 19 to 22 below must be done before any evidence is called and, subject to subsection (3) below and section 23 below, with the accused present in court.

(3) The court may proceed in the absence of the accused in accordance with such of the provisions of sections 19 to 22 below as are applicable in the circumstances if the court considers that by reason of his disorderly conduct before the court it is not practicable for the proceedings to be conducted in his presence; and subsections (3) to (5) of section 23 below, so far as applicable, shall have effect in relation to proceedings conducted in the absence of the accused by virtue of this subsection (references in those subsections to the person representing the accused being for this purpose read as references to the person, if any, representing him).

(4) A magistrates' court proceeding under sections 19 to 23 below may adjourn the proceedings at any time, and on doing so on any occasion when the accused is present may remand the accused, and shall remand him if—

(a) on the occasion on which he first appeared, or was brought, before the court to answer to the information he was in custody or, having been released on bail, surrendered to the custody of the court; or

(b) he has been remanded at any time in the course of proceedings on the information;

and where the court remands the accused, the time fixed for the resumption of the proceedings shall be that at which he is required to appear or be brought before the court in pursuance of the remand or would be required to be brought before the court but for section 128(3A) below.

(5) The functions of a magistrates' court under sections 19 to 23 below may be discharged by a single justice, but this subsection shall not be taken as authorising—

(a) the summary trial of an information (otherwise than in accordance with section 20(7) below); or

(b) the imposition of a sentence,

by a magistrates' court composed of fewer than two justices.

19 Decision as to allocation

(1) The court shall decide whether the offence appears to it more suitable for summary trial or for trial on indictment.

(2) Before making a decision under this section, the court—

    (a) shall give the prosecution an opportunity to inform the court of the accused's previous convictions (if any); and

    (b) shall give the prosecution and the accused an opportunity to make representations as to whether summary trial or trial on indictment would be more suitable.

(3) In making a decision under this section, the court shall consider—

    (a) whether the sentence which a magistrates' court would have power to impose for the offence would be adequate; and

    (b) any representations made by the prosecution or the accused under subsection (2)(b) above,

and shall have regard to any allocation guidelines (or revised allocation guidelines) issued as definitive guidelines under section 170 of the Criminal Justice Act 2003.

(4) Where—

    (a) the accused is charged with two or more offences; and

    (b) it appears to the court that the charges for the offences could be joined in the same indictment or that the offences arise out of the same or connected circumstances,

subsection (3)(a) above shall have effect as if references to the sentence which a magistrates' court would have power to impose for the offence were a reference to the maximum aggregate sentence which a magistrates' court would have power to impose for all of the offences taken together.

(5) In this section any reference to a previous conviction is a reference to—

    (a) a previous conviction by a court in the United Kingdom; or

    (b) a previous finding of guilt in—

        (i) any proceedings under the Army Act 1955, the Air Force Act 1955 or the Naval Discipline Act 1957 (whether before a court-martial or any other court or person authorised under any of those Acts to award a punishment in respect of any offence); or

        (ii) any proceedings before a Standing Civilian Court.

(6) If, in respect of the offence, the court receives a notice under section 51B or 51C of the Crime and Disorder Act 1998 (which relate to serious or complex fraud cases and to certain cases involving children respectively), the preceding provisions of this section and sections 20, 20A and 21 below shall not apply, and the court shall proceed in relation to the offence in accordance with section 51(1) of that Act.

20 Procedure where summary trial appears more suitable

(1) If the court decides under section 19 above that the offence appears to it more suitable for summary trial, the following provisions of this section shall apply (unless they are excluded by section 23 below).

(2) The court shall explain to the accused in ordinary language—

    (a) that it appears to the court more suitable for him to be tried summarily for the offence;

    (b) that he can either consent to be so tried or, if he wishes, be tried on indictment; and

    (c) that if he is tried summarily and is convicted by the court, he may be committed for sentence to the Crown Court under section 3 or (if applicable) section 3A of the Powers of Criminal Courts (Sentencing) Act 2000 if the court is of such opinion as is mentioned in subsection (2) of the applicable section.

(3) The accused may then request an indication ("an indication of sentence") of whether a custodial sentence or non-custodial sentence would be more likely to be imposed if he were to be tried summarily for the offence and to plead guilty.

(4) If the accused requests an indication of sentence, the court may, but need not, give such an indication.

(5) If the accused requests and the court gives an indication of sentence, the court shall ask the accused whether he wishes, on the basis of the indication, to reconsider the indication of plea which was given, or is taken to have been given, under section 17A or 17B above.

(6) If the accused indicates that he wishes to reconsider the indication under section 17A or 17B above, the court shall ask the accused whether (if the offence were to proceed to trial) he would plead guilty or not guilty.

(7) If the accused indicates that he would plead guilty the court shall proceed as if—

    (a) the proceedings constituted from that time the summary trial of the information; and

    (b) section 9(1) above were complied with and he pleaded guilty under it.

(8) Subsection (9) below applies where—

    (a) the court does not give an indication of sentence (whether because the accused does not request one or because the court does not agree to give one);

    (b) the accused either—

        (i) does not indicate, in accordance with subsection (5) above, that he wishes; or

        (ii) indicates, in accordance with subsection (5) above, that he does not wish,

to reconsider the indication of plea under section 17A or 17B above; or

    (c) the accused does not indicate, in accordance with subsection (6) above, that he would plead guilty.

(9) The court shall ask the accused whether he consents to be tried summarily or wishes to be tried on indictment and—

    (a) if he consents to be tried summarily, shall proceed to the summary trial of the information; and

    (b) if he does not so consent, shall proceed in relation to the offence in accordance with section 51(1) of the Crime and Disorder Act 1998.

20A Procedure where summary trial appears more suitable: supplementary

(1) Where the case is dealt with in accordance with section 20(7) above, no court (whether a magistrates' court or not) may impose a custodial sentence for the offence unless such a sentence was indicated in the indication of sentence referred to in section 20 above.

(2) Subsection (1) above is subject to sections 3A(4), 4(8) and 5(3) of the Powers of Criminal Courts (Sentencing) Act 2000.

(3) Except as provided in subsection (1) above—

    (a) an indication of sentence shall not be binding on any court (whether a magistrates' court or not); and

    (b) no sentence may be challenged or be the subject of appeal in any court on the ground that it is not consistent with an indication of sentence.

(4) Subject to section 20(7) above, the following shall not for any purpose be taken to constitute the taking of a plea—

    (a) asking the accused under section 20 above whether (if the offence were to proceed to trial) he would plead guilty or not guilty; or

    (b) an indication by the accused under that section of how he would plead.

(5) Where the court gives an indication of sentence under section 20 above, it shall cause each such indication to be entered in the register.

(6) In this section and in section 20 above, references to a custodial sentence are to a custodial sentence within the meaning of section 76 of the Powers of Criminal Courts (Sentencing) Act 2000, and references to a non-custodial sentence shall be construed accordingly.

21 Procedure where trial on indictment appears more suitable

If the court decides under section 19 above that the offence appears to it more suitable for trial on indictment, the court shall tell the accused that the court has decided that it is more suitable for him to be tried on indictment, and shall proceed in relation to the offence in accordance with section 51(1) of the Crime and Disorder Act 1998.

25.— Power to change from summary trial to committal proceedings, and vice versa.

(1) Subsections (2) to (2D) below shall have effect where a person who has attained the age of 18 years appears or is brought before a magistrates' court on an information charging him with an offence triable either way.

(2) Where the court is required under section 20(9) above to proceed to the summary trial of the information, the prosecution may apply to the court for the offence to be tried on indictment instead.

(2A) An application under subsection (2) above—

 (a) must be made before the summary trial begins; and

 (b) must be dealt with by the court before any other application or issue in relation to the summary trial is dealt with.

(2B) The court may grant an application under subsection (2) above but only if it is satisfied that the sentence which a magistrates' court would have power to impose for the offence would be inadequate.

(2C) Where—

 (a) the accused is charged on the same occasion with two or more offences; and

 (b) it appears to the court that they constitute or form part of a series of two or more offences of the same or a similar character,

subsection (2B) above shall have effect as if references to the sentence which a magistrates' court would have power to impose for the offence were a reference to the maximum aggregate sentence which a magistrates' court would have power to impose for all of the offences taken together.

(2D) Where the court grants an application under subsection (2) above, it shall proceed in relation to the offence in accordance with section 51(1) of the Crime and Disorder Act 1998.

Power to commit to crown court for sentence

Where a defendant has been convicted of an either-way offence, they may be committed to the Crown Court for sentence in the following situations:

(a) *Indication of guilty plea under the plea before venue procedure when first asked–s.3 PCC(S)A 2000*

A defendant may be committed to the Crown Court for sentence where they or their legal representative has indicated an intention to plead guilty under the plea before venue provisions when first asked, and the court considers that the offence, or the combination of one or more offences associated with it, is "so serious that the Crown Court should, in the court's opinion, have the power to deal with the offender in any way it could deal with him if he had been convicted on indictment".

Section 3 PCC(S)A 2000 is amended such that the wording of the provision is different from the previous version of s.3 ("so serious that greater punishment should be inflicted for the offence than the court has power to impose"). The reference to violent and sexual offences has been deleted. However, the practical effect of the change is likely to be minimal.

(b) *Conviction after trial–s.3 PCC(S) A 2000*

This power should not ordinarily be used where the defendant has reconsidered the indication of plea and pleads guilty following an indication of sentence, or is convicted after summary trial because the allocation decision has been made already in those cases. Legally it is still available, but the court will need to justify changing the original decision based on matters that have since come to light. This will be rare.

(c) **Defendant is a dangerous offender–s.3A PCC(S)A 2000**

Where the defendant has been convicted of a specified offence within the meaning of s.224 CJA 2003 and it appears to the court that there is a significant risk to members of the public of serious harm occasioned by the commission by them of further specified offences such that they qualify for a sentence of imprisonment for public protection or an extended sentence, the court must commit for sentence, irrespective of the route by which the defendant has been convicted in the magistrates' court.

(d) **Defendant has been sent to the Crown Court for trial for related offence(s)–s.4 PCC(S)A 2000**

Where the court has sent the defendant to the Crown Court for trial for one or more related offences and the defendant indicates an intention to plead guilty to an either-way offence, the court may commit for sentence to the Crown Court. The court does not need to find that its powers of sentence are inadequate.

A defendant may be committed under this provision where they have reconsidered the plea and indicated an intention to plead guilty following an indication of sentence. The indication of sentence shall not be binding on any court in relation to the decision to commit for sentence and any decision cannot be challenged or appealed against on the grounds that it is inconsistent with that indication.

In this situation, the Crown Court must sentence for the either-way offence within the powers of the magistrates' courts unless:

- the defendant has been convicted of one or more of the related offences for which they have been sent for trial; or
- the magistrates' court has stated that, in its opinion, it also had power to commit for sentence because the offence(s) are so serious that the Crown Court should have power to deal with the defendant as if they had been convicted on indictment or (if applicable) under the dangerous offender provisions.

(e) **Defendant has been committed for sentence under ss.3, 3A or 4 PCC(S)A 2000 and is to be sentenced for other offences–s.6 PCC(S)A 2000**

Where the court commits a defendant under ss.3, 3A or 4 PCC(S)A 2000 see the preceding paragraphs, the court can also commit other offences for sentence under s.6 PCC(S)A 2000, i.e. any offence whatsoever for which the magistrates' court has power to deal with the defendant where the relevant offence is an indictable offence, or, where the relevant offence is a summary offence, any offence punishable with imprisonment or disqualification under the Road Traffic Offenders Act 1988.

On committal for sentence under ss.3, 3A or 4 PCC(S)A 2000, the Crown Court "shall enquire into the circumstances of the case and may deal with the offender in any way in which it could deal with him if he had just been convicted of the offence on indictment before the court".

Powers of Criminal Courts (Sentencing) Act 2000, ss 3, 3A, 4 and 6

3.— Committal for sentence on summary trial of offence triable either way.

(1) Subject to subsection (4) below, this section applies where on the summary trial of an offence triable either way a person aged 18 or over is convicted of the offence.

(2) If the court is of the opinion—

    (a) that the offence or the combination of the offence and one or more offences associated with it was so serious that greater punishment should be inflicted for the offence than the court has power to impose, or

(b) in the case of a violent or sexual offence, that a custodial sentence for a term longer than the court has power to impose is necessary to protect the public from serious harm from him,

the court may commit the offender in custody or on bail to the Crown Court for sentence in accordance with section 5(1) below.

(3) Where the court commits a person under subsection (2) above, section 6 below (which enables a magistrates' court, where it commits a person under this section in respect of an offence, also to commit him to the Crown Court to be dealt with in respect of certain other offences) shall apply accordingly.

(4) This section does not apply in relation to an offence as regards which this section is excluded by section 33 of the Magistrates' Courts Act 1980 (certain offences where value involved is small).

(5) The preceding provisions of this section shall apply in relation to a corporation as if—

(a) the corporation were an individual aged 18 or over; and

(b) in subsection (2) above, paragraph (b) and the words "in custody or on bail" were omitted.

3A Committal for sentence of dangerous adult offenders

(1) This section applies where on the summary trial of a specified offence triable either way a person aged 18 or over is convicted of the offence.

(2) If, in relation to the offence, it appears to the court that the criteria for the imposition of a sentence under section 225(3) or 227(2) of the Criminal Justice Act 2003 would be met, the court must commit the offender in custody or on bail to the Crown Court for sentence in accordance with section 5(1) below.

(3) Where the court commits a person under subsection (2) above, section 6 below (which enables a magistrates' court, where it commits a person under this section in respect of an offence, also to commit him to the Crown Court to be dealt with in respect of certain other offences) shall apply accordingly.

(4) In reaching any decision under or taking any step contemplated by this section—

(a) the court shall not be bound by any indication of sentence given in respect of the offence under section 20 of the Magistrates' Courts Act 1980 (procedure where summary trial appears more suitable); and

(b) nothing the court does under this section may be challenged or be the subject of any appeal in any court on the ground that it is not consistent with an indication of sentence.

(5) Nothing in this section shall prevent the court from committing an offender convicted of a specified offence to the Crown Court for sentence under section 3 above if the provisions of that section are satisfied.

(6) In this section, references to a specified offence are to a specified offence within the meaning of section 224 of the Criminal Justice Act 2003.

4.— Committal for sentence on indication of guilty plea to offence triable either way.

(1) This section applies where—

(a) a person aged 18 or over appears or is brought before a magistrates' court ("the court") on an information charging him with an offence triable either way ("the offence");

(b) he or (where applicable) his representative indicates under section 17A, 17B or 20(7) of the Magistrates' Courts Act 1980 that he would plead guilty if the offence were to proceed to trial; and

(c) proceeding as if section 9(1) of that Act were complied with and he pleaded guilty under it, the court convicts him of the offence.

(1A)   But this section does not apply to an offence as regards which this section is excluded by section 17D of that Act (certain offences where value involved is small).

(2)   If the court has sent the offender to the Crown Court for trial for one or more related offences, that is to say, one or more offences which, in its opinion, are related to the offence, it may commit him in custody or on bail to the Crown Court to be dealt with in respect of the offence in accordance with section 5(1) below.

(3)   If the power conferred by subsection (2) above is not exercisable but the court is still to determine to, or to determine whether to, send the offender to the Crown Court for trial under section 51 or 51A of the Crime and Disorder Act 1998 for one or more related offences—

    (a)   it shall adjourn the proceedings relating to the offence until after it has made those determinations; and

    (b)   if it sends the offender to the Crown Court for trial for one or more related offences, it may then exercise that power.

(4)   Where the court—

    (a)   under subsection (2) above commits the offender to the Crown Court to be dealt with in respect of the offence, and

    (b)   does not state that, in its opinion, it also has power so to commit him under section 3(2) or, as the case may be, section 3A(2) above,

section 5(1) below shall not apply unless he is convicted before the Crown Court of one or more of the related offences.

(5)   Where section 5(1) below does not apply, the Crown Court may deal with the offender in respect of the offence in any way in which the magistrates' court could deal with him if it had just convicted him of the offence.

(6)   Where the court commits a person under subsection (2) above, section 6 below (which enables a magistrates' court, where it commits a person under this section in respect of an offence, also to commit him to the Crown Court to be dealt with in respect of certain other offences) shall apply accordingly.

(7)   For the purposes of this section one offence is related to another if, were they both to be prosecuted on indictment, the charges for them could be joined in the same indictment.

(8)   In reaching any decision under or taking any step contemplated by this section—

    (a)   the court shall not be bound by any indication of sentence given in respect of the offence under section 20 of the Magistrates' Courts Act 1980 (procedure where summary trial appears more suitable); and

    (b)   nothing the court does under this section may be challenged or be the subject of any appeal in any court on the ground that it is not consistent with an indication of sentence.

6.— Committal for sentence in certain cases where offender committed in respect of another offence.

(1)   This section applies where a magistrates' court ("the committing court") commits a person in custody or on bail to the Crown Court under any enactment mentioned in subsection (4) below to be sentenced or otherwise dealt with in respect of an offence ("the relevant offence").

(2)   Where this section applies and the relevant offence is an indictable offence, the committing court may also commit the offender, in custody or on bail as the case may require, to the Crown Court to be dealt with in respect of any other offence whatsoever in respect of which the committing court has power to deal with him (being an offence of which he has been convicted by that or any other court).

(3)   Where this section applies and the relevant offence is a summary offence, the committing court may commit the offender, in custody or on bail as the case may require, to the

Crown Court to be dealt with in respect of—

(a) any other offence of which the committing court has convicted him, being either—
  (i) an offence punishable with imprisonment; or
  (ii) an offence in respect of which the committing court has a power or duty to order him to be disqualified under section 34, 35 or 36 of the Road Traffic Offenders Act 1988 (disqualification for certain motoring offences); or

(b) any suspended sentence in respect of which the committing court has under paragraph 11(1) of Schedule 12 to the Criminal Justice Act 2003 power to deal with him.

(4) The enactments referred to in subsection (1) above are—

(a) the Vagrancy Act 1824 (incorrigible rogues);

(b) sections 3 to 4A above (committal for sentence for offences triable either way);

(c) section 13(5) below (conditionally discharged person convicted of further offence);

[...]

(e) paragraph 11(2) of Schedule 12 to the Criminal Justice Act 2003 (committal to Crown Court where offender convicted during operational period of suspended sentence).

Allocation—new procedure for adults

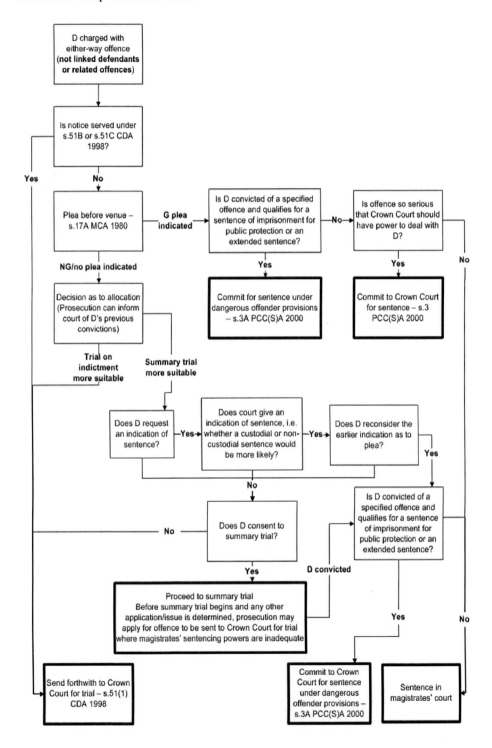

AMENDMENT OF INFORMATION

Prosecutors do not have an unfettered right to seek to amend charges that are not subject to any limitation of time (ie indictable and indictable only charges). Amendments should be granted where the application is judged to be proper and appropriate (*R v Redbridge Justices, ex p Whitehouse* [1992] 94 CAR 332). In *Director of Public Prosecutions v Hammerton* [2009] EWHC 921 (Admin) the court applauded a refusal to amend a charge alleging an either-way offence with one triable summarily only, when the application had been made on the day that the original offence was due to be committed to the Crown Court for trial. Reflecting the substantial change in attitude required by all parties in order to make the criminal justice system more effective, the court observed: "All the cases cited to me pre-date the Criminal Procedure Rules. The courts, including the magistrates' courts, now have the Criminal Procedure Rules to apply and in particular they have the overriding objective to consider. That is something the magistrates clearly would have had in mind. It is, therefore, not for the Crown Prosecution Service simply to assume to itself the way in which a proceeding will be conducted. For example, as the magistrates here noted, there had been ample time for the Crown Prosecution Service to assess the position before the date of actual committal. The magistrates' courts are concerned with the speedy and efficient administration of justice (also evidenced, for example, by the successful introduction of the CJSSS scheme throughout magistrates' courts in England and Wales). It is wholly unsurprising, to my mind, that the magistrates here were thoroughly dissatisfied with the last minute nature of this application.

...

where a lesser charge is to be substituted, first, it must be proper and appropriate to the facts of the case; secondly the application should be made promptly and not left until the last minute, at all events without any proper explanation; and, thirdly, an eye should also be kept on considerations of the good administration of justice and the wider picture: as the facts of this case illustrate, by reason of the situation of any co-accused."

The effect of *Hammerton* is arguably being overstated by defence advocates and a careful reading of the case will reveal a decision peculiar to its own facts and falling well short of providing any kind of precedent for future cases. It is notable that many of the features of *Hammerton* can be seen in earlier decisions such as *R (Crown Prosecution Service) v Everest* [2005] EWHC 1124 (Admin).

APPEARANCE BY COUNSEL OR SOLICITOR

A party represented by solicitor or counsel is deemed not to be absent from court, but this does not excuse the defendant from court where any enactment or condition of recognizance requires his attendance (Magistrates' Courts Act 1980, s 122). Lawyers need to be careful to distinguish between cases where there is no requirement for a defendant to appear in person, and those where there is, albeit in some cases with the power to proceed in absence under s 122 should the court see fit. A defendant is required to be at court: When on bail; for the purposes of plea before venue, committal or sending for trial and for the purposes of imposing a community or custodial sentence.

AUTREFOIS ACQUIT AND AUTREFOIS CONVICT

Burden: The burden of proof falls on the defendant, to be discharged at the civil standard (*Coughlan* (1976) 63 Cr App R 33). The essence of the plea is that the defendant has previously been 'put in jeopardy'. Autrefois is a plea in bar that can be raised in the magistrates' court when a person has previously been convicted or acquitted of the charge before the court (or a charge based on the same facts). The rule does not apply to stop a prosecution in relation to a matter that has resulted in a police caution (*Director of Public Prosecutions v Alexander* [2010] EWHC 2266

(Admin)), civil contempt proceedings (*Crown Prosecution Service v Tweddell* [2001] EWHC 188 (Admin)), or dismissal for want of prosecution (*R v Willesden Justices ex p Clemmings* (1988) 87 Cr App R 280). It is proper for the prosecution to seek to charge a conspiracy based on the same facts as the substantive matter to which the defendant has previously pleaded (see for example *Dwyer* [2012] EWCA Crim 10; *Ali* [2011] EWCA Crim 1260). **Dismissal of information:** In most cases the dismissal of a previous information will found a solid basis for arguing autrefois convict (*R (A) v South Staffordshire Magistrates' Court* (2007) 171 JP 36).

BAIL

Legislation: The full text of the Bail Act 1976 is reproduced in Appendix 12.

Murder Cases

A magistrates' court has no power to grant bail in relation to a defendant who is charged with murder (whether charged alone or with additional charges). Bail must be refused and the bail position determined by a crown court judge. In the event that a defendant is before the court in respect to a breach of bail which is not proven, the court has no power to re-bail on the same conditions as before, as the original bail came to an end on arrest, and a re-bail is a grant of bail that is now prohibited in relation to murder. A court has the power to bail in respect to attempted murder and conspiracy to murder.

Coroners and Justice Act 2009, s 115

(1) A person charged with murder may not be granted bail except by order of a judge of the Crown Court.

(2) Subsections (3) and (4) apply where a person appears or is brought before a magistrates' court charged with murder.

(3) A judge of the Crown Court must make a decision about bail in respect of the person as soon as reasonably practicable and, in any event, within the period of 48 hours beginning with the day after the day on which the person appears or is brought before the magistrates' court.

(4) The magistrates' court must, if necessary for the purposes of subsection (3), commit the person to custody to be brought before a judge of the Crown Court.

(5) For the purposes of subsections (3) and (4), it is immaterial whether the magistrates' court—

    (a) sends the person to the Crown Court for trial, or

    (b) adjourns proceedings under section 52(5) of the Crime and Disorder Act 1998 (c. 37) and remands the person.

(6) In this section a reference to a person charged with murder includes a person charged with murder and one or more other offences.

(7) For the purposes of subsection (3), when calculating the period of 48 hours Saturdays, Sundays, Christmas Day, Good Friday and bank holidays are to be excluded.

Treason Cases

Only a High Court Judge (or the Secretary of State) can grant bail in a murder case. It is theoretically possible for a High Court Judge to sit in a magistrates' court, but extremely unlikely. Therefore bail must be refused in most cases (Magistrates' Courts Act 1980, s 41).

The right to bail, or presumption in favour of bail

In certain cases there is a right to bail (section 4 of the 1976 Act) unless an exception to bail is established (Sch 1 of the 1976 Act), there are also some statutory qualifications to that right.

Where the statutory right to bail does not apply the court can refuse bail without recourse to any of the statutory exceptions (but note that there is a body of case law which must be considered).

The presumption in favour of bail does not apply:

- in extradition proceedings where the person is alleged to have been convicted of the offence or in connection with a warrant issued in the Republic of Ireland;
- following committal to the Crown Court for sentence or for breach of a Crown Court order;
- after conviction, unless the proceedings are adjourned for inquiries to be made or a report to be prepared for sentence;
- on appeal against conviction or sentence;
- following a breach of bail.

Qualifications to the general right to bail:

- Murder and Treason (see above).
- When the Criminal Justice and Public Order Act 1994, s 25 applies (although the provisions within in relation to murder are otiose so far as the magistrates' court is concerned).
- The Criminal Justice Act 2003, s 14 applies. The section is partially in force and applies only where the defendant is charged with an offence carrying life imprisonment, detention during Her Majesty's pleasure or custody for life (SI 2006/3217). If that offence was committed whilst on bail then he may not be granted bail unless the court is satisfied that there is no significant risk of him committing an offence while on bail. If the defendant is under 18 years the provision is different in that the court must simply give weight to the fact that the defendant was previously on bail.
- The Criminal Justice Act 2003, s 15 applies. The section applies in the same way as section 14 above (and is limited to the same offences), save that it is concerned with when a defendant on bail for an offence that carries life imprisonment fails to surrender to bail.

Criminal Justice and Public Order Act 1994, s 25

(1) A person who in any proceedings has been charged with or convicted of an offence to which this section applies in circumstances to which it applies shall be granted bail in those proceedings only if the court or, as the case may be, the constable considering the grant of bail is satisfied that there are exceptional circumstances which justify it.

(2) This section applies, subject to subsection (3) below, to the following offences, that is to say—

(a) murder;

(b) attempted murder;

(c) manslaughter;

(d) rape under the law of Scotland;

(e) an offence under section 1 of the Sexual Offences Act 1956 (rape);

(f) an offence under section 1 of the Sexual Offences Act 2003 (rape);

(g) an offence under section 2 of that Act (assault by penetration);

(h) an offence under section 4 of that Act (causing a person to engage in sexual activity without consent), where the activity caused involved penetration within subsection (4)(a) to (d) of that section;

(i) an offence under section 5 of that Act (rape of a child under 13);

(j) an offence under section 6 of that Act (assault of a child under 13 by penetration);

(k) an offence under section 8 of that Act (causing or inciting a child under 13 to engage in sexual activity), where an activity involving penetration within subsection (3)(a) to (d) of that section was caused;

(l) an offence under section 30 of that Act (sexual activity with a person with a mental disorder impeding choice), where the touching involved penetration within subsection (3)(a) to (d) of that section;

(m) an offence under section 31 of that Act (causing or inciting a person, with a mental disorder impeding choice, to engage in sexual activity), where an activity involving penetration within subsection (3)(a) to (d) of that section was caused;

    (ma) an offence under Article 5 of the Sexual Offences (Northern Ireland) Order 2008 (rape);

    (mb) an offence under Article 6 of that Order (assault by penetration);

    (mc) an offence under Article 8 of that Order (causing a person to engage in sexual activity without consent) where the activity caused involved penetration within paragraph (4)(a) to (d) of that Article;

    (md) an offence under Article 12 of that Order (rape of a child under 13);

    (me) an offence under Article 13 of that Order (assault of a child under 13 by penetration);

    (mf) an offence under Article 15 of that Order (causing or inciting a child under 13 to engage in sexual activity) where an activity involving penetration within paragraph (2)(a) to (d) of that Article was caused;

    (mg) an offence under Article 43 of that Order (sexual activity with a person with a mental disorder impeding choice) where the touching involved penetration within paragraph (3)(a) to (d) of that Article;

    (mh) an offence under Article 44 of that Order (causing or inciting a person, with a mental disorder impeding choice, to engage in sexual activity) where an activity involving penetration within paragraph (3)(a) to (d) of that Article was caused;

    (n) an attempt to commit an offence within any of paragraphs (d) to (mh).

(3)   This section applies in the circumstances described in subsection (3A) or (3B) only.

(3A)   This section applies where—

    (a) the person has been previously convicted by or before a court in any part of the United Kingdom of any offence within subsection (2) or of culpable homicide, and

    (b) if that previous conviction is one of manslaughter or culpable homicide—

      (i) the person was then a child or young person, and was sentenced to long-term detention under any of the relevant enactments, or

      (ii) the person was not then a child or young person, and was sentenced to imprisonment or detention.

(3B)   This section applies where—

    (a) the person has been previously convicted by or before a court in another member State of any relevant foreign offence corresponding to an offence within subsection (2) or to culpable homicide, and

    (b) if the previous conviction is of a relevant foreign offence corresponding to the offence of manslaughter or culpable homicide—

      (i) the person was then a child or young person, and was sentenced to detention for a period in excess of 2 years, or

      (ii) the person was not then a child or young person, and was sentenced to detention.

(4)   This section applies whether or not an appeal is pending against conviction or sentence.

(5)   In this section—

"conviction" includes—

    (a) a finding that a person is not guilty by reason of insanity;

    (b) a finding under section 4A(3) of the Criminal Procedure (Insanity) Act 1964 (cases of unfitness to plead) that a person did the act or made the omission charged against him; and

    (c) a conviction of an offence for which an order is made discharging the offender absolutely or conditionally;

and "convicted" shall be construed accordingly;

"the relevant enactments" means—

(a) as respects England and Wales, section 91 of the Powers of Criminal Courts (Sentencing) Act 2000;

(b) as respects Scotland, sections 205(1) to (3) and 208 of the Criminal Procedure (Scotland) Act 1995;

(c) as respects Northern Ireland, section 73(2) of the Children and Young Persons Act (Northern Ireland) 1968; and

"relevant foreign offence", in relation to a member State other than the United Kingdom, means an offence under the law in force in that member State.

(5A) For the purposes of subsection (3B), a relevant foreign offence corresponds to another offence if the relevant foreign offence would have constituted that other offence if it had been done in any part of the United Kingdom at the time when the relevant foreign offence was committed.

(6) This section does not apply in relation to proceedings instituted before its commencement.

Criminal Justice Act 2003, ss 14–15

14 Offences committed on bail

(1) For paragraph 2A of Part 1 of Schedule 1 to the 1976 Act (defendant need not be granted bail where he was on bail on date of offence) there is substituted—

"2A

(1) If the defendant falls within this paragraph he may not be granted bail unless the court is satisfied that there is no significant risk of his committing an offence while on bail (whether subject to conditions or not).

(2) The defendant falls within this paragraph if—

(a) he is aged 18 or over, and

(b) it appears to the court that he was on bail in criminal proceedings on the date of the offence."

(2) After paragraph 9 of that Part there is inserted—

"9AA

(1) This paragraph applies if—

(a) the defendant is under the age of 18, and

(b) it appears to the court that he was on bail in criminal proceedings on the date of the offence.

(2) In deciding for the purposes of paragraph 2(1) of this Part of this Schedule whether it is satisfied that there are substantial grounds for believing that the defendant, if released on bail (whether subject to conditions or not), would commit an offence while on bail, the court shall give particular weight to the fact that the defendant was on bail in criminal proceedings on the date of the offence."

15 Absconding by persons released on bail

(1) For paragraph 6 of Part 1 of Schedule 1 to the 1976 Act (defendant need not be granted bail if having been released on bail he has been arrested in pursuance of section 7) there is substituted—

"6

(1) If the defendant falls within this paragraph, he may not be granted bail unless the court is satisfied that there is no significant risk that, if released on bail (whether subject to conditions or not), he would fail to surrender to custody.

(2) Subject to sub-paragraph (3) below, the defendant falls within this paragraph if—

(a) he is aged 18 or over, and

    (b) it appears to the court that, having been released on bail in or in connection with the proceedings for the offence, he failed to surrender to custody.

(3)   Where it appears to the court that the defendant had reasonable cause for his failure to surrender to custody, he does not fall within this paragraph unless it also appears to the court that he failed to surrender to custody at the appointed place as soon as reasonably practicable after the appointed time.

(4)   For the purposes of sub-paragraph (3) above, a failure to give to the defendant a copy of the record of the decision to grant him bail shall not constitute a reasonable cause for his failure to surrender to custody."

(2)   After paragraph 9AA of that Part (inserted by section 14(2)) there is inserted—

"9AB

(1)   Subject to sub-paragraph (2) below, this paragraph applies if—

    (a) the defendant is under the age of 18, and
    (b) it appears to the court that, having been released on bail in or in connection with the proceedings for the offence, he failed to surrender to custody.

(2)   Where it appears to the court that the defendant had reasonable cause for his failure to surrender to custody, this paragraph does not apply unless it also appears to the court that he failed to surrender to custody at the appointed place as soon as reasonably practicable after the appointed time.

(3)   In deciding for the purposes of paragraph 2(1) of this Part of this Schedule whether it is satisfied that there are substantial grounds for believing that the defendant, if released on bail (whether subject to conditions or not), would fail to surrender to custody, the court shall give particular weight to—

    (a) where the defendant did not have reasonable cause for his failure to surrender to custody, the fact that he failed to surrender to custody, or
    (b) where he did have reasonable cause for his failure to surrender to custody, the fact that he failed to surrender to custody at the appointed place as soon as reasonably practicable after the appointed time.

(4)   For the purposes of this paragraph, a failure to give to the defendant a copy of the record of the decision to grant him bail shall not constitute a reasonable cause for his failure to surrender to custody."

(3)   In section 6 of the 1976 Act (offence of absconding by person released on bail) after subsection (9) there is inserted—

"(10) Section 127 of the Magistrates' Courts Act 1980 shall not apply in relation to an offence under subsection (1) or (2) above.

(11) Where a person has been released on bail in criminal proceedings and that bail was granted by a constable, a magistrates' court shall not try that person for an offence under subsection (1) or (2) above in relation to that bail (the "relevant offence") unless either or both of subsections (12) and (13) below applies.

(12) This subsection applies if an information is laid for the relevant offence within 6 months from the time of the commission of the relevant offence.

(13) This subsection applies if an information is laid for the relevant offence no later than 3 months from the time of the occurrence of the first of the events mentioned in subsection (14) below to occur after the commission of the relevant offence.

(14) Those events are—

    (a) the person surrenders to custody at the appointed place;
    (b) the person is arrested, or attends at a police station, in connection with the relevant offence or the offence for which he was granted bail;

(c) the person appears or is brought before a court in connection with the relevant offence or the offence for which he was granted bail."

General exceptions to the right to bail

The general exceptions to the right to bail are contained in the Bail Act 1976, sch 1, and are either generic grounds for refusal or dependent on the type of offence for which the defendant is charged.

Generic grounds:

- The defendant need not be granted bail (Sch 1 para 2) if the court is satisfied that there are substantial grounds for believing that the defendant, if released on bail (whether subject to conditions or not) would—
  - ◦ fail to surrender to custody, or
  - ◦ commit an offence while on bail, or
  - ◦ interfere with witnesses or otherwise obstruct the course of justice, whether in relation to himself or any other person.
- The defendant is aged 18 or over and has committed an offence whilst on bail, unless the court is satisfied that there is no significant risk of him committing an offence whilst on bail (sch 1 para 2A).
- The defendant need not be granted bail in connection with extradition proceedings if— (a) the conduct constituting the offence would, if carried out by the defendant in England and Wales, constitute an indictable offence or an offence triable either way; and (b) it appears to the court that the defendant was on bail on the date of the offence (sch 1 para 2B).
- The court is satisfied that the defendant should be kept in custody for his own protection or, if he is a child or young person, for his own welfare (sch 1 para 3).
- The defendant is a serving prison (sch 1 para 4).
- There is insufficient information on which to make a decision (sch 1 para 5).
- Following a failure to surrender in the proceedings (sch 1 para 6):

(1) If the defendant falls within this paragraph, he may not be granted bail unless the court is satisfied that there is no significant risk that, if released on bail (whether subject to conditions or not), he would fail to surrender to custody.

(2) Subject to sub-paragraph (3) below, the defendant falls within this paragraph if—

    (a) he is aged 18 or over, and

    (b) it appears to the court that, having been released on bail in or in connection with the proceedings for the offence, he failed to surrender to custody.

(3) Where it appears to the court that the defendant had reasonable cause for his failure to surrender to custody, he does not fall within this paragraph unless it also appears to the court that he failed to surrender to custody at the appointed place as soon as reasonably practicable after the appointed time.

(4) For the purposes of sub-paragraph (3) above, a failure to give to the defendant a copy of the record of the decision to grant him bail shall not constitute a reasonable cause for his failure to surrender to custody.

- Where a person has tested positive for class A drugs and is refusing to cooperate with treatment (Bail Act 1976, sch 1 paras 6A, 6B and 6C). In such cases bail cannot be granted unless the court is satisfied that there is no significant risk of an offence being committed on bail.
- Where his case is adjourned for inquiries or a report, the defendant need not be granted bail if it appears to the court that it would be impracticable to complete the inquiries or make the report without keeping the defendant in custody (sch 1 para 7).

Summary only offences:

Limitations on the above exceptions of bail are detailed in Sch 1 Parts 1A and 2. The effect is as follows:

Summary only imprisonable offences

Bail can only be refused on one or more of the following grounds:

- failure to surrender (if the defendant has previously failed to surrender);
- commission of further offences (if the instant offence was committed on bail);
- fear of commission of offences likely to cause another person to suffer or fear of physical or mental injury;
- the defendant's own protection (for his own welfare if a child);
- the defendant is serving custody;
- fear of failure to surrender, commission of offences, interference with witnesses, or obstruction of justice (if the defendant has been arrested for breach of bail in respect of the instant offence); and
- lack of sufficient information.

Summary only non-imprisonable offences

Bail can only be denied if there has been a previous failure to surrender in the proceedings and the court believes that if granted bail he would fail to surrender again, or:

- for the defendant's own protection (for his own welfare if a child);
- where the defendant is already in custody;
- following a breach of bail, or the defendant absconding, there are substantial grounds for believing that if released on bail the defendant would:
    - (a) fail to surrender;
    - (b) commit further offences; or
    - (c) interfere with witnesses or otherwise obstruct the course of justice.

Conditional bail

Conditional bail can be imposed if the court believes there to be a risk that:

- the defendant will fail to surrender;
- the defendant will commit an offence while on bail;
- the defendant would interfere with witnesses or obstruct justice;
- the defendant would not cooperate with the making of pre-sentence or other reports; or
- the defendant would not attend appointments with his legal adviser.

A person granted bail on a charge of murder must be required to undergo a psychiatric examination (Bail Act 1976, s 3(6A)).

Electronic monitoring

Section 3AA deals with electronic monitoring for children and young persons; section 3AB deals with adults; and section 3AC is applicable to all defendants.

Prosecution appeals against the grant of bail

The Bail (Amendment) Act 1993 allows a prosecutor to appeal the grant of bail in any case where the offence is imprisonable. The prosecution must have objected to bail, and following the grant of bail, must orally in court state their intention to appeal the decision. A written notice must be served on both the court and defendant within two hours of the oral notice having been given. A delay of five minutes in giving an oral indication to the court (and after the defendant had been taken from the courtroom) was deemed to comply with the Act in *R v Isleworth Crown Court, ex p Clarke* [1998] 1 Cr App R 257. In *R (Jeffrey) v Crown Court at Warwick* [2003] Crim LR 190, a written notice was served three minutes late due to no fault on the part of the prosecutor. A challenge to the validity of that service failed and the court suggested that section 1(7) of the Act should have read into it the following words:

… unless such failure was caused by circumstances outside the control of the prosecution and not due to any fault on its part.

Service of the written notice on a jailer who hands the notice to a defendant suffices, and solicitors who accept such notices do so on the implicit understanding that they will be immediately communicated to the defendant.

Breach of bail

Following an alleged breach of bail, the defendant must be brought before a magistrates' court within 24 hours of arrest. This means that the hearing must commence at court within those 24 hours, and any delay must result in the defendant's automatic release from custody (*R v Governor of Glen Parva Young Offender Institution, ex p G (A Minor)* [1998] 2 Cr App R 349). A court can, however, bring a defendant into the dock and then adjourn the hearing until later in the court list (*R (Hussein) v Derby Magistrates' Court* [2001] 1 WLR 254), subject to the proviso that the breach must be resolved within the 24-hour period. A magistrates' court has no power simply to commit an offender to the Crown Court in order for the breach to be decided (*R v Teeside Magistrates' Court, ex p Ellison* (2001) 165 JP 355).

Only one magistrate needs deal with an alleged bail breach and there is no requirement for formal evidence to be called by prosecution or defence. There is no defence of 'reasonable excuse' in relation to the breaking of bail conditions (*R (Vickers) v West London Magistrates' Court* [2004] Crim LR 63), although the reasons for breach would be relevant to the determination of whether or not to grant bail.

In *R v Liverpool Justices, ex p Director of Public Prosecutions* (1992) 95 Cr App R 222, the court laid down the following guidance for a court to follow when considering bail breaches:

Strict rules of evidence did not apply and hearsay was admissible; the court must consider the type of evidence called and take account of the fact that there had been no cross-examination;

the prosecution and defence can call witnesses if they so wish, and the other party has the right to cross-examine; the defendant has a right to give oral evidence.

In practice a statement will be read to the court, it follows as a result of the above that no issue in relation to hearsay arises (*R (Thomas) v Greenwich Magistrates' Court* [2009] EWHC 1180 (Admin)).

If the breach is not proved the defendant must be released on the same conditions as existed previously. If the breach is proved that does not mean an automatic remand into custody, it is simply a factor to be considered when the court decides on whether or not it should rebail.

Appeal against conditional bail

If a defendant is dissatisfied with the conditions of bail he may appeal to the Crown Court, provided that he has first applied to a magistrates' court to vary those conditions and has been unsuccessful. An appeal only lies in relation to the following conditions:

* residence (but not in relation to any bail hostel);
* surety or security;
* curfew;
* non-contact.

Appeal against refusal of bail

Following full argument in the magistrates' court (and a certificate of full argument having been issued) an appeal lies as of right to the Crown Court.

There is no longer any appeal route to the High Court, save in an exceptional case by way of judicial review.

CASE MANAGEMENT, GENERALLY

Ambush defence:

There is now a substantial body of case law on this topic, for example *Gleeson* [2003] EWCA Crim 3357:

"Just as a defendant should not be penalised for errors of his legal representatives in the conduct of his defence if he is unfairly prejudiced by them, so also should a prosecution not be frustrated by errors of the prosecutor, unless such errors have irremediably rendered a fair trial for the defendant impossible. For defence advocates to seek to take advantage of such errors by deliberately delaying identification of an issue of fact or law in the case until the last possible moment is, in our view, no longer acceptable, given the legislative and procedural changes to our criminal justice process in recent years. Indeed, we consider it to be contrary to the requirement on an accused in section 5(6) of the 1996 Act, in particular paragraph (b), to indicate "the matters on which he takes issue with the prosecution", and to their professional duty to the court – and not in the legitimate interests of the defendant.

In this context we take the opportunity to repeat and adopt the extra-judicial sentiments of one of us in the Report of the Criminal Courts Review (October 2001), in paragraph 154 of Chapter 10:

"To the extent that the prosecution may legitimately wish to fill possible holes in its case once issues have been identified by the defence statement, it is understandable why as a matter of tactics a defendant might prefer to keep his case close to his chest. But that is not a valid reason for preventing a full and fair hearing on the issues canvassed at the trial. A criminal trial is not a game under which a guilty defendant should be provided with a sporting chance. It is a search for truth in accordance with the twin principles that the prosecution must prove its case and that a defendant is not obliged to inculpate himself, the object being to convict the guilty and acquit the innocent. Requiring a defendant to indicate in advance what he disputes about the prosecution case offends neither of those principles.""

This extends to issues that only arise during the case, eg *Penner* [2010] EWCA Crim 1155:

"So this case is an ample demonstration of why it is essential that counsel at the PCMH stage carefully examine and identify the issues. As counsel in this case failed to do so, when the point, as he tells us, occurred to him in the course of cross-examination, it was then his duty to have identified it to the judge, before going any further with his cross-examination. He should not have left the matter for half time. He should have told the judge that there was a new issue and asked the judge how this matter should be dealt with.

That would have enabled counsel for the Crown to take the opportunity of looking at the law and the presumptions and provisions of the Sex Offenders Act to which we have referred. It is no longer possible to have cases conducted in the way in which this case was conducted by counsel for the appellant, where points occur to someone and then an attempt is made to ambush the prosecution by a submission of no case to answer. The Divisional Court made clear in the Chorley Justices case [2006] EWHC 1795 (Admin) that trial by ambush was no longer permissible. It is a regrettable fact that this court has again had to make that position clear. It is important to do so in this case, because if counsel had identified the issue, even if it occurred to him late (in a proper manner and not by means of submission at half time) then the Crown would have had an opportunity, if there had been any evidence in this case, to correct and bring before the trial court proper evidence. It is no longer permissible for the ambush of the type that it might be suggested happened in this case, to be performed in the future. We add those merely by way of observations. The appeal fails simply because, had the true position been put before this court, leave to appeal would never have been granted."

Costs sanctions: See *SVS Solicitors* [2012] EWCA Crim 319.

Duty to actively case manage:

In *Jisl* [2004] EWCA Crim 696 it was held:

"After an earlier trial which had taken place in 1998, this trial took place in the summer of 2001. By the time the retrial started we recognise that its management had already been fixed, virtually immutably, into pre-determined patterns. The observations which follow are not intended to be critical of the trial judge. Rather, they are an attempt to explain that since the date of this trial arrangements for case management by trial judges have changed, and to emphasise the urgent necessity that these changes and their potential impact are fully and widely understood.

The starting point is simple. Justice must be done. The defendant is entitled to a fair trial: and, which is sometimes overlooked, the prosecution is equally entitled to a reasonable opportunity to present the evidence against the defendant. It is not however a concomitant of the entitlement to a fair trial that either or both sides are further entitled to take as much time as they like, or for that matter, as long as counsel and solicitors or the defendants themselves think appropriate. Resources are limited. The funding for courts and judges, for prosecuting and the vast majority of defence lawyers is dependent on public money, for which there are many competing demands. Time itself is a resource. Every day unnecessarily used, while the trial meanders sluggishly to its eventual conclusion, represents another day's stressful waiting for the remaining witnesses and the jurors in that particular trial, and no less important, continuing and increasing tension and worry for another defendant or defendants, some of whom are remanded in custody, and the witnesses in trials which are waiting their turn to be listed. It follows that the sensible use of time requires judicial management and control.

[...] in R v Chaaban [2003] EWCA Crim 1012 this Court endeavoured to explain the principle:

"35. ... The trial judge has always been responsible for managing the trial. That is one of his most important functions. To perform it he has to be alert to the needs of everyone involved in the case. That obviously includes, but it is not limited to, the interests of the defendant. It extends to the prosecution, the complainant, to every witness (whichever side is to call the witness), to the jury, or if the jury has not been sworn, to jurors in waiting. Finally, the judge should not overlook the community's interest that justice should be done without unnecessary delay. A fair balance has to be struck between all these interests.

...

37. ... nowadays, as part of his responsibility for managing the trial, the judge is expected to control the timetable and to manage the available time. Time is not unlimited. No one should assume that trials can continue to take as long or use up as much time as either or both sides may wish, or think, or assert, they need. The entitlement to a fair trial is not inconsistent with proper judicial control over the use of time. At the risk of stating the obvious, every trial which takes longer than it reasonably should is wasteful of limited resources. It also results in delays to justice in cases still waiting to be tried, adding to the tension and distress of victims, defendants, particularly those in custody awaiting trial, and witnesses. Most important of all it does nothing to assist the jury to reach a true verdict on the evidence.

38. In principle, the trial judge should exercise firm control over the timetable, where necessary, making clear in advance and throughout the trial that the timetable will be subject to appropriate constraints. With such necessary even-handedness and flexibility as the interests of the justice require as the case unfolds, the judge is entitled to direct that the trial is expected to conclude by a specific date and to exercise his powers to see that it does."

The principle therefore, is not in doubt. This appeal enables us to re-emphasise that its practical application depends on the determination of trial judges and the co-operation of the legal profession. Active, hands on, case management, both pre-trial and throughout the trial itself, is now regarded as an essential part of the judge's duty. The profession must understand that this has become and will remain part of the normal trial process, and that cases must be prepared and conducted accordingly.

The issues in this particular trial were identified at a very early stage, indeed during the course of the previous trial itself. In relation to each of the defendants, in a single word, the issue was knowledge. And indeed, the issue in most trials is equally readily identified.

Once the issue has been identified, in a case of any substance at all, (and this particular case was undoubtedly a case of substance and difficulty) the judge should consider whether to direct a timetable to cover pre-trial steps, and eventually the conduct of the trial itself, not rigid, nor immutable, and fully recognising that during the trial at any rate the unexpected must be treated as normal, and making due allowance for it in the interests of justice. To enable the trial judge to manage the case in a way which is fair to every participant, pre-trial, the potential problems as well as the possible areas for time saving, should be canvassed. In short, a sensible informed discussion about the future management of the case and the most convenient way to present the evidence, whether disputed or not, and where appropriate, with admissions by one or other or both sides, should enable the judge to make a fully informed analysis of the future timetable, and the proper conduct of the trial. The objective is not haste and rush, but greater efficiency and better use of limited resources by closer identification of and focus on critical rather than peripheral issues. When trial judges act in accordance with these principles, the directions they give, and where appropriate, the timetables they prescribe in the exercise of their case management responsibilities, will be supported in this Court. Criticism is more likely to be addressed to those who ignore them."

Other sanctions: The court has the power, in the event of a rule breach, to stop expert evidence being adduced (eg *Ensor* [2009] EWCA Crim 2519), prohibit use of bad character evidence (eg *Musone* [2007] EWCA Crim 1237) and to stop the prosecution from relying on further evidence (eg *Owens* [2006] EWCA Crim 2206).

Time constraints: The court has power to limit oral and written argument (*Kay* [2006] EWCA Crim 835) and control the limits of cross-examination (*Butt* [2005] EWCA Crim 805).

Criminal Procedure Rules 2012, r 1–3

Part 1: The overriding objective

1.1.—(1) The overriding objective of this new code is that criminal cases be dealt with justly.
    (2) Dealing with a criminal case justly includes—

       (a) acquitting the innocent and convicting the guilty;
       (b) dealing with the prosecution and the defence fairly;
       (c) recognising the rights of a defendant, particularly those under Article 6 of the European Convention on Human Rights;
       (d) respecting the interests of witnesses, victims and jurors and keeping them informed of the progress of the case;
       (e) dealing with the case efficiently and expeditiously;
       (f) ensuring that appropriate information is available to the court when bail and sentence are considered; and
       (g) dealing with the case in ways that take into account
          (i) the gravity of the offence alleged,
          (ii) the complexity of what is in issue,
          (iii) the severity of the consequences for the defendant and others affected, and
          (iv) the needs of other cases.

The duty of the participants in a criminal case

1.2.—(1) Each participant, in the conduct of each case, must

       (a) prepare and conduct the case in accordance with the overriding objective;
       (b) comply with these Rules, practice directions and directions made by the court; and
       (c) at once inform the court and all parties of any significant failure (whether or not that participant is responsible for that failure) to take any procedural step required by

these Rules, any practice direction or any direction of the court. A failure is significant if it might hinder the court in furthering the overriding objective.

(2)   Anyone involved in any way with a criminal case is a participant in its conduct for the purposes of this rule.

The application by the court of the overriding objective

1.3.   The court must further the overriding objective in particular when—

(a)   exercising any power given to it by legislation (including these Rules);

(b)   applying any practice direction; or

(c)   interpreting any rule or practice direction.

Part 2: When the Rules apply

2.1.—(1) In general, the Criminal Procedure Rules apply—

(a)   in all criminal cases in magistrates' courts and in the Crown Court; and

(b)   in all cases in the criminal division of the Court of Appeal.

(2)   If a rule applies only in one or two of those courts, the rule makes that clear.

(3)   The Rules apply on and after 1st October, 2012, but unless the court otherwise directs they do not affect a right or duty existing under The Criminal Procedure Rules 2011.

(4)   Rule 9.6, and the rules in Section 3 of Part 9 (Allocation and sending for trial), apply only where there have come into force the amendments made by Schedule 3 to the Criminal Justice Act 2003 (Allocation of cases triable either way, and sending cases to the Crown Court, etc.) which confer the powers to which those rules apply.

Definitions

2.2.—(1) In these Rules, unless the context makes it clear that something different is meant:

'business day' means any day except Saturday, Sunday, Christmas Day, Boxing Day, Good Friday, Easter Monday or a bank holiday;

'court' means a tribunal with jurisdiction over criminal cases. It includes a judge, recorder, District Judge (Magistrates' Court), lay justice and, when exercising their judicial powers, the Registrar of Criminal Appeals, a justices' clerk or assistant clerk;

'court officer' means the appropriate member of the staff of a court;

'justices' legal adviser' means a justices' clerk or an assistant to a justices' clerk;

'live link' means an arrangement by which a person can see and hear, and be seen and heard by, the court when that person is not in court;

'Practice Direction' means the Lord Chief Justice's Consolidated Criminal Practice Direction, as amended, and 'Criminal Costs Practice Direction' means the Lord Chief Justice's Practice Direction (Costs in Criminal Proceedings), as amended;

'public interest ruling' means a ruling about whether it is in the public interest to disclose prosecution material under sections 3(6), 7A(8) or 8(5) of the Criminal Procedure and Investigations Act 1996(6); and

'Registrar' means the Registrar of Criminal Appeals or a court officer acting with the Registrar's authority.

(2) Definitions of some other expressions are in the rules in which they apply.

References to Acts of Parliament and to Statutory Instruments

2.3. In these Rules, where a rule refers to an Act of Parliament or to subordinate legislation by title and year, subsequent references to that Act or to that legislation in the rule are shortened: so, for example, after a reference to the Criminal Procedure and Investigations Act 1996 that Act is called 'the 1996 Act'; and after a reference to The Criminal Procedure and Investigations Act 1996 (Defence Disclosure Time Limits) Regulations 2011 those Regulations are called 'the 2011 Regulations'.

Representatives

2.4.—(1) Under these Rules, unless the context makes it clear that something different is meant, anything that a party may or must do may be done—

    (a) by a legal representative on that party's behalf;

    (b) by a person with the corporation's written authority, where that party is a corporation;

    (c) with the help of a parent, guardian or other suitable supporting adult where that party is a defendant—

        (i) who is under 18, or

        (ii) whose understanding of what the case involves is limited.

(2) Anyone with a prosecutor's authority to do so may, on that prosecutor's behalf—

    (a) serve on the magistrates' court officer, or present to a magistrates' court, an information under section 1 of the Magistrates' Courts Act 1980(9); or

    (b) issue a written charge and requisition under section 29 of the Criminal Justice Act 2003(10).

Part 3: The scope of this Part

3.1. This Part applies to the management of each case in a magistrates' court and in the Crown Court (including an appeal to the Crown Court) until the conclusion of that case.

The duty of the court

3.2.—(1) The court must further the overriding objective by actively managing the case.

(2) Active case management includes—

    (a) the early identification of the real issues;

    (b) the early identification of the needs of witnesses;

    (c) achieving certainty as to what must be done, by whom, and when, in particular by the early setting of a timetable for the progress of the case;

    (d) monitoring the progress of the case and compliance with directions;

    (e) ensuring that evidence, whether disputed or not, is presented in the shortest and clearest way;

    (f) discouraging delay, dealing with as many aspects of the case as possible on the same occasion, and avoiding unnecessary hearings;

    (g) encouraging the participants to co-operate in the progression of the case; and

    (h) making use of technology.

(3) The court must actively manage the case by giving any direction appropriate to the needs of that case as early as possible.

The duty of the parties

3.3. Each party must—

    (a) actively assist the court in fulfilling its duty under rule 3.2, without or if necessary with a direction; and

    (b) apply for a direction if needed to further the overriding objective.

Case progression officers and their duties

3.4.—(1) At the beginning of the case each party must, unless the court otherwise directs

    (a) nominate an individual responsible for progressing that case; and

    (b) tell other parties and the court who he is and how to contact him.

(2) In fulfilling its duty under rule 3.2, the court must where appropriate—

    (a) nominate a court officer responsible for progressing the case; and

    (b) make sure the parties know who he is and how to contact him.

(3) In this Part a person nominated under this rule is called a case progression officer.

(4) A case progression officer must—

    (a) monitor compliance with directions;

    (b) make sure that the court is kept informed of events that may affect the progress of that case;

    (c) make sure that he can be contacted promptly about the case during ordinary business hours;

    (d) act promptly and reasonably in response to communications about the case; and

    (e) if he will be unavailable, appoint a substitute to fulfil his duties and inform the other case progression officers.

The court's case management powers

3.5.—(1) In fulfilling its duty under rule 3.2 the court may give any direction and take any step actively to manage a case unless that direction or step would be inconsistent with legislation, including these Rules.

(2) In particular, the court may—

    (a) nominate a judge, magistrate or justices' legal adviser to manage the case;

    (b) give a direction on its own initiative or on application by a party;

    (c) ask or allow a party to propose a direction;

    (d) for the purpose of giving directions, receive applications and representations by letter, by telephone or by any other means of electronic communication, and conduct a hearing by such means;

    (e) give a direction—

        (i) at a hearing, in public or in private, or

        (ii) without a hearing;

    (f) fix, postpone, bring forward, extend, cancel or adjourn a hearing;

    (g) shorten or extend (even after it has expired) a time limit fixed by a direction;

    (h) require that issues in the case should be—

        (i) identified in writing,

        (ii) determined separately, and decide in what order they will be determined; and

    (i) specify the consequences of failing to comply with a direction.

(3) A magistrates' court may give a direction that will apply in the Crown Court if the case is to continue there.

(4) The Crown Court may give a direction that will apply in a magistrates' court if the case is to continue there.

(5) Any power to give a direction under this Part includes a power to vary or revoke that direction.

(6) If a party fails to comply with a rule or a direction, the court may—

    (a) fix, postpone, bring forward, extend, cancel or adjourn a hearing;

    (b) exercise its powers to make a costs order; and

    (c) impose such other sanction as may be appropriate.

Application to vary a direction

3.6.—(1) A party may apply to vary a direction if—

    (a) the court gave it without a hearing;

    (b) the court gave it at a hearing in his absence; or

    (c) circumstances have changed.

(2) A party who applies to vary a direction must—

    (a) apply as soon as practicable after he becomes aware of the grounds for doing so; and

    (b) give as much notice to the other parties as the nature and urgency of his application permits.

Agreement to vary a time limit fixed by a direction

3.7.—(1) The parties may agree to vary a time limit fixed by a direction, but only if—

    (a) the variation will not—
        (i)   affect the date of any hearing that has been fixed, or
        (ii) significantly affect the progress of the case in any other way;
    (b) the court has not prohibited variation by agreement; and
    (c) the court's case progression officer is promptly informed.

  (2) The court's case progression officer must refer the agreement to the court if he doubts the condition in paragraph (1)(a) is satisfied.

Case preparation and progression

3.8.—(1) At every hearing, if a case cannot be concluded there and then the court must give directions so that it can be concluded at the next hearing or as soon as possible after that.

  (2) At every hearing the court must, where relevant—

    (a) if the defendant is absent, decide whether to proceed nonetheless;
    (b) take the defendant's plea (unless already done) or if no plea can be taken then find out whether the defendant is likely to plead guilty or not guilty;
    (c) set, follow or revise a timetable for the progress of the case, which may include a timetable for any hearing including the trial or (in the Crown Court) the appeal;
    (d) in giving directions, ensure continuity in relation to the court and to the parties' representatives where that is appropriate and practicable; and
    (e) where a direction has not been complied with, find out why, identify who was responsible, and take appropriate action.

  (3) In order to prepare for a trial in the Crown Court, the court must conduct a plea and case management hearing unless the circumstances make that unnecessary.

  (4) In order to prepare for the trial, the court must take every reasonable step to encourage and to facilitate the attendance of witnesses when they are needed.

Readiness for trial or appeal

3.9.—(1) This rule applies to a party's preparation for trial or appeal, and in this rule and rule 3.10 trial includes any hearing at which evidence will be introduced.

  (2) In fulfilling his duty under rule 3.3, each party must—

    (a) comply with directions given by the court;
    (b) take every reasonable step to make sure his witnesses will attend when they are needed;
    (c) make appropriate arrangements to present any written or other material; and
    (d) promptly inform the court and the other parties of anything that may
        (i)   affect the date or duration of the trial or appeal, or
        (ii) significantly affect the progress of the case in any other way.

  (3) The court may require a party to give a certificate of readiness.

Conduct of a trial or an appeal

3.10. In order to manage a trial or an appeal, the court—

    (a) must establish, with the active assistance of the parties, what are the disputed issues;
    (b) must consider setting a timetable that—
        (i)   takes account of those issues and of any timetable proposed by a party, and
        (ii) may limit the duration of any stage of the hearing;
    (c) may require a party to identify—
        (i)   which witnesses that party wants to give evidence in person,
        (ii)   the order in which that party wants those witnesses to give their evidence,
        (iii) whether that party requires an order compelling the attendance of a witness,

(iv)   what arrangements are desirable to facilitate the giving of evidence by a witness,

(v)   what arrangements are desirable to facilitate the participation of any other person, including the defendant,

(vi)   what written evidence that party intends to introduce,

(vii) what other material, if any, that person intends to make available to the court in the presentation of the case, and

(viii) whether that party intends to raise any point of law that could affect the conduct of the trial or appeal; and

(d) may limit—

(i)   the examination, cross-examination or re-examination of a witness, and

(ii)   the duration of any stage of the hearing.

Case management forms and records

3.11.—(1) The case management forms set out in the Practice Direction must be used, and where there is no form then no specific formality is required.

(2)   The court must make available to the parties a record of directions given.

(3)   Where a person is entitled or required to attend a hearing, the court officer must give as much notice as reasonably practicable to—

(a) that person; and

(b) that person's custodian (if any).

CHANGE OF PLEA

If after an unequivocal plea of guilty has been made, it becomes apparent that the defendant did not appreciate the elements of the offence to which he was pleading guilty, then it is likely to be appropriate to permit him to withdraw his plea–see *R v South Tameside Magistrates' Court, ex p Rowland* [1983] 3 All ER 689 at p. 692 per Glidewell LJ. Such a situation should be rare, for it is unlikely to arise where the defendant is represented and, where he is not, it is the duty of the court to make sure that the nature of the offence is made clear to him before a plea of guilty is accepted. In *S v Recorder of Manchester* [1971] AC 481 the court held:

"The duty of any court to clear the innocent must be equal or superior in importance to its duty to convict and punish the guilty. Guilt may be proved by evidence. But it also may be confessed. The court will, however, have great concern if any doubt exists as to whether a confession was intended or whether it ought really ever to have been made."

The case of *R v Croydon Youth Court, ex p Director of Public Prosecutions* [1997] 2 Cr App R 411 appears to suggest that the Magistrates' Court Act 1980, s 142 cannot be utilised in order to set aside an unequivocal plea. In *R (Williamson) v City of Westminster Magistrates' Court* [2012] EWHC 1444 (Admin) the court held:

"We accept that there may be circumstances in which section 142(2) could be used to allow an unequivocal guilty plea to be set aside. Examples which spring to mind include cases in which a guilty plea had been entered to an offence unknown to the law. Surprising though it may seem, such errors do occur in particular in connection with repealed legislation. That would fall comfortably within the language of mistake. They may include cases where a jurisdictional bar was not appreciated by the defendant relating, for example, to a time limit or the identity of a prosecutor. There may be cases in which the proceedings were, in truth, a nullity. We would not exclude the possibility that section 142(2) would be apt to deal with a case in which circumstances developed after a guilty plea and sentence which led the prosecution to conclude that the conviction should not be sustained."

Criminal Procedure Rules 2012, r 37.9

37.9.—(1) This rule applies where the defendant wants to withdraw a guilty plea.

(2)   The defendant must apply to do so—

(a) as soon as practicable after becoming aware of the reasons for doing so; and

(b) before sentence.

(3) Unless the court otherwise directs, the application must be in writing and the defendant must

serve it on—

(a) the court officer; and

(b) the prosecutor.

(4) The application must—

(a) explain why it would be unjust not to allow the defendant to withdraw the guilty plea;

(b) identify—

(i) any witness that the defendant wants to call, and

(ii) any other proposed evidence; and

(c) say whether the defendant waives legal professional privilege, giving any relevant name

and date.

CLERKS RETIRING WITH JUSTICES

Consolidated Criminal Practice Direction, part V.55

(V.55.1)

A Justice clerk is responsible for:

(a) the legal advice tendered to the justices within the area;

(b) the performance of any of the functions set out below by any member of his staff acting as legal adviser;

(c) ensuring that competent advice is available to justices when the Justice clerk is not personally present in court; and

(d) the effective delivery of case management and the reduction of unnecessary delay.

(V.55.2)

Where a person other than the Justice clerk (a 'legal adviser'), who is authorised to do so, performs any of the functions referred to in this direction he will have the same responsibilities as the Justice clerk. The legal adviser may consult the Justice clerk or other person authorised by the Justice clerk for that purpose before tendering advice to the bench. If the Justice clerk or that person gives any advice directly to the bench, he should give the parties or their advocates an opportunity of repeating any relevant submissions prior to the advice being given.

(V.55.3)

It shall be the responsibility of the legal adviser to provide the justices with any advice they require properly to perform their functions, whether or not the justices have requested that advice, on:

(a) questions of law (including European Court of Human Rights jurisprudence and those matters set out in section 2(1) of the Human Rights Act 1998);

(b) questions of mixed law and fact;

(c) matters of practice and procedure;

(d) the range of penalties available;

(e) any relevant decisions of the superior courts or other guidelines;

(f) other issues relevant to the matter before the court; and

(g) the appropriate decision-making structure to be applied in any given case.

In addition to advising the justices it shall be the legal adviser's responsibility to assist the court, where appropriate, as to the formulation of reasons and the recording of those reasons.

(V.55.4)

A Justice clerk or legal adviser must not play any part in making findings of fact, but may assist the bench by reminding them of the evidence, using any notes of the proceedings for this purpose.

(V.55.5)

A Justice clerk or legal adviser may ask questions of witnesses and the parties in order to clarify the evidence and any issues in the case. A legal adviser has a duty to ensure that every case is conducted fairly.

(V.55.6)

When advising the justices the Justice clerk or legal adviser, whether or not previously in court, should:

(a) ensure that he is aware of the relevant facts; and
(b) provide the parties with the information necessary to enable the parties to make any representations they wish as to the advice before it is given.

(V.55.7)

At any time justices are entitled to receive advice to assist them in discharging their responsibilities. If they are in any doubt as to the evidence which has been given, they should seek the aid of their legal adviser, referring to his notes as appropriate. This should ordinarily be done in open court. Where the justices request their adviser to join them in the retiring room, this request should be made in the presence of the parties in court. Any legal advice given to the justices other than in open court should be clearly stated to be provisional and the adviser should subsequently repeat the substance of the advice in open court and give the parties an opportunity to make any representations they wish on that provisional advice. The legal adviser should then state in open court whether the provisional advice is confirmed or if it is varied the nature of the variation.

(V.55.8)

The performance of a legal adviser may be appraised by a person authorised by the magistrates' courts committee to do so. For that purpose the appraiser may be present in the Justice retiring room. The content of the appraisal is confidential, but the fact that an appraisal has taken place, and the presence of the appraiser in the retiring room, should be briefly explained in open court.

(V.55.9)

The legal adviser is under a duty to assist unrepresented parties to present their case, but must do so without appearing to become an advocate for the party concerned.

(V.55.10)

The role of legal advisers in fine default proceedings or any other proceedings for the enforcement of financial orders, obligations or penalties is to assist the court. They must not act in an adversarial or partisan manner. With the agreement of the justices a legal adviser may ask questions of the defaulter to elicit information which the justices will require to make an adjudication, for example to facilitate his explanation for the default. A legal adviser may also advise the justices in the normal way as to the options open to them in dealing with the case. It would be inappropriate for the legal adviser to set out to establish wilful refusal or neglect or any other type of culpable behaviour, to offer an opinion on the facts, or to urge a particular course of action upon the justices. The duty of impartiality is the paramount consideration for the legal adviser at all times, and this takes precedence over any role he may have as a collecting officer. The appointment of other staff to 'prosecute' the case for the collecting officer is not essential to ensure compliance with the law, including the Human Rights Act 1998. Whether to make such appointments is a matter for the Justice chief executive.

CONSENT TO PROSECUTE

Consent to prosecute is necessary in a number of cases, but lack of consent does not invalidate arrest, charge or remand (Prosecution of Offences Act 1985, s 25(2)), if any further action is taken prior to consent it can be possibly be cured by consent being obtained and the procedure (eg allocation) being repeated (*Lambert* [2009] 2 Cr App R 32). In *Lambert* the court left open the question of what relief might be available if a conviction were to be secured absent consent having been obtained. The consent of the Director of Public Prosecutions can be given by any crown prosecutor (Prosecution of Offences Act 1985, s 1(7)).

CONSTITUTION OF THE COURT

A District Judge may sit alone (Courts Act 2003, s 26). Magistrates and Justice clerks have more limited powers when sitting alone and at least 2 magistrates (Magistrates' Courts Act 1980, s 121) are required to hear a trial, with a maximum of 3 sitting on any one case (Justices of the Peace (Size and Chairmanship of Bench) Rules 2005). A single justice cannot impose imprisonment exceeding 14 days, or impose a fine more than £1 (MCA 1980, s 121(5)). If a magistrate absents themselves from part of proceedings he may not later act any further therein. **Open justice**: Subject to the provisions of any enactment to the contrary, a magistrates' court must sit in open court if it is (a) trying summarily an information for an indictable offence, (b) trying an information for a summary offence, (c) imposing imprisonment, (d) hearing a complaint, or (e) holding an inquiry into the means of an offender for the purposes of section 82 (MCA 1980, s 121(4)). **Trial benches**: Where the trial of an information is adjourned after the accused has been convicted and before he is sentenced or otherwise dealt with, the court which sentences or deals with him need not be composed of the same justices as that which convicted him; but, where among the justices composing the court which sentences or deals with an offender there are any who were not sitting when he was convicted, the court which sentences or deals with the offender shall before doing so make such inquiry into the facts and circumstances of the case as will enable the justices who were not sitting when the offender was convicted to be fully acquainted with those facts and circumstances (MCA 1980, s 121(7)).

CUSTODY TIME LIMITS

Unless an extension is granted a person cannot be detained in custody for more than 56 days from date of first appearance to trial, or 70 from first appearance to committal proceedings taking place. Each separate offence attracts its own time limit (*R v Wirral Magistrates' Court ex p Meikle* [1990] Crim LR 801). Time runs from midnight on the first day to midnight on the last day. There is no power to extend a time limit once it has expired (*R v Sheffield Justices ex p Turner* [1991] 2 WLR 987. Any extension is to be decided on the balance of probabilities. There is extensive case law on this topic including the key authorities of *R v Crown Court at Manchester ex p MacDonald* [1999] 1 All ER 805 and *R (Raeside) v Crown Court at Luton* [2012] EWHC 1064 (Admin) where it was held:

> "This case demonstrates again the necessity of treating the CTL in each case and any application to extend it in the very serious manner required of the statutory provisions which Parliament, consistent with the long tradition of the common law, has enacted to ensure cases are tried speedily and those who have not been convicted are not deprived of their liberty beyond the time specified without good reason. A person should not to be deprived of his liberty where the State cannot meet the duty to try him speedily and within the time limit specified without detailed evidence that is then subject to vigorous and stringent examination to see if the State has established good and sufficient cause to deprive him of his liberty beyond that time limit".

It is almost inconceivable that a lack of judicial resources or court availability would in the magistrates' court suffice as a good and sufficient cause to extend custody time limits.

Prosecution of Offences Act 1985, ss 22(3), (5), (6) and (6A)

(3) The appropriate court may, at any time before the expiry of a time limit imposed by the regulations, extend, or further extend, that limit; but the court shall not do so unless it is satisfied—

    (a) that the need for the extension is due to—

        (i) the illness or absence of the accused, a necessary witness, a judge or a magistrate;

        (ii) a postponement which is occasioned by the ordering by the court of separate trials in the case of two or more accused or two or more offences; or

        (iii) some other good and sufficient cause; and

    (b) that the prosecution has acted with all due diligence and expedition.

(4) [...]

(5) Where—

    (a) a person escapes from the custody of a magistrates' court or the Crown Court before the expiry of a custody time limit which applies in his case; or

    (b) a person who has been released on bail in consequence of the expiry of a custody time limit—

        (i) fails to surrender himself into the custody of the court at the appointed time; or

        (ii) is arrested by a constable on a ground mentioned in section 7(3)(b) of the Bail Act 1976 (breach, or likely breach, of conditions of bail);

the regulations shall, so far as they provide for any custody time limit in relation to the preliminary stage in question, be disregarded.

(6) Subsection (6A) below applies where —

    (a) a person escapes from the custody of a magistrates' court or the Crown Court; or

    (b) a person who has been released on bail fails to surrender himself into the custody of the court at the appointed time;

and is accordingly unlawfully at large for any period.

(6A) The following, namely—

    (a) the period for which the person is unlawfully at large; and

    (b) such additional period (if any) as the appropriate court may direct, having regard to the disruption of the prosecution occasioned by—

        (i) the person's escape or failure to surrender; and

        (ii) the length of the period mentioned in paragraph (a) above,

shall be disregarded, so far as the offence in question is concerned, for the purposes of the overall time limit which applies in his case in relation to the stage which the proceedings have reached at the time of the escape or, as the case may be, at the appointed time.

DEATH OF DEFENDANT

The court should receive such evidence as to make it satisfied that the defendant has died, but there appears to be no particular formality required. The prosecution will then either withdraw proceedings or offer no evidence. Proceedings ought not to be adjourned sine die.

DEFECTIVE INFORMATION, SUMMONS OR WARRANT

Despite the apparently clear wording of section 123 its effect has given rise to a considerable body of case law. Essentially, there are defects that do not invalidate the process and can be left without the need for amendment, defects that do not invalidate the proceedings yet require an amendment (and adjournment if necessary to avoid prejudice), and defects that are so fundamental that it is improper to proceed further (so for example it is not proper to amend an information that alleges an offence not known to law with one that is (*Garman v Plaice* [1969] 1 All ER 62). The presence of a person at court, otherwise than to challenge the process on the basis of an irregularity, cures any defect in process. It is the obligation of the court to bring any such defect to the defendant's attention as he cannot exercise a waiver in relation to matters of which he has no knowledge (*R v Essex Justices, ex p Perkins* [1927] 2 KB 475).

Magistrates' Courts Act 1980, s 123

(1) No objection shall be allowed to any information or complaint, or to any summons or warrant to procure the presence of the defendant, for any defect in it in substance or in form, or for any variance between it and the evidence adduced on behalf of the prosecutor or complainant at the hearing of the information or complaint.

(2) If it appears to a magistrates' court that any variance between a summons or warrant and the evidence adduced on behalf of the prosecutor or complainant is such that the defendant has been misled by the variance, the court shall, on the application of the defendant, adjourn the hearing.

DISCLOSURE

General Duty on Prosecution and defence to Disclose

Initial disclosure of the prosecution case in order to assist the defendant prior to the entering of a plea is now contained in CrPR Rule 21. There are also specific provisions (for which see below) dealing with discrete areas of disclosure, such as expert evidence. General disclosure prior to trial is however less regulated save that the extent of the disclosure that is necessary to ensure there is a fair trial will depend on the evidence and the issues in the case (*Filmer v Director of Public Prosecutions* [2006] EWHC 3450 (Admin)). The Attorney General's Guidelines on Disclosure (April 2005) at para 57 state:

> "The prosecutor should, in addition to complying with the obligations under the Act, provide to the defence all evidence upon which the Crown proposes to rely in a summary trial. Such provision should allow the accused and their legal advisers sufficient time properly to consider the evidence before it is called."

There are various statutory requirements requiring defence disclosure, and in addition there is now a substantial volume of case law that supports the proposition that the defence cannot keep its case concealed until the last minute in order to take maximum advantage (so called ambush defences). Failure to abide by both letter and spirit of the criminal procedure rules will in all likelihood result in an adjournment at best and a wasted costs order at worse. In *Director of Public Prosecutions v Chorley Justices* [2006] EWHC 1795 (Admin) the court held:

> "In April 2005 the Criminal Procedure Rules came into effect. By 15th April they were in force. They have effected a sea change in the way in which cases should be conducted, but it appears from what has happened in this case that not everyone has appreciated the fundamental change to the conduct of cases in the Magistrates' Courts that has been brought about by the rules. The rules make clear that the overriding objective is that criminal cases be dealt with justly; that includes acquitting the innocent and convicting the guilty, dealing with the prosecution and the defence fairly, respecting the interests of witnesses, dealing with the case efficiently and expeditiously, and also, of great importance,

dealing with the case in a way that takes into account the gravity of the offence, the complexity of what is in issue, the severity of the consequences to the defendant and others affected and the needs of other cases. Rule 1.2 imposes upon the duty of participants in a criminal case to prepare and conduct the case in accordance with the overriding objective, to comply with the rules and, importantly, to inform the court and all parties of any significant failure, whether or not the participant is responsible for that failure, to take any procedural step required by the rules. Rule 3.2 imposes upon the court a duty to further that overriding objective by actively managing the case. The pertinent part relevant to what happened in this case is the early identification of the real issues. It is, it seems to us, clear that what should have happened is that at the first hearing of a case of this kind, after the entry of the plea of not guilty, the defendant should have been asked first what was in issue. At that stage and at the first hearing, he should then have been asked what witnesses did he need."

In *Malcolm v Director of Public Prosecutions* [2007] EWHC 363 (Admin) the court said:

"In my judgment, [Counsel's] submissions, which emphasised the obligation of the prosecution to prove its case in its entirety before closing its case, and certainly before end of the final speech for the defence, had an anachronistic, and obsolete, ring. Criminal trials are no longer to be treated as a game, in which each move is final and any omission by the prosecution leads to its failure. It is the duty of the defence to make its defence and the issues it raises clear to the prosecution and to the court at an early stage. That duty is implicit in rule 3.3 of the Criminal Procedure Rules, which requires the parties actively to assist the exercise by the court of its case management powers, the exercise of which requires early identification of the real issues. Even in a relatively straightforward trial such as the present, in the magistrates' court (where there is not yet any requirement of a defence statement or a pre-trial review), it is the duty of the defence to make the real issues clear at the latest before the prosecution closes its case."

Initial Details of Prosecution Case

Criminal Procedure Rules 2012, r 21 provides:

When this Part applies

21.1.—(1) This Part applies in a magistrates' court, where the offence is one that can be tried in a magistrates' court.

    (2) The court may direct that, for a specified period, this Part will not apply—

        (a) to any case in that court; or

        (b) to any specified category of case.

[Note. An offence may be classified as—

        (a) one that can be tried only in a magistrates' court (in other legislation, described as triable only summarily);

        (b) one that can be tried either in a magistrates' court or in the Crown Court (in other legislation, described as triable either way); or

        (c) one that can be tried only in the Crown Court (in other legislation, described as triable only on indictment).

See the definitions contained in Schedule 1 to the Interpretation Act 1978. In some circumstances, the Crown Court can try an offence that usually can be tried only in a magistrates' court.

This Part does not apply where an offence can be tried only in the Crown Court. In such a case, details are served on the defendant after the case is sent for trial. Part 9 contains relevant rules.]

Providing initial details of the prosecution case

21.2. The prosecutor must provide initial details of the prosecution case by—

(a) serving those details on the court officer; and

(b) making those details available to the defendant,

at, or before, the beginning of the day of the first hearing.

Content of initial details

21.3. Initial details of the prosecution case must include—

(a) a summary of the evidence on which that case will be based; or

(b) any statement, document or extract setting out facts or other matters on which that case will be based; or

(c) any combination of such a summary, statement, document or extract; and

(d) the defendant's previous convictions.

An absence of initial disclosure will not necessarily give rise to an adjournment, nor will it be a reason to delay the entering of plea in many instances. Where a failure to disclose leads to unfairness an adjournment may be granted by the court, and continued failure to serve initial details of prosecution case might exceptionally support an application to stay the case for abuse of process (*Willesden Justices ex p Clemings* (87) Cr App R 280).

Expert Evidence

A party who is contemplating the instruction of an expert and the service of expert evidence should notify the court of that fact at the earliest possible juncture. In *Ensor* [2009] EWCA Crim 2519 the court held:

> "it is incumbent upon both prosecution and defence parties to criminal trials to alert the court and the other side at the earliest practical moment if it is intending or may be intending to adduce expert evidence. That should be done if possible at a PCMH. If it cannot be done then it must be done as soon as the possibility becomes live. The nearer the start of the trial, the greater the urgency in informing the court and other side of the possibility of adducing expert evidence so that appropriate steps can be taken by the court and the other side to manage the expert evidence in an efficient way."

Breach: A failure to comply with the CrPR may in appropriate cases result in the exclusion of expert evidence (eg *Writtle v Director of Public Prosecutions* 173 JP 244). The Criminal Procedure and Investigations Act 1996, s 6D (not yet in force) will require parties to formally disclose the details of defence experts instructed by an accused:

Criminal Procedure and Investigations Act 1996, s 6D

(1) If the accused instructs a person with a view to his providing any expert opinion for possible use as evidence at the trial of the accused, he must give to the court and the prosecutor a notice specifying the person's name and address.

(2) A notice does not have to be given under this section specifying the name and address of a person whose name and address have already been given under section 6C.

(3) A notice under this section must be given during the period which, by virtue of section 12, is the relevant period for this section.

Criminal Procedure Rules 2012, r 33 applies to expert evidence:

Reference to expert

33.1. A reference to an 'expert' in this Part is a reference to a person who is required to give or prepare expert evidence for the purpose of criminal proceedings, including evidence required to determine fitness to plead or for the purpose of sentencing.

[Note. Expert medical evidence may be required to determine fitness to plead under section 4 of the Criminal Procedure (Insanity) Act 1964. It may be required also under section 11 of the Powers of Criminal Courts (Sentencing) Act 2000(3), under Part III of the Mental Health Act

1983 or under Part 12 of the Criminal Justice Act 2003. Those Acts contain requirements about the qualification of medical experts.]

Expert's duty to the court

33.2.—(1) An expert must help the court to achieve the overriding objective by giving objective, unbiased opinion on matters within his expertise.

   (2)   This duty overrides any obligation to the person from whom he receives instructions or by whom he is paid.
   (3)   This duty includes an obligation to inform all parties and the court if the expert's opinion changes from that contained in a report served as evidence or given in a statement.

Content of expert's report

33.3.—(1) An expert's report must—

   (a) give details of the expert's qualifications, relevant experience and accreditation;
   (b) give details of any literature or other information which the expert has relied on in making the report;
   (c) contain a statement setting out the substance of all facts given to the expert which are material to the opinions expressed in the report, or upon which those opinions are based;
   (d) make clear which of the facts stated in the report are within the expert's own knowledge;
   (e) say who carried out any examination, measurement, test or experiment which the expert has used for the report and—
      (i)   give the qualifications, relevant experience and accreditation of that person,
      (ii) say whether or not the examination, measurement, test or experiment was carried out under the expert's supervision, and
      (iii) summarise the findings on which the expert relies;
   (f) where there is a range of opinion on the matters dealt with in the report—
      (i)   summarise the range of opinion, and
      (ii) give reasons for his own opinion;
   (g) if the expert is not able to give his opinion without qualification, state the qualification;
   (h) contain a summary of the conclusions reached;
   (i) contain a statement that the expert understands his duty to the court, and has complied and will continue to comply with that duty; and
   (j) contain the same declaration of truth as a witness statement.

   (2)   Only sub-paragraphs (i) and (j) of rule 33.3(1) apply to a summary by an expert of his conclusions served in advance of that expert's report.

[Note. Part 27 contains rules about witness statements. Declarations of truth in witness statements are required by section 9 of the Criminal Justice Act 1967 and section 5B of the Magistrates' Courts Act 1980. A party who accepts another party's expert's conclusions may admit them as facts under section 10 of the Criminal Justice Act 1967. Evidence of examinations etc. on which an expert relies may be admissible under section 127 of the Criminal Justice Act 2003.]

Service of expert evidence

33.4.—(1) A party who wants to introduce expert evidence must—

      (a) serve it on—
         (i)   the court officer, and
         (ii) each other party;
      (b) serve it—
         (i)   as soon as practicable, and in any event
         (ii) with any application in support of which that party relies on that evidence; and

    (c) if another party so requires, give that party a copy of, or a reasonable opportunity to inspect—

        (i)   a record of any examination, measurement, test or experiment on which the expert's findings and opinion are based, or that were carried out in the course of reaching those findings and opinion, and

        (ii) anything on which any such examination, measurement, test or experiment was carried out.

(2) A party may not introduce expert evidence if that party has not complied with this rule, unless–

    (a) every other party agrees; or

    (b) the court gives permission.

[Note. Under section 81 of the Police and Criminal Evidence Act 1984, and under section 20(3) of the Criminal Procedure and Investigations Act 1996, rules may—

    (a) require the disclosure of expert evidence before it is introduced as part of a party's case; and

    (b) prohibit its introduction without the court's permission, if it was not disclosed as required.]

Expert to be informed of service of report

33.5. A party who serves on another party or on the court a report by an expert must, at once, inform that expert of that fact.

Pre-hearing discussion of expert evidence

33.6.—(1) This rule applies where more than one party wants to introduce expert evidence.

  (2) The court may direct the experts to—

    (a) discuss the expert issues in the proceedings; and

    (b) prepare a statement for the court of the matters on which they agree and disagree, giving their reasons.

  (3) Except for that statement, the content of that discussion must not be referred to without the court's permission.

  (4) A party may not introduce expert evidence without the court's permission if the expert has not complied with a direction under this rule.

[Note. At a pre-trial hearing, a court may make binding rulings about the admissibility of evidence and about questions of law under section 9 of the Criminal Justice Act 1987; sections 31 and 40 of the Criminal Procedure and Investigations Act 1996; and section 8A of the Magistrates' Courts Act 1980.]

Court's power to direct that evidence is to be given by a single joint expert

33.7.—(1) Where more than one defendant wants to introduce expert evidence on an issue at trial, the court may direct that the evidence on that issue is to be given by one expert only.

  (2) Where the co-defendants cannot agree who should be the expert, the court may—

    (a) select the expert from a list prepared or identified by them; or

    (b) direct that the expert be selected in another way.

Instructions to a single joint expert

33.8.—(1) Where the court gives a direction under rule 33.7 for a single joint expert to be used, each of the co-defendants may give instructions to the expert.

  (2) When a co-defendant gives instructions to the expert he must, at the same time, send a copy of the instructions to the other co-defendant(s).

  (3) The court may give directions about—

    (a) the payment of the expert's fees and expenses; and

    (b) any examination, measurement, test or experiment which the expert wishes to carry out.

(4) The court may, before an expert is instructed, limit the amount that can be paid by way of fees and expenses to the expert.

(5) Unless the court otherwise directs, the instructing co-defendants are jointly and severally liable for the payment of the expert's fees and expenses.

Court's power to vary requirements under this Part

33.9.—(1) The court may—

    (a) extend (even after it has expired) a time limit under this Part;

    (b) allow the introduction of expert evidence which omits a detail required by this Part.

(2) A party who wants an extension of time must—

    (a) apply when serving the expert evidence for which it is required; and

    (b) explain the delay.

Proof by Written Statement

The bracketed words in section 9(1) are disregarded in respect to those areas where as of 18 June 2012 committal proceedings are abolished. **Effect:** In *Lister v Quaife* (1982) 75 Cr App R 313 it was held: The contents of the statements read are evidence in the case just as if, and only to the extent as if, the makers of those statements had been called as witnesses in the trial and given the evidence contained in the statements. If no challenge is made to that evidence and the defendant then goes on to give contradictory evidence (having failed to put his case to the witness whose evidence was agreed) no doubt strong comment could be made that nothing had been put to the witness. If the Crown find a defendant giving evidence which is inconsistent with evidence set out in the section 9 statements which have not been the subject of a notice under paragraph (*d*) of subsection (2), they always have the right, as does the court of its own motion, to apply for or to order an adjournment in order that the maker of the statement shall attend to give evidence. In certain circumstances it may very well be that a court would take the view that if such an application was made by the Crown, not only would justice require that such an adjournment should be granted but that justice would also require that the costs thrown away by any such adjournment should be paid by the defendant, it having been the failure to take appropriate steps to ensure that the proper procedure, namely that a defendant's case is put to prosecution witnesses, was followed in the circumstances of that case. Legal representatives of defendants in criminal cases, whether before the justices or indeed in the Crown Court, should observe the well-known practice that they do put their case to witnesses for the prosecution, and the failure to give a notice under section 9 (2) (*d*) is not to be used as any sort of device whereby they can have the defendant present, giving evidence in person, but avoid the presence of the witnesses whose statements under section 9 have been served and merely hear those statements read out in court. **Strict adherence:** If the statement read does not accord with the declaration (for example there are less pages than stated), the statement will be inadmissible (*Patterson v Director of Public Prosecutions* [1990] RTR 329), although in many cases the interests of justice will require the case to be adjourned so that the party seeking to introduce the evidence can remedy any defect in this respect.

Criminal Justice Act 1967, s 9

(1) In any criminal proceedings, [other than committal proceedings], a written statement by any person shall, if such of the conditions mentioned in the next following subsection as are applicable are satisfied, be admissible as evidence to the like extent as oral evidence to the like effect by that person.

(2) The said conditions are—

    (a) the statement purports to be signed by the person who made it;

(b) the statement contains a declaration by that person to the effect that it is true to the best of his knowledge and belief and that he made the statement knowing that, if it were tendered in evidence, he would be liable to prosecution if he wilfully stated in it anything which he knew to be false or did not believe to be true;

(c) before the hearing at which the statement is tendered in evidence, a copy of the statement is served, by or on behalf of the party proposing to tender it, on each of the other parties to the proceedings; and

(d) none of the other parties or their solicitors, within seven days from the service of the copy of the statement, serves a notice on the party so proposing objecting to the statement being tendered in evidence under this section:

Provided that the conditions mentioned in paragraphs (c) and (d) of this subsection shall not apply if the parties agree before or during the hearing that the statement shall be so tendered.

(3) The following provisions shall also have effect in relation to any written statement tendered in evidence under this section, that is to say—

(a) if the statement is made by a person under the age of eighteen, it shall give his age;

(b) if it is made by a person who cannot read it, it shall be read to him before he signs it and shall be accompanied by a declaration by the person who so read the statement to the effect that it was so read; and

(c) if it refers to any other document as an exhibit, the copy served on any other party to the proceedings under paragraph (c) of the last foregoing subsection shall be accompanied by a copy of that document or by such information as may be necessary in order to enable the party on whom it is served to inspect that document or a copy thereof.

(4) Notwithstanding that a written statement made by any person may be admissible as evidence by virtue of this section—

(a) the party by whom or on whose behalf a copy of the statement was served may call that person to give evidence; and

(b) the court may, of its own motion or on the application of any party to the proceedings, require that person to attend before the court and give evidence.

(5) An application under paragraph (b) of the last foregoing subsection to a court other than a magistrates' court may be made before the hearing and on any such application the powers of the court shall be exercisable

(a) by a puisne judge of the High Court, a Circuit judge or Recorder sitting alone; or

(b) subject to subsection (5A), by a qualifying judge advocate (within the meaning of the Senior Courts Act 1981) sitting alone.

(5A) Subsection (5)(b) applies only where the application in question is to the Crown Court.

(6) So much of any statement as is admitted in evidence by virtue of this section shall, unless the court otherwise directs, be read aloud at the hearing and where the court so directs an account shall be given orally of so much of any statement as is not read aloud.

(7) Any document or object referred to as an exhibit and identified in a written statement tendered in evidence under this section shall be treated as if it had been produced as an exhibit and identified in court by the maker of the statement.

(8) A document required by this section to be served on any person may be served—

(a) by delivering it to him or to his solicitor; or

(b) by addressing it to him and leaving it at his usual or last known place of abode or place of business or by addressing it to his solicitor and leaving it at his office; or

(c) by sending it in a registered letter or by the recorded delivery service or by first class post addressed to him at his usual or last known place of abode or place of business or addressed to his solicitor at his office; or

(d) in the case of a body corporate, by delivering it to the secretary or clerk of the body at its registered or principal office or sending it in a registered letter or by the recorded delivery service or by first class post addressed to the Secretary or clerk of that body at that office; and in paragraph (d) of this subsection references to the secretary, in relation to a limited liability partnership, are to any designated member of the limited liability partnership.

Unused Material, Prosecution Disclosure Of

Legislation: Relevant parts of the Criminal Procedure and Investigations Act 1996 are reproduced in Appendix 6.

The prosecutions duty (which extends to a private prosecutor, see section 2(3) and *R v Belmarsh Magistrates' Court, ex p Watts* [1999] 2 Cr App R 188) is to serve on the defence unused material which might reasonably be considered to undermine the prosecution case or assist the defence case. That duty is a continuing one and the prosecutor will pay particular regard to new information presented as a result of defence disclosure, and in particular the service of any defence statement. In *H* [2004] 2 AC 134 the court held: "If material does not weaken the prosecution case or strengthen that of the defendant, there is no requirement to disclose it. For this purpose the parties' respective cases should not be restrictively analysed. But they must be carefully analysed, to ascertain the specific facts the prosecution seek to establish and the specific grounds on which the charges are resisted. The trial process is not well served if the defence are permitted to make general and unspecified allegations and then seek far-reaching disclosure in the hope that material may turn up to make them good. Neutral material or material damaging to the defendant need not be disclosed and should not be brought to the attention of the court. Only in truly borderline cases should the prosecution seek a judicial ruling on the disclosability of material in its hands. If the material contains information which the prosecution would prefer that the defendant did not have, on forensic as opposed to public interest grounds, that will suggest that the material is disclosable. If the disclosure test is faithfully applied, the occasions on which a judge will be obliged to recuse himself because he has been privately shown material damning to the defendant will, as the Court of Appeal envisaged [...], be very exceptional indeed".

Common law: The 1996 Act is triggered upon the defendant entering a not-guilty plea, but that does not absolve the prosecution of its common law duties of disclosure in the interests of fairness (see *R v Director of Public Prosecutions ex p Lee* [1999] 2 Cr App R 304; *R (Johnson) v Stratford Magistrates' Court* [2003] EWHC 353 (Admin)). In *Lee* the court held (para 9): The 1996 Act does not specifically address the period between arrest and committal, and whereas in most cases prosecution disclosure can wait until after committal without jeopardising the defendant's right to a fair trial the prosecutor must always be alive to the need to make advance disclosure of material of which he is aware (either from his own consideration of the papers or because his attention has been drawn to it by the defence) and which he, as a responsible prosecutor, recognises should be disclosed at an earlier stage. Examples canvassed before us were — (a) Previous convictions of a complainant or deceased if that information could reasonably be expected to assist the defence when applying for bail; (b) Material which might enable a defendant to make a pre-committal application to stay the proceedings as an abuse of process: (c) Material which might enable a defendant to submit that he should only be committed for trial on a lesser charge, or perhaps that he should not be committed for trial at all: (d) Material which will enable the defendant and his legal advisors to make preparations for trial which may be significantly less effective if disclosure is delayed (e.g. names of eye witnesses who the prosecution do not intend to use).

Post-conviction: Disclosure obligation continues post-conviction both as a result of common law and the Attorney General's Guidelines. In *Nunn v Chief Constable of Suffolk Constabulary* [2012] EWHC 1186 (Admin) the court set out very limited the extent of the common law obligations.

Defence Disclosure–Default

The consequences of default are dealt with under section 11 of the Act. It is not permissible to punish a breach of the rules by way of contempt (*Rochford* [2010] EWCA Crim 1928, nor by denying the party its right to call witnesses (*R (Tinnion) v Reading Crown Court* 174 JP 36; *Ullah* [2011] EWCA Crim 3275). Wasted costs may follow against the defendant, and his legal advisors (if they are complicit in the breach) (*SVS Solicitors* [2012] EWCA Crim 319). Late service of a defence statement does not deprive the defendant of an application being made under section 8 of the 1996 Act (*Director of Public Prosecutions v Wood and McGillicuddy* [2005] EWHC 2986 (QB)).

Criminal Procedure and Investigations Act 1996, s 11

(1)   This section applies in the three cases set out in subsections (2), (3) and (4).

(2)   The first case is where section 5 applies and the accused—

    (a)   fails to give an initial defence statement,

    (b)   gives an initial defence statement but does so after the end of the period which, by virtue of section 12, is the relevant period for section 5,

    (c)   is required by section 6B to give either an updated defence statement or a statement of the kind mentioned in subsection (4) of that section but fails to do so,

    (d)   gives an updated defence statement or a statement of the kind mentioned in section 6B(4) but does so after the end of the period which, by virtue of section 12, is the relevant period for section 6B,

    (e)   sets out inconsistent defences in his defence statement, or

    (f)   at his trial—

        (i)   puts forward a defence which was not mentioned in his defence statement or is different from any defence set out in that statement,

        (ii)   relies on a matter (or any particular of any matter of fact) which, in breach of the requirements imposed by or under section 6A, was not mentioned in his defence statement,

        (iii) adduces evidence in support of an alibi without having given particulars of the alibi in his defence statement, or

        (iv) calls a witness to give evidence in support of an alibi without having complied with section 6A(2)(a) or (b) as regards the witness in his defence statement.

(3)   The second case is where section 6 applies, the accused gives an initial defence statement, and the accused—

    (a)   gives the initial defence statement after the end of the period which, by virtue of section 12, is the relevant period for section 6, or

    (b)   does any of the things mentioned in paragraphs (c) to (f) of subsection (2).

(4)   The third case is where the accused—

    (a)   gives a witness notice but does so after the end of the period which, by virtue of section 12, is the relevant period for section 6C, or

    (b)   at his trial calls a witness (other than himself) not included, or not adequately identified, in a witness notice.

(5)   Where this section applies—

    (a)   the court or any other party may make such comment as appears appropriate;

    (b)   the court or jury may draw such inferences as appear proper in deciding whether the accused is guilty of the offence concerned.

(6)   Where—

    (a)   this section applies by virtue of subsection (2)(f)(ii) (including that provision as it applies by virtue of subsection (3)(b)), and

    (b) the matter which was not mentioned is a point of law (including any point as to the admissibility of evidence or an abuse of process) or an authority,

comment by another party under subsection (5)(a) may be made only with the leave of the court.

(7)   Where this section applies by virtue of subsection (4), comment by another party under subsection (5)(a) may be made only with the leave of the court.

(8)   Where the accused puts forward a defence which is different from any defence set out in his defence statement, in doing anything under subsection (5) or in deciding whether to do anything under it the court shall have regard—

    (a) to the extent of the differences in the defences, and

    (b) to whether there is any justification for it.

(9)   Where the accused calls a witness whom he has failed to include, or to identify adequately, in a witness notice, in doing anything under subsection (5) or in deciding whether to do anything under it the court shall have regard to whether there is any justification for the failure.

(10) A person shall not be convicted of an offence solely on an inference drawn under subsection (5).

(12) In this section—

    (a) "initial defence statement" means a defence statement given under section 5 or 6;

    (b) "updated defence statement" means a defence statement given under section 6B;

    (c) a reference simply to an accused's "defence statement" is a reference—

        (i)   where he has given only an initial defence statement, to that statement;

        (ii) where he has given both an initial and an updated defence statement, to the updated defence statement;

        (iii) where he has given both an initial defence statement and a statement of the kind mentioned in section 6B(4), to the initial defence statement;

    (d) a reference to evidence in support of an alibi shall be construed in accordance with section 6A(3);

    (e) "witness notice" means a notice given under section 6C.

Defence Statement

There is no duty on a defendant in summary proceedings to serve a defence statement. The prosecutions continuing duty to keep disclosure under review (s 7A) is engaged when a defence statement is served (albeit not exclusively so), and therefore in some cases there may be an advantage in serving a statement voluntarily. In summary proceedings a defence statement should be served (where the defendant wishes to voluntarily do so) within 14 days of the prosecution complying or purporting to comply with its initial duty of disclosure (SI 2011/209). Note that section 6B is not currently in force.

Criminal Procedure and Investigations Act 1996, ss 6, 6A, 6B, 6E

6.— Voluntary disclosure by accused.

(1)   This section applies where—

    (a) this Part applies by virtue of section 1(1), and

    (b) the prosecutor complies with section 3 or purports to comply with it.

(2)   The accused—

    (a) may give a defence statement to the prosecutor, and

    (b) if he does so, must also give such a statement to the court.

(4)   If the accused gives a defence statement under this section he must give it during the period which, by virtue of section 12 is the relevant period for this section.

6A Contents of defence statement

(1) For the purposes of this Part a defence statement is a written statement—

    (a) setting out the nature of the accused's defence, including any particular defences on which he intends to rely,

    (b) indicating the matters of fact on which he takes issue with the prosecution,

    (c) setting out, in the case of each such matter, why he takes issue with the prosecution,

    (ca) setting out particulars of the matters of fact on which he intends to rely for the purposes of his defence, and

    (d) indicating any point of law (including any point as to the admissibility of evidence or an abuse of process) which he wishes to take, and any authority on which he intends to rely for that purpose.

(2) A defence statement that discloses an alibi must give particulars of it, including—

    (a) the name, address and date of birth of any witness the accused believes is able to give evidence in support of the alibi, or as many of those details as are known to the accused when the statement is given;

    (b) any information in the accused's possession which might be of material assistance in identifying or finding any such witness in whose case any of the details mentioned in paragraph (a) are not known to the accused when the statement is given.

(3) For the purposes of this section evidence in support of an alibi is evidence tending to show that by reason of the presence of the accused at a particular place or in a particular area at a particular time he was not, or was unlikely to have been, at the place where the offence is alleged to have been committed at the time of its alleged commission.

(4) The Secretary of State may by regulations make provision as to the details of the matters that, by virtue of subsection (1), are to be included in defence statements.

6B Updated disclosure by accused

(1) Where the accused has, before the beginning of the relevant period for this section, given a defence statement under section 5 or 6, he must during that period give to the court and the prosecutor either—

    (a) a defence statement under this section (an "updated defence statement"), or

    (b) a statement of the kind mentioned in subsection (4).

(2) The relevant period for this section is determined under section 12.

(3) An updated defence statement must comply with the requirements imposed by or under section 6A by reference to the state of affairs at the time when the statement is given.

(4) Instead of an updated defence statement, the accused may give a written statement stating that he has no changes to make to the defence statement which was given under section 5 or 6.

(5) Where there are other accused in the proceedings and the court so orders, the accused must also give either an updated defence statement or a statement of the kind mentioned in subsection (4), within such period as may be specified by the court, to each other accused so specified.

(6) The court may make an order under subsection (5) either of its own motion or on the application of any party.

6E Disclosure by accused: further provisions

(1) Where an accused's solicitor purports to give on behalf of the accused—

    (a) a defence statement under section 5, 6 or 6B, or

    (b) a statement of the kind mentioned in section 6B(4),

the statement shall, unless the contrary is proved, be deemed to be given with the authority of the accused.

(2) If it appears to the judge at a pre-trial hearing that an accused has failed to comply fully with section 5, 6B or 6C, so that there is a possibility of comment being made or inferences drawn under section 11(5), he shall warn the accused accordingly.

(3) In subsection (2) "pre-trial hearing" has the same meaning as in Part 4 (see section 39).

(4) The judge in a trial before a judge and jury—

    (a) may direct that the jury be given a copy of any defence statement, and

    (b) if he does so, may direct that it be edited so as not to include references to matters evidence of which would be inadmissible.

(5) A direction under subsection (4)—

    (a) may be made either of the judge's own motion or on the application of any party;

    (b) may be made only if the judge is of the opinion that seeing a copy of the defence statement would help the jury to understand the case or to resolve any issue in the case.

(6) The reference in subsection (4) to a defence statement is a reference—

    (a) where the accused has given only an initial defence statement (that is, a defence statement given under section 5 or 6), to that statement;

    (b) where he has given both an initial defence statement and an updated defence statement (that is, a defence statement given under section 6B), to the updated defence statement;

    (c) where he has given both an initial defence statement and a statement of the kind mentioned in section 6B(4), to the initial defence statement.

Notice of Intention to Call Defence Witnesses

In summary proceedings witness requirements should be served within 14 days of the prosecution complying or purporting to comply with its initial duty of disclosure (SI 2011/209). CrPR 22 applies.

Criminal Procedure and Investigations Act 1996, s 6C

(1) The accused must give to the court and the prosecutor a notice indicating whether he intends to call any persons (other than himself) as witnesses at his trial and, if so—

    (a) giving the name, address and date of birth of each such proposed witness, or as many of those details as are known to the accused when the notice is given;

    (b) providing any information in the accused's possession which might be of material assistance in identifying or finding any such proposed witness in whose case any of the details mentioned in paragraph (a) are not known to the accused when the notice is given.

(2) Details do not have to be given under this section to the extent that they have already been given under section 6A(2).

(3) The accused must give a notice under this section during the period which, by virtue of section 12, is the relevant period for this section.

(4) If, following the giving of a notice under this section, the accused—

    (a) decides to call a person (other than himself) who is not included in the notice as a proposed witness, or decides not to call a person who is so included, or

    (b) discovers any information which, under subsection (1), he would have had to include in the notice if he had been aware of it when giving the notice,

he must give an appropriately amended notice to the court and the prosecutor.

Application by Accused for Disclosure

Criminal Procedure and Investigations Act 1996, s 8

(1) This section applies where the accused has given a defence statement under section 5, 6 or 6B and the prosecutor has complied with section 7A(5) or has purported to comply with it or has failed to comply with it.

(2) If the accused has at any time reasonable cause to believe that there is prosecution material which is required by section 7A to be disclosed to him and has not been, he may apply to the court for an order requiring the prosecutor to disclose it to him.

(3) For the purposes of this section prosecution material is material—

   (a) which is in the prosecutor's possession and came into his possession in connection with the case for the prosecution against the accused.

   (b) which, in pursuance of a code operative under Part II, he has inspected in connection with the case for the prosecution against the accused, or

   (c) which falls within subsection (4).

(4) Material falls within this subsection if in pursuance of a code operative under Part II the prosecutor must, if he asks for the material, be given a copy of it or be allowed to inspect it in connection with the case for the prosecution against the accused.

(5) Material must not be disclosed under this section to the extent that the court, on an application by the prosecutor, concludes it is not in the public interest to disclose it and orders accordingly.

(6) Material must not be disclosed under this section to the extent that it is material the disclosure of which is prohibited by section 17 of the Regulation of Investigatory Powers Act 2000.

EARLY ADMINISTRATIVE HEARINGS

Crime and Disorder Act 1998, s 50

(1) Where a person ("the accused") has been charged with an offence at a police station, the magistrates' court before whom he appears or is brought for the first time in relation to the charge may consist of a single justice.

(2) At a hearing conducted by a single justice under this section the accused shall be asked whether he wishes to be granted a right to representation funded by the Legal Services Commission as part of the Criminal Defence Service.

(2A) Where the accused wishes to be granted such a right, the Legal Services Commission shall decide whether or not to grant him that right.

(3) At such a hearing the single justice—

   (a) may exercise, subject to subsection (2) above, such of his powers as a single justice as he thinks fit; and

   (b) on adjourning the hearing, may remand the accused in custody or on bail.

(4) This section applies in relation to a justices' clerk as it applies in relation to a single justice; but nothing in subsection (3)(b) above authorises such a clerk to remand the accused in custody or, without the consent of the prosecutor and the accused, to remand the accused on bail on conditions other than those (if any) previously imposed.

(4A) A hearing conducted by a single justice under this section may be—

   (a) adjourned to enable the decision mentioned in subsection (2A) above to be taken, and

   (b) subsequently resumed by a single justice.

EXTRADITION

Jurisdiction

The Extradition Act 2003 outlines the procedures to be adopted during the extradition process. The Magistrates' Court Act 1980, s 142 does not extend to extradition proceedings (*R (Klimeto) v City of Westminter Magistrates' Court* [2012] EWHC 2051 (Admin)). The power to extradite rests with the Senior Magistrate and authorised District Judges, and cases are generally only heard at Westminster Magistrates' Court. This section details the initial checks that a solicitor or barrister should make when seized of the case for the first time. Unless absolutely satisfied that extradition can properly proceed unopposed under Part 1 of the Act, recourse should be had to the detailed practitioner works.

Countries are divided into category 1 (Part 1 Extraditions) and category 2 countries (Part 2 Extraditions). Category 1 states utilize the European Arrest Warrant procedure, and extradition will generally be ordered save in the most exceptional circumstances. More robust evidential protections are in place in relation to most category 2 states. In addition, the United Kingdom also has special arrangements in place with certain states, for example the United States of America.

Part 1 Extradition

The following states have been designated under Part 1 of the 2003 Act:

Austria, Belgium, Bulgaria, Cyprus, Czech Republic, Denmark, Estonia, Finland, France, Germany, Gibraltar, Greece, Hungary, Ireland, Italy, Latvia, Lithuania, Luxembourg, Malta, the Netherlands, Poland, Portugal, Romania, Slovakia, Slovenia, Spain, and Sweden.

Following the issuing of an arrest warrant the police will execute that warrant and bring the individual before the court.

The arrest warrant should be in the standard format and detail the statutory particulars as required under section 2 of the Act.

Part 2 Extradition

The following states have been designated under Part 2 of the 2003 Act:

Albania, Algeria, Andorra, Antigua and Barbuda, Argentina, Armenia, Australia, Azerbaijan, The Bahamas, Bangladesh, Barbados, Belize, Bolivia, Bosnia and Herzegovina, Botswana, Brazil, Brunei, Canada, Chile, Colombia, Cook Islands, Croatia, Cuba, Dominica, Ecuador, El Salvador, Fiji, The Gambia, Georgia, Ghana, Grenada, Guatemala, Guyana, Hong Kong Special Administrative Region, Haiti, Iceland, India, Iraq, Israel, Jamaica, Kenya, Kiribati, Lesotho, Liberia, Libya, Liechtenstein, Macedonia (FYR), Malawi, Malaysia, Maldives, Mauritius, Mexico, Moldova, Monaco, Montenegro, Nauru, New Zealand, Nicaragua, Nigeria, Norway, Panama, Papua New Guinea, Paraguay, Peru, Russian Federation, Saint Christopher and Nevis, Saint Lucia, Saint Vincent and the Grenadines, San Marino, Serbia, Seychelles, Sierra Leone, Singapore, Solomon Islands, South Africa, Sri Lanka, Swaziland, Switzerland, Tanzania, Thailand, Tonga, Trinidad and Tobago, Turkey, Tuvalu, Uganda, Ukraine, the United Arab Emirates, the United States of America, Uruguay, Vanuatu, Western Samoa, Zambia, and Zimbabwe.

A request for an arrest warrant is made to the Secretary of State and will result in the wanted person being brought before the court pursuant to an arrest warrant being issued by the court (s 71).

The warrant should comply with section 70 of the Act, but it is a matter for the Secretary of the State as opposed to the court, to determine whether it does so comply.

Funding

Extradition work is funded under the Standard Criminal Contract and an application for representation should be made in the usual way. Extradition proceedings are the only proceedings in the magistrates' court that allow for representation by Queen's Counsel. It is rare for legal aid to be refused on merits. If a case cannot be dealt with by the duty solicitor an adjournment for the grant of legal aid will in most cases be necessary (*Stopyra v Poland* [2012] EWHC 1787 (Admin)).

Timing of appearance

In the case of a provisional arrest warrant the first appearance must be within 48 hours of arrest (weekends and holidays excepted). In all other cases the appearance must be as soon as is practicable. A failure to comply should lead to the person's discharge. Section 4(2) requires service of the warrant. The initial hearing can be adjourned to a later date.

Extradition Act 2003, ss 4–6

4 Person arrested under Part 1 warrant

(1) This section applies if a person is arrested under a Part 1 warrant.

(2) A copy of the warrant must be given to the person as soon as practicable after his arrest.

(3) The person must be brought as soon as practicable before the appropriate judge.

(4) If subsection (2) is not complied with and the person applies to the judge to be discharged, the judge may order his discharge.

(5) If subsection (3) is not complied with and the person applies to the judge to be discharged, the judge must order his discharge.

(6) A person arrested under the warrant must be treated as continuing in legal custody until he is brought before the appropriate judge under subsection (3) or he is discharged under sub-section (4) or (5).

5 Provisional arrest

(1) A constable, a customs officer or a service policeman may arrest a person without a warrant if he has reasonable grounds for believing—

    (a) that a Part 1 warrant has been or will be issued in respect of the person by an authority of a category 1 territory, and

    (b) that the authority has the function of issuing arrest warrants in the category 1 territory.

(2) A constable or a customs officer may arrest a person under subsection (1) in any part of the United Kingdom.

(3) A service policeman may arrest a person under subsection (1) only if the person is subject to service law or is a civilian subject to service discipline.

(4) If a service policeman has power to arrest a person under subsection (1) he may exercise the power anywhere.

6 Person arrested under section 5

(1) This section applies if a person is arrested under section 5.

(2) The person must be brought before the appropriate judge within 48 hours starting with the time when the person is arrested.

(2A) The documents specified in subsection (4) must be produced to the judge within 48 hours starting with the time when the person is arrested but this is subject to any extension under subsection (3B).

(2B) Subsection (3) applies if—

    (a) the person has been brought before the judge in compliance with subsection (2); but

    (b) documents have not been produced to the judge in compliance with subsection (2A).

(3) The person must be brought before the judge when the documents are produced to the judge.

(3A) While the person is before the judge in pursuance of subsection (2), the authority of the category 1 territory may apply to the judge for an extension of the 48 hour period mentioned in subsection (2A) by a further 48 hours.

(3B)   The judge may grant an extension if the judge decides that subsection (2A) could not reasonably be complied with within the initial 48 hour period.

(3C)   The judge must decide whether that subsection could reasonably be so complied with on a balance of probabilities.

(3D)   Notice of an application under subsection (3A) must be given in accordance with rules of court.

(4)   The documents are—

    (a) a Part 1 warrant in respect of the person;
    (b) a certificate under section 2 in respect of the warrant.

(5)   A copy of the warrant must be given to the person as soon as practicable after his arrest.

(5A)   Subsection (5B) applies if—

    (a) the person is before the judge in pursuance of subsection (2); and
    (b) the documents specified in subsection (4) have not been produced to the judge.

(5B)   The judge must remand the person in custody or on bail (subject to subsection (6)).

(6)   If subsection (2), (2A) or (3) is not complied with and the person applies to the judge to be discharged, the judge must order his discharge.

(7)   If subsection (5) is not complied with and the person applies to the judge to be discharged, the judge may order his discharge.

(8)   The person must be treated as continuing in legal custody until he is brought before the appropriate judge under subsection (2) or he is discharged under subsection (6) or (7).

(8A)   In calculating a period of 48 hours for the purposes of this section no account is to be taken of—

    (a) any Saturday or Sunday;
    (b) Christmas Day;
    (c) Good Friday; or
    (d) any day falling within subsection (8B).

(8B)   The following days fall within this subsection—

    (a) in Scotland, any day prescribed under section 8(2) of the Criminal Procedure (Scotland) Act 1995 as a court holiday in the court of the appropriate judge;
    (b) in any part of the United Kingdom, any day that is a bank holiday under the Banking and Financial Dealings Act 1971 in that part of the United Kingdom.

(9)   Subsection (10) applies if—

    (a) a person is arrested under section 5 on the basis of a belief that a Part 1 warrant has been or will be issued in respect of him;
    (b) the person is discharged under subsection (6) or (7).

(10)   The person must not be arrested again under section 5 on the basis of a belief relating to the same Part 1 warrant.

Identity

If identity is not admitted the requesting state must be in a position to prove it on a balance of probabilities (ss 7, 78). Some examples of identification methods include: photographic or video evidence; possession of (or proximity to) papers bearing the same or essentially the same details; unusual name; fingerprints; admissions.

Consent

A person who is legally represented (or is ineligible for legal aid, has declined it, or has had it withdrawn) may consent to extradition, but such consent cannot be revoked.

Consent should only be given when the legal adviser is satisfied that none of the statutory or other bars to extradition are at issue (for which see below).

If consent to extradition is not given the Judge will set the appropriate timetable:

Part 1 states: 21 days from arrest, or a later date if it is in the interests of justice (Extradition Act 2003, s 8).

Part 2 states: not later than two months from first appearance, or a later date if it is in the interests of justice (Extradition Act 2003, s 75).

Age

Relevant law: Extradition Act 2003, s 15

There can be no extradition in respect to a child less than 10 years of age.

Double jeopardy

Relevant law:

Extradition Act 2003, ss 12, 80

12. A person's extradition to a category 1 territory is barred by reason of the rule against double jeopardy if (and only if) it appears that he would be entitled to be discharged under any rule of law relating to previous acquittal or conviction on the assumption—

    (a) that the conduct constituting the extradition offence constituted an offence in the part of the United Kingdom where the judge exercises jurisdiction;

    (b) that the person were charged with the extradition offence in that part of the United Kingdom.

80. A person's extradition to a category 2 territory is barred by reason of the rule against double jeopardy if (and only if) it appears that he would be entitled to be discharged under any rule of law relating to previous acquittal or conviction if he were charged with the extradition offence in the part of the United Kingdom where the judge exercises his jurisdiction.

Cases: *Germany v Altun* [2011] EWHC 397 (Admin). *Fofana v Thubin* [2006] EWHC 744 (Admin).

Earlier extradition

Relevant law:

Extradition Act 2003, s18

A person's extradition to a category 1 territory is barred by reason of his earlier extradition to the United Kingdom from another category 1 territory if (and only if)—

    (a) the person was extradited to the United Kingdom from another category 1 territory (the extraditing territory);

    (b) under arrangements between the United Kingdom and the extraditing territory, that territory's consent is required to the person's extradition from the United Kingdom to the category 1 territory in respect of the extradition offence under consideration;

    (c) that consent has not been given on behalf of the extraditing territory.

Extraneous considerations

Relevant law: Extradition Act 2003, ss 13, 81

The effect of this section is to bar a person's extradition if it appears that the Part 1 warrant (although purporting to be issued in respect of the extradition offence) has actually been issued for the purpose of prosecuting or punishing him for reasons of his race, religion, nationality, gender, sexual orientation or political opinions. His extradition would also be barred if it appears that he would be prejudiced at trial, or his liberty restricted, for any of the same reasons. For a recent case involving Turkey, see *Konuksever v Turkey* [2012] EWHC 2166 (Admin)).

Hostage taking

Relevant law: Extradition Act 2003, ss 16, 83

A person's extradition to a category 1 territory is barred by reason of hostage-taking considerations if (and only if) the territory is a party to the Hostage-taking Convention and it appears that (a) if extradited he might be prejudiced at his trial because communication between him and the appropriate authorities would not be possible, and (b) the act or omission constituting the extradition offence also constitutes an offence under section 1 of the Taking of Hostages Act 1982 or an attempt to commit such an offence.

Passage of time

Relevant law: Extradition Act 2003, ss 14, 82

Cases: Extradition will be barred if due to passage of time it would be unjust or oppressive to order extradition. In *Kakis v Government of* Cyprus [1978] 1 WLR 779 the court held:

> " 'Unjust' I regard as directed primarily to the risk of prejudice to the accused in the conduct of the trial itself, 'oppressive' as directed to hardship to the accused resulting from change in his circumstances that have occurred during the period to be taken into consideration; but there is room for overlapping, and between them they would cover all cases where to return him would not be fair. Delay in the commencement or conduct of extradition proceedings which is brought about by the accused himself by fleeing the country, concealing his whereabouts or evading arrest cannot, in my view, be relied upon as a ground for holding it to be either unjust or oppressive to return him. Any difficulties that he may encounter in the conduct of his defence in consequence of the delay due to such causes are of his own choice and making. Save in the most exceptional circumstances it would be neither unjust nor oppressive that he should be required to accept them. As respects delay which is not brought about by the acts of the accused himself, however, the question of where responsibility lies for the delay is not generally relevant. What matters is not so much the cause of such delay as its effect; or, rather, the effects of those events which would not have happened before the trial of the accused if it had taken place with ordinary promptitude. So where the application for discharge under section 8(3) is based upon the "passage of time" under paragraph (b) and not on absence of good faith under paragraph (c), the court is not normally concerned with what could be an invidious task of considering whether mere inaction of the requisitioning government or its prosecuting authorities which resulted in delay was blameworthy or otherwise."

Oppression could be established by reasons that on their own would not amount to oppression but cumulatively did so (*Italy v Merico* [2011] EWHC 1857 (Admin)).

Speciality

Relevant law: Extradition Act 2003, ss 17, 95

Cases: The speciality rule is a long-standing protection in extradition. It prohibits a person from being prosecuted in the requesting territory after his extradition for an offence committed before his extradition. The exceptions to this rule are where the offence is that in respect of which he was extradited, where the consent of the requested state is obtained or the person has had an opportunity to leave the country to which he was extradited but has failed to do so.

Asylum claim

Relevant law: Extradition Act 2003, ss 39, 40, 41

Cases: A person with refugee status in the UK cannot be extradited (*Poland v Dytlow* [2009] EWHC 1009 (Admin)). If asylum had been claimed prior to the extradition request being issued, there was no bar to extradition under the act (*Dos Santos v Portugal* [2010] EWHC 1815 (Admin)). It was held in *Dos Santos* that the court was not obliged to delay extradition proceedings pending determination of the outstanding asylum claim. In *Chichvarkin v Secretary of State for the Home Department* [2011] EWCA Civ 91 the court doubted [at 61] the correctness of a court refusing a stay in order that an asylum claim be determined, particularly where the claim also involved human rights issues.

Competing claims for extradition

Relevant law:

Extradition Act 2003, ss 22, 88, 90

22 Person charged with offence in United Kingdom

(1) This section applies if at any time in the extradition hearing the judge is informed that the person in respect of whom the Part 1 warrant is issued is charged with an offence in the United Kingdom.

(2) The judge must adjourn the extradition hearing until one of these occurs—

    (a) the charge is disposed of;

    (b) the charge is withdrawn;

    (c) proceedings in respect of the charge are discontinued;

    (d) an order is made for the charge to lie on the file, or in relation to Scotland, the diet is deserted pro loco et tempore .

(3) If a sentence of imprisonment or another form of detention is imposed in respect of the offence charged, the judge may adjourn the extradition hearing until the person is released from detention pursuant to the sentence (whether on licence or otherwise).

(4) If before he adjourns the extradition hearing under subsection (2) the judge has decided under section 11 whether the person's extradition is barred by reason of the rule against double jeopardy, the judge must decide that question again after the resumption of the hearing.

88 Person charged with offence in United Kingdom

(1) This section applies if at any time in the extradition hearing the judge is informed that the person is charged with an offence in the United Kingdom.

(2) The judge must adjourn the extradition hearing until one of these occurs—

    (a) the charge is disposed of;

    (b) the charge is withdrawn;

    (c) proceedings in respect of the charge are discontinued;

    (d) an order is made for the charge to lie on the file, or in relation to Scotland, the diet is deserted pro loco et tempore .

(3) If a sentence of imprisonment or another form of detention is imposed in respect of the offence charged, the judge may adjourn the extradition hearing until the person is released from detention pursuant to the sentence (whether on licence or otherwise).

(4) If before he adjourns the extradition hearing under subsection (2) the judge has decided under section 79 whether the person's extradition is barred by reason of the rule against double jeopardy, the judge must decide that question again after the resumption of the hearing.

90 Competing extradition claim

(1) This section applies if at any time in the extradition hearing the judge is informed that the conditions in subsection (2) or (3) are met.

(2) The conditions are that—

    (a) the Secretary of State has received another valid request for the person's extradition to a category 2 territory;

    (b) the other request has not been disposed of;

    (c) the Secretary of State has made an order under section 126(2) for further proceedings on the request under consideration to be deferred until the other request has been disposed of.

(3) The conditions are that—

(a) a certificate has been issued under section 2 in respect of a Part 1 warrant issued in respect of the person;

(b) the warrant has not been disposed of;

(c) the Secretary of State has made an order under section 179(2) for further proceedings on the request to be deferred until the warrant has been disposed of.

(4) The judge must remand the person in custody or on bail.

(5) If the person is remanded in custody, the appropriate judge may later grant bail.

Convictions in absence

Relevant law: Extradition Act 2003, ss 20, 86

Unless the applicant voluntarily absented himself from the proceedings, conviction in absence acts as a bar to extradition.

Human rights considerations

Relevant law: Extradition Act 2003, ss 21, 87

Cases: The purpose of the Council Framework Decision 2009/948/JHA is to prevent dual litigation of issues in member states, accordingly the correct forum for an article 8 issue to be decided is the receiving state (when that state is a party to the framework agreement) (eg *Williams v France*, unreported, 4 July 2012). It will be rare that an article 8 issue would bar extradition (*Norris v United States* [2010] UKSC 9). The rights of children in the context of article 8 was considered in *HH v Italy; PH v Italy; FK v Poland* [2012] UKSC 25. Extradition to the United States where the applicant would be held subject to a 'civil commitment' order for sex offenders amounted to an article 5 violation, and unless the United States offered suitable undertakings the extradition would be blocked (*Sullivan v United States* [2012] EWHC 1680 (Admin)).

Person serving sentences

Relevant law: Extradition Act 2003, ss 23, 89

Cases: Proceedings can be adjourned if the person is serving a prison sentence. Given that extradition will only take place once the prison sentence is served it will be generally be appropriate to adjourn the proceedings (eg *R (Slator) v Bow Street Magistrates' Court* [2006] EWHC 2628 (Admin)).

Physical or mental health

Relevant law: Extradition Act 2003, 25, 91

Cases: A substantial risk of suicide would make extradition oppressive (*Jansons v Latvia* [2009] EWHC 1845 (Admin)). In *Wrobel v Poland* [2011] EWHC 374 (Admin) it was held:

> "In deciding what risk is sufficiently great to result in such a finding it must be borne in mind, firstly, that there is a public interest in giving effect to treaty obligations (see Howes and also Norris [2010] 2 AC 487); secondly, that it should be assumed, at any rate in a European arrest warrant case under Part 1 [...] that the requesting state has the facilities to cope with and treat mental illness. Whether or not the treatment is, in all respects, as good as the appellant might receive in London is not to the point. Thirdly, a high threshold has to be surmounted in order to show oppression. Finally, in a case based on the risk of suicide there must, [...] be independent and convincing evidence of a very high risk of suicide if the fugitive is returned."

Bail

Usual Bail Act considerations apply, although there is no presumption in favour of bail in conviction cases. A security or surety is generally required.

FITNESS TO PLEAD

In a strict legal sense the issue of fitness to plead does not arise in the magistrates' court as the relevant legislation does not provide for any summary procedures. However, if the accused is being tried for an either-way or indictable offence, and it is shown that the accused did the act or made the omission charged, he can be made subject to a hospital order. The same provisions apply to the youth court (*R (on the application of P) v Barking Youth Court* (2002) EWHC 734 (Admin)). A magistrates' court (so far as an adult offender is concerned) has no power to determine fitness to plead in relation to an indictable only offence (*R v Chippenham Magistrates' Court, ex p Thompson* (1996) 160 JP 207).

Diversion

The Crown Prosecution Service has issued the following guidance which is to be considered before prosecuting an offender (or if the prosecution has commenced, before dealing further with the offender); Advocates should ensure that in an appropriate case the reviewing lawyer is reminded of the principles below, before any more formal route to disposal is considered:

"The Code for Crown Prosecutors states that alternatives to prosecution should be considered when deciding whether a case should be prosecuted. Rehabilitative, reparative and restorative processes can be considered, and alternatives to prosecution for adult offenders include a simple caution and conditional caution.

The National Standards for Cautioning require that the following conditions are met before a simple caution may be administered by the police:

- there is a realistic prospect of conviction;
- the offender admits the offence; and
- the offender (or appropriate adult) understands the significance of a caution and gives informed consent to being cautioned.

The National Standards for Conditional Cautioning require that the following conditions are met before a conditional caution may be administered:

- there is enough evidence to bring charges and it is in the public interest to do so;
- the offender has admitted the offence and is aged 18 or over;
- the offender agrees to accept the caution and to carry out the conditions;
- the most likely outcome of attending court would have been a small fine, compensation, conditional discharge or a community penalty at the lower end of the scale; and
- the use of reparative or rehabilitative conditions is felt to be the most effective way of dealing with the offending behaviour and/or recompensing the victim.

A caution or conditional caution will not be appropriate if there is any doubt about the reliability of any admissions made or if the defendant's level of understanding prevents him or her from understanding the significance of the caution or conditional caution and giving informed consent. It should not be assumed that all mentally disordered offenders are ineligible for cautioning or conditional cautioning, but there is no definition of or restriction on the particular form of mental or psychological condition or disorder that may make an admission unreliable (*Walker* [1998] Crim LR 211).

Where a caution or conditional caution is inappropriate, the only alternative to prosecution is to take no further action. In considering whether the public interest requires a prosecution, prosecutors should inquire whether:

- the police or Social Services have used their powers under sections 135 or 136 Mental Health Act 1983;
- the defendant has been admitted to hospital for assessment or treatment under sections 2 or 3 Mental Health Act 1983;
- the defendant is receiving supervised community treatment under a Community Treatment Order made under section 17A Mental Health Act 1983;

- the offender has been admitted to hospital as an informal patient under section 131 Mental Health Act 1983; or
- an order for guardianship under section 7 Mental Health Act 1983 has been made.

However, the existence of a mental disorder is only one of the factors to be taken into account when deciding whether the public interest requires a prosecution. The seriousness or the persistence of the offending behaviour, the views of the victim and any responsible clinician should also be considered.

The fact that a person is receiving compulsory treatment under the Mental Health Act 1983, or as an informal patient under section 131 Mental Health Act 1983, does not prevent a prosecution. However, a prosecution must not be pursued solely to treat and manage a mental disorder. The decision to prosecute or divert a patient receiving treatment under the Mental Health Act 1983 should be informed by additional information, including:

medical reports from the responsible clinician to explain the nature and degree of the disorder or disability, and any relationship between the disorder and the treatment and behaviour of the offender; and

any other relevant information from hospital staff about the treatment and behaviour of the patient, including the treatment regime and any history of similar and recent behaviour.

Where the patient is alleged to have assaulted a member of staff, prosecutors should refer to the NHS/SMS/CPS Memorandum of Understanding on the Effective Prosecution of cases involving Violence and Abuse Against any Member of NHS staff."

Stages:

- Issue of mental disorder raised–established by *up to date* medical reports (see *Blouet v Bath and Wansdyke Magistrates' Court* [2009] EWHC 759 (Admin)).
- If there is a possibility that a section 37 order will be made, adjourn to establish whether the accused did the act or made the omission charged.
- Obtain requisite medical assessment.
- Make hospital order.

The prosecution will only be required to prove the actus reus of the offence (*Antoine* [2000] 2 All ER 208, HL). If the prosecution cannot prove the act or omission the defendant must be discharged. Insanity is available as a defence in the magistrates' court, but the defendant does not have an absolute right to having the issue determined at trial if the court feels that a disposal under section 37(3) of the Mental Health Act 1983 might be more appropriate (*R (Singh) v Stratford Magistrates' Court* [2007] EWHC 1582 (Admin)). In the event that an order made under section 37 no longer serve any further purpose a court is entitled to reopen the matter under section 142 MCA and try the defendant (*R (Bartram) v Southend Magistrates' Court* [2004] EWHCA 2691 (Admin)).

In order to decide whether the person should be tried or made subject to the fitness to plead procedure the court may need to consider the report of a medical practitioner, and a remand to hospital under section 11 of the Powers of Criminal Courts (Sentencing) Act 2000 will be necessary in most cases:

Powers of Criminal Courts (Sentencing) Act 2000, s 11

(1) If, on the trial by a magistrates' court of an offence punishable on summary conviction with imprisonment, the court—

    (a) is satisfied that the accused did the act or made the omission charged, but

    (b) is of the opinion that an inquiry ought to be made into his physical or mental condition before the method of dealing with him is determined,

the court shall adjourn the case to enable a medical examination and report to be made, and shall remand him.

(2) An adjournment under subsection (1) above shall not be for more than three weeks at a time where the court remands the accused in custody, nor for more than four weeks at a time where it remands him on bail.

(3) Where on an adjournment under subsection (1) above the accused is remanded on bail, the court shall impose conditions under paragraph (d) of section 3(6) of the Bail Act 1976 and the requirements imposed as conditions under that paragraph shall be or shall include requirements that the accused—

(a) undergo medical examination by a registered medical practitioner or, where the inquiry is into his mental condition and the court so directs, two such practitioners; and

(b) for that purpose attend such an institution or place, or on such practitioner, as the court directs and, where the inquiry is into his mental condition, comply with any other directions which may be given to him for that purpose by any person specified by the court or by a person of any class so specified.

Subject to having obtained two satisfactory reports (the court can remand under section 35 for that purpose) the court can then go on to make a hospital order under section 37(3):

Mental Health Act 1983, s 37(3)

Where a person is charged before a magistrates' court with any act or omission as an offence and the court would have power, on convicting him of that offence, to make an order under subsection (1) above in his case, then, if the court is satisfied that the accused did the act or made the omission charged, the court may, if it thinks fit, make such an order without convicting him.

HANDCUFFS

Handcuffs are only permitted if there is a risk of violence or escape (*Vrastides* [1998] Crim LR 251, CA). Only in the most exceptional case should handcuffs be permitted while a defendant was giving evidence. Once a defendant is in the custody of the court the question of handcuffs is one for the court and not security personnel, a court should determine the issue before a defendant is brought into the dock (*Rollinson* (1996) 161 JP 107), unless a decision has been made previously and there is no change in circumstances (*R v Cambridge Justices, ex p Peacock* (1992) 161 JP 113, DC). ECHR Article 3 does not bite if handcuffing has been imposed in connection with lawful detention, provided the force and public exposure does not exceed that which is reasonably considered necessary by the public authority carrying out the handcuffing. (*R (JB) v GSL Limited* [2007] EWHC 2227 (Admin))

Test: It is for the applicant to show that reasonable grounds exist for their use. A response that 'it was usual practice' to make an application when the prisoner had an escape marker recorded against him was not acceptable and the court should either be given detailed information on which to make a decision, or in its absence should request it (*Horden* [2009] EWCA Crim 288).

The CPS has issued the following guidance to prosecutors:

"The rights of the suspects need to be balanced against public safety, and legitimate reasons put forward for handcuffing in court. Any derogations from these principles must be strictly justified. Consistent with this approach, other methods of countering any risk of escape or violence should be explored to ensure the least risk of prejudice to the suspect. This may include, for example, the presence of covertly armed police officers in court or a use of a specially protected dock. Applications for handcuffs are becoming common. It is the role of the prosecutor to make representations to the court for the handcuffing of a prisoner based on information provided by the police or court security officers. It would not be appropriate for a prosecutor to comment upon the decision to seek an order or to advise on the safety of a particular person, other than to advise on the legal parameters of the court's discretion. Therefore, a prosecutor should not advise whether a particular defendant should be handcuffed but may refuse to assist the police or security staff where an application would be outside the court's discretion. A prosecutor may also refuse to make an application where s/he is not satisfied about the nature or extent of information provided by the police or Securicor when requested to make an application.

It is not appropriate for anyone other than the prosecutor to make a direct application to the court.

To maintain consistency of approach, all requests should be channelled through the prosecutor and the application should be made, wherever possible, before the defendant is brought into court. There is nothing, however, to prevent an application being made once the court is sitting or the suspect is in the dock.

Prosecutors need to carefully examine requests to make applications for handcuffs to be worn in court, and to ensure that there are sufficient grounds for making such applications.

A court is not bound to consider the application afresh at each subsequent hearing (R v Cambridge Justices, ex p Peacock (1992) 156 JP 895), but if there has been a change in circumstances, such as a defendant withdrawing his initial consent following a change of representation, the court should consider the matter afresh (*Monk* [2004] EWCA Crim 1256)."

ISSUING OF SUMMONSES AND WARRANTS

A warrant should only be issued where it is believed that a summons alone would be ineffectual, or where the matter is very serious in nature (*O'Brien v Brabner* (1885) 49 JPN 227).

Magistrates' Courts Act 1980, s 1

(1) On an information being laid before a justice of the peace that a person has, or is suspected of having, committed an offence, the justice may issue–

    (a) a summons directed to that person requiring him to appear before a magistrates' court to answer the information, or

    (b) a warrant to arrest that person and bring him before a magistrates' court.

    [...]

(3) No warrant shall be issued under this section unless the information is in writing.

(4) No warrant shall be issued under this section for the arrest of any person who has attained the age of 18 years unless—

    (a) the offence to which the warrant relates is an indictable offence or is punishable with imprisonment, or

    (b) the person's address is not sufficiently established for a summons to be served on him.

(4A) Where a person who is not a public prosecutor lays an information before a justice of the peace in respect of an offence to which this subsection applies, no warrant shall be issued under this section without the consent of the Director of Public Prosecutions .

(4B) In subsection (4A) "public prosecutor" has the same meaning as in section 29 of the Criminal Justice Act 2003.

(4C) Subsection (4A) applies to—

    (a) a qualifying offence which is alleged to have been committed outside the United Kingdom, or

    (b) an ancillary offence relating to a qualifying offence where it is alleged that the qualifying offence was, or would have been, committed outside the United Kingdom.

(4D) In subsection (4C) "qualifying offence" means any of the following—

    (a) piracy or an offence under section 2 of the Piracy Act 1837 (piracy where murder is attempted);

(b) an offence under section 1 of the Geneva Conventions Act 1957 (grave breaches of Geneva conventions);

(c) an offence which (disregarding the provisions of the Suppression of Terrorism Act 1978, the Nuclear Material (Offences) Act 1983, the United Nations Personnel Act 1997 and the Terrorism Act 2000) would not be an offence apart from section 1 of the Internationally Protected Persons Act 1978 (attacks and threats of attacks on protected persons);

(d) an offence under section 1 of the Taking of Hostages Act 1982 (hostage-taking);

(e) an offence under section 1, 2 or 6 of the Aviation Security Act 1982 (hijacking etc);

(f) an offence which (disregarding the provisions of the Internationally Protected Persons Act 1978, the Suppression of Terrorism Act 1978, the United Nations Personnel Act 1997 and the Terrorism Act 2000) would not be an offence apart from sections 1 to 2A of the Nuclear Material (Offences) Act 1983 (offences relating to nuclear material);

(g) an offence under section 134 of the Criminal Justice Act 1988 (torture);

(h) an offence under section 1 of the Aviation and Maritime Security Act 1990 (endangering safety at aerodromes);

(i) an offence under sections 9 to 14 of that Act (hijacking ships etc);

(j) an offence which (disregarding the provisions of the Internationally Protected Persons Act 1978, the Suppression of Terrorism Act 1978, the Nuclear Material (Offences) Act 1983 and the Terrorism Act 2000) would not be an offence apart from sections 1 to 3 of the United Nations Personnel Act 1997 (attacks on UN workers etc).

(4E) In subsection (4C) "ancillary offence", in relation to an offence, means—

(a) an offence under Part 2 of the Serious Crime Act 2007 (encouraging or assisting crime) in relation to the offence (including, in relation to times before the commencement of that Part, an offence of incitement);

(b) attempting or conspiring to commit the offence.

[...]

(6) Where the offence charged is an indictable offence, a warrant under this section may be issued at any time notwithstanding that a summons has previously been issued.

(7) A justice of the peace may issue a summons or warrant under this section upon an information being laid before him notwithstanding any enactment requiring the information to be laid before two or more justices.

MISBEHAVIOUR AT COURT

Magistrates' Courts Act 1980, s 4(4)(a)

(4) Examining justices may allow evidence to be tendered before them in the absence of the accused if—

(a) they consider that by reason of his disorderly conduct before them it is not practicable for the evidence to be tendered in his presence.

Magistrates' Courts Act 1980, s 18(3)

(3) The court may proceed in the absence of the accused in accordance with such of the provisions of sections 19 to 22 below as are applicable in the circumstances if the court considers that by reason of his disorderly conduct before the court it is not practicable for the proceedings to be conducted in his presence; and subsections (3) to (5) of section 23 below, so far as applicable, shall have effect in relation to proceedings conducted in the absence of the accused by virtue of this subsection (references in those subsections to the

person representing the accused being for this purpose read as references to the person, if any, representing him).

Contempt of Court Act 1981, s 12

(1)   A magistrates' court has jurisdiction under this section to deal with any person who—

      (a) wilfully insults the justice or justices, any witness before or officer of the court or any solicitor or counsel having business in the court, during his or their sitting or attendance in court or in going to or returning from the court; or

      (b) wilfully interrupts the proceedings of the court or otherwise misbehaves in court.

(2)   In any such case the court may order any officer of the court, or any constable, to take the offender into custody and detain him until the rising of the court; and the court may, if it thinks fit, commit the offender to custody for a specified period not exceeding one month or impose on him a fine not exceeding £2,500, or both.

(2A)   A fine imposed under subsection (2) above shall be deemed, for the purposes of any enactment, to be a sum adjudged to be paid by a conviction.

(4)   A magistrates' court may at any time revoke an order of committal made under subsection (2) and, if the offender is in custody, order his discharge.

(5)   Section 135 of the Powers of Criminal Courts (Sentencing) Act 2000 (limit on fines in respect of young persons) and the following provisions of the Magistrates' Courts Act 1980 apply in relation to an order under this section as they apply in relation to a sentence on conviction or finding of guilty of an offence; and those provisions of the Magistrates' Courts Act 1980 are section 36 (restriction on fines in respect of young persons); sections 75 to 91 (enforcement); section 108 (appeal to Crown Court); section 136 (overnight detention in default of payment); and section 142(1) (power to rectify mistakes).

Consolidated Criminal Practice Direction, part V.54

General

(V.54.1)

Section 12 of the Contempt of Court Act 1981 gives magistrates' courts the power to detain until the court rises, someone, whether a defendant or another person present in court, who wilfully insults anyone specified in section 12 or who interrupts proceedings. In any such case, the court may order any officer of the court, or any constable, to take the offender into custody and detain him until the rising of the court; and the court may, if it thinks fit, commit the offender to custody for a specified period not exceeding one month or impose a fine not exceeding level 4 on the standard scale or both. This power can be used to stop disruption of their proceedings. Detention is until the person can be conveniently dealt with without disruption of the proceedings. Prior to the court using the power the offender should be warned to desist or face the prospect of being detained.

(V.54.2)

Magistrates' courts also have the power to commit to custody any person attending or brought before a magistrates' court who refuses without just cause to be sworn or to give evidence under section 97(4) of the Magistrates' Courts Act 1980, until the expiration of such period not exceeding one month as may be specified in the warrant or until he sooner gives evidence or produces the document or thing, or impose on him a fine not exceeding £2,500, or both.

(V.54.3)

In the exercise of any of these powers, as soon as is practical, and in any event prior to an offender being proceeded against, an offender should be told of the conduct which it is alleged to constitute his offending in clear terms. When making an order under section 12 the justices should state their findings of fact as to the contempt.

(V.54.4)

Exceptional situations require exceptional treatment. While this direction deals with the generality of situations, there will be a minority of situations where the application of the direction will not be consistent with achieving justice in the special circumstances of the particular case. Where this is the situation, the compliance with the direction should be modified so far as is necessary so as to accord with the interests of justice.

(V.54.5)

The power to bind persons over to be of good behaviour in respect of their conduct in court should cease to be exercised.

Contempt consisting of wilfully insulting anyone specified in section 12 or interrupting proceedings

(V.54.6)

In the case of someone who wilfully insults anyone specified in section 12 or interrupts proceedings, if an offender expresses a willingness to apologise for his misconduct, he should be brought back before the court at the earliest convenient moment in order to make the apology and to give undertakings to the court to refrain from further misbehaviour.

(V.54.7)

In the majority of cases, an apology and a promise as to future conduct should be sufficient for justices to order an offender's release. However, there are likely to be certain cases where the nature and seriousness of the misconduct requires the justices to consider using their powers under section 12(2) of the Contempt of Court 1981 Act either to fine or to order the offender's committal to custody.

Where an offender is detained for contempt of court

(V.54.8)

Anyone detained under either of these provisions in paragraphs V.54.1 or V.54.2 should be seen by the duty solicitor or another legal representative and be represented in proceedings if they so wish. Public funding should generally be granted to cover representation. The offender must be afforded adequate time and facilities in order to prepare his case. The matter should be resolved the same day if at all possible.

(V.54.9)

The offender should be brought back before the court before the justices conclude their daily business. The justices should ensure that he understands the nature of the proceedings, including his opportunity to apologise or give evidence and the alternative of them exercising their powers.

(V.54.10)

Having heard from the offender's solicitor, the justices should decide whether to take further action.

Sentencing of an offender who admits being in contempt

(V.54.11)

If an offence of contempt is admitted the justices should consider whether they are able to proceed on the day or whether to adjourn to allow further reflection. The matter should be dealt with on the same day if at all possible. If the justices are of the view to adjourn they should generally grant the offender bail unless one or more of the exceptions to the right to bail in the Bail Act 1976 are made out.

(V.54.12)

When they come to sentence the offender where the offence has been admitted, the justices should first ask the offender if he has any objection to them dealing with the matter. If there is any objection to the justices dealing with the matter a differently constituted panel should hear the proceedings. If the offender's conduct was directed to the justices, it will not be appropriate for the same bench to deal with the matter.

(V.54.13)

The justices should consider whether an order for the offender's discharge is appropriate, taking into account any time spent on remand, whether the offence was admitted and the seriousness of the contempt. Any period of committal should be for the shortest time commensurate with the interests of preserving good order in the administration of justice.

Trial of the issue where the contempt is not admitted

(V.54.14)

Where the contempt is not admitted the justices' powers are limited to making arrangements for a trial to take place. They should not at this stage make findings against the offender.

(V.54.15)

In the case of a contested contempt the trial should take place at the earliest opportunity and should be before a bench of justices other than those before whom the alleged contempt took place. If a trial of the issue can take place on the day such arrangements should be made taking into account the offender's rights under Article 6 of the European Convention for the Protection of Human Rights and Fundamental Freedoms (Rome, 4 November 1950; TS 71 (1953); Cmd 8969). If the trial cannot take place that day the justices should again bail the offender unless there are grounds under the Bail Act 1976 to remand him in custody.

(V.54.16)

The offender is entitled to call and examine witnesses where evidence is relevant. If the offender is found by the court to have committed contempt the court should again consider first whether an order for his discharge from custody is sufficient to bring proceedings to an end. The justices should also allow the offender a further opportunity to apologise for his contempt or to make representations. If the justices are of the view that they must exercise their powers to commit to custody under section12(2) of the 1981 Act, they must take into account any time spent on remand and the nature and seriousness of the contempt. Any period of committal should be for the shortest period of time commensurate with the interests of preserving good order in the administration of justice.

NON-APPEARANCE OF PARTIES

Cases: In *Director of Public Prosecutions v Shuttleworth* [2002] EWHC 621 (Admin) the court dismissed a case for want of prosecution where despite the defendant indicating that she would be pleading guilty the prosecution had no file at court. The court held:

> "Prior to plea, the question of the prosecution's ability to open the case or to call evidence does not arise. There was enough information in court, in the Court Agenda which was in the hands of the court clerk and the Crown Prosecutor, to allow the plea of Miss Shuttleworth to be taken. Had she entered a not guilty plea, the case would have been put off for trial. Had she, as was clearly anticipated, entered a guilty plea, the court would have moved to the stage of the trial process set out in section 9(3) of the Act. The magistrates would have to consider whether to convict without hearing evidence and whether they were in a position to proceed to sentence. If they were, it would be at the stage of having to open the case that the prosecution would be in difficulties. Though physically present in court, the prosecution would not be in a position to proceed, due to the absence of the file. At that stage the appropriate course would have been to adjourn the case and the magistrates could have considered whether any order for costs should be made in respect

of the additional adjourned hearing. It follows that, in my judgment, in the circumstances of this case the magistrates were not entitled to dismiss the information under section 15(1) when they did...I would add three points, which do not necessarily arise in this case but may be of general application. One can understand the frustration and perhaps irritation of benches when faced by the absence of a prosecution file, which might cause delay in their court and may necessitate the adjournment of a case to a future date. However, section 15(1) of the Magistrates' Court Act 1980 is not a provision which should be used as a punitive or disciplinary provision against the Crown Prosecution Service. That is not the purpose of that section. Secondly, where through fault an additional hearing is necessitated, the magistrates may consider whether there are costs implications for the defaulting party. Thirdly, it is entirely appropriate for magistrates to consider, as the magistrates did in this case, the position of the defendant and the legitimate expectations of a defendant to be dealt with promptly. However, there are other interests which must also be borne in mind. There is, for example, the general public interest in prosecuting and convicting offenders. There is also the more particular interest of those people who may be personally affected by the alleged offence. In the context of the kind of offence that Miss Shuttleworth is alleged to have committed, it may be that a member of the public had suffered personal injury as a result of the alleged offence, or suffered damage to property. To that member of the public the proper prosecution and, if appropriate, conviction of an offender might be a very significant event. In so far as these interests may be in competition one with the other a proper balance must be struck."

In *R v Dudley Justices' ex p Director of Public Prosecutions* (1992) 156 JPN 618 the court held that it was wrong to dismiss proceedings for want of prosecution when the fault lay with court listings.

The power to dismiss proceedings is not a punitive measure, see *R v Hendon Justices' ex p Director of Public Prosecutions* [1994] QB 167 and *London Borough of Bromley v Bromley Magistrates' Court* 175 JP 179. In the absence of either party good practice is to adjourn for a short period in order to make enquiries.

Re instituting proceedings: In *Holmes v Campbell* (1998) 162 JP 655 the court quashed a decision to stay re-instituted proceedings as an abuse of process where the original decision to dismiss the proceedings for want of prosecution was a nullity.

Magistrates' Courts Act 1980, ss 15–16

15.— Non-appearance of prosecutor.

(1) Where at the time and place appointed for the trial or adjourned trial of an information the accused appears or is brought before the court and the prosecutor does not appear, the court may dismiss the information or, if evidence has been received on a previous occasion, proceed in the absence of the prosecutor.

(2) Where, instead of dismissing the information or proceeding in the absence of the prosecutor, the court adjourns the trial, it shall not remand the accused in custody unless he has been brought from custody or cannot be remanded on bail by reason of his failure to find sureties.

16. Non-appearance of both parties.

Subject to section 11(3) and (4) and to section 12 above, where at the time and place appointed for the trial or adjourned trial of an information neither the prosecutor nor the accused appears, the court may dismiss the information or, if evidence has been received on a previous occasion, proceed in their

PERSON

Includes a body of persons corporate or unincorporate (Interpretation Act 1978, Sch 1). Accordingly, and unless the statute provides otherwise, such persons can be prosecuted for offences.

POWERS EXERCISABLE BY JUSTICES' CLERKS AND THEIR ASSISTANTS

Justices' Clerks Rules 2005, sch 1

- The laying of an information or the making of a complaint, other than an information or complaint substantiated on oath.
- The issue of any summons, including a witness summons.
- The issue of a warrant of arrest, whether or not endorsed for bail, for failure to surrender to the court, where there is no objection on behalf of the accused.
- The marking of an information as withdrawn.
- The dismissing of an information, or the discharging of an accused in respect of an information, or the discharging of an accused in respect of an information, where no evidence is offered by the prosecution.
- The making of an order for the payment of defence costs out of central funds.
- The adjournment of the hearing of a complaint if the parties to the complaint consent to the complaint being adjourned.
- The extending of bail on the same conditions as those (if any) previously imposed, or, with the consent of the prosecutor and the accused, the imposing or varying of conditions of bail.
- The further adjournment of criminal proceedings with the consent of the prosecutor and the accused, if but only if,
    - (a) the accused, not having been remanded on the previous adjournment, is not remanded on the further adjournment; or
    - (b) the accused, having been remanded on bail on the previous adjournment, is remanded on bail on the like terms and conditions, or, with the consent of the prosecutor and the accused, on other terms and conditions.
- The further adjournment of criminal proceedings, where there has been no objection by the prosecutor, where the accused, having been remanded on bail on the previous adjournment, is remanded on bail on the like terms and conditions in his absence.
- And, The remand of the accused on bail in his absence at the time of further adjourning the proceedings in pursuance of [the paragraph] above.
- The appointment of a later time at which a person, who has been granted bail under the Police and Criminal Evidence Act 1984 subject to a duty to appear before a magistrates' court, is to appear, and the enlargement of any sureties for that person at that time, in accordance with section 43(1) of the Magistrates' Courts Act 1980, provided there is no objection by the prosecutor.
- Where a person has been granted police bail to appear at a magistrates' court, the appointment of an earlier time for his appearance.
- The committal of a person for trial on bail in accordance with section 6(2) and (3)(b) of the Magistrates' Courts Act 1980 where, having been remanded on bail on the previous adjournment, he is released on bail on the like terms and conditions.
- The asking of an accused whether he pleads guilty or not guilty to a charge, after having stated to him the substance of the information laid against him.
- The fixing or setting aside of a date, time and place for the trial of an information.
- The making of a direction in accordance with rule 93A(7) or (8) of the Magistrates' Courts Rules 19811.

- The giving, variation or revocation of directions for the conduct of a criminal trial, including directions as to the following matters, namely–
- the timetable for proceedings;
- the attendance of the parties;
- the service of documents (including summaries of any legal arguments relied on by the parties);
- the manner in which evidence is to be given.
- With the consent of the parties, the giving, variation or revocation of orders for separate or joint trials in the case of two or more accused or two or more informations.
- The extension, with the consent of the accused, of an overall time limit under section 22 of the Prosecution of Offences Act 1985.
- The request of a pre-sentence report following a plea of guilty.
- The request of a medical report and, for that purpose, the remand of an accused on bail on the same conditions as those (if any) previously imposed, or, with the consent of the prosecutor and the accused, on other conditions.
- The remitting of an offender to another court for sentence.
- Where an accused has been convicted of an offence, the making of an order for him to produce his driving licence.
- The giving of consent for another magistrates' court to deal with an offender for an earlier offence in respect of which, after the offender had attained the age of eighteen years, a court had made an order for conditional discharge, where the justices' clerk is the clerk of the court which made the order, or in the case of a community rehabilitation order, of that court or the supervising court.
- The amending, in accordance with paragraph 15 of Schedule 3 to the Powers of Criminal Courts (Sentencing) Act 2000, of a community rehabilitation order or community punishment order by substituting for the local justice area specified in the order the other area in which the offender proposes to reside or is residing.
- The varying, in accordance with paragraph 5(1) of Schedule 5 to the Powers of Criminal Courts (Sentencing) Act 2000, of an attendance centre order by–
- (a) varying the day or hour specified in the order for the offender's first attendance at the relevant attendance centre; or
- (b) substituting for the relevant attendance centre an attendance centre which the justices' clerk is satisfied is reasonably accessible to the offender, having regard to his age, the means of access available to him and any other circumstances.
- The signing of a certificate given to the Crown Court under paragraph 4(6) of Schedule 3 to the Powers of Criminal Courts (Sentencing) Act 2000 as to non-compliance with a community order.
- The acceptance under section 14 of the Magistrates Courts Act 1980 of service of such a statutory declaration as is mentioned in subsection (3) of that section.
- The issue of a warrant of distress.
- The allowing of further time for payment of a sum enforceable by a magistrates' court.
- The varying of the number of instalments payable, the amount of any instalment payable and the date on which any instalment becomes payable where a magistrates' court has ordered that a sum adjudged to be paid shall be paid by instalments.
- The making of a transfer of fine order under section 89 of the Magistrates' Courts Act 1980.
- The making of an order before an enquiry into the means of a person under section 82 of the Magistrates' Courts Act 1980 that that person shall furnish to the court a statement of his means under section 84 of that Act.
- The fixing under section 86(3) of the Magistrates' Courts Act 1980 of a later day in substitution for a day previously fixed for the appearance of an offender to enable an enquiry into his means to be made under section 82 of that Act or to enable a hearing required by section 82(5) of that Act to be held.

- The making or withdrawal of an application to the Secretary of State, pursuant to the Fines (Deductions from Income Support) Regulations 1992 1, for deductions to be made from an offender's income support.
- The doing of such other things as are required or permitted to be done by a magistrates' court under the Fines (Deductions from Income Support) Regulations 1992.

PRE-TRIAL RULINGS

Note: The bracketed words in s 8B(6)(a) are deleted in the 12 areas where committal proceedings have been abolished. **Generally:** Because of the binding nature of these rulings, it is not open to a later bench simply to reverse the ruling because it would have reached a different conclusion. In *Brett v Director of Public Prosecutions* [2009] EWHC 440 (Admin), the court took a far less restrictive approach than that taken in previous cases in holding a judge to have erred in feeling that he was bound by a previous ruling under section 8A of the Magistrates' Courts Act 1980. What is certainly clear from pre- and post-section 8A case law, is that a later court cannot simply annul a previous decision on the sole ground that it simply disagrees with it (*Crown Prosecution Service v Gloucester Justices and Loveridge* [2008] EWHC 1488 (Admin)). In R *(Jones) v South East Surrey Local Justice Area*, unreported, 12 March 2010, the court having previously disallowed a prosecution application to adjourn, later granted it due to the fact that the information presented on the renewed application was different, and that it was in the interests of justice that the previous ruling be reversed. Where the court acts of its own motion to vary a previous ruling, the grounds for discharge or variation are simply the interests of justice, and where an application is made by a party, there is an additional requirement for proof of material change of circumstances (*Crown Prosecution Service v Gloucester Justices and Alan Loveridge* [2008] EWHC 1488 (Admin)).

Magistrates' Courts Act 1980, ss 8A–8B

8A Power to make rulings at pre-trial hearing

(1) For the purposes of this section a hearing is a pre-trial hearing if—

    (a) it relates to an information—

        (i)   which is to be tried summarily, and

        (ii)   to which the accused has pleaded not guilty, and

    (b) it takes place before the start of the trial.

(2) [...]

(3) At a pre-trial hearing, a magistrates' court may make a ruling as to any matter mentioned in subsection (4) if—

    (a) the condition in subsection (5) is met,

    (b) the court has given the parties an opportunity to be heard, and

    (c) it appears to the court that it is in the interests of justice to make the ruling.

(4) The matters are—

    (a) any question as to the admissibility of evidence;

    (b) any other question of law relating to the case.

(5) [...]

(6) A ruling may be made under this section—

    (a) on an application by a party to the case, or

    (b) of the court's own motion.

(7) For the purposes of this section and section 8B, references to the prosecutor are to any person acting as prosecutor, whether an individual or body.

8B Effect of rulings at pre-trial hearing

(1) Subject to subsections (3) and (6), a ruling under section 8A has binding effect from the time it is made until the case against the accused or, if there is more than one, against each of them, is disposed of.

(2) The case against an accused is disposed of if—

 (a) he is acquitted or convicted,

 (b) the prosecutor decides not to proceed with the case against him, or

 (c) the information is dismissed.

(3) A magistrates' court may discharge or vary (or further vary) a ruling under section 8A if—

 (a) the condition in section 8A(5) is met,

 (b) the court has given the parties an opportunity to be heard, and

 (c) it appears to the court that it is in the interests of justice to do so.

(4) The court may act under subsection (3)—

 (a) on an application by a party to the case, or

 (b) of its own motion.

(5) No application may be made under subsection (4)(a) unless there has been a material change of circumstances since the ruling was made or, if a previous application has been made, since the application (or last application) was made.

(6) A ruling under section 8A is discharged in relation to an accused if—

 (a) the magistrates' court commits or sends him to the Crown Court for trial for the offence charged in the information, or

 (b) a count charging him with the offence is included in an indictment by virtue of section 40 of the Criminal Justice Act 1988.

PRIVATE PROSECUTIONS

An individual enjoys the right to bring a private prosecution (Prosecution of Offences Act 1985, s 6(1)). If proceedings in relation to the criminal conduct alleged have already been started by a public prosecutor, a court should only in special circumstances (such as apparent bad faith on the part of the public prosecutor) allow a private prosecutor to initiate further proceedings (*R v Tower Bridge Stipendiary Magistrate, ex p Chaudhry* [1994] RTR 113). Special circumstances are not however required where the proceedings brought by the public prosecutor have been discontinued (*R (Charlson) v Guildford Magistrates' Court* [2007] RTR 1). A private prosecutor is not bound by the same considerations as a public prosecutor (eg public interest test) (*Ewing v Davis* [2007] 1 WLR 3223), although if the Director of Public Prosecutions takes over the right to conduct a private prosecution (Prosecution of Offences Act 1985, s 6(2)) he will rightfully apply those considerations when deciding whether or not to continue the proceedings (*R (Gujra) v Crown Prosecution Service* [2011] EWHC 472 (Admin)). Where an offender has accepted a police caution on the basis that he would not be prosecuted, a private prosecution will thereafter be an abuse of process (*Jones v Whalley* [2007] AC 63). In *R (Dacre) v Westminster Magistrates' Court* [2008] ECHC 1667 (Admin) the prosecutor had assisted in creating the circumstances that led to the criminality alleged, as such it was held to be an abuse of process to proceed with the prosecution. The mere presence of an indirect or improper motive in launching a prosecution did not necessarily vitiate it; and a court should be slow to halt such a prosecution in the case of mixed motives unless the conduct was truly oppressive (*Bow Street Metropolitan Stipendiary Magistrate and Anor v ex p South Coast Shipping Company Limited and Others* [1993] QB 645).

REMAND PERIODS

Prior to conviction

- Remand to police cells for three days.
- Remand to custody for maximum of eight clear days on first remand.
- Subsequent remand to custody for up to 28 clear days provided the next stage in the proceedings will be dealt with. If it is known that the next stage cannot be dealt with in that period, then eight-day remands will have to follow until such time as completion of the next stage within 28 days is achievable.
- Subsequent remand to custody for 28 clear days if the defendant is already in custody serving a sentence and will not be released before that date.
- Remand on bail for eight days, or longer if the defendant consents.
- Following a committal or sending to the Crown Court, the magistrates have the power to adjourn for a period up to the date of trial (so the normal eight-day limit on first remand does not apply). It is important to note that the expression 'remand' has a particular meaning within the 1980 Act, and the court is not remanding a person when it commits or sends someone for trial—therefore when a court sends a person for trial during their first appearance it can do so in custody for a period in excess of eight days.

Section 129 of the Magistrates' Courts Act 1980 allows for the remands of persons not produced before the court due to illness or accident. The court must have 'solid grounds' to justify an opinion that failure to be produced was due to illness or accident (*R v Liverpool Justices, ex p Grogan* The Times, 8 October 1990).

Post conviction

- Maximum three weeks if in custody, four weeks if on bail.

REPORTING RESTRICTIONS

Legislation: Restriction on reporting are imposed either automatically (as in the case of proceedings in the youth court, s 49 of the 1933 Act) or by order of the court (section 39 of the 1933 Act or section 4(2) Contempt of Court Act 1981). **Documents:** The right to report proceedings extends to documents used in those proceedings, and proper disclosure should be made (*R (Guardian News and Media Ltd) v Westminster Magistrates' Court* [2012] EWCA Civ 420). For the practical application of the Guardian News case see *R v King*, Birmingham Crown Court, 1 May 2012. **Lifting of reporting restrictions:** It has been said that the reporting of youth cases will be very rare (*McKerry v Teesdale and Wear Valley Justice* [2000] Crim LR), and that principle remains true today, despite a more aggressive approach by the press designed to promote the greater reporting of criminal cases. In *R v Winchester Crown Court* [2000] 1 Cr App R 11 Simon Brown LJ distilled the following propositions from earlier cases:

i) In deciding whether to impose or thereafter to lift reporting restrictions, the court will consider whether there are good reasons for naming the defendant;

ii) In reaching that decision, the court will give considerable weight to the age of the offender and to the potential damage to any young person of public identification as a criminal before the offender has the benefit or burden of adulthood;

iii) By virtue of section 44 of the 1933 Act, the court must "have regard to the welfare of the child or young person";

iv) The prospect of being named in court with the accompanying disgrace is a powerful deterrent and the naming of a defendant in the context of his punishment serves as a deterrent to others. These deterrents are proper objectives for the court to seek;

v) There is a strong public interest in open justice and in the public knowing as much as possible about what has happened in court, including the identity of those who have committed crime;

vi) The weight to be attributed to the different factors may shift at different stages of the proceedings and, in particular, after the defendant has been found, or pleads, guilty and is sentenced. It may then be appropriate to place greater weight on the interest of the public in knowing the identity of those who have committed crimes, particularly serious and detestable crimes;

vii) The fact that an appeal has been made may be a material consideration.

In Y v Aylesbury Crown Court [2012] EWHC 1140 (Admin) the court stated:

"In most cases the good reason upon which the defendant child or young person will rely is his or her welfare. Section 44 of the Children and Young Persons Act 1933 requires the court to have regard to his or her welfare when deciding a section 39 application. Having regard to the mandatory requirement of section 44, it is probably unnecessary to consider Article 8. Because the defendant is a child or young person and not an adult, his or her future progress may well be assisted by restricting publication. Publication could well have a significant effect on the prospects and opportunities of the young person, and, therefore, on the likelihood of effective integration into society. Identifying a defendant in the media may constitute an additional and disproportionate punishment on the child or young person. In rare cases (and not in this case) the child or young person may be at serious personal risk if identified. In reaching the decision upon an application by a defendant to restrict publication under section 39, the court must, in addition to having regard to the welfare of the child, have regard to the public interest and to Article 10 of the ECHR. Amongst the possible public interests is the public interest in knowing the outcome of proceedings in court and the public interest in the valuable deterrent effect that the identification of those guilty of at least serious crimes may have on others".

Contempt of Court Act 1981, s 4(2)

(2) In any such proceedings the court may, where it appears to be necessary for avoiding a substantial risk of prejudice to the administration of justice in those proceedings, or in any other proceedings pending or imminent, order that the publication of any report of the proceedings, or any part of the proceedings, be postponed for such period as the court thinks necessary for that purpose.

Children and Young Persons Act 1933, s 39

(1) In relation to any proceedings in any court, the court may direct that—

(a) no newspaper report of the proceedings shall reveal the name, address or school, or include any particulars calculated to lead to the identification, of any child or young person concerned in the proceedings, either as being the person by or against or in respect of whom the proceedings are taken, or as being a witness therein:

(b) no picture shall be published in any newspaper as being or including a picture of any child or young person so concerned in the proceedings as aforesaid;

except in so far (if at all) as may be permitted by the direction of the court.

(2) Any person who publishes any matter in contravention of any such direction shall on summary conviction be liable in respect of each offence to a fine not exceeding level 5 on the standard scale.

Children and Young Persons Act 1933, s49

(1) The following prohibitions apply (subject to subsection (5) below) in relation to any proceedings to which this section applies, that is to say—

(a) no report shall be published which reveals the name, address or school of any child or young person concerned in the proceedings or includes any particulars likely to lead to the identification of any child or young person concerned in the proceedings; and

(b) no picture shall be published or included in a programme service as being or including a picture of any child or young person concerned in the proceedings.

(2) The proceedings to which this section applies are—

    (a) proceedings in a youth court;

    (b) proceedings on appeal from a youth court (including proceedings by way of case stated);

    (c) proceedings in a magistrates' court under Schedule 2 to the Criminal Justice and Immigration Act 2008 (proceedings for breach, revocation or amendment of youth rehabilitation orders);

    (d) proceedings on appeal from a magistrates' court arising out of any proceedings mentioned in paragraph (c) (including proceedings by way of case stated).

(3) The reports to which this section applies are reports in a newspaper and reports included in a programme service; and similarly as respects pictures.

(4) For the purposes of this section a child or young person is "concerned" in any proceedings whether as being the person against or in respect of whom the proceedings are taken or as being a witness in the proceedings.

(4A) If a court is satisfied that it is in the public interest to do so, it may, in relation to a child or young person who has been convicted of an offence, by order dispense to any specified extent with the requirements of this section in relation to any proceedings before it to which this section applies by virtue of subsection (2)(a) or (b) above, being proceedings relating to—

    (a) the prosecution or conviction of the offender for the offence;

    (b) the manner in which he, or his parent or guardian, should be dealt with in respect of the offence;

    (c) the enforcement, amendment, variation, revocation or discharge of any order made in respect of the offence;

    (d) where an attendance centre order is made in respect of the offence, the enforcement of any rules made under section 222(1)(d) or (e) of the Criminal Justice Act 2003; or

    (e) where a detention and training order is made, the enforcement of any requirements imposed under section 103(6)(b) of the Powers of Criminal Courts (Sentencing) Act 2000.

(4B) A court shall not exercise its power under subsection (4A) above without—

    (a) affording the parties to the proceedings an opportunity to make representations; and

    (b) taking into account any representations which are duly made.

(5) Subject to subsection (7) below, a court may, in relation to proceedings before it to which this section applies, by order dispense to any specified extent with the requirements of this section in relation to a child or young person who is concerned in the proceedings if it is satisfied—

    (a) that it is appropriate to do so for the purpose of avoiding injustice to the child or young person; or

    (b) that, as respects a child or young person to whom this paragraph applies who is unlawfully at large, it is necessary to dispense with those requirements for the purpose of apprehending him and bringing him before a court or returning him to the place in which he was in custody.

(6) Paragraph (b) of subsection (5) above applies to any child or young person who is charged with or has been convicted of—

    (a) a violent offence,

    (b) a sexual offence, or

    (c) an offence punishable in the case of a person aged 21 or over with imprisonment for fourteen years or more.

(7) The court shall not exercise its power under subsection (5)(b) above—

(a) except in pursuance of an application by or on behalf of the Director of Public Prosecutions ; and

(b) unless notice of the application has been given by the Director of Public Prosecutions to any legal representative of the child or young person.

(8) The court's power under subsection (5) above may be exercised by a single justice.

(9) If a report or picture is published or included in a programme service in contravention of subsection (1) above, the following persons, that is to say—

(a) in the case of publication of a written report or a picture as part of a newspaper, any proprietor, editor or publisher of the newspaper;

(b) in the case of the inclusion of a report or picture in a programme service, any body corporate which provides the service and any person having functions in relation to the programme corresponding to those of an editor of a newspaper,

shall be liable on summary conviction to a fine not exceeding level 5 on the standard scale.

(10) In any proceedings under Schedule 2 to the Criminal Justice and Immigration Act 2008 (proceedings for breach, revocation or amendment of youth rehabilitation orders) before a magistrates' court other than a youth court or on appeal from such a court it shall be the duty of the magistrates' court or the appellate court to announce in the course of the proceedings that this section applies to the proceedings; and if the court fails to do so this section shall not apply to the proceedings.

(11) In this section—

[...]

"programme" and "programme service" have the same meaning as in the Broadcasting Act 1990;

"sexual offence" means an offence listed in Part 2 of Schedule 15 to the Criminal Justice Act 2003;

"specified" means specified in an order under this section;

"violent offence" means an offence listed in Part 1 of Schedule 15 to the Criminal Justice Act 2003;

and a person who, having been granted bail, is liable to arrest (whether with or without a warrant) shall be treated as unlawfully at large.

RIGHTS OF AUDIENCE

A defendant may represent himself (although there are provisions preventing him from cross-examining witnesses in certain cases), and a lay person may conduct a private prosecution (Prosecution of Offences Act 1985, s 6(1)). A court may permit a Mckenzie Friend to assist a defendant in person must this does not extend to a general right to conduct advocacy in the proceedings (see: R (Koli) v Maidstone Crown Court [2011] EWHC 2821 (Admin), but note that the extempore ruling in relation to this point does not appear in the official transcript). Legally qualified persons authorised to practice under the Legal Services Act 2007 and in accordance with the rules of their regulator are permitted to address the court, as are a number of non-legally qualified individuals with more limited rights of audience, most notably associate prosecutors (Prosecution of Offences Act 1985, s 7A) and many employed in local government. Police Officers (or civilian staff) are empowered (presumably at common law) to assist the court in dealing with certain offences that result in a guilty plea, generally motoring matters (Prosecution of Offences Act 1985 (Specified Proceedings) Order 1999 (SI 1999/904); also see The Prosecution of Offences Act 1985 (Specified Proceedings) (Amendment) Order 2012 (SI 2012/1635); this Order amends the 1999 Order with the effect that proceedings do not cease to be specified where a magistrates' court begins to receive evidence, provided that the court does so in defined circumstances. The first of these is where the accused has not appeared, and the court proceeds in his absence. The second is where evidence is read out in the case of an accused who has indicated a guilty plea by post–this maintains the position under the existing Order. The third is where evidence is received for the purposes of the court's consideration of whether an accused who has been convicted of repeated motoring offences should be spared obligatory disqualification under the "totting up" provisions. In general such evidence concerns the exceptional hardship that disqualification would cause to the accused.

SERVICE OF SUMMONS OUT OF TIME

Magistrates' Courts Act 1980, s 46

Where any enactment requires, expressly or by implication, that a summons in respect of an offence shall be issued or served within a specified period after the commission of the offence, and service of the summons may under rules of court be effected by post, then, if under the rules service of the summons is not treated as proved, but it is shown that a letter containing the summons was posted at such time as to enable it to be delivered in the ordinary course of post within that period, a second summons may be issued on the same information; and the enactment shall have effect, in relation to that summons, as if the specified period were a period running from the return day of the original summons.

SITTING TIMES

Save when the Lord Chancellor directs otherwise a court can sit at any location and on any day and at any time (Courts Act 2003, s 30(8)).

SOVEREIGN AND DIPLOMATIC IMMUNITY

Certain persons enjoy immunity from prosecution (and therefore the proceedings against them are void, *Madan* [1961] Crim LR 253) provided that their arrival into the UK has been notified to the Foreign Office (*R v Lambeth Justices ex p Yusufu* [1985] Crim LR 510). Diplomatic immunity can be waived by the home government if it so wishes. British citizens may also enjoy immunity when acting in their capacity as an agent to the foreign mission. **See generally:** Diplomatic Privileges Act 1964 and *R v Bow Street Stipendiary Magistrate ex p Pinochet (No 3)* 1 AC 147, HL; Commonwealth Secretariat Act 1966; Consular Relations act 1968; European Court of Human Rights (Immunities and Privileges) Order 2000 (SI 2000/1817); International Organisations Act 1968, s 6; Visiting Forces Act 1952, s 3. Whether a person is visiting as part of a special mission is one to be determined by the UK Government and not the courts (*Bat v Germany* [2011] EWHC 2029 (Admin)).

STATUTORY DECLARATION

A statutory declaration, certifying that the defendant was not aware of the proceedings, should be made on the prescribed form (see CrPR 37.11). The effect of the declaration is to void the proceedings (*Singh v Director of Public Prosecutions* [1999] RTR 424), including all penalties flowing from conviction. If the prosecution wishes to continue with the case it is not necessary to issue fresh proceedings.

Magistrates' Courts Act 1980, s 14

(1) Where a summons has been issued under section 1 above and a magistrates' court has begun to try the information to which the summons relates, then, if—

(a) the accused, at any time during or after the trial, makes a statutory declaration that he did not know of the summons or the proceedings until a date specified in the declaration, being a date after the court has begun to try the information; and

(b) within 21 days of that date the declaration is served on the designated officer for the court,

without prejudice to the validity of the information, the summons and all subsequent proceedings shall be void.

(2) For the purposes of subsection (1) above a statutory declaration shall be deemed to be duly served on the designated officer if it is delivered to him, or left at his office, or is sent in a registered letter or by the recorded delivery service addressed to him at his office.

(3) If on the application of the accused it appears to a magistrates' court (which for this purpose may be composed of a single justice) that it was not reasonable to expect the accused to serve such a statutory declaration as is mentioned in subsection (1) above within the period allowed by that subsection, the court may accept service of such a declaration by the accused after that period has expired; and a statutory declaration accepted under this subsection shall be deemed to have been served as required by that subsection.

(4) Where any proceedings have become void by virtue of subsection (1) above, the information shall not be tried again by any of the same justices.

TERMINATING PROCEEDINGS

The prosecution may withdraw proceedings if no plea has been taken, or discontinue post plea (subject to the proceedings still being at a preliminary stage) or offer no evidence.

Prosecution of Offences Act 1985, s 23

23.— Discontinuance of proceedings in magistrates' courts.

(1) Where the Director of Public Prosecutions has the conduct of proceedings for an offence, this section applies in relation to the preliminary stages of those proceedings.

(2) In this section, "preliminary stage" in relation to proceedings for an offence does not include—

(a) any stage of the proceedings after the court has begun to hear evidence for the prosecution at a summary trial of the offence; or

(b) any stage of the proceedings after the accused has been sent for trial for the offence.

(3) Where, at any time during the preliminary stages of the proceedings, the Director gives notice under this section to the [designated officer for] 2 the court that he does not want the proceedings to continue, they shall be discontinued with effect from the giving of that notice but may be revived by notice given by the accused under subsection (7) below.

(4) Where, in the case of a person charged with an offence after being taken into custody without a warrant, the Director gives him notice, at a time when no magistrates' court has been informed of the charge, that the proceedings against him are discontinued, they shall be discontinued with effect from the giving of that notice.

(5) The Director shall, in any notice given under subsection (3) above, give reasons for not wanting the proceedings to continue.

(6) On giving any notice under subsection (3) above the Director shall inform the accused of the notice and of the accused's right to require the proceedings to be continued; but the Director shall not be obliged to give the accused any indication of his reasons for not wanting the proceedings to continue.

(7) Where the Director has given notice under subsection (3) above, the accused shall, if he wants the proceedings to continue, give notice to that effect to the designated officer for

the court within the prescribed period; and where notice is so given the proceedings shall continue as if no notice had been given by the Director under subsection (3) above.

(8) Where the designated officer for the court has been so notified by the accused he shall inform the Director.

(9) The discontinuance of any proceedings by virtue of this section shall not prevent the institution of fresh proceedings in respect of the same offence.

(10) In this section "prescribed" means prescribed by Criminal Procedure Rules.

TERRITORIAL JURISDICTION

Unless statute or common law provides otherwise the presumption is that offences committed outside of the jurisdiction are not triable in England and Wales (*Air India v Wiggins* (1980) 71 Cr App R 213), notable exceptions include murder by or of British subjects. **Aircraft**: The Civil Aviation Act 1982, s 92 provides for jurisdiction in relation to offences (which would be an offence if committed on land) occurring on any aircraft in British airspace which is destined to land here on its next stop, and offences that occur on board a British-controlled aircraft. There are a number of statutes creating offences specific to air travel. Consent of the Director of Public Prosecutions is needed for offences committed on aircraft which are not in UK airspace (s 92(2)). **Local government**: Generally speaking local authorities can only prosecute offences committed within the specific local government area, although consent to deal with prosecutions arising from acts in neighbouring areas can be sought . If in doubt as to the authority to prosecute, consideration should be given to sections 101 and 202 of the Local Government Act 1972 and the cases of *Brighton and Hove County Council v Woolworths* [2002] EWHC 2656 (Admin) and *R (Donnachie) v Cardiff Magistrates' Court* [2009] EWHC 489 (Admin). **Ships**: There are wide provisions covering offences by British Citizens and lesser liability for foreign national committing offences on any British ship on the high seas (Merchant Shipping Act 1995, s 281; see ss 286-290 for evidential provisions and Magistrates' Courts Act 1980, s 3A for scope).

TIME LIMITS FOR LAYING OF INFORMATION OR CHARGE

Time limitation runs only in relation to summary only offences and is generally a period of 6 months from date of offence. In computing that period the following rules apply: Month means calendar month (Interpretation Act 1978, Sch 1) and the date runs to the end of the same date in the next month (or the day earlier is there is no such date in that month) (*Dodds v Walker* [1981] 2 All ER 609). The date of the offence itself is excluded (*Verderers of the New Forest v Young* [2004] EWHC 2954 (Admin)). In relation to continuous offences the time runs from the last act (*Director of Public Prosecutions v Baker* [2004] EWHC 2782 (Admin)). Any doubt as to whether the proceedings are commenced in time is to be resolved in the defendant's favour (*Lloyd v Young* [1963] Crim LR 703) but prosecutors should not concede the point lightly as a case cannot be re-opened if the decision was made in error (*Verderers of the New Forest*) .

A number of offences that can only be tried summarily are, in certain circumstances, exempt from the six-month time bar. In relation to some offences time only runs from when an offence is 'discovered' by the prosecutor, which means when there was a reasonable belief that an offence had been committed (*Tesco Stores Limited v London Borough of Harrow* (2003) 167 JP 657, DC).

Amendments: An information can be amended outside of the 6 months' time-limit to charge a new summary only offence if the new offence is based on the same 'misdoing' (ie whether both offences arose from the same or substantially the same facts), and the amendment is in the interests of justice (*R v Scunthorpe Justices, ex p McPhee and Gallagher* (1998) 162 JP 635). It may not be in the interests of justice to permit an offence with a substantially greater penalty to be charged (eg *Shaw v Director of Public Prosecutions* [2007] EWHC 207 (Admin) where the potential penalty rose from a purely financial one to the risk of imprisonment). The amendment of a charge to substitute failing to provide a specimen of breath, with one of failing to provide a specimen of urine was held to be proper in *Williams v Director of Public Prosecutions* [2009] ECHC 2354 (Admin), although the court did allow the appeal as the alteration had not been made in a timely fashion (applying *Hammerton*). The imposition of a higher fine (if convicted of the new charge) would not in itself be enough to justify the refusal of an otherwise sound amendment (*R v Newcastle Upon Tyne Justices, ex p Poundstretcher*, unreported, 2 March 1998). An out of time amendment to allege a different defendant is not permissible (*Sainsbury's Supermarkets Ltd v HM Courts Service* [2006] EWHC 1749 (Admin)).

Magistrates' Courts Act 1980, s 127

(1) Except as otherwise expressly provided by any enactment and subject to subsection (2) below, a magistrates' court shall not try an information or hear a complaint unless the information was laid, or the complaint made, within 6 months from the time when the offence was committed, or the matter of complaint arose.

(2) Nothing in—

    (a) subsection (1) above; or

    (b) subject to subsection (4) below, any other enactment (however framed or worded) which, as regards any offence to which it applies, would but for this section impose a time-limit on the power of a magistrates' court to try an information summarily or impose a limitation on the time for taking summary proceedings,

shall apply in relation to any indictable offence.

TRANSFER OF CASES

Magistrates' Courts Act 1980, s 27A

(1) Where a person appears or is brought before a magistrates' court—

    (a) to be tried by the court for an offence, or

    (b) for the court to inquire into the offence as examining justices,

the court may transfer the matter to another magistrates' court.

(2) The court may transfer the matter before or after beginning the trial or inquiry.

(3) But if the court transfers the matter after it has begun to hear the evidence and the parties, the court to which the matter is transferred must begin hearing the evidence and the parties again.

(4) The power of the court under this section to transfer any matter must be exercised in accordance with any directions given under section 30(3) of the Courts Act 2003.

TRANSFER OF CERTAIN CASES INVOLVING CHILDREN

Note: Section 53 is repealed in the 12 areas where committal proceedings have been abolished.

Criminal Justice Act 1991, s 53

(1) If a person has been charged with an offence to which section 32(2) of the 1988 Act applies (sexual offences and offences involving violence or cruelty) and the Director of Public Prosecutions is of the opinion—

    (a) that the evidence of the offence would be sufficient for the person charged to be committed for trial;

    (b) that a child who is alleged—

        (i) to be a person against whom the offence was committed; or

        (ii) to have witnessed the commission of the offence,

will be called as a witness at the trial; and

      (c) that, for the purpose of avoiding any prejudice to the welfare of the child, the case should be taken over and proceeded with without delay by the Crown Court,

a notice ("notice of transfer") certifying that opinion may be given by or on behalf of the Director to the magistrates' court in whose jurisdiction the offence has been charged.

(2) A notice of transfer shall be given before the magistrates' court begins to inquire into the case as examining justices.

(3) On the giving of a notice of transfer the functions of the magistrates' court shall cease in relation to the case except as provided by paragraphs 2 and 3 of Schedule 6 to this Act or by [paragraph 2 of Schedule 3 to the Access to Justice Act 1999.

(4) The decision to give a notice of transfer shall not be subject to appeal or liable to be questioned in any court.

(5) Schedule 6 to this Act (which makes further provision in relation to notices of transfer) shall have effect.

(6) In this section "child" means a person who—

      (a) in the case of an offence falling within section 32(2)(a) or (b) of the 1988 Act, is under fourteen years of age or, if he was under that age when any such video recording as is mentioned in section 32A(2) of that Act was made in respect of him, is under fifteen years of age; or

      (b) in the case of an offence falling within section 32(2)(c) of that Act, is under seventeen years of age or, if he was under that age when any such video recording was made in respect of him, is under eighteen years of age.

(7) Any reference in subsection (6) above to an offence falling within paragraph (a), (b) or (c) of section 32(2) of that Act includes a reference to an offence which consists of attempting or conspiring to commit, or of aiding, abetting, counselling, procuring or inciting the commission of, an offence falling within that paragraph.

TRANSFER OF SERIOUS FRAUD CASES

Note: Sections 4 and 5 are repealed in the 12 areas where committal proceedings have been abolished. See: Allocation, Committal, Sending and Transfer for the relevant provisions in those areas.

Criminal Justice Act 1987, ss 4–5

4.— Notices of transfer and designated authorities.

(1) If—

      (a) a person has been charged with an indictable offence; and

      (b) in the opinion of an authority designated by subsection (2) below or of one of such an authority's officers acting on the authority's behalf the evidence of the offence charged—

          (i) would be sufficient for the person charged to be committed for trial; and

          (ii) reveals a case of fraud of such seriousness or complexity that it is appropriate that the management of the case should without delay be taken over by the Crown Court; and

      (c) before the magistrates' court in whose jurisdiction the offence has been charged begins to inquire into the case as examining justices the authority or one of the authority's officers acting on the authority's behalf gives the court a notice (in this Act referred to as a "notice of transfer") certifying that opinion.

the functions of the magistrates' court shall cease in relation to the case, except as provided by section 5(3), (7A) and (8) below and by paragraph 2 of Schedule 3 to the Access to Justice Act 1999.

(2) The authorities mentioned in subsection (1) above (in this Act referred to as "designated authorities") are—

(a) the Director of Public Prosecutions ;
(b) the Director of the Serious Fraud Office;
(c) the Commissioners of Inland Revenue;
(d) the Commissioners of Customs and Excise; and
(e) the Secretary of State.

(3) A designated authority's decision to give notice of transfer shall not be subject to appeal or liable to be questioned in any court.

(4) This section and sections 5 and 6 below shall not apply in any case in which section 51 of the Crime and Disorder Act 1998 (no committal proceedings for indictable-only offences) applies.

5.— Notices of transfer—procedure.

(1) A notice of transfer shall specify the proposed place of trial and in selecting that place the designated authority shall have regard to the considerations to which section 7 of the Magistrates' Courts Act 1980 requires a magistrates' court committing a person for trial to have regard when selecting the place at which he is to be tried.

(2) A notice of transfer shall specify the charge or charges to which it relates and include or be accompanied by such additional matter as regulations under subsection (9) below may require.

(3) If a magistrates' court has remanded a person to whom a notice of transfer relates in custody, it shall have power, subject to section 4 of the Bail Act 1976 and regulations under section 22 of the Prosecution of Offences Act 1985—

(a) to order that he shall be safely kept in custody until delivered in due course of law; or
(b) to release him on bail in accordance with the Bail Act 1976, that is to say, by directing him to appear before the Crown Court for trial;

and where his release on bail is conditional on his providing one or more surety or sureties and, in accordance with section 8(3) of the Bail Act 1976, the court fixes the amount in which the surety is to be bound with a view to his entering into his recognizance subsequently in accordance with subsections (4) and (5) or (6) of that section, the court shall in the meantime make an order such as is mentioned in paragraph (a) of this subsection.

(4) If the conditions specified in subsection (5) below are satisfied, a court may exercise the powers conferred by subsection (3) above in relation to a person charged without his being brought before it in any case in which by virtue of section 128(3A) of the Magistrates' Courts Act 1980 it would have power further to remand him on an adjournment such as is mentioned in that subsection.

(5) The conditions mentioned in subsection (4) above are—

(a) that the person in question has given his written consent to the powers conferred by subsection (3) above being exercised without his being brought before the court; and
(b) that the court is satisfied that, when he gave his consent, he knew that the notice of transfer had been issued.

(6) Where notice of transfer is given after a person to whom it relates has been remanded on bail to appear before a magistrates' court on an appointed day, the requirement that he shall so appear shall cease on the giving of the notice, unless the notice states that it is to continue.

(7) Where the requirement that a person to whom the notice of transfer relates shall appear before a magistrates' court ceases by virtue of subsection (6) above, it shall be his duty to appear before the Crown Court at the place specified by the notice of transfer as the

proposed place of trial or at any place substituted for it by a direction under section 76 of the Senior Courts Act 1981.

(7A) If the notice states that the requirement is to continue, when a person to whom the notice relates appears before the magistrates' court, the court shall have—

(a) the powers and duty conferred on a magistrates' court by subsection (3) above, but subject as there provided; and

(b) power to enlarge, in the surety's absence, a recognizance conditioned in accordance with section 128(4)(a) of the Magistrates' Courts Act 1980 so that the surety is bound to secure that the person charged appears also before the Crown Court.

(8) For the purposes of the Criminal Procedure (Attendance of Witnesses) Act 1965—

(a) any magistrates' court for the petty sessions area for which the court from which a case was transferred sits shall be treated as examining magistrates; and

(b) a person indicated in the notice of transfer as a proposed witness; shall be treated as a person who has been examined by the court.

(9) The Attorney General—

(a) shall by regulations make provision requiring the giving of a copy of a notice of transfer, together with copies of the documents containing the evidence (including oral evidence) on which any charge to which it relates is based—

(i) to any person to whom the notice of transfer relates; and

(ii) to the Crown Court sitting at the place specified by the notice of transfer as the proposed place of trial; and

(b) may by regulations make such further provision in relation to notices of transfer, including provision as to the duties of a designated authority in relation to such notices, as appears to him to be appropriate.

(9A) Regulations under subsection (9)(a) above may provide that there shall be no requirement for copies of documents to accompany the copy of the notice of transfer if they are referred to, in documents sent with the notice of transfer, as having already been supplied.

(10) The power to make regulations conferred by subsection (9) above shall be exercisable by statutory instrument subject to annulment in pursuance of a resolution of either House of Parliament.

(11) Any such regulations may make different provision with respect to different cases or classes of case.

VIDEO LINK

Crime and Disorder Act 1998, ss 57A–F

57A Introductory

(1) This Part–

(a) applies to preliminary hearings and sentencing hearings in the course of proceedings for an offence and enforcement hearings relating to confiscation orders; and

(b) enables the court in the circumstances provided for in sections 57B, 57C, 57E and 57F to direct the use of a live link for securing the accused's attendance at a hearing to which this Part applies.

(2) The accused is to be treated as present in court when, by virtue of a live link direction under this Part, he attends a hearing through a live link.

(3) In this Part–

"confiscation order" means an order made under—

(a) section 71 of the Criminal Justice Act 1988;

(b) section 2 of the Drug Trafficking Act 1994; or

(c) section 6 of the Proceeds of Crime Act 2002;

"custody"–

(a) includes local authority accommodation to which a person is remanded or committed by virtue of section 23 of the Children and Young Persons Act 1969; but

(b) does not include police detention;

"enforcement hearing" means a hearing under section 82 of the Magistrates' Courts Act 1980 to consider the issuing of a warrant of committal or to inquire into a person's means;

"live link" means an arrangement by which a person (when not in the place where the hearing is being held) is able to see and hear, and to be seen and heard by, the court during a hearing (and for this purpose any impairment of eyesight or hearing is to be disregarded);

"police detention" has the meaning given by section 118(2) of the Police and Criminal Evidence Act 1984;

"preliminary hearing" means a hearing in the proceedings held before the start of the trial (within the meaning of subsection (11A) or (11B) of section 22 of the 1985 Act) including, in the case of proceedings in the Crown Court, a preparatory hearing held under–

(a) section 7 of the Criminal Justice Act 1987 (cases of serious or complex fraud); or

(b) section 29 of the Criminal Procedure and Investigations Act 1996 (other serious, complex or lengthy cases);

"sentencing hearing" means any hearing following conviction which is held for the purpose of–

(a) proceedings relating to the giving or rescinding of a direction under section 57E;

(b) proceedings (in a magistrates' court) relating to committal to the Crown Court for sentencing; or

(c) sentencing the offender or determining how the court should deal with him in respect of the offence.

57B Use of live link at preliminary hearings where accused is in custody

(1) This section applies in relation to a preliminary hearing in a magistrates' court or the Crown Court.

(2) Where it appears to the court before which the preliminary hearing is to take place that the accused is likely to be held in custody during the hearing, the court may give a live link direction under this section in relation to the attendance of the accused at the hearing.

(3) A live link direction under this section is a direction requiring the accused, if he is being held in custody during the hearing, to attend it through a live link from the place at which he is being held.

(4) If a hearing takes place in relation to the giving or rescinding of such a direction, the court may require or permit a person attending the hearing to do so through a live link.

(5) The court shall not give or rescind such a direction (whether at a hearing or otherwise) unless the parties to the proceedings have been given the opportunity to make representations.

(6) If in a case where it has power to do so a magistrates' court decides not to give a live link direction under this section, it must–

(a) state in open court its reasons for not doing so; and

(b) cause those reasons to be entered in the register of its proceedings.

(7) The following functions of a magistrates' court under this section may be discharged by a single justice—

(a) giving a live link direction under this section;

(b) rescinding a live link direction before a preliminary hearing begins; and

(c) requiring or permitting a person to attend by live link a hearing about a matter within paragraph (a) or (b).

57C Use of live link at preliminary hearings where accused is at police station

(1)   This section applies in relation to a preliminary hearing in a magistrates' court.

(2)   Where subsection (3) or (4) applies to the accused, the court may give a live link direction in relation to his attendance at the preliminary hearing.

(3)   This subsection applies to the accused if–

(a) he is in police detention at a police station in connection with the offence; and

(b) it appears to the court that he is likely to remain at that station in police detention until the beginning of the preliminary hearing.

(4)   This subsection applies to the accused if he is at a police station in answer to live link bail in connection with the offence.

(5)   A live link direction under this section is a direction requiring the accused to attend the preliminary hearing through a live link from the police station.

(6)   But a direction given in relation to an accused to whom subsection (3) applies has no effect if he does not remain in police detention at the police station until the beginning of the preliminary hearing.

(6A)   A live link direction under this section may not be given unless the court is satisfied that it is not contrary to the interests of justice to give the direction.

[...]

(8)   A magistrates' court may rescind a live link direction under this section at any time during a hearing to which it relates.

(9)   A magistrates' court may require or permit–

[...]

(b) any party to the proceedings who wishes to make representations in relation to the giving or rescission of a live link direction under this section to do so through a live link.

(10)   Where a live link direction under this section is given in relation to an accused person who is answering to live link bail he is to be treated as having surrendered to the custody of the court (as from the time when the direction is given).

(11)   In this section, "live link bail" means bail granted under Part 4 of the Police and Criminal Evidence Act 1984 subject to the duty mentioned in section 47(3)(b) of that Act.

57D Continued use of live link for sentencing hearing following a preliminary hearing

(1)   Subsection (2) applies where–

(a) a live link direction under section 57B or 57C is in force;

(b) the accused is attending a preliminary hearing through a live link by virtue of the direction;

(c) the court convicts him of the offence in the course of that hearing (whether by virtue of a guilty plea or an indication of an intention to plead guilty); and

(d) the court proposes to continue the hearing as a sentencing hearing in relation to the offence.

(2)   The accused may continue to attend through the live link by virtue of the direction if–

(a) the hearing is continued as a sentencing hearing in relation to the offence; and

[...]

(c) the court is satisfied that [the accused continuing to attend through the live link is not contrary to the interests of justice.

(3)   But the accused may not give oral evidence through the live link during a continued hearing under subsection (2) unless–

[...]

    (b) the court is satisfied that it is not contrary to the interests of justice for him to give it in that way.

57E Use of live link in sentencing hearings

(1) This section applies where the accused is convicted of the offence.

(2) If it appears to the court by or before which the accused is convicted that it is likely that he will be held in custody during any sentencing hearing for the offence, the court may give a live link direction under this section in relation to that hearing.

(3) A live link direction under this section is a direction requiring the accused, if he is being held in custody during the hearing, to attend it through a live link from the place at which he is being held.

(4) Such a direction–

    (a) may be given by the court of its own motion or on an application by a party; and

    (b) may be given in relation to all subsequent sentencing hearings before the court or to such hearing or hearings as may be specified or described in the direction.

(5) The court may not give such a direction unless–

[...]

    (b) the court is satisfied that it is not contrary to the interests of justice to give the direction.

(6) The court may rescind such a direction at any time before or during a hearing to which it relates if it appears to the court to be in the interests of justice to do so (but this does not affect the court's power to give a further live link direction in relation to the offender).

The court may exercise this power of its own motion or on an application by a party.

(7) The offender may not give oral evidence while attending a hearing through a live link by virtue of this section unless–

[...]

    (b) the court is satisfied that it is not contrary to the interests of justice for him to give it in that way.

(8) The court must–

    (a) state in open court its reasons for refusing an application for, or for the rescission of, a live link direction under this section; and

    (b) if it is a magistrates' court, cause those reasons to be entered in the register of its proceedings.

57F Use of live link in certain enforcement hearings

(1) This section applies where—

    (a) a confiscation order is made against a person; and

    (b) the amount required to be paid under the order is not paid when it is required to be paid.

(2) If it appears to the court before which an enforcement hearing relating to the confiscation order is to take place that it is likely that the person will be held in custody at the time of the hearing, the court may give a live link direction under this section in relation to that hearing.

(3) A live link direction under this section is a direction requiring the person, if the person is being held in custody at the time of the hearing, to attend it through a live link from the place at which the person is being held.

(4) Such a direction—

    (a) may be given by the court of its own motion or on an application by a party; and

    (b) may be given in relation to all subsequent enforcement hearings before the court or to such hearing or hearings as may be specified or described in the direction.

(5) The court may rescind a live link direction under this section at any time before or during a hearing to which it relates.

(6) The court may not give or rescind a live link direction under this section (whether at a hearing or otherwise) unless the parties to the proceedings have been given the opportunity to make representations.

(7) If a hearing takes place in relation to the giving or rescinding of such a direction, the court may require or permit any party to the proceedings who wishes to make representations in relation to the giving or rescission of a live link direction under this section to do so through a live link.

(8) The person may not give oral evidence while attending a hearing through a live link by virtue of this section unless the court is satisfied that it is not contrary to the interests of justice for the person to give it that way.

(9) If in a case where it has power to do so a court decides not to give a live link direction under this section, it must—

    (a) state in open court its reasons for not doing so; and

    (b) cause those reasons to be entered in the register of its proceedings.

(10) The following functions of a magistrates' court under this section may be discharged by a single justice—

    (a) giving a live link direction under this section;

    (b) rescinding a live link direction before a preliminary hearing begins; and

    (c) requiring or permitting a person to attend by live link a hearing about a matter within paragraph (a) or (b).

Extradition Act 2003, ss 206A–C

206A Use of live links at certain hearings

(1) This section applies in relation to—

    (a) a hearing before the appropriate judge in proceedings under Part 1, other than—

        (i) an extradition hearing within the meaning of that Part;

        (ii) a hearing under section 54 or 56, and

    (b) a hearing before the appropriate judge in proceedings under Part 2, other than an extradition hearing within the meaning of that Part.

(2) If satisfied that the person affected by an extradition claim is likely to be in custody during the hearing, the appropriate judge may give a live link direction at any time before the hearing.

(3) A live link direction is a direction that, if the person is being held in custody at the time of the hearing, any attendance at the hearing is to be through a live link from the place at which the person is held.

(4) Such a direction—

    (a) may be given on the appropriate judge's own motion or on the application of a party to the proceedings, and

    (b) may be given in relation to all subsequent hearings to which this section applies, or to such hearing or hearings to which this section applies as may be specified or described in the direction.

(5) The appropriate judge may give such a direction only if satisfied that it is not contrary to the interests of justice to give the direction.

(6) A person affected by an extradition claim is to be treated as present in court when, by virtue of a live link direction, the person attends a hearing through a live link.

206B Live links: supplementary

(1) The appropriate judge may rescind a live link direction at any time before or during a hearing to which it relates.

(2) The appropriate judge must not give a live link direction or rescind such a direction unless the parties to the proceedings have been given the opportunity to make representations.

(3) If a hearing takes place in relation to the giving or rescinding of a live link direction, the appropriate judge may require or permit any party to the proceedings who wishes to make representations to do so through a live link.

(4) If in a case where an appropriate judge has power to give a live link direction but decides not to do so, the appropriate judge must—

    (a) state in open court the reasons for not doing so, and

    (b) cause those reasons to be entered in the register of proceedings.

(5) Subsection (7) applies if—

    (a) an application for a live link direction is made under section 206A(4) in relation to a qualifying hearing but the application is refused, or

    (b) a live link direction is given in relation to a qualifying hearing but the direction is rescinded before the hearing takes place.

(6) A hearing is a qualifying hearing—

    (a) in relation to proceedings under Part 1, if it is a hearing by virtue of which section 4(3) would be complied with;

    (b) in relation to proceedings under Part 2, if it is a hearing by virtue of which section 72(3) or 74(3) would be complied with.

(7) The requirement in section 4(3), 72(3) or 74(3) (as the case requires) to bring the person as soon as practicable before the appropriate judge is to be read as a requirement to bring the person before that judge as soon as practicable after the application is refused or the direction is rescinded.

206C Live links: interpretation

(1) This section applies for the purposes of section 206A and subsections (2) and (3) also apply for the purposes of section 206B.

(2) In relation to proceedings under Part 1, section 67 applies for determining the appropriate judge.

(3) In relation to proceedings under Part 2, section 139 applies for determining the appropriate judge.

(4) A person is affected by an extradition claim if—

    (a) a Part 1 warrant is issued in respect of the person;

    (b) the person is arrested under section 5;

    (c) a request for the person's extradition is made; or

    (d) a warrant under section 73 is issued in respect of the person.

(5) References to being in custody include—

    (a) in England and Wales, references to being in police detention within the meaning of the Police and Criminal Evidence Act 1984;

    (b) in Northern Ireland, references to being in police detention within the meaning of the Police and Criminal Evidence (Northern Ireland) Order 1989;

    (c) in Scotland, references to detention under section 14 of the Criminal Procedure (Scotland) Act 1995.

(6) "Live link" means an arrangement by which a person, while absent from the place where the hearing is being held, is able—

(a) to see and hear the appropriate judge, and other persons,

(b) to be seen and heard by the judge, other persons,

and for this purpose any impairment of eyesight or hearing is to be disregarded.

WARRANTS

Warrant, Execution Out of Jurisdiction

A warrant may be issued with or without being backed for bail. A warrant remains in force until executed or ceases to have effect due to statutory provision and can be executed in England, Wales, Scotland, Northern Ireland, the Isle of Man and the Channel Islands (Magistrates' Courts Act 1980, ss 125, 126).

Magistrates' Courts Act 1980, s 13

(1)   Subject to the provisions of this section, where the court, instead of proceeding in the absence of the accused, adjourns or further adjourns the trial, the court may issue a warrant for his arrest.

(2)   Where a summons has been issued, the court shall not issue a warrant under this section unless the condition in subsection (2A) below or that in subsection (2B) below is fulfilled.

(2A)   The condition in this subsection is that it is proved to the satisfaction of the court, on oath or in such other manner as may be prescribed, that the summons was served on the accused within what appears to the court to be a reasonable time before the trial or adjourned trial.

(2B)   The condition in this subsection is that—

(a) the adjournment now being made is a second or subsequent adjournment of the trial.

(b) the accused was present on the last (or only) occasion when the trial was adjourned, and

(c) on that occasion the court determined the time for the hearing at which the adjournment is now being made.

(3)   A warrant for the arrest of any person who has attained the age of 18 shall not be issued under this section unless—

(a) [...] the offence to which the warrant relates is punishable with imprisonment, or

(b) the court, having convicted the accused, proposes to impose a disqualification on him.

(3A)   A warrant for the arrest of any person who has not attained the age of 18 shall not be issued under this section unless—

(a) the offence to which the warrant relates is punishable, in the case of a person who has attained the age of 18, with imprisonment, or

(b) the court, having convicted the accused, proposes to impose a disqualification on him.

(4)   This section shall not apply to an adjournment on the occasion of the accused's conviction in his absence under subsection (5) of section 12 above or to an adjournment required by subsection (9) of that section..

WRITTEN CHARGE AND REQUISITION

Availability: The Criminal Justice Act 2003 (Commencement No. 27) Order 2012 brings in the procedure to charge and requisition in relation to all prosecutions undertaken by the CPS or Serious Fraud Office.

Criminal Justice Act 2003, ss 29, 30

29 New method of instituting proceedings

(1) A public prosecutor may institute criminal proceedings against a person by issuing a document (a "written charge") which charges the person with an offence.

(2) Where a public prosecutor issues a written charge, it must at the same time issue a document (a "requisition") which requires the person to appear before a magistrates' court to answer the written charge.

(3) The written charge and requisition must be served on the person concerned, and a copy of both must be served on the court named in the requisition.

(4) In consequence of subsections (1) to (3), a public prosecutor is not to have the power to lay an information for the purpose of obtaining the issue of a summons under section 1 of the Magistrates' Courts Act 1980 (c. 43).

(5) In this section "public prosecutor" means—

(a) a police force or a person authorised by a police force to institute criminal proceedings,

(b) the Director of the Serious Fraud Office or a person authorised by him to institute criminal proceedings,

(c) the Director of Public Prosecutions or a person authorised by him to institute criminal proceedings,

(ca) the Director of Revenue and Customs Prosecutions or a person authorised by him to institute criminal proceedings,

(cb) the Director General of the Serious Organised Crime Agency or a person authorised by him to institute criminal proceedings;

(d) the Attorney General or a person authorised by him to institute criminal proceedings,

(e) a Secretary of State or a person authorised by a Secretary of State to institute criminal proceedings,

(f) the Commissioners of Inland Revenue or a person authorised by them to institute criminal proceedings,

(g) the Commissioners of Customs and Excise or a person authorised by them to institute criminal proceedings, or

(h) a person specified in an order made by the Secretary of State for the purposes of this section or a person authorised by such a person to institute criminal proceedings.

(6) In subsection (5) "police force" has the meaning given by section 3(3) of the Prosecution of Offences Act 1985 (c. 23).

30 Further provision about new method

(1) Criminal Procedure Rules may make—

(a) provision as to the form, content, recording, authentication and service of written charges or requisitions, and

(b) such other provision in relation to written charges or requisitions as appears to the Criminal Procedure Rule Committee to be necessary or expedient.

(2) Without limiting subsection (1), the provision which may be made by virtue of that subsection includes provision—

(a) which applies (with or without modifications), or which disapplies, the provision of any enactment relating to the service of documents,

(b) for or in connection with the issue of further requisitions.

[...]

(4) Nothing in section 29 affects—

(a) the power of a public prosecutor to lay an information for the purpose of obtaining the issue of a warrant under section 1 of the Magistrates' Courts Act 1980 (c. 43),

(b) the power of a person who is not a public prosecutor to lay an information for the purpose of obtaining the issue of a summons or warrant under section 1 of that Act, or

(c) any power to charge a person with an offence whilst he is in custody.

(5) Except where the context otherwise requires, in any enactment contained in an Act passed before this Act—

(a) any reference (however expressed) which is or includes a reference to an information within the meaning of section 1 of the Magistrates' Courts Act 1980 (c.43) (or to the laying of such an information) is to be read as including a reference to a written charge (or to the issue of a written charge),

(b) any reference (however expressed) which is or includes a reference to a summons under section 1 of the Magistrates' Courts Act 1980 (or to a justice of the peace issuing such a summons) is to be read as including a reference to a requisition (or to a public prosecutor issuing a requisition).

(6) Subsection (5) does not apply to section 1 of the Magistrates' Courts Act 1980.

(7) The reference in subsection (5) to an enactment contained in an Act passed before this Act includes a reference to an enactment contained in that Act as a result of an amendment to that Act made by this Act or by any other Act passed in the same Session as this Act.

(8) In this section "public prosecutor", "requisition" and "written charge" have the same meaning as in section 29.

PART D EVIDENCE

ADVERSE INFERENCES

Common Law: An inference can be made if a statement is made in the presence of the defendant and he ought reasonably to have issued a denial (*Christie* [1914] AC 545). In *Parkes* [1976] 1 WLR 1251 it was said that such conduct could only be admitted where the person making the statement and the defendant were on even terms: "the whole admissibility of statements of this kind rests upon the consideration that if a charge is made against a person in that person's presence it is reasonable to expect that he or she will immediately deny it, and that the absence of such a denial is some evidence of an admission on the part of the person charged, and of the truth of the charge. Undoubtedly, when persons are speaking on even terms, and a charge is made, and the person charged says nothing, and expresses no indignation, and does nothing to repel the charge, that is some evidence to show that he admits the charge to be true". **Failing to mention facts when questioned or charged:** Legal advice to remain silent will not of itself prevent an inference (*Condron* [1996] EWCA Crim 1129; *Beckles* [2004] EWCA Crim 2766), but lack of disclosure, or complexity of the disclosure might in some cases (*Roble* [1997] EWCA Crim 118). In *Howell* [2003] EWCA Crim 1 the court held:

> "The kind of circumstance which may most likely justify silence will be such matters as the suspect's condition (ill-health, in particular mental disability; confusion; intoxication; shock, and so forth–of course we are not laying down an authoritative list), or his inability genuinely to recollect events without reference to documents which are not to hand, or communication with other persons who may be able to assist his recollection. There must always be soundly based objective reasons for silence, sufficiently cogent and telling to weigh in the balance against the clear public interest in an account being given by the suspect to the police. Solicitors bearing the important responsibility of giving advice to suspects at police stations must always have that in mind".

In *Argent* [1996] EWCA Crim 1728 the court set out the following conditions to be met before an inference could be drawn:

> "He first is that there must be proceedings against a person for an offence; that condition must necessarily be satisfied before section 34(2)(d) can bite and plainly it was satisfied here. The second condition is that the alleged failure must occur before a defendant is charged. That condition also was satisfied here. The third condition is that the alleged failure must occur during questioning under caution by a constable. The requirement that the questioning should be by a constable is not strictly a condition, as is evident from section 34(4), but here the alleged failure did occur during questioning by a constable, Detective Constable Armstrong, and the appellant had been properly cautioned. The fourth condition is that the constable's questioning must be directed to trying to discover whether or by whom the alleged offence had been committed. The fifth condition is that the alleged failure by the defendant must be to mention any fact relied on in his defence in those proceedings. That raises two questions of fact: first, is there some fact which the defendant has relied on in his defence; and secondly, did the defendant fail to mention it to the constable when he was being questioned in accordance with the section? Being questions of fact these questions are for the jury as the tribunal of fact to resolve. The sixth condition is that the appellant failed to mention a fact which in the circumstances existing at the time the accused could reasonably have been expected to mention when so questioned. The time referred to is the time of questioning, and account must be taken of all the relevant circumstances existing at that time. The courts should not construe the expression

"in the circumstances" restrictively: matters such as time of day, the defendant's age, experience, mental capacity, state of health, sobriety, tiredness, knowledge, personality and legal advice are all part of the relevant circumstances; and those are only examples of things which may be relevant. When reference is made to "the accused" attention is directed not to some hypothetical, reasonable accused of ordinary phlegm and fortitude but to the actual accused with such qualities, apprehensions, knowledge and advice as he is shown to have had at the time. It is for the jury to decide whether the fact (or facts) which the defendant has relied on in his defence in the criminal trial, but which he had not mentioned when questioned under caution before charge by the constable investigating the alleged offence for which the defendant is being tried, is (or are) a fact (or facts) which in the circumstances as they actually existed the actual defendant could reasonably have been expected to mention. Like so many other questions in criminal trials this is a question to be resolved by the jury in the exercise of their collective common-sense, experience and understanding of human nature. Sometimes they may conclude that it was reasonable for the defendant to have held his peace for a host of reasons, such as that he was tired, ill, frightened, drunk, drugged, unable to understand what was going on, suspicious of the police, afraid that his answer would not be fairly recorded, worried at committing himself without legal advice, acting on legal advice, or some other reason accepted by the jury. In other cases the jury may conclude, after hearing all that the defendant and his witnesses may have to say about the reasons for failing to mention the fact or facts in issue, that he could reasonably have been expected to do so. This is an issue on which the judge may, and usually should, give appropriate directions. But he should ordinarily leave the issue to the jury to decide. Only rarely would it be right for the judge to direct the jury that they should, or should not, draw the appropriate inference".

Good cause to remain silent: Not being able to remember the events in questions does not amount to a good reason not to give evidence (*Charisma* [2009] EWCA Crim 2345). In *R (Director of Public Prosecutions) v Kavanagh* [2005] EWHC 820 (Admin) the court held:

(1) There must be an evidential basis for any determination by the court that it is undesirable for the defendant to give evidence (see *Cowan* [1996] QB 373). A statement or a submission by an advocate does not constitute evidence at all, let alone the kind of evidence on which a court can properly conclude that it is undesirable for a defendant to give evidence.

(2) It is not sufficient that the defendant suffers from some physical or mental condition. The mental condition must be such that makes it undesirable for him to give evidence. The fact that he may have some difficulty in giving evidence, for example, is insufficient to justify a conclusion that it is undesirable for the defendant to give evidence. Many, if not most, difficulties that a defendant, or indeed any other witness, may have in giving evidence, are matters to be taken into account by the judge of fact, be it magistrates or a jury, in assessing the reliability of his evidence. It does not justify a comprehensive failure to give evidence. It may go as to the weight of evidence, not as to the decision whether or not it is undesirable for him to give evidence.

(3) The court will draw an inference against a defendant in circumstances where, to use the language of the standard direction, (a) the prosecution's case is so strong that it clearly calls for an answer by him, and (b), that the only sensible explanation for his silence is that he has no answer or none that would bear examination.

Criminal Justice and Public Order Act 1994, ss 34, 35, 36, 37

4.— Effect of accused's failure to mention facts when questioned or charged.

(1) Where, in any proceedings against a person for an offence, evidence is given that the accused—

(a) at any time before he was charged with the offence, on being questioned under caution by a constable trying to discover whether or by whom the offence had been committed, failed to mention any fact relied on in his defence in those proceedings; or

    (b)   on being charged with the offence or officially informed that he might be prosecuted for it, failed to mention any such fact,

being a fact which in the circumstances existing at the time the accused could reasonably have been expected to mention when so questioned, charged or informed, as the case may be, subsection (2) below applies.

    (2)   Where this subsection applies—

        (a)   a magistrates' court inquiring into the offence as examining justices;

        (b)   a judge, in deciding whether to grant an application made by the accused under paragraph 2 of Schedule 3 to the Crime and Disorder Act 1998;

        (c)   the court, in determining whether there is a case to answer; and

        (d)   the court or jury, in determining whether the accused is guilty of the offence charged,

may draw such inferences from the failure as appear proper.

    (2A)   Where the accused was at an authorised place of detention at the time of the failure, subsections (1) and (2) above do not apply if he had not been allowed an opportunity to consult a solicitor prior to being questioned, charged or informed as mentioned in subsection (1) above.

    (3)   Subject to any directions by the court, evidence tending to establish the failure may be given before or after evidence tending to establish the fact which the accused is alleged to have failed to mention.

    (4)   This section applies in relation to questioning by persons (other than constables) charged with the duty of investigating offences or charging offenders as it applies in relation to questioning by constables; and in subsection (1) above "officially informed" means informed by a constable or any such person.

    (5)   This section does not—

        (a)   prejudice the admissibility in evidence of the silence or other reaction of the accused in the face of anything said in his presence relating to the conduct in respect of which he is charged, in so far as evidence thereof would be admissible apart from this section; or

        (b)   preclude the drawing of any inference from any such silence or other reaction of the accused which could properly be drawn apart from this section.

    (6)   This section does not apply in relation to a failure to mention a fact if the failure occurred before the commencement of this section.

35.— Effect of accused's silence at trial.

    (1)   At the trial of any person for an offence, subsections (2) and (3) below apply unless—

        (a)   the accused's guilt is not in issue; or

        (b)   it appears to the court that the physical or mental condition of the accused makes it undesirable for him to give evidence;

but subsection (2) below does not apply if, at the conclusion of the evidence for the prosecution, his legal representative informs the court that the accused will give evidence or, where he is unrepresented, the court ascertains from him that he will give evidence.

    (2)   Where this subsection applies, the court shall, at the conclusion of the evidence for the prosecution, satisfy itself (in the case of proceedings on indictment with a jury, in the presence of the jury) that the accused is aware that the stage has been reached at which evidence can be given for the defence and that he can, if he wishes, give evidence and that, if he chooses not to give evidence, or having been sworn, without good cause refuses to answer any question, it will be permissible for the court or jury to draw such inferences

as appear proper from his failure to give evidence or his refusal, without good cause, to answer any question.

(3) Where this subsection applies, the court or jury, in determining whether the accused is guilty of the offence charged, may draw such inferences as appear proper from the failure of the accused to give evidence or his refusal, without good cause, to answer any question.

(4) This section does not render the accused compellable to give evidence on his own behalf, and he shall accordingly not be guilty of contempt of court by reason of a failure to do so.

(5) For the purposes of this section a person who, having been sworn, refuses to answer any question shall be taken to do so without good cause unless—

(a) he is entitled to refuse to answer the question by virtue of any enactment, whenever passed or made, or on the ground of privilege; or

(b) the court in the exercise of its general discretion excuses him from answering it.

(7) This section applies—

(a) in relation to proceedings on indictment for an offence, only if the person charged with the offence is arraigned on or after the commencement of this section;

(b) in relation to proceedings in a magistrates' court, only if the time when the court begins to receive evidence in the proceedings falls after the commencement of this section.

36.— Effect of accused's failure or refusal to account for objects, substances or marks.

(1) Where—

(a) a person is arrested by a constable, and there is—
   (i) on his person; or
   (ii) in or on his clothing or footwear; or
   (iii) otherwise in his possession; or
   (iv) in any place in which he is at the time of his arrest,

any object, substance or mark, or there is any mark on any such object; and

(b) that or another constable investigating the case reasonably believes that the presence of the object, substance or mark may be attributable to the participation of the person arrested in the commission of an offence specified by the constable; and

(c) the constable informs the person arrested that he so believes, and requests him to account for the presence of the object, substance or mark; and

(d) the person fails or refuses to do so,

then if, in any proceedings against the person for the offence so specified, evidence of those matters is given, subsection (2) below applies.

(2) Where this subsection applies—

(b) a judge, in deciding whether to grant an application made by the accused under paragraph 2 of Schedule 3 to the Crime and Disorder Act 1998;

(c) the court, in determining whether there is a case to answer; and

(d) the court or jury, in determining whether the accused is guilty of the offence charged,

may draw such inferences from the failure or refusal as appear proper.

(3) Subsections (1) and (2) above apply to the condition of clothing or footwear as they apply to a substance or mark thereon.

(4) Subsections (1) and (2) above do not apply unless the accused was told in ordinary language by the constable when making the request mentioned in subsection (1)(c) above what the effect of this section would be if he failed or refused to comply with the request.

(4A) Where the accused was at an authorised place of detention at the time of the failure or refusal, subsections (1) and (2) above do not apply if he had not been allowed an opportunity to consult a solicitor prior to the request being made.

(5) This section applies in relation to officers of customs and excise as it applies in relation to constables.

(6) This section does not preclude the drawing of any inference from a failure or refusal of the accused to account for the presence of an object, substance or mark or from the condition of clothing or footwear which could properly be drawn apart from this section.

(7) This section does not apply in relation to a failure or refusal which occurred before the commencement of this section.

37.— Effect of accused's failure or refusal to account for presence at a particular place.

(1) Where—

    (a) a person arrested by a constable was found by him at a place at or about the time the offence for which he was arrested is alleged to have been committed; and

    (b) that or another constable investigating the offence reasonably believes that the presence of the person at that place and at that time may be attributable to his participation in the commission of the offence; and

    (c) the constable informs the person that he so believes, and requests him to account for that presence; and

    (d) the person fails or refuses to do so,

then if, in any proceedings against the person for the offence, evidence of those matters is given, subsection (2) below applies.

(2) Where this subsection applies—

    (b) a judge, in deciding whether to grant an application made by the accused under paragraph 2 of Schedule 3 to the Crime and Disorder Act 1998;

    (c) the court, in determining whether there is a case to answer; and

    (d) the court or jury, in determining whether the accused is guilty of the offence charged,

may draw such inferences from the failure or refusal as appear proper.

(3) Subsections (1) and (2) do not apply unless the accused was told in ordinary language by the constable when making the request mentioned in subsection (1)(c) above what the effect of this section would be if he failed or refused to comply with the request.

(3A) Where the accused was at an authorised place of detention at the time of the failure or refusal, subsections (1) and (2) do not apply if he had not been allowed an opportunity to consult a solicitor prior to the request being made.

(4) This section applies in relation to officers of customs and excise as it applies in relation to constables.

(5) This section does not preclude the drawing of any inference from a failure or refusal of the accused to account for his presence at a place which could properly be drawn apart from this section.

(6) This section does not apply in relation to a failure or refusal which occurred before the commencement of this section.

BAD CHARACTER

See: Character Evidence–Bad Character

BURDEN AND STANDARD OF PROOF

The standard of proof is the criminal standard when the burden is borne by the prosecution (*Woolmington v Director of Public Prosecutions* [1935] AC 462), this means not only in relation to proving an element of an offence, but also in rebutting a defence raised by the defendant. The evidential burden of raising defences falls on the defendant–the prosecution then having to disprove the defence, although in some cases the legal burden falls on the defence, albeit at the civil standard of proof (*Carr-Briant* [1943] KB 607). So far as the magistrates' court is concerned the 1980 Act prescribes when the legal burden of proving a defence falls on the defendant himself:

Magistrates' Courts Act 1980, s 101

Where the defendant to an information or complaint relies for his defence on any exception, exemption, proviso, excuse or qualification, whether or not it accompanies the description of the offence or matter of complaint in the enactment creating the offence or on which the complaint is founded, the burden of proving the exception, exemption, proviso, excuse or qualification shall be on him; and this notwithstanding that the information or complaint contains an allegation negativing the exception, exemption, proviso, excuse or qualification.

BYELAWS

Local Government Act 1972, s 238

The production of a printed copy of a byelaw purporting to be made by a local authority, the Greater London Authority, an Integrated Transport Authority for an integrated transport area in England or a combined authority upon which is endorsed a certificate purporting to be signed by the proper officer of the authority stating—

(a) that the byelaw was made by the authority;
(b) that the copy is a true copy of the byelaw;
(c) that on a specified date the byelaw was confirmed by the authority named in the certificate or, as the case may require, was sent to the Secretary of State and has not been disallowed;
(d) the date, if any, fixed by the confirming authority for the coming into operation of the byelaw;

shall be prima facie evidence of the facts stated in the certificate, and without proof of the handwriting or official position of any person purporting to sign the certificate.

CHALLENGING ADMISSIBILITY OF EVIDENCE

The procedure for challenging admissibility of evidence has been discussed in a large number of cases, many reaching contradictory conclusions. The situation appears to be that an argument as to the admissibility of a confession should be held on a voir dire (*Liverpool Juvenile Court, ex p R* [1988] QB 1), as such a challenge to such evidence at committal proceedings (*Oxford City Justices ex p Berry* [1988] QB 507). An application to exclude under section 78 PACE 1984 will not necessarily be determined on voir dire (*Vel v Owen* [1987] Crim LR 496); general guidance was given in *Halawa v Federation Against Copyright Theft* [1995] 1 Cr App R 21 as to how magistrates' should arrive at the correct procedure:

"A proper understanding of the factors relevant to securing that the trial is fair and just to both sides will, in my judgment, lead in some cases to a decision by magistrates that, if the accused wishes to proceed by way of a trial within a trial, he should be allowed to do so. I take that view because, if evidence has been, or may have been, obtained in such circumstances that, having regard to all the circumstances, the admission of the evidence would have such an adverse effect on the fairness of the proceedings that the court ought not to admit it, the accused should, unless there are good reasons to take a different course, have the opportunity to secure the exclusion of that unfair evidence before he is required to give evidence on the main issues. If he is unfairly denied that opportunity, his right to remain silent on the main issues is impaired.

In most cases of trial in a Magistrates' court, the better course will be for the whole of the prosecution case to be heard, including the disputed evidence, before any trial within a trial should be held. Unless the prosecutor is content that some part of the prosecution case for this purpose be excluded, fairness to the prosecutor requires that it all be before the court.

In order to decide what course to take the court would, in my view, be entitled to ask the defendant the extent of the issues which would be addressed by the evidence of the accused in the trial within a trial. If the issues are limited to the circumstances in which the evidence was obtained, as in this case the question of whether the accused was cautioned, there would in most cases be no apparent reason why the accused should not be heard as on a voire dire. If the defendant intends to give evidence in contradiction of some part of the prosecution's account of "all the circumstances", upon which he could properly be cross examined in the voire dire, it would be open to the court to conclude, in a proper case, that the proceedings on the voire dire would be or might be protracted and would introduce issues which would have to be re-examined in the remaining stages of the trial if a prima facie case is held to have been established; and that, in all the circumstances, the securing of a just trial to both sides did not require the holding of a trial within a trial. For that purpose the court would be entitled to take notice of the nature and extent of the cross examination of the prosecution witnesses for an understanding of the extent of any dispute as to "all the circumstances."

The Court must permit the giving of evidence on a voire dire if representation is made in a Magistrates' court that a confession was not voluntary under section 76. If that course is followed, it would mean, [...], that an alternative contention in the same case, based on section 78, i.e., that if the admission is proved to have been admissible because voluntary, it should be excluded as unfair because of breaches of the Code of Practice, would also be examined on the same voire dire at the same time."

CHARACTER EVIDENCE–GOOD CHARACTER

A defendant is entitled to adduce evidence of his good character, which will be relevant to propensity (in all cases) and credibility where he has given evidence in his own defence. Good character may be lost if the defendant has been cautioned for an offence, although the court retains a wide discretion in this respect (*Maillet* [2005] EWCA Crim 3159). There is a general discretion to treat a person of good character where the convictions are not relevant (eg very old) or where they are spent (*Nye* (1982) 75 Cr App R 247). The standard good character direction to be found in *Vye* [1993] 1 WLR 471 may be modified in an appropriate case. Where one defendant is of good character but a co-defendant is not, the defendant of good character is entitled to an appropriate direction (*Olu* [2010] EWCA Crim 2975). The following principles emerge from *Vye*:

(1) A direction as to the relevance of his good character to a defendant's credibility is to be given where he has testified or made pre-trial answers or statements [but should statements must be wholly culpatory or mixed, see *Aziz* [1996] 1 AC 41].

(2) A direction as to the relevance of his good character to the likelihood of his having committed the offence charged is to be given, whether or not he has testified, or made pre-trial answers or statements.

(3) Where defendant A of good character is jointly tried with defendant B of bad character, (1) and (2) still apply.

CHARACTER EVIDENCE–BAD CHARACTER

Bad character: 'Snapping' at a partner and aggression falling short of violence not bad character (*Osbourne*, The Times, April 24, 2007); Taking on overdose not reprehensible behavior (*Hall-Chung* (2007) 151 SJ 1020); Mere giving of a warning under the Protection from Harassment Act 1997 not admissible (*Dalby* [2012] EWCA Crim 701); Mere fact of fixed penalty notice (for disorder) not admissible (*Hamer* [2010] EWCA Crim 2053); Unsubstantiated crime report not admissible (*Braithwaite* [2010] EWCA Crim 1082); Police caution admissible, but see *Olu and* *others* [2010] EWCA Crim 2975; Evidence of telling lies and taking drugs found to be admissible (*AJC* [2006] EWCA Crim 284); Offence for which W awaiting trial might be admissible (*Dunn* [2005] EWCA Crim 1416).

Basic principles: *Hanson* [2005] EWCA Crim 824:

"Where propensity to commit the offence is relied upon there are thus essentially three questions to be considered:

1. Does the history of conviction(s) establish a propensity to commit offences of the kind charged?

2. Does that propensity make it more likely that the defendant committed the offence charged?

3. Is it unjust to rely on the conviction(s) of the same description or category; and, in any event, will the proceedings be unfair if they are admitted?

There is no minimum number of events necessary to demonstrate such a propensity. The fewer the number of convictions the weaker is likely to be the evidence of propensity. A single previous conviction for an offence of the same description or category will often not show propensity. But it may do so where, for example, it shows a tendency to unusual behaviour or where its circumstances demonstrate probative force in relation to the offence charged (compare *Director of Public Prosecutions v P* [1991] 2 AC 447 at 460E to 461A). Child sexual abuse or fire setting are comparatively clear examples of such unusual behaviour but we attempt no exhaustive list. Circumstances demonstrating probative force are not confined to those sharing striking similarity. So, a single conviction for shoplifting, will not, without more, be admissible to show propensity to steal. But if the modus operandi has significant features shared by the offence charged it may show propensity.

In a conviction case, the decisions required of the trial judge under section 101(3) and section 103(3), though not identical, are closely related. It so to be noted that wording of section 101(3) – "must not admit" – is stronger than the comparable provision in section 78 of the Police and Criminal Evidence Act 1984 – "may refuse to allow". When considering what is just under section 103(3), and the fairness of the proceedings under section 101(3), the judge may, among other factors, take into consideration the degree of similarity between the previous conviction and the offence charged, albeit they are both within the same description or prescribed category. For example, theft and assault occasioning actual bodily harm may each embrace a wide spectrum of conduct. This does not however mean that what used to be referred as striking similarity must be shown before convictions become admissible. The judge may also take into consideration the respective gravity of the past and present offences. He or she must always consider the strength of the prosecution case. If there is no or very little other evidence against a defendant, it is unlikely to be just to admit his previous convictions, whatever they are.

In principle, if there is a substantial gap between the dates of commission of and conviction for the earlier offences, we would regard the date of commission as generally being of more significance than the date of conviction when assessing admissibility. Old convictions, with no special feature shared with the offence charged, are likely seriously to affect the fairness of proceedings adversely, unless, despite their age, it can properly be said that they show a continuing propensity.

In principle, if there is a substantial gap between the dates of commission of and conviction for the earlier offences, we would regard the date of commission as generally being of more significance than the date of conviction when assessing admissibility. Old convictions, with no special feature shared with the offence charged, are likely seriously to affect the fairness of proceedings adversely, unless, despite their age, it can properly be said that they show a continuing propensity.

Propensity to untruthfulness, this, as it seems to us, is not the same as propensity to dishonesty. It is to be assumed, bearing in mind the frequency with which the words honest and dishonest appear in the criminal law, that Parliament deliberately chose the word "untruthful" to convey a different meaning, reflecting a defendant's account of his behaviour, or lies told when committing an offence. Previous convictions, whether for offences of dishonesty or otherwise, are therefore only likely to be capable of showing a propensity to be untruthful where, in the present case, truthfulness is an issue and, in the earlier case, either there was a plea of not guilty and the defendant gave an account, on arrest, in interview, or in evidence, which the jury must have disbelieved, or the way in which the offence was committed shows a propensity for untruthfulness, for example, by the making of false representations. The observations made above in paragraph 9 as to the number of convictions apply equally here.

In cases of the kind we are considering, it is the Crown which begins the process of applying to adduce evidence of bad character. It must specify the relevant gateways. The form of application (BC2), prescribed by Rule 23E, inserted into the Crown Court Rules 1982 by Statutory Instrument 2004 No 2991 (L18) requires that the Crown set out "a description of the bad character evidence and how it is to be adduced or elicited in the proceedings including the names of any relevant witnesses." Form BC 3, similarly prescribed for the use of the defence, calls for particulars of why it is contended that the evidence ought not to be admitted. It follows from what we have already said that, in a conviction case the Crown needs to decide, at the time of giving notice of the application, whether it proposes to rely simply upon the fact of conviction or also upon the circumstances of it. The former may be enough when the circumstances of the conviction are sufficiently apparent from its description, to justify a finding that it can establish propensity, either to commit an offence of the kind charged or to be untruthful and that the requirements of section 103(3) and 101(3) can, subject to any particular matter raised on behalf of the defendant, be satisfied. For example, a succession of convictions for dwelling-house burglary, where the same is now charged, may well call for no further evidence than proof of the fact of the convictions. But where, as will often be the case, the Crown needs and proposes to rely on the circumstances of the previous convictions, those circumstances and the manner in which they are to be proved must be set out in the application. There is a similar obligation of frankness upon the defendant, which will be reinforced by the general obligation contained in the new Criminal Procedure Rules to give active assistance to the court in its case management (see rule 3.3). Routine applications by defendants for disclosure of the circumstances of previous convictions are likely to be met by a requirement that the request be justified by identification of the reason why it is said that those circumstances may show the convictions to be inadmissible. We would expect the relevant circumstances of previous convictions generally to be capable of agreement, and that, subject to the trial judge's ruling as to admissibility, they will be put before the jury by way of admission. Even where the circumstances are genuinely in dispute, we would expect the minimum indisputable facts to be thus admitted. It will be very rare indeed for it to be necessary for the judge to hear evidence before ruling on admissibility under this Act.

Our final general observation is that, in any case in which evidence of bad character is admitted to show propensity, whether to commit offences or to be untruthful the judge in summing-up should warn the jury clearly against placing undue reliance on previous convictions. Evidence of bad character cannot be used simply to bolster a weak case, or to prejudice the minds of a jury against a defendant. In particular, the jury should be directed; that they should not conclude that the defendant is guilty or untruthful merely because he has these convictions. That, although the convictions may show a propensity, this does not mean that he has committed this offence or been untruthful in this case; that whether they in fact show a propensity is for them to decide; that they must take into account what the defendant has said about his previous convictions; and that, although they are entitled, if they find propensity as shown, to take this into account when determining guilt, propensity is only one relevant factor and they must assess its significance in the light of all the other evidence in the case".

Criminal Procedure Rules: Rule 35 applies. **Common law rules:** In so far as evidence is admissible under section 98(a) and (b) of the Act, common law rules continue to apply (*Apabhai* [2011]

EWHC Crim 917). **Context of the case as a whole** (s 101(1)): "This assessment is, by definition, highly fact-sensitive in each case. It is an assessment of whether the evidence in question substantially goes to show (prove) the point which the applicant wishes to prove on the issue in question. The issue will often, but not always, be either the propensity of the person against whom the application is made to behave in a particular way, or his credibility. The probative value of the evidence advanced falls to be assessed in the context of the case as a whole. That means that it may in some cases be appropriate to consider whether or not it adds significantly to other more probative evidence directed to the same issue" (*Braithwaite* [2010] EWCA Crim 1082; also see *Phillips* [2011] EWCA Crim 2935). **Evidence in relation to one count might be admissible as bad character in relation to another:** *Freeman* [2008] EWCA Crim 1863. **Credibility** s 100(1)(b)(i): This is a matter in issue in proceedings (*S (Andrew)*, unreported, April 28, 2006). **Attack on victim's character:** Sexual promiscuity (*Renda* [2005] EWCA Crim 2826);

Criminal Justice Act 2003, ss 98–110, 112

98 "Bad character"

References in this Chapter to evidence of a person's "bad character" are to evidence of, or of a disposition towards, misconduct on his part, other than evidence which—

    (a) has to do with the alleged facts of the offence with which the defendant is charged, or

    (b) is evidence of misconduct in connection with the investigation or prosecution of that offence.

99 Abolition of common law rules

    (1) The common law rules governing the admissibility of evidence of bad character in criminal proceedings are abolished.

    (2) Subsection (1) is subject to section 118(1) in so far as it preserves the rule under which in criminal proceedings a person's reputation is admissible for the purposes of proving his bad character.

100 Non-defendant's bad character

    (1) In criminal proceedings evidence of the bad character of a person other than the defendant is admissible if and only if—

        (a) it is important explanatory evidence,

        (b) it has substantial probative value in relation to a matter which—

            (i) is a matter in issue in the proceedings, and

            (ii) is of substantial importance in the context of the case as a whole,

or

        (c) all parties to the proceedings agree to the evidence being admissible.

    (2) For the purposes of subsection (1)(a) evidence is important explanatory evidence if—

        (a) without it, the court or jury would find it impossible or difficult properly to understand other evidence in the case, and

        (b) its value for understanding the case as a whole is substantial.

    (3) In assessing the probative value of evidence for the purposes of subsection (1)(b) the court must have regard to the following factors (and to any others it considers relevant)—

        (a) the nature and number of the events, or other things, to which the evidence relates;

        (b) when those events or things are alleged to have happened or existed;

        (c) where—

            (i) the evidence is evidence of a person's misconduct, and

            (ii) it is suggested that the evidence has probative value by reason of similarity between that misconduct and other alleged misconduct, the nature and extent of the similarities and the dissimilarities between each of the alleged instances of misconduct;

    (d) where—

        (i)   the evidence is evidence of a person's misconduct,

        (ii) it is suggested that that person is also responsible for the misconduct charged, and

        (iii) the identity of the person responsible for the misconduct charged is disputed,

the extent to which the evidence shows or tends to show that the same person was responsible each time.

  (4)   Except where subsection (1)(c) applies, evidence of the bad character of a person other than the defendant must not be given without leave of the court.

101 Defendant's bad character

  (1)   In criminal proceedings evidence of the defendant's bad character is admissible if, but only if—

    (a) all parties to the proceedings agree to the evidence being admissible,

    (b) the evidence is adduced by the defendant himself or is given in answer to a question asked by him in cross-examination and intended to elicit it,

    (c) it is important explanatory evidence,

    (d) it is relevant to an important matter in issue between the defendant and the prosecution,

    (e) it has substantial probative value in relation to an important matter in issue between the defendant and a co-defendant,

    (f) it is evidence to correct a false impression given by the defendant, or

    (g) the defendant has made an attack on another person's character.

  (2)   Sections 102 to 106 contain provision supplementing subsection (1).

  (3)   The court must not admit evidence under subsection (1)(d) or (g) if, on an application by the defendant to exclude it, it appears to the court that the admission of the evidence would have such an adverse effect on the fairness of the proceedings that the court ought not to admit it.

  (4)   On an application to exclude evidence under subsection (3) the court must have regard, in particular, to the length of time between the matters to which that evidence relates and the matters which form the subject of the offence charged.

102 "Important explanatory evidence"

For the purposes of section 101(1)(c) evidence is important explanatory evidence if—

    (a) without it, the court or jury would find it impossible or difficult properly to understand other evidence in the case, and

    (b) its value for understanding the case as a whole is substantial.

103 "Matter in issue between the defendant and the prosecution"

  (1)   For the purposes of section 101(1)(d) the matters in issue between the defendant and the prosecution include—

    (a) the question whether the defendant has a propensity to commit offences of the kind with which he is charged, except where his having such a propensity makes it no more likely that he is guilty of the offence;

    (b) the question whether the defendant has a propensity to be untruthful, except where it is not suggested that the defendant's case is untruthful in any respect.

  (2)   Where subsection (1)(a) applies, a defendant's propensity to commit offences of the kind with which he is charged may (without prejudice to any other way of doing so) be established by evidence that he has been convicted of—

(a) an offence of the same description as the one with which he is charged, or

(b) an offence of the same category as the one with which he is charged.

(3) Subsection (2) does not apply in the case of a particular defendant if the court is satisfied, by reason of the length of time since the conviction or for any other reason, that it would be unjust for it to apply in his case.

(4) For the purposes of subsection (2)—

(a) two offences are of the same description as each other if the statement of the offence in a written charge or indictment would, in each case, be in the same terms;

(b) two offences are of the same category as each other if they belong to the same category of offences prescribed for the purposes of this section by an order made by the Secretary of State.

(5) A category prescribed by an order under subsection (4)(b) must consist of offences of the same type.

(6) Only prosecution evidence is admissible under section 101(1)(d).

(7) Where—

(a) a defendant has been convicted of an offence under the law of any country outside England and Wales ("the previous offence"), and

(b) the previous offence would constitute an offence under the law of England and Wales ("the corresponding offence") if it were done in England and Wales at the time of the trial for the offence with which the defendant is now charged ("the current offence"),

subsection (8) applies for the purpose of determining if the previous offence and the current offence are of the same description or category.

(8) For the purposes of subsection (2)—

(a) the previous offence is of the same description as the current offence if the corresponding offence is of that same description, as set out in subsection (4)(a);

(b) the previous offence is of the same category as the current offence if the current offence and the corresponding offence belong to the same category of offences prescribed as mentioned in subsection (4)(b).

(9) For the purposes of subsection (10) "foreign service offence" means an offence which—

(a) was the subject of proceedings under the service law of a country outside the United Kingdom, and

(b) would constitute an offence under the law of England and Wales or a service offence ("the corresponding domestic offence") if it were done in England and Wales by a member of Her Majesty's forces at the time of the trial for the offence with which the defendant is now charged ("the current offence").

(10) Where a defendant has been found guilty of a foreign service offence ("the previous service offence"), for the purposes of subsection (2)—

(a) the previous service offence is an offence of the same description as the current offence if the corresponding domestic offence is of that same description, as set out in subsection (4)(a);

(b) the previous service offence is an offence of the same category as the current offence if the current offence and the corresponding domestic offence belong to the same category of offences prescribed as mentioned in subsection (4)(b).

(11) In this section—

"Her Majesty's forces" has the same meaning as in the Armed Forces Act 2006;

"service law", in relation to a country outside the United Kingdom, means the law governing all or any of the naval, military or air forces of that country.

104 "Matter in issue between the defendant and a co-defendant"

(1) Evidence which is relevant to the question whether the defendant has a propensity to be untruthful is admissible on that basis under section 101(1)(e) only if the nature or conduct of his defence is such as to undermine the codefendant's defence.

(2) Only evidence—

    (a) which is to be (or has been) adduced by the co-defendant, or

    (b) which a witness is to be invited to give (or has given) in cross-examination by the co-defendant,

is admissible under section 101(1)(e).

105 "Evidence to correct a false impression"

(1) For the purposes of section 101(1)(f)—

    (a) the defendant gives a false impression if he is responsible for the making of an express or implied assertion which is apt to give the court or jury a false or misleading impression about the defendant;

    (b) evidence to correct such an impression is evidence which has probative value in correcting it.

(2) A defendant is treated as being responsible for the making of an assertion if—

    (a) the assertion is made by the defendant in the proceedings (whether or not in evidence given by him),

    (b) the assertion was made by the defendant—

        (i) on being questioned under caution, before charge, about the offence with which he is charged, or

        (ii) on being charged with the offence or officially informed that he might be prosecuted for it,

and evidence of the assertion is given in the proceedings,

    (c) the assertion is made by a witness called by the defendant,

    (d) the assertion is made by any witness in cross-examination in response to a question asked by the defendant that is intended to elicit it, or is likely to do so, or

    (e) the assertion was made by any person out of court, and the defendant adduces evidence of it in the proceedings.

(3) A defendant who would otherwise be treated as responsible for the making of an assertion shall not be so treated if, or to the extent that, he withdraws it or disassociates himself from it.

(4) Where it appears to the court that a defendant, by means of his conduct (other than the giving of evidence) in the proceedings, is seeking to give the court or jury an impression about himself that is false or misleading, the court may if it appears just to do so treat the defendant as being responsible for the making of an assertion which is apt to give that impression.

(5) In subsection (4) "conduct" includes appearance or dress.

(6) Evidence is admissible under section 101(1)(f) only if it goes no further than is necessary to correct the false impression.

(7) Only prosecution evidence is admissible under section 101(1)(f).

106 "Attack on another person's character"

(1) For the purposes of section 101(1)(g) a defendant makes an attack on another person's character if—

    (a) he adduces evidence attacking the other person's character,

    (b) he (or any legal representative appointed under section 38(4) of the Youth Justice and Criminal Evidence Act 1999 (c. 23) to cross-examine a witness in his interests) asks questions in cross-examination that are intended to elicit such evidence, or are likely to do so, or

(c) evidence is given of an imputation about the other person made by the defendant—

    (i) on being questioned under caution, before charge, about the offence with which he is charged, or

    (ii) on being charged with the offence or officially informed that he might be prosecuted for it.

(2) In subsection (1) "evidence attacking the other person's character" means evidence to the effect that the other person—

    (a) has committed an offence (whether a different offence from the one with which the defendant is charged or the same one), or

    (b) has behaved, or is disposed to behave, in a reprehensible way;

and "imputation about the other person" means an assertion to that effect.

(3) Only prosecution evidence is admissible under section 101(1)(g).

107 Stopping the case where evidence contaminated

(1) If on a defendant's trial before a judge and jury for an offence—

    (a) evidence of his bad character has been admitted under any of paragraphs (c) to (g) of section 101(1), and

    (b) the court is satisfied at any time after the close of the case for the prosecution that—

        (i) the evidence is contaminated, and

        (ii) the contamination is such that, considering the importance of the evidence to the case against the defendant, his conviction of the offence would be unsafe,

the court must either direct the jury to acquit the defendant of the offence or, if it considers that there ought to be a retrial, discharge the jury.

(2) Where—

    (a) a jury is directed under subsection (1) to acquit a defendant of an offence, and

    (b) the circumstances are such that, apart from this subsection, the defendant could if acquitted of that offence be found guilty of another offence,

the defendant may not be found guilty of that other offence if the court is satisfied as mentioned in subsection (1)(b) in respect of it.

(3) If—

    (a) a jury is required to determine under section 4A(2) of the Criminal Procedure (Insanity) Act 1964 (c. 84) whether a person charged on an indictment with an offence did the act or made the omission charged,

    (b) evidence of the person's bad character has been admitted under any of paragraphs (c) to (g) of section 101(1), and

    (c) the court is satisfied at any time after the close of the case for the prosecution that—

        (i) the evidence is contaminated, and

        (ii) the contamination is such that, considering the importance of the evidence to the case against the person, a finding that he did the act or made the omission would be unsafe,

the court must either direct the jury to acquit the defendant of the offence or, if it considers that there ought to be a rehearing, discharge the jury.

(4) This section does not prejudice any other power a court may have to direct a jury to acquit a person of an offence or to discharge a jury.

(5) For the purposes of this section a person's evidence is contaminated where—

    (a) as a result of an agreement or understanding between the person and one or more others, or

(b) as a result of the person being aware of anything alleged by one or more others whose evidence may be, or has been, given in the proceedings,

the evidence is false or misleading in any respect, or is different from what it would otherwise have been.

108 Offences committed by defendant when a child

(1) Section 16(2) and (3) of the Children and Young Persons Act 1963 (c. 37) (offences committed by person under 14 disregarded for purposes of evidence relating to previous convictions) shall cease to have effect.

(2) In proceedings for an offence committed or alleged to have been committed by the defendant when aged 21 or over, evidence of his conviction for an offence when under the age of 14 is not admissible unless—

(a) both of the offences are triable only on indictment, and

(b) the court is satisfied that the interests of justice require the evidence to be admissible.

(2A) Subsection (2B) applies where—

(a) the defendant has been convicted of an offence under the law of any country outside England and Wales ("the previous offence"), and

(b) the previous offence would constitute an offence under the law of England and Wales ("the corresponding offence") if it were done in England and Wales at the time of the proceedings for the offence with which the defendant is now charged.

(2B) For the purposes of subsection (2), the previous offence is to be regarded as triable only on indictment if the corresponding offence is so triable.

(3) Subsection (2) applies in addition to section 101.

109 Assumption of truth in assessment of relevance or probative value

(1) Subject to subsection (2), a reference in this Chapter to the relevance or probative value of evidence is a reference to its relevance or probative value on the assumption that it is true.

(2) In assessing the relevance or probative value of an item of evidence for any purpose of this Chapter, a court need not assume that the evidence is true if it appears, on the basis of any material before the court (including any evidence it decides to hear on the matter), that no court or jury could reasonably find it to be true.

110 Court's duty to give reasons for rulings

(1) Where the court makes a relevant ruling—

(a) it must state in open court (but in the absence of the jury, if there is one) its reasons for the ruling;

(b) if it is a magistrates' court, it must cause the ruling and the reasons for it to be entered in the register of the court's proceedings.

(2) In this section "relevant ruling" means—

(a) a ruling on whether an item of evidence is evidence of a person's bad character;

(b) a ruling on whether an item of such evidence is admissible under section 100 or 101 (including a ruling on an application under section 101(3));

(c) a ruling under section 107.

112 Interpretation of Chapter 1

(1) In this Chapter—

"bad character "is to be read in accordance with section 98;

"criminal proceedings" means criminal proceedings in relation to which the strict rules of evidence apply;

"defendant", in relation to criminal proceedings, means a person charged with an offence in those proceedings; and "co-defendant", in relation to a defendant, means a person charged with an offence in the same proceedings;

"important matter" means a matter of substantial importance in the context of the case as a whole;

"misconduct" means the commission of an offence or other reprehensible behaviour;

"offence" includes a service offence;

"probative value", and "relevant" (in relation to an item of evidence), are to be read in accordance with section 109;

"prosecution evidence" means evidence which is to be (or has been) adduced by the prosecution, or which a witness is to be invited to give (or has given) in cross-examination by the prosecution;

"service offence" has the same meaning as in the Armed Forces Act 2006;

"written charge" has the same meaning as in section 29 and also includes an information.

(2) Where a defendant is charged with two or more offences in the same criminal proceedings, this Chapter (except section 101(3)) has effect as if each offence were charged in separate proceedings; and references to the offence with which the defendant is charged are to be read accordingly.

(3) Nothing in this Chapter affects the exclusion of evidence—

(a) under the rule in section 3 of the Criminal Procedure Act 1865 (c. 18) against a party impeaching the credit of his own witness by general evidence of bad character,

(b) under section 41 of the Youth Justice and Criminal Evidence Act 1999 (c. 23) (restriction on evidence or questions about complainant's sexual history), or

(c) on grounds other than the fact that it is evidence of a person's bad character.

CIRCUMSTANTIAL EVIDENCE

In *Taylor, Weaver and Donovan* (1930) 21 C r App R 20 it was said:

"I has been said that the evidence against the applicants is circumstantial: so it is, but circumstantial evidence is very often the best. It is evidence of surrounding circumstances which, by undesigned coincidence, is capable of proving a proposition with the accuracy of mathematics. It is no derogation of evidence to say that it is circumstantial".

Circumstantial evidence is not an inferior form of evidence but it must be scrutinised so as to ensure against fabrication, and to ensure that there are no other co-existing circumstances which would weaken or destroy the inference to be drawn from such evidence (*Teper* [1952] AC 480).

COMPETENT AND COMPELLABLE WITNESSES

Basic rule: At every stage in criminal proceedings all persons are (whatever their age) competent to give evidence (Youth Justice and Criminal Evidence Act 1999, s 53). **Defendant:** Competent but not compellable. If a defendant pleads guilty he becomes a compellable witness (*Boal* [1965] 1 QB 402). **Spouse:** The spouse or civil partner of a defendant is a competent witness, but is only compellable in accordance with section 80 PACE 1984. **Test:** In *B* [2010] EWCA Crim 4 the court held:

"These statutory provisions are not limited to the evidence of children. They apply to individuals of unsound mind. They apply to the infirm. The question in each case is whether the individual witness, or, as in this case, the individual child, is competent to give evidence in the particular trial. The question is entirely witness or child specific. There are no presumptions or preconceptions. The witness need not understand the special importance that the truth should be told in court, and the witness need not understand every single question or give a readily understood answer to every question. Many competent adult witnesses would fail such a competency test. Dealing with it broadly and fairly, provided the witness can understand the questions put to him and can also provide understandable answers, he or she is competent. If the witness cannot understand the questions or his answers to questions which he understands cannot themselves be understood he is not. The questions come, of course, from both sides. If the child is called as a witness by the prosecution he or she must have the ability to understand the questions put to him by the defence as well as the prosecution and to provide answers to them which are understandable. The provisions of the statute are clear and unequivocal, and do not require reinterpretation. (R v MacPherson [2006] 1 CAR 30: R v Powell [2006] 1 CAR 31: R v M [2008] EWCA Crim 2751 and R v Malicki [2009] EWCA Crim 365.)

…although the distinction is a fine one, whenever the competency question is addressed, what is required is not the exercise of a discretion but the making of a judgment, that is whether the witness fulfils the statutory criteria. In short, it is not open to the judge to create or impose some additional but non-statutory criteria based on the approach of earlier generations to the evidence of small children. In particular, although the chronological age of the child will inevitably help to inform the judicial decision about competency, in the end the decision is a decision about the individual child and his or her competence to give evidence in the particular trial.

We emphasise that in our collective experience the age of a witness is not determinative on his or her ability to give truthful and accurate evidence. Like adults some children will provide truthful and accurate testimony, and some will not. However children are not miniature adults, but children, and to be treated and judged for what they are, not what they will, in years ahead, grow to be. Therefore, although due allowance must be made in the trial process for the fact that they are children with, for example, a shorter attention span than most adults, none of the characteristics of childhood, and none of the special measures which apply to the evidence of children carry with them the implicit stigma that children should be deemed in advance to be somehow less reliable than adults. The purpose of the trial process is to identify the evidence which is reliable and that which is not, whether it comes from an adult or a child. If competent, as defined by the statutory criteria, in the context of credibility in the forensic process, the child witness starts off on the basis of equality with every other witness. In trial by jury, his or her credibility is to be assessed by the jury, taking into account every specific personal characteristic which may bear on the issue of credibility, along with the rest of the available evidence.

The judge determines the competency question, by distinguishing carefully between the issues of competence and credibility. At the stage when the competency question is determined the judge is not deciding whether a witness is or will be telling the truth and giving accurate evidence. Provided the witness is competent, the weight to be attached to the evidence is for the jury.

The trial process must, of course, and increasingly has, catered for the needs of child witnesses, as indeed it has increasingly catered for the use of adult witnesses whose evidence in former years would not have been heard, by, for example, the now well understood and valuable use of intermediaries. In short, the competency test is not failed because the forensic techniques of the advocate (in particular in relation to cross-examination) or the processes of the court (for example, in relation to the patient expenditure of time) have to be adapted to enable the child to give the best evidence of which he or she is capable. At the same time the right of the defendant to a fair trial must be undiminished. When the issue is whether the child is lying or mistaken in claiming that the defendant behaved indecently towards him or her, it should not be over-problematic for the advocate to formulate short, simple questions which put the essential elements of the defendant's case to the witness, and fully to ventilate before the jury the areas of evidence which bear on the child's credibility. Aspects of evidence which undermine or are believed to undermine the child's credibility must, of course, be revealed to the jury, but it is not necessarily appropriate for them to form the subject matter of detailed cross-examination of the child and the advocate may have to forego much of the kind of contemporary cross-examination which consists of no more than comment on matters which will be before the jury in any event from different sources. Notwithstanding some of the difficulties, when all is said and done, the witness whose cross-examination is in contemplation is a child, sometimes very young, and it should not take very lengthy cross-examination to demonstrate, when it is the case, that the child may indeed be fabricating, or fantasising, or imagining, or reciting a well rehearsed untruthful script, learned by rote, or simply just suggestible, or contaminated by or in collusion with others to make false allegations, or making assertions in language which is beyond his or her level of comprehension, and therefore likely to be derived from another source. Comment on the evidence, including comment on evidence which may bear adversely on the credibility of the child, should be addressed after the child has finished giving evidence.

The competency test may be re-analysed at the end of the child's evidence. This extra statutory jurisdiction is a judicial creation, clearly established in a number of decisions of this court (R v MacPherson: R v Powell: R v M: R v Malicki; see to the contrary effect Director of Public Prosecutions v R [2007] EWHC 1842 (Admin)), where it was emphasised that an asserted loss of memory by a witness does not necessarily justify the conclusion that the appropriate level of understanding is absent.) If we were inclined to do so, and we are not, it would be too late to question this jurisdiction. This second test should be viewed as an element in the defendant's entitlement to a fair trial, at which he must be, and must have been, provided with a reasonable opportunity to challenge the allegations against him, a valuable adjunct to the process, just because it provides an additional safeguard for the defendant. If the child witness has been unable to provide intelligible answers to questions in cross-examination (as in Powell) or a meaningful cross-examination was impossible (as in Malicki) the first competency decision will not have produced a fair trial, and in that event, the evidence admitted on the basis of a competency decision which turned out to be wrong could reasonably be excluded under section 78 of the 1984 Act. The second test should be seen in that context, but, and it is an important but, the judge is not addressing credibility questions at that stage of the process any more than he was when conducting the first competency test."

Youth Justice and Criminal Evidence Act 1999, s 54

(1) Any question whether a witness in criminal proceedings is competent to give evidence in the proceedings, whether raised—

  (a) by a party to the proceedings, or
  (b) by the court of its own motion,

shall be determined by the court in accordance with this section.

(2) It is for the party calling the witness to satisfy the court that, on a balance of probabilities, the witness is competent to give evidence in the proceedings.

(3) In determining the question mentioned in subsection (1) the court shall treat the witness as having the benefit of any directions under section 19 which the court has given, or proposes to give, in relation to the witness.

(4) Any proceedings held for the determination of the question shall take place in the absence of the jury (if there is one).

(5) Expert evidence may be received on the question.

(6) Any questioning of the witness (where the court considers that necessary) shall be conducted by the court in the presence of the parties.

Police and Criminal Evidence Act 1984, s 80

[...]

(2) In any proceedings the spouse or civil partner of a person charged in the proceedings shall, subject to subsection (4) below, be compellable to give evidence on behalf of that person.

(2A) In any proceedings the spouse or civil partner of a person charged in the proceedings shall, subject to subsection (4) below, be compellable—

(a) to give evidence on behalf of any other person charged in the proceedings but only in respect of any specified offence with which that other person is charged; or

(b) to give evidence for the prosecution but only in respect of any specified offence with which any person is charged in the proceedings.

(3) In relation to the spouse or civil partner of a person charged in any proceedings, an offence is a specified offence for the purposes of subsection (2A) above if—

(a) it involves an assault on, or injury or a threat of injury to, the spouse or civil partner or a person who was at the material time under the age of 16;

(b) it is a sexual offence alleged to have been committed in respect of a person who was at the material time under that age; or

(c) it consists of attempting or conspiring to commit, or of aiding, abetting, counselling, procuring or inciting the commission of, an offence falling within paragraph (a) or (b) above.

(4) No person who is charged in any proceedings shall be compellable by virtue of subsection (2) or (2A) above to give evidence in the proceedings.

(4A) References in this section to a person charged in any proceedings do not include a person who is not, or is no longer, liable to be convicted of any offence in the proceedings (whether as a result of pleading guilty or for any other reason).

(5) In any proceedings a person who has been but is no longer married to the accused shall be compellable to give evidence as if that person and the accused had never been married.

(5A) In any proceedings a person who has been but is no longer the civil partner of the accused shall be compellable to give evidence as if that person and the accused had never been civil partners.

(6) Where in any proceedings the age of any person at any time is material for the purposes of subsection (3) above, his age at the material time shall for the purposes of that provision be deemed to be or to have been that which appears to the court to be or to have been his age at that time.

(7) In subsection (3)(b) above "sexual offence" means an offence under the Protection of Children Act 1978[or Part 1 of the Sexual Offences Act 2003.

(9) Section 1(d) of the Criminal Evidence Act 1898 (communications between husband and wife) and section 43(1) of the Matrimonial Causes Act 1965 (evidence as to marital intercourse) shall cease to have effect.

CONVICTIONS AND ACQUITTALS, PROOF OF

Police and Criminal Evidence Act 1984, ss 73, 74, 75

73.— Proof of convictions and acquittals.

(1) Where in any proceedings the fact that a person has in the United Kingdom or any other member State been convicted or acquitted of an offence otherwise than by a Service court is admissible in evidence, it may be proved by producing a certificate of conviction or, as the case may be, of acquittal relating to that offence, and proving that the person named in the certificate as having been convicted or acquitted of the offence is the person whose conviction or acquittal of the offence is to be proved.

(2) For the purposes of this section a certificate of conviction or of acquittal—

(a) shall, as regards a conviction or acquittal on indictment, consist of a certificate, signed by the proper officer of the court where the conviction or acquittal took place, giving the substance and effect (omitting the formal parts) of the indictment and of the conviction or acquittal; and

(b) shall, as regards a conviction or acquittal on a summary trial, consist of a copy of the conviction or of the dismissal of the information, signed by the proper officer of the court where the conviction or acquittal took place or by the proper officer of the court, if any, to which a memorandum of the conviction or acquittal was sent; and

(c) shall, as regards a conviction or acquittal by a court in a member State (other than the United Kingdom), consist of a certificate, signed by the proper officer of the court where the conviction or acquittal took place, giving details of the offence, of the conviction or acquittal, and of any sentence;

and a document purporting to be a duly signed certificate of conviction or acquittal under this section shall be taken to be such a certificate unless the contrary is proved.

(3) In subsection (2) above "proper officer" means—

(a) in relation to a magistrates' court in England and Wales, the designated officer for the court; and

(b) in relation to any other court in the United Kingdom, the clerk of the court, his deputy or any other person having custody of the court record, and

(c) in relation to any court in another member State ("the EU court"), a person who would be the proper officer of the EU court if that court were in the United Kingdom.

(4) The method of proving a conviction or acquittal authorised by this section shall be in addition to and not to the exclusion of any other authorised manner of proving a conviction or acquittal.

74.— Conviction as evidence of commission of offence.

(1) In any proceedings the fact that a person other than the accused has been convicted of an offence by or before any court in the United Kingdom or any other member State or by a Service court outside the United Kingdom shall be admissible in evidence for the purpose of proving that that person committed that offence, where evidence of his having done so is admissible, whether or not any other evidence of his having committed that offence is given.

(2) In any proceedings in which by virtue of this section a person other than the accused is proved to have been convicted of an offence by or before any court in the United Kingdom or any other member State or by a Service court outside the United Kingdom, he shall be taken to have committed that offence unless the contrary is proved.

(3) In any proceedings where evidence is admissible of the fact that the accused has committed an offence, if the accused is proved to have been convicted of the offence—

(a) by or before any court in the United Kingdom or any other member State; or

(b) by a Service court outside the United Kingdom,

he shall be taken to have committed that offence unless the contrary is proved.

(4) Nothing in this section shall prejudice—

(a) the admissibility in evidence of any conviction which would be admissible apart from this section; or

(b) the operation of any enactment whereby a conviction or a finding of fact in any proceedings is for the purposes of any other proceedings made conclusive evidence of any fact.

75.— Provisions supplementary to section 74.

(1) Where evidence that a person has been convicted of an offence is admissible by virtue of section 74 above, then without prejudice to the reception of any other admissible evidence for the purpose of identifying the facts on which the conviction was based—

(a) the contents of any document which is admissible as evidence of the conviction; and

(b) the contents of—

(i) the information, complaint, indictment or charge-sheet on which the person in question was convicted, or

(ii) in the case of a conviction of an offence by a court in a member State (other than the United Kingdom), any document produced in relation to the proceedings for that offence which fulfils a purpose similar to any document or documents specified in sub-paragraph (i),

shall be admissible in evidence for that purpose.

(2) Where in any proceedings the contents of any document are admissible in evidence by virtue of subsection (1) above, a copy of that document, or of the material part of it, purporting to be certified or otherwise authenticated by or on behalf of the court or authority having custody of that document shall be admissible in evidence and shall be taken to be a true copy of that document or part unless the contrary is shown.

(3) Nothing in any of the following—

(a) section 14 of the Powers of Criminal Courts (Sentencing) Act 2000 (under which a conviction leading to probation or discharge is to be disregarded except as mentioned in that section);

(aa) section 187 of the Armed Forces Act 2006 (which makes similar provision in respect of service convictions);

(b) section 247 of the Criminal Procedure (Scotland) Act 1995 (which makes similar provision in respect of convictions on indictment in Scotland); and

(c) section 8 of the Probation Act (Northern Ireland) 1950 (which corresponds to section 13 of the Powers of Criminal Courts Act 1973) or any legislation which is in force in Northern Ireland for the time being and corresponds to that section,

shall affect the operation of section 74 above; and for the purposes of that section any order made by a court of summary jurisdiction in Scotland under section 228 or section 246(3) of the said Act of 1995 shall be treated as a conviction.

(4) Nothing in section 74 above shall be construed as rendering admissible in any proceedings evidence of any conviction other than a subsisting one.

CORROBORATION

With the exception of very few offences (most notably speeding) there is no requirement for corroborative evidence in order to prove guilt. In some cases (albeit rare) a Judge enjoys the discretion to give a warning in relation to uncorroborated evidence, and in the magistrates' court that warning applies equally to justices when deciding guilt. In *Makanjuola* [1995] 1 WLR 1348 the court held:

"it is clear that to carry on giving "discretionary" warnings generally and in the same terms as were previously obligatory would be contrary to the policy and purpose of the Act. Whether, as a matter of discretion, a judge should give any warning and if so its strength and terms must depend upon the content and manner of the witness's evidence, the circumstances of the case and the issues raised. The judge will often consider that no special warning is required at all. Where, however the witness has been shown to be unreliable, he or she may consider it necessary to urge caution. In a more extreme case, if the witness is shown to have lied, to have made previous false complaints, or to bear the defendant some grudge, a stronger warning may be thought appropriate and the judge may suggest it would be wise to look for some supporting material before acting on the impugned witness's evidence. We stress that these observations are merely illustrative of some, not all, of the factors which judges may take into account in measuring where a witness stands in the scale of reliability and what response they should make at that level in their directions to the jury. We also stress that judges are not required to conform to any formula and this Court would be slow to interfere with the exercise of discretion by a trial judge who has the advantage of assessing the manner of a witness's evidence as well as its content".

FORMAL ADMISSIONS

Criminal Justice Act 1967, s 10

(1) Subject to the provisions of this section, any fact of which oral evidence may be given in any criminal proceedings may be admitted for the purpose of those proceedings by or on behalf of the prosecutor or defendant, and the admission by any party of any such fact under this section shall as against that party be conclusive evidence in those proceedings of the fact admitted.

(2) An admission under this section—

(a) may be made before or at the proceedings;

(b) if made otherwise than in court, shall be in writing;

(c) if made in writing by an individual, shall purport to be signed by the person making it and, if so made by a body corporate, shall purport to be signed by a director or manager, or the secretary or clerk, or some other similar officer of the body corporate;

(d) if made on behalf of a defendant who is an individual, shall be made by his counsel or solicitor;

(e) if made at any state before the trial by a defendant who is an individual, must be approved by his counsel or solicitor (whether at the time it was made or subsequently) before or at the proceedings in question.

(3) An admission under this section for the purpose of proceedings relating to any matter shall be treated as an admission for the purpose of any subsequent criminal proceedings relating to that matter (including any appeal or retrial).

(4) An admission under this section may with the leave of the court be withdrawn in the proceedings for the purpose of which it is made or any subsequent criminal proceedings relating to the same matter.

HEARSAY

Criminal Procedure Rules: Rule 34 applies.

Party responsible (wholly or partially) for the absence of a witness: the principle underlying section 116(5) is that a person who is responsible for the absence of the witness whose hearsay evidence he wishes to rely on should not be allowed to benefit from the fact that the witness is unavailable to give evidence in person if he brought that situation about deliberately (*Rowley* [2012] EWCA Crim 1434). **Previous statements of a witness** (s 120): In *Chinn* [2012] EWCA Crim 501 the court set out the principles to be applied. **Matter stated:** In *Twist* [2011] EWCA Crim 1143 the court set out the relevant principles–reproduced in Appendix 7. **Admissions by agents:** Admissibility at common law is preserved, see *R (Firth) v Epping Magistrates' Court* [2011] EWHC 288 (Admin) for the admission of a case management form completed by counsel during committal proceedings, and *Newell* [2012] EWCA Crim 650 where it was held: "Where statements are made on the form which are not made under the section relating to admissions, such statements should be made without the risk that they would be used at trial as statements of the defendant admissible in evidence against the defendant, provided the advocate follows the letter and the spirit of the Criminal Procedure Rules". **Agreement to admit:** Any agreement to admit should be communicated to the trial judge (*J* []2010] 2 Cr App R 2). Agreement can be inferred where there is no objection from a represented party (*Williams v Vehicle and Operator Services Agency* [2008] EWHC 849 (Admin)). **Anonymous witness:** The hearsay evidence of an anonymous person cannot be admitted (*Ford* [2010] EWCA Crim 2250). **Absent witness and section 114:** The use of section 114 will rarely be appropriate as a means of circumventing section 116 (*Freeman* [2010] EWCA Crim 1197; for an appropriate case see: *Musone* [2007] 2 Cr App R 29). Its use may be appropriate in the case of a competent but not compellable witness (eg spouse) (*ED* [2010] EWCA

Crim 1213; *Horsnell* [2012] EWCA Crim 227). **Sole and decisive evidence:** In *Al-Khawaja and Tahery*, ECHR (App Nos 26766/05 and 22228/06), it was held:

"Where a hearsay statement is the sole or decisive evidence against a defendant, its admission as evidence will not automatically result in a breach of Article 6(1). At the same time where a conviction is based solely or decisively on the evidence of absent witnesses, the Court must subject the proceedings to the most searching scrutiny. Because of the dangers of the admission of such evidence, it would constitute a very important factor to balance in the scales, to use the words of Lord Mance in R v Davis ... and one which would require sufficient counterbalancing factors, including the existence of strong procedural safeguards. The question in each case is whether there are sufficient counterbalancing factors in place, including measures that permit a fair and proper assessment of the reliability of that evidence to take place. This would permit a conviction to be based on such evidence only if it is sufficiently reliable given its importance in the case".

Also see: *Horncastle* [2009] UKSC 14.

Criminal Justice Act 2003, ss 114-127, 129, 133, 134

114 Admissibility of hearsay evidence

(1) In criminal proceedings a statement not made in oral evidence in the proceedings is admissible as evidence of any matter stated if, but only if—

    (a) any provision of this Chapter or any other statutory provision makes it admissible,

    (b) any rule of law preserved by section 118 makes it admissible,

    (c) all parties to the proceedings agree to it being admissible, or

    (d) the court is satisfied that it is in the interests of justice for it to be admissible.

(2) In deciding whether a statement not made in oral evidence should be admitted under subsection (1)(d), the court must have regard to the following factors (and to any others it considers relevant)—

    (a) how much probative value the statement has (assuming it to be true) in relation to a matter in issue in the proceedings, or how valuable it is for the understanding of other evidence in the case;

    (b) what other evidence has been, or can be, given on the matter or evidence mentioned in paragraph (a);

    (c) how important the matter or evidence mentioned in paragraph (a) is in the context of the case as a whole;

    (d) the circumstances in which the statement was made;

    (e) how reliable the maker of the statement appears to be;

    (f) how reliable the evidence of the making of the statement appears to be;

    (g) whether oral evidence of the matter stated can be given and, if not, why it cannot;

    (h) the amount of difficulty involved in challenging the statement;

    (i) the extent to which that difficulty would be likely to prejudice the party facing it.

(3) Nothing in this Chapter affects the exclusion of evidence of a statement on grounds other than the fact that it is a statement not made in oral evidence in the proceedings.

115 Statements and matters stated

(1) In this Chapter references to a statement or to a matter stated are to be read as follows.

(2) A statement is any representation of fact or opinion made by a person by whatever means; and it includes a representation made in a sketch, photofit or other pictorial form.

(3) A matter stated is one to which this Chapter applies if (and only if) the purpose, or one of the purposes, of the person making the statement appears to the court to have been—

    (a) to cause another person to believe the matter, or

    (b) to cause another person to act or a machine to operate on the basis that the matter is as stated.

116 Cases where a witness is unavailable

(1) In criminal proceedings a statement not made in oral evidence in the proceedings is admissible as evidence of any matter stated if—

    (a) oral evidence given in the proceedings by the person who made the statement would be admissible as evidence of that matter,

    (b) the person who made the statement (the relevant person) is identified to the court's satisfaction, and

    (c) any of the five conditions mentioned in subsection (2) is satisfied.

(2) The conditions are—

    (a) that the relevant person is dead;

    (b) that the relevant person is unfit to be a witness because of his bodily or mental condition;

    (c) that the relevant person is outside the United Kingdom and it is not reasonably practicable to secure his attendance;

    (d) that the relevant person cannot be found although such steps as it is reasonably practicable to take to find him have been taken;

    (e) that through fear the relevant person does not give (or does not continue to give) oral evidence in the proceedings, either at all or in connection with the subject matter of the statement, and the court gives leave for the statement to be given in evidence.

(3) For the purposes of subsection (2)(e) "fear" is to be widely construed and (for example) includes fear of the death or injury of another person or of financial loss.

(4) Leave may be given under subsection (2)(e) only if the court considers that the statement ought to be admitted in the interests of justice, having regard—

    (a) to the statement's contents,

    (b) to any risk that its admission or exclusion will result in unfairness to any party to the proceedings (and in particular to how difficult it will be to challenge the statement if the relevant person does not give oral evidence),

    (c) in appropriate cases, to the fact that a direction under section 19 of the Youth Justice and Criminal Evidence Act 1999 (c. 23) (special measures for the giving of evidence by fearful witnesses etc) could be made in relation to the relevant person, and

    (d) to any other relevant circumstances.

(5) A condition set out in any paragraph of subsection (2) which is in fact satisfied is to be treated as not satisfied if it is shown that the circumstances described in that paragraph are caused—

    (a) by the person in support of whose case it is sought to give the statement in evidence, or

    (b) by a person acting on his behalf,

in order to prevent the relevant person giving oral evidence in the proceedings (whether at all or in connection with the subject matter of the statement).

117 Business and other documents

(1) In criminal proceedings a statement contained in a document is admissible as evidence of any matter stated if—

    (a) oral evidence given in the proceedings would be admissible as evidence of that matter,

    (b) the requirements of subsection (2) are satisfied, and

    (c) the requirements of subsection (5) are satisfied, in a case where subsection (4) requires them to be.

(2) The requirements of this subsection are satisfied if—

(a) the document or the part containing the statement was created or received by a person in the course of a trade, business, profession or other occupation, or as the holder of a paid or unpaid office,

(b) the person who supplied the information contained in the statement (the relevant person) had or may reasonably be supposed to have had personal knowledge of the matters dealt with, and

(c) each person (if any) through whom the information was supplied from the relevant person to the person mentioned in paragraph (a) received the information in the course of a trade, business, profession or other occupation, or as the holder of a paid or unpaid office.

(3) The persons mentioned in paragraphs (a) and (b) of subsection (2) may be the same person.

(4) The additional requirements of subsection (5) must be satisfied if the statement—

(a) was prepared for the purposes of pending or contemplated criminal proceedings, or for a criminal investigation, but

(b) was not obtained pursuant to a request under section 7 of the Crime (International Co-operation) Act 2003 (c. 32) or an order under paragraph 6 of Schedule 13 to the Criminal Justice Act 1988 (c. 33) (which relate to overseas evidence).

(5) The requirements of this subsection are satisfied if—

(a) any of the five conditions mentioned in section 116(2) is satisfied (absence of relevant person etc), or

(b) the relevant person cannot reasonably be expected to have any recollection of the matters dealt with in the statement (having regard to the length of time since he supplied the information and all other circumstances).

(6) A statement is not admissible under this section if the court makes a direction to that effect under subsection (7).

(7) The court may make a direction under this subsection if satisfied that the statement's reliability as evidence for the purpose for which it is tendered is doubtful in view of—

(a) its contents,

(b) the source of the information contained in it,

(c) the way in which or the circumstances in which the information was supplied or received, or

(d) the way in which or the circumstances in which the document concerned was created or received.

118 Preservation of certain common law categories of admissibility

(1) The following rules of law are preserved.

1 Public information etc

Any rule of law under which in criminal proceedings—(a) published works dealing with matters of a public nature (such as histories, scientific works, dictionaries and maps) are admissible as evidence of facts of a public nature stated in them,

(b) public documents (such as public registers, and returns made under public authority with respect to matters of public interest) are admissible as evidence of facts stated in them,

(c) records (such as the records of certain courts, treaties, Crown grants, pardons and commissions) are admissible as evidence of facts stated in them, or

(d) evidence relating to a person's age or date or place of birth may be given by a person without personal knowledge of the matter.

2 Reputation as to character

Any rule of law under which in criminal proceedings evidence of a person's reputation is admissible for the purpose of proving his good or bad character.

Note

The rule is preserved only so far as it allows the court to treat such evidence as proving the matter concerned.

3 Reputation or family tradition

Any rule of law under which in criminal proceedings evidence of reputation or family tradition is admissible for the purpose of proving or disproving—(a) pedigree or the existence of a marriage,

> (b) the existence of any public or general right, or
> (c) the identity of any person or thing.

119 Inconsistent statements

(1) If in criminal proceedings a person gives oral evidence and—

> (a) he admits making a previous inconsistent statement, or
> (b) a previous inconsistent statement made by him is proved by virtue of section 3, 4 or 5 the Criminal Procedure Act 1865 (c. 18),

the statement is admissible as evidence of any matter stated of which oral evidence by him would be admissible.

(2) If in criminal proceedings evidence of an inconsistent statement by any person is given under section 124(2)(c), the statement is admissible as evidence of any matter stated in it of which oral evidence by that person would be admissible.

120 Other previous statements of witnesses

(1) This section applies where a person (the witness) is called to give evidence in criminal proceedings.

(2) If a previous statement by the witness is admitted as evidence to rebut a suggestion that his oral evidence has been fabricated, that statement is admissible as evidence of any matter stated of which oral evidence by the witness would be admissible.

(3) A statement made by the witness in a document—

> (a) which is used by him to refresh his memory while giving evidence,
> (b) on which he is cross-examined, and
> (c) which as a consequence is received in evidence in the proceedings,

is admissible as evidence of any matter stated of which oral evidence by him would be admissible.

(4) A previous statement by the witness is admissible as evidence of any matter stated of which oral evidence by him would be admissible, if—

> (a) any of the following three conditions is satisfied, and
> (b) while giving evidence the witness indicates that to the best of his belief he made the statement, and that to the best of his belief it states the truth.

(5) The first condition is that the statement identifies or describes a person, object or place.

(6) The second condition is that the statement was made by the witness when the matters stated were fresh in his memory but he does not remember them, and cannot reasonably be expected to remember them, well enough to give oral evidence of them in the proceedings.

(7) The third condition is that—

> (a) the witness claims to be a person against whom an offence has been committed,
> (b) the offence is one to which the proceedings relate,
> (c) the statement consists of a complaint made by the witness (whether to a person in authority or not) about conduct which would, if proved, constitute the offence or part of the offence,
> (e) the complaint was not made as a result of a threat or a promise, and
> (f) before the statement is adduced the witness gives oral evidence in connection with its subject matter.

(8) For the purposes of subsection (7) the fact that the complaint was elicited (for example, by a leading question) is irrelevant unless a threat or a promise was involved.

121 Additional requirement for admissibility of multiple hearsay

(1) A hearsay statement is not admissible to prove the fact that an earlier hearsay statement was made unless—

(a) either of the statements is admissible under section 117, 119 or 120,

(b) all parties to the proceedings so agree, or

(c) the court is satisfied that the value of the evidence in question, taking into account how reliable the statements appear to be, is so high that the interests of justice require the later statement to be admissible for that purpose.

(2) In this section "hearsay statement" means a statement, not made in oral evidence, that is relied on as evidence of a matter stated in it.

122 Documents produced as exhibits

(1) This section applies if on a trial before a judge and jury for an offence—

(a) a statement made in a document is admitted in evidence under section 119 or 120, and

(b) the document or a copy of it is produced as an exhibit.

(2) The exhibit must not accompany the jury when they retire to consider their verdict unless—

(a) the court considers it appropriate, or

(b) all the parties to the proceedings agree that it should accompany the jury.

123 Capability to make statement

(1) Nothing in section 116, 119 or 120 makes a statement admissible as evidence if it was made by a person who did not have the required capability at the time when he made the statement.

(2) Nothing in section 117 makes a statement admissible as evidence if any person who, in order for the requirements of section 117(2) to be satisfied, must at any time have supplied or received the information concerned or created or received the document or part concerned—

(a) did not have the required capability at that time, or

(b) cannot be identified but cannot reasonably be assumed to have had the required capability at that time.

(3) For the purposes of this section a person has the required capability if he is capable of—

(a) understanding questions put to him about the matters stated, and

(b) giving answers to such questions which can be understood.

(4) Where by reason of this section there is an issue as to whether a person had the required capability when he made a statement—

(a) proceedings held for the determination of the issue must take place in the absence of the jury (if there is one);

(b) in determining the issue the court may receive expert evidence and evidence from any person to whom the statement in question was made;

(c) the burden of proof on the issue lies on the party seeking to adduce the statement, and the standard of proof is the balance of probabilities.

124 Credibility

(1) This section applies if in criminal proceedings—

(a) a statement not made in oral evidence in the proceedings is admitted as evidence of a matter stated, and

(b) the maker of the statement does not give oral evidence in connection with the subject matter of the statement.

(2) In such a case—

(a) any evidence which (if he had given such evidence) would have been admissible as relevant to his credibility as a witness is so admissible in the proceedings;

(b) evidence may with the court's leave be given of any matter which (if he had given such evidence) could have been put to him in crossexamination as relevant to his credibility as a witness but of which evidence could not have been adduced by the cross-examining party;

(c) evidence tending to prove that he made (at whatever time) any other statement inconsistent with the statement admitted as evidence is admissible for the purpose of showing that he contradicted himself.

(3) If as a result of evidence admitted under this section an allegation is made against the maker of a statement, the court may permit a party to lead additional evidence of such description as the court may specify for the purposes of denying or answering the allegation.

(4) In the case of a statement in a document which is admitted as evidence under section 117 each person who, in order for the statement to be admissible, must have supplied or received the information concerned or created or received the document or part concerned is to be treated as the maker of the statement for the purposes of subsections (1) to (3) above.

125 Stopping the case where evidence is unconvincing

(1) If on a defendant's trial before a judge and jury for an offence the court is satisfied at any time after the close of the case for the prosecution that—

(a) the case against the defendant is based wholly or partly on a statement not made in oral evidence in the proceedings, and

(b) the evidence provided by the statement is so unconvincing that, considering its importance to the case against the defendant, his conviction of the offence would be unsafe,

the court must either direct the jury to acquit the defendant of the offence or, if it considers that there ought to be a retrial, discharge the jury.

(2) Where—

(a) a jury is directed under subsection (1) to acquit a defendant of an offence, and

(b) the circumstances are such that, apart from this subsection, the defendant could if acquitted of that offence be found guilty of another offence,

the defendant may not be found guilty of that other offence if the court is satisfied as mentioned in subsection (1) in respect of it.

(3) If—

(a) a jury is required to determine under section 4A(2) of the Criminal Procedure (Insanity) Act 1964 (c. 84) whether a person charged on an indictment with an offence did the act or made the omission charged, and

(b) the court is satisfied as mentioned in subsection (1) above at any time after the close of the case for the prosecution that—

(i) the case against the defendant is based wholly or partly on a statement not made in oral evidence in the proceedings, and

(ii) the evidence provided by the statement is so unconvincing that, considering its importance to the case against the person, a finding that he did the act or made the omission would be unsafe, the court must either direct the jury to acquit the defendant of the offence or, if it considers that there ought to be a rehearing, discharge the jury.

(4) This section does not prejudice any other power a court may have to direct a jury to acquit a person of an offence or to discharge a jury.

126 Court's general discretion to exclude evidence

(1) In criminal proceedings the court may refuse to admit a statement as evidence of a matter stated if—

    (a) the statement was made otherwise than in oral evidence in the proceedings, and

    (b) the court is satisfied that the case for excluding the statement, taking account of the danger that to admit it would result in undue waste of time, substantially outweighs the case for admitting it, taking account of the value of the evidence.

(2) Nothing in this Chapter prejudices—

    (a) any power of a court to exclude evidence under section 78 of the Police and Criminal Evidence Act 1984 (c. 60) (exclusion of unfair evidence), or

    (b) any other power of a court to exclude evidence at its discretion (whether by preventing questions from being put or otherwise).

127 Expert evidence: preparatory work

(1) This section applies if—

    (a) a statement has been prepared for the purposes of criminal proceedings,

    (b) the person who prepared the statement had or may reasonably be supposed to have had personal knowledge of the matters stated,

    (c) notice is given under the appropriate rules that another person (the expert) will in evidence given in the proceedings orally or under section 9 of the Criminal Justice Act 1967 (c. 80) base an opinion or inference on the statement, and

    (d) the notice gives the name of the person who prepared the statement and the nature of the matters stated.

(2) In evidence given in the proceedings the expert may base an opinion or inference on the statement.

(3) If evidence based on the statement is given under subsection (2) the statement is to be treated as evidence of what it states.

(4) This section does not apply if the court, on an application by a party to the proceedings, orders that it is not in the interests of justice that it should apply.

(5) The matters to be considered by the court in deciding whether to make an order under subsection (4) include—

    (a) the expense of calling as a witness the person who prepared the statement;

    (b) whether relevant evidence could be given by that person which could not be given by the expert;

    (c) whether that person can reasonably be expected to remember the matters stated well enough to give oral evidence of them.

(6) Subsections (1) to (5) apply to a statement prepared for the purposes of a criminal investigation as they apply to a statement prepared for the purposes of criminal proceedings, and in such a case references to the proceedings are to criminal proceedings arising from the investigation.

(7) The appropriate rules are Criminal Procedure Rules made by virtue of —

    (a) section 81 of the Police and Criminal Evidence Act 1984 (advance notice of expert evidence in Crown Court), or

    (b) section 20(3) of the Criminal Procedure and Investigations Act 1996 (c. 25) (advance notice of expert evidence in magistrates' courts).

129 Representations other than by a person

(1) Where a representation of any fact—

(a) is made otherwise than by a person, but

(b) depends for its accuracy on information supplied (directly or indirectly) by a person,

the representation is not admissible in criminal proceedings as evidence of the fact unless it is proved that the information was accurate.

(2) Subsection (1) does not affect the operation of the presumption that a mechanical device has been properly set or calibrated.

133 Proof of statements in documents

Where a statement in a document is admissible as evidence in criminal proceedings, the statement may be proved by producing either—

(a) the document, or

(b) (whether or not the document exists) a copy of the document or of the material part of it,

authenticated in whatever way the court may approve.

134 Interpretation of Chapter 2

(1) In this Chapter—

"copy", in relation to a document, means anything on to which information recorded in the document has been copied, by whatever means and whether directly or indirectly;

"criminal proceedings" means criminal proceedings in relation to which the strict rules of evidence apply;

"defendant", in relation to criminal proceedings, means a person charged with an offence in those proceedings;

"document" means anything in which information of any description is recorded;

"oral evidence" includes evidence which, by reason of any disability, disorder or other impairment, a person called as a witness gives in writing or by signs or by way of any device;

"statutory provision" means any provision contained in, or in an instrument made under, this or any other Act, including any Act passed after this Act.

(2) Section 115 (statements and matters stated) contains other general interpretative provisions.

(3) Where a defendant is charged with two or more offences in the same criminal proceedings, this Chapter has effect as if each offence were charged in separate proceedings.

IDENTIFICATION

Proving a previous conviction

This is necessary in certain cases (eg to demonstrate that the defendant was a disqualified driver) and is proved by evidencing the court record and proving (if it is not admitted) that the defendant is the person referred to in that memorandum. In *Pattison v Director of Public Prosecutions* [2005] EWHC 2938 (Admin) the court held (adopting *Derwentside Justices ex p Heaviside* [1996] RTR 384):

"It is clear that proof according to the provision involves two evidential stages: (1) the production of the certificate of conviction and (2) proof to the criminal standard that the person to whom that certificate relates is the accused. As to (2), the proof contemplated by the subsection is not limited to particular defined methods of proof. For example, proof by an admission by or on behalf of the accused or by the evidence of finger prints or by someone who was present in court at the time the person was convicted and disqualified being present to give evidence. The evidential issue is at large; proof to the criminal standard will be required that the person to whom the certificate relates is the person then and there before the court". The court went on to say: "The principle which emerges from the cases is that it will normally be possible to establish a prima facie case on the basis of consistency of details between the accused and the person named on the memorandum of conviction. If the accused calls no evidence to contradict that prima facie case it will be open to the court to be satisfied that identity has been proved", and finally: "The following principles can be distilled from the cases:

(a) As with any other essential element of an offence, the prosecution must prove to the criminal standard that the person accused was a disqualified driver. (b) It can be proved by any admissible means such as an admission (even a non-formal one) by the accused that he was a disqualified driver. (c) If a certificate of conviction is relied upon pursuant to section 73 of PACE then it is an essential element of the prosecution case that the accused is proved to the criminal standard to be the person named on that certificate. (d) Three clear ways which this can be proved are the three ways identified in *Heaviside*. (e) There is, however, no prescribed way that this must be proved. It too can be proved by any admissible means. (f) An example of such means is a match between the personal details of the accused on the one hand and the personal details recorded on the certificate of conviction on the other hand. (g) Even in a case where the personal details such as the name of the accused are not uncommon, a match will be sufficient for a prima facie case.

(h) In the absence of any evidence contradicting this prima facie case the evidence will be sufficient for the court to convict. (i) The failure of the accused to give any contradictory evidence in rebuttal will be a matter to take into account. If it is proper and fair to do so and a warning has been given, it can additionally give rise to an adverse inference under section 35(2) of the Criminal Justice and Public Order Act 1994."

In *R (Howe) v South Durham Magistrates' Court* [2005] RTR 4 the court upheld a conviction based on the testimony of the defendant's solicitor who had been summonsed to court in order to confirm that the defendant in the instant case was the same defendant referred to in the memorandum of conviction (as the solicitor had represented the defendant in those proceedings). An argument that such a procedure offended legal privilege was rejected.

Proof by fingerprints

The issues here are similar to above in that the fingerprints taken at the scene must match those held centrally, and the crown must prove that the fingerprints held centrally are actually the fingerprints of the defendant. The defence are entitled to, but rarely do, put the crown to strict proof on the issue (*Chappell v Director of Public Prosecutions* (1989) 89 Cr App R 82). In Chappell the court held: "The justices were wrong to hold that the defendant's failure in the course of his evidence specifically to deny that the fingerprints were his could amount to evidence that in fact they were. Nor in my view did, or could, his replies in evidence to the effect that he could not explain the fingerprints, or that he did not know how "his" fingerprints were found to be on the envelope, amount to an admission that in fact the fingerprints were his. The position was that, by his plea, the defendant had denied the charge and thereby plainly put in issue the evidence relied on by the prosecution unless or until it was the subject of express admission. Standards of proof in a criminal trial are strict. Each step in the prosecution must be formally proved by calling the appropriate witness or making proper use of any statutory provisions which permit proof by other means than oral evidence. Of course the express admission of a witness in answer to a question concerning facts relied on by the prosecution may assist to prove his guilt, and of course inferences may be drawn, without direct proof or specific admission, as to the occurrence of events not directly witnessed or formally proved by witnesses called for the prosecution as part of its case. However, wherever the defendant by his plea denies that he was the offender and the evidence relied on by the prosecution to establish identity is the linking of forensic evidence, such as fingerprint evidence, to the defendant, the only proper course is to prove the case by evidence of a comparison made with fingerprints proved to have been taken from the defendant. Quite apart from this obvious and general requirement, on the facts of this case I fail to see how a statement by the defendant in cross-examination to the effect that he could not explain the fingerprints, or even "his" fingerprints, alleged to have been found on the envelope, could properly be said to amount to an admission that they were in fact his".

Identification by image comparison

In *Attorney General's Reference (No 2 of 2002)* [2002] EWCA Crim 2373 the court held: a jury can be invited to conclude, that the defendant committed the offence on the basis of a photographic image from the scene of the crime: (i) where the photographic image is sufficiently clear, the jury can compare it with the defendant sitting in the dock (Dodson & Williams); (ii) where a witness knows the defendant sufficiently well to recognise him as the offender depicted in the photographic image, he can give evidence of this (Fowden & White, Kajalave v Noble, Grimer, Caldwell & Dixon and Blenkinsop); and this may be so even if the photographic image is no longer available for the jury (Taylor v The Chief Constable of Chester); (iii) where a witness who does not know the defendant spends substantial time viewing and analysing photographic images from the scene, thereby acquiring special knowledge which the jury does not have, he can give evidence of identification based on a comparison between those images and a reasonably contemporary photograph of the defendant, provided that the images and the photograph are available to the jury (Clare & Peach); (iv) a suitably qualified expert with facial mapping skills can give opinion evidence of identification based on a comparison between images from the scene, (whether expertly enhanced or not and a reasonably contemporary photograph of the defendant, provided the images and the photograph are available for the jury (*Stockwell* 97 Cr App R 260, *Clarke* [1995] 2 Cr App R 425 and *Hookway* [1999] Crim LR 750)".

Dock identification

Dock identification has been upheld in relation to road traffic matters tried summarily, subject to the following (*Karia v Director of Public Prosecutions* [2002] EWHC 2175 (Admin)): "It is not a breach of the Human Rights Act or Article 6 of the European Convention for the court to expect, and in that sense require, an accused to indicate prior to trial that identification as the driver is in issue. In the absence of such prior indication, it is fair to permit the prosecution to seek and rely on a dock identification of the accused as the driver for the purpose, as was stated in Barnes, of preventing an unmeritorious, purely formal objection being taken to the prosecution case and an unmeritorious submission of no case to answer being made at the close of the prosecution evidence".

Turnbull direction

In *Turnbull* [1977] QB 244 the court held: "First, whenever the case against an accused depends wholly or substantially on the correctness of one or more identifications of the accused which the defence alleges to be mistaken, the judge should warn the jury of the special need for caution before convicting the accused in reliance on the correctness of the identification or identifications. In addition he should instruct them as to the reason for the need for such a warning and should make some reference to the possibility that a mistaken witness can be a convincing one and that a number of such witnesses can all be mistaken. Provided this is done in clear terms the judge need not use any particular form of words.

Secondly, the judge should direct the jury to examine closely the circumstances in which the identification by each witness came to be made. How long did the witness have the accused under observation? At what distance? In what light? Was the observation impeded in any way, as for example, by passing traffic or a press of people? Had the witness ever seen the accused before? How often? If only occasionally, had he any special reason for remembering the accused? How long elapsed between the original observation and the subsequent identification to the police? Was there any material discrepancy between the description of the accused given to the police by the witness when first seen by them and his actual appearance? If in any case, whether it is being dealt with summarily or on indictment, the prosecution have reason to believe that there is such a material discrepancy they should supply the accused or his legal advisers with particulars of the description the police were first given. In all cases if the accused asks to be given particulars of such descriptions, the prosecution should supply them. Finally, he should remind the jury of any specific weaknesses which had appeared in the identification evidence. Recognition may be more reliable than identification of a stranger; but even when the witness is purporting to recognise someone whom he knows, the jury should be reminded that mistakes in recognition of close relatives and friends are sometimes made.

All these matters go to the quality of the identification evidence. If the quality is good and remains good at the close of the accused's case, the danger of a mistaken identification is lessened; but the poorer the quality, the greater the danger. When, in the judgment of the trial judge, the quality of the identifying evidence is poor, as for example when it depends solely on a fleeting glance or on a longer observation made in difficult conditions, the situation is very different. The judge should then withdraw the case from the jury and direct an acquittal unless there is other evidence which goes to support the correctness of the identification".

JUDICIAL NOTICE

In *Mullen v London Borough of Hackney* [1997] 1 WLR 1103 it was said:

"It is well established that courts may take judicial notice of various matters when they are so notorious, or clearly established, or susceptible of demonstration by reference to a readily obtainable and authoritative source that evidence of their existence is unnecessary. Generally, matters directed by statute, or which have been so noticed by the well established practice or precedence of the court, must be recognised by the judges; but beyond this, they have a wide discretion and may notice much which they cannot be required to notice. The matters noticeable may include facts which are in issue or relevant to the issue; and the notice is in some cases conclusive and in others merely prima facie and rebuttable; Moreover, a judge may rely on his own local knowledge where he does so "properly and within reasonable limits". This judicial function appears to be acceptable where "the type of knowledge is of a quite general character and is not liable to be varied by specific individual characteristics of the individual case". This test allows a judge to use what might be called "special (or local) general knowledge""

PHOTOGRAPH OR SKETCH DRAWING

It is not necessary to call as a witness the person who made the photograph or drawing, only one that can testify as to its accuracy (*Tolson* (1864) 4 F&F 103). In *Attwater* [2010] EWCA Crim 2399 the court held: "There is a distinction between showing a photograph to a witness and exhibiting it. [It is] right to say that you cannot normally exhibit a photograph until it has been proved. On the other hand, provided the judge is satisfied that there will be evidence to prove the photograph, then the advocate must be entitled to put it to a witness". In many instances evidence to prove the photograph might be obtained from the very same witness.

PUBLIC INTEREST IMMUNITY

If issues of public interest immunity arise in a case triable on indictment this will generally be sufficient reason in itself to decline jurisdiction if the issues raised are of a level of complexity not generally within the experience of the court. In *H and C* [2004] AC 134 the court held:

"The appellants raised the question whether special counsel should routinely be appointed on the rare occasions when PII applications fall to be made in magistrates' courts. In this context attention was drawn to two authorities: R v Stipendiary Magistrate for Norfolk,

Ex p Taylor (1997) 161 JP 773 , and R (Director of Public Prosecutions) v Acton Youth Court [2001] EWHC Admin 402, [2001] 1 WLR 1828 . The first of these cases must now be read subject to two qualifications: first, that the test for disclosure is now that laid down in the 1996 Act and not the earlier test of relevance on which the judgment was based (see p 777G); and secondly that the test of apparent bias laid down in R v Gough [1993] AC 646 has now been restated by the House in Porter v Magill [2001] UKHL 67, [2002] 2 AC 357 , 494, paragraphs 102–103. In the second case the relevant principles were correctly applied. If PII applications are confined, as they should be, to material which undermines the prosecution case or strengthens that of the defence, the bench will not be alerted to material damaging to the defendant. If it is, the principles which should govern the court's decision whether to recuse itself are the same as in the case of any other tribunal of fact, but the court's duty of continuing review ordinarily militates in favour of continuing the proceedings before the court which determines the PII application. If a case raises complex and contentious PII issues, and the court has discretion to send the case to the crown court for trial, the magistrates' court should carefully consider whether those issues are best resolved in the crown court. The occasions on which it will be appropriate to appoint special counsel in the magistrates' court will be even rarer than in the crown court."

UNFAIRLY OR ILLEGALLY OBTAINED EVIDENCE

Confession: "confession", includes any statement wholly or partly adverse to the person who made it, whether made to a person in authority or not and whether made in words or otherwise (*Police and Criminal Evidence Act 1984*, s 82(1)). Evidence in criminal proceedings (*McGregor* [1968] 1 QB 371). Conduct (eg running away from police) or acting adversely to an allegation (*Parkes* 64 Cr App R 25). Withdrawn guilty plea (*Johnson* 171 JP 574). Mitigation advanced by a legal representative (*Turner* (1975) 61 Cr App R 67). Unsigned court documents (eg section 172 admission form) (*Mawdsley v Chief Constable of Cheshire* [2004] 1 All ER 58). Statements that are wholly exculpatory are not confessions (*Sat-Bhambra* (1988) 88 Cr App R 55). **Unreliable:** The court should apply the following test (*Barry* (1991) 95 Cr App R 384): "The first step was to identify the thing said or done. The second step was then to ask whether what was said and done was likely in the circumstances to render unreliable a confession made in consequence. The test is objective. But all the circumstances had to be taken into account, including the circumstances affecting the defendant himself. The final step: Have the prosecution proved beyond reasonable doubt that the confession was not obtained in consequence of the things said or done? This is a question of fact to be approached in a commonsense way".

Police and Criminal Evidence Act 1984, ss 76, 76A, 77, 78

76.— Confessions.

(1) In any proceedings a confession made by an accused person may be given in evidence against him in so far as it is relevant to any matter in issue in the proceedings and is not excluded by the court in pursuance of this section.

(2) If, in any proceedings where the prosecution proposes to give in evidence a confession made by an accused person, it is represented to the court that the confession was or may have been obtained—

   (a) by oppression of the person who made it; or

   (b) in consequence of anything said or done which was likely, in the circumstances existing at the time, to render unreliable any confession which might be made by him in consequence thereof,

the court shall not allow the confession to be given in evidence against him except in so far as the prosecution proves to the court beyond reasonable doubt that the confession (notwithstanding that it may be true) was not obtained as aforesaid.

(3) In any proceedings where the prosecution proposes to give in evidence a confession made by an accused person, the court may of its own motion require the prosecution, as a condition of allowing it to do so, to prove that the confession was not obtained as mentioned in subsection (2) above.

(4) The fact that a confession is wholly or partly excluded in pursuance of this section shall not affect the admissibility in evidence—

   (a) of any facts discovered as a result of the confession; or

   (b) where the confession is relevant as showing that the accused speaks, writes or expresses himself in a particular way, of so much of the confession as is necessary to show that he does so.

(5) Evidence that a fact to which this subsection applies was discovered as a result of a statement made by an accused person shall not be admissible unless evidence of how it was discovered is given by him or on his behalf.

(6) Subsection (5) above applies—

   (a) to any fact discovered as a result of a confession which is wholly excluded in pursuance of this section; and

   (b) to any fact discovered as a result of a confession which is partly so excluded, if the fact is discovered as a result of the excluded part of the confession.

(7) Nothing in Part VII of this Act shall prejudice the admissibility of a confession made by an accused person.

(8) In this section "oppression" includes torture, inhuman or degrading treatment, and the use or threat of violence (whether or not amounting to torture).

76A Confessions may be given in evidence for co-accused

(1) In any proceedings a confession made by an accused person may be given in evidence for another person charged in the same proceedings (a co-accused) in so far as it is relevant to any matter in issue in the proceedings and is not excluded by the court in pursuance of this section.

(2) If, in any proceedings where a co-accused proposes to give in evidence a confession made by an accused person, it is represented to the court that the confession was or may have been obtained—

   (a) by oppression of the person who made it; or

   (b) in consequence of anything said or done which was likely, in the circumstances existing at the time, to render unreliable any confession which might be made by him in consequence thereof,

the court shall not allow the confession to be given in evidence for the co-accused except in so far as it is proved to the court on the balance of probabilities that the confession (notwithstanding that it may be true) was not so obtained.

(3) Before allowing a confession made by an accused person to be given in evidence for a co-accused in any proceedings, the court may of its own motion require the fact that the confession was not obtained as mentioned in subsection (2) above to be proved in the proceedings on the balance of probabilities.

(4) The fact that a confession is wholly or partly excluded in pursuance of this section shall not affect the admissibility in evidence—

   (a) of any facts discovered as a result of the confession; or

   (b) where the confession is relevant as showing that the accused speaks, writes or expresses himself in a particular way, of so much of the confession as is necessary to show that he does so.

(5) Evidence that a fact to which this subsection applies was discovered as a result of a statement made by an accused person shall not be admissible unless evidence of how it was discovered is given by him or on his behalf.

(6) Subsection (5) above applies—

    (a) to any fact discovered as a result of a confession which is wholly excluded in pursuance of this section; and

    (b) to any fact discovered as a result of a confession which is partly so excluded, if the fact is discovered as a result of the excluded part of the confession.

(7) In this section "oppression" includes torture, inhuman or degrading treatment, and the use or threat of violence (whether or not amounting to torture).

77.— Confessions by mentally handicapped persons.

(1) Without prejudice to the general duty of the court at a trial on indictment with a jury to direct the jury on any matter on which it appears to the court appropriate to do so, where at such a trial—

    (a) the case against the accused depends wholly or substantially on a confession by him; and

    (b) the court is satisfied—

        (i) that he is mentally handicapped; and

        (ii) that the confession was not made in the presence of an independent person,

the court shall warn the jury that there is special need for caution before convicting the accused in reliance on the confession, and shall explain that the need arises because of the circumstances mentioned in paragraphs (a) and (b) above.

(2) In any case where at the summary trial of a person for an offence it appears to the court that a warning under subsection (1) above would be required if the trial were on indictment with a jury, the court shall treat the case as one in which there is a special need for caution before convicting the accused on his confession.

(2A) In any case where at the trial on indictment without a jury of a person for an offence it appears to the court that a warning under subsection (1) above would be required if the trial were with a jury, the court shall treat the case as one in which there is a special need for caution before convicting the accused on his confession.

(3) In this section—

"independent person" does not include a police officer or a person employed for, or engaged on, police purposes;

"mentally handicapped", in relation to a person, means that he is in a state of arrested or incomplete development of mind which includes significant impairment of intelligence and social functioning; and

"police purposes" has the meaning assigned to it by section 101(2) of the Police Act 1996.

78.— Exclusion of unfair evidence.

(1) In any proceedings the court may refuse to allow evidence on which the prosecution proposes to rely to be given if it appears to the court that, having regard to all the circumstances, including the circumstances in which the evidence was obtained, the admission of the evidence would have such an adverse effect on the fairness of the proceedings that the court ought not to admit it.

(2) Nothing in this section shall prejudice any rule of law requiring a court to exclude evidence.

WITNESS COACHING

Witness coaching is forbidden, but witness familiarisation is permitted (*Momodou* [2005] EWCA Crim 177 (at para 61).

PART E TRIAL

AIDS TO COMMUNICATION

See: 'Special Measures' for general principles to be applied.

Youth Justice and Criminal Evidence Act 1999, s 30

A special measures direction may provide for the witness, while giving evidence (whether by testimony in court or otherwise), to be provided with such device as the court considers appropriate with a view to enabling questions or answers to be communicated to or by the witness despite any disability or disorder or other impairment which the witness has or suffers from.

APPEALS AGAINST CONVICTION AND SENTENCE

Time limit: Unless leave is granted by the crown court to hear an appeal out of time, an appeal must be lodged within 21 days of sentence, this is the case even if the appeal is against conviction and sentence is adjourned to a later date. An appeal out of time must be lodged at the magistrates' court explaining the reasons for delay and why an extension ought to be granted. **Appeals following a guilty plea:** If a defendant pleads guilty he can only appeal his sentence, unless it is successfully argued (at the crown court) that the guilty plea was equivocal (*R v Rochdale Justices ex p Allwork* 73 Cr App R 319). **Criminal procedure rules:** Rule 63.10 applies (see below) and an appeal must be lodged on the approved form. **Abandonment:** See CrPR 63.8 and Magistrates' Courts Act 1980, s 109. **Legal aid:** Magistrates' court legal aid does not extend to cover an appeal; a fresh application should be submitted to the relevant magistrates' court. Financial eligibility is slightly different (and more favourable to the appellant) in respect to crown court appeals to a client may be eligible for assistance in the crown court even though not eligible on means in the magistrates' court **Bail:** See Part E Bail Pending Appeal. Suspension of sentence pending appeal: with the exception of bail and suspension of driving disqualifications (if granted) a sentence takes effect notwithstanding that an appeal notice has been lodged (see *Greater Manchester Probation Service ex p Bent* (1996) 160 JP 297). **Case stated:** If an appeal by way of case stated is lodged any right of appeal to the crown court is lost.

Magistrates' Courts Act 1980, s 108

(1)   A person convicted by a magistrates' court may appeal to the Crown Court—

    (a) if he pleaded guilty, against his sentence;
    (b) if he did not, against the conviction or sentence.

(1A)   Section 14 of the Powers of Criminal Courts (Sentencing) Act 2000 (under which a conviction of an offence for which an order for conditional or absolute discharge is made is deemed not to be a conviction except for certain purposes) shall not prevent an appeal under this Act, whether against conviction or otherwise.

(2)   A person sentenced by a magistrates' court for an offence in respect of which an order for conditional discharge has been previously made may appeal to the Crown Court against the sentence.

(3)   In this section "sentence" includes any order made on conviction by a magistrates' court, not being—

    (b) an order for the payment of costs;
    (c) an order under section 37(1) of the Animal Welfare Act 2006 (which enables a court to order the destruction of an animal); or

(d) an order made in pursuance of any enactment under which the court has no discretion as to the making of the order or its terms

and also includes a declaration of relevance, within the meaning of section 23 of 9 the Football Spectators Act 1989.

(4) Subsection (3)(d) above does not prevent an appeal against a surcharge imposed under section 161A of the Criminal Justice Act 2003.

Criminal Procedure Rules 2012, r 63.2, 63.3, 63.8

Service of appeal notice

63.2.—(1) An appellant must serve an appeal notice on—

    (a) the magistrates' court officer; and
    (b) every other party.

(2) The appellant must serve the appeal notice—

    (a) as soon after the decision appealed against as the appellant wants; but
    (b) not more than 21 days after—
        (i) sentence or the date sentence is deferred, whichever is earlier, if the appeal is against

conviction or against a finding of guilt,

        (ii) sentence, if the appeal is against sentence, or
        (iii) the order or failure to make an order about which the appellant wants to appeal, in

any other case.

(3) The appellant must serve with the appeal notice any application for the following, with

reasons—

    (a) an extension of the time limit under this rule, if the appeal notice is late;
    (b) bail pending appeal, if the appellant is in custody;
    (c) the suspension of any disqualification imposed in the case, where the magistrates' court

or the Crown Court can order such a suspension pending appeal.

(4) Where both the magistrates' court and the Crown Court can suspend a disqualification

pending appeal, an application for its suspension must indicate by which court the appellant wants the application determined.

Form of appeal notice

63.3. The appeal notice must be in writing and must—

    (a) specify—
        (i) the conviction or finding of guilt,
        (ii) the sentence, or
        (iii) the order, or the failure to make an order
        about which the appellant wants to appeal;
    (b) summarise the issues;
    (c) in an appeal against conviction—
        (i) identify the prosecution witnesses whom the appellant will want to question if they

are called to give oral evidence, and

        (ii) say how long the trial lasted in the magistrates' court and how long the appeal is likely to last in the Crown Court;

> (d) in an appeal against a finding that the appellant insulted someone or interrupted

proceedings in the magistrates' court, attach—

>> (i) the magistrates' court's written findings of fact, and
>> (ii) the appellant's response to those findings;

> (e) say whether the appellant has asked the magistrates' court to reconsider the case; and
> (f) include a list of those on whom the appellant has served the appeal notice.

Abandoning an appeal

63.8.—(1) The appellant—

> (a) may abandon an appeal without the Crown Court's permission, by serving a notice of

abandonment on—

>> (i) the magistrates' court officer,
>> (ii) the Crown Court officer, and
>> (iii) every other party

before the hearing of the appeal begins; but

> (b) after the hearing of the appeal begins, may only abandon the appeal with the Crown

Court's permission.

> (2) A notice of abandonment must be signed by or on behalf of the appellant.
> (3) Where an appellant who is on bail pending appeal abandons an appeal—

>> (a) the appellant must surrender to custody as directed by the magistrates' court officer; and
>> (b) any conditions of bail apply until then.

BAIL PENDING APPEAL

Appeal to crown court or by case stated: There is no right to bail pending appeal and the starting point is that bail will not be granted. Where the appeal is against conviction and the defendant was convicted after trial many courts will look more favourably on bail pending appeal, particularly when the custodial sentence is short. This is simply due to the fact that the defendant has an automatic right to a rehearing in the crown court. In *Imdad Shah* (1980) 144 JP 460, the court rejected an argument that bail should be granted where the sentence was a short one and there was a risk that the sentence would be served prior to the appeal being heard. The court ruled that in such cases an early listing should be sought. By way of contrast in *R (G) v Inner London Crown Court* [2003] EWHC 2715 (Admin) the applicant successfully judicially reviewed a decision by a Crown Court to refuse bail in a 'short sentence' case. **Judicial review:** A magistrates' court has no power to grant bail pending a judicial review, application should be made to the High Court.

Magistrates' Courts Act 1980, s 113

> (1) Where a person has given notice of appeal to the Crown Court against the decision of a magistrates' court or has applied to a magistrates' court to state a case for the opinion of the High Court, then, if he is in custody, the magistrates' court may, subject to section 25 of the Criminal Justice and Public Order Act 1994 grant him bail.
> (2) If a person is granted bail under subsection (1) above, the time and place at which he is to appear (except in the event of the determination in respect of which the case is stated being reversed by the High Court) shall be—

(a) if he has given notice of appeal, the Crown Court at the time appointed for the hearing of the appeal;

(b) if he has applied for the statement of a case, the magistrates' court at such time within 10 days after the judgment of the High Court has been given as may be specified by the magistrates' court;

and any recognizance that may be taken from him or from any surety for him shall be conditioned accordingly.

(3) Subsection (1) above shall not apply where the accused has been committed to the Crown Court for sentence under section 37 above or section 3 of the Powers of Criminal Courts (Sentencing) Act 2000.

(4) Section 37(6) of the Criminal Justice Act 1948 (which relates to the currency of a sentence while a person is released on bail by the High Court) shall apply to a person released on bail by a magistrates' court under this section pending the hearing of a case stated as it applies to a person released on bail by the High Court under section 22 of the Criminal Justice Act 1967.

CLOSING SPEECH

The prosecution may make a closing speech where (i) the defendant is represented by a legal representative, or (ii) whether represented or not, the defendant has introduced evidence other than his or her own (CrPR 37.3). Where a defendant is represented but has not given evidence a prosecutor should rarely make a closing speech (*Bryant* [1979] QB 108). The same principle applies where there is more than one defendant, one who has called evidence and the other not, ie the prosecutor should restrict his speech to arguments in relation to the defendant who has adduced evidence. There is no prohibition on any party making representations on matters of law raised by another party.

CORPORATE DEFENDANTS

Magistrates' Courts Act 1980, Sch 3, paras 2–3

2. A representative may on behalf of a corporation—

(a) make before examining justices such representations as could be made by an accused who is not a corporation;.

(b) consent to the corporation being tried summarily;

(c) enter a plea of guilty or not guilty on the trial by a magistrates' court of an information.

3.—

(1) Where a representative appears, any requirement of this Act that anything shall be done in the presence of the accused, or shall be read or said to the accused, shall be construed as a requirement that that thing shall be done in the presence of the representative or read or said to the representative.

(2) Where a representative does not appear, any such requirement, and any requirement that the consent of the accused shall be obtained for summary trial, shall not apply.

CROSS-EXAMINATION

Generally: The right to cross-examine is not conditional on evidence having been given in chief. If the evidence of a witness is inconsistent with the case being advanced by the defendant, the defendant's case must 'be put' that witness. This rule is best explained by *R (Wilkinson) v Director of Public Prosecutions* (2003) 167 JP 229 where it was held:

"It is undoubtedly the professional obligation of an advocate acting for the defence to put to prosecution witnesses conflicts between the defence case and the evidence given by the prosecution witness in question in order to give the prosecution witness an opportunity to comment on what is put: Whether it is the possibility of a mistake or whether it is that the prosecution witness is lying, whether his recollection is incorrect, whether he has been confused or whatever. The position in relation to the defence case is somewhat different. By the time the defence comes to give evidence, the prosecution evidence has been given, the defence are aware of what evidence has been given and the defence are able, therefore, in chief, to ask witnesses whether or not they agree with prosecution evidence and to comment on it. It is nonetheless the professional duty of the advocate acting for the defence to make it clear what evidence is rejected or disputed. That is particularly important where a trial takes place before a jury. It is less important where the trial takes place before a professional legally qualified judge who may be expected to be aware of what the issues are in a case."

Where it is known that a defendant will not himself give evidence there are limits placed on what advocates can put to witnesses. In *O'Neill* (1950) 34 Cr App R 108 the court held:

"In this case a violent attack was made on the police. It was suggested that they had done improper things, and indeed, Ackers repeats that suggestion in his notice of appeal. The applicants had the opportunity of going into the box at the trial and explaining and supporting what they had instructed their counsel to say. They did not dare to go into the box and, therefore, counsel, who knew that they were not going into the box, ought not to have made these suggestions against the police. It is one thing to cross-examine properly and temperately with regard to credit, though it is very dangerous to do so unless you have material on which to cross-examine, and with which you can confront the witness. It is, however, entirely wrong to make suggestions as were made in this case, namely that the police beat "the prisoners until they made confessions, and then, when there is the chance for the prisoners to substantiate what has been said by going into the box, for counsel not to call them. The Court hopes that notice will be taken of this, and that counsel will refrain, if they do not intend to call their client, from making charges which, if true, form a defence but which, if there is nothing to support them, ought not to be pursued."

Co-defendants: Defendants are cross-examined in the order they appear on the indictment (or in the magistrates' court, the court list). **Collateral issues:** A party is not entitled to seek to adduce evidence to rebut answers given in relation to collateral issues. Matters that go merely to credit are always a collateral issue. In *Funderburk* [1990] 90 Cr App R 466 the court held:

"... as relevance is a matter of degree in each case, the question in reality is whether or not the evidence is or is not sufficiently relevant. For in order to keep criminal trials within bounds and to assist the jury in concentrating on what matters and not being distracted by marginal events, it is necessary in the interests of justice to avoid multiplicity of issues where possible. In every case this is a matter for the trial judge and on the way the case is put before him."

There are however 5 exceptions to the rule in relation to rebuttal of collateral issues, namely: (1) Evidence to establish bias or partiality; (2) Evidence of bad character; (3) Evidence to establish reputation for untruthfulness; (4) Medical evidence affecting going to the reliability of the witnesses evidence, and (5) Evidence adduced under the Criminal Justice Act 2003, s 124.

EXAMINATION IN CHIEF

Purpose: A witness may be called to answer open questions intended to elicit evidence which is relevant and probative to the case being advanced. **Formalities:** A witness should be asked to identify himself by name. It is not proper (unless it is otherwise relevant to a matter in issue) to ask a witness to state his home or work address. **Leading questions:** Leading questions are not permitted unless they relate to matters that are not in dispute or there is agreement that they can be asked. As a matter of courtesy an advocate should inform the court of any such agreement reached so that the court knows whether this rule of evidence is being breached or not. A hostile witness may be asked leading questions.

HOSTILE WITNESS

Timing of application: Whilst unusual, an application can be made during re-examination of a witness (*Powell* [1995] Crim LR 592). **Treatment of witnesses' evidence:** Save possibly in the most exceptional cases, once a witness has been treated as hostile some warning should be given to the jury about approaching his evidence with caution. The nature of the warning will obviously be dependent on the particular facts of the case (*Greene* [2009] EWCA Crim 2282). **Effect of previous statement:** A previous statement does not become evidence simply because a hostile witness was examined on its content (unless of course he adopts the content–*Golder* [1960] 1 WLR 1169), note however that effective use can be made of Criminal Justice Act 2003, s 119 provided that the conditions in that section are properly satisfied, noting also that section 125 of the 2003 Act operates as an effective safeguard (see *Gibbons* [2008] EWCA Crim 1574).

Criminal Procedure Act 1865, s 3

A party producing a witness shall not be allowed to impeach his credit by general evidence of bad character; but he may, in case the witness shall in the opinion of the judge prove adverse, contradict him by other evidence, or, by leave of the judge, prove that he has made at other times a statement inconsistent with his present testimony; but before such last-mentioned proof can be given the circumstances of the supposed statement, sufficient to designate the particular occasion, must be mentioned to the witness, and he must be asked whether or not he has made such statement.

IDENTITY OF PARTIES

Magistrates should be identified by name, but the court retains discretion to refuse this information if it is believed that it is being sought for a mischievous nature (*Felixtowe Justices ex p Leigh* [1987] QB 582). Solicitors and counsel acting for parties in proceedings should also be willing, absent good reason otherwise, to give their name to an interested party.

INTERMEDIARY

A court may authorise the use of an intermediary (by virtue of a special measures direction) in respect of any witness with the exception of the defendant. The Coroners and Justice Act 2009, s 104 will provide for, once in force, the provision of intermediaries for defendants. A court has a common law power to approve the use of an intermediary in order to ensure a fair trial, but has no power to authorise payment of the same out of central funds (*C v Sevenoaks Youth Court* [2009] EWHC 3088 (Admin)). In *Cox* [2012] EWCA Crim 549 the court held:

> "We immediately acknowledge the valuable contribution made to the administration of justice by the use of intermediaries in appropriate cases. We recognise that there are occasions when the use of an intermediary would improve the trial process. That, however, is far from saying that whenever the process would be improved by the availability of an intermediary, it is mandatory for an intermediary to be made available. It can, after all, sometimes be overlooked that as part of their general responsibilities judges are expected to deal with specific communication problems faced by any defendant or any individual witness (whether a witness for the prosecution or the defence) as part and parcel of their ordinary control of the judicial process. When necessary, the processes have to be adapted

to ensure that a particular individual is not disadvantaged as a result of personal difficulties, whatever form they may take. In short, the overall responsibility of the trial judge for the fairness of the trial has not been altered because of the increased availability of intermediaries, or indeed the wide band of possible special measures now enshrined in statute. In the context of a defendant with communication problems, when every sensible step taken to identify an available intermediary has been unsuccessful, the next stage is not for the proceedings to be stayed, which [...] would represent a gross unfairness to the complainant, but for the judge to make an informed assessment of whether the absence of an intermediary would make the proposed trial an unfair trial. It would, in fact, be a most unusual case for a defendant who is fit to plead to be found to be so disadvantaged by his condition that a properly brought prosecution would have to be stayed."

Youth Justice and Criminal Evidence Act 1999, s 29

(1) A special measures direction may provide for any examination of the witness (however and wherever conducted) to be conducted through an interpreter or other person approved by the court for the purposes of this section ("an intermediary").

(2) The function of an intermediary is to communicate—

    (a) to the witness, questions put to the witness, and

    (b) to any person asking such questions, the answers given by the witness in reply to them,

and to explain such questions or answers so far as necessary to enable them to be understood by the witness or person in question.

(3) Any examination of the witness in pursuance of subsection (1) must take place in the presence of such persons as Criminal Procedure Rules or the direction may provide, but in circumstances in which—

    (a) the judge or justices (or both) and legal representatives acting in the proceedings are able to see and hear the examination of the witness and to communicate with the intermediary, and

    (b) (except in the case of a video recorded examination) the jury (if there is one) are able to see and hear the examination of the witness.

(4) Where two or more legal representatives are acting for a party to the proceedings, subsection (3)(a) is to be regarded as satisfied in relation to those representatives if at all material times it is satisfied in relation to at least one of them.

(5) A person may not act as an intermediary in a particular case except after making a declaration, in such form as may be prescribed by Criminal Procedure Rules, that he will faithfully perform his function as intermediary.

(6) Subsection (1) does not apply to an interview of the witness which is recorded by means of a video recording with a view to its admission as evidence in chief of the witness; but a special measures direction may provide for such a recording to be admitted under section 27 if the interview was conducted through an intermediary and—

    (a) that person complied with subsection (5) before the interview began, and

    (b) the court's approval for the purposes of this section is given before the direction is given.

(7) Section 1 of the Perjury Act 1911 (perjury) shall apply in relation to a person acting as an intermediary as it applies in relation to a person lawfully sworn as an interpreter in a judicial proceeding; and for this purpose, where a person acts as an intermediary in any proceeding which is not a judicial proceeding for the purposes of that section, that proceeding shall be taken to be part of the judicial proceeding in which the witness's evidence is given.

MULTIPLE INFORMATIONS

Co-accused: An information may be laid alleging joint misconduct by more than one defendant (*R v Lipscombe ex p Biggins* (1862) 26 JP 244). The Criminal Procedure Rules 2012, r 14 do not apply to the magistrates' court but the principles to be applied are much the same. In *Chief Constable of Norfolk v Clayton* [1983] 2 AC 473 the court held:

"Where a defendant is charged on several informations and the facts are connected, for example motoring offences or several charges of shoplifting, I can see no reason why those informations should not, if the justices think fit, be heard together. Similarly, if two or mere defendants are charged on separate informations but the facts are connected. I can see no reason why they should not, if the justices think fit, be heard together. In the present cases there were separate informations against the husband and the wife and a joint information against them both. I can see no rational objection to all those informations being heard and determined together. Of course, when this question arises, as from time to time it will arise, justices will be well advised to inquire both of the prosecution and of the defence whether either side has any objection to all the informations being heard together. If consent is forthcoming on both sides there is no problem. If such consent is not forthcoming, the justices should then consider the rival submissions and, under any necessary advice from their clerk, rule as they think right in the overall interest of justice. If the defendant is absent or not represented, the justices, of course, should seek the views of the prosecution and again if necessary the advice of their clerk and then rule as they think fit in the overall interests of justice. Absence of consent, either express where the defendant is present or represented and objects or necessarily brought about by his absence or the absence of representation, should no longer in practice be regarded as a complete and automatic bar to hearing more than one information at the same time or information against more than one defendant charged on separate informations at the same time when in the justices' view the facts are sufficiently closely connected to justify this course and there is no risk of injustice to defendants by its adoption. Accordingly the justices should always ask themselves whether it would be fair and just to the defendant or defendants to allow a joint trial. Only if the answer is clearly in the affirmative should they order joint trial in the absence of consent by or on behalf of the defendant."

OVERSEAS WITNESS

A youth court, but not an adult magistrates' court, may receive evidence via video-link from a witness abroad (Criminal Justice Act 1988, s 32).

PHOTOGRAPHIC AND AUDIO RECORDINGS, TEXT COMMUNICATIONS

Photograph: Includes video recording (*Loveridge* [2001] 2 Cr App R 29). **Contempt:** In addition to the criminal offence created by this section, the court may instead proceed by way of contempt proceedings (*Vincent* [2004] EWCA Crim 1271). In recent years incidents have ranged from foreign visitors unwittingly finding themselves locked up in a court cell for a few hours pending determination of the contempt proceedings, to those intentionally taking photographs being imprisoned (eg *Thompson (Paul)*, Luton Crown Court, 23 September 2011–jailed for 2 months). **Text:** There is no law prohibiting text based communication live from court (eg Twitter), but a court retains a common law discretion to prevent this occurring. Guidance makes clear that there is no longer any need for representatives of the media/legal commentators to make an application to use text-based devices to communicate from court. Members of the public should make a formal or informal application if they wish to use these devices (*Practice Guidance: The use of live text-based forms of communication (including Twitter) from court for the purposes of fair and accurate reporting* [2011] 1 Cr App R 23).

Criminal Justice Act 1925, s 41

(1) No person shall—

    (a) take or attempt to take in any court any photograph, or with a view to publication make or attempt to make in any court any portrait or sketch, of any person, being a judge of the court or a juror or a witness in or a party to any proceedings before the court, whether civil or criminal; or

    (b) publish any photograph, portrait or sketch taken or made in contravention of the foregoing provisions of this section or any reproduction thereof;

and if any person acts in contravention of this section he shall, on summary conviction, be liable in respect of each offence to a fine not exceeding level 3 on the standard scale.

(2) For the purposes of this section—

    (a) the expression "court" means any court of justice (including the court of a coroner), apart from the Supreme Court;

    (b) the expression "Judge"includes, registrar, magistrate, justice and coroner:

    (c) a photograph, portrait or sketch shall be deemed to be a photograph, portrait or sketch taken or made in court if it is taken or made in the court-room or in the building or in the precincts of the building in which the court is held, or if it is a photograph, portrait or sketch taken or made of the person while he is entering or leaving the court-room or any such building or precincts as aforesaid.

Contempt of Court Act 1981, s 9

(1) Subject to subsection (4) below, it is a contempt of court—

    (a) to use in court, or bring into court for use, any tape recorder or other instrument for recording sound, except with the leave of the court;

    (b) to publish a recording of legal proceedings made by means of any such instrument, or any recording derived directly or indirectly from it, by playing it in the hearing of the public or any section of the public, or to dispose of it or any recording so derived, with a view to such publication;

    (c) to use any such recording in contravention of any conditions of leave granted under paragraph (a).

(2) Leave under paragraph (a) of subsection (1) may be granted or refused at the discretion of the court, and if granted may be granted subject to such conditions as the court thinks proper with respect to the use of any recording made pursuant to the leave; and where leave has been granted the court may at the like discretion withdraw or amend it either generally or in relation to any particular part of the proceedings.

(3) Without prejudice to any other power to deal with an act of contempt under paragraph (a) of subsection (1), the court may order the instrument, or any recording made with it, or both, to be forfeited; and any object so forfeited shall (unless the court otherwise determines on application by a person appearing to be the owner) be sold or otherwise disposed of in such manner as the court may direct.

(4) This section does not apply to the making or use of sound recordings for purposes of official transcripts of proceedings.

PLEA, GUILTY PLEA BY POST

Magistrates' Courts Act 1980, ss 12, 12A

12.— Non-appearance of accused; plea of guilty.

(1) This section shall apply where—

(a) a summons has been issued requiring a person to appear before a magistrates' court, other than a youth court, to answer to an information for a summary offence, not being—

[...]

(ii) an offence specified in an order made by the Secretary of State by statutory instrument; and

(b) the designated officer for the court is notified by or on behalf of the prosecutor that the documents mentioned in subsection (3) below have been served upon the accused with the summons.

(2) The reference in subsection (1)(a) above to the issue of a summons requiring a person to appear before a magistrates' court other than a youth court includes a reference to the issue of a summons requiring a person who has attained the age of 16 at the time when it is issued to appear before a youth court.

(3) The documents referred to in subsection (1)(b) above are—

(a) a notice containing such statement of the effect of this section as may be prescribed;

(b) either of the following, namely—

(i) a concise statement of such facts relating to the charge as will be placed before the court by the prosecutor if the accused pleads guilty without appearing before the court, or

(ii) a copy of such written statement or statements complying with subsections (2) (a) and (b) and (3) of section 9 of the Criminal Justice Act 1967 (proof by written statement) as will be so placed in those circumstances; and

(c) if any information relating to the accused will or may, in those circumstances, be placed before the court by or on behalf of the prosecutor, a notice containing or describing that information.

(4) Where the designated officer for the court receives a notification in writing purporting to be given by the accused or by a legal representative acting on his behalf that the accused desires to plead guilty without appearing before the court—

(a) the designated officer for the court shall inform the prosecutor of the receipt of the notification; and

(b) the following provisions of this section shall apply:

(5) If at the time and place appointed for the trial or adjourned trial of the information—

(a) the accused does not appear; and

(b) it is proved to the satisfaction of the court, on oath or in such manner as may be prescribed, that the documents mentioned in subsection (3) above have been served upon the accused with the summons,

the court may, subject to section 11(3) and (4) above and subsections (6) to (8) below, proceed to hear and dispose of the case in the absence of the accused, whether or not the prosecutor is also absent, in like manner as if both parties had appeared and the accused had pleaded guilty.

(6) If at any time before the hearing the designated officer for the court receives an indication in writing purporting to be given by or on behalf of the accused that he wishes to withdraw the notification—

(a) the designated officer for the court shall inform the prosecutor of the withdrawal; and

(b) the court shall deal with the information as if the notification had not been given.

(7) Before accepting the plea of guilty and convicting the accused under subsection (5) above, the court shall cause the following to be read out before the court by the clerk of the court, namely—

(a) in a case where a statement of facts as mentioned in subsection (3)(b)(i) above was served on the accused with the summons, that statement;

(aa) in a case where a statement or statements as mentioned in subsection (3)(b)(ii) above was served on the accused with the summons and the court does not otherwise direct, that statement or those statements;

(b) any information contained in a notice so served, and any information described in such a notice and produced by or on behalf of the prosecutor;

(c) the notification under subsection (4) above; and

(d) any submission received with the notification which the accused wishes to be brought to the attention of the court with a view to mitigation of sentence.

(7A) Where the court gives a direction under subsection (7)(aa) above the court shall cause an account to be given orally before the court by the clerk of the court of so much of any statement as is not read aloud.

(7B) Whether or not a direction under paragraph (aa) of subsection (7) above is given in relation to any statement served as mentioned in that paragraph the court need not cause to be read out the declaration required by section 9(2)(b) of the Criminal Justice Act 1967.

(8) If the court proceeds under subsection (5) above to hear and dispose of the case in the absence of the accused, the court shall not permit—

(a) any other statement with respect to any facts relating to the offence charged; or

(b) any other information relating to the accused,

to be made or placed before the court by or on behalf of the prosecutor except on a resumption of the trial after an adjournment under section 10(3) above.

(9) If the court decides not to proceed under subsection (5) above to hear and dispose of the case in the absence of the accused, it shall adjourn or further adjourn the trial for the purpose of dealing with the information as if the notification under subsection (4) above had not been given.

(10) In relation to an adjournment on the occasion of the accused's conviction in his absence under subsection (5) above or to an adjournment required by subsection (9) above, the notice required by section 10(2) above shall include notice of the reason for the adjournment.

(11) No notice shall be required by section 10(2) above in relation to an adjournment—

(a) which is for not more than 4 weeks; and

(b) the purpose of which is to enable the court to proceed under subsection (5) above at a later time.

[...]

12A.— Application of section 1 2 where accused appears.

(1) Where the [designated officer for] 2 the court has received such a notification as is mentioned in subsection (4) of section 12 above but the accused nevertheless appears before the court at the time and place appointed for the trial or adjourned trial, the court may, if he consents, proceed under subsection (5) of that section as if he were absent.

(2) Where the designated officer for the court has not received such a notification and the accused appears before the court at that time and place and informs the court that he desires to plead guilty, the court may, if he consents, proceed under section 12(5) above as if he were absent and the designated officer had received such a notification.

(3) For the purposes of subsections (1) and (2) above, subsections (6) to (11) of section 12 above shall apply with the modifications mentioned in subsection (4) or, as the case may be, subsection (5) below.

(4) The modifications for the purposes of subsection (1) above are that—

(a) before accepting the plea of guilty and convicting the accused under subsection (5) of section 12 above, the court shall afford the accused an opportunity to make an oral submission with a view to mitigation of sentence; and

(b) where he makes such a submission, subsection (7)(d) of that section shall not apply.

(5) The modifications for the purposes of subsection (2) above are that—

(a) subsection (6) of section 12 above shall apply as if any reference to the notification under subsection (4) of that section were a reference to the consent under subsection (2) above;

(b) subsection (7)(c) and (d) of that section shall not apply; and

(c) before accepting the plea of guilty and convicting the accused under subsection (5) of that section, the court shall afford the accused an opportunity to make an oral submission with a view to mitigation of sentence.

PLEA, TAKING OF

Where there is to be summary trial the court should proceed to take a plea (Magistrates' Courts Act 1980, s 9). If a defendant fails to plead then the court will proceed to summary trial (Magistrates' Courts Act 1980, s 9(2)). In essential case management, applying the Criminal Procedure Rules it is stated: 'At every hearing, (however early): Unless it has been done already, the court must take the defendant's plea [CrPR 3.8(2)(b)]. This obligation does not depend on the extent of advance information, service of evidence, disclosure of unused material, or the grant of legal aid.'

Where an unequivocal plea of guilty is entered the court may proceed to sentence. If there is a factual dispute that will materially affect sentence a *Newton* hearing may be held (see Part B Newton Hearing). **Change of plea:** See Part C Change of Plea.

Special rules apply to corporations:

Criminal Justice Act 1925, s 33

[...]

(3) On arraignment of a corporation, the corporation may, enter in writing by its representative a plea of guilty or not guilty, and if either the corporation does not appear by a representative or, though it does so appear, fails to enter as aforesaid any plea, the court shall order a plea of not guilty to be entered and the trial shall proceed as though the corporation had duly entered a plea of not guilty.

(4) Provision may be made by rules under the Indictments Act 1915 with respect to the service on any corporation charged with an indictable offence of any documents requiring to be served in connection with the proceedings.

[...]

(6) In this section the expression "representative" in relation to a corporation means a person duly appointed by the corporation to represent it for the purpose of doing any act or thing which the representative of a corporation is by this section authorized to do, but a person so appointed shall not, by virtue only of being so appointed, be qualified to act on behalf of the corporation before any court for any other purpose.

A representative for the purposes of this section need not be appointed under the seal of the corporation, and a statement in writing purporting to be signed by a managing director of the corporation, or by any person (by whatever name called) having, or being one of the persons having, the management of the affairs of the corporation, to the effect that the person named in the statement has been appointed as the representative of the corporation for the purposes of this section shall be admissible without further proof as prima facie evidence that that person has been so appointed.

PREVIOUS CONSISTENT STATEMENT

The effect of the Criminal Justice Act 2003, s 120 was considered in *Chinn* [2012] EWCA Crim 501, and the following propositions emerge:

(1) The wording of section 120(3) is a little difficult to follow. The opening words of it are "A statement made by a witness in a document-" . Then sub-paragraph (a) sets out the first condition–"which is used by him to refresh his memory while giving evidence" . The word "which" in that paragraph must refer back to "a document" , because it is the document which is used to refresh the witness's memory. Moreover, it is clear that this sub- paragraph contemplates that the document has to be used by the witness to refresh his memory while giving evidence in examination in chief, given the subsequent reference to cross-examination in sub-paragraph (b). Sub-paragraph (b) does not follow the old common law position in that it does not specifically stipulate that there must be cross-examination of a part of the document which was not used by the witness to refresh his memory. The sub-paragraph simply says "on which he is cross-examined" . The word "which" in that sub-paragraph must also refer to the document and, we think, to the whole document. Given the plain wording of that sub-paragraph there is no room for any implied limitation to a part of the document. We think that sub-paragraph (c) must be intended to reflect the common law rule that where there had been cross-examination then the document would become an exhibit in the trial; hence the words "in consequence [is] received in evidence in the proceedings" . Thus, consistently with sub-paragraphs (a) and (b), the word "which" in that sub-paragraph must also refer to the document as a whole. The last part of section 120(3) refers back to the first words of the sub-section. So the thing that "is admissible as evidence of any matter stated of which oral evidence by [the witness] would be admissible" must be the "statement made by the witness in a document...." . But if the document contains several "statements", plural, then those statements will be admissible as evidence of the matters stated in them of which oral evidence by the witness would be admissible, provided that those "statements" in the document were used by the witness to refresh his memory. The document itself will not be given to the jury, even though it is an exhibit, unless the court specifically permits it: see section 122.

(2) The above is consistent with the courts analysis of section 120(2) in Pashmfouroush [2006] EWCA Crim 2330.

(3) But what if a re-reading of a previous out of court document fails to refresh the witness's memory when giving oral evidence at the trial? It seems to us that in those circumstances section 120(3) cannot apply to make admissible as truth of the matters stated any or all of the statements made in the written document. This is for two principal reasons. First, section 120(3) contemplates that the witness does refresh his memory by examining the relevant statement in the out of court document. The effect of that is that his oral evidence about the facts of which he has refreshed his memory are admissible oral evidence in the normal way. The novelty in section 120(3) is that those statements in the document used to refresh the witness's evidence also become admissible evidence of the matters stated therein. Secondly, the situation where the witness has made a previous statement when the matters were fresh in his memory but he does not remember them at the time of the trial, even when he has attempted to refresh his memory, is dealt with specifically by section 120(4) and (6) . Those provisions contains particular conditions, which must be fulfilled before that previous statement becomes admissible as evidence of the matters stated. It would, in our view, subvert the statutory scheme if section 120(3) could be used to make a previous written statement admissible as evidence of the matters stated without requiring that the conditions set out in section 120(4) and (6) be fulfilled.

(4) We accept that the precise scope of section 120(5) is not entirely clear from the statutory wording. We do not like having to go back to the pre-existing common law to try and work

out the possible ambit of the sub-section, which is, after all, part of a new statutory code on hearsay evidence in criminal proceedings. But we accept that this exercise may assist in construing the sub-section. At common law a previous identification (particularly of the accused) was admissible as evidence of that fact at trial. Originally the rationale was that this could neutralise the argument that a witness only identified the accused because he was in the dock. The type of previous identification admissible was extended to out of court "photofits" by the complainant of the accused or a complainant's description that enabled a police artist to sketch the accused's likeness. But if a witness saw a lorry involved in an incident and noted its registration number, then gave the number to a policeman who had not seen the lorry, the evidence by the policeman of his note of the lorry's number plate was held by the Divisional Court to be inadmissible hearsay: see Jones v Metcalfe [1967] 1 WLR 1286 . We see some force in the argument that it cannot have been the intention of Parliament that section 120(5) could be so broad that it could be used to circumvent the safeguards set out in section 120(6) . However, in order to work out the precise scope of section 120(5) we think it is necessary to look more closely at its purpose. The previous statement of a witness will have identified or described a person, object or place that is connected with an alleged offence or other relevant event. A description of a person, object or place that is made in a vacuum is of no use in criminal proceedings. The description or identification has to be put in the relevant context because the person, or object or place is being described or identified for a particular purpose in the criminal proceedings. Thus the witness may say in the statement that it was Mr X who was at the ABC Bar on a certain day at a certain time. That statement identifies Mr X in this way because it is that identification at that place and time that is relevant; probably to an alleged offence at the ABC Bar at a particular time. The same must be true of an object and a place.

(5) Section 126(2) of the CJA provides that nothing in that Act prejudices the power of a court to exclude evidence under section 78 of the Police and Criminal Evidence Act 1984 ("PACE"). In certain circumstances, Eg where the only evidence of identification of an accused is that contained in a hearsay statement sought to be adduced by the prosecution under section 120(5) , the defence might argue that it should be excluded on the grounds that its admission would so adversely affect the fairness of the proceedings it should not be admitted.

(6) Further, in a suitable case, the judge has the power under section 125 of the CJA to stop a case after the close of the prosecution if he is satisfied that the case against the defendant is based solely or partly on a statement not made in oral evidence in the proceedings and that such evidence is "so unconvincing" that, considering its importance to the case against the defendant, his conviction of the offence would be unsafe.

(7) We do not accept that sections 120(4) and (6) were intended to apply only when the matters sought to be adduced are "routine". There is nothing in the statutory wording to limit the scope of the provisions in that way. Nor is that limitation referred to in the Law Commission's report. The admissibility of previous statements under section 120(4) and (6) will depend solely on whether the statutory criteria, as analysed above, have been fulfilled.

Criminal Justice Act 2003, s 120

(1) This section applies where a person (the witness) is called to give evidence in criminal proceedings.

(2) If a previous statement by the witness is admitted as evidence to rebut a suggestion that his oral evidence has been fabricated, that statement is admissible as evidence of any matter stated of which oral evidence by the witness would be admissible.

(3) A statement made by the witness in a document—

    (a) which is used by him to refresh his memory while giving evidence,

    (b) on which he is cross-examined, and

(c) which as a consequence is received in evidence in the proceedings,

is admissible as evidence of any matter stated of which oral evidence by him would be admissible.

(4) A previous statement by the witness is admissible as evidence of any matter stated of which oral evidence by him would be admissible, if—

(a) any of the following three conditions is satisfied, and

(b) while giving evidence the witness indicates that to the best of his belief he made the statement, and that to the best of his belief it states the truth.

(5) The first condition is that the statement identifies or describes a person, object or place.

(6) The second condition is that the statement was made by the witness when the matters stated were fresh in his memory but he does not remember them, and cannot reasonably be expected to remember them, well enough to give oral evidence of them in the proceedings.

(7) The third condition is that—

(a) the witness claims to be a person against whom an offence has been committed,

(b) the offence is one to which the proceedings relate,

(c) the statement consists of a complaint made by the witness (whether to a person in authority or not) about conduct which would, if proved, constitute the offence or part of the offence,

[...]

(e) the complaint was not made as a result of a threat or a promise, and

(f) before the statement is adduced the witness gives oral evidence in connection with its subject matter.

(8) For the purposes of subsection (7) the fact that the complaint was elicited (for example, by a leading question) is irrelevant unless a threat or a promise was involved.

PREVIOUS INCONSISTENT STATEMENT

Procedure: The fact of inconsistency should be put to the witness, first having been asked whether he is fact did make that statement. It is not necessary that the statement be shown to the witness (*Anderson* 21 Cr App R 178). The witness should be asked which account is true. If the earlier statement is denied it can be proved (section 4 of the 1865 Act). Due to section 119 of the 2003 Act the earlier statement is admitted as truth of its content. An advocate needs to take great care when putting a previous inconsistent statement to a witness in order to avoid the whole statement being exhibited, which is an undesirable outcome in most cases. Current testimony can and should be tested against what was said on earlier occasions but the testing needs to be done selectively, and with precision (*Hewins*, Unreported, 15 February 1999).

Criminal Procedure Act 1865, ss 4, 5

4. As to proof of contradictory statements of adverse witness.

If a witness, upon cross-examination as to a former statement made by him relative to the subject matter of the indictment or proceeding, and inconsistent with his present testimony, does not distinctly admit that he has made such statement, proof may be given that he did in fact make it; but before such proof can be given the circumstances of the supposed statement, sufficient to designate the particular occasion, must be mentioned to the witness, and he must be asked whether or not he has made such statement.

5. Cross-examinations as to previous statements in writing.

A witness may be cross-examined as to previous statements made by him in writing, or reduced into writing, relative to the subject matter of the indictment or proceeding, without such writing being shown to him; but if it is intended to contradict such witness by the writing, his attention must, before such contradictory proof can be given, be called to those parts of the writing which are to be used for the purpose of so contradicting him:

Provided always, that it shall be competent for the judge, at any time during the trial, to require the production of the writing for his inspection, and he may thereupon make such use of it for the purposes of the trial as he may think fit.

Criminal Justice Act 2003, s 119

(1) If in criminal proceedings a person gives oral evidence and—

    (a) he admits making a previous inconsistent statement, or

    (b) a previous inconsistent statement made by him is proved by virtue of section 3, 4 or 5 the Criminal Procedure Act 1865 (c. 18),

the statement is admissible as evidence of any matter stated of which oral evidence by him would be admissible.

(2) If in criminal proceedings evidence of an inconsistent statement by any person is given under section 124(2)(c), the statement is admissible as evidence of any matter stated in it of which oral evidence by that person would be admissible.

PROHIBITION ON CROSS-EXAMINATION, PREVIOUS SEXUAL HISTORY

Youth Justice and Criminal Evidence Act 1999, ss 41–43

41.— Restriction on evidence or questions about complainant's sexual history.

(1) If at a trial a person is charged with a sexual offence, then, except with the leave of the court—

    (a) no evidence may be adduced, and

    (b) no question may be asked in cross-examination,

by or on behalf of any accused at the trial, about any sexual behaviour of the complainant.

(2) The court may give leave in relation to any evidence or question only on an application made by or on behalf of an accused, and may not give such leave unless it is satisfied—

    (a) that subsection (3) or (5) applies, and

    (b) that a refusal of leave might have the result of rendering unsafe a conclusion of the jury or (as the case may be) the court on any relevant issue in the case.

(3) This subsection applies if the evidence or question relates to a relevant issue in the case and either—

    (a) that issue is not an issue of consent; or

    (b) it is an issue of consent and the sexual behaviour of the complainant to which the evidence or question relates is alleged to have taken place at or about the same time as the event which is the subject matter of the charge against the accused; or

    (c) it is an issue of consent and the sexual behaviour of the complainant to which the evidence or question relates is alleged to have been, in any respect, so similar—

        (i) to any sexual behaviour of the complainant which (according to evidence adduced or to be adduced by or on behalf of the accused) took place as part of the event which is the subject matter of the charge against the accused, or

        (ii) to any other sexual behaviour of the complainant which (according to such evidence) took place at or about the same time as that event,

that the similarity cannot reasonably be explained as a coincidence.

(4) For the purposes of subsection (3) no evidence or question shall be regarded as relating to a relevant issue in the case if it appears to the court to be reasonable to assume that the

purpose (or main purpose) for which it would be adduced or asked is to establish or elicit material for impugning the credibility of the complainant as a witness.

(5) This subsection applies if the evidence or question—

(a) relates to any evidence adduced by the prosecution about any sexual behaviour of the complainant; and

(b) in the opinion of the court, would go no further than is necessary to enable the evidence adduced by the prosecution to be rebutted or explained by or on behalf of the accused.

(6) For the purposes of subsections (3) and (5) the evidence or question must relate to a specific instance (or specific instances) of alleged sexual behaviour on the part of the complainant (and accordingly nothing in those subsections is capable of applying in relation to the evidence or question to the extent that it does not so relate).

(7) Where this section applies in relation to a trial by virtue of the fact that one or more of a number of persons charged in the proceedings is or are charged with a sexual offence—

(a) it shall cease to apply in relation to the trial if the prosecutor decides not to proceed with the case against that person or those persons in respect of that charge; but

(b) it shall not cease to do so in the event of that person or those persons pleading guilty to, or being convicted of, that charge.

(8) Nothing in this section authorises any evidence to be adduced or any question to be asked which cannot be adduced or asked apart from this section.

42.— Interpretation and application of section 41.

(1) In section 41—

(a) "relevant issue in the case" means any issue falling to be proved by the prosecution or defence in the trial of the accused;

(b) "issue of consent" means any issue whether the complainant in fact consented to the conduct constituting the offence with which the accused is charged (and accordingly does not include any issue as to the belief of the accused that the complainant so consented);

(c) "sexual behaviour" means any sexual behaviour or other sexual experience, whether or not involving any accused or other person, but excluding (except in section 41(3) (c)(i) and (5)(a)) anything alleged to have taken place as part of the event which is the subject matter of the charge against the accused; and

(d) subject to any order made under subsection (2), "sexual offence" shall be construed in accordance with section 62.

(2) The Secretary of State may by order make such provision as he considers appropriate for adding or removing, for the purposes of section 41, any offence to or from the offences which are sexual offences for the purposes of this Act by virtue of section 62.

(3) Section 41 applies in relation to the following proceedings as it applies to a trial, namely—

(c) the hearing of an application under paragraph 2(1) of Schedule 3 to the Crime and Disorder Act 1998 (application to dismiss charge by person sent for trial under section 51 or 51A of that Act),

(d) any hearing held, between conviction and sentencing, for the purpose of determining matters relevant to the court's decision as to how the accused is to be dealt with, and

(e) the hearing of an appeal,

and references (in section 41 or this section) to a person charged with an offence accordingly include a person convicted of an offence.

43.— Procedure on applications under section 41.

(1) An application for leave shall be heard in private and in the absence of the complainant.

In this section "leave" means leave under section 41.

(2) Where such an application has been determined, the court must state in open court (but in the absence of the jury, if there is one)—

(a) its reasons for giving, or refusing, leave, and

(b) if it gives leave, the extent to which evidence may be adduced or questions asked in pursuance of the leave,

and, if it is a magistrates' court, must cause those matters to be entered in the register of its proceedings.

(3) [Criminal Procedure Rules] 1 may make provision—

(a) requiring applications for leave to specify, in relation to each item of evidence or question to which they relate, particulars of the grounds on which it is asserted that leave should be given by virtue of subsection (3) or (5) of section 41;

(b) enabling the court to request a party to the proceedings to provide the court with information which it considers would assist it in determining an application for leave;

(c) for the manner in which confidential or sensitive information is to be treated in connection with such an application, and in particular as to its being disclosed to, or withheld from, parties to the proceedings.

PROHIBITION ON CROSS-EXAMINATION, WITNESSES BY DEFENDANT

Generally: The Youth Justice and Criminal Evidence Act 1999 contains a number of provisions which act to curtail cross-examination by the defendant personally. In such cases the court has power to appoint a legal representative for the purposes of cross-examination in cases where the accused is not otherwise represented. Detailed guidance to assist advocates is set out in Appendix 8. **Payment**: Appointed legal representatives are remunerated from central funds at a rate to be taxed (Prosecution of Offences Act 1985, s 19(3)(e)). **Criminal Procedure Rules**: Rule 31 applies.

Youth Justice and Criminal Evidence Act 1999, ss 34, 35, 36, 37, 38

34. Complainants in proceedings for sexual offences.

No person charged with a sexual offence may in any criminal proceedings cross-examine in person a witness who is the complainant, either—

(a) in connection with that offence, or

(b) in connection with any other offence (of whatever nature) with which that person is charged in the proceedings.

35.— Child complainants and other child witnesses.

(1) No person charged with an offence to which this section applies may in any criminal proceedings cross-examine in person a protected witness, either—

(a) in connection with that offence, or

(b) in connection with any other offence (of whatever nature) with which that person is charged in the proceedings.

(2) For the purposes of subsection (1) a "protected witness" is a witness who—

(a) either is the complainant or is alleged to have been a witness to the commission of the offence to which this section applies, and

(b) either is a child or falls to be cross-examined after giving evidence in chief (whether wholly or in part)—

(i) by means of a video recording made (for the purposes of section 27) at a time when the witness was a child, or

(ii)   in any other way at any such time.

(3)   The offences to which this section applies are—

(a) any offence under—

...

(iva) any of sections 33 to 36 of the Sexual Offences Act 1956,
(v)   the Protection of Children Act 1978, or
(vi) Part 1 of the Sexual Offences Act 2003 or any relevant superseded enactment;

(b) kidnapping, false imprisonment or an offence under section 1 or 2 of the Child Abduction Act 1984;
(c) any offence under section 1 of the Children and Young Persons Act 1933;
(d) any offence (not within any of the preceding paragraphs) which involves an assault on, or injury or a threat of injury to, any person.

(3A)   In subsection (3)(a)(vi) "relevant superseded enactment" means—

(a) any of sections 1 to 32 of the Sexual Offences Act 1956;
(b) the Indecency with Children Act 1960;
(c) the Sexual Offences Act 1967;
(d) section 54 of the Criminal Law Act 1977.

(4)   In this section "child" means—

(a) where the offence falls within subsection (3)(a), a person under the age of 18 ; or
(b) where the offence falls within subsection (3)(b), (c) or (d), a person under the age of 14.

(5)   For the purposes of this section "witness" includes a witness who is charged with an offence in the proceedings.

36.— Direction prohibiting accused from cross-examining particular witness

(1)   This section applies where, in a case where neither of sections 34 and 35 operates to prevent an accused in any criminal proceedings from cross-examining a witness in person—

(a) the prosecutor makes an application for the court to give a direction under this section in relation to the witness, or
(b) the court of its own motion raises the issue whether such a direction should be given.

(2)   If it appears to the court—

(a) that the quality of evidence given by the witness on cross-examination—

(i)   is likely to be diminished if the cross-examination (or further cross-examination) is conducted by the accused in person, and
(ii)   would be likely to be improved if a direction were given under this section, and

(b) that it would not be contrary to the interests of justice to give such a direction,

the court may give a direction prohibiting the accused from cross-examining (or further cross-examining) the witness in person.

(3)   In determining whether subsection (2)(a) applies in the case of a witness the court must have regard, in particular, to—

(a) any views expressed by the witness as to whether or not the witness is content to be cross-examined by the accused in person;
(b) the nature of the questions likely to be asked, having regard to the issues in the proceedings and the defence case advanced so far (if any);
(c) any behaviour on the part of the accused at any stage of the proceedings, both generally and in relation to the witness;
(d) any relationship (of whatever nature) between the witness and the accused;

(e) whether any person (other than the accused) is or has at any time been charged in the proceedings with a sexual offence or an offence to which section 35 applies, and (if so) whether section 34 or 35 operates or would have operated to prevent that person from cross-examining the witness in person;

(f) any direction under section 19 which the court has given, or proposes to give, in relation to the witness.

(4) For the purposes of this section—

(a) "witness", in relation to an accused, does not include any other person who is charged with an offence in the proceedings; and

(b) any reference to the quality of a witness's evidence shall be construed in accordance with section 16(5).

37.— Further provisions about directions under section 36.

(1) Subject to subsection (2), a direction has binding effect from the time it is made until the witness to whom it applies is discharged.

In this section "direction" means a direction under section 36.

(2) The court may discharge a direction if it appears to the court to be in the interests of justice to do so, and may do so either—

(a) on an application made by a party to the proceedings, if there has been a material change of circumstances since the relevant time, or

(b) of its own motion.

(3) In subsection (2) "the relevant time" means—

(a) the time when the direction was given, or

(b) if a previous application has been made under that subsection, the time when the application (or last application) was made.

(4) The court must state in open court its reasons for—

(a) giving, or

(b) refusing an application for, or for the discharge of, or

(c) discharging,

a direction and, if it is a magistrates' court, must cause them to be entered in the register of its proceedings.

(5) Criminal Procedure Rules may make provision—

(a) for uncontested applications to be determined by the court without a hearing;

(b) for preventing the renewal of an unsuccessful application for a direction except where there has been a material change of circumstances;

(c) for expert evidence to be given in connection with an application for, or for discharging, a direction;

(d) for the manner in which confidential or sensitive information is to be treated in connection with such an application and in particular as to its being disclosed to, or withheld from, a party to the proceedings.

38.— Defence representation for purposes of cross-examination.

(1) This section applies where an accused is prevented from cross-examining a witness in person by virtue of section 34, 35 or 36.

(2) Where it appears to the court that this section applies, it must—

(a) invite the accused to arrange for a legal representative to act for him for the purpose of cross-examining the witness; and

(b) require the accused to notify the court, by the end of such period as it may specify, whether a legal representative is to act for him for that purpose.

(3) If by the end of the period mentioned in subsection (2)(b) either—

    (a) the accused has notified the court that no legal representative is to act for him for the purpose of cross-examining the witness, or

    (b) no notification has been received by the court and it appears to the court that no legal representative is to so act,

the court must consider whether it is necessary in the interests of justice for the witness to be cross-examined by a legal representative appointed to represent the interests of the accused.

(4) If the court decides that it is necessary in the interests of justice for the witness to be so cross-examined, the court must appoint a qualified legal representative (chosen by the court) to cross-examine the witness in the interests of the accused.

(5) A person so appointed shall not be responsible to the accused.

(6) Criminal Procedure Rules may make provision—

    (a) as to the time when, and the manner in which, subsection (2) is to be complied with;

    (b) in connection with the appointment of a legal representative under subsection (4), and in particular for securing that a person so appointed is provided with evidence or other material relating to the proceedings.

(7) Criminal Procedure Rules made in pursuance of subsection (6)(b) may make provision for the application, with such modifications as are specified in the rules, of any of the provisions of—

    (a) Part I of the Criminal Procedure and Investigations Act 1996 (disclosure of material in connection with criminal proceedings), or

    (b) the Sexual Offences (Protected Material) Act 1997.

(8) For the purposes of this section—

    (a) any reference to cross-examination includes (in a case where a direction is given under section 36 after the accused has begun cross-examining the witness) a reference to further cross-examination; and

    (b) "qualified legal representative" means a legal representative who has a right of audience (within the meaning of the Courts and Legal Services Act 1990) in relation to the proceedings before the court.

PROHIBITION ON SPEAKING TO WITNESS DURING EVIDENCE

Unless leave of the court is sought a party should not speak to its own witness once evidence has started and prior to its conclusion. If leave is granted the advocate should make clear the extent of the proposed discussion and that he wishes to retain any right he might have to re-examine that witness (*Reading and West Berkshire Stipendiary Magistrates. Ex p Dyas* (2000) 164 JP 117).

REBUTTAL, EVIDENCE IN

Rebuttal evidence ought only to be admitted where the issue to be addressed was not properly foreseen (which is a matter for the court to determine). In *Milliken* (1969) 53 Cr App R 330 the court held:

    "Where evidence sought to be introduced in rebuttal is itself evidence probative of the guilt of the defendant and when it is reasonably foreseeable by the prosecution that some gap in the proof of guilt needs to be filled by evidence called for the prosecution, then generally speaking the court is likely to rule against the closing of any such gap by rebuttal evidence; but ... the evidence here was not evidence in any sense probative of guilt of the defendant, since it really consisted of no more than the denials of the accusations of conspiracy and concoction of the charge made by the defendant in his own evidence ... the evidence was to disprove the truth of the defence which itself consisted of an affirmative attack on the credibility and honesty of the police officer."

RE-EXAMINATION

Re-examination is restricted to questioning on matters relating only to evidence raised in cross-examination (*The Queen's Case* (1820) 2 B & B 284). A court has a general discretion to permit new matters to be put where the interests of justice require it.

RE-OPENING CASE

Evidence should be called before each party's case is concluded (*Pilcher* 60 Cr App R 1). Recent authorities have shown a general approval of additional evidence being called in order to prevent so called 'ambush defences' or cases falling on technicalities. In *Malcolm v Director of Public Prosecutions* [2007] EWHC 363 (Admin) the court held:

"The obligation of the prosecution to prove its case in its entirety before closing its case, and certainly before end of the final speech for the defence, [has] an anachronistic, and obsolete, ring. Criminal trials are no longer to be treated as a game, in which each move is final and any omission by the prosecution leads to its failure. It is the duty of the defence to make its defence and the issues it raises clear to the prosecution and to the court at an early stage. That duty is implicit in rule 3.3 of the Criminal Procedure Rules, which requires the parties actively to assist the exercise by the court of its case management powers, the exercise of which requires early identification of the real issues. Even in a relatively straightforward trial such as the present, in the magistrates' court (where there is not yet any requirement of a defence statement or a pre-trial review), it is the duty of the defence to make the real issues clear at the latest before the prosecution closes its case. In *R v Pydar Justices ex p Foster* [1995] 160 JP 87 at 90B Curtis J. commented on the submission that a defending advocate was entitled to "keep his powder dry". He said: "Without any doubt whatsoever, it is the duty of a defending advocate properly to lay the ground for a submission, either by cross examination or, if appropriate, by calling evidence.""

In *R (CPS) v Norwich Magistrates' Court* [2011] EWHC 82 (Admin) the court made clear that the power to reopen did not depend on any issue of 'ambush' or gamesmanship and extends to cases where (as in this case for example) identification as an issue in the case was not made clear:

"If the defence was going to take a positive point on identification, it was incumbent on it to flag the point at an early stage, not to wait until the close of the prosecution case before raising it for the first time in a submission of no case. It should have been expressed during the case management process and included in terms in the trial information form. That is all the more obvious in the environment in which the parties now operate by reference to the Criminal Procedure Rules and the overriding objective. Even if there had been an omission to deal with it at that earlier stage, it ought to have been raised very clearly when the prosecuting advocate opened the case by telling the magistrates that there was no issue over identification. It was not appropriate, as it seems to me, simply to sit tight and to raise it at the end of the prosecution case by way of a submission of no case."

RE-OPENING CONVICTION

Section 142 MCA 1980 relates to criminal proceedings and has no application to other areas of magistrates' court jurisdiction such as liability orders (*Liverpool City Council v Plemora Distribution Limited* [2002] EWHC 2467 (Admin)) and detention and forfeiture in relation to proceeds of crime. Further, the court enjoys no common law jurisdiction to reopen civil matters such as an anti-social behaviour order (*Samuda v Birmingham Justices* [2008] EWHC 205 (Admin)). Persons made subject to a hospital order under section 37(3) of the Mental Health Act 1983 fall within the definition of 'offender', and a person can use section 142 to reopen a hearing determining the issue under the Mental Health Act (*R (Bartram) v Southend Magistrates' Court* [2004] EWHC 2691 (Admin)). An order to commit an offender to prison for non-satisfaction of a confiscation order made under the Proceeds of Crime Act 2002 in the Crown Court is capable of being reopened.

The court has power to revisit the issue of a warrant following nonpayment of fines. A court does not have the power to rescind a costs order made in favour of a defendant who was not convicted as the section related only to orders post conviction (*Coles v East Penwith Justices* The Times, 27 July 1998).

The nature of the remedy afforded under this Act is akin to a 'slip rule', allowing a court to rectify a clear mistake or injustice. An applicant who had entered an unequivocal plea of guilty cannot apply to reopen plea under this section (*R v Croydon Youth Court, ex p Director of Public Prosecutions* [1997] 2 Cr App R 411). Section 142 should not be used to advance new arguments, nor should it be used as an 'appeal' mechanism against an earlier decision (*Zykin v Crown Prosecution Service* [2009] EWHC 1469 (Admin)). Applications based on a change of law between conviction and application should not be entertained under normal principles of finality of judgment.

A prosecutor cannot apply to reopen proceedings that have previously been withdrawn (*R (Green and Green Scaffolding Ltd) v Staines Magistrates' Court* (2008) 172 JP 353).

Applications: An application may be made orally or in writing; the applicant does not have to attend the hearing. All parties must be given notice of the application and be heard if they so wish. Section 142(1A) and (2A) set out the instances when a remedy under this provision is denied on account of an alternative avenue of appeal having been taken.

There is no statutory time limit on reopening but the former 28-day rule should act as a salutary guideline. Applications made much beyond this date might be properly refused on interests of justice grounds as 'Delay in matters of this sort is always harmful, memories fade, records may be lost and the essence of doing justice is that it should be done expeditiously' (*R v Ealing Magistrates' Court, ex p Sahota* The Times, 9 December 1997). It is not, however, a decisive factor. It is not enough for the magistrates simply to say that the length of time is such that it is no longer proper to open the case under section 142. More substantial reasoning than that has to be given, so that the applicant (and any court on appeal) can understand why it is no longer proper to deal with the matter.

Applications can be made by both defence and prosecution, but the exercise of such discretion in favour of a prosecutor will be rare, and can never extend to the overturning of an acquittal. A prosecutor could properly make an application to reopen where the court had erroneously failed to impose penalty points or some other appropriate order. Similarly, if the court had been unaware of factors relevant to sentence it could be invited to reopen sentence, even if that meant a risk that it would be increased. However, if it is appropriate for the powers under section 142 to be used to increase sentence, then the power must be exercised very speedily (*R (Holme) v Liverpool Magistrates' Court* [2004] EWHC 3131 (Admin); in this case the court declined to allow the prosecution to exercise the power. Advocates facing this type of application should refer to the full judgment).

A defendant who had been convicted in absence can properly attempt to reopen under this section. Culpability on the part of the offender is relevant to whether it is in the interests of justice to reopen, but it is not determinative. It will normally be in the interests of justice for a defendant to be able to defend himself, and unless the evidence indicates that his absence from trial is deliberate and voluntary, a rehearing would normally be the appropriate course (*R (Morsby) v*

Tower Bridge Magistrates' Court [2007] EWHC 2766 (Admin)). Any inconvenience to the court in allowing a reopening can never outweigh the interests of justice (*R (Blick) v Doncaster Magistrates' Court* (2008) 172 JP 651).

Interests of justice: Justices are given wide discretion in determining what are relevant factors in relation to interests of justice, but decisions must be based on sound judicial reasoning. A defendant's late arrival at court was held not to be a proper ground, in itself, to refuse a rehearing (*R v Camber-well Green Magistrates' Court, ex p Ibrahim* (1984) 148 JP 400). Factors a court ought to consider include:

- why the convicted person did not appear at the original trial (if that was the case);
- timeliness of the application;
- reason for any delay;
- importance of the decision being questioned—note that the importance to all parties, including defendant, prosecution, and other interested parties (such as victim), should be assessed;
- inconvenience and prejudice caused to opposing parties;
- whether a more appropriate appeal remedy is available. It will not be appropriate to allow a reopening where a defendant is denied a right of appeal due to an unequivocal guilty plea (*R v Croydon Youth Court, ex p Director of Public Prosecutions* [1997] 2 Cr App R 411).

In addition, the court must always consider rule 1 of the Criminal Procedure Rules and the overriding objective.

Effect of reopening: A conviction will be set aside, as will any sentence or ancillary orders flowing from it. The matter is treated as adjourned for trial. Justices who sat on the original hearing, or the hearing to reopen, cannot sit on the adjourned trial. The prosecution retain the right to offer no evidence and the court lacks power to insist that a prosecutor proceeds with the case (*R (Rhodes-Presley) v South Worcestershire Magistrates' Court* [2008] EWHC 2700 (Admin)).

If a sentence or order is reopened, the court may vary or rescind the original finding and substitute any other lawful sentence or order that would have been available to the court at the original hearing. The new orders take effect from the date of the old order unless the court directs otherwise. A court must be careful not to offend against any legitimate expectation given to the offender (*Jane v Broome* The Times, 2 November 1988).

Magistrates' Courts Act 1980, s 142

(1) A magistrates' court may vary or rescind a sentence or other order imposed or made by it when dealing with an offender if it appears to the court to be in the interests of justice to do so, and it is hereby declared that this power extends to replacing a sentence or order which for any reason appears to be invalid by another which the court has power to impose or make.

(1A) The power conferred on a magistrates' court by subsection (1) above shall not be exercisable in relation to any sentence or order imposed or made by it when dealing with an offender if—

    (a) the Crown Court has determined an appeal against—

        (i) that sentence or order;

        (ii) the conviction in respect of which that sentence or order was imposed or made; or

        (iii) any other sentence or order imposed or made by the magistrates' court when dealing with the offender in respect of that conviction (including a sentence or order replaced by that sentence or order); or

    (b) the High Court has determined a case stated for the opinion of that court on any question arising in any proceeding leading to or resulting from the imposition or making of the sentence or order.

(2) Where a person is convicted by a magistrates' court and it subsequently appears to the court that it would be in the interests of justice that the case should be heard again by different justices, the court may so direct.

(2A) The power conferred on a magistrates' court by subsection (2) above shall not be exercisable in relation to a conviction if—

(a) the Crown Court has determined an appeal against—
   (i) the conviction; or
   (ii) any sentence or order imposed or made by the magistrates' court when dealing with the offender in respect of the conviction; or
(b) the High Court has determined a case stated for the opinion of that court on any question arising in any proceeding leading to or resulting from the conviction.

(3) Where a court gives a direction under subsection (2) above—

(a) the conviction and any sentence or other order imposed or made in consequence thereof shall be of no effect; and
(b) section 10(4) above shall apply as if the trial of the person in question had been adjourned.

(4) [repealed]

(5) Where a sentence or order is varied under subsection (1) above, the sentence or other order, as so varied, shall take effect from the beginning of the day on which it was originally imposed or made, unless the court otherwise directs.

REFRESHING MEMORY

In *Chinn* [2012] EWCA Crim 501 the court held:

"Section 139 reformulates the circumstances in which a person giving oral evidence in criminal proceedings about any matter may refresh his memory of that matter from a document made or verified by him at a previous time. It is generally accepted that the statutory provisions enlarge the previous common law rules".

In *Mangena* [2009] EWCA Crim 2535 it was held that it is not necessary that the witness '*has first stumbled*' on his evidence.

Criminal Justice Act 2003, s 139

(1) A person giving oral evidence in criminal proceedings about any matter may, at any stage in the course of doing so, refresh his memory of it from a document made or verified by him at an earlier time if—

(a) he states in his oral evidence that the document records his recollection of the matter at that earlier time, and
(b) his recollection of the matter is likely to have been significantly better at that time than it is at the time of his oral evidence.

(2) Where—

(a) a person giving oral evidence in criminal proceedings about any matter has previously given an oral account, of which a sound recording was made, and he states in that evidence that the account represented his recollection of the matter at that time,
(b) his recollection of the matter is likely to have been significantly better at the time of the previous account than it is at the time of his oral evidence, and
(c) a transcript has been made of the sound recording,

he may, at any stage in the course of giving his evidence, refresh his memory of the matter from that transcript.

SPECIAL MEASURES

Relevant offence: Relevant offences for the purposes of section 17(5) are listed in Appendix 9.
General principles: Individual measures that are available are outlined in separate sections in this part. The Act, despite excluding the defendant from many special measures protections, is compliant with the ECHR (*R (S) v Waltham Forest Youth Court* [2004] EWHC 715 (Admin); *R (D) v Camberwell Green Youth Court* [2005] UKHL 4).

Overview of special measures that are available in the magistrates' court:

	Section 16 witnesses (children and vulnerable adults)	Section 17 witnesses (intimidated/ fear or distress)
Section 23 screening witness from accused	Full availability	Full availability
Section 24 evidence via live link	Full availability	Full availability
Section 25 evidence given in private	Full availability	Full availability
Section 26 removal of wigs/gowns	Not applicable	Not applicable
Section 27 video recorded evidence in chief	Full availability	Not available
Section 28 video recorded cross-examination and re-examination	Not available	Not available
Section 29 examination through an intermediary	Full availability	Not applicable
Section 30 aids to communication	Full availability	Not applicable.

Youth Justice and Criminal Evidence Act 1999, ss 16–23

16.— Witnesses eligible for assistance on grounds of age or incapacity.

(1) For the purposes of this Chapter a witness in criminal proceedings (other than the accused) is eligible for assistance by virtue of this section—

    (a) if under the age of 18 at the time of the hearing; or

    (b) if the court considers that the quality of evidence given by the witness is likely to be diminished by reason of any circumstances falling within subsection (2).

(2) The circumstances falling within this subsection are—

    (a) that the witness—

        (i) suffers from mental disorder within the meaning of the Mental Health Act 1983, or

        (ii) otherwise has a significant impairment of intelligence and social functioning;

    (b) that the witness has a physical disability or is suffering from a physical disorder.

(3) In subsection (1)(a) "the time of the hearing", in relation to a witness, means the time when it falls to the court to make a determination for the purposes of section 19(2) in relation to the witness.

(4) In determining whether a witness falls within subsection (1)(b) the court must consider any views expressed by the witness.

(5) In this Chapter references to the quality of a witness's evidence are to its quality in terms of completeness, coherence and accuracy; and for this purpose "coherence" refers to a witness's ability in giving evidence to give answers which address the questions put to the witness and can be understood both individually and collectively.

17.— Witnesses eligible for assistance on grounds of fear or distress about testifying.

(1) For the purposes of this Chapter a witness in criminal proceedings (other than the accused) is eligible for assistance by virtue of this subsection if the court is satisfied that the quality of evidence given by the witness is likely to be diminished by reason of fear or distress on the part of the witness in connection with testifying in the proceedings.

(2) In determining whether a witness falls within subsection (1) the court must take into account, in particular—

    (a) the nature and alleged circumstances of the offence to which the proceedings relate;

    (b) the age of the witness;

    (c) such of the following matters as appear to the court to be relevant, namely—

        (i) the social and cultural background and ethnic origins of the witness,

        (ii) the domestic and employment circumstances of the witness, and

        (iii) any religious beliefs or political opinions of the witness;

    (d) any behaviour towards the witness on the part of—

        (i) the accused,

        (ii) members of the family or associates of the accused, or

        (iii) any other person who is likely to be an accused or a witness in the proceedings.

(3) In determining that question the court must in addition consider any views expressed by the witness.

(4) Where the complainant in respect of a sexual offence is a witness in proceedings relating to that offence (or to that offence and any other offences), the witness is eligible for assistance in relation to those proceedings by virtue of this subsection unless the witness has informed the court of the witness' wish not to be so eligible by virtue of this subsection.

(5) A witness in proceedings relating to a relevant offence (or to a relevant offence and any other offences) is eligible for assistance in relation to those proceedings by virtue of this subsection unless the witness has informed the court of the witness's wish not to be so eligible by virtue of this subsection.

(6) For the purposes of subsection (5) an offence is a relevant offence if it is an offence described in Schedule 1A.

(7) The Secretary of State may by order amend Schedule 1A.

18.— Special measures available to eligible witnesses

(1) For the purposes of this Chapter—

    (a) the provision which may be made by a special measures direction by virtue of each of sections 23 to 30 is a special measure available in relation to a witness eligible for assistance by virtue of section 16; and

    (b) the provision which may be made by such a direction by virtue of each of sections 23 to 28 is a special measure available in relation to a witness eligible for assistance by virtue of section 17;

but this subsection has effect subject to subsection (2).

(2) Where (apart from this subsection) a special measure would, in accordance with subsection (1)(a) or (b), be available in relation to a witness in any proceedings, it shall not be taken by a court to be available in relation to the witness unless—

    (a) the court has been notified by the Secretary of State that relevant arrangements may be made available in the area in which it appears to the court that the proceedings will take place, and

    (b) the notice has not been withdrawn.

(3) In subsection (2) "relevant arrangements" means arrangements for implementing the measure in question which cover the witness and the proceedings in question.

(4) The withdrawal of a notice under that subsection relating to a special measure shall not affect the availability of that measure in relation to a witness if a special measures direction providing for that measure to apply to the witness's evidence has been made by the court before the notice is withdrawn.

(5) The Secretary of State may by order make such amendments of this Chapter as he considers appropriate for altering the special measures which, in accordance with subsection (1)(a) or (b), are available in relation to a witness eligible for assistance by virtue of section 16 or (as the case may be) section 17, whether—

    (a) by modifying the provisions relating to any measure for the time being available in relation to such a witness,

    (b) by the addition—

        (i) (with or without modifications) of any measure which is for the time being available in relation to a witness eligible for assistance by virtue of the other of those sections, or

        (ii) of any new measure, or

    (c) by the removal of any measure.

19.— Special measures direction relating to eligible witness.

(1) This section applies where in any criminal proceedings—

    (a) a party to the proceedings makes an application for the court to give a direction under this section in relation to a witness in the proceedings other than the accused, or

    (b) the court of its own motion raises the issue whether such a direction should be given.

(2) Where the court determines that the witness is eligible for assistance by virtue of section 16 or 17, the court must then—

    (a) determine whether any of the special measures available in relation to the witness (or any combination of them) would, in its opinion, be likely to improve the quality of evidence given by the witness; and

    (b) if so—

        (i) determine which of those measures (or combination of them) would, in its opinion, be likely to maximise so far as practicable the quality of such evidence; and

        (ii) give a direction under this section providing for the measure or measures so determined to apply to evidence given by the witness.

(3) In determining for the purposes of this Chapter whether any special measure or measures would or would not be likely to improve, or to maximise so far as practicable, the quality of evidence given by the witness, the court must consider all the circumstances of the case, including in particular—

    (a) any views expressed by the witness; and

    (b) whether the measure or measures might tend to inhibit such evidence being effectively tested by a party to the proceedings.

(4) A special measures direction must specify particulars of the provision made by the direction in respect of each special measure which is to apply to the witness's evidence.

(5) In this Chapter "special measures direction" means a direction under this section.

(6) Nothing in this Chapter is to be regarded as affecting any power of a court to make an order or give leave of any description (in the exercise of its inherent jurisdiction or otherwise)—

    (a) in relation to a witness who is not an eligible witness, or

    (b) in relation to an eligible witness where (as, for example, in a case where a foreign language interpreter is to be provided) the order is made or the leave is given otherwise than by reason of the fact that the witness is an eligible witness.

20.— Further provisions about directions: general.

(1) Subject to subsection (2) and section 21(8), a special measures direction has binding effect from the time it is made until the proceedings for the purposes of which it is made are either—

(a) determined (by acquittal, conviction or otherwise), or

(b) abandoned,

in relation to the accused or (if there is more than one) in relation to each of the accused.

(2) The court may discharge or vary (or further vary) a special measures direction if it appears to the court to be in the interests of justice to do so, and may do so either—

(a) on an application made by a party to the proceedings, if there has been a material change of circumstances since the relevant time, or

(b) of its own motion.

(3) In subsection (2) "the relevant time" means —

(a) the time when the direction was given, or

(b) if a previous application has been made under that subsection, the time when the application (or last application) was made.

(4) Nothing in section 24(2) and (3), 27(4) to (7) or 28(4) to (6) is to be regarded as affecting the power of the court to vary or discharge a special measures direction under subsection (2).

(5) The court must state in open court its reasons for—

(a) giving or varying,

(b) refusing an application for, or for the variation or discharge of, or

(c) discharging,

a special measures direction and, if it is a magistrates' court, must cause them to be entered in the register of its proceedings.

(6) Criminal Procedure Rules may make provision—

(a) for uncontested applications to be determined by the court without a hearing;

(b) for preventing the renewal of an unsuccessful application for a special measures direction except where there has been a material change of circumstances;

(c) for expert evidence to be given in connection with an application for, or for varying or discharging, such a direction;

(d) for the manner in which confidential or sensitive information is to be treated in connection with such an application and in particular as to its being disclosed to, or withheld from, a party to the proceedings.

21.— Special provisions relating to child witnesses.

(1) For the purposes of this section—

(a) a witness in criminal proceedings is a "child witness" if he is an eligible witness by reason of section 16(1)(a) (whether or not he is an eligible witness by reason of any other provision of section 16 or 17); and

[...]

(c) a "relevant recording", in relation to a child witness, is a video recording of an interview of the witness made with a view to its admission as evidence in chief of the witness.

(2) Where the court, in making a determination for the purposes of section 19(2), determines that a witness in criminal proceedings is a child witness, the court must—

(a) first have regard to subsections (3) to (4C) below; and

(b) then have regard to section 19(2);

and for the purposes of section 19(2), as it then applies to the witness, any special measures required to be applied in relation to him by virtue of this section shall be treated as if they were measures determined by the court, pursuant to section 19(2)(a) and (b)(i), to be ones that (whether on their own or with any other special measures) would be likely to maximise, so far as practicable, the quality of his evidence.

(3) The primary rule in the case of a child witness is that the court must give a special measures direction in relation to the witness which complies with the following requirements—

(a) it must provide for any relevant recording to be admitted under section 27 (video recorded evidence in chief); and

(b) it must provide for any evidence given by the witness in the proceedings which is not given by means of a video recording (whether in chief or otherwise) to be given by means of a live link in accordance with section 24.

(4) The primary rule is subject to the following limitations—

(a) the requirement contained in subsection (3)(a) or (b) has effect subject to the availability (within the meaning of section 18(2)) of the special measure in question in relation to the witness;

(b) the requirement contained in subsection (3)(a) also has effect subject to section 27(2);

(ba) if the witness informs the court of the witness's wish that the rule should not apply or should apply only in part, the rule does not apply to the extent that the court is satisfied that not complying with the rule would not diminish the quality of the witness's evidence; and

(c) the rule does not apply to the extent that the court is satisfied that compliance with it would not be likely to maximise the quality of the witness's evidence so far as practicable (whether because the application to that evidence of one or more other special measures available in relation to the witness would have that result or for any other reason).

(4A) Where as a consequence of all or part of the primary rule being disapplied under subsection (4)(ba) a witness's evidence or any part of it would fall to be given as testimony in court, the court must give a special measures direction making such provision as is described in section 23 for the evidence or that part of it.

(4B) The requirement in subsection (4A) is subject to the following limitations—

(a) if the witness informs the court of the witness's wish that the requirement in subsection (4A) should not apply, the requirement does not apply to the extent that the court is satisfied that not complying with it would not diminish the quality of the witness's evidence; and

(b) the requirement does not apply to the extent that the court is satisfied that making such a provision would not be likely to maximise the quality of the witness's evidence so far as practicable (whether because the application to that evidence of one or more other special measures available in relation to the witness would have that result or for any other reason).

(4C) In making a decision under subsection (4)(ba) or (4B)(a), the court must take into account the following factors (and any others it considers relevant)—

(a) the age and maturity of the witness;

(b) the ability of the witness to understand the consequences of giving evidence otherwise than in accordance with the requirements in subsection (3) or (as the case may be) in accordance with the requirement in subsection (4A);

(c) the relationship (if any) between the witness and the accused;

(d) the witness's social and cultural background and ethnic origins;

(e) the nature and alleged circumstances of the offence to which the proceedings relate.

[...]

(8) Where a special measures direction is given in relation to a child witness who is an eligible witness by reason only of section 16(1)(a), then—

(a) subject to subsection (9) below, and

(b) except where the witness has already begun to give evidence in the proceedings,

the direction shall cease to have effect at the time when the witness attains the age of 18.

(9) Where a special measures direction is given in relation to a child witness who is an eligible witness by reason only of section 16(1)(a) and—

(a) the direction provides—

(i) for any relevant recording to be admitted under section 27 as evidence in chief of the witness, or

(ii) for the special measure available under section 28 to apply in relation to the witness, and

(b) if it provides for that special measure to so apply, the witness is still under the age of 18 when the video recording is made for the purposes of section 28,

then, so far as it provides as mentioned in paragraph (a)(i) or (ii) above, the direction shall continue to have effect in accordance with section 20(1) even though the witness subsequently attains that age.

22.— Extension of provisions of section 21 to certain witnesses over 18.

(1) For the purposes of this section—

(a) a witness in criminal proceedings (other than the accused) is a "qualifying witness" if he—

(i) is not an eligible witness at the time of the hearing (as defined by section 16(3)), but

(ii) was under the age of [18] 2 when a relevant recording was made; and

[...]

(c) a "relevant recording", in relation to a witness, is a video recording of an interview of the witness made with a view to its admission as evidence in chief of the witness.

(2) Subsections (2) to (4) and (4C) of section 21, so far as relating to the giving of a direction complying with the requirement contained in section 21(3)(a), apply to a qualifying witness in respect of the relevant recording as they apply to a child witness (within the meaning of that section).

22A Special provisions relating to sexual offences

(1) This section applies where in criminal proceedings relating to a sexual offence (or to a sexual offence and other offences) the complainant in respect of that offence is a witness in the proceedings.

(2) This section does not apply if the place of trial is a magistrates' court.

(3) This section does not apply if the complainant is an eligible witness by reason of section 16(1)(a) (whether or not the complainant is an eligible witness by reason of any other provision of section 16 or 17).

(4) If a party to the proceedings makes an application under section 19(1)(a) for a special measures direction in relation to the complainant, the party may request that the direction provide for any relevant recording to be admitted under section 27 (video recorded evidence in chief).

(5) Subsection (6) applies if—

(a) a party to the proceedings makes a request under subsection (4) with respect to the complainant, and

(b) the court determines for the purposes of section 19(2) that the complainant is eligible for assistance by virtue of section 16(1)(b) or 17.

(6)   The court must—

(a) first have regard to subsections (7) to (9); and

(b) then have regard to section 19(2);

and for the purposes of section 19(2), as it then applies to the complainant, any special measure required to be applied in relation to the complainant by virtue of this section is to be treated as if it were a measure determined by the court, pursuant to section 19(2)(a) and (b)(i), to be one that (whether on its own or with any other special measures) would be likely to maximise, so far as practicable, the quality of the complainant's evidence.

(7)   The court must give a special measures direction in relation to the complainant that provides for any relevant recording to be admitted under section 27.

(8)   The requirement in subsection (7) has effect subject to section 27(2).

(9)   The requirement in subsection (7) does not apply to the extent that the court is satisfied that compliance with it would not be likely to maximise the quality of the complainant's evidence so far as practicable (whether because the application to that evidence of one or more other special measures available in relation to the complainant would have that result or for any other reason).

(10) In this section "relevant recording", in relation to a complainant, is a video recording of an interview of the complainant made with a view to its admission as the evidence in chief of the complainant.

23.— Screening witness from accused.

(1)   A special measures direction may provide for the witness, while giving testimony or being sworn in court, to be prevented by means of a screen or other arrangement from seeing the accused.

(2)   But the screen or other arrangement must not prevent the witness from being able to see, and to be seen by—

(a) the judge or justices (or both) and the jury (if there is one);

(b) legal representatives acting in the proceedings; and

(c) any interpreter or other person appointed (in pursuance of the direction or otherwise) to assist the witness.

(3)   Where two or more legal representatives are acting for a party to the proceedings, subsection (2)(b) is to be regarded as satisfied in relation to those representatives if the witness is able at all material times to see and be seen by at least one of them.

SUBMISSION OF NO CASE TO ANSWER

Alternative charge: If conviction on an alternative charge is possible (for which see: Verdicts And Alternative Verdicts) a court can proceed to consider guilt on that charge having found no case to answer in relation to the substantive matter (*R (H) v Liverpool Youth Court* [2001] Crim LR 487). **Test:** In *R v Galbraith* (1981) 73 Cr App R 124 the court laid down the following test:

(1)   If there is no evidence that the crime alleged has been committed by the defendant, there is no difficulty. The judge will of course stop the case.

(2)   The difficulty arises where there is some evidence but it is of a tenuous character, for example because of inherent weakness or vagueness or because it is inconsistent with other evidence. (a) Where the judge comes to the conclusion that the prosecution evidence, taken at its highest, is such that a jury properly directed could not properly

convict upon it, it is his duty, upon a submission being made, to stop the case. (b) Where however the prosecution evidence is such that its strength or weakness depends on the view to be taken of a witness's reliability, or other matters which are generally speaking within the province of the jury and where on one possible view of the facts there is evidence upon which a jury could properly come to the conclusion that the defendant is guilty, then the judge should allow the matter to be tried by the jury. It follows that we think the second of the two schools of thought is to be preferred.

SUMMARY TRIAL, SEQUENCE OF EVENTS

Criminal Procedure Rules 2012, r 37 provides:

37.3.—(1) This rule applies—

    (a) if the defendant has—
        (i)   entered a plea of not guilty, or
        (ii) not entered a plea; or
    (b) if, in either case, it appears to the court that there may be grounds for making a hospital order without convicting the defendant.

(2) If a not guilty plea was taken on a previous occasion, the Justice legal adviser or the court must ask the defendant to confirm that plea.

(3) In the following sequence—

    (a) the prosecutor may summarise the prosecution case, identifying the relevant law and facts;
    (b) the prosecutor must introduce the evidence on which the prosecution case relies;
    (c) at the conclusion of the prosecution case, on the defendant's application or on its own initiative, the court—
        (i)   may acquit on the ground that the prosecution evidence is insufficient for any reasonable court properly to convict, but
        (ii) must not do so unless the prosecutor has had an opportunity to make representations;
    (d) the Justice legal adviser or the court must explain, in terms the defendant can understand (with help, if necessary)—
        (i)   the right to give evidence, and
        (ii) the potential effect of not doing so at all, or of refusing to answer a question while doing so;
    (e) the defendant may introduce evidence;
    (f) a party may introduce further evidence if it is then admissible (for example, because it is in rebuttal of evidence already introduced);
    (g) the prosecutor may make final representations in support of the prosecution case, where—
        (i)   the defendant is represented by a legal representative, or
        (ii) whether represented or not, the defendant has introduced evidence other than his or her own; and
    (h) the defendant may make final representations in support of the defence case.

(4) Where a party wants to introduce evidence or make representations after that party's opportunity to do so under paragraph (3), the court—

    (a) may refuse to receive any such evidence or representations; and
    (b) must not receive any such evidence or representations after it has announced its verdict.

(5) If the court—

    (a) convicts the defendant; or

    (b) makes a hospital order instead of doing so,

it must give sufficient reasons to explain its decision.

    (6) If the court acquits the defendant, it may—

        (a) give an explanation of its decision; and

        (b) exercise any power it has to make—

           (i)   a civil behaviour order,

           (ii)   a costs order.

[Note. See section 9 of the Magistrates' Courts Act 1980.

Under section 37(3) of the Mental Health Act 1983(2), if the court is satisfied that the defendant did the act or made the omission alleged, then it may make a hospital order without convicting the defendant.

Under section 35 of the Criminal Justice and Public Order Act 1994, the court may draw such inferences as appear proper from a defendant's failure to give evidence, or refusal without good cause to answer a question while doing so. The procedure set out in rule 37.3(3)(d) is prescribed by that section.

The admissibility of evidence that a party introduces is governed by rules of evidence.

Section 2 of the Criminal Procedure Act 1865(4) and section 3 of the Criminal Evidence Act 1898(5) restrict the circumstances in which the prosecutor may make final representations without the court's permission.

See rule 37.10 for the procedure if the court convicts the defendant.

Part 50 contains rules about civil behaviour orders after verdict or finding.]

SWEARING OF A WITNESS

All witnesses aged 14 and over must be sworn before they are permitted to give evidence. In rare circumstances unsworn evidence can be received. In *Kemble* [1990] 91 Cr App R 178 the appellant appealed on the ground that the witness (a Muslim) has elected to be sworn using the New Testament as opposed to the Koran. The court held:

> "The question of whether the administration of an oath is lawful does not depend upon what may be the considerable intricacies of the particular religion which is adhered to by the witness. It concerns two matters and two matters only in our judgment. First of all, is the oath an oath which appears to the court to be binding on the conscience of the witness? And if so, secondly, and most importantly, is it an oath which the witness himself considers to be binding upon his conscience."

Youth Justice and Criminal Evidence Act 1999, ss 55–57

55.— Determining whether witness to be sworn.

    (1) Any question whether a witness in criminal proceedings may be sworn for the purpose of giving evidence on oath, whether raised—

        (a) by a party to the proceedings, or

        (b) by the court of its own motion,

shall be determined by the court in accordance with this section.

    (2) The witness may not be sworn for that purpose unless—

        (a) he has attained the age of 14, and

        (b) he has a sufficient appreciation of the solemnity of the occasion and of the particular responsibility to tell the truth which is involved in taking an oath.

(3) The witness shall, if he is able to give intelligible testimony, be presumed to have a sufficient appreciation of those matters if no evidence tending to show the contrary is adduced (by any party).

(4) If any such evidence is adduced, it is for the party seeking to have the witness sworn to satisfy the court that, on a balance of probabilities, the witness has attained the age of 14 and has a sufficient appreciation of the matters mentioned in subsection (2)(b).

(5) Any proceedings held for the determination of the question mentioned in subsection (1) shall take place in the absence of the jury (if there is one).

(6) Expert evidence may be received on the question.

(7) Any questioning of the witness (where the court considers that necessary) shall be conducted by the court in the presence of the parties.

(8) For the purposes of this section a person is able to give intelligible testimony if he is able to—

(a) understand questions put to him as a witness, and

(b) give answers to them which can be understood.

56.— Reception of unsworn evidence.

(1) Subsections (2) and (3) apply to a person (of any age) who—

(a) is competent to give evidence in criminal proceedings, but

(b) (by virtue of section 55(2)) is not permitted to be sworn for the purpose of giving evidence on oath in such proceedings.

(2) The evidence in criminal proceedings of a person to whom this subsection applies shall be given unsworn.

(3) A deposition of unsworn evidence given by a person to whom this subsection applies may be taken for the purposes of criminal proceedings as if that evidence had been given on oath.

(4) A court in criminal proceedings shall accordingly receive in evidence any evidence given unsworn in pursuance of subsection (2) or (3).

(5) Where a person ("the witness") who is competent to give evidence in criminal proceedings gives evidence in such proceedings unsworn, no conviction, verdict or finding in those proceedings shall be taken to be unsafe for the purposes of any of sections 2(1), 13(1) and 16(1) of the Criminal Appeal Act 1968 (grounds for allowing appeals) by reason only that it appears to the Court of Appeal that the witness was a person falling within section 55(2) (and should accordingly have given his evidence on oath).

57.— Penalty for giving false unsworn evidence.

(1) This section applies where a person gives unsworn evidence in criminal proceedings in pursuance of section 56(2) or (3).

(2) If such a person wilfully gives false evidence in such circumstances that, had the evidence been given on oath, he would have been guilty of perjury, he shall be guilty of an offence and liable on summary conviction to—

(a) imprisonment for a term not exceeding 6 months, or

(b) a fine not exceeding £1,000,

or both.

(3) In relation to a person under the age of 14, subsection (2) shall have effect as if for the words following "on summary conviction" there were substituted "to a fine not exceeding £250".

VIEW OF LOCUS

A court may deem it necessary to view a particular location. Care should be taken to ensure fairness and to that end arrangements should be made for all parties to be in attendance at the same time, and it would be improper for the prosecutor to travel alone with magistrates' to the scene (*Ely Justices, ex p Burgess* 157 JP 484). It is not proper for one magistrate on his own volition to visit the scene and purport to report back his findings (*R (Broxbourne Borough County Council) v North and East Hertfordshire Magistrates' Court* [2009] EWHC 695 (Admin)). In *M v Director of Public Prosecutions* [2009] 2 Cr App R 12 the court held:

> "Before any court embarks upon any view is that there is absolute clarity about precisely what is to happen on such a view, about who is to stand in what position, about what (if any) objects should be placed in a specific position and about who will do what. None of this should happen at the scene of a view, which should be conducted without discussion for the very reasons identified in this case, namely that otherwise not all involved can participate."

VERDICTS AND ALTERNATIVE VERDICTS

A court can return either a unanimous or majority decision. Where there are an equal number of magistrates and the decision is split there will need to be a retrial (*R v Redbridge Justice ex p Ram* [1992] 94 Cr App R 127). Reasons: Brief reasons should be given for the verdict (see *Brent Justice, ex p McGowan* (2002) 166 JP 29). **Alternative verdicts:** Save as provided for by statute, a court cannot return a conviction on an alternative basis. **Trying alternative charges:** Given the limitations in relation to alternative charges prosecutors should carefully consider whether an alternative count should be tried. Where this procedure is adopted and the court convicts on one count the other charge should be withdrawn or adjourned sine die (*Director of Public Prosecutions v Gane* 155 JP 846; *Clarke v CPS* [2007] EWHC 2228 (Admin)).

Road Traffic Offenders Act 1988, s 24; the effect of this section is:

Offence charged (RTA 1988, section)	Alternative (RTA 1988, section)
1	2 or 3
2	3
2B	3
3A	2B, 3, 4(1), 5(1)(a), 7(6) or 7A(6)
4(1)	4(2)
5(1)(a)	5(1)(b)
28	29

Theft Act 1968, s 12A(5) provides for the court convicting a defendant of the basic offence as a statutory alternative.

VIDEO RECORDED EVIDENCE

See: 'Special Measures' for general principles to be applied. **Commencement:** Section 28 and section 137 were not in force at the time of writing. **Transcript:** The transcript of the video evidence should not normally be exhibited (and accordingly magistrates' should not retire with a copy when retiring to consider their decision as to guilt or innocence) (*Popescu* [2010] EWCA Crim 1230). **Inadmissible parts of video evidence:** It is permissible for inadmissible evidence to be adduced if to edit it out would be detrimental to the understanding of the remainder (*R (CPS) v*

Brentford Youth Court [2003] EWHC 2409 (Admin)). Breach of good practice: A breach of good practice so far as video evidence is concerned will not automatically render it inadmissible. In *Hanton* [2005] EWCA Crim 2009 the court held:

"It was for the jury to decide, having considered the Guidance and the points made [in relation to breaches of that guidance], whether they were sure that the evidence given by [the witness] in the video-recorded interview was reliable and accurate."

Youth Justice and Criminal Evidence Act 1999, ss 27, 28

27.— Video recorded evidence in chief.

(1) A special measures direction may provide for a video recording of an interview of the witness to be admitted as evidence in chief of the witness.

(2) A special measures direction may, however, not provide for a video recording, or a part of such a recording, to be admitted under this section if the court is of the opinion, having regard to all the circumstances of the case, that in the interests of justice the recording, or that part of it, should not be so admitted.

(3) In considering for the purposes of subsection (2) whether any part of a recording should not be admitted under this section, the court must consider whether any prejudice to the accused which might result from that part being so admitted is outweighed by the desirability of showing the whole, or substantially the whole, of the recorded interview.

(4) Where a special measures direction provides for a recording to be admitted under this section, the court may nevertheless subsequently direct that it is not to be so admitted if—

    (a) it appears to the court that—

        (i) the witness will not be available for cross-examination (whether conducted in the ordinary way or in accordance with any such direction), and

        (ii) the parties to the proceedings have not agreed that there is no need for the witness to be so available; or

    (b) any Criminal Procedure Rules requiring disclosure of the circumstances in which the recording was made have not been complied with to the satisfaction of the court.

(5) Where a recording is admitted under this section—

    (a) the witness must be called by the party tendering it in evidence, unless—

        (i) a special measures direction provides for the witness's evidence on cross-examination to be given in any recording admissible under section 28, or

        (ii) the parties to the proceedings have agreed as mentioned in subsection (4)(a)(ii); and

    (b) the witness may not without the permission of the court give evidence in chief otherwise than by means of the recording as to any matter which, in the opinion of the court, is dealt with in the witness's recorded testimony.

(6) Where in accordance with subsection (2) a special measures direction provides for part only of a recording to be admitted under this section, references in subsections (4) and (5) to the recording or to the witness's recorded testimony are references to the part of the recording or testimony which is to be so admitted.

(7) The court may give permission for the purposes of subsection (5)(b) if it appears to the court to be in the interests of justice to do so, and may do so either—

    (a) on an application by a party to the proceedings, or

    (b) of its own motion.

(9) The court may, in giving permission for the purposes of [subsection (5)(b)] 7 , direct that the evidence in question is to be given by the witness by means of a live link.

(9A) If the court directs under subsection (9) that evidence is to be given by live link, it may also make such provision in that direction as it could make under section 24(1A) in a special measures direction.

[...]

(11) Nothing in this section affects the admissibility of any video recording which would be admissible apart from this section.

28.— Video recorded cross-examination or re-examination.

(1) Where a special measures direction provides for a video recording to be admitted under section 27 as evidence in chief of the witness, the direction may also provide—

    (a) for any cross-examination of the witness, and any re-examination, to be recorded by means of a video recording; and

    (b) for such a recording to be admitted, so far as it relates to any such cross-examination or re-examination, as evidence of the witness under cross-examination or on re-examination, as the case may be.

(2) Such a recording must be made in the presence of such persons as Criminal Procedure Rules or the direction may provide and in the absence of the accused, but in circumstances in which—

    (a) the judge or justices (or both) and legal representatives acting in the proceedings are able to see and hear the examination of the witness and to communicate with the persons in whose presence the recording is being made, and

    (b) the accused is able to see and hear any such examination and to communicate with any legal representative acting for him.

(3) Where two or more legal representatives are acting for a party to the proceedings, subsection (2)(a) and (b) are to be regarded as satisfied in relation to those representatives if at all material times they are satisfied in relation to at least one of them.

(4) Where a special measures direction provides for a recording to be admitted under this section, the court may nevertheless subsequently direct that it is not to be so admitted if any requirement of subsection (2) or Criminal Procedure Rules or the direction has not been complied with to the satisfaction of the court.

(5) Where in pursuance of subsection (1) a recording has been made of any examination of the witness, the witness may not be subsequently cross-examined or re-examined in respect of any evidence given by the witness in the proceedings (whether in any recording admissible under section 27 or this section or otherwise than in such a recording) unless the court gives a further special measures direction making such provision as is mentioned in subsection (1)(a) and (b) in relation to any subsequent cross-examination, and re-examination, of the witness.

(6) The court may only give such a further direction if it appears to the court—

    (a) that the proposed cross-examination is sought by a party to the proceedings as a result of that party having become aware, since the time when the original recording was made in pursuance of subsection (1), of a matter which that party could not with reasonable diligence have ascertained by then, or

    (b) that for any other reason it is in the interests of justice to give the further direction.

(7) Nothing in this section shall be read as applying in relation to any cross-examination of the witness by the accused in person (in a case where the accused is to be able to conduct any such cross-examination).

Criminal Justice Act 2003, ss 137, 138, 140

137 Evidence by video recording

(1) This section applies where—

(a) a person is called as a witness in proceedings for an offence triable only on indictment, or for a prescribed offence triable either way,

(b) the person claims to have witnessed (whether visually or in any other way)—

    (i) events alleged by the prosecution to include conduct constituting the offence or part of the offence, or

    (ii) events closely connected with such events,

(c) he has previously given an account of the events in question (whether in response to questions asked or otherwise),

(d) the account was given at a time when those events were fresh in the person's memory (or would have been, assuming the truth of the claim mentioned in paragraph (b)),

(e) a video recording was made of the account,

(f) the court has made a direction that the recording should be admitted as evidence in chief of the witness, and the direction has not been rescinded, and

(g) the recording is played in the proceedings in accordance with the direction.

(2) If, or to the extent that, the witness in his oral evidence in the proceedings asserts the truth of the statements made by him in the recorded account, they shall be treated as if made by him in that evidence.

(3) A direction under subsection (1)(f)—

    (a) may not be made in relation to a recorded account given by the defendant;

    (b) may be made only if it appears to the court that—

        (i) the witness's recollection of the events in question is likely to have been significantly better when he gave the recorded account than it will be when he gives oral evidence in the proceedings, and

        (ii) it is in the interests of justice for the recording to be admitted, having regard in particular to the matters mentioned in subsection (4).

(4) Those matters are—

    (a) the interval between the time of the events in question and the time when the recorded account was made;

    (b) any other factors that might affect the reliability of what the witness said in that account;

    (c) the quality of the recording;

    (d) any views of the witness as to whether his evidence in chief should be given orally or by means of the recording.

(5) For the purposes of subsection (2) it does not matter if the statements in the recorded account were not made on oath.

(6) In this section "prescribed" means of a description specified in an order made by the Secretary of State.

138 Video evidence: further provisions

[...]

(2) The reference in subsection (1)(f) of section 137 to the admission of a recording includes a reference to the admission of part of the recording; and references in that section and this one to the video recording or to the witness's recorded account shall, where appropriate, be read accordingly.

(3) In considering whether any part of a recording should be not admitted under section 137, the court must consider—

    (a) whether admitting that part would carry a risk of prejudice to the defendant, and

    (b) if so, whether the interests of justice nevertheless require it to be admitted in view of the desirability of showing the whole, or substantially the whole, of the recorded interview.

(4) A court may not make a direction under section 137(1)(f) in relation to any proceedings unless—

    (a) the Secretary of State has notified the court that arrangements can be made, in the area in which it appears to the court that the proceedings will take place, for implementing directions under that section, and

    (b) the notice has not been withdrawn.

(5) Nothing in section 137 affects the admissibility of any video recording which would be admissible apart from that section.

140 Interpretation of Chapter 3

In this Chapter—

"criminal proceedings" means criminal proceedings in relation to which the strict rules of evidence apply;

"defendant", in relation to criminal proceedings, means a person charged with an offence in those proceedings;

"document" means anything in which information of any description is recorded, but not including any recording of sounds or moving images;

"oral evidence" includes evidence which, by reason of any disability, disorder or other impairment, a person called as a witness gives in writing or by signs or by way of any device;

"video recording" means any recording, on any medium, from which a moving image may by any means be produced, and includes the accompanying sound-track.

WITNESS ANONYMITY ORDER

CrPr: Rule 29 applies. **Test:** See *Mayers* [2008] EWCA Crim 2989 and *Chisholm* [2010] EWCA Crim 258. In *Powar* [2009] EWCA Crim 594 it was held:

> "The calling of anonymous witnesses must not become a routine event in the prosecution of serious crime but we reject the submission that witness anonymity orders should be confined to cases of terrorism or gangland killings. The intimidation of witnesses has become an ugly feature of contemporary life; ... 'the climate of fear in these cases is like a cancer'; this fear serves 'to silence, blind and deafen witnesses'; without witnesses justice cannot be done".

Coroners and Justice Act 2009, ss 86-92

86 Witness anonymity orders

(1) In this Chapter a "witness anonymity order" is an order made by a court that requires such specified measures to be taken in relation to a witness in criminal proceedings as the court considers appropriate to ensure that the identity of the witness is not disclosed in or in connection with the proceedings.

(2) The kinds of measures that may be required to be taken in relation to a witness include measures for securing one or more of the following—

    (a) that the witness's name and other identifying details may be—
        (i) withheld;
        (ii) removed from materials disclosed to any party to the proceedings;

    (b) that the witness may use a pseudonym;

    (c) that the witness is not asked questions of any specified description that might lead to the identification of the witness;

    (d) that the witness is screened to any specified extent;

    (e) that the witness's voice is subjected to modulation to any specified extent.

(3) Subsection (2) does not affect the generality of subsection (1).

(4) Nothing in this section authorises the court to require—

    (a) the witness to be screened to such an extent that the witness cannot be seen by—

        (i) the judge or other members of the court (if any), or

        (ii) the jury (if there is one);

    (b) the witness's voice to be modulated to such an extent that the witness's natural voice cannot be heard by any persons within paragraph (a)(i) or (ii).

(5) In this section "specified" means specified in the witness anonymity order concerned.

87 Applications

(1) An application for a witness anonymity order to be made in relation to a witness in criminal proceedings may be made to the court by the prosecutor or the defendant.

(2) Where an application is made by the prosecutor, the prosecutor—

    (a) must (unless the court directs otherwise) inform the court of the identity of the witness, but

    (b) is not required to disclose in connection with the application—

        (i) the identity of the witness, or

        (ii) any information that might enable the witness to be identified, to any other party to the proceedings or his or her legal representatives.

(3) Where an application is made by the defendant, the defendant—

    (a) must inform the court and the prosecutor of the identity of the witness, but

    (b) (if there is more than one defendant) is not required to disclose in connection with the application—

        (i) the identity of the witness, or

        (ii) any information that might enable the witness to be identified,

to any other defendant or his or her legal representatives.

(4) Accordingly, where the prosecutor or the defendant proposes to make an application under this section in respect of a witness, any relevant material which is disclosed by or on behalf of that party before the determination of the application may be disclosed in such a way as to prevent—

    (a) the identity of the witness, or

    (b) any information that might enable the witness to be identified,

from being disclosed except as required by subsection (2)(a) or (3)(a).

(5) "Relevant material" means any document or other material which falls to be disclosed, or is sought to be relied on, by or on behalf of the party concerned in connection with the proceedings or proceedings preliminary to them.

(6) The court must give every party to the proceedings the opportunity to be heard on an application under this section.

(7) But subsection (6) does not prevent the court from hearing one or more parties in the absence of a defendant and his or her legal representatives, if it appears to the court to be appropriate to do so in the circumstances of the case.

(8) Nothing in this section is to be taken as restricting any power to make rules of court.

88 Conditions for making order

(1) This section applies where an application is made for a witness anonymity order to be made in relation to a witness in criminal proceedings.

(2) The court may make such an order only if it is satisfied that Conditions A to C below are met.

(3) Condition A is that the proposed order is necessary—

(a) in order to protect the safety of the witness or another person or to prevent any serious damage to property, or

(b) in order to prevent real harm to the public interest (whether affecting the carrying on of any activities in the public interest or the safety of a person involved in carrying on such activities, or otherwise).

(4) Condition B is that, having regard to all the circumstances, the effect of the proposed order would be consistent with the defendant receiving a fair trial.

(5) Condition C is that the importance of the witness's testimony is such that in the interests of justice the witness ought to testify and—

(a) the witness would not testify if the proposed order were not made, or

(b) there would be real harm to the public interest if the witness were to testify without the proposed order being made.

(6) In determining whether the proposed order is necessary for the purpose mentioned in subsection (3)(a), the court must have regard (in particular) to any reasonable fear on the part of the witness—

(a) that the witness or another person would suffer death or injury, or

(b) that there would be serious damage to property,

if the witness were to be identified.

89 Relevant considerations

(1) When deciding whether Conditions A to C in section 88 are met in the case of an application for a witness anonymity order, the court must have regard to—

(a) the considerations mentioned in subsection (2) below, and

(b) such other matters as the court considers relevant.

(2) The considerations are—

(a) the general right of a defendant in criminal proceedings to know the identity of a witness in the proceedings;

(b) the extent to which the credibility of the witness concerned would be a relevant factor when the weight of his or her evidence comes to be assessed;

(c) whether evidence given by the witness might be the sole or decisive evidence implicating the defendant;

(d) whether the witness's evidence could be properly tested (whether on grounds of credibility or otherwise) without his or her identity being disclosed;

(e) whether there is any reason to believe that the witness—

(i) has a tendency to be dishonest, or

(ii) has any motive to be dishonest in the circumstances of the case,

having regard (in particular) to any previous convictions of the witness and to any relationship between the witness and the defendant or any associates of the defendant;

(f) whether it would be reasonably practicable to protect the witness by any means other than by making a witness anonymity order specifying the measures that are under consideration by the court.

90 Warning to jury

(1) Subsection (2) applies where, on a trial on indictment with a jury, any evidence has been given by a witness at a time when a witness anonymity order applied to the witness.

(2) The judge must give the jury such warning as the judge considers appropriate to ensure that the fact that the order was made in relation to the witness does not prejudice the defendant.

91 Discharge or variation of order

(1) A court that has made a witness anonymity order in relation to any criminal proceedings may in those proceedings subsequently discharge or vary (or further vary) the order if it appears to the court to be appropriate to do so in view of the provisions of sections 88 and 89 that apply to the making of an order.

(2) The court may do so—

(a) on an application made by a party to the proceedings if there has been a material change of circumstances since the relevant time, or

(b) on its own initiative.

(3) The court must give every party to the proceedings the opportunity to be heard—

(a) before determining an application made to it under subsection (2);

(b) before discharging or varying the order on its own initiative.

(4) But subsection (3) does not prevent the court hearing one or more of the parties to the proceedings in the absence of a defendant in the proceedings and his or her legal representatives, if it appears to the court to be appropriate to do so in the circumstances of the case.

(5) "The relevant time" means—

(a) the time when the order was made, or

(b) if a previous application has been made under subsection (2), the time when the application (or the last application) was made.

92 Discharge or variation after proceedings

(1) This section applies if—

(a) a court has made a witness anonymity order in relation to a witness in criminal proceedings ("the old proceedings"), and

(b) the old proceedings have come to an end.

(2) The court that made the order may discharge or vary (or further vary) the order if it appears to the court to be appropriate to do so in view of—

(a) the provisions of sections 88 and 89 that apply to the making of a witness anonymity order, and

(b) such other matters as the court considers relevant.

(3) The court may do so—

(a) on an application made by a party to the old proceedings if there has been a material change of circumstances since the relevant time, or

(b) on an application made by the witness if there has been a material change of circumstances since the relevant time.

(4) The court may not determine an application made to it under subsection (3) unless in the case of each of the parties to the old proceedings and the witness—

(a) it has given the person the opportunity to be heard, or

(b) it is satisfied that it is not reasonably practicable to communicate with the person.

(5) Subsection (4) does not prevent the court hearing one or more of the persons mentioned in that subsection in the absence of a person who was a defendant in the old proceedings and that person's legal representatives, if it appears to the court to be appropriate to do so in the circumstances of the case.

(6) "The relevant time" means—

(a) the time when the old proceedings came to an end, or

(b) if a previous application has been made under subsection (3), the time when the application (or the last application) was made.

WITNESS CALLED BY COURT

A court has the power to call a witness itself in circumstances where the opposing party is able to properly not call that witness, but it is in the interests of justice that the witness be available for the other party to cross-examine (eg *Haringey Justice ex p Director of Public Prosecutions* [1996] 2 Cr App R 119). **Questioning:** Where a party is legally represented the better course of action is to leave questioning of the witness to the advocate. There is no objection to questioning that is necessary in order to clarify evidence already given. In *Hulusi* (1974) 58 Cr App R 378 the court held:

> "It has been recognised always that it is wrong for a judge to descend into the arena and give the impression of acting as advocate. Not only is it wrong but very often a judge can do more harm than leaving it to experienced counsel. Whether his interventions in any case give ground for quashing a conviction is not only a matter of degree, but depends to what the interventions are directed and what their effect may be. Interventions to clear up ambiguities, interventions to enable the judge to make certain that he is making an accurate note, are of course perfectly justified. But the interventions which give rise to a quashing of a conviction are really threefold; those which invite the jury to disbelieve the evidence for the defence which is put to the jury in such strong terms that it cannot be cured by the common formula that the facts are for the jury and you, the members of the jury, must disregard anything that I, the judge, may have said with which you disagree. The second ground giving rise to a quashing of a conviction is where the interventions have made it really impossible for counsel for the defence to do his or her duty in properly presenting the defence, and thirdly, cases where the interventions have had the effect of preventing the prisoner himself from doing himself justice and telling the story in his own way."

WITNESS, EVIDENCE GIVEN IN PRIVATE

See: 'Special Measures' for general principles to be applied.

Youth Justice and Criminal Evidence Act 1999, s 25

25.— Evidence given in private.

(1) A special measures direction may provide for the exclusion from the court, during the giving of the witness's evidence, of persons of any description specified in the direction.

(2) The persons who may be so excluded do not include—

    (a) the accused,

    (b) legal representatives acting in the proceedings, or

    (c) any interpreter or other person appointed (in pursuance of the direction or otherwise) to assist the witness.

(3) A special measures direction providing for representatives of news gathering or reporting organisations to be so excluded shall be expressed not to apply to one named person who—

    (a) is a representative of such an organisation, and

    (b) has been nominated for the purpose by one or more such organisations,

unless it appears to the court that no such nomination has been made.

(4) A special measures direction may only provide for the exclusion of persons under this section where—

    (a) the proceedings relate to a sexual offence; or

    (b) it appears to the court that there are reasonable grounds for believing that any person other than the accused has sought, or will seek, to intimidate the witness in connection with testifying in the proceedings.

(5) Any proceedings from which persons are excluded under this section (whether or not those persons include representatives of news gathering or reporting organisations) shall nevertheless be taken to be held in public for the purposes of any privilege or exemption from liability available in respect of fair, accurate and contemporaneous reports of legal proceedings held in public.

WITNESS, EVIDENCE VIA LIVE LINK

See: 'Special Measures' for general principles to be applied.

Youth Justice and Criminal Evidence Act 1999, ss 24, 33A

24.— Evidence by live link.

(1) A special measures direction may provide for the witness to give evidence by means of a live link.

(1A) Such a direction may also provide for a specified person to accompany the witness while the witness is giving evidence by live link.

(1B) In determining who may accompany the witness, the court must have regard to the wishes of the witness.

(2) Where a direction provides for the witness to give evidence by means of a live link, the witness may not give evidence in any other way without the permission of the court.

(3) The court may give permission for the purposes of subsection (2) if it appears to the court to be in the interests of justice to do so, and may do so either—

(a) on an application by a party to the proceedings, if there has been a material change of circumstances since the relevant time, or

(b) of its own motion.

(4) In subsection (3) "the relevant time" means —

(a) the time when the direction was given, or

(b) if a previous application has been made under that subsection, the time when the application (or last application) was made.

[...]

(8) In this Chapter "live link" means a live television link or other arrangement whereby a witness, while absent from the courtroom or other place where the proceedings are being held, is able to see and hear a person there and to be seen and heard by the persons specified in section 23(2)(a) to (c).

33A Live link directions

(1) This section applies to any proceedings (whether in a magistrates' court or before the Crown Court) against a person for an offence.

(2) The court may, on the application of the accused, give a live link direction if it is satisfied–

(a) that the conditions in subsection (4) or, as the case may be, subsection (5) are met in relation to the accused, and

(b) that it is in the interests of justice for the accused to give evidence through a live link.

(3) A live link direction is a direction that any oral evidence to be given before the court by the accused is to be given through a live link.

(4) Where the accused is aged under 18 when the application is made, the conditions are that–

(a) his ability to participate effectively in the proceedings as a witness giving oral evidence in court is compromised by his level of intellectual ability or social functioning, and

(b) use of a live link would enable him to participate more effectively in the proceedings as a witness (whether by improving the quality of his evidence or otherwise).

(5) Where the accused has attained the age of 18 at that time, the conditions are that–

(a) he suffers from a mental disorder (within the meaning of the Mental Health Act 1983) or otherwise has a significant impairment of intelligence and social function,

(b) he is for that reason unable to participate effectively in the proceedings as a witness giving oral evidence in court, and

(c) use of a live link would enable him to participate more effectively in the proceedings as a witness (whether by improving the quality of his evidence or otherwise).

(6) While a live link direction has effect the accused may not give oral evidence before the court in the proceedings otherwise than through a live link.

(7) The court may discharge a live link direction at any time before or during any hearing to which it applies if it appears to the court to be in the interests of justice to do so (but this does not affect the power to give a further live link direction in relation to the accused).

The court may exercise this power of its own motion or on an application by a party.

(8) The court must state in open court its reasons for–

(a) giving or discharging a live link direction, or

(b) refusing an application for or for the discharge of a live link direction,

and, if it is a magistrates' court, it must cause those reasons to be entered in the register of its proceedings.

Criminal Justice Act 2003, ss 51, 52, 53

51 Live links in criminal proceedings

(1) A witness (other than the defendant) may, if the court so directs, give evidence through a live link in the following criminal proceedings.

(2) They are—

(a) a summary trial,

[...]

(f) a hearing before a magistrates' court or the Crown Court which is held after the defendant has entered a plea of guilty, and

(g) a hearing before the Court of Appeal under section 80 of this Act.

(3) A direction may be given under this section—

(a) on an application by a party to the proceedings, or

(b) of the court's own motion.

(4) But a direction may not be given under this section unless—

(a) the court is satisfied that it is in the interests of the efficient or effective administration of justice for the person concerned to give evidence in the proceedings through a live link,

(b) it has been notified by the Secretary of State that suitable facilities for receiving evidence through a live link are available in the area in which it appears to the court that the proceedings will take place, and

(c) that notification has not been withdrawn.

(5) The withdrawal of such a notification is not to affect a direction given under this section before that withdrawal.

(6) In deciding whether to give a direction under this section the court must consider all the circumstances of the case.

(7) Those circumstances include in particular—

(a) the availability of the witness,

(b) the need for the witness to attend in person,

(c) the importance of the witness's evidence to the proceedings,

(d) the views of the witness,

(e) the suitability of the facilities at the place where the witness would give evidence through a live link,

(f) whether a direction might tend to inhibit any party to the proceedings from effectively testing the witness's evidence.

(8) The court must state in open court its reasons for refusing an application for a direction under this section and, if it is a magistrates' court, must cause them to be entered in the register of its proceedings.

52 Effect of, and rescission of, direction

(1) Subsection (2) applies where the court gives a direction under section 51 for a person to give evidence through a live link in particular proceedings.

(2) The person concerned may not give evidence in those proceedings after the direction is given otherwise than through a live link (but this is subject to the following provisions of this section).

(3) The court may rescind a direction under section 51 if it appears to the court to be in the interests of justice to do so.

(4) Where it does so, the person concerned shall cease to be able to give evidence in the proceedings through a live link, but this does not prevent the court from giving a further direction under section 51 in relation to him.

(5) A direction under section 51 may be rescinded under subsection (3)—

(a) on an application by a party to the proceedings, or

(b) of the court's own motion.

(6) But an application may not be made under subsection (5)(a) unless there has been a material change of circumstances since the direction was given.

(7) The court must state in open court its reasons—

(a) for rescinding a direction under section 51, or

(b) for refusing an application to rescind such a direction,

and, if it is a magistrates' court, must cause them to be entered in the register of its proceedings.

53 Magistrates' courts permitted to sit at other locations

(1) This section applies where—

(a) a magistrates' court is minded to give a direction under section 51 for evidence to be given through a live link in proceedings before the court, and

(b) suitable facilities for receiving such evidence are not available at any place at which the court can (apart from subsection (2)) lawfully sit.

(2) The court may sit for the purposes of the whole or any part of the proceedings at any place at which such facilities are available and which has been authorised by a direction under section 30 of the Courts Act 2003.

(3) If the place mentioned in subsection (2) is outside the local justice area in which the justices act it shall be deemed to be in that area for the purpose of the jurisdiction of the justices acting in that area.

WITNESS, FOR THE DEFENCE

The defendant may give evidence if he chooses, and whether or not he gives evidence he can call other persons to give evidence on his behalf. The defendant should only be called to give evidence before any other defence witness, unless leave of the court is granted to call evidence out of sequence (which will be rare) (Police and Criminal Evidence Act 1984, s 79). In *Cook* [2005] EWCA Crim 2011 the court set out the general principles to be applied:

1. The Judge has a discretionary power to allow the recall of a witness or a defendant at any stage of the trial subsequent to his initial evidence and prior to the summing up for the putting of such questions as the exigencies of justice require–see Sullivan [1922] 16 Cr. App. R.ep 121 and McKenna 40 Cr. App. R.ep 65 .

2. Once a defendant has made himself a witness, he is liable, like any other witness, to be recalled for the purpose of answering such questions as the judge permits to be put to him.

3. A judge will permit a defendant to be recalled only to deal with matters which have arisen since he gave evidence if he could not reasonably have anticipated them and if it appears to be in the interests of justice that he should be recalled.

4. A judge should never permit a defendant to be recalled so that he may resile from evidence already given and advance a new version of events where that version was available to him when he was first in the witness box.

Recall: Exceptionally a defendant may be recalled to give further evidence in accordance with the above principles (eg *Reid* [2010] EWCA Crim 1478). **Location:** A defendant should give evidence from the witness box just like any other witness (*R v Farnham Justices, ex p Gibson* [1991] RTR 309). **Security:** Any security measures necessary in order to prevent escape should be done as discretely as possible (eg custody personnel at the door of the court as opposed to adjacent to the defendant); Handcuffs will only be permissible in the most exceptional circumstances (See Part C Handcuffs).

WITNESS, FOR THE PROSECUTION

The prosecution must call or tender for cross-examination those witnesses whose statements have been served on the defence. In *Russell-Jones* [195] 1 Cr App R 538 the court held:

(1) Generally speaking the prosecution must have at court all the witnesses named on the back of the indictment (nowadays those whose statements have been served as witnesses on whom the prosecution intend to rely), if the defence want those witnesses to attend. In deciding which statements to serve, the prosecution has an unfettered discretion, but must normally disclose material statements not served.

(2) The prosecution enjoy a discretion whether to call, or tender, any witness it requires to attend, but the discretion is not unfettered.

(3) The first principle which limits this discretion is that it must be exercised in the interests of justice, so as to promote a fair trial. See per Lord Parker C.J. in Oliva . See also per Fullagar J. in Ziems v. The Prothonotary of the Supreme Court of New South Wales (1957) 97 C.L.R. 279 , 292:

"The present case, however, seems to me to call for a reminder that the discretion should be exercised with due regard to traditional considerations of fairness."

The dictum of Lord Thankerton in the Palestine case "the court will not interfere with the exercise of that discretion, unless, perhaps, it can be shown that the prosecutor has been influenced by some oblique motive" does not mean that the Court will only interfere if the prosecutor has acted out of malice; it means that the prosecutor must call his mind to his overall duty of fairness, as a minister of justice. Were he not to do so, he would have been moved by a consideration not relevant to his proper task—in that sense, an oblique motive.

Clearly, however, to say merely that the prosecutor must act fairly gives little guidance as to how the discretion should be exercised in practice; and there are further limiting principles.

(4) The next principle is that the prosecution ought normally to call or offer to call all the witnesses who give direct evidence of the primary facts of the case, unless for good

reason, in any instance, the prosecutor regards the witness's evidence as unworthy of belief. In most cases the jury should have available all of that evidence as to what actually happened, which the prosecution, when serving statements, considered to be material, even if there are inconsistencies between one witness and another. The defence cannot always be expected to call for themselves witnesses of the primary facts whom the prosecution has discarded. For example, the evidence they may give, albeit at variance with other evidence called by the Crown, may well be detrimental to the defence case. If what a witness of the primary facts has to say is properly regarded by the prosecution as being incapable of belief, or as some of the authorities say "incredible", then his evidence cannot help the jury assess the overall picture of the crucial events; hence, it is not unfair that he should not be called.

This limitation of the prosecution's discretion, which requires witnesses of the central facts to be called, is supported by what was said by Lord Roche in Seneviratne . This is also the sense in which, as it seems to us, Lord Hewart C.J.'s observation in Harris [1927] 2 K.B. 587 , 590 should be read.

(1) It is for the prosecution to decide which witnesses give direct evidence of the primary facts of the case. A prosecutor may reasonably take the view that what a particular witness has to say is at best marginal.

(2) The prosecutor is also, as we have said, the primary judge of whether or not a witness to the material events is incredible, or unworthy of belief. It goes without saying that he could not properly condemn a witness as incredible merely because, for example, he gives an account at variance with that of a larger number of witnesses, and one which is less favourable to the prosecution case than that of the others.

(3) A prosecutor properly exercising his discretion will not therefore be obliged to proffer a witness merely in order to give the defence material with which to attack the credit of other witnesses on whom the Crown relies. To hold otherwise would, in truth, be to assert that the prosecution are obliged to call a witness for no purpose other than to assist the defence in its endeavour to destroy the Crown's own case. No sensible rule of justice could require such a stance to be taken.

(4) Plainly, what we have said should not be regarded as a lexicon or rule book to cover all cases in which a prosecutor is called upon to exercise this discretion. There may be special situations to which we have not adverted; and in every case, it is important to emphasise, the judgment to be made is primarily that of the prosecutor, and, in general, the court will only interfere with it if he has gone wrong in principle.

WITNESS, SCREENING FROM ACCUSED

See: 'Special Measures' for general principles to be applied.

Youth Justice and Criminal Evidence Act 1999, s 23

(1) A special measures direction may provide for the witness, while giving testimony or being sworn in court, to be prevented by means of a screen or other arrangement from seeing the accused.

(2) But the screen or other arrangement must not prevent the witness from being able to see, and to be seen by—

(a) the judge or justices (or both) and the jury (if there is one);
(b) legal representatives acting in the proceedings; and
(c) any interpreter or other person appointed (in pursuance of the direction or otherwise) to assist the witness.

(3) Where two or more legal representatives are acting for a party to the proceedings, subsection (2)(b) is to be regarded as satisfied in relation to those representatives if the witness is able at all material times to see and be seen by at least one of them.

WITNESS SUMMONS

CrPR: Rule 28 applies. **Fishing expedition:** When issuing a summons in order to obtain documentary evidence the evidence sought must be properly particularised as the summons procedure is not akin to civil discovery. The evidence must be admissible per se (*R v Reading Justice ex p Berkshire County Council* [1996] 1 Cr App R 239), and not simply requested for the purposes of cross-examination alone (*R v Skegness Magistrates' Court, ex p Cardy* [1985] RTR 49). **ECHR:** Where disclosure impacts upon the rights of individuals (eg medical records) the court must carry out a balancing exercise when deciding whether to issue a summons (for a summary of the relevant principles see *TB v The Crown Court at Stafford* [2006] EWHC 1645 (Admin)).

Magistrates' Courts Act 1980, s 97

(1)   Where a justice of the peace is satisfied that—

    (a) any person in England or Wales is likely to be able to give material evidence, or produce any document or thing likely to be material evidence, at the summary trial of an information or hearing of a complaint or of an application in family proceedings by a magistrates' court, and

    (b) it is in the interests of justice to issue a summons under this subsection to secure the attendance of that person to give evidence or produce the document or thing,

the justice shall issue a summons directed to that person requiring him to attend before the court at the time and place appointed in the summons to give evidence or to produce the document or thing.

(2)   If a justice of the peace is satisfied by evidence on oath of the matters mentioned in subsection (1) above, and also that it is probable that a summons under that subsection would not procure the attendance of the person in question, the justice may instead of issuing a summons issue a warrant to arrest that person and bring him before such a court as aforesaid at a time and place specified in the warrant; but a warrant shall not be issued under this subsection where the attendance is required for the hearing of a complaint or of an application [in family proceedings.

(2A) A summons may also be issued under subsection (1) above if the justice is satisfied that the person in question is outside the British Islands but no warrant shall be issued under subsection (2) above unless the justice is satisfied by evidence on oath that the person in question is in England or Wales.

(2B) A justice may refuse to issue a summons under subsection (1) above in relation to the summary trial of an information if he is not satisfied that an application for the summons was made by a party to the case as soon as reasonably practicable after the accused pleaded not guilty.

(2C) In relation to the summary trial of an information, subsection (2) above shall have effect as if the reference to the matters mentioned in subsection (1) above included a reference to the matter mentioned in subsection (2B) above.

(3)   On the failure of any person to attend before a magistrates' court in answer to a summons under this section, if—

    (a) the court is satisfied by evidence on oath that he is likely to be able to give material evidence or produce any document or thing likely to be material evidence in the proceedings; and

    (b) it is proved on oath, or in such other manner as may be prescribed, that he has been duly served with the summons, and that a reasonable sum has been paid or tendered to him for costs and expenses; and

    (c) it appears to the court that there is no just excuse for the failure,

the court may issue a warrant to arrest him and bring him before the court at a time and place specified in the warrant.

(4) If any person attending or brought before a magistrates' court refuses without just excuse to be sworn or give evidence, or to produce any document or thing, the court may commit him to custody until the expiration of such period not exceeding one month as may be specified in the warrant or until he sooner gives evidence or produces the document or thing or impose on him a fine not exceeding £2,500 or both.

(5) A fine imposed under subsection (4) above shall be deemed, for the purposes of any enactment, to be a sum adjudged to be paid by a conviction..

Criminal Procedure Rules 2012, r 28

28.1.—(1) This Part applies in magistrates' courts and in the Crown Court where—

    (a) a party wants the court to issue a witness summons, warrant or order under—
        (i) section 97 of the Magistrates' Courts Act 1980,
        (ii) section 2 of the Criminal Procedure (Attendance of Witnesses) Act 1965, or
        (iii) section 7 of the Bankers' Books Evidence Act 1879;
    (b) the court considers the issue of such a summons, warrant or order on its own initiative as if a party had applied; or
    (c) one of those listed in rule 28.7 wants the court to withdraw such a summons, warrant or order.

(2) A reference to a 'witness' in this Part is a reference to a person to whom such a summons, warrant or order is directed.

28.2.—(1) The court may issue or withdraw a witness summons, warrant or order with or without a hearing.

(2) A hearing under this Part must be in private unless the court otherwise directs.

28.3.—(1) A party who wants the court to issue a witness summons, warrant or order must apply as soon as practicable after becoming aware of the grounds for doing so.

(2) The party applying must—

    (a) identify the proposed witness;
    (b) explain—
        (i) what evidence the proposed witness can give or produce,
        (ii) why it is likely to be material evidence, and
        (iii) why it would be in the interests of justice to issue a summons, order or warrant as

appropriate.

(3) The application may be made orally unless—

    (a) rule 28.5 applies; or
    (b) the court otherwise directs.

28.4.—(1) An application in writing under rule 28.3 must be in the form set out in the Practice Direction, containing the same declaration of truth as a witness statement.

(2) The party applying must serve the application—

    (a) in every case, on the court officer and as directed by the court; and
    (b) as required by rule 28.5, if that rule applies.

28.5.—(1) This rule applies to an application under rule 28.3 for a witness summons requiring the proposed witness—

    (a) to produce in evidence a document or thing; or
    (b) to give evidence about information apparently held in confidence, that relates to another person.

(2) The application must be in writing in the form required by rule 28.4.

(3) The party applying must serve the application—

    (a) on the proposed witness, unless the court otherwise directs; and

    (b) on one or more of the following, if the court so directs—

        (i) a person to whom the proposed evidence relates,

        (ii) another party.

(4) The court must not issue a witness summons where this rule applies unless—

    (a) everyone served with the application has had at least 14 days in which to make

representations, including representations about whether there should be a hearing of the application before the summons is issued; and

    (b) the court is satisfied that it has been able to take adequate account of the duties and rights, including rights of confidentiality, of the proposed witness and of any person to whom the proposed evidence relates.

(5) This rule does not apply to an application for an order to produce in evidence a copy of an entry in a banker's book.

28.6.—(1) This rule applies where a person served with an application for a witness summons requiring the proposed witness to produce in evidence a document or thing objects to its production on the ground that—

    (a) it is not likely to be material evidence; or

    (b) even if it is likely to be material evidence, the duties or rights, including rights of confidentiality, of the proposed witness or of any person to whom the document or thing

relates, outweigh the reasons for issuing a summons.

(2) The court may require the proposed witness to make the document or thing available for the objection to be assessed.

(3) The court may invite—

    (a) the proposed witness or any representative of the proposed witness; or

    (b) a person to whom the document or thing relates or any representative of such a person,

to help the court assess the objection.

28.7.—(1) The court may withdraw a witness summons, warrant or order if one of the following applies for it to be withdrawn—

    (a) the party who applied for it, on the ground that it no longer is needed;

    (b) the witness, on the grounds that—

        (i) he was not aware of any application for it, and

        (ii) he cannot give or produce evidence likely to be material evidence, or

        (iii) even if he can, his duties or rights, including rights of confidentiality, or those of any

person to whom the evidence relates, outweigh the reasons for the issue of the summons, warrant or order; or

    (c) any person to whom the proposed evidence relates, on the grounds that—

        (i) he was not aware of any application for it, and

        (ii) that evidence is not likely to be material evidence, or

        (iii) even if it is, his duties or rights, including rights of confidentiality, or those of the

witness, outweigh the reasons for the issue of the summons, warrant or order.

(2) A person applying under the rule must—

    (a) apply in writing as soon as practicable after becoming aware of the grounds for doing so, explaining why he wants the summons, warrant or order to be withdrawn; and

    (b) serve the application on the court officer and as appropriate on—

        (i) the witness,

        (ii) the party who applied for the summons, warrant or order, and

        (iii) any other person who he knows was served with the application for the summons,

warrant or order.

    (3) Rule 28.6 applies to an application under this rule that concerns a document or thing to be

produced in evidence.

28.8.—(1) The court may—

    (a) shorten or extend (even after it has expired) a time limit under this Part; and

    (b) where a rule or direction requires an application under this Part to be in writing, allow

that application to be made orally instead.

    (2) Someone who wants the court to allow an application to be made orally under paragraph (1)(b) of this rule must—

    (a) give as much notice as the urgency of his application permits to those on whom he would otherwise have served an application in writing; and

    (b) in doing so explain the reasons for the application and for wanting the court to consider it orally.

PART F YOUTH COURT

AGE OF OFFENDER

It is the duty of a youth court to determine age when a young person is brought before the court. In most cases there is no dispute and a simple confirmation of the youth's date of birth will suffice. The court is, however, able to hear evidence on the issue. If the age is later found to be incorrect this has no bearing on any orders made by the court. Section 99(1) of the Children and Young Persons Act 1933 provides:

Children and Young Persons Act 1933, s 99

(1) Where a person, whether charged with an offence or not, is brought before any court otherwise than for the purpose of giving evidence, and it appears to the court that he is a child or young person, the court shall make due inquiry as to the age of that person, and for that purpose shall take such evidence as may be forthcoming at the hearing of the case, but an order or judgment of the court shall not be invalidated by any subsequent proof that the age of that person has not been correctly stated to the court, and the age presumed or declared by the court to be the age of the person so brought before it shall, for the purposes of this Act, be deemed to be the true age of that person, and, where it appears to the court that the person so brought before it has attained the age of eighteen years, that person shall for the purposes of this Act be deemed not to be a child or young person.

(2) Where in any charge or indictment for any offence under this Act or any of the offences mentioned in the First Schedule to this Act except as provided in that Schedule, it is alleged that the person by or in respect of whom the offence was committed was a child or young person or was under or had attained any specified age, and he appears to the court to have been at the date of the commission of the alleged offence a child or young person, or to have been under or to have attained the specified age, as the case may be, he shall for the purposes of this Act be presumed at that date to have been a child or young person or to have been under or to have attained that age, as the case may be, unless the contrary is proved.

(3) Where, in any charge or indictment for any offence under this Act or any of the offences mentioned in the First Schedule to this Act, it is alleged that the person in respect of whom the offence was committed was a child or was a young person, it shall not be a defence to prove that the person alleged to have been a child was a young person or the person alleged to have been a young person was a child in any case where the acts constituting the alleged offence would equally have been an offence if committed in respect of a young person or child respectively.

(4) Where a person is charged with an offence under this Act in respect of a person apparently under a specified age it shall be a defence to prove that the person was actually of or over that age.

The following scenarios detail what happens when a youth becomes an adult post charge:

- D aged 17 years is bailed to the youth court on a date when he would be 18 years of age. In this instance the proceedings had not begun as he had not appeared before the court, accordingly the court lacked jurisdiction to try D (*R v Amersham Juvenile Court, ex p Wilson* [1981] 2 All ER 315).
- D aged 17 is bailed to the youth court on a date when he would still be 17. D fails to appear at court, and the arrest warrant is executed only later when he is 18 years of age. In this

instance no court has jurisdiction, D will have to be recharged to an adult court (*R v Uxbridge Youth Court, ex p H* [1998] EWHC Admin 342).

- D aged 17 appears before the youth court. After he has attained 18 years the prosecution lay an alternative charge against D arising out of the same facts. Any new charge, even one based on the same facts, must commence in an adult court if the defendant is aged 18 years or over (*R v Chelsea Justices, ex p Director of Public Prosecutions* [1963] 3 All ER 657).

- D aged 17 years appears before the youth court. Section 24(1) of the Magistrates' Courts Act 1980 does not apply in his case, and before he is put to plea he attains 18 years. In this case D is entitled in an appropriate case to elect Crown Court trial (*R v Islington North Juvenile Court, ex p Daley* [1983] 1 AC 347; see also *R v Lewes Juvenile Court, ex p Turner* (1984) 149 JP 186).

- D aged 17 years appears before the youth court. During the proceedings he attains 18 years of age. In this instance the court may continue to deal with the case (Children and Young Persons Act 1963, s 29(1)). Crucially, section 29 extends to the imposition of any sentence that would have been available to the court had the defendant not turned 18, for example, a referral order (see *A v Director of Public Prosecutions* [2002] 2 Cr App R (S) 88). Provided that the court has not begun to hear prosecution evidence it can instead exercise its discretion to remit D to the adult court (Crime and Disorder Act 1998, s 47(1)). Section 29 provides:

Children and Young Persons Act 1963, s 29

(1) Where proceedings in respect of a young person are begun [under section 1 of the Children and Young Persons Act 1969 or for an offence] and he attains the age of seventeen before the conclusion of the proceedings, the court may deal with the case and make any order which it could have made if he had not attained that age.

AGE OF OFFENDER–SENTENCING

See Part B Age of Offender.

AIMS OF YOUTH JUSTICE SYSTEM

Children and Young Persons Act 1933, s 44

(1) Every court in dealing with a child or young person who is brought before it, either as an offender or otherwise, shall have regard to the welfare of the child or young person and shall in a proper case take steps for removing him from undesirable surroundings, and for securing that proper provision is made for his education and training.

Crime and Disorder Act 1998, s 37

(1) It shall be the principal aim of the youth justice system to prevent offending by children and young persons.

(2) In addition to any other duty to which they are subject, it shall be the duty of all persons and bodies carrying out functions in relation to the youth justice system to have regard to that aim.

ALLOCATION, COMMITTAL, SENDING AND TRANSFER–OLD PROVISIONS

Note: On 18 June 2012 substantial changes to these provisions took effect in 12 criminal justices areas. See the next section for those revisions.

Homicide and other offences that cannot be tried in the youth court

In relation to the following matters the court does not have jurisdiction to try the offence(s) and the proceedings will be adjourned for committal proceedings:

- An offence of murder, attempted murder, manslaughter, causing or allowing the death of a child or vulnerable adult, or infanticide must be committed to the Crown Court for trial (Magistrates' Courts Act 1980, s 24(1)), along with any other offences with which he is charged at the same time if the charges for both offences could be joined in the same indictment (Magistrates' Courts Act 1980, s 24(1A)).
- Offences falling within section 51A of the Firearms Act 1968 provided the youth was aged at least 16 years at the date of offence (see below).
- An offence falling within section 29(3) of the Violent Crime Reduction Act 2006 (minimum sentences in certain cases of using someone to mind a weapon) would apply if he were convicted of the offence (see below).

Firearms Act 1968, s 51A

(1) This section applies where—

    (a) an individual is convicted of—

        (i) an offence under section 5(1)(a), (ab), (aba), (ac), (ad), (ae), (af) or (c) of this Act,

        (ii) an offence under section 5(1A)(a) of this Act, or

        (iii) an offence under any of the provisions of this Act listed in subsection (1A) in respect of a firearm or ammunition specified in section 5(1)(a), (ab), (aba), (ac), (ad), (ae), (af) or (c) or section 5(1A) (a) of this Act, and

    (b) the offence was committed after the commencement of this section and at a time when he was aged 16 or over.

(1A) The provisions are—

    (a) section 16 (possession of firearm with intent to injure);

    (b) section 16A (possession of firearm with intent to cause fear of violence);

    (c) section 17 (use of firearm to resist arrest);

    (d) section 18 (carrying firearm with criminal intent);

    (e) section 19 (carrying a firearm in a public place);

    (f) section 20(1) (trespassing in a building with firearm).

(2) The court shall impose an appropriate custodial sentence (or order for detention) for a term of at least the required minimum term (with or without a fine) unless the court is of the opinion that there are exceptional circumstances relating to the offence or to the offender which justify its not doing so.

(3) Where an offence is found to have been committed over a period of two or more days, or at some time during a period of two or more days, it shall be taken for the purposes of this section to have been committed on the last of those days.

(4) In this section 'appropriate custodial sentence (or order for detention)' means—

    (a) in relation to England and Wales—

        (i) in the case of an offender who is aged 18 or over when convicted, a sentence of imprisonment, and

        (iii) in the case of an offender who is aged under 18 at that time, a sentence of detention under section 91 of the Powers of Criminal Courts (Sentencing) Act 2000;

    (b) in relation to Scotland—

        (i) in the case of an offender who is aged 21 or over when convicted, a sentence of imprisonment,

        (ii) in the case of an offender who is aged under 21 at that time (not being an offender mentioned in sub-paragraph (iii)), a sentence of detention under section 207 of the Criminal Procedure (Scotland) Act 1995, and

(iii) in the case of an offender who is aged under 18 at that time and is subject to a supervision requirement, an order for detention under section 44, or sentence of detention under section 208, of that Act.

(5) In this section 'the required minimum term' means—

(a) in relation to England and Wales—

(i) in the case of an offender who was aged 18 or over when he committed the offence, five years, and

(ii) in the case of an offender who was under 18 at that time, three years, and

(b) in relation to Scotland—

(i) in the case of an offender who was aged 21 or over when he committed the offence, five years, and

(ii) in the case of an offender who was aged under 21 at that time, three years.

Violent Crime Reduction Act 2006, s 29(3)

(3) Where—

(a) at the time of the offence, the offender was aged 16 or over, and

(b) the dangerous weapon in respect of which the offence was committed was a firearm mentioned in section 5(1)(a) to (af) or (c) or section 5(1A) (a) of the 1968 Act (firearms possession of which attracts a minimum sentence),

the offender shall be liable, on conviction on indictment, to imprisonment for a term not exceeding 10 years or to a fine, or to both.

Youth charged with an adult

If a youth is jointly charged with an indictable only offence, the youth will be sent to the Crown Court with the adult unless it is not in the interests of justice to do so (this will be rare). Note that the youth does not have to be charged, or appear at court, at the same time. Any related either-way or summary offences will be sent alongside.

If a youth is jointly charged with an either-way offence the venue will be dictated by the adult. If the adult pleads guilty, the charge will be put to the youth (the youth has no right to elect Crown Court trial). If the adult pleads not guilty, the youth will be tried at the same venue as the adult (unless on election it is not in the interests of justice to try the youth with the adult).

Youth charged alone (or only with other youths)

If the youth is charged alone he will appear for trial in the youth court unless the offence is one of homicide or is a grave crime.

Grave crimes:

Homicide etc: Is the defendant charged with offence of homicide or a firearms offence that carries a mandatory minimum sentence?	Yes—proceed to committal proceedings	No—consider grave crimes
Grave crimes: Is the defendant charged with one of the offences listed below this table AND a sentence of more than two years' detention would be a real possibility if he was convicted?	Yes—proceed to committal proceedings	No—proceed to summary trial

List of potential grave crimes:

- an offence punishable in the case of a person aged 21 or over with imprisonment for 14 years or more, not being an offence the sentence for which is fixed by law; or

- an offence under section 3 of the Sexual Offences Act 2003 (in this section, 'the 2003 Act') (sexual assault); or
- an offence under section 13 of the 2003 Act (child sex offences committed by children or young persons); or
- an offence under section 25 of the 2003 Act (sexual activity with a child family member); or
- an offence under section 26 of the 2003 Act (inciting a child family member to engage in sexual activity); or
- under subsection (1)(a), (ab), (aba), (ac), (ad), (ae), (af), or (c) of section 5 of the Firearms Act 1968 (prohibited weapons); or under subsection (1A)(a) of that section; or
- under subsection (1)(a), (ab), (aba), (ac), (ad), (ae), (af), or (c) of section 5 of the Firearms Act 1968 (prohibited weapons); or under subsection (1A)(a) of that section; or
- under section 51A(1A)(b), (e), or (f) of that Act and was committed in respect of a firearm or ammunition specified in section 5(1) (a), (ab), (aba), (ac), (ad), (ae), (af), or (c) or section 5(1A)(a) of that Act; or
- an offence under section 28 of the Violent Crime Reduction Act 2006 (using someone to mind a weapon).

In determining whether a sentence of more than two years would be imposed the court should ask itself what sentence was realistically possible bearing in mind the sentencing range (*Crown Prosecution Service v Newcastle Upon Tyne Youth Court* [2010] EWHC 2773 (Admin)).

Dangerous offenders

A court can send the youth for trial at the Crown Court if it is believed that the dangerous offender provisions will apply:

Powers of Criminal Courts (Sentencing) Act 2000, s 3C

(1) This section applies where on the summary trial of a specified offence a person aged under 18 is convicted of the offence.

(2) If, in relation to the offence, it appears to the court that the criteria for the imposition of a sentence under section 226(3) or 228(2) of the Criminal Justice Act 2003 would be met, the court must commit the offender in custody or on bail to the Crown Court for sentence in accordance with section 5A(1) below.

(3) Where the court commits a person under subsection (2) above, section 6 below (which enables a magistrates' court, where it commits a person under this section in respect of an offence, also to commit him to the Crown Court to be dealt with in respect of certain other offences) shall apply accordingly.

(4) Nothing in this section shall prevent the court from committing a specified offence to the Crown Court for sentence under section 3B above if the provisions of that section are satisfied.

(5) In this section, references to a specified offence are to a specified offence within the meaning of section 224 of the Criminal Justice Act 2003.

Dangerousness: See Appendix 1 for an overview flowchart and a list of specified offences. This provision, rarely used in practice due to the 'grave crime' provisions allows a youth court to commit a dangerous young offender to the crown court for sentence. The Sentencing Guidelines Council has issued this general guidance:

'The court should be particularly rigorous before concluding that a youth is a dangerous offender. When assessing likely future conduct and whether it may give rise to a significant risk of serious harm, the court should consider the offender's level of maturity and that he or she may change and develop in a shorter period of time than an adult. When assessing the risk of the offender committing further specified offences, a young person is less likely than an adult to have an extensive criminal record. Accordingly, when preparing a pre-sentence report, the Youth Offending Team looks not only at the offender's previous convictions but also at any evidence of violence or sexual aggression at home, at school or amongst the offender's peer group that may not have resulted in a conviction. The Youth Justice Board anticipates that normally the court would find a youth to be a dangerous offender only if he or she was assessed in a pre-sentence report to pose a very high risk of serious harm or, in a small number of cases and due to specific circumstances, a high risk of serious harm. However, the court is not bound by the assessment of risk in the pre-sentence report; it does not follow automatically that, because an offender has been assessed as posing a high risk or very high risk of serious harm, he or she is a dangerous offender.'

In *Crown Prosecution Service v South East Surrey Youth Court* [2006] 2 Cr App R (S) 26 it was held that the following provisions should apply:

(i) the policy of the legislature is that those who are under 18 should, wherever possible, be tried in a Youth Court, which is best designed for their specific needs;

(ii) the guidance given by the Court of Appeal, in particular in paragraph 17 of the judgment in *Lang & Ors* [2006] 2 Cr App R (S) 3, particularly in (iv) in relation to non-serious specified offences;

(iii) the need, in relation to those under 18, to be particularly rigorous before concluding that there is a significant risk of serious harm by the commission of further offences: such a conclusion is unlikely to be appropriate in the absence of a pre-sentence report following assessment by a young offender team;

(iv) in most cases where a non-serious specified offence is charged, an assessment of dangerousness will not be appropriate until after conviction, when, if the dangerousness criteria are met, the defendant can be committed to the Crown Court for sentence;

(v) when a youth under 18 is jointly charged with an adult, an exercise of judgement will be called for by the Youth Court when assessing the competing presumptions in favour of (a) joint trial of those jointly charged and (b) the trial of youths in the Youth Court. Factors relevant to that judgement will include the age and maturity of the youth, the comparative culpability in relation to the offence and the previous convictions of the two, and whether the trial can be severed without either injustice or undue inconvenience to witnesses.

ALLOCATION, COMMITTAL, SENDING AND TRANSFER–NEW PROVISIONS

Note: The guidance in this section is largely drawn from training materials issued to justices clerks (© Copyright). The provisions in this section apply only in these criminal justice areas as of 18 June 2012 (see section above for old provisions):

Bath and Wansdyke; Berkshire; Bristol; Liverpool and Knowsley; North Avon; North Hampshire; North Somerset; Ormskirk; Sefton; St Helens; Wigan and Leigh; and Wirral.

Overview: See the end of this section for an overview flowchart.

Policy intention: It is still the intention that cases remain in the youth court unless crown court trial is necessary (Magistrates' Courts Act 1980, s 24(1)). A new section 51A Crime and Disorder Act 1998 provides for the sending of defendants to the crown court in certain circumstances, including when a child or young person is charged with an adult. There is also a revised procedure for indication as to plea.

Cases that must be sent for trial forthwith:

In the following instances a youth shall be sent for trial forthwith:

(1) Homicide offences (Crime and Disorder Act 1998, ss 51A(3)(a) and (12)(a)).

(2) Certain firearms offences (Firearms Act 1968, s 51A(1) and Crime and Disorder Act 1998, ss 51A(3)(a) and (12)(a)). See below for Section 51A of the Firearms Act and the list of applicable offences. Note that offences under Violent Crime Reduction Act 2006, s 28 are also included in this section.

(3) Notices in serious or complex fraud cases (Crime and Disorder Act 1998, s 51A(3)(c)).

(4) Notices in certain cases involving children (Crime and Disorder Act 1998, s 51A(3)(c)).

(5) Dangerousness (Crime and Disorder Act 1998, s 51A(3)(d)). If the offence is a specified offence then it must be sent to the crown court if it appears to the court that the criteria for the imposition of a sentence for public protection or an extended sentence would be met.

Dangerousness: See Appendix 1 for an overview flowchart and a list of specified offences. This provision, rarely used in practice due to the 'grave crime' provisions allows a youth court to commit a dangerous young offender to the crown court for sentence. The Sentencing Guidelines Council has issued this general guidance:

'The court should be particularly rigorous before concluding that a youth is a dangerous offender. When assessing likely future conduct and whether it may give rise to a significant risk of serious harm, the court should consider the offender's level of maturity and that he or she may change and develop in a shorter period of time than an adult. When assessing the risk of the offender committing further specified offences, a young person is less likely than an adult to have an extensive criminal record. Accordingly, when preparing a pre-sentence report, the Youth Offending Team looks not only at the offender's previous convictions but also at any evidence of violence or sexual aggression at home, at school or amongst the offender's peer group that may not have resulted in a conviction. The Youth Justice Board anticipates that normally the court would find a youth to be a dangerous offender only if he or she was assessed in a pre-sentence report to pose a very high risk of serious harm or, in a small number of cases and due to specific circumstances, a high risk of serious harm. However, the court is not bound by the assessment of risk in the pre-sentence report; it does not follow automatically that, because an offender has been assessed as posing a high risk or very high risk of serious harm, he or she is a dangerous offender.'

In *Crown Prosecution Service v South East Surrey Youth Court* [2006] 2 Cr App R (S) 26 it was held that the following provisions should apply:

(i) the policy of the legislature is that those who are under 18 should, wherever possible, be tried in a Youth Court, which is best designed for their specific needs;

(ii) the guidance given by the Court of Appeal, in particular in paragraph 17 of the judgment in *Lang & Ors* [2006] 2 Cr App R (S) 3, particularly in (iv) in relation to non-serious specified offences;

(iii) the need, in relation to those under 18, to be particularly rigorous before concluding that there is a significant risk of serious harm by the commission of further offences: such a conclusion is unlikely to be appropriate in the absence of a pre-sentence report following assessment by a young offender team;

(iv) in most cases where a non-serious specified offence is charged, an assessment of dangerousness will not be appropriate until after conviction, when, if the dangerousness criteria are met, the defendant can be committed to the Crown Court for sentence;

(v) when a youth under 18 is jointly charged with an adult, an exercise of judgement will be called for by the Youth Court when assessing the competing presumptions in favour of (a) joint trial of those jointly charged and (b) the trial of youths in the Youth Court. Factors relevant to that judgement will include the age and maturity of the youth, the comparative culpability in relation to the offence and the previous convictions of the two, and whether the trial can be severed without either injustice or undue inconvenience to witnesses.

Cases where a plea before venue procedure shall take place:

In the following instances the court must follow the plea before venue procedure outline in the Magistrates' Courts Act 1980, s 24A. In all other cases the court will simply take a plea and proceed to summary trial or sentence as appropriate:

(1) The offence is an indictable offence and the youth is charged jointly with an adult defendant who has been sent to the crown court for trial, or is charged with an indictable offence that is related to that offence (Crime and Disorder Act 1998, s 51(7));

(2) The youth is charged with an indictable or summary offence where they have been sent for trial under the above provision for a related offence (Crime and Disorder Act 1998, s 51(8));

(3) The youth is charged with a grave crime (Crime and Disorder Act 1998, s 51A(3)(b)). Grave crimes are as described in the Powers of Criminal Courts (Sentencing) Act 2000, s 91(1) as:

(a) an offence punishable in the case of a person aged 21 or over with imprisonment for 14 years or more, not being an offence the sentence for which is fixed by law; or

(b) an offence under section 3 of the Sexual Offences Act 2003 (in this section, "the 2003 Act") (sexual assault); or

(c) an offence under section 13 of the 2003 Act (child sex offences committed by children or young persons); or

(d) an offence under section 25 of the 2003 Act (sexual activity with a child family member); or

(e) an offence under section 26 of the 2003 Act (inciting a child family member to engage in sexual activity).

(4) The youth is charged with an indictable or summary offence which is related to an offence for which they are, on the same day, being sent for trial (Crime and Disorder Act 1998, s 51A(4)).

New plea before venue procedure:

(a) *Taking an indication of plea*

The charge should be written down and read to the defendant.

The court should explain to the defendant that they may indicate whether (if the offence were to proceed to trial) they would plead guilty or not guilty, and that, if they indicate a plea of guilty, they may be:

- committed to the Crown Court for sentence (Powers of Criminal Courts (Sentencing) Act 2000, s 3B) if the offence is punishable with long term detention for grave crimes; or
- (if the defendant is charged with a specified offence and the court considers that they qualify for a sentence of detention for public protection or an extended sentence) committed to the Crown Court for sentence under the dangerous offender provisions (Powers of Criminal Courts (Sentencing) Act 2000, s 3C).

The new s.24B MCA 1980 provides that the plea before venue procedure may take place in the absence of a legally represented defendant if it is not practicable for the proceedings to be conducted in the defendant's presence by reason of their disorderly conduct. The matters will be put to, and pleas taken from, the legal representative–*(b)* and *(c)* below would apply.

(b) *Indication of a guilty plea by defendant*

If the defendant indicates a guilty plea, they are treated as having been tried summarily and convicted. The court may proceed to deal with them, or commit for sentence as a grave crime or dangerous offender (Powers of Criminal Courts (Sentencing) Act 2000, ss 3B, 3C).

(c) *Defendant pleads not guilty or fails to indicate a plea*

Where the defendant fails to indicate a plea, they shall be taken to indicate a not guilty plea.

Where the defendant indicates a not guilty plea or is taken to indicate a not guilty plea, the court must determine whether to proceed to summary trial or to send the defendant to the Crown Court for trial.

The defendant may be sent to the Crown Court for trial where there is power to sentence the defendant to long-term detention under s.91 PCC(S) Act 2000 for the offence (other than a specified offence where the dangerous offender provisions apply) and the court considers that if they are found guilty of the offence it ought to be possible to impose a sentence of detention under s.91 (Crime and Disorder Act 1998, s 51A(3)(b)).

NB: there is no provision for the defendant to request an indication of sentence from the court as is the case with adult defendants.

(d) *Linked offences and sending for trial–s.51A(4) and (5) CDA 1998*

If a youth is sent to the Crown Court for trial for one or more offences, it may at the same time or on a subsequent occasion send them to the Crown Court for trial for any related indictable offence or summary offence punishable with imprisonment or disqualification from driving.

(e) *Youth charged jointly with an adult sent for trial–s.51(7) CDA 1998 as substituted by Sch.3, para.18 CJA 2003*

Where:

- the court sends an adult defendant A (not a youth) for trial;
- a youth Y appears before the court on the same or a subsequent occasion charged jointly with A with an indictable offence; and
- that offence appears to the court to be related to an offence for which A was sent for trial,

the court shall also send Y to the Crown Court for trial for the indictable offence if it considers it necessary in the interests of justice to do so. First, however, the defendant will be asked to indicate a plea. If a guilty plea is indicated, sending to the Crown Court for trial will be avoided.

Where the youth has been sent for trial under s.51(7) CDA 1998, the court may send them for trial for any related indictable offence, or related summary offences punishable with imprisonment or disqualification.

Magistrates' Courts Act 1980, ss 24, 24A, 24B

24.— Summary trial of information against child or young persons for indictable offence.

(1) Where a person under the age of 18 years appears or is brought before a magistrates' court on an information charging him with an indictable offence he shall, subject to sections 51 and 51A of the Crime and Disorder Act 1998 and to sections 24A and 24B below, be tried summarily.

24A Child or young person to indicate intention as to plea in certain cases

(1) This section applies where—

(a) a person under the age of 18 years appears or is brought before a magistrates' court on an information charging him with an offence other than one falling within section 51A(12) of the Crime and Disorder Act 1998 ("the 1998 Act"); and

(b) but for the application of the following provisions of this section, the court would be required at that stage, by virtue of section 51(7) or (8) or 51A(3)(b), (4) or (5) of the 1998 Act to determine, in relation to the offence, whether to send the person to the

Crown Court for trial (or to determine any matter, the effect of which would be to determine whether he is sent to the Crown Court for trial).

(2) Where this section applies, the court shall, before proceeding to make any such determination as is referred to in subsection (1)(b) above (the "relevant determination"), follow the procedure set out in this section.

(3) Everything that the court is required to do under the following provisions of this section must be done with the accused person in court.

(4) The court shall cause the charge to be written down, if this has not already been done, and to be read to the accused.

(5) The court shall then explain to the accused in ordinary language that he may indicate whether (if the offence were to proceed to trial) he would plead guilty or not guilty, and that if he indicates that he would plead guilty—

(a) the court must proceed as mentioned in subsection (7) below; and

(b) (in cases where the offence is one mentioned in section 91(1) of the Powers of Criminal Courts (Sentencing) Act 2000) he may be sent to the Crown Court for sentencing under section 3B or (if applicable) 3C of that Act if the court is of such opinion as is mentioned in subsection (2) of the applicable section.

(6) The court shall then ask the accused whether (if the offence were to proceed to trial) he would plead guilty or not guilty.

(7) If the accused indicates that he would plead guilty, the court shall proceed as if—

(a) the proceedings constituted from the beginning the summary trial of the information; and

(b) section 9(1) above was complied with and he pleaded guilty under it,

and, accordingly, the court shall not (and shall not be required to) proceed to make the relevant determination or to proceed further under section 51 or (as the case may be) section 51A of the 1998 Act in relation to the offence.

(8) If the accused indicates that he would plead not guilty, the court shall proceed to make the relevant determination and this section shall cease to apply.

(9) If the accused in fact fails to indicate how he would plead, for the purposes of this section he shall be taken to indicate that he would plead not guilty.

(10) Subject to subsection (7) above, the following shall not for any purpose be taken to constitute the taking of a plea—

(a) asking the accused under this section whether (if the offence were to proceed to trial) he would plead guilty or not guilty;

(b) an indication by the accused under this section of how he would plead.

24B Intention as to plea by child or young person: absence of accused

(1) This section shall have effect where—

(a) a person under the age of 18 years appears or is brought before a magistrates' court on an information charging him with an offence other than one falling within section 51A(12) of the Crime and Disorder Act 1998;

(b) but for the application of the following provisions of this section, the court would be required at that stage to make one of the determinations referred to in paragraph (b) of section 24A(1) above ("the relevant determination");

(c) the accused is represented by a legal representative;

(d) the court considers that by reason of the accused's disorderly conduct before the court it is not practicable for proceedings under section 24A above to be conducted in his presence; and

(e) the court considers that it should proceed in the absence of the accused.

(2) In such a case—

 (a) the court shall cause the charge to be written down, if this has not already been done, and to be read to the representative;

 (b) the court shall ask the representative whether (if the offence were to proceed to trial) the accused would plead guilty or not guilty;

 (c) if the representative indicates that the accused would plead guilty the court shall proceed as if the proceedings constituted from the beginning the summary trial of the information, and as if section 9(1) above was complied with and the accused pleaded guilty under it;

 (d) if the representative indicates that the accused would plead not guilty the court shall proceed to make the relevant determination and this section shall cease to apply.

(3) If the representative in fact fails to indicate how the accused would plead, for the purposes of this section he shall be taken to indicate that the accused would plead not guilty.

(4) Subject to subsection (2)(c) above, the following shall not for any purpose be taken to constitute the taking of a plea—

 (a) asking the representative under this section whether (if the offence were to proceed to trial) the accused would plead guilty or not guilty;

 (b) an indication by the representative under this section of how the accused would plead.

Crime and Disorder Act 1998, ss 51, 51A

51 Sending cases to the Crown Court: adults

(1) Where an adult appears or is brought before a magistrates' court ("the court") charged with an offence and any of the conditions mentioned in subsection (2) below is satisfied, the court shall send him forthwith to the Crown Court for trial for the offence.

(2) Those conditions are—

 (a) that the offence is an offence triable only on indictment other than one in respect of which notice has been given under section 51B or 51C below;

 (b) that the offence is an either-way offence and the court is required under section 20(9) (b), 21, 23(4)(b) or (5) or 25(2D) of the Magistrates' Courts Act 1980 to proceed in relation to the offence in accordance with subsection (1) above;

 (c) that notice is given to the court under section 51B or 51C below in respect of the offence.

(3) Where the court sends an adult for trial under subsection (1) above, it shall at the same time send him to the Crown Court for trial for any either-way or summary offence with which he is charged and which—

 (a) (if it is an either-way offence) appears to the court to be related to the offence mentioned in subsection (1) above; or

 (b) (if it is a summary offence) appears to the court to be related to the offence mentioned in subsection (1) above or to the either-way offence, and which fulfils the requisite condition (as defined in subsection (11) below).

(4) Where an adult who has been sent for trial under subsection (1) above subsequently appears or is brought before a magistrates' court charged with an either-way or summary offence which—

 (a) appears to the court to be related to the offence mentioned in subsection (1) above; and

 (b) (in the case of a summary offence) fulfils the requisite condition,

the court may send him forthwith to the Crown Court for trial for the either-way or summary offence.

(5) Where—

    (a) the court sends an adult ("A") for trial under subsection (1) or (3) above;

    (b) another adult appears or is brought before the court on the same or a subsequent occasion charged jointly with A with an either-way offence; and

    (c) that offence appears to the court to be related to an offence for which A was sent for trial under subsection (1) or (3) above,

the court shall where it is the same occasion, and may where it is a subsequent occasion, send the other adult forthwith to the Crown Court for trial for the either-way offence.

(6) Where the court sends an adult for trial under subsection (5) above, it shall at the same time send him to the Crown Court for trial for any either-way or summary offence with which he is charged and which—

    (a) (if it is an either-way offence) appears to the court to be related to the offence for which he is sent for trial; and

    (b) (if it is a summary offence) appears to the court to be related to the offence for which he is sent for trial or to the either-way offence, and which fulfils the requisite condition.

(7) Where—

    (a) the court sends an adult ("A") for trial under subsection (1), (3) or (5) above; and

    (b) a child or young person appears or is brought before the court on the same or a subsequent occasion charged jointly with A with an indictable offence for which A is sent for trial under subsection (1), (3) or (5) above, or an indictable offence which appears to the court to be related to that offence,

the court shall, if it considers it necessary in the interests of justice to do so, send the child or young person forthwith to the Crown Court for trial for the indictable offence.

(8) Where the court sends a child or young person for trial under subsection (7) above, it may at the same time send him to the Crown Court for trial for any indictable or summary offence with which he is charged and which—

    (a) (if it is an indictable offence) appears to the court to be related to the offence for which he is sent for trial; and

    (b) (if it is a summary offence) appears to the court to be related to the offence for which he is sent for trial or to the indictable offence, and which fulfils the requisite condition.

(9) Subsections (7) and (8) above are subject to sections 24A and 24B of the Magistrates' Courts Act 1980 (which provide for certain cases involving children and young persons to be tried summarily).

(10) The trial of the information charging any summary offence for which a person is sent for trial under this section shall be treated as if the court had adjourned it under section 10 of the 1980 Act and had not fixed the time and place for its resumption.

(11) A summary offence fulfils the requisite condition if it is punishable with imprisonment or involves obligatory or discretionary disqualification from driving.

(12) In the case of an adult charged with an offence—

    (a) if the offence satisfies paragraph (c) of subsection (2) above, the offence shall be dealt with under subsection (1) above and not under any other provision of this section or section 51A below;

    (b) subject to paragraph (a) above, if the offence is one in respect of which the court is required to, or would decide to, send the adult to the Crown Court under—

        (i) subsection (5) above; or

        (ii) subsection (6) of section 51A below,

the offence shall be dealt with under that subsection and not under any other provision of this section or section 51A below.

(13)   The functions of a magistrates' court under this section, and its related functions under section 51D below, may be discharged by a single justice.

51A Sending cases to the Crown Court: children and young persons

(1)   This section is subject to sections 24A and 24B of the Magistrates' Courts Act 1980 (which provide for certain offences involving children or young persons to be tried summarily).

(2)   Where a child or young person appears or is brought before a magistrates' court ("the court") charged with an offence and any of the conditions mentioned in subsection (3) below is satisfied, the court shall send him forthwith to the Crown Court for trial for the offence.

(3)   Those conditions are—

(a)   that the offence falls within subsection (12) below;

(b)   that the offence is such as is mentioned in subsection (1) of section 91 of the Powers of Criminal Courts (Sentencing) Act 2000 (other than one mentioned in paragraph (d) below in relation to which it appears to the court as mentioned there) and the court considers that if he is found guilty of the offence it ought to be possible to sentence him in pursuance of subsection (3) of that section;

(c)   that notice is given to the court under section 51B or 51C below in respect of the offence;

(d)   that the offence is a specified offence (within the meaning of section 224 of the Criminal Justice Act 2003) and it appears to the court that if he is found guilty of the offence the criteria for the imposition of a sentence under section 226(3) or 228(2) of that Act would be met.

(4)   Where the court sends a child or young person for trial under subsection (2) above, it may at the same time send him to the Crown Court for trial for any indictable or summary offence with which he is charged and which—

(a)   (if it is an indictable offence) appears to the court to be related to the offence mentioned in subsection (2) above; or

(b)   (if it is a summary offence) appears to the court to be related to the offence mentioned in subsection (2) above or to the indictable offence, and which fulfils the requisite condition (as defined in subsection (9) below).

(5)   Where a child or young person who has been sent for trial under subsection (2) above subsequently appears or is brought before a magistrates' court charged with an indictable or summary offence which—

(a)   appears to the court to be related to the offence mentioned in subsection (2) above; and

(b)   (in the case of a summary offence) fulfils the requisite condition,

the court may send him forthwith to the Crown Court for trial for the indictable or summary offence.

(6)   Where—

(a)   the court sends a child or young person ("C") for trial under subsection (2) or (4) above; and

(b)   an adult appears or is brought before the court on the same or a subsequent occasion charged jointly with C with an either-way offence for which C is sent for trial under subsection (2) or (4) above, or an either-way offence which appears to the court to be related to that offence, the court shall where it is the same occasion, and may where it is a subsequent occasion, send the adult forthwith to the Crown Court for trial for the either-way offence.

(7) Where the court sends an adult for trial under subsection (6) above, it shall at the same time send him to the Crown Court for trial for any either-way or summary offence with which he is charged and which—

(a) (if it is an either-way offence) appears to the court to be related to the offence for which he was sent for trial; and

(b) (if it is a summary offence) appears to the court to be related to the offence for which he was sent for trial or to the either way offence, and which fulfils the requisite condition.

(8) The trial of the information charging any summary offence for which a person is sent for trial under this section shall be treated as if the court had adjourned it under section 10 of the 1980 Act and had not fixed the time and place for its resumption.

(9) A summary offence fulfils the requisite condition if it is punishable with imprisonment or involves obligatory or discretionary disqualification from driving.

(10) In the case of a child or young person charged with an offence—

(a) if the offence satisfies any of the conditions in subsection (3) above, the offence shall be dealt with under subsection (2) above and not under any other provision of this section or section 51 above;

(b) subject to paragraph (a) above, if the offence is one in respect of which the requirements of subsection (7) of section 51 above for sending the child or young person to the Crown Court are satisfied, the offence shall be dealt with under that subsection and not under any other provision of this section or section 51 above.

(11) The functions of a magistrates' court under this section, and its related functions under section 51D below, may be discharged by a single justice.

(12) An offence falls within this subsection if—

(a) it is an offence of homicide;

(b) each of the requirements of section 51A(1) of the Firearms Act 1968 would be satisfied with respect to—

(i) the offence; and

(ii) the person charged with it,

if he were convicted of the offence ; or

(c) section 29(3) of Violent Crime Reduction Act 2006 (minimum sentences in certain cases of using someone to mind a weapon) would apply if he were convicted of the offence.

Firearms Act 1968, s 51A

(1) This section applies where—

(a) an individual is convicted of—

(i) an offence under section 5(1)(a), (ab), (aba), (ac), (ad), (ae), (af) or (c) of this Act,

(ii) an offence under section 5(1A)(a) of this Act, or

(iii) an offence under any of the provisions of this Act listed in subsection (1A) in respect of a firearm or ammunition specified in section 5(1)(a), (ab), (aba), (ac), (ad), (ae), (af) or (c) or section 5(1A)(a) of this Act, and

(b) the offence was committed after the commencement of this section and at a time when he was aged 16 or over.

(1A) The provisions are–

(a) section 16 (possession of firearm with intent to injure);

(b) section 16A (possession of firearm with intent to cause fear of violence);

(c) section 17 (use of firearm to resist arrest);

(d) section 18 (carrying firearm with criminal intent);

(e) section 19 (carrying a firearm in a public place);

(f) section 20(1) (trespassing in a building with firearm).

(2) The court shall impose an appropriate custodial sentence (or order for detention) for a term of at least the required minimum term (with or without a fine) unless the court is of the opinion that there are exceptional circumstances relating to the offence or to the offender which justify its not doing so.

(3) Where an offence is found to have been committed over a period of two or more days, or at some time during a period of two or more days, it shall be taken for the purposes of this section to have been committed on the last of those days.

(4) In this section "appropriate custodial sentence (or order for detention)" means—

(a) in relation to England and Wales—

(i) in the case of an offender who is aged 18 or over when convicted, a sentence of imprisonment, and

(ii) in the case of an offender who is aged under 18 at that time, a sentence of detention under section 91 of the Powers of Criminal Courts (Sentencing) Act 2000;

(b) in relation to Scotland—

(i) in the case of an offender who is aged 21 or over when convicted, a sentence of imprisonment,

(ii) in the case of an offender who is aged under 21 at that time (not being an offender mentioned in sub-paragraph (iii)), a sentence of detention under section 207 of the Criminal Procedure (Scotland) Act 1995, and

(iii) in the case of an offender who is aged under 18 at that time and is subject to a supervision requirement, an order for detention under section 44, or sentence of detention under section 208, of that Act.

(5) In this section "the required minimum term" means—

(a) in relation to England and Wales—

(i) in the case of an offender who was aged 18 or over when he committed the offence, five years, and

(ii) in the case of an offender who was under 18 at that time, three years, and

(b) in relation to Scotland—

(i) in the case of an offender who was aged 21 or over when he committed the offence, five years, and

(ii) in the case of an offender who was aged under 21 at that time, three years.

Violent Crime Reduction Act 2006, s 29(3)

(3) Where—

(a) at the time of the offence, the offender was aged 16 or over, and

(b) the dangerous weapon in respect of which the offence was committed was a firearm mentioned in section 5(1)(a) to (af) or (c) or section 5(1A) (a) of the 1968 Act (firearms possession of which attracts a minimum sentence),

the offender shall be liable, on conviction on indictment, to imprisonment for a term not exceeding 10 years or to a fine, or to both.

Power to commit a youth to the crown court for sentence

A defendant under 18 years who has been found guilty may be committed to the Crown Court for sentence as follows.

(a) *Sentence of long-term detention–s.3B PCC(S)A 2000*

A youth may be committed for sentence when they have indicated an intention to plead guilty to an offence mentioned in s.91 PCC(S)A 2000, and the court is of the opinion that the offence, or the combination of the offence and one or more offences associated with it, is such that the Crown Court should have power to sentence the defendant to long-term detention under s.91.

NB: this power applies only where the defendant indicates an intention to plead guilty. It does not apply where the defendant indicates a not guilty plea or no plea, the court decides to proceed to summary trial, and the defendant subsequently pleads guilty or is found guilty after trial.

(b) *Dangerous offender provisions–s.3C PCC(S)A 2000*

Where a defendant has been convicted of a specified offence on summary trial and it appears to the court that the criteria for the imposition of a sentence of detention for public protection or an extended sentence would be met, the court **must** commit them to the Crown Court for sentence.

A defendant cannot be committed for sentence under both ss.3B and 3C PCC(S)A 2000 for the same offence. However, s.3C PCC(S)A 2000 does not prevent a court from committing an offence under s.3B if those provisions are satisfied.

(c) *Guilty pleas to related offences following sending for trial for a grave crime–s.4A PCC(S)A 2000*

Where a defendant has been sent to the Crown Court for trial in relation to a grave crime and indicates an intention to plead guilty to other related offences, the court may commit them to the Crown Court for sentence on those other matters. In this situation, the Crown Court must sentence for the related offence within the powers of the magistrates' courts unless:

- the defendant has been found guilty of one or more of the related offences for which they have been committed for trial; or
- the magistrates' court has stated that, in its opinion, it also had power to commit for sentence under s.3B(2) or s.3C(2) PCC(S) Act 2000.

(d) *Defendant has been committed for sentence under ss.3B, 3C or 4A PCC(S)A 2000 and is to be sentenced for other offences–s.6 PCC(S)A 2000*

Where the court commits a defendant under ss. 3B, 3C or 4A PCC(S)A 2000 see preceding paragraphs, the court can also commit other offences for sentence under s.6 PCC(S)A 2000, i.e. any offence whatsoever for which the magistrates' court has power to deal with the defendant where the relevant offence is an indictable offence, or, where the relevant offence is a summary offence, any offence punishable with imprisonment or disqualification under the Road Traffic Offenders Act 1988.

On committal for sentence under ss.3B, 3C or 4A PCC(S)A 2000, the Crown Court "shall enquire into the circumstances of the case and may deal with the offender in any way in which it could deal with him if he had just been found guilty of the offence on indictment before the court" but in respect of s.4A only, if the court had stated it had power to commit under ss.3B(2) or 3C(2).

Powers of Criminal Courts (Sentencing) Act 2000, ss 3B, 3C, 4A and 6

3B Committal for sentence on indication of guilty plea by child or young person

(1) This section applies where—

(a) a person aged under 18 appears or is brought before a magistrates' court ("the court") on an information charging him with an offence mentioned in subsection (1) of section 91 below ("the offence");

(b) he or his representative indicates under section 24A or (as the case may be) 24B of the

Magistrates' Courts Act 1980 (child or young person to indicate intention as to plea in certain cases) that he would plead guilty if the offence were to proceed to trial; and

(c) proceeding as if section 9(1) of that Act were complied with and he pleaded guilty under it, the court convicts him of the offence.

(2) If the court is of the opinion that—

(a) the offence; or

(b) the combination of the offence and one or more offences associated with it,

was such that the Crown Court should, in the court's opinion, have power to deal with the offender as if the provisions of section 91(3) below applied, the court may commit him in custody or on bail to the Crown Court for sentence in accordance with section 5A(1) below.

(3) Where the court commits a person under subsection (2) above, section 6 below (which enables a magistrates' court, where it commits a person under this section in respect of an offence, also to commit him to the Crown Court to be dealt with in respect of certain other offences) shall apply accordingly.

3C Committal for sentence of dangerous young offenders

(1) This section applies where on the summary trial of a specified offence a person aged under 18 is convicted of the offence.

(2) If, in relation to the offence, it appears to the court that the criteria for the imposition of a sentence under section 226(3) or 228(2) of the Criminal Justice Act 2003 would be met, the court must commit the offender in custody or on bail to the Crown Court for sentence in accordance with section 5A(1) below.

(3) Where the court commits a person under subsection (2) above, section 6 below (which enables a magistrates' court, where it commits a person under this section in respect of an offence, also to commit him to the Crown Court to be dealt with in respect of certain other offences) shall apply accordingly.

(4) Nothing in this section shall prevent the court from committing a specified offence to the Crown Court for sentence under section 3B above if the provisions of that section are satisfied.

(5) In this section, references to a specified offence are to a specified offence within the meaning of section 224 of the Criminal Justice Act 2003.

4A Committal for sentence on indication of guilty plea by child or young person with related offences

(1) This section applies where—

(a) a person aged under 18 appears or brought before a magistrates' court ("the court") on an information charging him with an offence mentioned in subsection (1) of section 91 below ("the offence");

(b) he or his representative indicates under section 24A or (as the case may be) 24B of the Magistrates' Courts Act 1980 (child or young person to indicate intention as to plea in certain cases) that he would plead guilty if the offence were to proceed to trial; and

(c) proceeding as if section 9(1) of that Act were complied with and he pleaded guilty under it, the court convicts him of the offence.

(2) If the court has sent the offender to the Crown Court for trial for one or more related offences, that is to say one or more offences which, in its opinion, are related to the offence, it may commit him in custody or on bail to the Crown Court to be dealt with in respect of the offence in accordance with section 5A(1) below.

(3) If the power conferred by subsection (2) above is not exercisable but the court is still to determine to, or to determine whether to, send the offender to the Crown Court for trial under section 51 or 51A of the Crime and Disorder Act 1998 for one or more related offences—

(a) it shall adjourn the proceedings relating to the offence until after it has made those determinations; and

(b) if it sends the offender to the Crown Court for trial for one or more related offences, it may then exercise that power.

(4) Where the court—

(a) under subsection (2) above commits the offender to the Crown Court to be dealt with in respect of the offence; and

(b) does not state that, in its opinion, it also has power so to commit him under section 3B(2) or, as the case may be, section 3C(2) above,

section 5A(1) below shall not apply unless he is convicted before the Crown Court of one or more of the related offences.

(5) Where section 5A(1) below does not apply, the Crown Court may deal with the offender in respect of the offence in any way in which the magistrates' court could deal with him if it had just convicted him of the offence.

(6) Where the court commits a person under subsection (2) above, section 6 below (which enables a magistrates' court, where it commits a person under this section in respect of an offence, also to commit him to the Crown Court to be dealt with in respect of certain other offences) shall apply accordingly.

(7) Section 4(7) above applies for the purposes of this section as it applies for the purposes of that section.

6.— Committal for sentence in certain cases where offender committed in respect of another offence.

(1) This section applies where a magistrates' court ("the committing court") commits a person in custody or on bail to the Crown Court under any enactment mentioned in subsection (4) below to be sentenced or otherwise dealt with in respect of an offence ("the relevant offence").

(2) Where this section applies and the relevant offence is an indictable offence, the committing court may also commit the offender, in custody or on bail as the case may require, to the Crown Court to be dealt with in respect of any other offence whatsoever in respect of which the committing court has power to deal with him (being an offence of which he has been convicted by that or any other court).

(3) Where this section applies and the relevant offence is a summary offence, the committing court may commit the offender, in custody or on bail as the case may require, to the Crown Court to be dealt with in respect of—

(a) any other offence of which the committing court has convicted him, being either—

(i) an offence punishable with imprisonment; or

(ii) an offence in respect of which the committing court has a power or duty to order him to be disqualified under section 34, 35 or 36 of the Road Traffic Offenders Act 1988 (disqualification for certain motoring offences); or

(b) any suspended sentence in respect of which the committing court has under paragraph 11(1) of Schedule 12 to the Criminal Justice Act 2003 power to deal with him.

(4) The enactments referred to in subsection (1) above are—

(a) the Vagrancy Act 1824 (incorrigible rogues);

(b) sections 3 to 4A above (committal for sentence for offences triable either way);

(c) section 13(5) below (conditionally discharged person convicted of further offence);

[...]

(e) paragraph 11(2) of Schedule 12 to the Criminal Justice Act 2003 (committal to Crown Court where offender convicted during operational period of suspended sentence).

New allocation procedure for a young defendant:

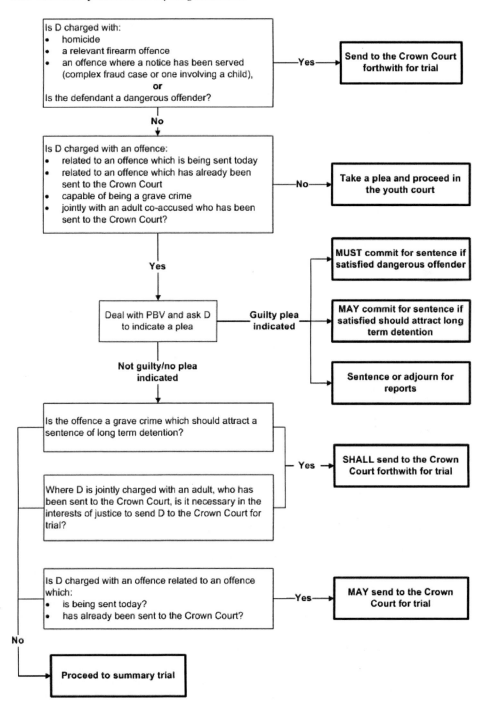

ATTENDANCE OF PARENT OR GUARDIAN

Children and Young Persons Act 1933, s 34A

(1) Where a child or young person is charged with an offence or is for any other reason brought before a court, the court—

(a) may in any case; and

(b) shall in the case of a child or a young person who is under the age of sixteen years,

require a person who is a parent or guardian of his to attend at the court during all the stages of the proceedings, unless and to the extent that the court is satisfied that it would be unreasonable to require such attendance, having regard to the circumstances of the case.

(2) In relation to a child or young person for whom a local authority have parental responsibility and who—

(a) is in their care; or

(b) is provided with accommodation by them in the exercise of any functions (in particular those under the Children Act 1989) which are social services functions within the meaning of the Local Authority Social Services Act 1970,

the reference in subsection (1) above to a person who is a parent or guardian of his shall be construed as a reference to that authority or, where he is allowed to live with such a person, as including such a reference.

In this subsection 'local authority' and 'parental responsibility' have the same meanings as in the Children Act 1989.

BAIL

Provision of bail for juveniles

The provision of bail for juveniles (below the age of 17) is almost exactly the same as for adults, save that age determines where the juvenile will be remanded to if bail is refused. In the case of a youth charged with murder, where the court has no power to grant bail, the court will still determine to where the youth is remanded (*R (A) v Lewisham Youth Court* [2011] EWHC 1193 (Admin)).

Forthcoming changes: The Legal Aid, Sentencing and Punishment of Offenders Act 2012 makes substantial changes in relation to bail, much of which is concerned with the remand of children. The legislative changes, not in force at the time of writing are detailed in Appendix 11.

Remand will be local authority accommodation unless

(1) boy or girl aged 10 or 11 and the local authority can apply for a secure accommodation order under section 25 of the Children Act 1989;

(2) girl aged 12–16 or boy aged 12–14 AND security requirement met. In that case remand will be to secure accommodation;

(3) boy aged 15 or 16 AND security requirement met AND vulnerable AND place available in secure accommodation. In that case remand will be to secure accommodation;

(4) boy aged 15 or 16 AND security requirement met AND either the boy is not vulnerable, or is vulnerable but there is no secure accommodation available. In that case remand will be to remand centre or prison.

Security requirement

In order to impose a security requirement the following conditions must be met where the juvenile is:

• charged with a violent or sexual offence, or an offence which for an adult is punishable with imprisonment of 14 years or more; or

- charged with or has been convicted of one or more imprisonable offences, which, together with any other imprisonable offences of which he has been convicted in any proceedings, amount to (or would amount to if he were convicted for the offences with which he is charged) a recent history of repeatedly committing imprisonable offences while remanded on bail or to local authority accommodation.

AND, in either case where:

the court is of the opinion, after considering all the options for the remand of the person, that only remanding him to local authority accommodation with a security requirement would be adequate—

    (a) to protect the public from really serious harm from him; or

    (b) to prevent the commission by him of imprisonable offences.

The juvenile must be legally represented (or have refused representation) before the court can impose a security requirement.

Vulnerability criteria

Children and Young Persons Act 1969, s 23

(1)   Where—

    (a) a court remands a child or young person charged with or convicted of one or more offences or commits him for trial or sentence; and

    (b) he is not released on bail,

the remand or committal shall be to local authority accommodation; and in the following provisions of this section (except subsection (1A)), any reference (however expressed) to a remand shall be construed as including a reference to a committal.

(1A)   Where a court remands a child or young person in connection with extradition proceedings and he is not released on bail the remand shall be to local authority accommodation.

(2)   A court remanding a person to local authority accommodation shall designate the local authority who are to receive him; and that authority shall be—

    (a) in the case of a person who is being looked after by a local authority, that authority; and

    (b) in any other case, the local authority in whose area it appears to the court that he resides or the offence or one of the offences was committed.

(3)   Where a person is remanded to local authority accommodation, it shall be lawful for any person acting on behalf of the designated authority to detain him.

(4)   Subject to subsections (5), (5ZA) and (5A) below, a court remanding a person to local authority accommodation may, after consultation with the designated authority, require that authority to comply with a security requirement, that is to say, a requirement that the person in question be placed and kept in secure accommodation.

(5)   A court shall not impose a security requirement in relation to a person remanded in accordance with subsection (1) above except in respect of a child who has attained the age of twelve, or a young person, who (in either case) is of a prescribed description , and then only if—

    (a) he is charged with or has been convicted of a violent or sexual offence, or an offence punishable in the case of an adult with imprisonment for a term of fourteen years or more; or

    (b) he is charged with or has been convicted of one or more imprisonable offences which, together with any other imprisonable offences of which he has been convicted in any proceedings–

        (i) amount, or

(ii)   would, if he were convicted of the offences with which he is charged, amount,

to a recent history of repeatedly committing imprisonable offences while remanded on bail or to local authority accommodation,

and (in either case) the condition set out in subsection (5AA) below is satisfied.

(5ZA) A court shall not impose a security requirement in relation to a person remanded in accordance with subsection (1A) above unless—

(a) he has attained the age of twelve and is of a prescribed description;
(b) one or both of the conditions set out in subsection (5ZB) below is satisfied; and
(c) the condition set out in subsection (5AA) below is satisfied.

(5ZB) The conditions mentioned in subsection (5ZA)(b) above are—

(a) that the conduct constituting the offence to which the extradition proceedings relate would if committed in the United Kingdom constitute an offence punishable in the case of an adult with imprisonment for a term of fourteen years or more;
(b) that the person has previously absconded from the extradition proceedings or from proceedings in the United Kingdom or the requesting territory which relate to the conduct constituting the offence to which the extradition proceedings relate.

(5ZC) For the purposes of subsection (5ZB) above a person has absconded from proceedings if in relation to those proceedings—

(a) he has been released subject to a requirement to surrender to custody at a particular time and he has failed to surrender to custody at that time, or
(b) he has surrendered into the custody of a court and he has at any time absented himself from the court without its leave.

(5AA) The condition mentioned in subsections (5) and (5ZA) above is that the court is of the opinion, after considering all the options for the remand of the person, that only remanding him to local authority accommodation with a security requirement would be adequate–

(a) to protect the public from serious harm from him; or
(b) to prevent the commission by him of imprisonable offences.

(5A)   A court shall not impose a security requirement in respect of a child or young person who is not legally represented in the court unless—

(a) he was granted a right to representation funded by the Legal Services Commission as part of the Criminal Defence Service but the right was withdrawn because of his conduct [or because it appeared that his financial resources were such that he was not eligible to be granted such a right;
(aa) he applied for such representation and the application was refused because it appeared that his financial resources were such that he was not eligible to be granted a right to it; or
(b) having been informed of his right to apply for such representation and had the opportunity to do so, he refused or failed to apply.

(6)   Where a court imposes a security requirement in respect of a person, it shall be its duty—

(a) to state in open court that it is of such opinion as is mentioned in subsection (5AA) above; and
(b) to explain to him in open court and in ordinary language why it is of that opinion;

and a magistrates' court shall cause a reason stated by it under paragraph (b) above to be specified in the warrant of commitment and to be entered in the register.

(7) Subject to section 23AA below, a court remanding a person to local authority accommodation without imposing a security requirement may, after consultation with the designated authority, require that person to comply with —

(a) any such conditions as could be imposed under section 3(6) of the Bail Act 1976 (c. 63) if he were then being granted bail; and

(b) any conditions imposed for the purpose of securing the electronic monitoring of his compliance with any other condition imposed under this subsection.

(7A) Where a person is remanded to local authority accommodation and a security requirement is imposed in respect of him–

(a) the designated local authority may, with the consent of the Secretary of State, arrange for the person to be detained, for the whole or any part of the period of the remand or committal, in a secure training centre; and

(b) his detention there pursuant to the arrangements shall be lawful.

(7B) Arrangements under subsection (7A) above may include provision for payments to be made by the authority to the Secretary of State.

(8) Where a court imposes on a person any such conditions as are mentioned in subsection (7) above, it shall be its duty to explain to him in open court and in ordinary language why it is imposing those conditions; and a magistrates' court shall cause a reason stated by it under this subsection to be specified in the warrant of commitment and to be entered in the register.

(9) A court remanding a person to local authority accommodation without imposing a security requirement may, after consultation with the designated authority, impose on that authority requirements—

(a) for securing compliance with any conditions imposed on that person under subsection (7) above; or

(b) stipulating that he shall not be placed with a named person.

(10) Where a person is remanded to local authority accommodation, a relevant court—

(a) may, on the application of the designated authority, impose on that person any such conditions as could be imposed under subsection (7) above if the court were then remanding him to such accommodation; and

(b) where it does so, may impose on that authority any requirements for securing compliance with the conditions so imposed.

(11) Where a person is remanded to local authority accommodation, a relevant court may, on the application of the designated authority or that person, vary or revoke any conditions or requirements imposed under subsection (7), (9) or (10) above.

(12) In this section—

"children's home" has the same meaning as in the Care Standards Act 2000;

'court' and 'magistrates' court' include a justice;

"extradition proceedings" means proceedings under the Extradition Act 2003;

'imprisonable offence' means an offence punishable in the case of an adult with imprisonment;

"prescribed description" means a description prescribed by reference to age or sex or both by an order of the Secretary of State;

"relevant court"—

(a) in relation to a person remanded to local authority accommodation under subsection (1) above, means the court by which he was so remanded, or any magistrates' court having jurisdiction in the place where he is for the time being;

    (b) in relation to a person remanded to local authority accommodation under subsection (1A) above, means the court by which he was so remanded.

"requesting territory" means the territory to which a person's extradition is sought in extradition proceedings;

'secure accommodation' means accommodation which is provided in a children's home in respect of which a person is registered under Part II of the Care Standards Act 2000 for the purpose of restricting liberty, and is approved for that purpose by the Secretary of State or the National Assembly for Wales;

"sexual offence" means an offence specified in Part 2 of Schedule 15 to the Criminal Justice Act 2003;

"violent offence" means murder or an offence specified in Part 1 of Schedule 15 to the Criminal Justice Act 2003;

'young person' means a person who has attained the age of fourteen years and is under the age of seventeen years.

but, for the purposes of the definition of "secure accommodation", "local authority accommodation" includes any accommodation falling within section 61(2) of the Criminal Justice Act 1991.

(13)   In this section—

    (a) any reference to a person who is being looked after by a local authority shall be construed in accordance with section 22 of the Children Act 1989;

    (b) any reference to consultation shall be construed as a reference to such consultation (if any) as is reasonably practicable in all the circumstances of the case; and

    (c) any reference, in relation to a person charged with or convicted of a violent or sexual offence, to protecting the public from serious harm from him shall be construed as a reference to protecting members of the public from death or serious personal injury, whether physical or psychological, occasioned by further such offences committed by him.

(14)   This section has effect subject to—

    [...]

    (b) section 128(7) of that Act (remands to the custody of a constable for periods of not more than three days),

but section 128(7) shall have effect in relation to a child or young person as if for the reference to three clear days there were substituted a reference to twenty-four hours

This section (in particular s 23(5)) applies to a person if the court is of opinion that, by reason of his physical or emotional immaturity or a propensity of his to harm himself, it would be undesirable for him to be remanded to a remand centre or a prison.

Advocates should insist on seeing the assessment of vulnerability carried out by the Youth Offending Team (an *Asset* assessment). The key factors from this assessment that determine the vulnerability of a young person, and therefore influence what type of custodial establishment they are placed in, include:

- risk of self-harm;
- having been bullied, abused, neglected, or depressed;
- separation, loss, or care episodes;
- risk-taking;
- substance misuse;
- other health-related needs;
- ability to cope in a young offender institution or other custodial establishment.

Conditions

A court can impose the same conditions as it could in the case of an adult. Conditions can also be imposed on the local authority.

Applications for secure accommodation

An application for secure remand under the Children Act 1989, s 25 in relation to a ten- or 11-year-old must be made to the Family Proceedings Court and cannot be remunerated under criminal legal aid. Remand must not exceed 28 days (although subsequent applications can be made).

An application under this section is also available where the secure accommodation requirements set out above are not met in relation to a child 12 years or above (*Re G (A Child) (Secure Accommodation Order)* (2001) FLR 884). In this instance the Children (Secure Accommodation) Regulations 1991, r 6(2) provides that a court cannot securely remand unless the child is likely to abscond from such accommodation or the child is likely to injure himself or other people if he is kept in any other accommodation.

Section 25 of the Children Act 1989 provides:

Children Act 1989, s 25

(1) Subject to the following provisions of this section, a child who is being looked after by a local authority may not be placed, and, if placed, may not be kept, in accommodation provided for the purpose of restricting liberty ('secure accommodation') unless it appears—

    (a) that—

        (i) he has a history of absconding and is likely to abscond from any other description of accommodation; and

        (ii) if he absconds, he is likely to suffer significant harm; or

    (b) that if he is kept in any other description of accommodation he is likely to injure himself or other persons.

(2) The appropriate national authority may by regulations—

    (a) specify a maximum period—

        (i) beyond which a child may not be kept in secure accommodation without the authority of the court; and

        (ii) for which the court may authorise a child to be kept in secure accommodation;

    (b) empower the court from time to time to authorise a child to be kept in secure accommodation for such further period as the regulations may specify; and

    (c) provide that applications to the court under this section shall be made only by local authorities.

(3) It shall be the duty of a court hearing an application under this section to determine whether any relevant criteria for keeping a child in secure accommodation are satisfied in his case.

(4) If a court determines that any such criteria are satisfied, it shall make an order authorising the child to be kept in secure accommodation and specifying the maximum period for which he may be so kept.

(5) On any adjournment of the hearing of an application under this section, a court may make an interim order permitting the child to be kept during the period of the adjournment in secure accommodation.

(6) No court shall exercise the powers conferred by this section in respect of a child who is not legally represented in that court unless, having been informed of his right to apply for representation funded by the Legal Services Commission as part of the Community Legal Service or Criminal Defence Service and having had the opportunity to do so, he refused or failed to apply.

(7) The appropriate national authority may by regulations provide that—

    (a) this section shall or shall not apply to any description of children specified in the regulations;

    (b) this section shall have effect in relation to children of a description specified in the regulations subject to such modifications as may be so specified;

    (c) such other provisions as may be so specified shall have effect for the purpose of determining whether a child of a description specified in the regulations may be placed or kept in secure accommodation.

(8) The giving of an authorisation under this section shall not prejudice any power of any court in England and Wales or Scotland to give directions relating to the child to whom the authorisation relates.

(9) This section is subject to section 20(8).

DOLI INCAPAX

The presumption of doli incapax was abolished by the Crime and Disorder Act 1998, s 34 (*T* [2008] 3 WLR 923).

INTELLECTUAL CAPACITY

The elements of a fair trial, so far as capacity is concerned are:

- Defendant has to understand what he is said to have done wrong;
- The court has to be satisfied that the claimant when he had done wrong by act or omission had the means of knowing that was wrong;
- The Defendant had to understand what, if any, defences were available to him;
- He had to have a reasonable opportunity to make relevant representations if he wished;
- He had to have the opportunity to consider what representation he wished to make once he understood the issues involved.

In *Crown Prosecution Service v P* [2007] EWHC 946 (Admin) the court held that the following procedure ought to be adopted in order to determine an issue as to capacity:

    (a) It may, particularly in the case of a young child with mental health or disability problems, be thought preferable to proceed by way of civil proceedings seeking a care or supervision order under the Children Act 1989, rather than to embark on a prosecution.

    (b) A stay for an abuse of process may be appropriate in an exceptional case.

    (c) Medical evidence will rarely provide the whole answer to the question of whether the child ought to be tried for a criminal offence. This is an issue which the court has to decide, not the doctors, although of course the medical evidence may be of great importance. But, the medical evidence must almost always be set in the context of other evidence relating to the child, which may well bear upon the issues of his understanding, mental capacity and ability to participate effectively in a trial. [eg] evidence of what the child is said to have done, how the child reacted when arrested (if he was) and how he behaved and what he said when interviewed (if he was). Other factors may also be relevant to the decision that the court has to take. If a trial begins, the court will wish to ensure that the child understands each stage of the process. That may involve some direct exchanges between the district judge or chairman of the bench and the child. The child's responses may well assist the court in deciding on the child's level of understanding. Further it may become apparent from the way in which the trial is conducted that the child's representative does or does not have adequate instructions on which to cross-examine witnesses. The court must be willing, in an appropriate case, to disagree with and reject the medical opinion. It is the court's opinion of the child's level of understanding which must determine whether a criminal trial proceeds. Accordingly, in most cases, the medical evidence should be considered as part of the evidence in the case and not as the sole evidence on a freestanding application. Although the medical evidence might on its own appear quite strong, when other matters are considered the court might conclude that the defendant's understanding and ability to take part in the trial are greater than were suggested by the doctors and that, with proper assistance from his legal adviser and suitable adjustments to the procedure of the court, the trial can properly proceed to a conclusion.

(d) If the court concludes that the defendant lacks capacity, consideration should be given to proceeding by way of a fact finding hearing.

INTERMEDIARY

See Part E–Intermediary.

JURISDICTION AND CONSTITUTION

Save where otherwise provided for (eg youth appearing with an adult) the youth court enjoys exclusive jurisdiction over those aged under 18 years in regard to criminal matters (freestanding applications for anti-social behaviour orders (ASBOs) and other civil matters must be made to an adult magistrates' court). In law, a youth court is simply a magistrates' court constituted in a particular manner:

Children and Young Persons Act 1933, s 45(1)–(3)

(1) Magistrates' courts—

(a) constituted in accordance with this section or section 66 of the Courts Act 2003 (judges having powers of District Judges (Magistrates' Courts)), and

(b) sitting for the purpose of—

(i) hearing any charge against a child or young person, or

(ii) exercising any other jurisdiction conferred on youth courts by or under this or any other Act, are to be known as youth courts.

(2) A justice of the peace is not qualified to sit as a member of a youth court for the purpose of dealing with any proceedings unless he has an authorisation extending to the proceedings.

(3) He has an authorisation extending to the proceedings only if he has been authorised by the Lord Chief Justice, with the concurrence of the Lord Chancellor, to sit as a member of a youth court to deal with—

(a) proceedings of that description, or

(b) all proceedings dealt with by youth courts.

Constitution

In the absence of unforeseen circumstances a youth court should be constituted either of a District Judge (sitting alone or exceptionally with lay justices) or of three magistrates one of whom must be male and one of whom must be female. If the court is proposing to sit in any other combination it should make that clear to the parties and invite representations (*R v Birmingham Justices, ex p F* (1999) 163 JP 523).

OPEN JUSTICE

Access to the youth court is restricted under section 47(2) of the Children and Young Persons Act 1933:

Children and Young Persons Act 1933, s 47(2)

(2) No person shall be present at any sitting of a youth court except—

    (a) members and officers of the court;

    (b) parties to the case before the court, their solicitors and counsel, and witnesses and other persons directly concerned in that case;

    (c) bonâ fide representatives of newspapers or news agencies;

    (d) such other persons as the court may specially authorise to be present.

PRE-CHARGE NOTIFICATION

The Children and Young Persons Act 1969, ss 5 and 34(2) stipulate that the local authority and probation service must be informed when a young person is to be prosecuted. A failure to so notify is not however fatal to the proceedings and the sections have been held to be discretionary, not mandatory (*Director of Public Prosecutions v Cottier* [1996] 3 All ER 126).

SENTENCING OVERVIEW

Age (last birthday)	10–13	14	15	16–17
Absolute discharge	Y	Y	Y	Y
Conditional discharge (note that a conditional discharge cannot be imposed if the offender has received a final warning in the previous 24 months unless exceptional circumstances are found). A conditional discharge in respect to a youth can be for a maximum period of 3 years.	Y	Y	Y	Y
Referral order (for a period of between 3 and 12 months)	Y	Y	Y	Y
Fine	Y: maximum £250. Order must be made against parent/ guardian unless unreasonable in the circumstances	Y: maximum £1,000. Order must be made against parent/ guardian unless unreasonable in the circumstances	Y: maximum £1,000. Order must be made against parent/ guardian unless unreasonable in the circumstances	Y: maximum £1,000
Compensation order	Y	Y	Y	Y
Costs	Y	Y	Y	Y
Reparation order (max 24 hours)	Y	Y	Y	Y

Youth rehabilitation order	Y (but cannot impose residence requirement or unpaid work). Can only impose ISSR or fostering if persistent offender	Y (but cannot impose residence requirement or unpaid work). Can only impose ISSR or fostering if persistent offender	Y (but cannot impose residence requirement or unpaid work).	Y
Detention and training order (period of 4, 6, 8, 10, 12, 18, or 24 months)	10 or 11 years: No 12 or 13 years: Yes if persistent offender	14-year-old if persistent offender	Y	Y

PART G LEGAL AID

ADJOURNMENT PENDING CONSIDERATION OF GRANT OF REPRESENTATION

In *Berry Trade Ltd v Moussavi* [2002] EWCA Civ 477 the court held that an adjournment ought normally to be granted in order that the applicant's timely application for legal aid be considered. Similarly, in *Stopyra v Poland* [2012] EWHC 1787 (Admin) the court held:

"...delays occasioned by means testing which are not occasioned by the fault of the requested person or his legal advisers, cannot be held against the requested person. Indeed, as we have said, it would be unjust in cases where the initial advice of a duty solicitor (under a properly funded scheme) is insufficient, to proceed either (a) to obtain the consent of the requested person to extradition or (b) with the extradition hearing itself, unless and until the means testing procedure is completed and adequate time to advise and obtain evidence has been afforded".

APPEALS AGAINST REFUSAL OF REPRESENTATION

A refusal on the basis of ineligibility due to means must be made to the appropriate authority (ie HMCTS acting on behalf of the LSC). An appeal against refusal on the basis that the interests of justice test is not satisfied is made to the court. A court will often be considering appeals at the conclusion of the proceedings when the outcome is known. The court should ensure that the application is not judged with the benefit of hindsight. In *Horseferry Road Magistrates' Court, ex p Punatar and Co* [2002] EWHC 1196 (Admin) the court was dealing with a case where when the solicitors were originally instructed the defendant faced an imprisonable offence, that offence being amended to a non-imprisonable one during the proceedings. The court held:

"The right time to look at this question, it seems to me, is the time when solicitors are deciding either that there is no real risk of imprisonment and so no reason to expect a right of representation to be granted, in which case they will tell clients that they are on their own, or that there is such a risk and that the expenditure of time and effort and costs in applying for the grant will be justified, whether or not it is ultimately successful."

Interest of Justice: Loss of liberty is to be judged not against the maximum penalty that might be imposed, but against the likely penalty on conviction (*Highgate Justices, ex p Lewis* [1977] Crim LR 611). A community penalty does amount to a loss of liberty (*Liverpool Magistrates' Court, ex p McGhee* (1994) 158 JP 275). Conviction for a sexual offence will normally justify the grant of representation (much will of course depend on the antecedent history of the defendant however) (*Brigg Justice ex p Lynch* (1984) 148 JP 214). Cases involving expert evidence (eg spiked drinks defence) will often meet the criteria for grant of representation (*Gravesend Magistrates' Court, ex p Baker* (1997) 161 JP 765). In a case where the defendant needs an interpreter, the test for grant of representation is likely to be met (*R (Matara) v Brent Magistrates' Court* [2005] EWHC 1829 (Admin)).

Criminal Defence Service (Representation Order: Appeals etc) Regulations 2006, r 4

(1) In this regulation "court" means the magistrates' court in which the proceedings in respect of which the individual is seeking a representation order are being or are to be heard and includes a single justice and a District Judge (Magistrates' Courts).

(2) Where the representation authority refuses to grant a representation order to an individual on the grounds that the interests of justice do not require such an order to be granted, the individual may renew the application for a representation order to that authority.

(3) The representation authority must grant the representation order or refuse the application.

(4) Where the representation authority refuses the application, the individual may appeal to the court against the refusal.

(5) The court must either—

(a) decide that it would be in the interests of justice for a representation order to be granted; or

(b) dismiss the appeal.

(6) Where the court makes a decision under paragraph (5)(a), the individual may apply to the representation authority for a representation order; and—

(a) if the individual states in writing, verified by a statement of truth, that the individual's financial resources have not changed since the date of the original application so as to make the individual financially ineligible for a representation order, the authority must grant such an order; or

(b) if the resources may have so changed, the representation authority must determine whether the individual is financially eligible to be granted a representation order in accordance with the Criminal Defence Service (Financial Eligibility) Regulations 2006 2 and, if the individual is so eligible, must grant such an order.".

EXTENT OF REPRESENTATION

Generally: A representation order extends to the services of a litigator and advocate (although counsel is paid under the General Criminal Contract from the monies paid to the litigator). An application can be made to extend the representation order to include representation in the magistrates' court by an advocate provided that the case is triable either-way or is indictable only (the practical effect of this is that the advocate is not paid from the litigator's standard fee). Only in the case of summary proceedings under the Extradition Act 2003 can a representation order be extended to cover the services of Queen's Counsel. The court has a power when sending a case of murder for trial to extend the representation order to include the services of Queen's Counsel at the crown court but this it is submitted that the court should rarely exercise as the crown court is in a better position to determine representation in such cases. **Equality of Arms:** There is no principle that entitles representation by counsel simply because the prosecution is so represented. **Desirable:** It is not sufficient that the case be unusually grave or difficult, as representation by an advocate must also be 'desirable'. In many cases (eg an uncontested committal) the nature of what is being done in the proceedings will mean that the test is not met (*R v Guildford Justice ex p Scott* [1975] Crim LR 286). There is no category of case (save for murder where there are no longer committal proceedings, for which see *R v Derby Justice ex p Kooner* (1970) 64 Cr App R 455) where the test will be automatically met, and in practice the grant of representation to cover an advocate will be rare. The fact that an individual litigator does not possess the necessary skills to conduct a case does not justify the grant of representation for advocate, representation should instead be transferred to a litigator who is competent to conduct the case. **Experts:** A court has no power to authorise or otherwise, the use of an expert in criminal proceedings. A court can however express its opinion on the matter (*Donnelly* [1998] Crim LR 131).

Criminal Defence Service (General) (No 2) Regulations 2001, r 12

(1) A representation order for the purposes of proceedings before a magistrates' court may only include representation by an advocate in the case of:

(a) any indictable offence, including an offence which is triable either way; or

(b) extradition hearings under the Extradition Act 2003

where the court is of the opinion that, because of circumstances which make the proceedings unusually grave or difficult, representation by both a litigator and an advocate would be desirable.

(2) A representation order for the purposes of proceedings before a magistrates' court may not include representation by an advocate other than as provided in paragraph (1).

(3) A representation order for the purposes of proceedings before a magistrates' court may provide for the services of a Queen's Counsel or of more than one advocate only—

(a) in extradition hearings under the Extradition Act 2003; and

(b) where the court is of the opinion that the assisted person could not be adequately represented except by a Queen's Counsel or by more than one advocate.

AMENDING THE ORDER

Representation is granted for the 'proceedings' and therefore encompasses all offences that are listed on the representation order when granted, and any subsequent charges that result from amendment or addition during the proceedings. Accordingly there is no longer any need (or indeed any power) to amend a representation order during the life of proceedings. If the nature of the proceedings or charges change, the court has the power to withdraw representation. Given the standard fee structure which operates in the magistrates' court there will rarely however be any benefit in revoking the order and it is a measure that is encountered only very rarely in practice.

Criminal Defence Service (General) (No 2) Regulations 2001, r 17

(1) Where any charge or proceedings against the assisted person are varied, the court before which the proceedings are heard or, in respect of any proceedings mentioned in regulation 3(2)(a) to (g), the Commission, must—

(a) consider whether the interests of justice continue to require that he be represented in respect of the varied charge or proceedings; and

(b) withdraw the representation order if the interests of justice do not so require.

(1A) The court before which the proceedings are heard or, in respect of any proceedings mentioned in regulation 3(2)(a) to (g), the Commission, must consider whether to withdraw the representation order in any of the following circumstances—

(a) where the assisted person declines to accept the order in the terms which are offered;

(b) otherwise at the request of the assisted person; or

(c) where the litigator named in the representation order declines to continue to represent the assisted person.;

(2) Where representation is withdrawn, the appropriate officer or the Commission, as appropriate, shall provide written notification to the assisted person and to the litigator (or, where there was no litigator assigned, to the advocate), who shall inform any assigned advocate (or, where notification is given to the advocate, any other assigned advocate).

(3) On any subsequent application by the assisted person for a representation order in respect of the same proceedings,

(a) he must declare the withdrawal of the previous representation order and the reason for it; and

(b) where the representation order was withdrawn in the circumstances set out in paragraph (1) or paragraph (1A)(a) or (b) and a representation order is subsequently granted, the court or the Commission, as appropriate, must select the same litigator, unless it considers that there are good reasons why it should select a different litigator .

CHANGE OF REPRESENTATION

A defendant does not enjoy an unfettered right to change representation, the conditions to be met for allowing such an change being contained in reg 16 of the 2001 regulations. In *Ashgar Khan* unreported, 10 July 2001, Birmingham Crown Court, a case that has been widely followed (and approved on a number of occasions by the Court of Appeal) it was held:

"It will not generally be sufficient to allege a lack of care or competence of existing representatives. As from 2nd April 2001 only those solicitors who have obtained a criminal franchise contract with the Legal Services Commission (LSC) are able to undertake work and obtain a representations order in criminal proceedings. Those franchises are only obtained after rigorous audit, inspection and control by the LSC, the Commission thereby satisfying itself that the professional standard of solicitors with franchises is of a high order. The court will infer from that fact that such solicitors do provide representation of good quality. Only in extremely rare circumstances, and where full particulars are given in the application, will a general ground of loss of confidence or incompetence be entertained. It must be further pointed out that it will not be sufficient simply to say that there is a breakdown in the relationship between solicitor and client. Many breakdowns are imagined rather than real or as the result of proper advice. This court will want to look to see what the cause of that is."

In *Ulcay* [2007] EWCA Crim 2379 the court held:

"The purpose of this part of the regulations is to ensure that the client does not manipulate the system, seeking to change his lawyers for dubious reasons which include, but are not limited to the fact that the lawyer offers sensible, but disagreeable advice to the client. Claims of a breakdown in the professional relationship between lawyer and client are frequently made by defendants, and they are often utterly spurious. If the judge intends to reject an application for a change of legal representative he may well explain to the defendant that the consequence may be that the case will continue without him being represented at public expense. The simple principle remains that the defendant is not entitled to manipulate the legal aid system and is no more entitled to abuse the process than the prosecution. If he chooses to terminate his lawyer's retainer for improper motives, the court is not bound to agree to an application for a change of representation."

In *Vyse* [2011] EWCA Crim 3255 the court held that earlier decisions, such as that in *Jisi*, unreported July 14, 2000:

"no longer have the force that they once did. Times have moved on. The courts have to be astute to ensure that public money is properly spent."

In *Iqbal* [2011] EWCA Crim 1294 the court held that where a breakdown of relationship was cited as the reason for transfer, details of that breakdown must be advanced to the court. In the absence of the solicitor from whom the transfer of representation is sought being given proper opportunity to make representations, the transfer is susceptible to being successfully challenged (*Clive Rees Solicitors v Swansea Magistrates' Court* [2011] EWHC 3155 (Admin)).

PART H COSTS

DEFENCE COSTS ORDER

Availability and rates: For proceedings commenced on or after 1 October 2012 defence costs, whether determined by the court or taxed, are to be paid at no more than rates prescribed by the Lord Chancellor (Costs in Criminal Cases (General) (Amendment) Regulations 2012). An order may only be made in favour of individuals (ie not companies and other entities). *Offence:* Section 16 only applies in relation to 'offences'. Costs order therefore cannot be made in respect to proceedings in relation to a breach of community order, nor to civil proceedings under the Proceeds of Crime Act 2002 (*Perinpanathan v City of Westminster Magistrates' Court* [2010] Civ 40), or in respect to freestanding applications for an anti-social behaviour order (*Manchester City Council v Manchester Magistrates' Court* [2009] EWHC 1866 (Admin)). It will be noted from the cases above that applications for costs under the Magistrates' Courts Act 1980, s 64 have met with little success, largely due to the effect of *City of Bradford MDC v Booth* [2000] EWHC 444 (Admin). **Timing:** An order can be made after the proceedings have concluded (*Bolton Justice ex p Wildish* (1983) 147 JP 309), and the court is entitled to reconsider the making of an order, either due to 'exceptional circumstances' or because of a failure on a party to make proper disclosure (whether willfully or not) (*Patel* [2012] EWCA Crim 1508). **Accused:** This is wide enough to cover costs paid by a parent or guardian (*Preston Crown Court, ex p Lancashire County Council* [1999] 1 WLR 142). **Acquittal:** Where a person is bound over (*Emohare v Thames Magistrates' Court* [2009] EWHC 689 (Admin), stayed for abuse of process (*R (on the application of R E Williams & Sons (Wholesale) Ltd) v Hereford Magistrates' Court*, unreported, 2 July 2008) or referred for a police caution (*R (Stoddard) v Oxfordshire Magistrates' Court* [2005] EWHC 2733 (Admin)) defence costs may still be granted. **Refusing costs:** In *R (Spiteri) v Basildon Crown Court* [2009] EWHC 665 (Admin), the applicant successfully appealed a refusal to make a defendant's costs order on the grounds that he was acquitted on a 'technicality'. It was held that a costs order could not be refused on the sole ground that the applicant had brought the proceedings upon himself, as more was required, such as the defendant having misled the prosecution as to the strength of the case against him. A similar point arose in *Dowler v MerseyRail* [2009] EWHC 558 (Admin), where the court ruled that when refusing costs courts should give reasons for the refusal contemporaneously with the ruling. In *R (Guney) v Central Criminal Court* [2011] EWHC 767 (Admin), a case involving the making of a Recovery of Defence Costs Order following an acquittal, the court discusses further the issue of a defendant who brings the proceedings upon himself and misleading the prosecution as to the strength of the case against him. The same principles will apply when a court is considering refusing a defence costs order. Where an appeal in the crown court was allowed as an 'act of mercy' costs were quite properly disallowed (*R (Pluckrose) v Snaresbrook Crown Court* [2009] EWHC 1506 (Admin)).

Prosecution of Offences Act 1985, s 16

(1) Where—

    (a) an information laid before a justice of the peace for any area, charging any person with an offence, is not proceeded with;

    (b) a magistrates' court inquiring into an indictable offence as examining justices determines not to commit the accused for trial;

    (c) a magistrates' court dealing summarily with an offence dismisses the information;

that court or, in a case falling within paragraph (a) above, a magistrates' court for that area, may make an order in favour of the accused for a payment to be made out of central funds in respect of his costs (a "defendant's costs order").

WITNESS COSTS

Witness costs are payable pursuant to The Costs in Criminal Cases (General) Regulations 1986, r 15, regardless of whether once he has attended court he actually proceeds to give oral evidence. The costs of a witness who attends solely for the purposes of giving character evidence can be granted only where the court certifies that his attendance was in the interests of justice.

COURT APPOINTED LEGAL REPRESENTATIVES

Costs are payable under the Prosecution of Offences Act 1985, s 19. The rates payable are not limited in the same way as those paid under a defence costs order.

WASTED COSTS

Jurisdiction: Orders that costs be paid by a 'party' the proceedings are made under section 19 of the Act. Orders against individual solicitors and counsel are made under section 19A (*Crown Court at Isleworth, ex p Montague and Co* [1990] COD 86). Costs against third-parties can be made under section 19B. For enforcement of such orders see Magistrates' Courts Act 1980, s 76. The principles to be applied when making an order under section 19A were set out in *Re A Barrister (Wasted Costs Order)* [1993] QB 293:

"1. There is a clear need for any judge or court intending to exercise the wasted costs jurisdiction to formulate carefully and concisely the complaint and grounds upon which such an order may be sought. These measures are Draconian, *295 and, as in contempt proceedings, the grounds must be clear and particular.

2. Where necessary a transcript of the relevant part of the proceedings under discussion should be available. And, in accordance with the rules, a transcript of any wasted costs hearing must be made.

3. A defendant involved in a case where such proceedings are contemplated should be present if, after discussion with counsel, it is thought that his interests may be affected. And he should certainly be present and represented if the matter might affect the course of his trial. Regulation 3B(2) furthermore requires that before a wasted costs order is made "the Court shall allow the legal or other representative and any party to the proceedings to make representations." There may be cases where it may be appropriate for counsel for the Crown to be present.

4. A three stage test or approach is recommended when a wasted costs order is contemplated:

    (i)   Has there been an improper, unreasonable or negligent act or omission?

    (ii) As a result have any costs been incurred by a party?

    (iii) If the answers to (i) and (ii) are yes; should the court exercise its discretion to disallow or order the representative to meet the whole or any part of the relevant costs, and if so what specific sum is involved?

5. It is inappropriate to propose any deal or settlement, such as was suggested in the present case, that the representative might forego fees. The judge should formally state his complaint, in chambers, and invite the representative to make his own comments. After any other party has been heard the judge should give his formal ruling. Discursive conversations such as took place in the present case may be unfair, and should certainly not take place.

6. As is indicated above the judge must specify the sum to be disallowed or ordered. Alternatively the relevant available procedure should be substituted, should it be impossible to fix the sum".

Improper, unreasonable or negligent: In *Ridehalgh v Horsefield* [1994] 3 WLR 462 these words were explained:

"Improper" means what it has been understood to mean in this context for at least half a century. The adjective covers, but is not confined to, conduct which would ordinarily be held to justify disbarment, striking off, suspension from practice or other serious professional penalty. It covers any significant breach of a substantial duty imposed by a relevant code of professional conduct. But it is not in our judgment limited to that. Conduct which would be regarded as improper according to the consensus of professional (including judicial) opinion can be fairly stigmatised as such whether or not it violates the letter of a professional code.

"Unreasonable" also means what it has been understood to mean in this context for at least half a century. The expression aptly describes conduct which is vexatious, designed to harass the other side rather than advance the resolution of the case, and it makes no difference that the conduct is the product of excessive zeal and not improper motive. But conduct cannot be described as unreasonable simply because it leads in the event to an unsuccessful result or because other more cautious legal representatives would have acted differently. The acid test is whether the conduct permits of a reasonable explanation. If so, the course adopted may be regarded as optimistic and as reflecting on a practitioner's judgment, but it is not unreasonable.

The term "negligent" was the most controversial of the three. It was argued that the 1990 Act, in this context as in others, used "negligent" as a term of art involving the well-known ingredients of duty, breach, causation and damage. Therefore, it was said, conduct cannot be regarded as negligent unless it involves an actionable breach of the legal representative's duty to his own client, to whom alone a duty is owed. We reject this approach. (1) As already noted, the predecessor of the present Order 62, rule 11 made reference to "reasonable competence". That expression does not invoke technical concepts of the law of negligence. It seems to us inconceivable that by changing the language Parliament intended to make it harder, rather than easier, for courts to make orders. (2) Since the applicant's right to a wasted costs order against a legal representative depends on showing that the latter is in breach of his duty to the court it makes no sense to superimpose a requirement under this head (but not in the case of impropriety or unreasonableness) that he is also in breach of his duty to his client.

Cases: Accepting a case (listed at 10am) in another town is a negligent act that justified the making of a wasted costs order when the advocate did not become available to attend a case listed for 2pm (*Henrys Solicitors* [2012] EWCA Crim 1480). In *Angela Taylor Solicitors* [2008] EWCA Crim 3085 a failure of a solicitor to ensure that proper procedures were in place to receive and act upon urgent fax communications was an error "...but to characterise it as a "serious error", or more importantly "serious misconduct", in our judgment, went too far. Accordingly this appeal is, for that reason, allowed". A solicitor who is complicit in a client's failure to abide by the criminal procedure rules runs the risk of a wasted costs application (*SVS Solicitors* [2012] EWCA Crim 319). It is normally inappropriate (other than in an extraordinary case) to make a wasted costs order against the prosecution in respect to a legally aided defendant as it merely involves the transfer of monies from one arm of government to another (*Oxford City Justice, ex p Chief Constable for Thames Valley Police*, The Times April 24 1987). It is doubtful whether the principle in *Oxford Justice* remains good law, particularly given the current pressures on legal aid. There are numerous reported cases (particularly in respect to immigration law cases) where the court has order costs be paid where the effect is to pass monies across different government funds.

Prosecution of Offences Act 1985, ss 19, 19A, 19B

19.— Provision for orders as to costs in other circumstances.

(1) The Lord Chancellor may by regulations make provision empowering magistrates' courts, the Crown Court and the Court of Appeal, in any case where the court is satisfied

that one party to criminal proceedings has incurred costs as a result of an unnecessary or improper act or omission by, or on behalf of, another party to the proceedings, to make an order as to the payment of those costs.

[...]

19A.— Costs against legal representatives etc.

(1) In any criminal proceedings—

    (a) the Court of Appeal;
    (b) the Crown Court; or
    (c) a magistrates' court,

may disallow, or (as the case may be) order the legal or other representative concerned to meet, the whole of any wasted costs or such part of them as may be determined in accordance with regulations.

(2) Regulations shall provide that a legal or other representative against whom action is taken by a magistrates' court under subsection (1) may appeal to the Crown Court and that a legal or other representative against whom action is taken by the Crown Court under subsection (1) may appeal to the Court of Appeal.

(3) In this section—

"legal or other representative", in relation to any proceedings, means a person who is exercising a right of audience, or a right to conduct litigation, on behalf of any party to the proceedings;

"regulations" means regulations made by the Lord Chancellor; and

"wasted costs" means any costs incurred by a party—

    (a) as a result of any improper, unreasonable or negligent act or omission on the part of any representative or any employee of a representative; or
    (b) which, in the light of any such act or omission occurring after they were incurred, the court considers it is unreasonable to expect that party to pay.

19B Provision for award of costs against third parties

(1) The Lord Chancellor may by regulations make provision empowering magistrates' courts, the Crown Court and the Court of Appeal to make a third party costs order if the condition in subsection (3) is satisfied.

(2) A "third party costs order" is an order as to the payment of costs incurred by a party to criminal proceedings by a person who is not a party to those proceedings ("the third party").

(3) The condition is that–

    (a) there has been serious misconduct (whether or not constituting a contempt of court) by the third party, and
    (b) the court considers it appropriate, having regard to that misconduct, to make a third party costs order against him.

(4) Regulations made under this section may, in particular–

    (a) specify types of misconduct in respect of which a third party costs order may not be made;
    (b) allow the making of a third party costs order at any time;
    (c) make provision for any other order as to costs which has been made in respect of the proceedings to be varied on, or taken account of in, the making of a third party costs order;
    (d) make provision for account to be taken of any third party costs order in the making of any other order as to costs in respect of the proceedings.

(5) Regulations made under this section in relation to magistrates' courts must provide that the third party may appeal to the Crown Court against a third party costs order made by a magistrates' court.

(6) [...]

APPENDIX 1

DANGEROUS OFFENDERS

Criminal Justice Act 2003, Sch 15, Part 1 and Part 2

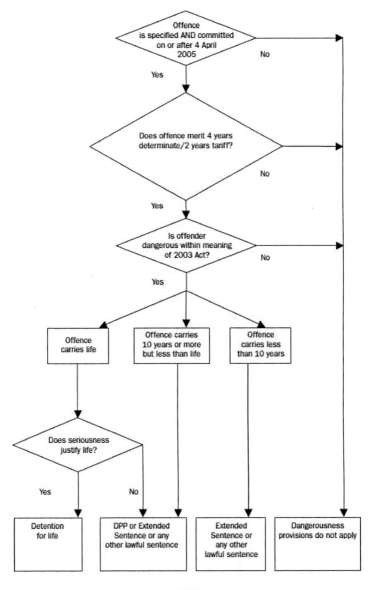

Part 1: Specified violent offences

1.   Manslaughter.

2.   Kidnapping.

3.   False imprisonment.

4.   An offence under section 4 of the Offences against the Person Act 1861 (c 100) (soliciting murder).

5.   An offence under section 16 of that Act (threats to kill).

6.   An offence under section 18 of that Act (wounding with intent to cause grievous bodily harm).

7.   An offence under section 20 of that Act (malicious wounding).

8.   An offence under section 21 of that Act (attempting to choke, suffocate, or strangle in order to commit or assist in committing an indictable offence).

9.   An offence under section 22 of that Act (using chloroform etc to commit or assist in the committing of any indictable offence).

10.   An offence under section 23 of that Act (maliciously administering poison etc so as to endanger life or inflict grievous bodily harm).

11.   An offence under section 27 of that Act (abandoning children).

12.   An offence under section 28 of that Act (causing bodily injury by explosives).

13.   An offence under section 29 of that Act (using explosives etc with intent to do grievous bodily harm).

14.   An offence under section 30 of that Act (placing explosives with intent to do bodily injury).

15.   An offence under section 31 of that Act (setting spring guns etc with intent to do grievous bodily harm).

16.   An offence under section 32 of that Act (endangering the safety of railway passengers).

17.   An offence under section 35 of that Act (injuring persons by furious driving).

18.   An offence under section 37 of that Act (assaulting officer preserving wreck).

19.   An offence under section 38 of that Act (assault with intent to resist arrest).

20.   An offence under section 47 of that Act (assault occasioning actual bodily harm).

21.   An offence under section 2 of the Explosive Substances Act 1883 (c 3) (causing explosion likely to endanger life or property).

22.   An offence under section 3 of that Act (attempt to cause explosion, or making or keeping explosive with intent to endanger life or property).

23.   An offence under section 1 of the Infant Life (Preservation) Act 1929 (c 34) (child destruction).

24.   An offence under section 1 of the Children and Young Persons Act 1933 (c 12) (cruelty to children).

25.   An offence under section 1 of the Infanticide Act 1938 (c 36) (infanticide).

26.   An offence under section 16 of the Firearms Act 1968 (c 27) (possession of firearm with intent to endanger life).

27.   An offence under section 16A of that Act (possession of firearm with intent to cause fear of violence).

28.   An offence under section 17(1) of that Act (use of firearm to resist arrest).

29.   An offence under section 17(2) of that Act (possession of firearm at time of committing or being arrested for offence specified in Schedule 1 to that Act).

30.   An offence under section 18 of that Act (carrying a firearm with criminal intent).

31. An offence under section 8 of the Theft Act 1968 (c 60) (robbery or assault with intent to rob).

32. An offence under section 9 of that Act of burglary with intent to—inflict grievous bodily harm on a person, or do unlawful damage to a building or anything in it.

33. An offence under section 10 of that Act (aggravated burglary).

34. An offence under section 12A of that Act (aggravated vehicle-taking) involving an accident which caused the death of any person.

35. An offence of arson under section 1 of the Criminal Damage Act 1971 (c 48).

36. An offence under section 1(2) of that Act (destroying or damaging property) other than an offence of arson.

37. An offence under section 1 of the Taking of Hostages Act 1982 (c 28) (hostage-taking).

38. An offence under section 1 of the Aviation Security Act 1982 (c 36) (hijacking).

39. An offence under section 2 of that Act (destroying, damaging or endangering safety of aircraft).

40. An offence under section 3 of that Act (other acts endangering or likely to endanger safety of aircraft).

41. An offence under section 4 of that Act (offences in relation to certain dangerous articles).

42. An offence under section 127 of the Mental Health Act 1983 (c 20) (ill-treatment of patients).

43. An offence under section 1 of the Prohibition of Female Circumcision Act 1985 (c 38) (prohibition of female circumcision).

44. An offence under section 1 of the Public Order Act 1986 (c 64) (riot).

45. An offence under section 2 of that Act (violent disorder).

46. An offence under section 3 of that Act (affray).

47. An offence under section 134 of the Criminal Justice Act 1988 (c 33) (torture).

48. An offence under section 1 of the Road Traffic Act 1988 (c 52) (causing death by dangerous driving).

49. An offence under section 3A of that Act (causing death by careless driving when under influence of drink or drugs).

50. An offence under section 1 of the Aviation and Maritime Security Act 1990 (c 31) (endangering safety at aerodromes).

51. An offence under section 9 of that Act (hijacking of ships).

52. An offence under section 10 of that Act (seizing or exercising control of fixed platforms).

53. An offence under section 11 of that Act (destroying fixed platforms or endangering their safety).

54. An offence under section 12 of that Act (other acts endangering or likely to endanger safe navigation).

55. An offence under section 13 of that Act (offences involving threats).

56. An offence under Part II of the Channel Tunnel (Security) Order 1994 (SI 1994/570) (offences relating to Channel Tunnel trains and the tunnel system).

57. An offence under section 4 of the Protection from Harassment Act 1997 (c 40) (putting people in fear of violence).

58. An offence under section 29 of the Crime and Disorder Act 1998 (c 37) (racially or religiously aggravated assaults).

59. An offence falling within section 31(1) (a) or (b) of that Act (racially or religiously aggravated offences under section 4 or 4A of the Public Order Act 1986 (c 64)).

59A. An offence under section 54 of the Terrorism Act 2000 (weapons training).

59B. An offence under section 56 of that Act (directing terrorist organisation).

59C. An offence under section 57 of that Act (possession of article for terrorist purposes).

59D. An offence under section 59 of that Act (inciting terrorism overseas).

60. An offence under section 51 or 52 of the International Criminal Court Act 2001 (c 17) (genocide, crimes against humanity, war crimes and related offences), other than one involving murder.

60A. An offence under section 47 of the Anti-terrorism, Crime and Security Act 2001 (use etc of nuclear weapons).

60B. An offence under section 50 of that Act (assisting or inducing certain weapons-related acts overseas).

60C. An offence under section 113 of that Act (use of noxious substance or thing to cause harm or intimidate).

61. An offence under section 1 of the Female Genital Mutilation Act 2003 (c 31) (female genital mutilation).

62. An offence under section 2 of that Act (assisting a girl to mutilate her own genitalia).

63. An offence under section 3 of that Act (assisting a non-UK person to mutilate overseas a girl's genitalia).

63A. An offence under section 5 of the Domestic Violence, Crime and Victims Act 2004 (causing or allowing a child or vulnerable adult to die or suffer serious physical harm).

63B. An offence under section 5 of the Terrorism Act 2006 (preparation of terrorist acts).

63C. An offence under section 6 of that Act (training for terrorism).

63D. An offence under section 9 of that Act (making or possession of radioactive device or material).

63E. An offence under section 10 of that Act (use of radioactive device or material for terrorist purposes etc).

63F. An offence under section 11 of that Act (terrorist threats relating to radioactive devices etc).

64. An offence of—

(a) aiding, abetting, counselling, procuring or inciting the commission of an offence specified in this Part of this Schedule,

(b) conspiring to commit an offence so specified, or

(c) attempting to commit an offence so specified.

65. An attempt to commit murder or a conspiracy to commit murder.

Part 2: specified sexual offences

66. An offence under section 1 of the Sexual Offences Act 1956 (c 69) (rape).

67. An offence under section 2 of that Act (procurement of woman by threats).

68. An offence under section 3 of that Act (procurement of woman by false pretences).

69. An offence under section 4 of that Act (administering drugs to obtain or facilitate intercourse).

70. An offence under section 5 of that Act (intercourse with girl under 13).

71. An offence under section 6 of that Act (intercourse with girl under 16).

72. An offence under section 7 of that Act (intercourse with a defective).

73.   An offence under section 9 of that Act (procurement of a defective).

74.   An offence under section 10 of that Act (incest by a man).

75.   An offence under section 11 of that Act (incest by a woman).

76.   An offence under section 14 of that Act (indecent assault on a woman).

77.   An offence under section 15 of that Act (indecent assault on a man).

78.   An offence under section 16 of that Act (assault with intent to commit buggery).

79.   An offence under section 17 of that Act (abduction of woman by force or for the sake of her property).

80.   An offence under section 19 of that Act (abduction of unmarried girl under 18 from parent or guardian).

81.   An offence under section 20 of that Act (abduction of unmarried girl under 16 from parent or guardian).

82.   An offence under section 21 of that Act (abduction of defective from parent or guardian).

83.   An offence under section 22 of that Act (causing prostitution of women).

84.   An offence under section 23 of that Act (procuration of girl under 21).

85.   An offence under section 24 of that Act (detention of woman in brothel).

86.   An offence under section 25 of that Act (permitting girl under 13 to use premises for intercourse).

87.   An offence under section 26 of that Act (permitting girl under 16 to use premises for intercourse).

88.   An offence under section 27 of that Act (permitting defective to use premises for intercourse).

89.   An offence under section 28 of that Act (causing or encouraging the prostitution of, intercourse with or indecent assault on girl under 16).

90.   An offence under section 29 of that Act (causing or encouraging prostitution of defective).

91.   An offence under section 32 of that Act (soliciting by men).

92.   An offence under section 33 of that Act (keeping a brothel).

93.   An offence under section 128 of the Mental Health Act 1959 (c 72) (sexual intercourse with patients).

94.   An offence under section 1 of the Indecency with Children Act 1960 (c 33) (indecent conduct towards young child).

95.   An offence under section 4 of the Sexual Offences Act 1967 (c 60) (procuring others to commit homosexual acts).

96.   An offence under section 5 of that Act (living on earnings of male prostitution).

97.   An offence under section 9 of the Theft Act 1968 (c 60) of burglary with intent to commit rape.

98.   An offence under section 54 of the Criminal Law Act 1977 (c 45) (inciting girl under 16 to have incestuous sexual intercourse).

99.   An offence under section 1 of the Protection of Children Act 1978 (c 37) (indecent photographs of children).

100. An offence under section 170 of the Customs and Excise Management Act 1979 (c 2) (penalty for fraudulent evasion of duty etc) in relation to goods prohibited to be imported under section 42 of the Customs Consolidation Act 1876 (c 36) (indecent or obscene articles).

101. An offence under section 160 of the Criminal Justice Act 1988 (c 33) (possession of indecent photograph of a child).

102. An offence under section 1 of the Sexual Offences Act 2003 (c 42) (rape).

103. An offence under section 2 of that Act (assault by penetration).

104. An offence under section 3 of that Act (sexual assault).

105. An offence under section 4 of that Act (causing a person to engage in sexual activity without consent).

106. An offence under section 5 of that Act (rape of a child under 13).

107. An offence under section 6 of that Act (assault of a child under 13 by penetration).

108. An offence under section 7 of that Act (sexual assault of a child under 13).

109. An offence under section 8 of that Act (causing or inciting a child under 13 to engage in sexual activity).

110. An offence under section 9 of that Act (sexual activity with a child).

111. An offence under section 10 of that Act (causing or inciting a child to engage in sexual activity).

112. An offence under section 11 of that Act (engaging in sexual activity in the presence of a child).

113. An offence under section 12 of that Act (causing a child to watch a sexual act).

114. An offence under section 13 of that Act (child sex offences committed by children or young persons).

115. An offence under section 14 of that Act (arranging or facilitating commission of a child sex offence).

116. An offence under section 15 of that Act (meeting a child following sexual grooming etc).

117. An offence under section 16 of that Act (abuse of position of trust: sexual activity with a child).

118. An offence under section 17 of that Act (abuse of position of trust: causing or inciting a child to engage in sexual activity).

119. An offence under section 18 of that Act (abuse of position of trust: sexual activity in the presence of a child).

120. An offence under section 19 of that Act (abuse of position of trust: causing a child to watch a sexual act).

121. An offence under section 25 of that Act (sexual activity with a child family member).

122. An offence under section 26 of that Act (inciting a child family member to engage in sexual activity).

123. An offence under section 30 of that Act (sexual activity with a person with a mental disorder impeding choice).

124. An offence under section 31 of that Act (causing or inciting a person with a mental disorder impeding choice to engage in sexual activity).

125. An offence under section 32 of that Act (engaging in sexual activity in the presence of a person with a mental disorder impeding choice).

126. An offence under section 33 of that Act (causing a person with a mental disorder impeding choice to watch a sexual act).

127. An offence under section 34 of that Act (inducement, threat or deception to procure sexual activity with a person with a mental disorder).

128. An offence under section 35 of that Act (causing a person with a mental disorder to engage in or agree to engage in sexual activity by inducement, threat or deception).

129. An offence under section 36 of that Act (engaging in sexual activity in the presence,

procured by inducement, threat or deception, of a person with a mental disorder).

130. An offence under section 37 of that Act (causing a person with a mental disorder to watch a sexual act by inducement, threat or deception).

131. An offence under section 38 of that Act (care workers: sexual activity with a person with a mental disorder).

132. An offence under section 39 of that Act (care workers: causing or inciting sexual activity).

133. An offence under section 40 of that Act (care workers: sexual activity in the presence of a person with a mental disorder).

134. An offence under section 41 of that Act (care workers: causing a person with a mental disorder to watch a sexual act).

135. An offence under section 47 of that Act (paying for sexual services of a child).

136. An offence under section 48 of that Act (causing or inciting child prostitution or pornography).

137. An offence under section 49 of that Act (controlling a child prostitute or a child involved in pornography).

138. An offence under section 50 of that Act (arranging or facilitating child prostitution or pornography).

139. An offence under section 52 of that Act (causing or inciting prostitution for gain).

140. An offence under section 53 of that Act (controlling prostitution for gain).

141. An offence under section 57 of that Act (trafficking into the UK for sexual exploitation).

142. An offence under section 58 of that Act (trafficking within the UK for sexual exploitation).

143. An offence under section 59 of that Act (trafficking out of the UK for sexual exploitation).

144. An offence under section 61 of that Act (administering a substance with intent).

145. An offence under section 62 of that Act (committing an offence with intent to commit a sexual offence).

146. An offence under section 63 of that Act (trespass with intent to commit a sexual offence).

147. An offence under section 64 of that Act (sex with an adult relative: penetration).

148. An offence under section 65 of that Act (sex with an adult relative: consenting to penetration).

149. An offence under section 66 of that Act (exposure).

150. An offence under section 67 of that Act (voyeurism).

151. An offence under section 69 of that Act (intercourse with an animal).

152. An offence under section 70 of that Act (sexual penetration of a corpse).

153. An offence of—

    (a) aiding, abetting, counselling, procuring or inciting the commission of an offence specified in this Part of this Schedule,
    (b) conspiring to commit an offence so specified, or
    (c) attempting to commit an offence so specified.

APPENDIX 2

MAGISTRATES' COURT SENTENCING GUIDELINES: FINES

Fine band starting points and ranges

In these guidelines, where the starting point or range for an offence is or includes a fine, it is expressed as one of three fine bands (A, B, or C). Each fine band has both a starting point and a range.

On some offence guidelines, both the starting point and the range are expressed as a single fine band; see, for example, careless driving, where the starting point and range for the first level of offence activity are 'fine band A'. This means that the starting point will be the starting point for fine band A (50 per cent of the offender's relevant weekly income) and the range will be the range for fine band A (25–75 per cent of relevant weekly income). On other guidelines, the range encompasses more than one fine band; see, for example, drunk and disorderly in a public place on page 55 of the Sentencing Guidelines, where the starting point for the second level of offence activity is 'fine band B' and the range is 'fine band A to fine band C'. This means that the starting point will be the starting point for fine band B (100 per cent of relevant weekly income) and the range will be the lowest point of the range for fine band A to the highest point of the range for fine band C (125–175 per cent of relevant weekly income).

1. The amount of a fine must reflect the seriousness of the offence.

2. The court must also take into account the financial circumstances of the offender; this applies whether it has the effect of increasing or reducing the fine. Normally a fine should be of an amount that is capable of being paid within 12 months.

3. The aim is for the fine to have an equal impact on offenders with different financial circumstances; it should be a hardship but should not force the offender below a reasonable 'subsistence' level.

4. The guidance below aims to establish a clear, consistent, and principled approach to the assessment of fines that will apply fairly in the majority of cases. However, it is impossible to anticipate every situation that may be encountered and in each case the court will need to exercise its judgement to ensure that the fine properly reflects the seriousness of the offence and takes into account the financial circumstances of the offender.

5. For the purpose of the offence guidelines, a fine is based on one of three bands (A, B, or C). The selection of the relevant fine band, and the position of the individual offence within that band, is determined by the seriousness of the offence.

	Starting point	Range
Fine band A	50% of relevant weekly income	25–75% of relevant weekly income
Fine band B	100% of relevant weekly income	75–125% of relevant weekly income
Fine band C	150% of relevant weekly income	125–175% of relevant weekly income

Definition of relevant weekly income

6. The seriousness of an offence determines the choice of fine band and the position of the offence within the range for that band. The offender's financial circumstances are taken into account by expressing that position as a proportion of the offender's relevant weekly income.

7. Where an offender is in receipt of income from employment or is self-employed and that income is more than £110 per week after deduction of tax and national insurance (or equivalent where the offender is self-employed), the actual income is the relevant weekly income.

8. Where an offender's only source of income is state benefit (including where there is relatively low additional income as permitted by the benefit regulations) or the offender is in receipt of income from employment or is self-employed but the amount of income after deduction of tax and national insurance is £110 or less, the relevant weekly income is deemed to be £110.

9. In calculating relevant weekly income, no account should be taken of tax credits, housing benefit, child benefit, or similar.

No reliable information

10. Where an offender has failed to provide information, or the court is not satisfied that it has been given sufficient reliable information, it is entitled to make such determination as it thinks fit regarding the financial circumstances of the offender. Any determination should be clearly stated on the court records for use in any subsequent variation or enforcement proceedings. In such cases, a record should also be made of the applicable fine band and the court's assessment of the position of the offence within that band based on the seriousness of the offence.

11. Where there is no information on which a determination can be made, the court should proceed on the basis of an assumed relevant weekly income of £350. This is derived from national median pre-tax earnings; a gross figure is used as, in the absence of financial information from the offender, it is not possible to calculate appropriate deductions.

12. Where there is some information that tends to suggest a significantly lower or higher income than the recommended £350 default sum, the court should make a determination based on that information.

13. A court is empowered to remit a fine in whole or part if the offender subsequently provides information as to means. The assessment of offence seriousness and, therefore, the appropriate fine band and the position of the offence within that band is not affected by the provision of this information.

Assessment of financial circumstances

14. While the initial consideration for the assessment of a fine is the offender's relevant weekly income, the court is required to take account of the offender's financial circumstances more broadly. Guidance on important parts of this assessment is set out below.

15. An offender's financial circumstances may have the effect of increasing or reducing the amount of the fine; however, they are not relevant to the assessment of offence seriousness. They should be considered separately from the selection of the appropriate fine band and the court's assessment of the position of the offence within the range for that band.

Out-of-the-ordinary expenses

16. In deciding the proportions of relevant weekly income that are the starting points and ranges for each fine band, account has been taken of reasonable living expenses. Accordingly, no further allowance should normally be made for these. In addition, no allowance should normally be made where the offender has dependants.

17. Outgoings will be relevant to the amount of the fine only where the expenditure is out of the ordinary and substantially reduces the ability to pay a financial penalty so that the requirement to pay a fine based on the standard approach would lead to undue hardship.

Unusually low outgoings

18. Where the offender's living expenses are substantially lower than would normally be expected, it may be appropriate to adjust the amount of the fine to reflect this. This may apply, for example, where an offender does not make any financial contribution towards his or her living costs.

Savings

19. Where an offender has savings these will not normally be relevant to the assessment of the amount of a fine although they may influence the decision on time to pay.

20. However, where an offender has little or no income but has substantial savings, the court may consider it appropriate to adjust the amount of the fine to reflect this.

Household has more than one source of income

21. Where the household of which the offender is a part has more than one source of income, the fine should normally be based on the income of the offender alone.

22. However, where the offender's part of the income is very small (or the offender is wholly dependent on the income of another), the court may have regard to the extent of the household's income and assets which will be available to meet any fine imposed on the offender.

Potential earning capacity

23. Where there is reason to believe that an offender's potential earning capacity is greater than his or her current income, the court may wish to adjust the amount of the fine to reflect this. This may apply, for example, where an unemployed offender states an expectation to gain paid employment within a short time. The basis for the calculation of fine should be recorded in order to ensure that there is a clear record for use in variation or enforcement proceedings.

High income offenders

24. Where the offender is in receipt of very high income, a fine based on a proportion of relevant weekly income may be disproportionately high when compared with the seriousness of the offence. In such cases, the court should adjust the fine to an appropriate level; as a general indication, in most cases the fine for a first time offender pleading not guilty should not exceed 75 per cent of the maximum fine.

Offence committed for 'commercial' purposes

25. Some offences are committed with the intention of gaining a significant commercial benefit. These often occur where, in order to carry out an activity lawfully, a person has to comply with certain processes which may be expensive. They include, for example, 'taxi-touting' (where unauthorized persons seek to operate as taxi drivers) and 'f y-tipping' (where the cost of lawful disposal is considerable).

26. In some of these cases, a fine based on the standard approach set out above may not reflect the level of financial gain achieved or sought through the of ending.

Accordingly:

    (a) where the offender has generated income or avoided expenditure to a level that can be calculated or estimated, the court may wish to consider that amount when determining the financial penalty;

    (b) where it is not possible to calculate or estimate that amount, the court may wish to draw on information from the enforcing authorities about the general costs of operating within the law.

Reduction for a guilty plea

27. Where a guilty plea has been entered, the amount of the fine should be reduced by the appropriate proportion.

Maximum fines

28. A fine must not exceed the statutory limit. Where this is expressed in terms of a 'level', the maxima are:

Level 1	£200
Level 2	£500
Level 3	£1,000
Level 4	£2,500
Level 5	£5,000

Victims' surcharge

29. Whenever a court imposes a fine in respect of an offence committed after 1 April 2007, it must order the offender to pay a surcharge of £15. [**Note:** See Part B Victim Surcharge].

30. Where the offender is of adequate means, the court must not reduce the fine to allow for imposition of the surcharge. Where the offender does not have sufficient means to pay the total financial penalty considered appropriate by the court, the order of priority is: compensation, surcharge, fine, costs.

31. Further guidance is set out in *Guidance on Victims Surcharge* issued by the Justice Clerks' Society and Magistrates' Association (30 March 2007).

Costs

32. Where the offender does not have sufficient means to pay the total financial penalty considered appropriate by the court, the order of priority is: compensation, surcharge, fine, costs.

Multiple offences

33. Where an offender is to be fined for two or more offences that arose out of the same incident, it will often be appropriate to impose on the most serious offence a fine which reflects the totality of the of ending where this can be achieved within the maximum penalty for that offence. 'No separate penalty' should be imposed for the other offences.

34. Where compensation is being ordered, that will need to be attributed to the relevant offence as will any necessary ancillary orders.

Fine bands D and E

35. Two further fine bands are provided to assist a court in calculating a fine where the offence and general circumstances would otherwise warrant a community order (band D) or a custodial sentence (band E) but the court has decided that it need not impose such a sentence and that a financial penalty is appropriate. See pages 160 and 163 of the *Magistrates' Court Sentencing Guidelines* for further guidance.

36. The following starting points and ranges apply:

	Starting point	Range
Band D	250% of relevant weekly income	200–300% of relevant weekly income
Band E	400% of relevant weekly income	300–500% of relevant weekly income

Imposition of fines with custodial sentences

37. A fine and a custodial sentence may be imposed for the same offence, although there will be few circumstances in which this is appropriate, particularly where the custodial sentence is to be served immediately. One example might be where an offender has profited financially from an offence but there is no obvious victim to whom compensation can be awarded. Combining these sentences is most likely to be appropriate only where the custodial sentence is short and/or the offender clearly has, or will have, the means to pay.

38. Care must be taken to ensure that the overall sentence is proportionate to the seriousness of the offence and that better-off offenders are not able to 'buy themselves out of custody'.

Payment

39. A fine is payable in full on the day on which it is imposed. The offender should always be asked for immediate payment when present in court and some payment on the day should be required wherever possible.

40. Where that is not possible, the court may, in certain circumstances, require the offender to be detained. More commonly, a court will allow payments to be made over a period set by the court:

    (a) if periodic payments are allowed, the fine should normally be payable within a maximum of 12 months. However, it may be unrealistic to expect those on very low incomes to maintain payments for as long as a year;

    (b) compensation should normally be payable within 12 months. However, in exceptional circumstances it may be appropriate to allow it to be paid over a period of up to three years.

41. Where fine bands D and E apply (see paras 35–36 above), it may be appropriate for the fine to be of an amount that is larger than can be repaid within 12 months. In such cases, the fine should normally be payable within a maximum of 18 months (band D) or two years (band E).

42. It is generally recognized that the maximum weekly payment by a person in receipt of state benefit should rarely exceed £5.

43. When allowing payment by instalments by an offender in receipt of earned income, the following approach may be useful. If the offender has dependants or larger than usual commitments, the weekly payment is likely to be decreased.

Net weekly income	Starting point for weekly payment
£60	£5
£120	£10
£200	£25
£250	£30
£300	£50
£400	£80

APPENDIX 3

SEXUAL OFFENCES ACT 2003, SCH 3

An offence under section 1 of the Sexual Offences Act 1956 (c. 69) (rape).

An offence under section 5 of that Act (intercourse with girl under 13).

An offence under section 6 of that Act (intercourse with girl under 16), if the offender was 20 or over.

An offence under section 10 of that Act (incest by a man), if the victim or (as the case may be) other party was under 18.

An offence under section 12 of that Act (buggery) if–

(a) the offender was 20 or over, and
(b) the victim or (as the case may be) other party was under 18.

An offence under section 13 of that Act (indecency between men) if–

(a) the offender was 20 or over, and
(b) the victim or (as the case may be) other party was under 18.

An offence under section 14 of that Act (indecent assault on a woman) if–

(a) the victim or (as the case may be) other party was under 18, or
(b) the offender, in respect of the offence or finding, is or has been–
    (i) sentenced to imprisonment for a term of at least 30 months; or
    (ii) admitted to a hospital subject to a restriction order.

An offence under section 15 of that Act (indecent assault on a man) if–

(a) the victim or (as the case may be) other party was under 18, or
(b) the offender, in respect of the offence or finding, is or has been–
    (i) sentenced to imprisonment for a term of at least 30 months; or
    (ii) admitted to a hospital subject to a restriction order.

An offence under section 16 of that Act (assault with intent to commit buggery), if the victim or (as the case may be) other party was under 18.

An offence under section 28 of that Act (causing or encouraging the prostitution of, intercourse with or indecent assault on girl under 16).

An offence under section 1 of the Indecency with Children Act 1960 (c. 33) (indecent conduct towards young child).

An offence under section 54 of the Criminal Law Act 1977 (c. 45) (inciting girl under 16 to have incestuous sexual intercourse).

An offence under section 1 of the Protection of Children Act 1978 (c. 37) (indecent photographs of children), if the indecent photographs or pseudo-photographs showed persons under 16 and–

(a) the conviction, finding or caution was before the commencement of this Part, or
(b) the offender–
    (i) was 18 or over, or

(ii)   is sentenced in respect of the offence to imprisonment for a term of at least 12 months.

An offence under section 170 of the Customs and Excise Management Act 1979 (c. 2) (penalty for fraudulent evasion of duty etc.) in relation to goods prohibited to be imported under section 42 of the Customs Consolidation Act 1876 (c. 36) (indecent or obscene articles), if the prohibited goods included indecent photographs of persons under 16 and–

(a)   the conviction, finding or caution was before the commencement of this Part, or
(b)   the offender–
  (i)   was 18 or over, or
  (ii)   is sentenced in respect of the offence to imprisonment for a term of at least 12 months.

An offence under section 160 of the Criminal Justice Act 1988 (c. 33) (possession of indecent photograph of a child), if the indecent photographs or pseudo-photographs showed persons under 16 and–

(a)   the conviction, finding or caution was before the commencement of this Part, or
(b)   the offender–
  (i)   was 18 or over, or
  (ii)   is sentenced in respect of the offence to imprisonment for a term of at least 12 months.

An offence under section 3 of the Sexual Offences (Amendment) Act 2000 (c. 44) (abuse of position of trust), if the offender was 20 or over.

An offence under section 1 or 2 of this Act (rape, assault by penetration).

An offence under section 3 of this Act (sexual assault) if–

(a)   where the offender was under 18, he is or has been sentenced, in respect of the offence, to imprisonment for a term of at least 12 months;
(b)   in any other case–
  (i)   the victim was under 18, or
  (ii)   the offender, in respect of the offence or finding, is or has been–

(a)   sentenced to a term of imprisonment,
(b)   detained in a hospital, or
(c)   made the subject of a community sentence of at least 12 months.

An offence under any of sections 4 to 6 of this Act (causing sexual activity without consent, rape of a child under 13, assault of a child under 13 by penetration).

An offence under section 7 of this Act (sexual assault of a child under 13) if the offender–

(a)   was 18 or over, or
(b)   is or has been sentenced in respect of the offence to imprisonment for a term of at least 12 months.

An offence under any of sections 8 to 12 of this Act (causing or inciting a child under 13 to engage in sexual activity, child sex offences committed by adults).

An offence under section 13 of this Act (child sex offences committed by children or young persons), if the offender is or has been sentenced, in respect of the offence, to imprisonment for a term of at least 12 months.

An offence under section 14 of this Act (arranging or facilitating the commission of a child sex offence) if the offender–

(a)   was 18 or over, or
(b)   is or has been sentenced, in respect of the offence, to imprisonment for a term of at least 12 months.

An offence under section 15 of this Act (meeting a child following sexual grooming etc).

An offence under any of sections 16 to 19 of this Act (abuse of a position of trust) if the offender, in respect of the offence, is or has been–

    (a) sentenced to a term of imprisonment,
    (b) detained in a hospital, or
    (c) made the subject of a community sentence of at least 12 months.

An offence under section 25 or 26 of this Act (familial child sex offences) if the offender–

    (a) was 18 or over, or
    (b) is or has been sentenced in respect of the offence to imprisonment for a term of at least 12 months.

An offence under any of sections 30 to 37 of this Act (offences against persons with a mental disorder impeding choice, inducements etc. to persons with mental disorder).

An offence under any of sections 38 to 41 of this Act (care workers for persons with mental disorder) if–

    (a) where the offender was under 18, he is or has been sentenced in respect of the offence to imprisonment for a term of at least 12 months;
    (b) in any other case, the offender, in respect of the offence or finding, is or has been–
        (i) sentenced to a term of imprisonment,
        (ii) detained in a hospital, or
        (iii) made the subject of a community sentence of at least 12 months.

An offence under section 47 of this Act (paying for sexual services of a child) if the victim or (as the case may be) other party was under 16, and the offender–

    (a) was 18 or over, or
    (b) is or has been sentenced in respect of the offence to imprisonment for a term of at least 12 months.

An offence under section 48 of this Act (causing or inciting child prostitution or pornography) if the offender–

    (a) was 18 or over, or
    (b) is or has been sentenced in respect of the offence to imprisonment for a term of at least 12 months.

An offence under section 49 of this Act (controlling a child prostitute or a child involved in pornography) if the offender–

    (a) was 18 or over, or
    (b) is or has been sentenced in respect of the offence to imprisonment for a term of at least 12 months.

An offence under section 50 of this Act (arranging or facilitating child prostitution or pornography) if the offender–

    (a) was 18 or over, or
    (b) is or has been sentenced in respect of the offence to imprisonment for a term of at least 12 months.

An offence under section 61 of this Act (administering a substance with intent).

An offence under section 62 or 63 of this Act (committing an offence or trespassing, with intent to commit a sexual offence) if–

    (a) where the offender was under 18, he is or has been sentenced in respect of the offence to imprisonment for a term of at least 12 months;
    (b) in any other case–

    (i)   the intended offence was an offence against a person under 18, or

    (ii) the offender, in respect of the offence or finding, is or has been–

    (a) sentenced to a term of imprisonment,

    (b) detained in a hospital, or

    (c) made the subject of a community sentence of at least 12 months.

An offence under section 64 or 65 of this Act (sex with an adult relative) if–

    (a) where the offender was under 18, he is or has been sentenced in respect of the offence to imprisonment for a term of at least 12 months;

    (b) in any other case, the offender, in respect of the offence or finding, is or has been–

        (i)   sentenced to a term of imprisonment, or

        (ii)   detained in a hospital.

An offence under section 66 of this Act (exposure) if–

    (a) where the offender was under 18, he is or has been sentenced in respect of the offence to imprisonment for a term of at least 12 months;

    (b) in any other case–

        (i)   the victim was under 18, or

        (ii)   the offender, in respect of the offence or finding, is or has been–

    (a) sentenced to a term of imprisonment,

    (b) detained in a hospital, or

    (c) made the subject of a community sentence of at least 12 months.

An offence under section 67 of this Act (voyeurism) if–

    (a) where the offender was under 18, he is or has been sentenced in respect of the offence to imprisonment for a term of at least 12 months;

    (b) in any other case–

    (i)   the victim was under 18, or

    (ii) the offender, in respect of the offence or finding, is or has been–

    (a) sentenced to a term of imprisonment,

    (b) detained in a hospital, or

    (c) made the subject of a community sentence of at least 12 months.

An offence under section 69 or 70 of this Act (intercourse with an animal, sexual penetration of a corpse) if–

    (a) where the offender was under 18, he is or has been sentenced in respect of the offence to imprisonment for a term of at least 12 months;

    (b) in any other case, the offender, in respect of the offence or finding, is or has been–

        (i)   sentenced to a term of imprisonment, or

        (ii)   detained in a hospital.

An offence under section 63 of the Criminal Justice and Immigration Act 2008 (possession of extreme pornographic images) if the offender—

    (a) was 18 or over, and

    (b) is sentenced in respect of the offence to imprisonment for a term of at least 2 years.

An offence under section 62(1) of the Coroners and Justice Act 2009 (possession of prohibited images of children) if the offender—

    (a) was 18 or over, and

    (b) is sentenced in respect of the offence to imprisonment for a term of at least 2 years.

APPENDIX 4

CRIMINAL JUSTICE ACT 2003, SCH 12

1 In this Schedule—

"the offender", in relation to a suspended sentence order, means the person in respect of whom the order is made;

"the local justice area concerned", in relation to a suspended sentence order, means the local justice area for the time being specified in the order;

"the responsible officer" has the meaning given by section 197.

2 In this Schedule—

    (a) any reference to a suspended sentence order being subject to review is a reference to such an order being subject to review in accordance with section 191(1)(b) or to a drug rehabilitation requirement of such an order being subject to review in accordance with section 210(1)(b);

    (b) any reference to the court responsible for a suspended sentence order which is subject to review is to be construed in accordance with section 191(3) or, as the case may be, 210(2).

3 Orders made on appeal

Where a suspended sentence order is made on appeal it is to be taken for the purposes of this Schedule to have been made by the Crown Court.

4 Duty to give warning in relation to community requirement

    (1) If the responsible officer is of the opinion that the offender has failed without reasonable excuse to comply with any of the community requirements of a suspended sentence order, the officer must give him a warning under this paragraph unless—

        (a) the offender has within the previous twelve months been given a warning under this paragraph in relation to a failure to comply with any of the community requirements of the order, or

        (b) the officer causes an information to be laid before a justice of the peace in respect of the failure.

    (2) A warning under this paragraph must—

        (a) describe the circumstances of the failure,

        (b) state that the failure is unacceptable, and

        (c) inform the offender that if within the next twelve months he again fails to comply with any requirement of the order, he will be liable to be brought before a court.

    (3) The responsible officer must, as soon as practicable after the warning has been given, record that fact.

    (4) In relation to any suspended sentence order which is made by the Crown Court and does not include a direction that any failure to comply with the community requirements of the order is to be dealt with by a magistrates' court, the reference in sub-paragraph (1)(b) to a justice of the peace is to be read as a reference to the Crown Court.

5 Breach of order after warning

(1)   If—

(a)   the responsible officer has given a warning under paragraph 4 to the offender in respect of a suspended sentence order, and

(b)   at any time within the twelve months beginning with the date on which the warning was given, the responsible officer is of the opinion that the offender has since that date failed without reasonable excuse to comply with any of the community requirements of the order,

the officer must cause an information to be laid before a justice of the peace in respect of the failure in question.

(2)   In relation to any suspended sentence order which is made by the Crown Court and does not include a direction that any failure to comply with the community requirements of the order is to be dealt with by a magistrates' court, the reference in sub-paragraph (1) to a justice of the peace is to be read as a reference to the Crown Court.

6 Issue of summons or warrant by justice of the peace

(1)   This paragraph applies to—

(a)   a suspended sentence order made by a magistrates' court, or

(b)   any suspended sentence order which was made by the Crown Court and includes a direction that any failure to comply with the community requirements of the order is to be dealt with by a magistrates' court.

(2)   If at any time while a suspended sentence order to which this paragraph applies is in force it appears on information to a justice of the peace that the offender has failed to comply with any of the community requirements of the order, the justice may—

(a)   issue a summons requiring the offender to appear at the place and time specified in it, or

(b)   if the information is in writing and on oath, issue a warrant for his arrest.

(3)   Any summons or warrant issued under this paragraph must direct the offender to appear or be brought—

(a)   in the case of a suspended sentence order which is subject to review, before the court responsible for the order,

[(b)   in any other case, before a magistrates' court acting in the local justice area in which the offender resides or, if it is not known where he resides, before a magistrates' court acting in the local justice area concerned.

(4)   Where a summons issued under sub-paragraph (2)(a) requires the offender to appear before a magistrates' court and the offender does not appear in answer to the summons, the magistrates' court may issue a warrant for the arrest of the offender.

7 [...]

8 Powers of court on breach of community requirement or conviction of further offence

(1)   This paragraph applies where—

(a)   it is proved to the satisfaction of a court before which an offender appears or is brought under paragraph 6 or 7 or by virtue of section 192(6) that he has failed without reasonable excuseto comply with any of the community requirements of the suspended sentence order, or

(b)   an offender is convicted of an offence committed during the operational period of a suspended sentence (other than one which has already taken effect) and either—

(i)   he is so convicted by or before a court having power under paragraph 11 to deal with him in respect of the suspended sentence, or (ii)　he subsequently appears or is brought before such a court.

(2)　The court must consider his case and deal with him in one of the following ways—

(a)　the court may order that the suspended sentence is to take effect with its original term unaltered,

(b)　the court may order that the sentence is to take effect [subject to the substitution for the original term of a lesser term,

(c)　the court may amend the order by doing any one or more of the following—

(i)　imposing more onerous community requirements which the court could include if it were then making the order,

(ii)　subject to subsections (3) and (4) of section 189, extending the supervision period, or

(iii)　subject to subsection (3) of that section, extending the operational period.

(3)　The court must make an order under sub-paragraph (2)(a) or (b) unless it is of the opinion that it would be unjust to do so in view of all the circumstances, including the matters mentioned in sub-paragraph (4); and where it is of that opinion the court must state its reasons.

(4)　The matters referred to in sub-paragraph (3) are—

(a)　the extent to which the offender has complied with the community requirements of the suspended sentence order, and

(b)　in a case falling within sub-paragraph (1)(b), the facts of the subsequent offence.

(4A)　Where a magistrates' court dealing with an offender under sub-paragraph (2)(c) would not otherwise have the power to amend the suspended sentence order under paragraph 14 (amendment by reason of change of residence), that paragraph has effect as if the references to the appropriate court were references to the court dealing with the offender.

(5)　Where a court deals with an offender under sub-paragraph (2) in respect of a suspended sentence, the appropriate officer of the court must notify the appropriate officer of the court which passed the sentence of the method adopted.

(6)　Where a suspended sentence order was made by the Crown Court and a magistrates' court would (apart from this sub-paragraph) be required to deal with the offender under sub-paragraph (2)(a), (b) or (c) it may instead commit him to custody or release him on bail until he can be brought or appear before the Crown Court.

(7)　A magistrates' court which deals with an offender's case under subparagraph (6) must send to the Crown Court—

(a)　a certificate signed by a justice of the peace certifying that the offender has failed to comply with the community requirements of the suspended sentence order in the respect specified in the certificate, and

(b)　such other particulars of the case as may be desirable;

and a certificate purporting to be so signed is admissible as evidence of the failure before the Crown Court.

(8)　In proceedings before the Crown Court under this paragraph any question whether the offender has failed to comply with the community requirements of the suspended sentence order and any question whether the offender has been convicted of an offence committed during the operational period of the suspended sentence is to be determined by the court and not by the verdict of a jury.

9　Further provisions as to order that suspended sentence is to take effect

(1)　When making an order under paragraph 8(2)(a) or (b) that a sentence is to take effect (with or without any variation of the original term), the court—

[...]

    (b) may order that the sentence is to take effect immediately or that the term of that sentence is to commence on the expiry of another term of imprisonment passed on the offender by that or another court.

(2) The power to make an order under sub-paragraph (1)(b) has effect subject to section 265 (restriction on consecutive sentences for released prisoners).

(3) For the purpose of any enactment conferring rights of appeal in criminal cases, any order made by the court under paragraph 8(2)(a) or (b) is to be treated as a sentence passed on the offender by that court for the offence for which the suspended sentence was passed.

10 Restriction of powers in paragraph 8 where treatment required

(1) An offender who is required by any of the following community requirements of a suspended sentence order—

    (a) a mental health treatment requirement,
    (b) a drug rehabilitation requirement, or
    (c) an alcohol treatment requirement,

to submit to treatment for his mental condition, or his dependency on or propensity to misuse drugs or alcohol, is not to be treated for the purposes of paragraph 8(1)(a) as having failed to comply with that requirement on the ground only that he had refused to undergo any surgical, electrical or other treatment if, in the opinion of the court, his refusal was reasonable having regard to all the circumstances.

(2) A court may not under paragraph 8(2)(c)(i) amend a mental health treatment requirement, a drug rehabilitation requirement or an alcohol treatment requirement unless the offender expresses his willingness to comply with the requirement as amended.

11 Court by which suspended sentence may be dealt with under paragraph 8(1)(b)

(1) An offender may be dealt with under paragraph 8(1)(b) in respect of a suspended sentence by the Crown Court or, where the sentence was passed by a magistrates' court, by any magistrates' court before which he appears or is brought.

(2) Where an offender is convicted by a magistrates' court of any offence and the court is satisfied that the offence was committed during the operational period of a suspended sentence passed by the Crown Court—

    (a) the court may, if it thinks fit, commit him in custody or on bail to the Crown Court, and
    (b) if it does not, must give written notice of the conviction to the appropriate officer of the Crown Court.

12 Procedure where court convicting of further offence does not deal with suspended sentence

(1) If it appears to the Crown Court, where that court has jurisdiction in accordance with sub-paragraph (2), or to a justice of the peace having jurisdiction in accordance with that sub-paragraph—

    (a) that an offender has been convicted in the United Kingdom of an offence committed during the operational period of a suspended sentence, and
    (b) that he has not been dealt with in respect of the suspended sentence,

that court or justice may, subject to the following provisions of this paragraph, issue a summons requiring the offender to appear at the place and time specified in it, or a warrant for his arrest.

(2) Jurisdiction for the purposes of sub-paragraph (1) may be exercised—

    (a) if the suspended sentence was passed by the Crown Court, by that court;
    (b) if it was passed by a magistrates' court, by a justice [acting in the local justice area in which the court acted.

(3) Where—

    (a) an offender is convicted in Scotland or Northern Ireland of an offence, and

    (b) the court is informed that the offence was committed during the operational period of a suspended sentence passed in England or Wales,

the court must give written notice of the conviction to the appropriate officer of the court by which the suspended sentence was passed.

  (4) Unless he is acting in consequence of a notice under sub-paragraph (3), a justice of the peace may not issue a summons under this paragraph except on information and may not issue a warrant under this paragraph except on information in writing and on oath.

  (5) A summons or warrant issued under this paragraph must direct the offender to appear or be brought before the court by which the suspended sentence was passed.

13

  (1) Where at any time while a suspended sentence order is in force, it appears to the appropriate court on the application of the offender or the responsible officer that, having regard to the circumstances which have arisen since the order was made, it would be in the interests of justice to do so, the court may cancel the community requirements of the suspended sentence order.

  (2) The circumstances in which the appropriate court may exercise its power under sub-paragraph (1) include the offender's making good progress or his responding satisfactorily to supervision.

  (3) In this paragraph "the appropriate court" means—(a) in the case of a suspended sentence order which is subject to review, the court responsible for the order,

    (b) in the case of a suspended sentence order which was made by the Crown Court and does not include any direction that any failure to comply with the community requirements of the order is to be dealt with by a magistrates' court, the Crown Court, and

    (c) in any other case, a magistrates' court acting in the local justice area concerned.

14

  (1) This paragraph applies where, at any time while a suspended sentence order is in force, the appropriate court is satisfied that the offender proposes to change, or has changed, his residence from the local justice area concerned to another local justice area.

  (2) Subject to sub-paragraphs (3) and (4), the appropriate court may, and on the application of the responsible officer must, amend the suspended sentence order by substituting the other local justice area for the area specified in the order.

  (3) The court may not amend under this paragraph a suspended sentence order which contains requirements which, in the opinion of the court, cannot be complied with unless the offender resides in the local justice area concerned unless, in accordance with paragraph 15 it either—

    (a) cancels those requirements, or

    (b) substitutes for those requirements other requirements which can be complied with if the offender does not reside in that area.

  (4) The court may not amend under this paragraph any suspended sentence order imposing a programme requirement unless it appears to the court that the accredited programme specified in the requirement is available in the other local justice area.

  (5) In this paragraph "the appropriate court" has the same meaning as in paragraph 13.

15

  (1) At any time during the supervision period, the appropriate court may, on the application of the offender or the responsible officer, by order amend any community requirement of a suspended sentence order—

    (a) by cancelling the requirement, or

    (b) by replacing it with a requirement of the same kind, which the court could include if it were then making the order.

(2) For the purposes of sub-paragraph (1)—

    (a) a requirement falling within any paragraph of section 190(1) is of the same kind as any other requirement falling within that paragraph, and

    (b) an electronic monitoring requirement is a requirement of the same kind as any requirement falling within section 190(1) to which it relates.

(3) The court may not under this paragraph amend a mental health treatment requirement, a drug rehabilitation requirement or an alcohol treatment requirement unless the offender expresses his willingness to comply with the requirement as amended.

(4) If the offender fails to express his willingness to comply with a mental health treatment requirement, drug rehabilitation requirement or alcohol treatment requirement as proposed to be amended by the court under this paragraph, the court may—

    (a) revoke the suspended sentence order and the suspended sentence to which it relates, and

    (b) deal with him, for the offence in respect of which the suspended sentence was imposed, in any way in which it could deal with him if he had just been convicted by or before the court of the offence.

(5) In dealing with the offender under sub-paragraph (4)(b), the court must take into account the extent to which the offender has complied with the requirements of the order.

(6) In this paragraph "the appropriate court" has the same meaning as in paragraph 13.

16

(1) Where the medical practitioner or other person by whom or under whose direction an offender is, in pursuance of any requirement to which this subparagraph applies, being treated for his mental condition or his dependency on or propensity to misuse drugs or alcohol—

    (a) is of the opinion mentioned in sub-paragraph (3), or

    (b) is for any reason unwilling to continue to treat or direct the treatment of the offender,

he must make a report in writing to that effect to the responsible officer and that officer must apply under paragraph 15 to the appropriate court for the variation or cancellation of the requirement.

(2) The requirements to which sub-paragraph (1) applies are—

    (a) a mental health treatment requirement,

    (b) a drug rehabilitation requirement, and

    (c) an alcohol treatment requirement.

(3) The opinion referred to in sub-paragraph (1) is—

    (a) that the treatment of the offender should be continued beyond the period specified in that behalf in the order,

    (b) that the offender needs different treatment,

    (c) that the offender is not susceptible to treatment, or

    (d) that the offender does not require further treatment.

(4) In this paragraph "the appropriate court" has the same meaning as in paragraph 13.

17

Where the responsible officer is of the opinion that a suspended sentence order imposing a drug rehabilitation requirement which is subject to review should be so amended as to provide for each periodic review (required by section 211) to be made without a hearing instead of at a review hearing, or vice versa, he must apply under paragraph 15 to the court responsible for the order for the variation of the order.

18

(1) Where—

(a) a suspended sentence order imposing an unpaid work requirement is in force in respect of the offender, and

(b) on the application of the offender or the responsible officer, it appears to the appropriate court that it would be in the interests of justice to do so having regard to circumstances which have arisen since the order was made,

the court may, in relation to the order, extend the period of twelve months specified in section 200(2).

(2) In this paragraph "the appropriate court" has the same meaning as in paragraph 13.

19

(1) No application may be made under paragraph 13, 15 or 18, and no order may be made under paragraph 14, while an appeal against the suspended sentence is pending.

(2) Sub-paragraph (1) does not apply to an application under paragraph 15 which—

(a) relates to a mental health treatment requirement, a drug rehabilitation requirement or an alcohol treatment requirement, and

(b) is made by the responsible officer with the consent of the offender.

20

(1) Subject to sub-paragraph (2), where a court proposes to exercise its powers under paragraph 15, otherwise than on the application of the offender, the court—

(a) must summon him to appear before the court, and

(b) if he does not appear in answer to the summons, may issue a warrant for his arrest.

(2) This paragraph does not apply to an order cancelling any community requirement of a suspended sentence order.

21

Paragraphs 8(2)(c) and 15(1)(b) have effect subject to the provisions mentioned in subsection (2) of section 190, and to subsections (3) and (5) of that section.

APPENDIX 5

SMITH [2011] EWCA 1772

Para 20–26

It is not appropriate to attempt to lay down a rule that one particular provision be adopted in all cases. The circumstances of cases vary greatly and orders must be tailored to them. That said, we set out some conclusions.

A blanket prohibition on computer use or internet access is impermissible. It is disproportionate because it restricts the defendant in the use of what is nowadays an essential part of everyday living for a large proportion of the public, as well as a requirement of much employment. Before the creation of the internet, if a defendant kept books of pictures of child pornography it would not have occurred to anyone to ban him from possession of all printed material. The internet is a modern equivalent.

Although the Hemsley formulation restricting internet use to job search, study, work, lawful recreation and purchases has its attractions, it seems to us on analysis to suffer from the same flaw, albeit less obviously. Even today, the legitimate use of the internet extends beyond these spheres of activity. Such a provision in a SOPO would, it seems, prevent a defendant from looking up the weather forecast, from planning a journey by accessing a map, from reading the news, from sending the electricity board his meter reading, from conducting his banking across the web unless paying charges for his account, and indeed from sending or receiving Email via the web, at least unless a strained meaning is given to 'lawful recreation'. The difficulties of defining the limits of that last expression seem to us another reason for avoiding this formulation. More, the speed of expansion of applications of the internet is such that it is simply impossible to predict what developments there will be within the foreseeable lifespan of a great many SOPOs, which would unexpectedly and unnecessarily, and therefore wrongly, be found to be prohibited.

Some courts have been attracted to a prohibition upon the possession of any computer or other device giving access to the internet without notification to the local police. It may be that this might occasionally be the only way of preventing offending, but the vast increase in the number and type of such devices makes it onerous both for defendants and the police. Its effect is, inter alia, to require the defendant to tell the police when he buys a new mobile telephone, or a play station for his children. It seems to us that in most cases the police will need to work on the basis that most defendants, like most people generally, will have some devices with internet access, and that a requirement that they be notified of it adds little of any value.

There are fewer difficulties about a prohibition on internet access without filtering software, but there is a clear risk that there may be uncertainty about exactly what is required and the policing of such a provision seems likely to be attended by some difficulty.

Of the formulations thus far devised and reported, the one which seems to us most likely to be effective is the one requiring the preservation of readable internet history coupled with submission to inspection on request. There is no need for the SOPO to invest the police with powers of forcible entry into private premises beyond the statutory ones which they already have. It is sufficient to prohibit use of the internet without submitting to inspection on request. If the defendant were to deny the officers sight of his computer, either in his home or by surrendering it to them, he would be in breach. One suitable form of such an order appears in <u>Smith</u> below.

Where the risk is not simply of downloading pornography but consists of or includes the use of chatlines or similar networks to groom young people for sexual purposes, it may well be appropriate to include a prohibition on communicating via the internet with any young person known or believed to be under the age of 16, coupled no doubt with a provision such as we mention in (v). In some such cases, it may be necessary to prohibit altogether the use of social networking sites or other forms of chatline or chatroom. See for an example Clarke's case, with which we deal below at paragraph 33(3).

Personal contact with children: age

Any provision in a SOPO must be tailored to the necessity to prevent sexual offending which causes serious harm to others. The majority of offences relating to children are committed only when the child is under the age of 16. The exceptions are offences committed under ss 16-19 Sexual Offences Act 2003 against those in respect of whom the defendant stands in a position of trust, as defined in section 21, together with family offences under ss 25 and 26. If the risk is genuinely of these latter offences, prohibitions on contact with children under 18 may be justified. Otherwise, if contact with children needs to be restricted, it should relate to those under 16, not under 18.

Personal contact with children: generally

Care must be taken in considering whether prohibitions on contact with children are really necessary. In Lea (supra) the defendant had been convicted of offences of viewing child pornography. The SOPO imposed contained provisions prohibiting him from having unsupervised contact with any child under the age of 16 except in the presence of a parent or appropriate adult, and from permitting any such person to be in any house where he lived or stayed. This court rejected the submission of the Crown that those provisions were justified in case the defendant graduated to contact offences. There was no indication whatever of any likelihood of such progression. The case is a good example of overuse of a SOPO. Preventive these orders are; it does not follow that anything is permissible. It is not legitimate to impose multiple prohibitions on a defendant just in case he commits a different kind of offence. There must be an identifiable risk of contact offences before this kind of prohibition can be justified.

Prohibitions on contact with children may however be necessary in some cases of predatory paedophiles who seek out children for sexual purposes. Even then, care must be taken with their terms. The defendant may have children of his own, or within his extended family. If his offences are within the family, or there is a risk that offences of that kind may be committed, then those children may need protection. But if they are not, and there is no sign of a risk that he may abuse his own family, it is both unnecessary and an infringement of the children's entitlement to family life to impose restrictions which extend to them. Even if there is a history of abuse within the family, any order ought ordinarily to be subject to any order made in family proceedings for the very good reason that part of the family court process may, if it is justified, involve carefully supervised rehabilitation of parent and child. In those cases where it really is necessary to impose a prohibition on contact with children (of whichever age) it is essential to include a saving for incidental contact such as is inherent in everyday life. Otherwise the defendant commits a criminal offence if he is dealt with by a 15 year old at a shop checkout, or has dealings with a child in other similarly inevitable circumstances. The inevitably imprecise nature of this essential saving is a further reason for exercising considerable caution before imposing a prohibition of this kind. One possible form providing for such a saving is set out in the case of Clarke below at paragraph 33(5).

Occupations or activities and children

Terms seem commonly to be included in SOPOs which prohibit the defendant from activities which are likely to bring him into contact with children. As to those our conclusions are as follows.

Such a term must be justified as required beyond the restrictions placed upon the defendant by the Independent Safeguarding Authority ("ISA") under the Safeguarding Vulnerable Groups Act 2006 ("SVGA"). If there is a real risk that he may undertake some activity outside the ISA prohibitions, then such a term may be justified. Otherwise it is not. What is covered by the SVGA needs examination in each case. The key provisions are to be found in s 5 and Schedule 4 Part 1, which defines regulated activities relating to children. Generally speaking, paragraph 2 prevents the defendant from engaging in any form of teaching, training or instruction of children, any form of care, advice, guidance or therapy, and from acting as a driver for children's activities. That will cover most unpaid as well as formal paid occupations which carry a risk of contact offences. It will for example cover football or other sports clubs and youth groups. We suggest that judges should ordinarily require the Crown to justify an application for a SOPO term relating to activity with children by demonstrating what the risk is which is not already catered for by the SVGA.

The age ought ordinarily to be under 16; free association with 16 and 17 year olds is not an offence. It is otherwise if the defendant would be in a position of trust, as defined by section 21 Sexual Offences Act 2003, but in the ordinary way no such position will be permitted by the SVGA restrictions.

Providing a draft

Arrangements for the provision of a draft order will necessarily vary from court to court. We say no more than that it is essential that there is a written draft, properly considered in advance of the sentencing hearing. The normal requirement should be that it is served on the court and the defendant before the sentencing hearing–we suggest not less than two clear days before but in any event not *at* the hearing. This will usually be possible because sentencing in such cases only occasionally follows immediately on conviction. Because the draft is likely to require amendment before it is issued by the court staff, it is sensible for it to be available in electronic as well as paper form. If a judge finds that insufficient time for consideration has been given, he has ample power to put the issue back to another hearing, but this is wasteful and the occasion for it ought to be avoided by prior service of the draft.

APPENDIX 6

PROSECUTION DISCLOSURE OF UNUSED MATERIAL

Extracts from the Criminal Procedure and Investigations Act 1996, ss 1, 2, 3, 4, 7A, 8, 10, 12, 13

Criminal Procedure and Investigations Act 1996, ss 1, 2, 3, 4, 7A, 8, 10, 12, 13

1.— Application of this Part.

(1) This Part applies where—

    (a) a person is charged with a summary offence in respect of which a court proceeds to summary trial and in respect of which he pleads not guilty,

    (b) a person who has attained the age of 18 is charged with an offence which is triable either way, in respect of which a court proceeds to summary trial and in respect of which he pleads not guilty, or

    (c) a person under the age of 18 is charged with an indictable offence in respect of which a court proceeds to summary trial and in respect of which he pleads not guilty.

(2) This Part also applies where—

[...]

    (cc) a person is charged with an offence for which he is sent for trial,

    (d) a count charging a person with a summary offence is included in an indictment under the authority of section 40 of the Criminal Justice Act 1988 (common assault etc.),

    (e) a bill of indictment charging a person with an indictable offence is preferred under the authority of section 2(2)(b) of the Administration of Justice (Miscellaneous Provisions) Act 1933 (bill preferred by direction of Court of Appeal, or by direction or with consent of a judge), or

    (f) a bill of indictment charging a person with an indictable offence is preferred under section 22B(3)(a) of the Prosecution of Offences Act 1985.

(3) This Part applies in relation to alleged offences into which no criminal investigation has begun before the appointed day.

(4) For the purposes of this section a criminal investigation is an investigation which police officers or other persons have a duty to conduct with a view to it being ascertained—

    (a) whether a person should be charged with an offence, or

    (b) whether a person charged with an offence is guilty of it.

(5) The reference in subsection (3) to the appointed day is to such day as is appointed for the purposes of this Part by the Secretary of State by order.

2.— General interpretation.

(1) References to the accused are to the person mentioned in section 1(1) or (2).

(2) Where there is more than one accused in any proceedings this Part applies separately in relation to each of the accused.

(3) References to the prosecutor are to any person acting as prosecutor, whether an individual or a body.

(4) References to material are to material of all kinds, and in particular include references to—

    (a) information, and

    (b) objects of all descriptions.

(5) References to recording information are to putting it in a durable or retrievable form (such as writing or tape).

(6) This section applies for the purposes of this Part.

3.— Initial duty of prosecutor to disclose

(1) The prosecutor must—

    (a) disclose to the accused any prosecution material which has not previously been disclosed to the accused and which [might reasonably be considered capable of undermining the case for the prosecution against the accused or of assisting the case for the accused, or

    (b) give to the accused a written statement that there is no material of a description mentioned in paragraph (a)

(2) For the purposes of this section prosecution material is material—

    (a) which is in the prosecutor's possession, and came into his possession in connection with the case for the prosecution against the accused, or

    (b) which, in pursuance of a code operative under Part II, he has inspected in connection with the case for the prosecution against the accused.

(3) Where material consists of information which has been recorded in any form the prosecutor discloses it for the purposes of this section—

    (a) by securing that a copy is made of it and that the copy is given to the accused, or

    (b) if in the prosecutor's opinion that is not practicable or not desirable, by allowing the accused to inspect it at a reasonable time and a reasonable place or by taking steps to secure that he is allowed to do so;

and a copy may be in such form as the prosecutor thinks fit and need not be in the same form as that in which the information has already been recorded.

(4) Where material consists of information which has not been recorded the prosecutor discloses it for the purposes of this section by securing that it is recorded in such form as he thinks fit and—

    (a) by securing that a copy is made of it and that the copy is given to the accused, or

    (b) if in the prosecutor's opinion that is not practicable or not desirable, by allowing the accused to inspect it at a reasonable time and a reasonable place or by taking steps to secure that he is allowed to do so.

(5) Where material does not consist of information the prosecutor discloses it for the purposes of this section by allowing the accused to inspect it at a reasonable time and a reasonable place or by taking steps to secure that he is allowed to do so.

(6) Material must not be disclosed under this section to the extent that the court, on an application by the prosecutor, concludes it is not in the public interest to disclose it and orders accordingly.

(7) Material must not be disclosed under this section to the extent that it is material the disclosure of which is prohibited by section 17 of the Regulation of Investigatory Powers Act 2000.

[...]

(8) The prosecutor must act under this section during the period which, by virtue of section 12, is the relevant period for this section.

4.— Initial duty to disclose: further provisions.

(1) This section applies where—

    (a) the prosecutor acts under section 3, and

    (b) before so doing he was given a document in pursuance of provision included, by virtue of section 24(3), in a code operative under Part II.

(2) In such a case the prosecutor must give the document to the accused at the same time as the prosecutor acts under section 3.

7A Continuing duty of prosecutor to disclose

(1) [...] This section applies at all times—

    (a) after the prosecutor has complied with section 3 or purported to comply with it, and

    (b) before the accused is acquitted or convicted or the prosecutor decides not to proceed with the case concerned.

(2) The prosecutor must keep under review the question whether at any given time (and, in particular, following the giving of a defence statement) there is prosecution material which—

    (a) might reasonably be considered capable of undermining the case for the prosecution against the accused or of assisting the case for the accused, and

    (b) has not been disclosed to the accused.

(3) If at any time there is any such material as is mentioned in subsection (2) the prosecutor must disclose it to the accused as soon as is reasonably practicable (or within the period mentioned in subsection (5)(a), where that applies).

(4) In applying subsection (2) by reference to any given time the state of affairs at that time (including the case for the prosecution as it stands at that time) must be taken into account.

(5) Where the accused gives a defence statement under section 5, 6 or 6B—

    (a) if as a result of that statement the prosecutor is required by this section to make any disclosure, or further disclosure, he must do so during the period which, by virtue of section 12, is the relevant period for this section;

    (b) if the prosecutor considers that he is not so required, he must during that period give to the accused a written statement to that effect.

(6) For the purposes of this section prosecution material is material—

    (a) which is in the prosecutor's possession and came into his possession in connection with the case for the prosecution against the accused, or

    (b) which, in pursuance of a code operative under Part 2, he has inspected in connection with the case for the prosecution against the accused.

(7) Subsections (3) to (5) of section 3 (method by which prosecutor discloses) apply for the purposes of this section as they apply for the purposes of that.

(8) Material must not be disclosed under this section to the extent that the court, on an application by the prosecutor, concludes it is not in the public interest to disclose it and orders accordingly.

(9) Material must not be disclosed under this section to the extent that it is material the disclosure of which is prohibited by section 17 of the Regulation of Investigatory Powers Act 2000 (c. 23).

8.— Application by accused for disclosure.

(1) This section applies where the accused has given a defence statement under section 5, 6 or 6B and the prosecutor has complied with section 7A(5) or has purported to comply with it or has failed to comply with it.

(2) If the accused has at any time reasonable cause to believe that there is prosecution material which is required by section 7A to be disclosed to him and has not been, he may apply to the court for an order requiring the prosecutor to disclose it to him.

(3) For the purposes of this section prosecution material is material—

    (a) which is in the prosecutor's possession and came into his possession in connection with the case for the prosecution against the accused.

    (b) which, in pursuance of a code operative under Part II, he has inspected in connection with the case for the prosecution against the accused, or

    (c) which falls within subsection (4).

(4) Material falls within this subsection if in pursuance of a code operative under Part II the prosecutor must, if he asks for the material, be given a copy of it or be allowed to inspect it in connection with the case for the prosecution against the accused.

(5) Material must not be disclosed under this section to the extent that the court, on an application by the prosecutor, concludes it is not in the public interest to disclose it and orders accordingly.

(6) Material must not be disclosed under this section to the extent that it is material the disclosure of which is prohibited by section 17 of the Regulation of Investigatory Powers Act 2000.

10.— Prosecutor's failure to observe time limits.

(1) This section applies if the prosecutor—

    (a) purports to act under section 3 after the end of the period which, by virtue of section 12, is the relevant period for section 3, or

    (b) purports to act under section 7A(5) after the end of the period which, by virtue of section 12, is the relevant period for section 7A.

(2) Subject to subsection (3) the failure to act during the period concerned does not on its own constitute grounds for staying the proceedings for abuse of process.

(3) Subsection (2) does not prevent the failure constituting such grounds if it involves such delay by the prosecutor that the accused is denied a fair trial.

12.— Time limits.

(1) This section has effect for the purpose of determining the relevant period for sections 3, 5, 6, 6B, 6C and 7A(5).

(2) Subject to subsection (3), the relevant period is a period beginning and ending with such days as the Secretary of State prescribes by regulations for the purposes of the section concerned.

(3) The regulations may do one or more of the following—

    (a) provide that the relevant period for any section shall if the court so orders be extended (or further extended) by so many days as the court specifies;

    (b) provide that the court may only make such an order if an application is made by a prescribed person and if any other prescribed conditions are fulfilled;

    (c) provide that an application may only be made if prescribed conditions are fulfilled;

    (d) provide that the number of days by which a period may be extended shall be entirely at the court's discretion;

    (e) provide that the number of days by which a period may be extended shall not exceed a prescribed number;

    (f) provide that there shall be no limit on the number of applications that may be made to extend a period;

    (g) provide that no more than a prescribed number of applications may be made to extend a period;

and references to the relevant period for a section shall be construed accordingly.

(4) Conditions mentioned in subsection (3) may be framed by reference to such factors as the Secretary of State thinks fit.

(5) Without prejudice to the generality of subsection (4), so far as the relevant period for section 3 or 7A(5) is concerned—

(a) conditions may be framed by reference to the nature or volume of the material concerned;

(b) the nature of material may be defined by reference to the prosecutor's belief that the question of non-disclosure on grounds of public interest may arise.

(6) In subsection (3) "prescribed" means prescribed by regulations under this section.

13.— Time limits: transitional.

(1) As regards a case in relation to which no regulations under section 12 have come into force for the purposes of section 3, section 3(8) shall have effect as if it read—

"(8) The prosecutor must act under this section as soon as is reasonably practicable after—

[...]

(ca) copies of the documents containing the evidence on which the charge or charges are based are served on the accused (where this Part applies by virtue of section 1(2)(cc)),

[...]

(d) the count is included in the indictment (where this Part applies by virtue of section 1(2)(d)), or

(e) the bill of indictment is preferred (where this Part applies by virtue of section 1(2)(e) or (f))."

(2) As regards a case in relation to which no regulations under section 12 have come into force for the purposes of section 7A, section 7A(5) shall have effect as if—

(a) in paragraph (a) for the words from ""during the period"" to the end, and

(b) in paragraph (b) for ""during that period"",

there were substituted " "as soon as is reasonably practicable after the accused gives the statement in question"".

APPENDIX 7

TWIST [2011] EWCA CRIM 1143

These four cases, which we have heard together, raise questions connected with the way in which the comparatively new rules upon hearsay contained in the Criminal Justice Act 2003 apply to communications made to, or by, the defendant. These cases all happen to concern text messages sent by mobile telephone. No doubt messages of that kind are frequently encountered at the moment, because they are currently a very popular form of communication. The principles, however, apply equally to all forms of communication. The overhearing, deliberate or accidental, of one or both ends of a communication is by no means new. A text message is, in the end, significantly different neither from an E-mail nor from a letter, nor from an overheard remark made to a person with whom the speaker is in conversation whether together in the same place or via telephone or other remote device. Sometimes the evidence is of one end of the conversation only, sometimes it is of both, and sometimes the evidence of one end includes reaction to the other speaker from which it may be possible to infer what the other has said.

Of the four cases which we have to decide, three are concerned with messages received by the defendant. In <u>Twist</u> and <u>Boothman</u> the indictment required proof of an intent to supply drugs. The messages received by the defendant were–or were contended to be - requests that he supply drugs. In <u>Tomlinson & Kelly</u> the indictment charged robbery and a key issue was whether the defendants had had a gun in their possession at a time when the alleged victim said that they had. The message received by one of the defendants was a request for a gun to be delivered to the sender. The fourth case, <u>Lowe</u>, differs because the messages relied on were outgoing messages sent by the defendant himself. He faced a charge of rape of his young girlfriend. The issue was consent, and in particular whether he had forced himself upon her in the course of a row, or had had consensual sexual intercourse with her, followed by an unconnected row. The messages were sent by him to the complainant in the ensuing two days and were contended by the Crown to amount either to confessions of rape or at least to significant admissions against interest helping to prove that there had been rape.

Although it employs the word sparingly, the Criminal Justice Act 2003 contains a complete code for hearsay in those criminal proceedings to which the strict rules of evidence apply (s 134). As is well known, the statute followed in time a comprehensive report of the Law Commission on hearsay (LC 245, 1997). It largely adopts the draft bill provided by the Commission, although there are some differences (not material to the present issue) between the bill and the statute as enacted. What is undoubted is that the Act abolishes the common law of hearsay except where it is expressly preserved; this court so held in <u>Singh</u> [2006] EWCA Crim 660; 2 Cr App R 12 at 201.

It is not necessary to set out most of the provisions of the Act. The key ones for this purpose are the opening words of section 114(1) and the whole of section 115. Whatever may be the position elsewhere in the Act, neither of these departs by so much as a comma from the Law Commission's draft bill.

Section 114(1) delineates the scope of the provisions which follow. Under the side-heading "Admissibility of hearsay evidence" it reads:

"(1)   In criminal proceedings a statement not made in oral evidence in the proceedings is admissible as evidence of any matter stated if, but only if—......."

and it then goes on to set out the well known four alternative bases of admission: statutory authorisation, preserved rule listed in section 118, the consent of all parties and the court's decision that it is in the interests of justice to admit the evidence. Thus the default position is that hearsay is inadmissible, unless it qualifies for admission under one or more of these four bases.

These important opening words of section 114 "admissible **as evidence of any matter stated**" demonstrate that the Act involves asking what it is that a party is seeking to prove. This is unsurprising. Most (but not all) communications will no doubt contain one or more matters stated, but it does not always follow that any is the matter which the party seeking to adduce the communication is setting out to try to prove, i.e. that the communication is proffered as evidence of that matter. He may sometimes be trying to prove simply that two people were in communication with each other, and not be concerned with the content at all. On other occasions he may be trying to prove the relationship between the parties to the communication but not be in the least concerned with the veracity of the content of it. And there may, of course, be occasions where what he seeks to prove is that a matter stated in the communications is indeed fact. The opening words of section 114 show that it is the last of these situations which engages the rules against hearsay.

Section 115 needs to be set out in full. It provides wholly new definitions of 'statement' and of 'matter stated.' It reads:

"(1) In this Chapter references to a statement or to a matter stated are to be read as follows.

(2)   A statement is any representation of fact or opinion made by a person by whatever means; and it includes a representation made in a sketch, photofit or other pictorial form.

(3)   A matter stated is one to which this Chapter applies if (and only if) the purpose, or one of the purposes, of the person making the statement appears to the court to have been—

(a) to cause another person to believe the matter, or

(b) to cause another person to act or a machine to operate on the basis that the matter is as stated."

Section 115(3) thus imposes a crucial limitation on the otherwise general expression "matter stated". It is not enough that the matter is stated. It is governed by the hearsay rules only if one of the purposes of the maker was as set out.

The Act does not use the expression "assertion". Instead it speaks of a "statement" and the "matter stated" in it. That seems likely to have been because its framers wished to avoid the complex philosophical arguments which beset the common law, as explained in <u>DIRECTOR OF PUBLIC PROSECUTIONS v Kearley</u> [1992] 2 AC 228, as to when an utterance contains an implied assertion. That was a case of telephone calls to the home of the defendant, all seeking the supply of drugs, on which the Crown sought to rely as evidence that he was in the habit of supplying them. The House of Lords held, by a majority, that the calls amounted to "implied assertions" that the defendant was a drug dealer and that they were for that reason hearsay. It was accepted by counsel in <u>R v Singh</u> [2006] EWCA Crim 660; [2006] 2 CR App R 12 at 201, and held by the court at paragraph 14, that the evident intention of the Act was to reverse <u>Kearley</u>. That is also apparent from the Law Commission report, see in particular paragraphs 7.20–22, 7.26–27 and 7.41. There is no trace of any change of policy in the statute and the policy is unsurprising. The principal underlying reason why hearsay evidence is only admissible in limited circumstances lies in the danger of concoction and the difficulty of testing or contradicting it when the speaker is not in court to be examined upon it. But as the Law Commission put it at paragraph 7.20:

"Where there is a substantial risk that an out-of-court assertion may have been deliberately fabricated, therefore, we think it right that the assertion should fall within the hearsay rule–whether it is express or implied. It follows that the rule should extend to any conduct which is intended to give the impression that a particular fact is true, and is adduced as evidence of that fact. But where that risk is not present–in other words, where the person from whose conduct a fact is to be inferred can safely be assumed to have believed that fact to be true–we do not think a court should be precluded from inferring that fact merely because that person may have been mistaken in believing it. And if that person did not intend anyone to infer it, it follows that that person cannot have been seeking to mislead."

In <u>Kearley</u> itself, at 248–249 Lord Bridge was one of those who felt that it was too late to modify judicially what he held to be the common law rule applying hearsay rules to implied assertions. He nevertheless recognised the same argument. He referred to the US federal rules of evidence which had abolished that rule and substituted one confining the concept of hearsay to express assertions and conduct intended to amount to assertion, which outcome was interpreted to mean that assertions had to be intended to persuade in order to be caught by the hearsay rule. He identified:

"...the only rational ground for excluding from the scope of the hearsay rule assertions which are not express but implied by the words and conduct of persons not called as witnesses. Put shortly, the speakers' words and conduct are motivated quite independently of any possible intention to mislead and are thus exempt from the suspicion attaching to express assertions and are, in that sense, self authenticating."

It is therefore helpful, as it seems to us, that the Act avoids the use of the expression "assertion" altogether, and with it the difficult concept of the "implied assertion". Instead, the Act concentrates the mind on the 'matter stated', which it is sought to prove. This is defined by reference to the purpose of the maker (ie usually the speaker or sender of the communication). The matter stated must be something which the maker intended someone (generally the recipient, since it is to him that the communication is addressed) to believe or to act upon: s 115(3).

The 'matter stated' will usually be a fact, but may also be an opinion: s 115(2). For convenience we shall refer hereafter to facts, but the same applies where the matter stated is an opinion.

There are therefore two questions which have to be addressed in most cases:

what is the matter which it is sought to prove ? (it must of course be a relevant matter), and

did the maker of the communication have the purpose of causing the recipient to believe or to act upon that matter ?

In addressing these questions, and the application of the Act generally, it needs to be remembered that to say that a communication is <u>evidence</u> of a fact (ie tends to prove it) is not the same as saying that that fact is the matter stated in the communication for the purposes of the Act.

If a buyer for a large chain store telephones the sales director of a manufacturer, with whom he routinely does business, and orders a supply of breakfast cereal or fashion jeans he is generally not representing as a fact or matter either (a) that the sales director's firm manufactures the flakes or the jeans or (b) that he the buyer works for the chain store. Crucially for the application of the Act, even if it be suggested that the order should be construed as an "implied assertion" of either fact (a) or fact (b), it will be beyond doubt in most cases that the caller does not have it as one of his purposes to cause the recipient to believe or act upon either of those facts. The recipient knows them very well. Those are simply the facts (or matters) which are common knowledge as between the parties to the call. Neither is, therefore, a matter stated in the call for the purpose of sections 114 and 115. The call is however <u>evidence</u> of both fact (a) and fact (b). It is not, no doubt, conclusive, at least if there is any realistic possibility of mistake, but it is undoubtedly evidence of those facts. Conversely, if the caller tells the recipient, perhaps in order to induce him to speed up the supply, that the buyers have already sold 5 tons of the goods, it <u>is</u> his purpose to induce the recipient to believe that fact. If that were the fact sought to be proved, the call would be hearsay evidence **of that matter.**

If there is a queue of young people outside a building at midnight, obviously waiting for an evening out, that is some evidence tending to prove that the building is being operated as a club, which may be the matter which it is sought to prove, perhaps in licensing proceedings. There is no statement of that matter for the purposes of the Act. If several of the queuers were heard to be telling others about last week's 'rave', the only way that could possibly be regarded as a statement of the fact that this was a club would be by treating it, artificially as it seems to us, as an implied assertion of that fact. But it makes no difference whether it is so treated or not, because none of the speakers would have the purpose of inducing any listener to believe or to act upon the fact that the place is a club, since that is simply a common basis for conversation, and all of them know it. Conversely, if the issue is not whether the place was a club, but rather whether there was a large event the previous week, the statement of the fact/matter that there had been such an event would indeed be caught by the hearsay rule; those who spoke of it were doing so with the purpose of inducing their hearers who had not been there to believe it. The out of court statement would indeed be hearsay evidence **of that matter.**

Some communications may contain no statement at all. If, for example, the communication does no more than ask a question, it is difficult to see how it contains any statement. A text message to someone asking "Will you have any crack tomorrow ?" seems to us to contain no statement at all. But even if it be analysed as containing an "implied assertion" that the recipient is a drug dealer, that fact is still not a "matter stated" for the purposes of sections 114 and 115(3) because the sender does not have any purpose to cause the recipient to believe that fact or to act upon the basis that it is true. They both know it, and it is the common basis of their communication.

Similarly, it is important when applying the statute to distinguish between:

the speaker wishing the hearer to act upon his **message**; and

the speaker wishing the hearer to act upon the basis that a **matter stated in the message is as stated (ie true).**

Only the second will bring into operation the hearsay rules. If the sender asks whether the recipient will have any crack tomorrow, he does indeed want the recipient to act on his message because he hopes to extract an answer to his question. Even more clearly he does so if he goes one step further and asks for crack to be sold to him tomorrow, because then he hopes to receive a supply. But in neither case does he have the purpose of causing the recipient of his message to believe that the recipient is a drug dealer, or to act on the basis that that is the truth.

Generally, therefore, it is likely to be helpful to approach the question whether the hearsay rules apply in this way:

identify what relevant fact (matter) it is sought to prove;

ask whether there is a statement of **that matter** in the communication. If no, then no question of hearsay arises (whatever other matters may be contained in the communication);

If yes, ask whether it was one of the purposes (not necessarily the only or dominant purpose) of the maker of the communication that the recipient, or any other person, should believe **that matter** or act upon it as true ? If yes, it is hearsay. If no, it is not.

The answers to these questions will be case-sensitive. The same communication may sometimes be hearsay and sometimes not, depending on the matter for which it is relied upon and the fact which it is sought to prove.

In addressing these questions, we would strongly recommend avoidance of the difficult concept of the "implied assertion". That was described by the Law Commission, rightly in our view, as "a somewhat unfortunate expression" (paragraph 7.7). As the Commission went on to point out:

> "First, it begs the question of whether the words or conduct in question *are* an assertion of the fact that they are adduced to prove. It is at least arguable that they are not assertive at

all, but directly probative–in which case it would follow that they should not be caught by the hearsay rule.

7.8 Second, the word "implied" is here used in an unusual sense. Normally it refers to a statement which is not expressly spoken or written but is intended to be understood from what is said or done. But where there *is* an assertion of the fact to be proved, it is immaterial whether that assertion is express or (in the ordinary sense) implied. An assertion of a fact is no less of an assertion because it is implicit in an express assertion of a different fact, or because it takes the form of nonverbal conduct such as a gesture. An assertion can therefore be implied (in the ordinary sense) without being what is described in the context of hearsay as an "implied assertion."

As we have sought to explain, it no longer matters whether a statement is analysed as containing an implicit (or "implied") assertion if the speaker's purpose does not include getting anyone else to accept it as true.

It is also important to remember that deciding whether one or more communications is or is not hearsay may not be the end of the issue of admissibility. Even if the communications are not relied upon for their hearsay content, as that is defined by the Act, that does not relieve the court of applying the usual tests for admissibility. The fact which it is sought to prove must be a relevant fact; otherwise the evidence is inadmissible on grounds of irrelevance. And secondly, it is necessary that that fact is indeed a legitimate conclusion to be drawn from the evidence. If, for example, the only thing which the communications are capable of proving is that the senders held an opinion that x was a fact, that would not generally be admissible as proof of fact x, though it would be admissible, if the issue were whether they believed x, to show that they did: see Kearley where this point was plainly made. If, on the other hand, it is a proper conclusion to draw from the evidence of a communication, or of a number of similar communications, not only that the sender held an opinion but also that there was an existing relationship between him and the recipient, for example of buyer and supplier, or otherwise that a relevant background fact plainly existed, then the evidence, assuming it is not within the Act's concept of hearsay, is admissible on that issue. What the evidence is capable of proving will depend on the facts of each case. It will be necessary, in some cases, for judges to focus the jury's attention carefully on what it is that the evidence is and is not capable of proving.

Further, to say that a communication is not hearsay and that it is admissible evidence tending to prove a fact, is not to say that it is unanswerable or conclusive. To take an example, a single message requesting the supply of drugs, or for that matter a gun, might have been misdirected by mistake, or might be based on a mistaken belief that the recipient is likely to be able to supply what is asked for. No doubt, the more similar messages there are, sent independently of one another, the more likely it is that they do prove the fact alleged, but that will depend on what possible alternative explanations there might be for the evidence. Whether a communication which is not hearsay does or does not prove the fact alleged is always a matter of weight for the jury.

It ought not to be thought that it makes little difference whether the court is dealing with hearsay or not. True, there is a discretion to admit hearsay evidence if satisfied that the interests of justice require it (section 114(1)(d) and (2)). Sometimes the contents of a communication may be admissible by this route even though hearsay. But:

i) admission under section 114(1)(d) is not routine, nor a matter of mere form; it requires careful thought, having due regard to (especially) reliability and the opportunity to test it: see for example R v Y [2008] 1 Cr App R 34 at 411, at paragraphs 56-62, and R v Z [2009] EWCA Crim 20 at paragraphs 20–24;

ii) there are different rules applicable to hearsay; see for example section 121 where there is multiple hearsay, the power contained in section 125 to stop a case dependent on hearsay if the evidence is so unconvincing that a conviction would be unsafe and the general discretion under s 126 to refuse to admit a statement on grounds of undue waste of time;

iii) if the maker(s) of the communication is or are unknown, that will be very relevant to whether their hearsay evidence ought to be admitted; we have not heard full argument upon this point and do not decide it; however, we draw attention to the fact that no anonymous witness order under ss 86–89 of the Coroners and Justice Act 2009 can be made in a case of fear in relation to evidence which is hearsay, because of the existence of s 116(1)(c) of the 2003 Act which requires the fearful witness whose hearsay is adduced to be identified: R v Mayers [2008] EWCA Crim 2989; [2009] 1 Cr App R 30; whilst there may be some forms of anonymous hearsay which are nevertheless admissible, such as business records or the statement of an unidentified agent of the defendant, the hearsay testimony of an anonymous witness may well fail the interests of justice test of admissibility; an example is Fox [2010] EWCA Crim 1280, where the contents of an anonymous 999 call were inadmissible as evidence that the facts reported were true; that case is a good example of a communication which certainly was relied upon for the accuracy of the matter stated in it and without, so it would appear, the limited circumstances of spontaneity which would permit admission under the principle of Andrews [1987] AC 281, one of the rules preserved in section 118.

Our understanding of the Act, set out above, was foreshadowed by Rose LJ in Singh [2006] EWCA Crim 660; 2 Cr App R 12 at 201. The court was there not considering a communication at all, but rather the note for himself that a mobile telephone user makes when he enters in the memory of his telephone the number of a contact. This was in similar case to a private diary entry which is written for oneself and no-one else; the maker of the entry has no purpose to cause anyone else to believe or act upon the truth of the entry—it is entirely for his own use and for that reason is not hearsay. It was therefore admissible evidence to tend to prove that the telephone number in question was used by the defendant, the person to whom the entry was attributed. But the court expressly considered the impact of the 2003 Act on Kearley. At paragraph 14 it said:

> "What was said by the callers in Kearley would now be admissible as direct evidence of the fact that there was a ready market for the supply of drugs from the premises, from which could be inferred an intention by the occupier to supply drugs. The view of the majority in Kearley, in relation to hearsay, has been set aside by the Act."

We were referred to R v Leonard [2009] EWCA Crim 1251. That case concerned incoming text messages received on the defendant's mobile telephone which commented upon the quality or quantity of drugs previously supplied. They were relied on by the Crown in a case in which the defendant was indicted for possession of drugs with intent to supply. The conclusion reached in the judgment (delivered by Aikens LJ) was that the messages were hearsay. But that case proceeded upon the basis, apparently accepted by the Crown, that (a) the quality/quantity of past supplies was a matter stated in the communications, and more importantly (b) that the Crown was seeking to prove that matter in order through that route to prove that the defendant was a dealer in drugs: see paragraph 36. Of course, if those two things were correct, it does indeed follow that the evidence is hearsay, because clearly the senders of the messages intended the defendant recipient to believe the comments about the goods. It would clearly have been different if the Crown had relied on the messages not to prove the quality of past supplies (and through this route that the defendant was a dealer) but merely to show that the relationship between the parties was one of drug customer and drug supplier, without any attempt to prove the quality of the past supplies. Some academic commentators have suggested that that was in reality what the Crown sought to do, but that was not the basis of the decision. We therefore do not think that Leonard compelled the reluctant assumption made in Bains [2010] EWCA Crim 873 that the text messages in that latter case were hearsay, but Bains in any event did not decide that point, referring simply to the concession made in Leonard. That it is crucial, as we have said above, to look carefully at what fact it is sought to prove, emerges clearly from considering Leonard alongside another decision of this court, not long afterwards, in which the judgment was also given by Aikens LJ: R v Chrysostomou [2010] EWCA Crim 1403. There the relevant texts appeared to be orders for drugs. They were relied upon to prove bad character rather than directly to prove the offence charged, which was not a drugs offence, but that feature does not affect the question of whether the evidence was hearsay or not: it would of course be very relevant to the discretion to exclude evidence tendered as to bad character (see section 101(3) Criminal Justice Act 2003). The court held that the evidence was not hearsay. It relied specifically at paragraph 28 on what it was the Crown was setting out to prove: not the contents of the messages but the state of affairs which they revealed. That is consistent with the analysis of the Act which we have endeavoured to set out. In the terms of our analysis, the matter sought to be proved was the relationship between the sender of the messages and the defendant. The sender did not have the purpose of getting the defendant to believe or act upon that matter; it was simply the common knowledge revealed by the messages.

R v MK [2007] EWCA Crim 3150 is clear support for our approach to the application of the statute. The Crown sought to prove that the defendant was guilty of offences of drug trafficking. Part of its evidence was of a telephone call made to him, in which a person who was known to be wishing to make a subsale of drugs enquired the defendant's price for amphetamine. This court allowed a Crown appeal against a ruling by the recorder that that conversation was inadmissible hearsay. It did so on the grounds that there was no representation in the call of the fact that the defendant was a supplier of drugs and that in any event the caller's purpose did not include getting the defendant to believe or act upon the truth of that fact. Although in Leonard doubt was expressed about the second of those propositions, it is perfectly clear that it was part of the decision and it was, in our view, plainly correct.

R v Elliott [2010] EWCA Crim 2378 is a further illustration of the correct approach. It was relevant for the Crown to prove that the defendant was an adherent to a gang. It sought to rely (inter alia) on some letters sent to him in prison which contained references to membership of the gang and symbols signifying the same. This court held that this evidence was not hearsay, because the authors of the letters did not have the purpose of causing the defendant to believe any representation that there might be, nor to act upon its truth. Common membership of the gang was simply the shared basis of the communications.

[Remaining paragraphs edited]

APPENDIX 8

Guidance: The Bar Council has issued the following guidance which is equally applicable to solicitors:

Commentary

1. The Criminal Bar Association has been asked by the General Management Committee of the Bar Council to draft brief guidance to assist with the issues which arise when the court appoints legal representatives to act on behalf of defendants and to consider whether a list of suitable counsel and solicitors should be drawn up from which the courts can make such appointments.

There have been previous reports written on this subject[1] and, although in practice, the appointment of counsel by the court is not likely to occur often, as a matter of common sense, when it does occur, it is likely to involve a defendant who is either not cooperating or who is 'playing the system' and such guidance will have to be interpreted liberally if the interests of the defendant are to be preserved and justice is seen to be done.

We have set out in full the background and statutory basis for these issues in order to explain why we have drafted the guidance in the terms we have. The draft guidance itself is annexed to the report.

2. The Background

2.1 The legislation which has provided for this procedure was passed as a result of two widely publicised cases in which a defendant acting in person cross-examined the complainant on an allegation of rape.[2] The Lord Chief Justice gave guidance (in the then absence of statutory reform) in the case of R v Brown (Milton) [1998] 2.Cr.App.R.364 to assist trial judges confronted with such a problem:

> 'It will often be desirable, before any question is asked by the defendant in cross-examination, for the trial judge to discuss the course of the proceedings with the defendant in the absence of the jury. The judge can then elicit the general nature of the defence and identify the specific points in the complainant's evidence with which the defendant takes issue and any points he wishes to put to her. If the defendant proposes to call witnesses in his own defence, the substance of their evidence can be elicited so that the complainant's observations on it may, so far as it is relevant, be invited.'

There was further guidance set out as to the steps to be taken to restrict repetition or the intimidation or humiliation of the witness by way of the defendant's dress, bearing, manner or questions.

2.2 Statutory restrictions on cross-examination of the complainant by a defendant in person charged with a sexual offence[3] were imposed by Section 34 of the Youth Justice and Criminal Evidence Act, 1999 (the Act) and this provision is now in force in respect of proceedings

---

[1] Peter Rook QC 27th January, 2001 and Nicholas Price QC March 2002
[2] R v Brown (Milton) [1998] 2Cr.App.R.364 and R v Ralston Edwards
[3] Defined in S.62 YJ&CEA, 1999

commencing on or after 4th September, 2000. This prohibition covers any other offence (of whatever nature) with which that person is charged in the proceedings.[4]

2.3 Section 34A of the Criminal Justice Act, 1988 prohibited cross-examination in person of child witnesses in certain cases and Section 35 of the Act extended this to include the alleged victims of kidnapping, false imprisonment and abduction. This prohibition also extends to cross-examination in respect of other offences with which a defendant is charged in the proceedings.[5]

2.4 There is a further power under Sections 36 and 37 of the Act to prohibit a defendant in person from cross-examining witnesses not covered by Sections 34 & 35 if the court is satisfied, first, that the quality of the witness's evidence is likely to be diminished if the defendant is allowed to proceed and improved if he is prohibited from doing so and secondly, that it would not be contrary to the interests of justice to give such a direction. These provisions came into force on the 24th July, 2002.

2.5 Section 38 of the Act makes provision for the appointment of a qualified legal representative for the purposes of cross-examination of a witness where an accused in person has been prevented from so doing by virtue of Section 34, 35 or 36.

3. Section 38

3.1 Section 38 allows the accused to have the opportunity of appointing his own legal representative to conduct the cross-examination on his behalf. If he does not, Section 38(4) of the Act specifies that where the court has decided that it is necessary in the interests of justice for the witness to be cross-examined by a court appointed legal representative, the court must appoint a qualified legal representative[6] (chosen by the court) to cross-examine the witness in the interests of the accused. A person so appointed shall not be responsible to the accused.[7] Any reference to cross-examination includes (in a case where a direction under Section 36 has been given after the accused has begun cross-examining the witness) a reference to further cross-examination.[8] Even after the appointment by the court under Section 38(4) of such a legal representative, the accused may arrange for that legal representative to be appointed to act for him and it is then as though he had done so at the outset under Section 38(2)(a) of the Act.[9]

The legal representative is then no longer the representative of the Court.

3.2 We have set out the statutory framework in some detail because the provisions themselves make it clear that there are the two underlying principles behind the appointment of such a legal representative, namely, that such an appointment is in the interests of justice and that the legal representative is appointed to represent the interests of the accused although not responsible to him. They may sound obvious principles but the tensions which are likely to flow from such a situation make any court appointed legal representative liable to face a number of extremely difficult decisions and it will be a testing task for the judge to ensure that the balance between the interests of justice and the interests of the accused is maintained. One of the obvious problems which we try to deal with in the guidance is the effect of disclosure material. This may well contain material which could properly be used in cross-examination where it was relevant but in the absence of specific issues identified by the defendant to the Court, it will be extremely difficult for its relevance to be assessed.

4. Code of Conduct

Paragraph 401(a) of the Code of Conduct has been amended to allow for a barrister in independent practice to be appointed by the court but it seems to us very likely that there will have to be other

---

[4] S.34(b) YJ&CEA, 1999
[5] S.35(b) YJ&CEA, 1999
[6] Defined in S.38(8)(b) as a legal representative who has a right of audience (within the meaning of the Courts and Legal Services Act 1990) in relation to the proceedings before the court
[7] S.38(5) YJ&CEA, 1999
[8] S.38(8)(b) YJ&CEA, 1999
[9] Crown Court Rules 1982 r 24D

amendments made since the role of court appointed counsel who is expressly not responsible to the defendant is quite different from the role of counsel appointed to represent the defendant. An example is under Paragraph 708(a) which deals with conduct in court and which requires that a barrister is personally responsible for the conduct and presentation of his case and must exercise personal judgement upon the substance and purpose of statements made and questions asked. This is likely to be very difficult since the questions asked are likely to be constrained by the judge who will ultimately be responsible for parameters of appropriate cross-examination.

It will also be very important that any court-appointed counsel is as clear as possible as to the purpose and the parameters of any questions to be asked since it is not difficult to foresee a situation where questions asked without instructions may receive answers which either make matters worse for the defendant or open up previously unexplored areas which the Crown may use to their advantage. This may be unavoidable but if both the judge and counsel are fully aware of the nature of the questions to be asked, the danger will be lessened and, if it occurs, counsel will not be at fault. A simple instruction from the court to 'test the evidence' will not be sufficient and the judge will have to be as specific as possible and counsel equally careful as to the questions asked to avoid unnecessarily exposing themselves to complaint from the defendant of unfairness.

5. List of Suitably Qualified Legal Representatives

5.1 As previously set out, 'qualified legal representative' is defined in Section 38(8)(b) as a 'legal representative who has a right of audience (within the meaning of the Courts and Legal Services Act, 1990) in relation to the proceedings before the Court'.

It is, in our view, essential that only legal representatives with the appropriate number of years experience (we suggest seven) in predominantly criminal law with previous experience of cross-examining complainants in sexual cases and children be considered for what is going to be a difficult task. Whilst these cases may not be restricted to allegations of sexual abuse, they are more likely to be generated by them. The Code of Conduct provisions would in any event apply to the Bar which would prevent counsel from accepting any instructions if to do so would cause him to be professionally embarrassed which includes having insufficient experience or competence to handle the matter.[10]

5.2 The task of appointing counsel is likely to be done on a practical level by the associate in consultation with the judge and perhaps the List Office. Who is appointed will depend on the stage at which the appointment is made. If it is early in the proceedings, there should be ample time to appoint an appropriate representative. In the absence of a list, this is likely to be from counsel who regularly appear in that court or who are well known. It seems to us there should at least be the opportunity for counsel to have their name on the list. It may be the appropriate course would be for all Chambers to be asked to provide a list of counsel with the appropriate experience who would like to be included on the list. Remuneration would have to be appropriate[11] because it will be necessary for counsel to familiarise themselves with all the material including unused which in these unusual circumstances should also be made available to the judge.

5.3 Although an appointment of a legal representative will normally terminate at the conclusion of the cross-examination,[12] there is provision for the court to determine otherwise and we consider that it may well be necessary for counsel to remain for the duration of the trial if case evidence is given by the defendant or another witness which needs to be put to the complainant who will then have to be recalled and re-cross-examined. This situation may arise where the defence is not known and the issues have not been fully identified because the defendant is being uncooperative and may have given a no comment interview. The cross-examination will have been based on the papers and, whilst obvious issues will have been covered, it may well be that the questions asked do not, in fact, cover the defendant's case as given from the witness box. To avoid

[10] Paragraph 603(a)
[11] S.40 YJ&CEA, 2002 makes provision for payment out of central funds
[12] Crown Court Rules 1982 r24C-(2)

the whole scenario becoming a sham, the defendant's case will have to be put to the complainant. It follows from this that counsel appointed by the court will have to be available for the whole trial as opposed to simply cross-examination. There is also the possibility that the judge may intervene during the trial to make a direction under Section 36 preventing the defendant from cross-examining other witnesses.

5.4 Such a list will need maintaining as well as setting up. Although there are a number of sources which could probably provide the relevant information, for example, the individual Bar Messes, the CBA, the circuit, none of these include solicitor advocates and although there may not presently be many with the necessary experience, the Law Society will need to be involved in this process to maintain equal opportunity for all those with suitable qualifications.

5.5 Once such a list is set up, it will be for the court to select the appropriate advocate and the cab-rank principle should apply to all approached, subject to an advocate feeling they are insufficiently experienced.

6. Duties of Court Appointed Legal Representative

6.1 It is expressly set out that the legal representative is not responsible to the defendant.[13] It follows that there will not be any meetings with the defendant nor any instructions taken directly from him unless he chooses to 'adopt' the court appointed representative as his own (see para 3.1).

6.2 Rules of court may make provision in particular for securing that the legal representative will be provided with 'evidence or other material relating to the proceedings'[14] and this can include disclosure of material in connection with criminal proceedings under Part 1 of the Criminal Procedure and Investigations Act, 1996.[15] It will be the duty of the legal representative to read all such material and watch any videos of disclosure interviews.

6.3 If the appointment is made at a relatively early stage in the proceedings, presence at preparatory hearings may seem sensible if there is to be a ruling on the admissibility of evidence or any similar ruling prior to the swearing of the jury and it may well be useful to attend simply to clarify the issues. It should be borne in mind, however, that the role of the legal representative is clearly intended to be limited to cross-examining witnesses whom the defendant is prohibited from cross-examining and although it may be thought that such a representative could be useful to the court in other areas, that does not seem to be intended by the legislation. Ultimately, it will be matter for the judge to decide and, no doubt if there is a point which can be properly taken on admissibility of a witness's evidence which is not dependent on the defendant's instructions, the legal representative will make the appropriate submissions, either of his own volition or at the invitation of the judge and these are areas which may well be identifiable at an early stage in the proceedings.

6.4 If it is possible, the legal representative should be present during the opening of the case to the jury and it is after this that there should be a hearing in the absence of the jury but in the presence of the defendant and both prosecuting counsel and the legal representative at which the judge will have to take steps to establish the issues in the case. Concern has been expressed that the defendant may refuse to tell the judge anything in the presence of prosecuting counsel and there is always the possibility that the defendant may inadvertently say something to the judge which could provide material in cross-examination. The problem is that prosecuting counsel has an ongoing duty of disclosure and they have to know what the defence is in order to comply with their duty. If the defendant makes it clear that he will not say anything if prosecuting counsel remains present, the Judge must decide what to do and this may well include explaining to the defendant the duty of the Crown and how limited the judge's powers are on disclosure without

---

[13] S.38(5) YJ&CEA, 1999
[14] S.38(6)(b) YJ&CEA, 1999
[15] S.38(7)(a) YJ&CEA, 1999

input from the Crown. Subject to that, if the Judge feels that the interests of justice are best served by a hearing in the absence of the Crown, then, no doubt, that is what he will do.

There are a number of possible scenarios:

(i) The defendant has given a full interview to the police setting out his defence. In this case, the defendant can simply be asked whether he will confirm the defence set out in the interview. If he does so, then it seems to us that the legal representative is justified in putting a positive case to the witness although no doubt in a moderate way. This will assist the jury to assess the credibility of the witness. If the defendant will not confirm that this is his defence, the witness should nonetheless be cross-examined on that basis but not as a positive case and any other relevant points need to be identified before cross-examination.

(ii) There is a defence statement setting out a defence. The same question can be asked but as the defendant will have presumably sacked whoever was responsible for that statement, care will need to be taken in putting that forward even if the defendant confirms that is his defence. There are often significant differences between an interview and a defence statement and all that will be required will be to give the witness the opportunity of dealing with any points made in either. It is important, however, that the cross-examination is not conducted in a way which invites scepticism because of how it is put as opposed to the actual content of the questions being put because the legal representative has been appointed to represent the interests of the defendant.

(iii) There is a no comment interview and no defence statement. Although the defendant can be asked by the judge if he will outline the points on which he takes issue in the case, it is not hard to foresee the scenario where a defendant is being completely uncooperative, no doubt wishing to make a point to the jury (which some may think has some force) that he has not been able to defend himself properly because he has been unable to cross-examine the main witness against him. In those circumstances, the legal representative is likely to be constrained by the issues which the judge directs are relevant as far as can be ascertained from the papers although no doubt the submissions of the legal representative will be sought. Once those issues have been identified, they should be explained to the defendant and he should again be asked whether he is now willing to indicate his defence. It should be noted that it is for the court to decide in the first place whether it is necessary in the interests of justice for the witness to be cross-examined by a legal representative appointed to represent the interests of the defendant and it is only if the court does so decide that a legal representative has to be appointed. Strictly speaking, if there is no sensible basis upon which a witness can be cross-examined, it may not be in the interests of justice for this to be done and it is open to the judge to refuse to appoint a legal representative to do so. This would be a brave decision to take and one which would seem likely to strike the average juror as unfair. The more likely scenario and the more sensible one would be for the legal representative to be invited to test the evidence as if a certain line of defence was being put forward but not putting any positive case to the witness.

(iv) Where the defendant refuses to be represented because of a psychiatric condition such as mental illness or a personality disorder. It is obvious in these very unfortunate cases that every effort should be made to persuade the defendant to be represented but that if they will not, then all proper and available lines of defence should be put to the witness and all proper legal arguments mounted.

6.5 Once the relevant areas of cross-examination have been identified, the legal representative must consider any proper legal arguments relevant to the cross-examination. This would include questions relating to the sexual history of the witness for which leave must be given or whether a particular line of cross-examination may lead to an application to adduce the defendant's previous convictions in the event of him giving evidence. We do not consider it is the duty of the legal representative to raise other legal arguments which are not relevant to cross-examination. It may be that such representatives would wish to ensure that either the court or the prosecution was made aware of such points to avoid a miscarriage of justice but it would not appear to be within the limited confines of their duty which is to cross-examine. There will no doubt be a strong temptation for the legal representative to be treated as amicus in the trial generally. We do not consider that to be appropriate unless the judge specifically requests that that role be adopted as it will be extremely difficult for the legal representative then to be confident that he or she is fully aware of the parameters of their role in the case. It would also be confusing for the jury who may well think that the defendant has actually got full representation even though he didn't want it.

6.6 There will be circumstances where the legal representative considers that it is in the interests of the defendant that they remain until the end of the evidence. If so, application should be made to the judge for leave to remain.

6.7 It may also be sensible for the defendant to be reminded at the end of the cross-examination that they can 'adopt' the legal representative. If that is done, there will need to be the opportunity for the defendant to give instructions and, if necessary, further cross-examination but care will have to be taken to prevent a defendant manipulating or appearing to manipulate the court process and also to prevent a witness being cross-examined more than is necessary.

7. It is our view that many of these decisions can only be taken on an individual case basis and will depend upon the sensible handling of the defendant by the judge. The legal representative will need to be alive to the limitations of their role and not to be beguiled into acting as the defendant's representative generally. There is a requirement in Section 40 of the Act that the judge gives such warning to the jury as he considers necessary to prevent prejudicial inferences being drawn either from the fact that the defendant is not cross-examining or (where this occurs) the fact that a court appointed representative has cross-examined on his behalf. It remains to be seen whether the difficult balance between maintaining the interests of justice whilst making sure that justice is being seen to be done can be achieved in practice.

Guidance for Court Appointed Legal Representatives

1. A court appointed legal representative will not meet privately with the defendant nor take instructions directly from the defendant.

2. All matters relevant to the cross-examination to be conducted by the legal representative will ordinarily be dealt with in open court in the presence of the prosecution and the defendant but in the absence of the jury.

3. The legal representative will be provided with the evidence in the case comprising all prosecution statements and exhibits and have access to unused material. It will be the duty of the legal representative to familiarise him/herself with the evidence and be in a position to assist the judge as to the likely material issues as disclosed on the papers.

4. Before the start of the trial, the judge will identify as far as possible the likely issues in the case. This will involve the prosecution and the legal representative and where possible, the defendant.

5. Where the defendant has given a full account in interview and has confirmed to the judge that this account is to be maintained at trial identifying, if appropriate, any material differences etc, the legal representative should prepare cross-examination on the basis of that defence. It is a matter for the legal representative's judgement in each case as to whether that is put forward as a positive defence in cross-examination or simply used as a basis for testing the evidence.

6. Where there is only a defence statement which the defendant has not confirmed as his defence, the legal representative should not put this forward as a positive defence. It should only be used as a basis from which to test the evidence of the witness.

7. Where there is only a defence statement but the judge has elicited from the defendant that this accurately represents his defence, the legal representative should prepare cross-examination on the basis of that defence but should not generally put it as a positive defence unless there is good reason so to do, for example, if the defendant indicates that the defence to a rape allegation is to be one of consent.

8. Where the defendant has made no comment in interview and there is no defence statement but the judge has elicited from the defendant what his defence is to be, the legal representative should prepare cross-examination on the basis of that defence but should not generally put it as a positive defence unless there is good reason so to do, for example, if the defendant indicates that the defence to a rape allegation is to be one of consent.

9. Where the defendant has made no comment in interview and there is no defence statement and declines to indicate what his defence is to be, the legal representative should prepare cross-examination in accordance with the directions of the judge after discussion with both prosecution and the legal representative as to the material issues in the case. This should not be put forward as a positive case. The only proper basis is to test the evidence of the witness on the specific areas identified by the judge.

10. Where the defendant has given an account in interview and/or his defence statement but has indicated that his defence is different and will not indicate in what way it differs, the same approach as in para 9 above should be followed.

11. Although the appointment by the court of a legal representative implies that the court considers that cross-examination of the relevant witness will be in the interests of the defendant, it is a matter for the legal representative to judge whether, in the event, it is in the interests of the defendant for there to be cross-examination as, for example, where the witness has not come up to proof on a material point.

12. It will be the duty of the legal representative to raise any points of law relevant to the conduct of the cross-examination prior to the cross-examination such as whether there are relevant and admissible questions on the witness's sexual history or whether a particular line of cross-examination is likely to result in the defendant's 'shield' being lost in the event of him giving evidence.

13. Whilst in the normal course of events, the appointment of the legal representative terminates at the conclusion of the cross-examination of the particular witness, the legal representative should consider whether there is a need for the appointment to remain until a later stage in the trial if, for example, it may be necessary for the witness to be recalled for further cross-examination and if there is, to make the appropriate application to the judge.

APPENDIX 9

RELEVANT OFFENCES (S 17(5) YJCEA 1999)

Youth Justice and Criminal Evidence Act 1999, sch 1A

(1) Murder in a case where it is alleged that a firearm or knife was used to cause the death in question.

(2) Manslaughter in a case where it is alleged that a firearm or knife was used to cause the death in question.

(3) Murder or manslaughter in a case (other than a case falling within paragraph 1 or 2) where it is alleged that—

the accused was carrying a firearm or knife at any time during the commission of the offence, and

a person other than the accused knew or believed at any time during the commission of the offence that the accused was carrying a firearm or knife.

(4) An offence under section 18 of the Offences against the Person Act 1861 (wounding with intent to cause grievous bodily harm etc) in a case where it is alleged that a firearm or knife was used to cause the wound or harm in question.

(5) An offence under section 20 of that Act (malicious wounding) in a case where it is alleged that a firearm or knife was used to cause the wound or inflict the harm in question.

(6) An offence under section 38 of that Act (assault with intent to resist arrest) in a case where it is alleged that a firearm or knife was used to carry out the assault in question.

(7) An offence under section 47 of the Offences against the Person Act 1861 (assault occasioning actual bodily harm) in a case where it is alleged that a firearm or knife was used to inflict the harm in question.

(8) An offence under section 18, 20, 38 or 47 of the Offences against the Person Act 1861 in a case (other than a case falling within any of paragraphs 4 to 7) where it is alleged that—

the accused was carrying a firearm or knife at any time during the commission of the offence, and

a person other than the accused knew or believed at any time during the commission of the offence that the accused was carrying a firearm or knife.

(9) An offence under section 1 of the Prevention of Crime Act 1953 (having an offensive weapon in a public place).

(10) An offence under section 1 of the Firearms Act 1968 (requirement of firearm certificate).

(11) An offence under section 2(1) of that Act (possession etc of a shot gun without a certificate).

(12) An offence under section 3 of that Act (business and other transactions with firearms and ammunition).

(13) An offence under section 4 of that Act (conversion of weapons).

(14) An offence under section 5(1) of that Act (weapons subject to general prohibition).

(15) An offence under section 5(1A) of that Act (ammunition subject to general prohibition).

(16) An offence under section 16 of that Act (possession with intent to injure).

(17) An offence under section 16A of that Act (possession with intent to cause fear of violence).

(18) An offence under section 17 of that Act (use of firearm to resist arrest).

(19) An offence under section 18 of that Act (carrying firearm with criminal intent).

(20) An offence under section 19 of that Act (carrying firearm in a public place).

(21) An offence under section 20 of that Act (trespassing with firearm).

(22) An offence under section 21 of that Act (possession of firearms by person previously convicted of crime).

(23) An offence under section 21A of that Act (firing an air weapon beyond premises).

(24) An offence under section 24A of that Act (supplying imitation firearms to minors).

(25) An offence under section 139 of the Criminal Justice Act 1988 (having article with blade or point in public place).

(26) An offence under section 139A of that Act (having article with blade or point (or offensive weapon) on school premises).

(27) An offence under section 28 of the Violent Crime Reduction Act 2006 (using someone to mind a weapon).

(28) An offence under section 32 of that Act (sales of air weapons by way of trade or business to be face to face).

(29) An offence under section 36 of that Act (manufacture, import and sale of realistic imitation firearms).

(30) A reference in any of paragraphs 1 to 8 to an offence ("offence A") includes—

a reference to an attempt to commit offence A in a case where it is alleged that it was attempted to commit offence A in the manner or circumstances described in that paragraph,

a reference to a conspiracy to commit offence A in a case where it is alleged that the conspiracy was to commit offence A in the manner or circumstances described in that paragraph,

a reference to an offence under Part 2 of the Serious Crime Act 2007 in relation to which offence A is the offence (or one of the offences) which the person intended or believed would be committed in a case where it is alleged that the person intended or believed offence A would be committed in the manner or circumstances described in that paragraph, and

a reference to aiding, abetting, counselling or procuring the commission of offence A in a case where it is alleged that offence A was committed, or the act or omission charged in respect of offence A was done or made, in the manner or circumstances described in that paragraph.

(31) A reference in any of paragraphs 9 to 29 to an offence ("offence A") includes—

a reference to an attempt to commit offence A,

a reference to a conspiracy to commit offence A,

a reference to an offence under Part 2 of the Serious Crime Act 2007 in relation to which offence A is the offence (or one of the offences) which the person intended or believed would be committed, and a reference to aiding, abetting, counselling or procuring the commission of offence A.

(32) In this Schedule—

(33) "firearm"has the meaning given by section 57 of the Firearms Act 1968;

(34) "knife"has the meaning given by section 10 of the Knives Act 1997.

APPENDIX 10

FRAUD GUIDELINE

Fraud—banking and insurance fraud, and obtaining credit through fraud, benefit fraud, and revenue fraud—factors to take into consideration

This guideline and accompanying notes are taken from the Sentencing Guidelines Council's definitive guideline *Sentencing for Fraud—Statutory Offences*, published 26 October 2009.

The starting points and ranges for fraud against HM Revenue and Customs, for benefit fraud and for banking and insurance and obtaining credit through fraud are the same since the seriousness of all offences of organisational fraud derives from the extent of the fraudulent activity (culpability) and the financial loss caused or likely to be caused (harm).

Key factors common to these types of fraud

(a) As the determinants of seriousness include the 'value of property or consequential loss involved', the table provides both a fixed amount (on which the starting point is based) and a band (on which the sentencing range is based). Where the value is larger or smaller than the amount on which the starting point is based, this should lead to upward or downward movement from the starting point as appropriate. Where the amount the offender intended to obtain cannot be established, the appropriate measure will be the amount that was likely to be achieved in all the circumstances. Where the offender was entitled to part or all of the amount obtained, the starting point should be based on the amount to which they were not entitled.

(b) A further determinant of seriousness is whether the fraud was a single fraudulent transaction or a multiple fraud. Where one false declaration or a failure to disclose a change in circumstances results in multiple payments, this should be regarded as multiple fraud.

(c) In general terms, the greater the loss, the more serious will be the offence. However, the financial value of the loss may not reflect the full extent of the harm caused. The court should also take into account; the impact of the offence on the victim (particularly where the loss may be significantly greater than the monetary value); harm to persons other than the direct victim (including the aggravation and stress of unscrambling the consequences of an offence); erosion of public confidence; and the difference between the loss intended and that which results (which may involve adjusting the assessment of seriousness to reflect the degree of loss caused).

(d) When the offending involves a number of people acting cooperatively, this will aggravate an offence as it indicates planning or professional activity, and may also increase the degree of loss caused or intended. The role of each offender is important in determining the appropriate level of seriousness and movement above or below the starting point within the applicable level.

(e) Use of another person's identity is an aggravating factor; the extent to which it aggravates an offence will be based on the degree of planning and the impact that the offence has had on the living victim or relatives of the deceased–whether the identity belongs to a living or deceased person is neutral for this purpose.

(f) Matters of offender mitigation which may be particularly relevant to these types of fraud include:

— *Voluntary cessation of offending*–a claim, supported by objective evidence, that an offender stopped offending before being apprehended should be treated as mitigation, particularly where accompanied by a genuine expression of remorse. The lapse of time since commission of the last offence is relevant to whether the claim is genuine, and reasons for the cessation will assist the court in determining whether it amounts to mitigation and if so, to what degree.

— *Complete and unprompted disclosure of the extent of the fraud*–An admission that a greater sum has been obtained than that known to the authorities ensures that an offender is sentenced for the complete extent of the fraud. This is ready co-operation with the authorities and should be treated as mitigation. Provision of information about others involved in the fraud should also be treated as mitigation. Generally, the earlier the disclosure is given and the higher the degree of assistance, the greater the allowance for mitigation.

— *Voluntary restitution*–the timing of the voluntary restitution will indicate the degree to which it reflects genuine remorse. Generally, the earlier the property or money is returned the greater the degree of mitigation the offender should receive. If circumstances beyond the control of the offender prevent return of defrauded items, the degree of mitigation will depend on the point in time at which, and the determination with which the offender tried to return the items.

— *Financial pressure*–financial pressure neither increases nor diminishes an offender's culpability. However, where such pressure is **exceptional** and not of the offender's own making, it may in very rare circumstances constitute mitigation.

(g) A court should be aware that a confiscation order is an important sanction. Such an order may only be made in the Crown Court. The court must commit the offender to the Crown Court where this is requested by the prosecution with a view to an order being considered.

(h) Ancillary orders should be considered in all cases, principally compensation, deprivation and disqualification from driving, as well as other powers particular to the type of offending behaviour.

Additional notes:

Banking and insurance fraud and obtaining credit through fraud

(i) A payment card or bank account fraud is unlikely to be committed in circumstances where the offender's intention was not fraudulent from the outset.

(ii) Use of another person's identity is a feature of nearly all payment card and bank account frauds since in most cases the offender claims to be the account holder or a person authorised to deal with the account. Courts should therefore increase the starting point to reflect the presence of this aggravating factor.

Benefit fraud

(i) This guideline is based on an understanding that the prosecutor will generally seek summary trial for appropriate benefit fraud cases involving sums up to £35,000.

(ii) The fact that defrauded sums may have been recovered is not relevant to the choice of the type of sentence to be imposed.

(iii) The court should have regard to personal and family circumstances of offenders which will vary greatly and may be particularly significant to sentencing this type of fraud.

Revenue fraud

(i) The proposals for the sentencing of revenue fraud take as a starting point an offender who acts intentionally. Where the offender has acted recklessly (relevant only to offences under the Value Added Tax Act 1994), courts should adjust the assessment of seriousness to take account of this lower level of culpability.

(ii) Payments to HMRC may be evaded in order to increase the profitability of a legitimate business or the level of an individual's legitimate remuneration; payments may be fraudulently obtained from HMRC without any underlying legitimate activity at all as in a Carousel Fraud. Although the type of harm is the same since both result in a loss to HMRC, where payment is sought from HMRC in such circumstances, culpability is likely to be higher. Accordingly, such offences are likely to be regarded as more serious.

All offences: Triable either way:

Maximum when tried summarily: Level 5 fine and/or 6 months

Maximum when tried on indictment: Fraud 10 years, other offences, 7 years

Offences under s. 112, Social Security Administration Act 1992 are not covered by this guideline.

This guideline does not apply to offences under s. 50 or s. 170, Customs and Excise Management Act 1979 which involve prohibited weapons and have a maximum penalty of 10 years.

Offence seriousness (culpability and harm)		
A. Identify the appropriate starting point		
Starting points based on first time offender pleading not guilty		
Examples of nature of activity	**Starting point**	**Range**
Single fraudulent transaction, not fraudulent from the outset	Value £2,500*—Band B fine Value £12,500*—Medium level community order Value £60,000*—12 weeks custody	Value less than £5,000—Band A fine to low level community order Value £5,000 to less than £20,000—Band B fine to 6 weeks custody Value £20,000 to less than £100,000—Medium level community order to Crown Court
Single fraudulent transaction, fraudulent from the outset	Value £2,500*—Low level community order Value £12,500*—High level community order Value £60,000*—26 weeks custody	Value less than £5,000—Band A fine to medium level community order Value £5,000 to less than £20,000—Band C fine to 18 weeks custody Value £20,000 to less than £100,000—6 weeks custody to Crown Court
Not fraudulent from the outset, **and either** • fraud carried out over a significant period of time or • multiple frauds **Where value exceeds £100,000**	Value £2,500*—Medium level community order Value £12,500*—6 weeks custody Value £60,000*—Crown Court Crown Court	Value less than £5,000—Band B fine to high level community order Value £5,000 to less than £20,000—Medium level community order to 26 weeks custody Value £20,000 to less than £100,000—12 weeks custody to Crown Court Crown Court Crown Court

Offence seriousness (culpability and harm)		
A. Identify the appropriate starting point		
Starting points based on first time offender pleading not guilty		
Examples of nature of activity	**Starting point**	**Range**
Fraudulent from the outset, **and either** • fraud carried out over a significant period of time or • multiple frauds **Where value £100,000 or more or fraud was professionally planned**	Value £2,500*—High level community order Value £12,500*—12 weeks custody Value £60,000*—Crown Court Crown Court	Value less than £5,000—Low level community order to 6 weeks custody Value £5,000 to less than £20,000—High level community order to Crown Court Value £20,000 to less than £100,000—18 weeks custody to Crown Court Crown Court

* Where the actual amount is greater or smaller than the value on which the starting point is based, that is likely to be one of the factors which will move the sentence within range (see (a) on page 62b)

Offence seriousness (culpability and harm)	
B. Consider the effect of aggravating and mitigating factors	
(other than those within examples above)	
Common aggravating and mitigating factors are identified in the pullout card—the following may be particularly relevant but **these lists are not exhaustive**	
Factors indicating higher culpability	**Factors indicating lower culpability**
1. Number involved in the offence and role of the offender 2. Making repeated importations, particularly in the face of warnings from the authorities 3. Dealing in goods with an additional health risk **Factors indicating greater degree of harm** 1. Use of another person's identity 2. Disposing of goods to under-aged purchasers	1. Peripheral involvement 2. Misleading or incomplete advice

Form a preliminary view of the appropriate sentence, then consider offender mitigation
Common factors are identified in the pullout card

Consider a reduction for a guilty plea

Consider ancillary orders
Refer to pages 168–174 (of the Magistrates' Court Sentencing Guidelines) for guidance on available ancillary orders

Decide sentence
Give reasons

Fraud—confidence—factors to take into consideration

This guideline and accompanying notes are taken from the Sentencing Guidelines Council's definitive guideline *Sentencing for Fraud—Statutory Offences*, published October 2009

Key factors

(a) This type of offending involves a victim transferring money and/or property as a result of being deceived or misled by the offender. An example of a simple confidence fraud is a person claiming to be collecting money for charity when, in fact, he or she intends to keep the money. Other examples of common confidence frauds are *Advance fee frauds* (such as lottery/prize draw scams and foreign money-making frauds) and *Fraudulent sales of goods and services* (where goods or services are never received/performed or are worth less than represented.

(b) As the determinants of seriousness include the 'value of property or consequential loss involved', the table provides both a fixed amount (on which the starting point is based) and a band (on which the sentencing range is based). Where the value is larger or smaller than the amount on which the starting point is based, this should lead to upward or downward movement as appropriate. Where the amount the offender intended to obtain cannot be established, the appropriate measure will be the amount that was likely to be achieved in all the circumstances.

(c) A further determinant of seriousness is whether the fraud was a single fraudulent transaction or a multiple fraud. Most confidence frauds will by their nature involve many actual or potential victims and multiple transactions and should be regarded as multiple fraud.

(d) Targeting a vulnerable victim is also a determinant of seriousness. A victim might be vulnerable as a result of old age, youth or disability. In addition, some victims of advance fee frauds may have personalities which make them 'vulnerable in a way and to a degree not typical of the general population' because they fall for scams many times and may be targeted using 'sucker lists' of people who have previously fallen victim to scams. Care should be taken to ensure that where targeting a vulnerable victim is used to determine the appropriate level of seriousness and starting point, that it is not used again as an aggravating factor to move within the sentencing range.

(e) In general terms, the greater the loss, the more serious will be the offence. However, the financial value of the loss may not reflect the full extent of the harm caused. The court should also take into account; the impact of the offence on the victim (particularly where the loss may be significantly greater than the monetary value); harm to persons other than the direct victim (including the aggravation and stress of unscrambling the consequences of an offence); erosion of public confidence; and the difference between the loss intended and that which results (which may involve adjusting the assessment of seriousness to reflect the degree of loss caused).

(f) When the offending involves a number of people acting co-operatively, this will aggravate an offence as it indicates planning or professional activity, and may also increase the degree of loss caused or intended. The role of each offender is important in determining the appropriate level of seriousness and movement above or below the starting point within the applicable level.

(g) Use of another person's identity is an aggravating factor; the extent to which it aggravates an offence will be based on the degree of planning and the impact that the offence has had on the living victim or relatives of the deceased–whether the identity belongs to a living or deceased person is neutral for this purpose.

(h) Matters of offender mitigation which may be particularly relevant to this type of fraud include:
— *Voluntary cessation of offending*–a claim, supported by objective evidence, that an offender stopped offending before being apprehended should be treated as

mitigation, particularly where accompanied by a genuine expression of remorse. The lapse of time since commission of the last offence is relevant to whether the claim is genuine, and reasons for the cessation will assist the court in determining whether it amounts to mitigation and if so, to what degree.

— *Complete and unprompted disclosure of the extent of the fraud*–an admission that a greater sum has been obtained than that known to the authorities ensures that an offender is sentenced for the complete extent of the fraud. This amounts to ready co-operation with the authorities and should be treated as mitigation. Provision of information about others involved in the fraud should also be treated as mitigation. Generally, the earlier the disclosure is given and the higher the degree of assistance, the greater the allowance for mitigation.

— *Voluntary restitution*–the timing of the voluntary restitution will indicate the degree to which it reflects genuine remorse. Generally, the earlier the property or money is returned the greater the degree of mitigation the offender should receive. If circumstances beyond the control of the offender prevent return of defrauded items, the degree of mitigation will depend on the point in time at which, and the determination with which the offender tried to return the items.

— *Financial pressure*–financial pressure neither increases nor diminishes an offender's culpability. However, where such pressure is **exceptional** and not of the offender's own making, it may in very rare circumstances constitute mitigation.

(i) A court should be aware that a confiscation order is an important sanction. Such an order may only be made in the Crown Court. The court must commit the offender to the Crown Court where this is requested by the prosecution with a view to an order being considered.

(j) Ancillary orders should be considered in all cases, principally compensation and deprivation.

All Offences: Triable either way:

Maximum when tried summarily: Level 5 fine and/or 6 months

Maximum when tried on indictment: Fraud 10 years, other offences, 7 years

Offence seriousness (culpability and harm)		
A. Identify the appropriate starting point		
Starting points based on first time offender pleading not guilty		
Examples of nature of activity	**Starting point**	**Range**
Single fraudulent transaction confidence fraud not targeting a vulnerable victim, and involving no or limited planning	Value £10,000*— Medium level community order Value £60,000*—12 weeks custody	Value less than £20,000—Band B fine to 6 weeks custody Value £20,000 to less than £100,000—Medium level community order to Crown Court
Single fraudulent transaction confidence fraud involving targeting of a vulnerable victim	Value £10,000*—6 weeks custody Value £60,000*—26 weeks custody	Value less than £20,000—Medium level community order to 26 weeks custody Value £20,000 to less than £100,000—High level community order to Crown Court

Offence seriousness (culpability and harm)

A. Identify the appropriate starting point

Starting points based on first time offender pleading not guilty

Examples of nature of activity	Starting point	Range
Lower scale advance fee fraud or other confidence fraud characterised by a degree of planning and/or multiple transactions	Value £10,000*—Crown Court Value £60,000*—Crown Court	Value less than £20,000—26 weeks custody to Crown Court Value £20,000 to less than £100,000—Crown Court
Large scale advance fee fraud or other confidence fraud involving the deliberate targeting of a large number of vulnerable victims	Value £10,000*—Crown Court Value £60,000*—Crown Court	Value less than £20,000—Crown Court Value £20,000 to less than £100,000—Crown Court

* Where the actual amount is greater or smaller than the value on which the starting point is based, that is likely to be one of the factors which will move the sentence within range (see (b) on page 62f)

Offence seriousness (culpability and harm)

B. Consider the effect of aggravating and mitigating factors

(other than those within examples above)

Common aggravating and mitigating factors are identified in the pullout card—the following may be particularly relevant but **these lists are not exhaustive**

Factors indicating higher culpability	Factors indicating lower culpability
1. Number involved in the offence and role of the offender 2. Offending carried out over a significant period of time **Factors indicating greater degree of harm** 1. Use of another person's identity 2. Offence has lasting effect on the victim	1. Peripheral involvement 2. Behaviour not fraudulent from the outset 3. Misleading or inaccurate advice

---

Form a preliminary view of the appropriate sentence, then consider offender mitigation

Common factors are identified in the pullout card

Consider a reduction for a guilty plea

Consider ancillary orders

Refer to pages 168–174 (of the Magistrates' Court Sentencing Guidelines) for guidance on available ancillary orders

---

Decide sentence

Give reasons

Fraud—possessing, making or supplying articles for use in fraud—factors to take into consideration

This guideline and accompanying notes are taken from the Sentencing Guidelines Council's definitive guideline *Sentencing for Fraud—Statutory Offences*, published 26 October 2009.

Key factors

(a) There are many ways in which offenders may commit this group of offences. 'Articles' will include any electronic programs or data stored electronically, false fronts for cash machines, computer programs for generating credit card numbers, lists of credit card or bank account details, 'sucker lists' and draft letters or emails for use in advance fee frauds.

(b) Offenders who possess, make or supply articles for use in fraud intend their actions to lead to a fraud, and therefore have the highest level of culpability. The three offences in this group all involve an element of planning (whether by the offender or by another person) which indicates a higher level of culpability; this has been incorporated into the proposed starting points.

(c) In relation to harm, the value of the fraud (either that intended by the offender where that can be ascertained, or that which was likely to be achieved) is not a determinant of seriousness for these offences but is a factor that should be taken into account in determining the appropriate sentence within the sentencing range.

(d) Whilst in many cases no financial harm will have been caused, in some cases, particularly where the 'article' is a list of credit card or bank account details, the victim(s) may have been inconvenienced despite not suffering any financial loss. In all cases, the harm must be judged in light of the offender's culpability.

(e) When the offending involves a number of people acting co-operatively, this will aggravate an offence as it indicates planning or professional activity, and may also increase the degree of loss caused or intended. The role of each offender is important in determining the appropriate level of seriousness and movement above or below the starting point within the applicable level.

(f) Matters of offender mitigation which may be particularly relevant to this type of fraud include:

— *Voluntary cessation of offending*–a claim, supported by objective evidence, that an offender stopped offending before being apprehended should be treated as mitigation, particularly where accompanied by a genuine expression of remorse. The lapse of time since commission of the last offence is relevant to whether the claim is genuine, and reasons for the cessation will assist the court in determining whether it amounts to mitigation and if so, to what degree.

— *Complete and unprompted disclosure of the extent of the fraud*–An admission that a greater sum has been obtained than that known to the authorities ensures that an offender is sentenced for the complete extent of the fraud. This amounts to ready co-operation with the authorities and should be treated as mitigation. Provision of information about others involved in the fraud should also be treated as mitigation. Generally, the earlier the disclosure is given and the higher the degree of assistance, the greater the allowance for mitigation.

— *Voluntary restitution*–the timing of the voluntary restitution will indicate the degree to which it reflects genuine remorse. Generally, the earlier the property or money is returned the greater the degree of mitigation the offender should receive. If circumstances beyond the control of the offender prevent return of defrauded items, the degree of mitigation will depend on the point in time at which, and the determination with which the offender tried to return the items.

— *Financial pressure*–financial pressure neither increases nor diminishes an offender's culpability. However, where such pressure is **exceptional** and not of the offender's own making, it may in very rare circumstances constitute mitigation.

(g) A court should be aware that a confiscation order is an important sanction. Such an order may only be made in the Crown Court. The court must commit the offender to the Crown Court where this is requested by the prosecution with a view to an order being considered.

(h) Ancillary orders should be considered in all cases, principally compensation and deprivation.

Possession of articles: Triable either way

Maximum when tried summarily: Level 5 fine and/or 6 months

Maximum when tried on indictment: 5 years

Making or supplying articles, and Fraud (s.1): Triable either way

Maximum when tried summarily: Level 5 fine and/or 6 months

Maximum when tried on indictment: 10 years

Offence seriousness (culpability and harm)
A. Identify the appropriate starting point
Starting points based on first time offender pleading not guilty

Examples of nature of activity	Starting point	Range
Possessing articles intended for use in a less extensive and less skillfully planned fraud Possessing articles for use in an extensive and skillfully planned fraud	Medium level community order Crown Court	Low level community order to 26 weeks custody 6 weeks custody to Crown Court
Making or adapting, supplying or offering to supply articles intended for use in a less extensive and less skillfully planned fraud Making or adapting, supplying or offering to supply articles for use in an extensive and skillfully planned fraud	26 weeks custody Crown Court	High level community order to Crown Court Crown Court

---

Offence seriousness (culpability and harm)
B. Consider the effect of aggravating and mitigating factors
(other than those within examples above)
Common aggravating and mitigating factors are identified in the pullout card—the following may be particularly relevant but **these lists are not exhaustive**

Factors indicating higher culpability	Factor indicating lower culpability
1. Number involved in the offence and role of the offender 2. Offending carried out over a significant period of time **Factors indicating greater degree of harm** 1. Use of another person's identity 2. Offence has lasting effect on the victim	1. Peripheral involvement

---

Form a preliminary view of the appropriate sentence, then consider offender mitigation
Common factors are identified in the pullout card

Consider a reduction for a guilty plea

Consider ancillary orders

Refer to pages 168–174 (of the Magistrates' Court Sentencing Guidelines) for guidance on available ancillary orders

Decide sentence

Give reasons

APPENDIX 11

Legal Aid, Sentencing and Punishment of Offenders Act 2012, ss 91-102

91 Remands of children otherwise than on bail

(1) This section applies where—

    (a) a court deals with a child charged with or convicted of one or more offences by remanding the child, and

    (b) the child is not released on bail.

(2) This section also applies where—

    (a) a court remands a child in connection with extradition proceedings, and

    (b) the child is not released on bail.

(3) Subject to subsection (4), the court must remand the child to local authority accommodation in accordance with section 92.

(4) The court may instead remand the child to youth detention accommodation in accordance with section 102 where—

    (a) in the case of a child remanded under subsection (1), the first or second set of conditions for such a remand (see sections 98 and 99) is met in relation to the child, or

    (b) in the case of a child remanded under subsection (2), the first or second set of conditions for such a remand in an extradition case (see sections 100 and 101) is met in relation to the child.

(5) This section is subject to section 128(7) of the Magistrates' Courts Act 1980 (remands to police detention for periods of not more than 3 days); but that provision has effect in relation to a child as if for the reference to 3 clear days there were substituted a reference to 24 hours.

(6) In this Chapter, "child" means a person under the age of 18.

(7) References in this Chapter (other than in relation to extradition proceedings) to the remand of a child include a reference to—

    (a) the sending of a child for trial, and

    (b) the committal of a child for sentence, and related expressions are to be construed accordingly.

(8) Before the insertion of section 51A of the Crime and Disorder Act 1998 (sending cases to the Crown Court: children and young persons) by Schedule 3 to the Criminal Justice Act 2003 is fully in force, subsection (7) has effect as if it also referred to the committal of a child for trial.

(9) Subsection (7) also applies to any provision of an Act other than this Act that refers (directly or indirectly) to the remand of a child under this section.

92 Remands to local authority accommodation

(1) A remand to local authority accommodation is a remand to accommodation provided by or on behalf of a local authority.

(2) A court that remands a child to local authority accommodation must designate the local authority that is to receive the child.

(3) That authority must be—

(a) in the case of a child who is being looked after by a local authority, that authority, and

(b) in any other case, the local authority in whose area it appears to the court that the child habitually resides or the offence or one of the offences was committed.

(4) The designated authority must—

(a) receive the child, and

(b) provide or arrange for the provision of accommodation for the child whilst the child is remanded to local authority accommodation.

(5) Where a child is remanded to local authority accommodation, it is lawful for any person acting on behalf of the designated authority to detain the child.

93 Conditions etc on remands to local authority accommodation

(1) A court remanding a child to local authority accommodation may require the child to comply with any conditions that could be imposed under section 3(6) of the Bail Act 1976 if the child were then being granted bail.

(2) The court may also require the child to comply with any conditions imposed for the purpose of securing the electronic monitoring of the child's compliance with the conditions imposed under subsection (1) if—

(a) in the case of a child remanded under section 91(1) (proceedings other than extradition proceedings), the requirements in section 94 are met, or

(b) in the case of a child remanded under section 91(2) (extradition proceedings), the requirements in section 95 are met.

(3) A court remanding a child to local authority accommodation may impose on the designated authority—

(a) requirements for securing compliance with any conditions imposed on the child under subsection (1) or (2), or

(b) requirements stipulating that the child must not be placed with a named person.

(4) A court may only impose a condition under subsection (1) or (2), or a requirement under subsection (3), after consultation with the designated authority.

(5) Where a child has been remanded to local authority accommodation, a relevant court—

(a) may, on the application of the designated authority, impose on that child any conditions that could be imposed under subsection (1) or (2) if the court were then remanding the child to local authority accommodation, and

(b) where it does so, may impose on the authority requirements for securing compliance with the conditions imposed under paragraph (a).

(6) Where a child has been remanded to local authority accommodation, a relevant court may, on the application of the designated authority or that child, vary or revoke any conditions or requirements imposed under this section (including as previously varied under this subsection).

(7) A court that imposes conditions on a child under this section or varies conditions so imposed—

(a) must explain to the child in open court and in ordinary language why it is imposing or varying those conditions, and

(b) if the court is a magistrates' court, must cause a reason given under paragraph (a) to be specified in the warrant of commitment and entered in the register.

(8) In this section "relevant court"—

    (a) in relation to a child remanded to local authority accommodation by virtue of section 91(1) (proceedings other than extradition proceedings), means—
        (i) the court by which the child was so remanded, or
        (ii) any magistrates' court that has jurisdiction in the place where the child is for the time being;

    (b) in relation to a child remanded to local authority accommodation by virtue of section 91(2) (extradition proceedings), means the court by which the child was so remanded.

(9) References in this section to consultation are to such consultation (if any) as is reasonably practicable in all the circumstances of the case.

94   Requirements for electronic monitoring

(1) The requirements referred to in section 93(2)(a) (requirements for imposing electronic monitoring condition: non-extradition cases) are those set out in subsections (2) to (6).

(2) The first requirement is that the child has reached the age of twelve.

(3) The second requirement is that the offence mentioned in section 91(1), or one or more of those offences, is an imprisonable offence.

(4) The third requirement is that—

    (a) the offence mentioned in section 91(1), or one or more of those offences, is a violent or sexual offence or an offence punishable in the case of an adult with imprisonment for a term of 14 years or more, or

    (b) the offence or offences mentioned in section 91(1), together with any other imprisonable offences of which the child has been convicted in any proceedings, amount or would, if the child were convicted of that offence or those offences, amount to a recent history of committing imprisonable offences while on bail or subject to a custodial remand.

(5) The fourth requirement is that the court is satisfied that the necessary provision for electronic monitoring can be made under arrangements currently available in each local justice area which is a relevant area.

(6) The fifth requirement is that a youth offending team has informed the court that, in its opinion, the imposition of an electronic monitoring condition will be suitable in the child's case.

(7) For the purposes of this section, a local justice area is a relevant area in relation to a proposed electronic monitoring condition if the court considers that it will not be practicable to secure the electronic monitoring in question unless electronic monitoring arrangements are available in that area.

(8) In this Chapter—

"electronic monitoring condition" means a condition imposed on a child remanded to local authority accommodation for the purpose of securing the electronic monitoring of the child's compliance with conditions imposed under section 93(1) or (5);

"imprisonable offence" means—

    (a) an offence punishable in the case of an adult with imprisonment, or

    (b) in relation to an offence of which a child has been accused or convicted outside England and Wales, an offence equivalent to an offence that, in England and Wales, is punishable in the case of an adult with imprisonment;

"sexual offence" means an offence specified in Part 2 of Schedule 15 to the Criminal Justice Act 2003;

"violent offence" means murder or an offence specified in Part 1 of Schedule 15 to the Criminal Justice Act 2003;

"youth offending team" means a team established under section 39 of the Crime and Disorder Act 1998.

   (9) References in this Chapter to a child being subject to a custodial remand are to the child being—

      (a) remanded to local authority accommodation or youth detention accommodation, or

      (b) subject to a form of custodial detention in a country or territory outside England and Wales while awaiting trial or sentence in that country or territory or during a trial in that country or territory.

  (10) The reference in subsection (9) to a child being remanded to local authority accommodation or youth detention accommodation includes—

      (a) a child being remanded to local authority accommodation under section 23 of the Children and Young Persons Act 1969, and

      (b) a child being remanded to prison under that section as modified by section 98 of the Crime and Disorder Act 1998 or under section 27 of the Criminal Justice Act 1948.

95 Requirements for electronic monitoring: extradition cases

   (1) The requirements referred to in section 93(2)(b) (requirements for imposing electronic monitoring condition: extradition cases) are those set out in subsections (2) to (6).

   (2) The first requirement is that the child has reached the age of twelve.

   (3) The second requirement is that the offence to which the extradition proceedings relate, or one or more of those offences, is an imprisonable offence.

   (4) The third requirement is that—

      (a) the conduct constituting the offence to which the extradition proceedings relate, or one or more of those offences, would, if committed in England and Wales, constitute a violent or sexual offence or an offence punishable in the case of an adult with imprisonment for a term of 14 years or more, or

      (b) the offence or offences to which the extradition proceedings relate, together with any other imprisonable offences of which the child has been convicted, amount or would, if the child were convicted of that offence or those offences, amount to a recent history of committing imprisonable offences while on bail or subject to a custodial remand.

   (5) The fourth requirement is that the court is satisfied that the necessary provision for electronic monitoring can be made under arrangements currently available in each local justice area which is a relevant area.

   (6) The fifth requirement is that a youth offending team has informed the court that, in its opinion, the imposition of an electronic monitoring condition will be suitable in the child's case.

   (7) For the purposes of this section, a local justice area is a relevant area in relation to a proposed electronic monitoring condition if the court considers that it will not be practicable to secure the electronic monitoring in question unless electronic monitoring arrangements are available in that area.

96 Further provisions about electronic monitoring

   (1) Where a court imposes an electronic monitoring condition, the condition must include provision making a person responsible for the monitoring.

   (2) A person who is made responsible by virtue of subsection (1) must be of a description specified in an order made by the Secretary of State.

   (3) The Secretary of State may make rules for regulating—

      (a) the electronic monitoring of compliance with conditions imposed under section 93(1) or (5), and

(b) in particular, the functions of persons made responsible by virtue of subsection (1) of this section.

(4) Rules under this section may make different provision for different cases.

(5) Any power of the Secretary of State to make an order or rules under this section is exercisable by statutory instrument.

(6) A statutory instrument containing rules under this section is subject to annulment in pursuance of a resolution of either House of Parliament.

97 Liability to arrest for breaking conditions of remand

(1) A child may be arrested without warrant by a constable if—

(a) the child has been remanded to local authority accommodation,

(b) conditions under section 93 have been imposed in respect of the child, and

(c) the constable has reasonable grounds for suspecting that the child has broken any of those conditions.

(2) Subject to subsection (3), a child arrested under subsection (1) must be brought before a justice of the peace—

(a) as soon as practicable, and

(b) in any event within the period of 24 hours beginning with the child's arrest.

(3) If the child was arrested during the period of 24 hours ending with the time appointed for the child to appear before the court in pursuance of the remand, the child must be brought before the court before which the child was to have appeared.

(4) In reckoning a period of 24 hours for the purposes of subsection (2) or (3), no account is to be taken of Christmas Day, Good Friday or any Sunday.

(5) If a justice of the peace before whom a child is brought under subsection (2) is of the opinion that the child has broken any condition imposed in respect of the child under section 93, the justice of the peace must remand the child.

(6) Section 91 applies to a child in relation to whom subsection (5) applies as if—

(a) except in a case within paragraph (b), the child was then charged with or convicted of the offence for which the child had been remanded, or

(b) in the case of a child remanded in connection with extradition proceedings, the child was then appearing before the justice of the peace in connection with those proceedings.

(7) If a justice of the peace before whom a child is brought under subsection (2) is not of the opinion mentioned in subsection (5), the justice of the peace must remand the child to the place to which the child had been remanded at the time of the child's arrest subject to the same conditions as those which had been imposed on the child at that time.

98 First set of conditions for a remand to youth detention accommodation

(1) For the purposes of section 91(4)(a), the first set of conditions for a remand to youth detention accommodation is met in relation to a child if each of the following is met in relation to the child—

(a) the age condition (see subsection (2)),

(b) the offence condition (see subsection (3)),

(c) the necessity condition (see subsection (4)), and

(d) the first or second legal representation condition (see subsections (5) and (6)).

(2) The age condition is that the child has reached the age of twelve.

(3) The offence condition is that the offence mentioned in section 91(1), or one or more of those offences—

(a) is a violent or sexual offence, or

(b) is an offence punishable in the case of an adult with imprisonment for a term of 14 years or more.

(4) The necessity condition is that the court is of the opinion, after considering all the options for the remand of the child, that only remanding the child to youth detention accommodation would be adequate—

(a) to protect the public from death or serious personal injury (whether physical or psychological) occasioned by further offences committed by the child, or

(b) to prevent the commission by the child of imprisonable offences.

(5) The first legal representation condition is that the child is legally represented before the court.

(6) The second legal representation condition is that the child is not legally represented before the court and—

(a) representation was provided to the child under Part 1 of this Act for the purposes of the proceedings, but was withdrawn—
   (i) because of the child's conduct, or
   (ii) because it appeared that the child's financial resources were such that the child was not eligible for such representation,

(b) the child applied for such representation and the application was refused because it appeared that the child's financial resources were such that the child was not eligible for such representation, or

(c) having been informed of the right to apply for such representation and having had the opportunity to do so, the child refused or failed to apply.

99 Second set of conditions for a remand to youth detention accommodation

(1) For the purposes of section 91(4)(a), the second set of conditions for a remand to youth detention accommodation is met in relation to a child if each of the following is met in relation to the child—

(a) the age condition (see subsection (2)),
(b) the sentencing condition (see subsection (3)),
(c) the offence condition (see subsection (4)),
(d) the first or second history condition or both (see subsections (5) and (6)),
(e) the necessity condition (see subsection (7)), and
(f) the first or second legal representation condition (see subsections (8) and (9)).

(2) The age condition is that the child has reached the age of twelve.

(3) The sentencing condition is that it appears to the court that there is a real prospect that the child will be sentenced to a custodial sentence for the offence mentioned in section 91(1) or one or more of those offences.

(4) The offence condition is that the offence mentioned in section 91(1), or one or more of those offences, is an imprisonable offence.

(5) The first history condition is that—

(a) the child has a recent history of absconding while subject to a custodial remand, and

(b) the offence mentioned in section 91(1), or one or more of those offences, is alleged to be or has been found to have been committed while the child was remanded to local authority accommodation or youth detention accommodation.

(6) The second history condition is that the offence or offences mentioned in section 91(1), together with any other imprisonable offences of which the child has been convicted in any proceedings, amount or would, if the child were convicted of that offence or those offences, amount to a recent history of committing imprisonable offences while on bail or subject to a custodial remand.

(7) The necessity condition is that the court is of the opinion, after considering all the options for the remand of the child, that only remanding the child to youth detention accommodation would be adequate—

    (a) to protect the public from death or serious personal injury (whether physical or psychological) occasioned by further offences committed by the child, or

    (b) to prevent the commission by the child of imprisonable offences.

(8) The first legal representation condition is that the child is legally represented before the court.

(9) The second legal representation condition is that the child is not legally represented before the court and—

    (a) representation was provided to the child under Part 1 of this Act for the purposes of the proceedings, but was withdrawn—

        (i) because of the child's conduct, or

        (ii) because it appeared that the child's financial resources were such that the child was not eligible for such representation,

    (b) the child applied for such representation and the application was refused because it appeared that the child's financial resources were such that the child was not eligible for such representation, or

    (c) having been informed of the right to apply for such representation and having had the opportunity to do so, the child refused or failed to apply.

(10) In this Chapter "custodial sentence" means a sentence or order mentioned in section 76(1) of the Powers of Criminal Courts (Sentencing) Act 2000.

(11) The reference in subsection (5)(b) to a child being remanded to local authority accommodation or youth detention accommodation includes—

    (a) a child being remanded to local authority accommodation under section 23 of the Children and Young Persons Act 1969, and

    (b) a child being remanded to prison under that section as modified by section 98 of the Crime and Disorder Act 1998 or under section 27 of the Criminal Justice Act 1948.

100 First set of conditions for a remand to youth detention accommodation: extradition cases

(1) For the purposes of section 91(4)(b), the first set of conditions for a remand to youth detention accommodation in an extradition case is met in relation to a child if each of the following is met in relation to the child—

    (a) the age condition (see subsection (2)),

    (b) the offence condition (see subsection (3)),

    (c) the necessity condition (see subsection (4)), and

    (d) the first or second legal representation condition (see subsections (5) and (6)).

(2) The age condition is that the child has reached the age of twelve.

(3) The offence condition is that the conduct constituting the offence to which the extradition proceedings relate, or one or more of those offences, would, if committed in England and Wales, constitute—

    (a) a violent or sexual offence, or

    (b) an offence punishable in the case of an adult with imprisonment for a term of 14 years or more.

(4) The necessity condition is that the court is of the opinion, after considering all the options for the remand of the child, that only remanding the child to youth detention accommodation would be adequate—

    (a) to protect the public from death or serious personal injury (whether physical or psychological) occasioned by further offences committed by the child, or

(b) to prevent the commission by the child of imprisonable offences.

(5) The first legal representation condition is that the child is legally represented before the court.

(6) The second legal representation condition is that the child is not legally represented before the court and—

(a) representation was provided to the child under Part 1 of this Act for the purposes of the proceedings, but was withdrawn—
    (i) because of the child's conduct, or
    (ii) because it appeared that the child's financial resources were such that the child was not eligible for such representation,

(b) the child applied for such representation and the application was refused because it appeared that the child's financial resources were such that the child was not eligible for such representation, or

(c) having been informed of the right to apply for such representation and having had the opportunity to do so, the child refused or failed to apply.

101 Second set of conditions for a remand to youth detention accommodation: extradition cases

(1) For the purposes of section 91(4)(b), the second set of conditions for a remand to youth detention accommodation in an extradition case is met in relation to a child if each of the following is met in relation to the child—

(a) the age condition (see subsection (2)),
(b) the sentencing condition (see subsection (3)),
(c) the offence condition (see subsection (4)),
(d) the first or second history condition or both (see subsections (5) and (6)),
(e) the necessity condition (see subsection (7)), and
(f) the first or second legal representation condition (see subsections (8) and (9)).

(2) The age condition is that the child has reached the age of twelve.

(3) The sentencing condition is that it appears to the court that, if the child were convicted in England and Wales of an offence equivalent to the offence to which the extradition proceedings relate or one or more of those offences, there would be a real prospect that the child would be sentenced to a custodial sentence for that offence or those offences.

(4) The offence condition is that the offence to which the extradition proceedings relate, or one or more of those offences, is an imprisonable offence.

(5) The first history condition is that—

(a) the child has a recent history of absconding while subject to a custodial remand, and
(b) the offence to which the extradition proceedings relate, or one or more of those offences, is alleged to be or has been found to have been committed while the child was subject to a custodial remand.

(6) The second history condition is that the offence or offences to which the extradition proceedings relate, together with any other imprisonable offences of which the child has been convicted, amount or would, if the child were convicted of that offence or those offences, amount to a recent history of committing imprisonable offences while on bail or subject to a custodial remand.

(7) The necessity condition is that the court is of the opinion, after considering all the options for the remand of the child, that only remanding the child to youth detention accommodation would be adequate—

(a) to protect the public from death or serious personal injury (whether physical or psychological) occasioned by further offences committed by the child, or
(b) to prevent the commission by the child of imprisonable offences.

(8) The first legal representation condition is that the child is legally represented before the court.

(9) The second legal representation condition is that the child is not legally represented before the court and—

(a) representation was provided to the child under Part 1 of this Act for the purposes of the proceedings, but was withdrawn—

    (i) because of the child's conduct, or

    (ii) because it appeared that the child's financial resources were such that the child was not eligible for such representation,

(b) the child applied for such representation and the application was refused because it appeared that the child's financial resources were such that the child was not eligible for such representation, or

(c) having been informed of the right to apply for such representation and having had the opportunity to do so, the child refused or failed to apply.

102 Remands to youth detention accommodation

(1) A remand to youth detention accommodation is a remand to such accommodation of a kind listed in subsection (2) as the Secretary of State directs in the child's case.

(2) Those kinds of accommodation are—

(a) a secure children's home,

(b) a secure training centre,

(c) a young offender institution, and

(d) accommodation, or accommodation of a description, for the time being specified by order under section 107(1)(e) of the Powers of Criminal Courts (Sentencing) Act 2000 (youth detention accommodation for purposes of detention and training order provisions).

(3) A child's detention in one of those kinds of accommodation pursuant to a remand to youth detention accommodation is lawful.

(4) Where a court remands a child to youth detention accommodation, the court must—

(a) state in open court that it is of the opinion mentioned in section 98(4), 99(7), 100(4) or 101(7) (as the case may be), and

(b) explain to the child in open court and in ordinary language why it is of that opinion.

(5) A magistrates' court must ensure a reason that it gives under subsection (4)(b)—

(a) is specified in the warrant of commitment, and

(b) is entered in the register.

(6) Where a court remands a child to youth detention accommodation, the court must designate a local authority as the designated authority for the child for the purposes of—

(a) subsection (8),

(b) regulations under section 103 (arrangements for remands), and

(c) section 104 (looked after child status).

(7) That authority must be—

(a) in the case of a child who is being looked after by a local authority, that authority, and

(b) in any other case, the local authority in whose area it appears to the court that the child habitually resides or the offence or one of the offences was committed.

(8) Before giving a direction under subsection (1), the Secretary of State must consult the designated authority.

(9)   A function of the Secretary of State under this section (other than the function of making regulations) is exercisable by the Youth Justice Board for England and Wales concurrently with the Secretary of State.

(10) The Secretary of State may by regulations provide that subsection (9) is not to apply, either generally or in relation to a particular description of case.

(11) In this Chapter "secure children's home" means accommodation which is provided in a children's home, within the meaning of the Care Standards Act 2000—

   (a) which provides accommodation for the purposes of restricting liberty, and
   (b) in respect of which a person is registered under Part 2 of that Act.

(12) Before the coming into force in relation to England of section 107(2) of the Health and Social Care (Community Health and Standards) Act 2003, subsection (11) has effect as if it defined "secure children's home" in relation to England as accommodation which—

   (a) is provided in a children's home, within the meaning of the Care Standards Act 2000, in respect of which a person is registered under Part 2 of that Act, and
   (b) is approved by the Secretary of State for the purpose of restricting the liberty of children.

APPENDIX 12

BAIL ACT 1976

1.— Meaning of "bail in criminal proceedings".

(1) In this Act "bail in criminal proceedings" means — (a) bail grantable in or in connection with proceedings for an offence to a person who is accused or convicted of the offence, or

  (b) bail grantable in connection with an offence to a person who is under arrest for the offence or for whose arrest for the offence a warrant (endorsed for bail) is being issued, or

  (c) bail grantable in connection with extradition proceedings in respect of an offence.

(2) In this Act "bail" means bail grantable under the law (including common law) for the time being in force.

(3) Except as provided by section 13(3) of this Act, this section does not apply to bail in or in connection with proceedings outside England and Wales.

[...]

(5) This section applies—

  (a) Whether the offence was committed in England or Wales or elsewhere, and

  (b) whether it is an offence under the law of England and Wales, or of any other country or territory.

(6) Bail in criminal proceedings shall be granted (and in particular shall be granted unconditionally or conditionally) in accordance with this Act.

2.— Other definitions.

(1) In this Act, unless the context otherwise requires, "conviction" includes— (a) a finding of guilt,

  (b) a finding that a person is not guilty by reason of insanity,

  (c) a finding under section 11(1) of the Powers of Criminal Courts (Sentencing) Act 2000 (remand for medical examination) that the person in question did the act or made the omission charged, and

  (d) a conviction of an offence for which an order is made discharging the offender] absolutely or conditionally

and "convicted" shall be construed accordingly.

(2) In this Act, unless the context otherwise requires—

"bail hostel" means premises for the accommodation of persons remanded on bail,

"child" means a person under the age of fourteen,

"court" includes a judge of a court, or a justice of the peace and, in the case of a specified court, includes a judge or (as the case may be) justice having powers to act in connection with proceedings before that court,

"Court Martial Appeal Rules" means rules made under section 49 of the Court Martial Appeals Act 1968, "extradition proceedings" means proceedings under the Extradition Act 2003,

"offence" includes an alleged offence,

"probation hostel" means premises for the accommodation of persons who may be required to reside there by a community order under section 177 of the Criminal Justice Act 2003,

"prosecutor", in relation to extradition proceedings, means the person acting on behalf of the territory to which extradition is sought;

"surrender to custody" means, in relation to a person released on bail, surrendering himself into the custody of the court or of the constable (according to the requirements of the grant of bail) at the time and place for the time being appointed for him to do so,

"vary", in relation to bail, means imposing further conditions after bail is granted, or varying or rescinding conditions,

"young person" means a person who has attained the age of fourteen and is under the age of seventeen.

(3) Where an enactment (whenever passed) which relates to bail in criminal proceedings refers to the person bailed appearing before a court it is to be construed unless the context otherwise requires as referring to his surrendering himself into the custody of the court.

(4) Any reference in this Act to any other enactment is a reference thereto as amended, and includes a reference thereto as extended or applied, by or under any other enactment, including this Act.

3.— General provisions.

(1) A person granted bail in criminal proceedings shall be under a duty to surrender to custody, and that duty is enforceable in accordance with section 6 of this Act.

(2) No recognizance for his surrender to custody shall be taken from him.

(3) Except as provided by this section—

    (a) no security for his surrender to custody shall be taken from him,

    (b) he shall not be required to provide a surety or sureties for his surrender to custody, and

    (c) no other requirement shall be imposed on him as a condition of bail.

(4) He may be required, before release on bail, to provide a surety or sureties to secure his surrender to custody.

(5) He may be required, before release on bail, to give security for his surrender to custody.

The security may be given by him or on his behalf.

(6) He may be required to comply, before release on bail or later, with such requirements as appear to the court to be necessary —

    (a) to secure that he surrenders to custody,

    (b) to secure that he does not commit an offence while on bail,

    (c) to secure that he does not interfere with witnesses or otherwise obstruct the course of justice whether in relation to himself or any other person,

    (ca) for his own protection or, if he is a child or young person, for his own welfare or in his own interests,

    (d) to secure that he makes himself available for the purpose of enabling inquiries or a report to be made to assist the court in dealing with him for the offence.

    (e) to secure that before the time appointed for him to surrender to custody, he attends an interview with a person who, for the purposes of the Legal Services Act 2007, is an authorised person in relation to an activity which constitutes the exercise of a right of audience or the conduct of litigation (within the meaning of that Act);

and, in any Act, "the normal powers to impose conditions of bail" means the powers to impose conditions under paragraph (a), (b) [, (c) or (ca)] 9 above.

(6ZAA)   The requirements which may be imposed under subsection (6) include electronic monitoring requirements.

The imposition of electronic monitoring requirements is subject to section 3AA (in the case of a child or young person), section 3AB (in the case of other persons) and section 3AC (in all cases).

(6ZAB)   In this section and sections 3AA to 3AC "electronic monitoring requirements" means requirements imposed for the purpose of securing the electronic monitoring of a person's compliance with any other requirement imposed on him as a condition of bail.

(6ZA)   Where he is required under subsection (6) above to reside in a bail hostel or probation hostel, he may also be required to comply with the rules of the hostel.

(6A)   In the case of a person accused of murder the court granting bail shall, unless it considers that satisfactory reports on his mental condition have already been obtained, impose as conditions of bail—

   (a) a requirement that the accused shall undergo examination by two medical practitioners, for the purpose of enabling such reports to be prepared; and

   (b) a requirement that he shall for that purpose attend such an institution or place as the court directs and comply with any other directions which may be given to him for that purpose by either of those practitioners.

(6B)   Of the medical practitioners referred to in subsection (6A) above at least one shall be practitioner approved for the purposes of section 12 of the Mental Health Act 1983.

(6C)   Subsection (6D) below applies where—

   (a) the court has been notified by the Secretary of State that arrangements for conducting a relevant assessment or, as the case may be, providing relevant follow-up have been made for the local justice area in which it appears to the court that the person referred to in subsection (6D) would reside if granted bail; and

   (b) the notice has not been withdrawn.

(6D)   In the case of a person ("P")—

   (a) in relation to whom paragraphs (a) to (c) of paragraph 6B(1) of Part 1 of Schedule 1 to this Act apply (including where P is a person to whom the provisions of Part 1A of Schedule 1 apply);

   (b) who, after analysis of the sample referred to in paragraph (b) of that paragraph, has been offered a relevant assessment or, if a relevant assessment has been carried out, has had relevant follow-up proposed to him; and

   (c) who has agreed to undergo the relevant assessment or, as the case may be, to participate in the relevant follow-up,

the court, if it grants bail, shall impose as a condition of bail that P both undergo the relevant assessment and participate in any relevant follow-up proposed to him or, if a relevant assessment has been carried out, that P participate in the relevant follow-up.

(6E)   In subsections (6C) and (6D) above—

   (a) "relevant assessment" means an assessment conducted by a suitably qualified person of whether P is dependent upon or has a propensity to misuse any specified Class A drugs;

   (b) "relevant follow-up" means, in a case where the person who conducted the relevant assessment believes P to have such a dependency or propensity, such further assessment, and such assistance or treatment (or both) in connection with the dependency or propensity, as the person who conducted the relevant assessment (or conducts any later assessment) considers to be appropriate in P's case,

and in paragraph (a) above "Class A drug" and "misuse" have the same meaning as in the Misuse of Drugs Act 1971, and "specified" (in relation to a Class A drug) has the same meaning as in Part 3 of the Criminal Justice and Court Services Act 2000.

(6F)   In subsection (6E)(a) above, "suitably qualified person" means a person who has such qualifications or experience as are from time to time specified by the Secretary of State for the purposes of this subsection.

(7)   If a parent or guardian of a child or young person consents to be surety for the child or young person for the purposes of this subsection, the parent or guardian may be required to secure that the child or young person complies with any requirement imposed on him by virtue of [subsection (6), (6ZAA) or (6A) above, but—

    (a) no requirement shall be imposed on the parent or the guardian of a young person by virtue of this subsection where it appears that the young person will attain the age of seventeen before the time to be appointed for him to surrender to custody; and

    (b) the parent or guardian shall not be required to secure compliance with any requirement to which his consent does not extend and shall not, in respect of those requirements to which his consent does extend, be bound in a sum greater than £50.

(8)   Where a court has granted bail in criminal proceedings that court or, where that court has sent a person on bail to the Crown Court for trial or committed him on bail to the Crown Court to be sentenced or otherwise dealt with, that court or the Crown Court may on application—

    (a) by or on behalf of the person to whom bail was granted, or
    (b) by the prosecutor or a constable,

vary the conditions of bail or impose conditions in respect of bail which has been granted unconditionally.

(9)   This section is subject to subsection (3) of section 11 of the Powers of Criminal Courts (Sentencing) Act 2000 (conditions of bail on remand for medical examination).

(10)   This section is subject, in its application to bail granted by a constable, to section 3A of this Act.

3A.— Conditions of bail in case of police bail.

(1)   Section 3 of this Act applies, in relation to bail granted by a custody officer under Part IV of the Police and Criminal Evidence Act 1984 or Part 3 of the Criminal Justice Act 2003 in cases where the normal powers to impose conditions of bail are available to him, subject to the following modifications.

(2)   Subsection (6) does not authorise the imposition of a requirement to reside in a bail hostel or any requirement under paragraph (d) or (e).

(3)   Subsections (6ZAA), (6ZA), and (6A) to (6F) shall be omitted.

(4)   For subsection (8), substitute the following—

"(8)   Where a custody officer has granted bail in criminal proceedings he or another custody officer serving at the same police station may, at the request of the person to whom it was granted, vary the conditions of bail; and in doing so he may impose conditions or more onerous conditions.".

(5)   Where a constable grants bail to a person no conditions shall be imposed under subsections (4), (5), (6) or (7) of section 3 of this Act unless it appears to the constable that it is necessary to do so —

    (a) for the purpose of preventing that person from failing to surrender to custody, or

(b) for the purpose of preventing that person from committing an offence while on bail, or

(c) for the purpose of preventing that person from interfering with witnesses or otherwise obstructing the course of justice, whether in relation to himself or any other person, or

(d) for that person's own protection or, if he is a child or young person, for his own welfare or in his own interests.

(6) Subsection (5) above also applies on any request to a custody officer under subsection (8) of section 3 of this Act to vary the conditions of bail.

3AA Conditions for the imposition of electronic monitoring requirements: children and young persons

(1) A court may not impose electronic monitoring requirements on a child or young person unless each of the following conditions is met.

(2) The first condition is that the child or young person has attained the age of twelve years.

(3) The second condition is that—

(a) the child or young person is charged with or has been convicted of a violent or sexual offence, or an offence punishable in the case of an adult with imprisonment for a term of fourteen years or more; or

(b) he is charged with or has been convicted of one or more imprisonable offences which, together with any other imprisonable offences of which he has been convicted in any proceedings—

(i) amount, or

(ii) would, if he were convicted of the offences with which he is charged, amount,

to a recent history of repeatedly committing imprisonable offences while remanded on bail or to local authority accommodation.

(4) The third condition is that the court is satisfied that the necessary provision for dealing with the person concerned can be made under arrangements for the electronic monitoring of persons released on bail that are currently available in each local justice area which is a relevant area.

(5) The fourth condition is that a youth offending team has informed the court that in its opinion the imposition of electronic monitoring requirements will be suitable in the case of the child or young person.

(11) In this section 'local authority accommodation' has the same meaning as in the Children and Young Persons Act 1969 (c. 54).

3AB Conditions for the imposition of electronic monitoring requirements: other persons

(1) A court may not impose electronic monitoring requirements on a person who has attained the age of seventeen unless each of the following conditions is met.

(2) The first condition is that the court is satisfied that without the electronic monitoring requirements the person would not be granted bail.

(3) The second condition is that the court is satisfied that the necessary provision for dealing with the person concerned can be made under arrangements for the electronic monitoring of persons released on bail that are currently available in each local justice area which is a relevant area.

(4) If the person is aged seventeen, the third condition is that a youth offending team has informed the court that in its opinion the imposition of electronic monitoring requirements will be suitable in his case.

3AC Electronic monitoring: general provisions

(1) Where a court imposes electronic monitoring requirements as a condition of bail, the requirements must include provision for making a person responsible for the monitoring.

(2) A person may not be made responsible for the electronic monitoring of a person on bail unless he is of a description specified in an order made by the Secretary of State.

(3) The Secretary of State may make rules for regulating—

(a) the electronic monitoring of persons on bail;

(b) without prejudice to the generality of paragraph (a), the functions of persons made responsible for such monitoring.

(4) The rules may make different provision for different cases.

(5) Any power of the Secretary of State to make an order or rules under this section is exercisable by statutory instrument.

(6) A statutory instrument containing rules under this section shall be subject to annulment in pursuance of a resolution of either House of Parliament.

(7) For the purposes of section 3AA or 3AB a local justice area is a relevant area in relation to a proposed electronic monitoring requirement if the court considers that it will not be practicable to secure the electronic monitoring in question unless electronic monitoring arrangements are available in that area.

(8) Nothing in sections 3, 3AA or 3AB is to be taken to require the Secretary of State to ensure that arrangements are made for the electronic monitoring of persons released on bail.

4.— General right to bail of accused persons and others.

(1) A person to whom this section applies shall be granted bail except as provided in Schedule 1 to this Act.

(2) This section applies to a person who is accused of an offence when—

(a) he appears or is brought before a magistrates' court or the Crown Court in the course of or in connection with proceedings for the offence, or

(b) he applies to a court for bail or for a variation of the conditions of bail in connection with the proceedings.

This subsection does not apply as respects proceedings on or after a person's conviction of the offence.

(2A) This section also applies to a person whose extradition is sought in respect of an offence, when—

(a) he appears or is brought before a court in the course of or in connection with extradition proceedings in respect of the offence, or

(b) he applies to a court for bail or for a variation of the conditions of bail in connection with the proceedings.

(2B) But subsection (2A) above does not apply if the person is alleged to have been convicted of the offence.

(3) This section also applies to a person who, having been convicted of an offence, appears or is brought before a magistrates' court or the Crown Court under—

(za) Schedule 1 to the Powers of Criminal Courts (Sentencing) Act 2000 (referral orders: referral back to appropriate court),

(zb) Schedule 8 to that Act (breach of reparation order),

(a) Schedule 2 to the Criminal Justice and Immigration Act 2008 (breach, revocation or amendment of youth rehabilitation orders),

(b) Part 2 of Schedule 8 to the Criminal Justice Act 2003 (breach of requirement of community order) , or

(c) the Schedule to the Street Offences Act 1959 (breach of orders under section 1(2A) of that Act).

(4) This section also applies to a person who has been convicted of an offence and whose

case is adjourned by the court for the purpose of enabling inquiries or a report to be made to assist the court in dealing with him for the offence.

(5) Schedule 1 to this Act also has effect as respects conditions of bail for a person to whom this section applies.

(6) In Schedule 1 to this Act "the defendant" means a person to whom this section applies and any reference to a defendant whose case is adjourned for inquiries or a report is a reference to a person to whom this section applies by virtue of subsection (4) above.

(7) This section is subject to section 41 of the Magistrates' Courts Act 1980 (restriction of bail by magistrates' court in cases of treason) and section 115(1) of the Coroners and Justice Act 2009 (bail decisions in murder cases to be made by Crown Court judge) .

(8) This section is subject to section 25 of the Criminal Justice and Public Order Act 1994 (exclusion of bail in cases of homicide and rape).3

(9) In taking any decisions required by Part I or II of Schedule 1 to this Act, the considerations to which the court is to have regard include, so far as relevant, any misuse of controlled drugs by the defendant ("controlled drugs" and "misuse" having the same meanings as in the Misuse of Drugs Act 1971).

5.— Supplementary provisions about decisions on bail.

(1) Subject to subsection (2) below, where—

(a) a court or constable grants bail in criminal proceedings, or

(b) a court withholds bail in criminal proceedings from a person to whom section 4 of this act applies, or

(c) a court, officer of a court or constable appoints a time or place or a different time or place for a person granted bail in criminal proceedings to surrender to custody, or

(d) a court or constable varies any conditions of bail or imposes conditions in respect of bail in criminal proceedings,

that court, officer or constable shall make a record of the decision in the prescribed manner and containing the prescribed particulars and, if requested to do so by the person in relation to whom the decision was taken, shall cause him to be given a copy of the record of the decision as soon as practicable after the record is made.

(2) Where bail in criminal proceedings is granted by endorsing a warrant of arrest for bail the constable who releases on bail the person arrested shall make the record required by subsection (1) above instead of the judge or justice who issued the warrant.

(2A) Where a magistrates' court or the Crown Court grants bail in criminal proceedings to a person to whom section 4 of this Act applies after hearing representations from the prosecutor in favour of withholding bail, then the court shall give reasons for granting bail.

(2B) A court which is by virtue of subsection (2A) above required to give reasons for its decision shall include a note of those reasons in the record of its decision and, if requested to do so by the prosecutor, shall cause the prosecutor to be given a copy of the record of the decision as soon as practicable after the record is made.

(3) Where a magistrates' court or the Crown Court—

(a) withholds bail in criminal proceedings, or

(b) imposes conditions in granting bail in criminal proceedings, or

(c) varies any conditions of bail or imposes conditions in respect of bail in criminal proceedings,

and does so in relation to a person to whom section 4 of this Act applies, then the court shall, give reasons for withholding bail or for imposing or varying the conditions.

(4) A court which is by virtue of subsection (3) above required to give reasons for its decision shall include a note of those reasons in the record of its decision and shall

(except in a case where, by virtue of subsection (5) below, this need not be done) give a copy of that note to the person in relation to whom the decision was taken.

(5)   The Crown Court need not give a copy of the note of the reasons for its decision to the person in relation to whom the decision was taken where that person has legal representation unless his legal representative requests the court to do so.

(6)   Where a magistrates' court withholds bail in criminal proceedings from a person who [does not have legal representation] 6 , the court shall—

(a) if it is sending him for trial to the Crown Court or if it issues a certificate under subsection (6A) below, inform him that he may apply to the Crown Court to be granted bail;

(6A) Where in criminal proceedings—

(a) a magistrates' court remands a person in custody under section 52(5) of the Crime and Disorder Act 1998, section 11 of the Powers of Criminal Courts (Sentencing) Act 2000 (remand for medical examination) or any of the following provisions of the Magistrates' Courts Act 1980—
(ii)   section 10 (adjournment of trial);
(iia) section 17C (intention as to plea: adjournment)
(iii) section 18 (initial procedure on information against adult for offence triable either way); or
(iv) section 24C (intention as to plea by child or young person: adjournment),

after hearing full argument on an application for bail from him; and

(b) either—
(i)   it has not previously heard such argument on an application for bail from him in those proceedings; or
(ii)   it has previously heard full argument from him on such an application but it is satisfied that there has been a change in his circumstances or that new considerations have been placed before it,

it shall be the duty of the court to issue a certificate in the prescribed form that they heard full argument on his application for bail before they refused the application.

(6B) Where the court issues a certificate under subsection (6A) above in a case to which paragraph (b)(ii) of that subsection applies, it shall state in the certificate the nature of the change of circumstances or the new considerations which caused it to hear a further fully argued bail application.

(6C) Where a court issues a certificate under subsection (6A) above it shall cause the person to whom it refuses bail to be given a copy of the certificate.

(7)   Where a person has given security in pursuance of section 3(5) above and a court is satisfied that he failed to surrender to custody then, unless it appears that he had reasonable cause for his failure, the court may order the forfeiture of the security.

(8)   If a court orders the forfeiture of a security under subsection (7) above, the court may declare that the forfeiture extends to such amount less than the full value of the security as it thinks fit to order.

(8A) An order under subsection (7) above shall, unless previously revoked, have effect at the end of twenty-one days beginning with the day on which it is made.

(8B) A court which has ordered the forfeiture of a security under subsection (7) above may, if satisfied on an application made by or on behalf of the person who gave it that he did after all have reasonable cause for his failure to surrender to custody, by order remit the forfeiture or declare that it extends to such amount less than the full value of the security as it thinks fit to order.

(8C) An application under subsection (8B) above may be made before or after the order for forfeiture has taken effect, but shall not be entertained unless the court is satisfied that the prosecution was given reasonable notice of the applicant's intention to make it.

(9) A security which has been ordered to be forfeited by a court under subsection (7) above shall, to the extent of the forfeiture—

(a) if it consists of money, be accounted for and paid in the same manner as a fine imposed by that court would be;

(b) if it does not consist of money, be enforced by such magistrates' court as may be specified in the order.

(9A) Where an order is made under subsection (8B) above after the order for forfeiture of the security in question has taken effect, any money which would have fallen to be repaid or paid over to the person who gave the security if the order under subsection (8B) had been made before the order for forfeiture took effect shall be repaid or paid over to him.

(10) In this section "prescribed" means, in relation to the decision of a court or an officer of a court, prescribed by Civil Procedure Rules, Court Martial Appeal Rules or Criminal Procedure Rules, as the case requires or, in relation to a decision of a constable, prescribed by direction of the Secretary of State .

(11) This section is subject, in its application to bail granted by a constable, to section 5A of this Act.

5A.— Supplementary provisions in cases of police bail.

(1) Section 5 of this Act applies, in relation to bail granted by a custody officer under Part IV of the Police and Criminal Evidence Act 1984 or Part 3 of the Criminal Justice Act 2003 in cases where the normal powers to impose conditions of bail are available to him, subject to the following modifications.

(1A) Subsections (2A) and (2B) shall be omitted.

(2) For subsection (3) substitute the following—

"(3) Where a custody officer, in relation to any person,—

(a) imposes conditions in granting bail in criminal proceedings, or

(b) varies any conditions of bail or imposes conditions in respect of bail in criminal proceedings,

the custody officer shall give reasons for imposing or varying the conditions.".

(3) For subsection (4) substitute the following—

"(4) A custody officer who is by virtue of subsection (3) above required to give reasons for his decision shall include a note of those reasons in the custody record and shall give a copy of that note to the person in relation to whom the decision was taken.".

(4) Subsections (5) and (6) shall be omitted.

5B.— Reconsideration of decisions granting bail.

(A1) This section applies in any of these cases—

(a) a magistrates' court has granted bail in criminal proceedings in connection with an offence to which this section applies or proceedings for such an offence;

(b) a constable has granted bail in criminal proceedings in connection with proceedings for such an offence;

(c) a magistrates' court or a constable has granted bail in connection with extradition proceedings.

(1) The court or the appropriate court in relation to the constable may, on application by the prosecutor for the decision to be reconsidered—

(a) vary the conditions of bail,

(b) impose conditions in respect of bail which has been granted unconditionally, or

(c) withhold bail.

(2) The offences to which this section applies are offences triable on indictment and offences triable either way.

(3) No application for the reconsideration of a decision under this section shall be made unless it is based on information which was not available to the court or constable when the decision was taken.

(4) Whether or not the person to whom the application relates appears before it, the magistrates' court shall take the decision in accordance with section 4(1) (and Schedule 1) of this Act.

(5) Where the decision of the court on a reconsideration under this section is to withhold bail from the person to whom it was originally granted the court shall—

 (a) if that person is before the court, remand him in custody, and

 (b) if that person is not before the court, order him to surrender himself forthwith into the custody of the court.

(6) Where a person surrenders himself into the custody of the court in compliance with an order under subsection (5) above, the court shall remand him in custody.

(7) A person who has been ordered to surrender to custody under subsection (5) above may be arrested without warrant by a constable if he fails without reasonable cause to surrender to custody in accordance with the order.

(8) A person arrested in pursuance of subsection (7) above shall be brought as soon as practicable, and in any event within 24 hours after his arrest, before a justice of the peace and the justice shall remand him in custody.

In reckoning for the purposes of this subsection any period of 24 hours, no account shall be taken of Christmas Day, Good Friday or any Sunday.

(8A) Where the court, on a reconsideration under this section, refuses to withhold bail from a relevant person after hearing representations from the prosecutor in favour of withholding bail, then the court shall give reasons for refusing to withhold bail.

(8B) In subsection (8A) above, "relevant person" means a person to whom section 4(1) (and Schedule 1) of this Act is applicable in accordance with subsection (4) above.

(8C) A court which is by virtue of subsection (8A) above required to give reasons for its decision shall include a note of those reasons in any record of its decision and, if requested to do so by the prosecutor, shall cause the prosecutor to be given a copy of any such record as soon as practicable after the record is made.

(9) Criminal Procedure Rules shall include provision—

 (a) requiring notice of an application under this section and of the grounds for it to be given to the person affected, including notice of the powers available to the court under it;

 (b) for securing that any representations made by the person affected (whether in writing or orally) are considered by the court before making its decision; and

 (c) designating the court which is the appropriate court in relation to the decision of any constable to grant bail.

6.— Offence of absconding by person released on bail.

(1) If a person who has been released on bail in criminal proceedings fails without reasonable cause to surrender to custody he shall be guilty of an offence.

(2) If a person who—

 (a) has been released on bail in criminal proceedings, and

 (b) having reasonable cause therefor, has failed to surrender to custody,

fails to surrender to custody at the appointed place as soon after the appointed time as is reasonably practicable he shall be guilty of an offence.

(3) It shall be for the accused to prove that he had reasonable cause for his failure to surrender to custody.

(4)   A failure to give to a person granted bail in criminal proceedings a copy of the record of the decision shall not constitute a reasonable cause for that person's failure to surrender to custody.

(5)   An offence under subsection (1) or (2) above shall be punishable either on summary conviction or as if it were a criminal contempt of court.

(6)   Where a magistrates' court convicts a person of an offence under subsection (1) or (2) above the court may, if it thinks—

    (a)   that the circumstances of the offence are such that greater punishment should be inflicted for that offence than the court has power to inflict, or

    (b)   in a case where it [sends] 1 that person for trial to the Crown Court for another offence, that it would be appropriate for him to be dealt with for the offence under subsection (1) or (2) above by the court before which he is tried for the other offence,

commit him in custody or on bail to the Crown Court for sentence.

(7)   A person who is convicted summarily of an offence under subsection (1) or (2) above and is not committed to the Crown Court for sentence shall be liable to imprisonment for a term not exceeding 3 months or to a fine not exceeding level 5 on the standard scale or to both and a person who is so committed for sentence or is dealt with as for such a contempt shall be liable to imprisonment for a term not exceeding 12 months or to a fine or to both.

(8)   In any proceedings for an offence under subsection (1) or (2) above a document purporting to be a copy of the part of the prescribed record which relates to the time and place appointed for the person specified in the record to surrender to custody and to be duly certified to be a true copy of that part of the record shall be evidence of the time and place appointed for that person to surrender to custody.

(9)   For the purposes of subsection (8) above—

    (a)   "the prescribed record" means the record of the decision of the court, officer or constable made in pursuance of section 5(1) of this Act;

    (b)   the copy of the prescribed record is duly certified if it is certified by the appropriate officer of the court or, as the case may be, by the constable who took the decision or a constable designated for the purpose by the officer in charge of the police station from which the person to whom the record relates was released;

    (c)   "the appropriate officer" of the court is—

        (i)   in the case of a magistrates' court, the designated officer for the court;

        (ii)   in the case of the Crown Court, such officer as may be designated for the purpose in accordance with arrangements made by the Lord Chancellor;

        (iii)   in the case of the High Court, such officer as may be designated for the purpose in accordance with arrangements made by the Lord Chancellor;

        (iv)   in the case of the Court of Appeal, the registrar of criminal appeals or such other officer as may be authorised by him to act for the purpose;

        (v)   in the case of the Court Martial Appeal Court , the registrar or such other officer as may be authorised by him to act for the purpose.

(10)   Section 127 of the Magistrates' Courts Act 1980 shall not apply in relation to an offence under subsection (1) or (2) above.

(11)   Where a person has been released on bail in criminal proceedings and that bail was granted by a constable, a magistrates' court shall not try that person for an offence under subsection (1) or (2) above in relation to that bail (the "relevant offence") unless either or both of subsections (12) and (13) below applies.

(12)   This subsection applies if an information is laid for the relevant offence within 6 months from the time of the commission of the relevant offence.

(13)   This subsection applies if an information is laid for the relevant offence no later than 3 months from the time of the occurrence of the first of the events mentioned in subsection (14) below to occur after the commission of the relevant offence.

(14) Those events are—

(a) the person surrenders to custody at the appointed place;

(b) the person is arrested, or attends at a police station, in connection with the relevant offence or the offence for which he was granted bail;

(c) the person appears or is brought before a court in connection with the relevant offence or the offence for which he was granted bail.

7.— Liability to arrest for absconding or breaking conditions of bail.

(1) If a person who has been released on bail in criminal proceedings and is under a duty to surrender into the custody of a court fails to surrender to custody at the time appointed for him to do so the court may issue a warrant for his arrest.

(1A) Subsection (1B) applies if—

(a) a person has been released on bail in connection with extradition proceedings,

(b) the person is under a duty to surrender into the custody of a constable, and

(c) the person fails to surrender to custody at the time appointed for him to do so.

(1B) A magistrates' court may issue a warrant for the person's arrest.

(2) If a person who has been released on bail in criminal proceedings absents himself from the court at any time after he has surrendered into the custody of the court and before the court is ready to begin or to resume the hearing of the proceedings, the court may issue a warrant for his arrest; but no warrant shall be issued under this subsection where that person is absent in accordance with leave given to him by or on behalf of the court.

(3) A person who has been released on bail in criminal proceedings and is under a duty to surrender into the custody of a court may be arrested without warrant by a constable—

(a) if the constable has reasonable grounds for believing that that person is not likely to surrender to custody;

(b) if the constable has reasonable grounds for believing that that person is likely to break any of the conditions of his bail or has reasonable grounds for suspecting that that person has broken any of those conditions; or

(c) in a case where that person was released on bail with one or more surety or sureties, if a surety notifies a constable in writing that that person is unlikely to surrender to custody and that for that reason the surety wishes to be relieved of his obligations as a surety.

(4) a person arrested in pursuance of subsection (3) above—

(a) shall, except where he was arrested within 24 hours of the time appointed for him to surrender to custody, be brought as soon as practicable and in any event within 24 hours after his arrest before a justice of the peace; and

(b) in the said excepted case shall be brought before the court at which he was to have surrendered to custody.

(4A) A person who has been released on bail in connection with extradition proceedings and is under a duty to surrender into the custody of a constable may be arrested without warrant by a constable on any of the grounds set out in paragraphs (a) to (c) of subsection (3).

(4B) A person arrested in pursuance of subsection (4A) above shall be brought as soon as practicable and in any event within 24 hours after his arrest before a justice of the peace for the petty sessions area in which he was arrested.

(5) A justice of the peace before whom a person is brought under subsection (4) or (4B) above may, subject to subsection (6) below, if of the opinion that that person—

(a) is not likely to surrender to custody, or

(b) has broken or is likely to break any condition of his bail, remand him in custody or commit him to custody, as the case may require, or alternatively, grant him bail subject to the same or to different conditions, but if not of that opinion shall grant him bail subject to the same conditions (if any) as were originally imposed.

(6) Where the person so brought before the justice is a child or young person and the justice does not grant him bail, subsection (5) above shall have effect subject to the provisions of section 23 of the Children and Young Persons Act 1969 (remands to the care of local authorities).

(7) In reckoning for the purposes of this section any period of 24 hours, no account shall be taken of Christmas Day, Good Friday or any Sunday.

(8) In the case of a person charged with murder or with murder and one or more other offences—

(a) subsections (4) and (5) have effect as if for " "justice of the peace" " there were substituted " "judge of the Crown Court"",

(b) subsection (6) has effect as if for " "justice" " (in both places) there were substituted " "judge" ", and

(c) subsection (7) has effect, for the purposes of subsection (4), as if at the end there were added "", Saturday or bank holiday.""

8.— Bail with sureties.

(1) This section applies where a person is granted bail in criminal proceedings on condition that he provides one or more surety or sureties for the purpose of securing that he surrenders to custody.

(2) In considering the suitability for that purpose of a proposed surety, regard may be had (amongst other things) to—

(a) the surety's financial resources;

(b) his character and any previous convictions of his; and

(c) his proximity (whether in point of kinship, place of residence or otherwise) to the person for whom he is to be surety.

(3) Where a court grants a person bail in criminal proceedings on such a condition but is unable to release him because no surety or no suitable surety is available, the court shall fix the amount in which the surety is to be bound and subsections (4) and (5) below, or in a case where the proposed surety resides in Scotland subsection (6) below, shall apply for the purpose of enabling the recognizance of the surety to be entered into subsequently.

(4) Where this subsection applies the recognizance of the surety may be entered into before such of the following persons or descriptions of persons as the court may by order specify or, if it makes no such order, before any of the following persons, that is to say—

(a) where the decision is taken by a magistrates' court, before a justice of the peace, a justices' clerk or a police officer who either is of the rank of inspector or above or is in charge of a police station or, if Criminal Procedure Rules so provide, by a person of such other description as is specified in the rules;

(b) where the decision is taken by the Crown Court, before any of the persons specified in paragraph (a) above or, if Criminal Procedure Rules so provide, by a person of such other description as is specified in the rules;

(c) where the decision is taken by the High Court or the Court of Appeal, before any of the persons specified in paragraph (a) above or, if Civil Procedure Rules or Criminal Procedure Rules so provide, by a person of such other description as is specified in the rules;

(d) where the decision is taken by the Court Martial Appeal Court , before any of the persons specified in paragraph (a) above or, if Court Martial Appeal Rules so provide, by a person of such other description as is specified in the rules;

and Civil Procedure Rules, Criminal Procedure Rules or Court Martial Appeal Rules may also prescribe the manner in which a recognizance which is to be entered into before such a person is to be entered into and the persons by whom and the manner in which the recognizance may be enforced.

(5) Where a surety seeks to enter into his recognizance before any person in accordance with subsection (4) above but that person declines to take his recognizance because he is not satisfied of the surety's suitability, the surety may apply to—

(a) the court which fixed the amount of the recognizance in which the surety was to be bound, or

(b) a magistrates' court,

for that court to take his recognizance and that court shall, if satisfied of his suitability, take his recognizance.

(6) Where this subsection applies, the court, if satisfied of the suitability of the proposed surety, may direct that arrangements be made for the recognizance of the surety to be entered into in Scotland before any constable, within the meaning of the Police (Scotland) Act 1967, having charge at any police office or station in like manner as the recognizance would be entered into in England or Wales.

(7) Where, in pursuance of subsection (4) or (6) above, a recognizance is entered into otherwise than before the court that fixed the amount of the recognizance, the same consequences shall follow as if it had been entered into before that court.

9.— Offence of agreeing to indemnify sureties in criminal proceedings.

(1) If a person agrees with another to indemnify that other against any liability which that other may incur as a surety to secure the surrender to custody of a person accused or convicted of or under arrest for an offence, he and that other person shall be guilty of an offence.

(2) An offence under subsection (1) above is committed whether the agreement is made before or after the person to be indemnified becomes a surety and whether or not he becomes a surety and whether the agreement contemplates compensation in money or in money's worth.

(3) Where a magistrates' court convicts a person of an offence under subsection (1) above the court may, if it thinks—

(a) that the circumstances of the offence are such that greater punishment should be inflicted for that offence than the court has power to inflict, or

(b) in a case where it sends that person for trial to the Crown Court for another offence, that it would be appropriate for him to be dealt with for the offence under subsection (1) above by the court before which he is tried for the other offence,

commit him in custody or on bail to the Crown Court for sentence.

(4) A person guilty of an offence under subsection (1) above shall be liable—

(a) on summary conviction, to imprisonment for a term not exceeding 3 months or to a fine not exceeding the prescribed sum or to both; or

(b) on conviction on indictment or if sentenced by the Crown Court on committal for sentence under subsection (3) above, to imprisonment for a term not exceeding 12 months or to a fine or to both.

(5) No proceedings for an offence under subsection (1) above shall be instituted except by or with the consent of the Director of Public Prosecutions .

9A Bail decisions relating to persons aged under 18 who are accused of offences mentioned in Schedule 2 to the Magistrates' Courts Act 1980

(1) This section applies whenever—

    (a) a magistrates' court is considering whether to withhold or grant bail in relation to a person aged under 18 who is accused of a scheduled offence; and

    (b) the trial of that offence has not begun.

(2) The court shall, before deciding whether to withhold or grant bail, consider whether, having regard to any representations made by the prosecutor or the accused person, the value involved does not exceed the relevant sum for the purposes of section 22.

(3) The duty in subsection (2) does not apply in relation to an offence if—

    (a) a determination under subsection (4) has already been made in relation to that offence; or

    (b) the accused person is, in relation to any other offence of which he is accused which is not a scheduled offence, a person to whom Part 1 of Schedule 1 to this Act applies.

(4) If where the duty in subsection (2) applies it appears to the court clear that, for the offence in question, the amount involved does not exceed the relevant sum, the court shall make a determination to that effect.

(5) In this section—

    (a) "relevant sum" has the same meaning as in section 22(1) of the Magistrates' Courts Act 1980 (certain either way offences to be tried summarily if value involved is less than the relevant sum);

    (b) "scheduled offence" means an offence mentioned in Schedule 2 to that Act (offences for which the value involved is relevant to the mode of trial); and

    (c) "the value involved" is to be construed in accordance with section 22(10) to (12) of that Act.

Schedule 1 PERSONS ENTITLED TO BAIL: SUPPLEMENTARY PROVISIONS

Part I DEFENDANTS ACCUSED OR CONVICTED OF IMPRISONABLE OFFENCES

Defendants to whom Part I applies

1

(1) Subject to sub-paragraph (2), the following provisions of this Part of this Schedule apply to the defendant if—

    (a) the offence or one of the offences of which he is accused or convicted in the proceedings is punishable with imprisonment, or

    (b) his extradition is sought in respect of an offence.

(2) But those provisions do not apply by virtue of sub-paragraph (1)(a) if the offence, or each of the offences punishable with imprisonment, is—

    (a) a summary offence; or

    (b) an offence mentioned in Schedule 2 to the Magistrates' Courts Act 1980 (offences for which the value involved is relevant to the mode of trial) in relation to which—

        (i) a determination has been made under section 22(2) of that Act (certain either way offences to be tried summarily if value involved is less than the relevant sum) that it is clear that the value does not exceed the relevant sum for the purposes of that section; or

        (ii) a determination has been made under section 9A(4) of this Act to the same effect.

2.

(1) The defendant need not be granted bail if the court is satisfied that there are substantial grounds for believing that the defendant, if released on bail (whether subject to conditions or not) would—

    (a) fail to surrender to custody, or

(b) commit an offence while on bail, or

(c) interfere with witnesses or otherwise obstruct the course of justice, whether in relation to himself or any other person.

(2) Where the defendant falls within one or more of paragraphs 2A, 6 and 6B of this Part of this Schedule, this paragraph shall not apply unless—

(a) where the defendant falls within paragraph 2A, the court is satisfied as mentioned in sub-paragraph (1) of that paragraph;

(b) where the defendant falls within paragraph 6, the court is satisfied as mentioned in sub-paragraph (1) of that paragraph;

(c) where the defendant falls within paragraph 6B, the court is satisfied as mentioned in paragraph 6A of this Part of this Schedule or paragraph 6A does not apply by virtue of paragraph 6C of this Part of this Schedule.

2A

(1) If the defendant falls within this paragraph he may not be granted bail unless the court is satisfied that there is no significant risk of his committing an offence while on bail (whether subject to conditions or not).

(2) The defendant falls within this paragraph if—

(a) he is aged 18 or over, and

(b) it appears to the court that he was on bail in criminal proceedings on the date of the offence.

2B

The defendant need not be granted bail in connection with extradition proceedings if—

(a) the conduct constituting the offence would, if carried out by the defendant in England and Wales, constitute an indictable offence or an offence triable either way; and

(b) it appears to the court that the defendant was on bail on the date of the offence.

3.

The defendant need not be granted bail if the court is satisfied that the defendant should be kept in custody for his own protection or, if he is a child or young person, for his own welfare.

4.

The defendant need not be granted bail if he is in custody in pursuance of a sentence of a court or a sentence imposed by an officer under the Armed Forces Act 2006.

5.

The defendant need not be granted bail where the court is satisfied that it has not been practicable to obtain sufficient information for the purpose of taking the decisions required by this Part of this Schedule for want of time since the institution of the proceedings against him.

6

(1) If the defendant falls within this paragraph, he may not be granted bail unless the court is satisfied that there is no significant risk that, if released on bail (whether subject to conditions or not), he would fail to surrender to custody.

(2) Subject to sub-paragraph (3) below, the defendant falls within this paragraph if—

(a) he is aged 18 or over, and

(b) it appears to the court that, having been released on bail in or in connection with the proceedings for the offence, he failed to surrender to custody.

(3) Where it appears to the court that the defendant had reasonable cause for his failure to surrender to custody, he does not fall within this paragraph unless it also appears to the

court that he failed to surrender to custody at the appointed place as soon as reasonably practicable after the appointed time.

(4) For the purposes of sub-paragraph (3) above, a failure to give to the defendant a copy of the record of the decision to grant him bail shall not constitute a reasonable cause for his failure to surrender to custody.

6ZA

If the defendant is charged with murder, the defendant may not be granted bail unless the court is of the opinion that there is no significant risk of the defendant committing, while on bail, an offence that would, or would be likely to, cause physical or mental injury to any person other than the defendant.

6A

Subject to paragraph 6C below, a defendant who falls within paragraph 6B below may not be granted bail unless the court is satisfied that there is no significant risk of his committing an offence while on bail (whether subject to conditions or not).

6B

(1) A defendant falls within this paragraph if—

    (a) he is aged 18 or over;

    (b) a sample taken—

        (i) under section 63B of the Police and Criminal Evidence Act 1984 (testing for presence of Class A drugs)   in connection with the offence; or

        (ii) under section 161 of the Criminal Justice Act 2003 (drug testing after conviction of an offence but before sentence),

has revealed the presence in his body of a specified Class A drug;

    (c) either the offence is one under section 5(2) or (3) of the Misuse of Drugs Act 1971 and relates to a specified Class A drug, or the court is satisfied that there are substantial grounds for believing—

        (i) that misuse by him of any specified Class A drug caused or contributed to the offence; or

        (ii) (even if it did not) that the offence was motivated wholly or partly by his intended misuse of such a drug; and

    (d) the condition set out in sub-paragraph (2) below is satisfied or (if the court is considering on a second or subsequent occasion whether or not to grant bail) has been, and continues to be, satisfied.

(2) The condition referred to is that after the taking and analysis of the sample—

    (a) a relevant assessment has been offered to the defendant but he does not agree to undergo it; or

    (b) he has undergone a relevant assessment, and relevant follow-up has been proposed to him, but he does not agree to participate in it.

(3) In this paragraph and paragraph 6C below—

    (a) "Class A drug" and "misuse" have the same meaning as in the Misuse of Drugs Act 1971;

    (b) "relevant assessment" and "relevant follow-up" have the meaning given by section 3(6E) of this Act;

    (c) "specified" (in relation to a Class A drug) has the same meaning as in Part 3 of the Criminal Justice and Court Services Act 2000.

6C

Paragraph 6A above does not apply unless—

    (a) the court has been notified by the Secretary of State that arrangements for conducting a relevant assessment or, as the case may be, providing relevant follow-up have been made for the local justice are in which it appears to the court that the defendant would reside if granted bail; and

    (b) the notice has not been withdrawn.

7.

Where his case is adjourned for inquiries or a report, the defendant need not be granted bail if it appears to the court that it would be impracticable to complete the inquiries or make the report without keeping the defendant in custody.

8.—

    (1) Subject to sub-paragraph (3) below, where the defendant is granted bail, no conditions shall be imposed under subsections (4) to (6B) or (7) (except subsection (6)(d) or (e)) of section 3 of this Act unless it appears to the court [that it is necessary to do so—

    [...]

        [(a) for the purpose of preventing the occurrence of any of the events mentioned in paragraph 2(1) of this Part of this Schedule, or

        (b) for the defendant's own protection or, if he is a child or young person, for his own welfare or in his own interests.

    [(1A) No condition shall be imposed under section 3(6)(d) of this Act unless it appears to be necessary to do so for the purpose of enabling inquiries or a report to be made.

    (2) Sub-paragraphs (1) and (1A) above also apply on any application to the court to vary the conditions of bail or to impose conditions in respect of bail which has been granted unconditionally.

    (3) The restriction imposed by [sub-paragraph (1A)] 6 above shall not [apply to the conditions required to be imposed under section 3(6A) of this Act or] 7 operate to override the direction in [section 11(3) of the Powers of Criminal Courts (Sentencing) Act 2000] 8 to a magistrates' court to impose conditions of bail under section 3(6)(d) of this Act of the description specified in [the said section 11(3)] 9 in the circumstances so specified.

9.

In taking the decisions required by paragraph 2(1) or, in deciding whether it is satisfied as mentioned in paragraph 2A(1), 6(1) or 6A or of the opinion mentioned in paragraph 6ZA, of this Part of this Schedule, the court shall have regard to such of the following considerations as appear to it to be relevant, that is to say—

    (a) the nature and seriousness of the offence or default (and the probable method of dealing with the defendant for it),

    (b) the character, antecedents, associations and community ties of the defendant,

    (c) the defendant's record as respects the fulfilment of his obligations under previous grants of bail in criminal proceedings,

    (d) except in the case of a defendant whose case is adjourned for inquiries or a report, the strength of the evidence of his having committed the offence or having defaulted,

    (e) if the court is satisfied that there are substantial grounds for believing that the defendant, if released on bail (whether subject to conditions or not), would commit an offence while on bail, the risk that the defendant may do so by engaging in conduct that would, or would be likely to, cause physical or mental injury to any person other than the defendant, as well as to any others which appear to be relevant.

9AB

    (1) Subject to sub-paragraph (2) below, this paragraph applies if—

        (a) the defendant is under the age of 18, and

(b) it appears to the court that, having been released on bail in or in connection with the proceedings for the offence, he failed to surrender to custody.

(2) Where it appears to the court that the defendant had reasonable cause for his failure to surrender to custody, this paragraph does not apply unless it also appears to the court that he failed to surrender to custody at the appointed place as soon as reasonably practicable after the appointed time.

(3) In deciding for the purposes of paragraph 2(1) of this Part of this Schedule whether it is satisfied that there are substantial grounds for believing that the defendant, if released on bail (whether subject to conditions or not), would fail to surrender to custody, the court shall give particular weight to—

(a) where the defendant did not have reasonable cause for his failure to surrender to custody, the fact that he failed to surrender to custody, or

(b) where he did have reasonable cause for his failure to surrender to custody, the fact that he failed to surrender to custody at the appointed place as soon as reasonably practicable after the appointed time.

(4) For the purposes of this paragraph, a failure to give to the defendant a copy of the record of the decision to grant him bail shall not constitute a reasonable cause for his failure to surrender to custody.

9B.

Where the court is considering exercising the power conferred by section 128A of the Magistrates' Courts Act 1980 (power to remand in custody for more than 8 clear days), it shall have regard to the total length of time which the accused would spend in custody if it were to exercise the power.

Part IA DEFENDANTS ACCUSED OR CONVICTED OF IMPRISONABLE OFFENCES TO WHICH PART 1 DOES NOT APPLY

1

The following provisions of this Part apply to the defendant if—

(a) the offence or one of the offences of which he is accused or convicted is punishable with imprisonment, but

(b) Part 1 does not apply to him by virtue of paragraph 1(2) of that Part.

2

The defendant need not be granted bail if—

(a) it appears to the court that, having been previously granted bail in criminal proceedings, he has failed to surrender to custody in accordance with his obligations under the grant of bail; and

(b) the court believes, in view of that failure, that the defendant, if released on bail (whether subject to conditions or not) would fail to surrender to custody.

3

The defendant need not be granted bail if—

(a) it appears to the court that the defendant was on bail in criminal proceedings on the date of the offence; and

(b) the court is satisfied that there are substantial grounds for believing that the defendant, if released on bail (whether subject to conditions or not) would commit an offence while on bail.

4

The defendant need not be granted bail if the court is satisfied that there are substantial grounds for believing that the defendant, if released on bail (whether subject to conditions or not), would commit an offence while on bail by engaging in conduct that would, or would be likely to, cause—

    (a) physical or mental injury to any person other than the defendant; or

    (b) any person other than the defendant to fear physical or mental injury.

5

The defendant need not be granted bail if the court is satisfied that the defendant should be kept in custody for his own protection or, if he is a child or young person, for his own welfare.

6

The defendant need not be granted bail if he is in custody in pursuance of a sentence of a court or a sentence imposed by an officer under the Armed Forces Act 2006.

7

The defendant need not be granted bail if—

    (a) having been released on bail in or in connection with the proceedings for the offence, he has been arrested in pursuance of section 7 of this Act; and

    (b) the court is satisfied that there are substantial grounds for believing that the defendant, if released on bail (whether subject to conditions or not) would fail to surrender to custody, commit an offence while on bail or interfere with witnesses or otherwise obstruct the course of justice (whether in relation to himself or any other person).

8

The defendant need not be granted bail where the court is satisfied that it has not been practicable to obtain sufficient information for the purpose of taking the decisions required by this Part of this Schedule for want of time since the institution of the proceedings against him.

9

Paragraphs 6A to 6C of Part 1 (exception applicable to drug users in certain areas and related provisions) apply to a defendant to whom this Part applies as they apply to a defendant to whom that Part applies.

Part II DEFENDANTS ACCUSED OR CONVICTED OF NON-IMPRISONABLE OFFENCES

1.

Where the offence or every offence of which the defendant is accused or convicted in the proceedings is one which is not punishable with imprisonment the following provisions of this Part of this Schedule apply.

2.

The defendant need not be granted bail if—

    (a) it appears to the court that, having been previously granted bail in criminal proceedings, he has failed to surrender to custody in accordance with his obligations under the grant of bail; and

    (b) the court believes, in view of that failure, that the defendant, if released on bail (whether subject to conditions or not) would fail to surrender to custody.

3.

The defendant need not be granted bail if the court is satisfied that the defendant should be kept in custody for his own protection or, if he is a child or young person, for his own welfare.

4.

The defendant need not be granted bail if he is in custody in pursuance of a sentence of a court or a sentence imposed by an officer under the Armed Forces Act 2006.

5

The defendant need not be granted bail if—

    (a) having been released on bail in or in connection with the proceedings for the offence, he has been arrested in pursuance of section 7 of this Act; and

    (b) the court is satisfied that there are substantial grounds for believing that the defendant, if released on bail (whether subject to conditions or not) would fail to surrender to custody, commit an offence on bail or interfere with witnesses or otherwise obstruct the course of justice (whether in relation to himself or any other person).

Part IIA DECISIONS WHERE BAIL REFUSED ON PREVIOUS HEARING

1.

If the court decides not to grant the defendant bail, it is the court's duty to consider, at each subsequent hearing while the defendant is a person to whom section 4 above applies and remains in custody, whether he ought to be granted bail.

2.

At the first hearing after that at which the court decided not to grant the defendant bail he may support an application for bail with any argument as to fact or law that he desires (whether or not he has advanced that argument previously).

3.

At subsequent hearings the court need not hear arguments as to fact or law which its has heard previously.